QMC　　　　365779 1

a30213 003657799

D1380956

DATE DUE FOR

ACCELERATED DEVELOPMENT IN SOUTHERN AFRICA

Also published by Macmillan
for S.A.I.I.A.

John Barratt and Michael Louw (editors)

International Aspects of Overpopulation

ACCELERATED DEVELOPMENT IN SOUTHERN AFRICA

Edited by

JOHN BARRATT
SIMON BRAND
DAVID S. COLLIER
and
KURT GLASER

MACMILLAN

QUEEN MARY
COLLEGE
LIBRARY

163884
HC 900

© South African Institute of International Affairs 1974

All rights reserved. No part of this publication
may be reproduced or transmitted, in any form
or by any means, without permission.

First published 1974,
in association with the Foundation for Foreign Affairs. Inc.,
the Rand Afrikaans University and the South African Institute of
International Affairs, by
THE MACMILLAN PRESS LTD
London and Basingstoke
Associated companies in New York
Dublin Melbourne Johannesburg and Madras

SBN 333 15395 2

Printed in Great Britain by
WESTERN PRINTING SERVICES LTD
Bristol

Contents

Foreword

The leaders of most of what is now widely known as the Third
World are aware of the vital need to accelerate the development
of their countries, and thus satisfy the rising expectations of their
peoples for a fuller life in the modern world. This applies as
much to Africa as to any other region of the world. But awareness of the need is only the beginning; the obstacles to development must be identified and understood; and ways and means
must then be found to overcome them. For many countries – far
behind on the road to modernisation – this process is not an easy
one. In Africa, in its second decade of independence, the success
stories are few, while many countries are still wrestling with basic
problems standing in the way of meaningful growth. Even in
South Africa – regarded as the most economically advanced
country on the continent – the pace of growth is uneven, and in
some areas development has hardly begun.

Underlying all the problems is often a lack of understanding
of what is involved in the concept of accelerated development.
It was in order to contribute to greater understanding that a conference was held in Johannesburg to consider the problems
encountered more particularly in the southern part of Africa,
while at the same time drawing from experience gained in other
parts of the world. In the belief that development is not simply
an economic question, the conference considered also the political
and social aspects. The results are set out in this volume, which
it is hoped will contribute not only to the greater understanding
required, but also to the finding of solutions to the many problems
in developing areas.

The proceedings of a previous conference held at Jan Smuts

House were edited by John Barratt and Michael Louw and published by the South African Institute of International Affairs in 1972, under the title *International Aspects of Overpopulation* (London, Macmillan) – a subject also of special concern to the developing countries. In the case of this present volume and the conference on which it is based, the Institute as the host organisation is most grateful for the fruitful co-operation of its two co-sponsors, the Foundation for Foreign Affairs, Inc., of Chicago and the Rand Afrikaans University in Johannesburg. We are pleased, too, to acknowledge the assistance of the Africa Institute of South Africa in the preparatory work for the Conference, and the generous support which the Institute and the University received, to help make the Conference possible, from several South African companies, namely the Anglo-American Corporation of South Africa Ltd., Anglo-Transvaal Consolidated Investment Co. Ltd, BP Southern Africa (Pty) Ltd, Leo Raphaely and Sons, Mobil Oil Southern Africa (Pty) Ltd, Murray and Stewart (Pty) Ltd, Rembrandt Tobacco Manufacturing Corporation, Roberts Construction Co. Ltd and Total South Africa (Pty) Ltd.

In addition, the Institute wishes to acknowledge with appreciation the assistance of the City Council of Johannesburg in regard to the Conference and the publication of this volume.

Finally, a sincere tribute must be paid to the late Dr Dean Terrill. As President of the Foundation for Foreign Affairs, he was a President of the Conference (together with Professor G. van N. Viljoen, Rector of the Rand Afrikaans University, and myself). His enthusiastic support was invaluable in ensuring the success of our joint undertaking, and his death, shortly after returning to the United States from South Africa, was a sad blow for the Foundation as well as for his many friends in South Africa. It is fitting to recall now his opening remarks at the Conference, when he drew attention to the fact that we are living in a period of great changes. In these critical times, he said, the welfare of mankind demanded 'a greater degree of understanding and compassionate co-operation' than was apparent throughout the world. He sincerely hoped that the results of the Conference – as they are now reflected in this volume – would 'lead to continually increasing co-operation between all who would participate in creating a greater and better and finer Southern Africa for each and all of its many and diverse peoples'. In that expression of hope all of us involved in the publication of this volume can fully share.

Leif Egeland

National Chairman S.A.I.I.A.

Preface

The articles in this volume are based on papers presented by the respective authors at a Conference held at Jan Smuts House, Johannesburg, from 21 March to 25 March 1972. The theme of the Conference was 'Accelerated Development in Southern Africa', and it was jointly sponsored by the Foundation for Foreign Affairs, Inc., the Rand Afrikaans University and the South African Institute of International Affairs. The participants included experts from Angola, Lesotho, Madagascar, Malawi, Moçambique, Rhodesia, South Africa and Swaziland, as well as from the United States, the United Kingdom and Germany. Among the South Africans participating – White and Black – were representatives of several Homeland governments, central government departments, universities and a number of private bodies, including commercial and industrial firms and organisations. The participation, therefore, reflected a wide cross-section of political and academic viewpoints, and included scholars, planners, development administrators and business executives.

The structure of this volume follows broadly the structure of the Conference itself. After the introductory chapter, Part One deals with certain basic dimensions of development in eight chapters and concludes with a ninth chapter on a subject of special relevance to the southern part of Africa, namely the problems of multi-ethnic societies. The three chapters of Part Two are concerned with international aspects of development. In Part Three there is an attempt to provide an overall evaluation, and to look at needs for the future. The Conference itself did not aim to reach concrete conclusions or recommendations, but many of the concerns and viewpoints which emerged during the discussions, regarding both the problems and opportunities, are reflected in the final part of this volume.

In addition to the main articles, brief comments by other participants – who in most cases were the lead-in discussants – are included at the end of each chapter, and in the case of the chapter on multi-ethnic societies a summary of the discussion which took place at the relevant session of the Conference is added. An annexure gives brief notes on all the contributors to this volume, as well as on the Editors.

Mention is made in Chapter Seven of the Education Workshop which preceded the main Conference. A report on the Workshop, with some additional material on education and training projects in the countries of Southern Africa, is being published separately.

The Editors wish to acknowledge with appreciation the assistance received from the staff of the S.A. Institute of International Affairs in the preparation of this volume for publication.

JOHN BARRATT
SIMON BRAND
DAVID S. COLLIER
KURT GLASER

Introduction

Basic Concepts and Goals of Development

The Goals, Strategy and Environment of Development

EDWARD W. WEIDNER

Millions of television viewers from around the world have watched the bright blue ball, known as earth, from the vastness of space. This novel and thrilling experience has changed many attitudes and reinforced others. It has influenced the course of affairs both from a practical or applied standpoint and from a philosophical or conceptual standpoint. The viewing of earth from afar symbolises a change in the way in which man views himself and his destiny in regard to the rest of his environment on the planet earth. This conceptual change has meaning for the way in which we view development.

THE MEANING OF DEVELOPMENT

Development means more of the good things of life. To the man on the street, development means the ability to attain his goals in life. To the man in the planning office, it means attaining more of the national goals. To the man in the ivory tower, it means that mankind maximises its happiness.

Development is fundamentally an equalitarian goal. It is equalitarian among the peoples of the world, and it is equalitarian within a given people. Most of the writing and discussion concerning development has alluded to the first of these goals. Thus we speak of the development of Ethiopia in comparison with the development of the United States, or the development of India in comparison with the development of the Republic of South Africa. International technical assistance has resulted in billions of dollars being transferred from the 'have' nations to the 'have not' nations. Comparative statistics on gross national products and per capita incomes are available, country by country. Indeed, in this age of nationalism, an equalitarian goal among the peoples of the world is both understandable and justified.

Increasingly, however the peoples of the world are given attention to equalitarian principles within nations. There was a time when it was fashionable to suggest that development necessarily meant a larger discrepancy between the well-to-do and the poverty classes within a particular country. This was understood to be natural and even inevitable in the development process. Whether it was natural or inevitable under certain conditions or not is today beside the point. There is a worldwide demand for all classes and all kinds of people to participate in development.

Nor is this equalitarian goal among a people simply a matter of *laissez-faire* or non-discrimination. The sweep of equalitarianism has moved on to much higher ground. It requires a positive affirmative action to make sure that such rounded development takes place. Thus in the United States, for example, affirmative action programmes are taking place not just in regard to poverty in general or in regard to particular racial minorities such as Blacks, American Indians, Spanish-speaking peoples and American Orientals. The principle of affirmative action has been extended to all kinds of subclassifications of individuals including those who might be discriminated against on the basis of their age, sex, national origin or religion. It is apparent that development within a country needs to be just as balanced among the various kinds of people found there, as international development needs to be balanced among the various nations of the world. And just as we have seen affirmative action among nations through technical assistance and economic aid, we are entering an era in which similar affirmative action will be taken more broadly by individual nations in regard to their various populations.

Of course, there are differences among individuals just as there are differences among nations. No two individuals are exactly alike. They may not be alike in regard to motivations or aspirations. They may not be alike in their manual or mental abilities. It would appear that no matter how hard we try to reduce these differences, some will always remain. Still, we are on the verge of a time when the secrets of the chemistry of the body, of the brain, and even of reproduction itself, are within our grasp in a way that they have not been previously. Chemistry aside, we can remove many of the differences among individuals far more effectively and quickly than we have ever been able to remove them previously. And within a decade or two, and certainly by the twenty-first century, we shall be on entirely new ground. Thus we must add to the concept of affirmative action the concept of reducing individual differences (in the sense of individual disabilities or inabilities) in a vigorous and forthright fashion. Unless we do so to the limit of our knowledge, we shall not truly embrace development in the full sense of the term.

To achieve development, we must also be more imaginative in reducing the differences among the nations of the world. Historical accident has played an important role in the distribution of people and resources on the face of the earth. Humanity can no longer justify differences in standards of living based upon exclusive control over particular resources. As we look upon the earth from the vastness of space, we are once again reminded of the oneness of our experience in this life. And yet there are great variations in what peoples of the world have done with the resources at their command. Somehow, incentive for each nation to do a better job with what it has must be maintained and enhanced, at the same time that more equality among nations is obtained.

Development means more of the good things of life and a greater fulfilment of individual happiness. It is not the false kind of happiness that might overtake a prisoner in a small cell as a result of being left alone, however. To be meaningful, such happiness must result from informed choice. Only when human beings know the range of alternative choices open to them, only when they have an idea of how to react to the alternatives they do perceive, can their definition of happiness be sufficiently unrestricted. Additionally, to be valid, such informed happiness must be well rounded. It is not enough to speak of material happiness or well-being. Nor is it enough to cite evidence of disease control without referring to problems of burgeoning population. Informed happiness must be thought of in a comprehensive way. It must be thought of in regard to a complete range of welfare values including culture and health as well as basic material well-being.

Above all, as we near the twenty-first century, we must not

get lost as human beings. Development that erases human identity is worse than meaningless. But identity that requires isolation from fellow-men is also meaningless. There is no identity in returning to the cave or the woods. There is no identity in being isolated at the North or South Pole, or in the islands of the South Seas. There is no identity in being a lost soul in a huge sprawling metropolis. True identity for our time requires a concept of men and women *in* society. The nature of the world's communication and transportation system and the very character of the limited spaceship, planet earth, demand a concept of development which considers man in society. Other men and women are a part of each person's environment. A person must seek individual identity in his relationship to other human beings. At the same time, there must be respect for, and interest in, the identity of others. Empathy is a very central requirement of development. The ability to project or imagine oneself in another's position or situation is a key to social change.

In 1966 this writer set down his thoughts on the meaning of development. It is an appropriate time to review these concepts, which were stated in terms of three dimensions of development:

First, a general distinction is now made between change in the output of a system and change in the system itself. Changes in the output of a system that are in the direction of greater quantity are frequently labelled growth, and those that are in the reverse direction, lack of growth or decline. Growth is essentially a quantitative concept. It does not make a qualitative distinction. . . .

A number of scholars of development administration have focused their attention on change in the social system, and particularly on change in the administrative system of a developing country, as a crucial variable. . . . Thus, four possibilities emerge: growth with system change, growth without system change, lack of growth (or decline) with system change, and lack of growth (or decline) with no system change.

Second, distinctions have been drawn among the different goals or outputs of an administrative system. . . .

Thus in common usage of the term, a rapidly developing country is a goal-oriented country, headed in the direction of modernity, with special emphasis on nation-building and socio-economic progress. This definition accords with the announced objectives of leaders of these nations. While specifics will vary and even be in dispute, the general direction is evident.

Returning to a consideration of the definition of development, we can now attempt a comprehensive statement. A more complete description of the development process would be growth, whether under conditions of system change or not, in the direction of modernity and particularly in the direction of nation-building and socio-economic progress. It is a reasonable hypothesis that in order for growth to proceed in this direction very far, system change in the form of increased differentiation and co-ordination, together with appropriate accompanying specialisation, would be required. . . .

Third, there is an inherently manipulative aspect to the term 'development'. It is commonly understood that those engaged in development work are consciously trying to bring about change in a particular direction. An assumption lies behind this common understanding: man can affect the environment of which he is a part as well as be affected by it. . . .

An assumption underlying the selection of goals in planning for national development is that achievement of modernity in general and nation-building and socio-economic progress in particular can be furthered by man through one means or another. . . . Since extensive progress toward achievement of these goals is likely to require major system change, it is also likely that most development on a major scale will be planned at least to the extent of encouraging environmental factors favourable to unplanned development.

Still, many of the accomplishments of any large organisation such as government are clearly not planned or even intended – at least by the authorities that be. And the underlying motivations for actions are normally very diverse and are by no means exclusively developmental or anti-developmental. It would be unduly restrictive to impute to any government or bureaucracy complete rationality and singleness or duality of purpose.[1]

As a result of this analysis, eight sets of conditions that might lead to development were listed (see Table 1).

TABLE I. Sets of conditions leading to development[2]

Type	Characteristics		
	Directional growth	*System change*	*Planned or intended*
1. Ideal	+	+	+
2. Short-run payoff	+	−	+
3. Long-run payoff	−	+	+
4. Failure	−	−	+
5. Environmental stimulus	+	+	−
6. Pragmatism	+	+	−
7. Crisis	−	+	−
8. Static society	−	−	−

These words were written barely six years ago, in 1966. Still, as reviewed today they seem strangely anachronistic. First of all, these passages indicate far too much concern with the nation-state. They are overly national in concept. They ignore the important international dimensions of development. They ignore the intimate human aspects of development.

They seem anachronistic to me for a second reason. The whole concept dates from before that giant step of mankind, travel to the moon. The big blue ball is not viewed in totality. The concepts of 'spaceship earth' have not permeated the discussion. Consequently the formulation seems narrow and restricted.

An understanding of the conditions leading to development as described in the 1966 grid would still prove useful to the scholar, analyst or planner. It is a legitimate formulation, as far as it goes. However, the need for broadening the study of development points to levels of analysis other than the purely national. A focus on equalitarianism in the development process as it relates to the individual and a focus on relations in and among nations suggests a framework for analysis incorporating these important dimensions. Thus, three grids instead of one would be necessary, incorporating the international, national and intra-national. These grids would be interrelated by a recognition of the overall concept of human interdependence, or human ecology, and the concept of a finite resource base in the long run. These concepts would serve as a lens through which any of the sets of conditions would be viewed, regardless of the level of analysis. Such changes would greatly modify the definitions earlier given to 'directional growth', 'system change' and 'planned or intended change', and would place them in a broader context.

THE DETERMINATION OF DEVELOPMENT GOALS

The literature of development is strangely formalistic in treating the determination of development goals. Almost all attention has been focused upon the role of planning commissions. More specifically, there has been a fixation on the five-year plan not only in the literature of the field but also in the halls of planning agencies.

Indeed, planning commissions and five-year plans can be useful. But their role is likely to be a modest one. A planning commission is most likely to be organised as a staff agency of the national executive. It can search out many facts on an overall nationwide basis. It can serve as a point through which plans of different government agencies funnel, and as a means of relating them one to another. It can even give expression to certain development goals rather effectively.

However, a reasonably objective view of planning commissions in different nations of the world would suggest that they are not in the mainstream of development. The writer recalls attending a conference in the mid-1960s. The purpose of the conference was to review the work of planning commissions and the effectiveness of five-year plans in South and South-east Asia. The unanimous conclusion of the forty to fifty Asians and Americans present, mostly economists, was that the work of the planning commissions was largely ineffective.

The conclusion of that seminar seemed shocking at first. As time passed, and reflection about the proceedings was possible, the conclusion seemed logical and almost inevitable. Planned development is of such importance in a country that it cannot be delegated to a planning commission, no matter how prestigious. Planning must be part of every agency. More importantly, planning is an integral part of the responsibility of every senior political officer of the government. Certainly, every cabinet officer and the chief executive and political leader of a country needs to have a major role in determining goals as well as in carrying them out. In neither political terms nor administrative terms can cabinet officers afford to delegate planning and development responsibility to members of a planning commission. The matter is too sensitive, the goals too fundamental to the entire political system, to permit such delegation. To a major political leader, the plans emanating from a planning commission are simply one additional input with which he has to deal. He must concern himself with his overall support base. He must work in such a manner that the various elements that make up that support base receive attention and participate actively in the development process. He must be conscious of the problem of appropriations, the marshalling of resources, and his interface with the whole parliamentary and political spectrum of the country. These are areas in which planning commissions have been abysmally weak. Because they have been weak, their master plans are just one of many inputs in the development process.

Such was the experience in the United States when, during the early 1940s, a national planning agency was abolished. Those interested in rational allocation of resources and the orderly processes of development were very unhappy. They thought that many of the things for which Franklin D. Roosevelt had fought were being thrust aside. They believed that the social and economic revolution of the country was at an end. They felt a 'business as usual' philosophy was carrying all before it. There was considerable dispirit. And yet, thirty years later, it is apparent that national planning and national development are among the crucial concerns of the nation and of the nation's leaders. Perhaps this was always so. And perhaps the planning board had to be eliminated because it interferred with the orderly selection of development goals in the combined administrative-political arena.

This does not mean that there should not be planning commissions attached to governments. It is only urged that planning commissions should be viewed simply as one means of securing staff aid in determining development goals. They will normally not be the crucial determiner of such goals *in fact*. Still, they can do many useful things for the political executives, particularly if their recommendations are flexible and are not interpreted as being a fixed prescription.

There are, then, three important considerations in setting development goals. First is that of legitimacy. Development goals must have a ring of legitimacy. Legitimacy may on occasion come through the actions of a planning commission. More likely, legitimacy will come through the political-legislative process, and by means of endorsement of goals by the nation's leaders. In the case of charismatic leaders, the legitimacy process may be simple. Through his charisma, the leader's ability to grant legitimacy to objectives is enhanced. His entourage will have at its command the levers of legitimacy. Examples are to be found in a number of the leaders of African nations, who were the principal figures in the revolutionary movements for independence, and have the aura of charisma.

Legitimacy does not often spring alone or substantially from the formal plans of the planning commission in any country, whether with or without charismatic leadership. For example, there has been substantial development in a number of countries that have governments controlled by modernising military leaders. Such leaders are frequently not charismatic in quality, even though strong in authority. Despite the substantial amount of power which they wield, these leaders have found it necessary to develop special techniques of legitimising their government policies in the eyes of the people. In regard to planning, they have found that commissions are only one means of legitimising development goals. Endorsement by military and government rank or brass, symbols of group support, ceremonial devices and *ad hoc* committees or arrangements have been other tools frequently used to enhance legitimacy.

Similarly, leaders that have come to power as the result of a high level of citizen participation in the political system have found it necessary to legitimise development goals in ways other than formally having them adopted by planning commissions. In particular, in those countries with strong legislative or parliamentary systems, planning must ultimately be sanctioned by the legislative body. It is at this juncture that development goals are given their ultimate legitimacy.

A second important consideration in the determination of development goals is the political interface of any governmental system. This is partly intertwined with the concept of legitimacy. However, it goes beyond legitimacy: political leaders need to assure themselves of an adequate support base. Consequently they cannot embrace development goals unless these goals are in line with urgent political necessities. It is at this point that neatly packaged plans for economic or social development are put aside. No one can be a statesman if he is not in power. Therefore, at a maximum, the role of a planning commission is that of proposer of development strategies and tactics. Political leaders take such suggestions and modify them in accordance with the political realities of any particular situation at any particular moment.

A third consideration is the possibility or likelihood of the development goals being achieved. Partly this is a matter of whether or not there are sufficient funds. Partly this is a matter of whether there is an administrative arm strong enough to implement such goals. And partly it is whether or not there is enough time and energy to meet a particular development goal according to a given schedule. Not everything can be done at once. A sense of timing is important both politically and administratively, as well as from the standpoint of presumed sequences of economic and social development.

Judgements of this nature are inherently those that are appropriate to a political leader. Thus the central point of determining development policy is that of the cabinet-level officers of a nation or of the governmental unit involved. A decision to carry through on particular development goals is a very sensitive thing. A leader must have his ear to the ground. If supporters are over-extending themselves, if the system is pushing too rapidly and thus disturbing certain influential elements in the country, if emergencies require resources to be allocated in alternative ways, if funding sources do not come through as expected, or if rival political forces change in relative strength, a halt may be called. These and other factors that affect the execution of programmes aimed at certain development goals will have crucial consequences for any given national plan.

Recently it has been fashionable to emphasise that development goals should be those of a nation itself, rather than goals specified or implied by a foreign power. This discussion has been particularly pronounced in regard to technical assistance and economic aid. Indeed, it is important that development goals be congenial to a particular country, as well as comfortable for its political leaders. Still, much of the impetus for a change comes from comparing one's situation with the situation of someone else. A country that looks inward entirely is likely to be a country that does not progress very rapidly. Competition and comparison with other countries are favourable factors for change, not unfavourable ones. Countries that are both similar and dissimilar to one's own can play an important role of stimulus. And it does not follow that a particular country will be like Egypt just because it compares itself with Egypt. Nor need it be like any other neighbour with which it compares itself.

STRATEGY FOR DEVELOPMENT

In order to achieve development goals, a unit of government is well advised to pursue one or more strategies for change. The strategies pursued are of necessity highly pragmatic. There is no single theory or set of theories that will give highly reliable guidance as to how to advance from a given condition to particular development goals. This is not to say that behavioural science and other branches of science are not relevant to decisions concerning strategy. It is to say that there are so many variables, and the situation is so complex, that it is not possible to prescribe strategies with any degree of certainty.

There is no one path to development. There are as many strategies for development as there are countries trying to achieve development. There is a wide variety represented in the vast continent of Africa. There is equal richness and variety in Asia, Latin America, North America and elsewhere. Partly, this variety is explained by the different styles of different political leaders and systems. Indira Gandhi follows a different strategy from Chou En-lai, for example, and both are different from Haile Selassie I in their approaches to development. While there are similarities among political systems and among systems of leadership, country to country, the impact of these variables on strategy for change are such that no two countries follow identical paths.

A political leader, however, need not be wafted from wave to wave depending upon the current and the wind. There are elements of strategies among which he can choose. One of the first choices to be made is between a balanced and an unbalanced strategy for development. A so-called balanced strategy implies that all sectors of society, all sectors of the economy and the various geographical portions of the country proceed towards development in rather steady and balanced fashion. Thus transportation, health, education, agriculture and public adminstration may go hand in hand at a rather steady pace. Extractive industries can be balanced by non-extractive industries. Handicrafts can be balanced by manufactured goods. The urban area can receive some attention, and the various rural areas can as well. For many years it was thought that to proceed in a balanced fashion was the most effective way of securing development. Of course, what is balance and what is unbalance can be defined in various ways.

In recent years there has been much evidence that an unbalanced strategy of development might yield more returns. In most of the developing areas, particularly in the rural sectors, there is substantial resistance to change. On occasion, this resistance extends into urban settlements as well. The general inability of the population to imagine the need for substantial change frequently poses a serious problem. Among those who are conscious of the kinds of benefits that change might bring, there may be quite a number who oppose particular changes simply because such changes are not in their own self-interest. Thus to proceed uniformly in trying to secure change at a relatively flat rate in different sectors can easily maximise opposition to development while minimising support.

Thus it is that leaders in many countries have come to favour change in one or more sectors over change in other sectors. For example, it is very possible that better health is one of the changes that is most palatable and the least unpalatable to a broad spectrum of people in a number of societies. Then why should not the government of such a country emphasise development goals in health? There would be much greater receptivity, the cost would be less than if all sectors were developed at a rapid rate, and political support might be enhanced. In addition, it is conceivable that if changes in health are successful and readily understood and appreciated, a consequence could be that demand would arise for changes in other areas. It is possible that with improvement in health there could be a demand for improvement in agriculture and education, for example. This, in turn, could spread to other sectors. The development of one part of the economy in an unbalanced fashion might readily stimulate demands for strengthening the economy in other areas. Thus there is not just a choice between a balanced and an unbalanced plan of development. There are alternative strategies within the unbalanced approach, since the 'lead' area of development might be quite different in one set of circumstances from that in another.

Closely allied to the problem of choosing between a balanced and an unbalanced strategy is a second choice: the problem of choosing between sequential and non-sequential development. Perhaps the simplest example of a sequential strategy occurs in education. It is quite obvious that unless elementary schools are developed, it is difficult to strengthen the secondary-school system. Similarly, if the secondary-school system has not been strengthened, it may be hard to strengthen universities properly. One element of education is sequentially related to other elements. The same is true in public administration. If a country launches upon a strategy of development that requires widespread government intervention and activity, it is quite obvious that its public administration system should first be strengthened. Rapid strides in the business area may be difficult without substantial strides in business administration. Certain kinds of economic development are unlikely of accomplishment unless the infrastructure of transportation and communication is strengthened. A basic adequacy in the utility area is important for widespread urban economic development.

It is apparent that sequential development is important in certain fields. Still, its significance has been substantially overplayed by some development theorists. There may be a temporary disturbing effect as one part of the country is developed without a desirable base or apparent precondition. Still, there may be sound political and other reasons why avoiding or postponing the base or precondition is a logical alternative. An example occurs at the writer's own university. In evolving towards attainment of a physical master plan, it is logical that buildings should be developed first, and then, as they are completed, the supporting roads, parking lots and landscaping be added. But the decision was made to go ahead with unneeded roads and parking lots because money was available. Had we waited two to four years, it is probable that the source of money would have disappeared. All this created some temporary dislocation, and indeed some criticism. But within four years of their completion all these roads and parking lots will be needed, and they will be available for use. It is even possible that their current availability has spurred certain other aspects of our development. Similarly in a nation-state. The development of a model seaport can act as an impetus to the development of other seaports. And a university, prematurely developed, can stimulate the demand for better secondary education. A secondary system, properly developed, can stimulate the demand for improvement in basic and elementary education.

A third choice may be made: choosing between a production and a consumption strategy. A production strategy means the postponement of immediate growth in the hope of making more fundamental changes in the economy and in the society. Such changes can lead to much higher consumption levels in the longer run. In short-range terms, a consumption policy may be a pleasant choice. It gives some immediate returns but may postpone future growth. There are obvious economic considerations in choosing between a production and a consumption emphasis. There are political considerations as well. No government chooses all of one or all of another. It will normally opt for a certain degree of one and a certain degree of another. The mix is one of the significant political decisions to be made each year in determining development strategies.

Fourthly, there is a choice between stability and dynamism. On occasion it is necessary or desirable to introduce changes that will have the least disruptive effect. On other occasions it may be desirable to introduce strategies that will have the most disruptive effect. There is a time for peace and solitude in any large organisation and in any society. There is a time for dynamic growth and change and fundamental realignments in the history of any group of people as well. Here again, the decision can only be made at the most senior levels of leadership. Just as in the selection of development goals, a government finds that in selecting development strategies it is dealing with the very fabric of its continued existence. The decisions must be made carefully and with full reflection of the political facts of life.

A fifth choice in strategy lies between a high degree of social control and heavy emphasis on private rights. This is not the same thing as socialism versus capitalism. Rather, it has to do with the social purpose or the private purpose of institutions, property and programmes. On the limited spaceship, planet earth, we may be entering a new era where social purposes are more encompassing than had previously been thought. Thus perhaps a private individual no longer has the right to fill in swampland and to build upon it. Perhaps a private person no longer has the right to log or destroy trees along a watershed or creek bed. Long ago it was determined that parents did not have the private right to deny their children education. The worldwide direction is clearly towards a broader definition of social purpose and a restriction of private rights. Still, there will be many variations in the balance between these two, country to country, from time to time. And the free-enterprise system can thrive under either set of conditions.

The value of comparison in determining development strategies can be great. Political leaders can learn much through comparative observation and analysis of various countries, or through similar investigations of regional and sectoral differences in their own nation. But while the value of comparison is well demonstrated, it is not appropriate to attach a similar value to imitation. When the wholesale transfer of plans, programmes, technologies or techniques is the method, failure is likely to be the result. Rather than adopting precise models, national leaders should consciously select successful techniques of development in different countries, areas or sectors that best meet their own particular needs. If the resulting transfer reflects thought and purpose, and the stimulus of comparison, great advantage can result.

Strategy for development is not based on an equilibrium notion of society. It is certainly not based on a static notion of society. It is definitely not based on a deterministic one either. Rather, the assumption behind developmental change is that men can influence the course of events by rational thought and action. In this regard, conscious choices among the five sets of alternatives just outlined are likely to be helpful and realistic. In fact, such choices are not so much among polar alternatives as they are choices along five continua. A choice of more or less in regard to each element, rather than a choice between two extremes, may be made.

THE ENVIRONMENT OF DEVELOPMENT

From a scholarly point of view, the strategies of development determine the independent variables, the goals of development are the dependent variables, and environmental circumstances are the intervening variables. In making comparisons among different development situations, a researcher or analyst is frequently at a loss. The intervening variables in any one development situation are not equivalent to the intervening variables in another. It is difficult even to classify environmental variables. Without attempting in any manner to be complete, I have selected five which seem to me to be of special significance.

First, the variable of literacy and technical training is everywhere recognised as a basic one. In fact, literacy is not only an environmental variable; it is also frequently a substantive goal of development. The effect of a high rate of literacy and a substantial degree of technical training is well demonstrated in the experience of Taiwan and South Korea after the Second World War. Because of emphasis on literacy and technical training, especially during the Japanese occupation, Taiwan and South Korea became prime development areas. Their progress during the last twenty-five years has been very impressive. In contrast, Indonesia, which had a low level of literacy and very little technical training under the Dutch, suffered badly in trying to move towards development. One of the intangibles, of course, is the inclination or desire of a country and its people for literacy and technical training. It is quite apparent, for example, that the Filipinos have a tremendous desire for education at all levels. This is one of their great assets in the push for development. It is one of the intervening variables that favours development in that situation. In another country the reverse may be the case, and the lack of inclination towards literacy, technical training and education becomes a drag on development efforts.

A second environmental variable is the extent of achievement and goal orientation in a country. Some peoples have a very substantial amount of goal or achievement orientation. There is high motivation and substantial initiative towards work and towards change. In other cultures, change is feared. The predominant religion may emphasise a satisfaction with the *status quo*. Much has been written about the Protestant ethic. There is little doubt that the Protestant ethic, understood in its broadest sense, impels a people towards change and towards development. The difference between some of the Spanish Dominican fathers in Latin America and some of the American Jesuit fathers in the Philippines is most marked. The Roman Catholic Jesuits in the Philippines have been good examples of the Protestant ethic in practice. Working side by side with Filipinos, they have had much impact on the progress which that nation has made.

Another dimension of achievement and goal orientation concerns the relative emphasis on competitiveness and co-operation in a society. This is not an either–or situation. Each society has elements of competitiveness and elements of co-operation. Both are necessary, in certain combinations, to impel a nation towards development goals. An over-emphasis on one or the other may frustrate the achievement of development goals.

In a real sense, achievement and goal orientation depend upon the religious and philosophical base of a country. This is not a matter of preferring one organised religion over another. It is a matter of emphasis, interpretation and application. Thus, one can find achievement and goal orientation in Islam, achievement and goal orientation in Catholicism and Protestantism, and achievement and goal orientation in Hebraic philosophy. With different interpretations of these great religions, one can end up with an emphasis on satisfaction with the *status quo*, and a waiting for the hereafter. It is not by chance that a number of leaders of the less developed countries have called for and supported a more modern interpretation of religious thought in order to give greater support to development goals.

A third environmental variable of great importance is the relative cohesiveness of a particular society. Perhaps a majority of the nations of the world have societies that are far from totally cohesive. While most countries do not evidence the violent divisions that have occurred in the former Congo or in Pakistan within recent memory, there still are substantial minorities in most nations in the world, whether of a racial, cultural or geographical nature. The cohesiveness of a society is not just measured in terms of minorities, however. It is also measured in regard to the satisfaction level of a people, the incentive they may have to change, and their desire to do so. If a substantial majority of people are determined to change, it becomes relatively easy for the leaders of a society to move forward in development matters. On the other hand, if the satisfaction level is high or, perhaps more properly put, if the dissatisfaction level is low, there may be little reward in leading a development programme. If a country or a polity is united in its dissatisfaction or satisfaction levels, one kind of development strategy can be pursued. If a country is substantially disunited in this respect, quite a different strategy or series of strategies may be developed. For example, political leaders may decide to move ahead with changes in that part of a country that has a high level of dissatisfaction. However, if dissatisfaction is centred in a political minority and not in part of the cluster that constitutes the base of power of those who have political leadership, the dissatisfaction may be ignored. But variations in the cohesive character of various societies are highly related to development results, and cannot be ignored.

It would be impossible to list environmental factors without speaking of a fourth variable, the bio-physical and population resources of countries. Certain areas are highly endowed with a valuable bio-physical base. Other regions are essentially deserts and have little to support life. Some countries have resources that are easily subject to exploitation and development, while others have resources that can be developed only with great pain and slowly, over a period of time. Perhaps the most critical element of all is the population/resource ratio. We are on the limited spaceship, planet earth. Those countries that do not have a well-thought-out population programme are like ostriches with heads in the sand. Indeed, in the long run, if national barriers remain as rigid as they are today, perhaps the population/resource ratio is as critical a variable in the ultimate development of a country as any. Science can change both parts of this ratio. But there are limits to that change both in regard to population and in regard to bio-physical resources. Environmental imperatives cannot be ignored.

Next summer (1972) there will be a conference on the environment in Stockholm. This conference symbolises the worldwide concern with the bio-physical aspects of the environment. It also dramatises a fifth element or variable of the environment: the relative state of depletion and pollution of natural resources in each country, and the rate of replenishing such resources.

There is a division in the world over the importance of bio-physical environmental control. In the less developed countries, it is frequently said that environmental control is primarily a problem of developed countries. It is argued that environmental concern is a plot on the part of the 'haves' against the 'have nots'. It is argued that it is presumptuous for developed countries to be prescriptive in these matters, since they obviously did not worry about the environment in the course of their own development. Some of these assertions are valid, or partially valid. But unfortunately for all countries of the world, the large blue ball is at a critical point in its existence. The less developed countries of the world are looking towards improving their lot at a time when there is a tremendous pressure of population worldwide, and a critical deterioration of the quality of the bio-physical environment. The depletion of soils, forests and other resources is appalling, even in some African countries. The minimising of pollution, the replenishing of resources and the husbanding of the entire bio-physical aspects of the earth is an essential element to every development plan as we approach the twenty-first century.

CONCLUSION

Reviewing the goals, strategies and environment of development, one is struck by the fact that development is directly and intimately associated with the highest political decisions of governments at all levels. It is not something that can be the monopoly of planning commissions or planning specialists. They are essential, and they perform useful tasks. But others are basically responsible for the selection of development goals and the selection of development strategies.

It is to political leadership that we must look. It is the political leaders at the Cabinet and legislative levels that must sense the necessity of moving ahead towards development goals. They must understand the nature of the country they represent. They must see the pitfalls as well as the opportunities of social change.

Development is based upon the assumption that man can control his own destiny. It is specifically not based upon a deterministic view of the social order. Still, there are substantial environmental conditions which intervene to make the attainment of any set of goals difficult.

But perhaps that is the challenge and the attractiveness of development. It is different for each government and each organisation. It is different for each set of leaders and each set of peoples. Ultimately, development is the manner in which man seeks his identity in concert with other human beings. It is the essence of the goal of man in society.

NOTES

1. Edward W. Weidner (ed.), *Development Administration in Asia* (Durham, N.C.: Duke Univ. Press, 1970) pp. 5–9.
2. Ibid.

Basic Concepts and Goals of Development: An Integral View

MICHAEL H. H. LOUW

1. INTRODUCTION

The era of development as a universal philosophy and as a vast national and international modern enterprise is essentially a post-war phenomenon. It is based on the confluence of two important new ideas: first, the concept of development planning as a means of consciously and rationally using the resources of a nation towards the attainment of specific objectives and bringing about development at a faster pace than that which an entirely free market economy would have produced. This idea, although it had previously existed as part of the general socialistic ideology, really acquired respectability and acceptance, even by non-socialist governments, during the post-war years of reconstruction in Europe. This period demonstrated in concrete terms, to the whole world, how effective the planned reconstruction of the damaged national economies of the countries which had been involved in the war could be.

The second idea, which is linked with the first, derives from the assumption that because a damaged or backward economy lacks at a critical moment the resources to give substance and content to its development, it should be assisted at the initial stage by loans, grants and such material resources as might be needed, from foreign sources. Again, the effective use of foreign aid for the miraculously fast reconstruction of the economies of the European countries convinced many people of the feasibility and desirability of foreign development assistance. By 1950 foreign aid policies had been initiated by the United States and by the United Nations, the latter gradually shifting its major budgetary resources towards multilateral international aid (at present 80 per cent), exemplified in the Development Decade of the 1960s and the Second Development Decade (D.D.2) of the 1970s. But the logic of foreign aid required the recipient country to prepare its own house to receive and absorb it, and this meant the systematic planning of its own economy and resource use, within which foreign aid would have an appropriate place.

It has become clear that in the international world of today, with the relative stagnation of a power-based pattern of international interaction, foreign aid for the development of countries which need and demand it has become an important new element in inter-state and international diplomacy, in which practically all states of the world participate in some form or another, either as donors or as recipients or, in many cases, as both. On the national level, development, i.e. a broad policy of raising the levels of living of a people, has become the prevalent answer to the 'revolution of rising expectations'. Thinking and action on these two levels have given rise to a vast new literature on theories and practices, which confirms the salience of development and aid as themes in modern political studies. It is noticeable, however, and perhaps understandable, that most studies deal with rather specific topics, areas or sectors, for example, economic development or educational planning or political modernisation, although there are obvious links between them. What is probably equally important is an overarching, integrative concept to link all the parts and strands of development, because it takes place in reality as an interrelated and dynamic process. It is the purpose of this paper to explore this area of integrative or holistic thinking on development, and the ways in which economic, social and political development are interrelated. It is intended to provide the policy-maker with a total, inclusive, conceptual framework to assist him on the policy level, in linking development ideas, proposals and demands, and, on the operational level, to relate, co-ordinate and evaluate specific agencies, sequences and activities.

One approach to the problem is the idea of a non-ideological 'science of development', exemplified by the viewpoint of Anderson, von der Mehden and Young, namely, that development is interdisciplinary in character, with the major relevant disciplines being economics, sociology and political science.[1] Development, according to them, could thus be studied comparatively in the economic, social and political spheres, although they concentrated on the political sector, in which they clarified three major problem areas: nation-building in the context of cultural pluralism, sustained domestic violence, and the widespread ideologies of revolution and socialism.[2] Finkle and Gable view 'society as a "master" social system made up of political, economic, religious and other subsystems', and modernisation as 'the multiple and interrelated transformations in all of the systems by which man organises his life and society'.[3] With such an inter-disciplinary and comparative approach, the interrelationships between action in the three sectors could be identified. Another widely used approach is the dynamic method of describing and comparing a generalised picture of an underdeveloped national condition (A) with a developed one (B) and seeing development as the process of moving from A to B, in many sectors and with many interrelationships, which can also be studied in interdisciplinary and in macro- and micro-terms. Often representative examples or models of real countries of the A and B types are used to identify the actual factors which caused development or, to complete the picture, decay or stagnation. A third idea is that of a 'global partnership'[4] which emphasises that in modern times nations and their development are mutually interdependent and that development as such has become a shared experience. The Pearson Report notes that in a 'village world we belong to a world community' and that the help given by rich to poor nations rests on a moral imperative: 'that it is only right for those who have to share with those who have not'.[5] The contemporary consensus may be said to view development as an interrelated process taking place on both national and international levels.

Being a process, development should also be seen in terms of time or sequences or phases. Many writers have tried to identify causes or stimuli of development and the socio-economic-political changes which they bring about, and have thus arrived at a generalised identification of phases. A well-known example is that of Rostow who identifies the following stages: the traditional society, the preconditions for 'take-off', the 'take-off', and finally sustained economic progress (the latter consisting of the drive to maturity and the age of high mass-consumption).[6] Among other phase interpretations are those based on the ratios of agricultural to industrial workers, on the substitution of traditional with modern institutions, levels of literacy and training, etc. In using these dynamic models one is then led to the next logical step, namely, what can and must be done to accelerate the process (this is, of course, assuming that acceleration is desirable). What are the key factors to stimulate necessary change and what are the investments which will have the largest and widest 'multiplier' effect?

Some preliminary generalisations may be made at this point: first, development is a complex process involving action in the economic, social and political spheres, all of which are autonomous in certain ways yet interdependent; second, the political system plays a decisive role in authoritatively determining the objectives of development, the allocation of resources and priorities in time; and third, development has become the concern also of the international community for humanitarian, political and practical reasons.

Today, after more than three decades of planned and internationally assisted development, a great deal of experience has been gained and it is perhaps appropriate to analyse this experience in terms of objectives, failures, achievements and the tasks ahead – in brief, to take stock of the development situation. It might be helpful to examine the essential nature of accelerated development in both theory and practice and its significance within the international context. These will be linked to the philosophy, implications and assumptions of development, the sectors for development, the international and Southern African contexts, the phases and types of development aid and the roles played by international, national, regional and private organisations. Finally, development action will be dealt with in its three essential stages of politicisation, legitimation and operationalisation.

2. SOME IMPLICATIONS OF DEVELOPMENT

(a) ASSUMPTIONS

The wide acceptance of development (or modernisation, to use the contemporary term) as a significant modern form of social change rests on a number of assumptions. These are, briefly: first, that much in the same manner as man has learnt to control and use his physical environment, we believe that he can also influence social and economic conditions in certain desired directions, namely, towards the attainment of higher levels of living, greater participation in government, etc. Second, and deriving from the former, we assume that we have adequate knowledge and criteria to identify and measure conditions of underdevelopment, stagnation and decay, and of the techniques, methods, sequences and strategies to direct development along desired channels, as well as to accelerate such development to reach a faster rate of social change than would otherwise have been the case. Third, we assume that development is not a mere mechanical or institutional process, but that it is related to values, at both the levels of objectives as well as of methods and operations, and that such values are and must be articulated at various stages and in appropriate manner by the major participants in the development process. Fourth, we assume that development, once initiated from a static point, goes through various phases and eventually becomes a self-sustaining and continuous process. It may cause disturbing and often unpleasant social changes and lead to higher levels of living but perhaps also to new and undesirable social conditions which require other social techniques for their solution, for example, overpopulation resulting from successful health measures and pollution of the environment resulting from industrialisation. Development is thus a nonterminal process which poses problems (albeit of a different order) even for highly developed countries. Fifth, there is today a shared belief among many nations that development is the major technique for preventing social and political unrest, raising the levels of living of impoverished peoples, and generally ensuring the basis of a stable and peaceful world order. Dag Hammarskjöld, for example, considered the economic development activities of the United Nations as essential to 'building the kind of world community in which . . . [political and military] crises will no longer be inevitable'.[7]

These basic assumptions and philosophies underlying the concept of development are important, because they are infused with values and beliefs, as well as concerned with the mechanics and strategies of the development process. They thus constitute the bases on which political debate about objectives, priorities and the use of resources takes place within national and international councils and on which decisions for development operations are made. In most cases this politicisation phase, i.e. debate and decision between alternatives and the search for consensus, is by far the most important one in the pattern of development action. By comparison, the other phases of legitimation and operationalisation of development involve fairly clear-cut and technical decisions.

(b) THE DEVELOPMENT SITUATION

The obvious point at which to start is to determine the condition of underdevelopment, or the traditional society, and identify its features, i.e. of what may be called situation A. If situation B is then assumed to be the condition of self-sustaining development, the task and challenge for the development enterprise is to effect those changes in the society to span, in terms of time and substance, the difference between A and B. This is an essential preliminary exercise for the policy-maker so that he would know the dimensions of his task. But of equal importance is also to be able to visualise the intermediate stages between A and B which may be called C, D and E. This concept of stages, which may be applied to sectors or programmes, is a useful one because it requires an evaluation of the progress of development at various points in time and a determination of whether the condition reached shows advance, a static situation, or a retrogressive or decaying situation. It should be remembered that the development process is complex, disruptive, often discontinuous and should be consciously managed.

The M.I.T. Study Group described the basic features of the traditional society as follows: it had a limited knowledge and was thus unable to generate a regular flow of inventions and innovations to adapt to new circumstances, agriculture had a preponderant role, a fatalism prevailed and the status of people remained at a static level.[8] The Pearson Report characterised underdevelopment as 'low levels of technology, high illiteracy rates, low savings ratios, high birth rates, inefficient public administration, political instability' – a vicious circle from which only a 'fortunate few might hope to escape'. It also pointed out that the approximately 100 less developed countries of the world were poor in money income but immensely diverse in culture, economic condition and social and political structure. Although the record of two decades of development is encouraging, it points out a number of new problems ahead: government structure should be reformed and made more adaptive to new conditions, the 'population dilemma' must be resolved, solutions must be found for unemployment and urbanisation problems, agriculture, nutrition, industry, research and development, education, foreign exchange (including the large burden of a foreign debt service) and the role of the private sector.[9]

On the operational level, the diagnostic task of identifying and measuring the condition of underdevelopment in a particular country would normally fall on the national planning agency, which is generally the only institution with a macro-approach to development. Its task is also to propose, on the basis of the evaluation of progress at various points in time, such new policies and strategies for real progress as may be necessary; it should be remembered that, prior to point B, the development process is, by definition, not yet self-sustaining or self-corrective.

(c) ROLES IN DEVELOPMENT

A number of important requirements for development, both explicit and implicit, may be noted. The condition for development should, first, be reasonably orderly and consistent to ensure that decisions which are made by government and by groups and individuals are not distorted by violence and uncertainty. Second, development is linked to a philosophy and an ultimate set of values and therefore the purposes to which it is linked have to be articulated. Third, people must be activated in collective action by leaders and innovators who articulate the objectives and strategies of development. The various roles played by ideas, people and institutions may be briefly noted.

In the realm of ideas, ideologies are perhaps most important today. An ideology provides an interpretation of history and of reality, a vision of the future and, in some cases, a strategy and a justification for violence and authoritarian government. Even if some ideologies, for example, Marxism-Leninism, which purport to be universal, are applied in a particular country, they also include, as most national ideologies do, features of the unique local situation and traditions, and for this reason they may provide a unifying idea to unite tribes or groups into a larger nation. The exponents (and often creators) of a national ideology are generally the intellectuals, political parties and political leaders, and their role in engendering a national consciousness, purposefulness, unity, and an élan for development action for a greater future, is crucial.

The intellectual has a unique role in this regard; he must offer philosophy of development with two major ingredients, in varying proportion or, if necessary, choices: first, a realistic position, which would accept slow and incremental improvements within the existing but evolving order, and second, a utopian position, which requires that the existing order be destroyed by violence and substituted with a new and more perfect one. He should also, as suggested by Mary Matossian, who calls him an 'assaulted intellectual', face the destruction of the traditional institutions and values of his people and the challenge of the modern West; he should also orient himself in three directions or relationships, i.e. to the West, to his people's past and to the masses of his people.[10] On this point Torres shows how, for example, the Western idea of democracy becomes something completely different when it becomes 'guided democracy' in some authoritarian non-Western states.[11] This also applies to socialism in some African states, which comes out as a programme for building a kind of welfare state. Anderson, von der Mehden and Young, for example, report that 'Above all, the faith in socialist techniques of transformation represents an almost supernatural persuasion of the capability of the state and its human armature, the public service, to order and control the economy', and point out how personal some interpretations of this idea and its other variant, 'developmental socialism', are.[12]

Related to ideology is the function of élites, which may be assumed to exist inevitably in every state and provide leadership in its various sectors. A most important function of élites is to provide the infrastructure for the top-level élite, namely, the governing élite. The governing élite in a developing state may be said to be committed to three major goals: maintaining its own regime, nation-building and socio-economic progress. This élite functions through individuals in various key positions who provide the policies, strategies, technical knowledge and decisions on the development process and its adjustments. According to Esman, governing élites '(*a*) set the goals and criteria of public policy, (*b*) initiate and supervise the execution of programmes contributing to nation-building and socio-economic development goals, (*c*) stimulate individual and group initiative and activity in the society, and (*d*) discipline competing claims on the political system according to developmental criteria fixed by the regime.'[13] The 'other élites' are generally supportive: the intellectual élite, for example, provides the governing élite with ideas, philosophies, policies and strategies; the professional élite with technical advice, insights and guidance on specific problems; the military élite with the monopoly of force to ensure the maintenance of the regime and public order (of course, in many cases where the military élite has taken over the reins of government it has itself become a modernising agent); the bureaucratic élite with policy advice and managerial skills for the implementation of development measures; and the party élites serve to make masses of people politically aware, to organise them into broad consensus groups, to aggregate and articulate demands and supports and to provide a leadership cadre from which leaders for government may be recruited.

Finally, government itself has perhaps the most crucial task of all in the sense that, as the overarching institution and with final authority over all other forms of activity, it has the two basic functions of making development possible: first, maintaining the condition of stability and the essential services for the orderly progression of development measures. (This is, of course, assuming that revolution, because of its tremendous human and material costs and the fact that it would also, as laboriously as the system it destroyed, have to build up a new governmental apparatus to handle its development measures, is rejected as a condition for development.) Second, it must initiate, provide the thrust, which includes a myriad decisions on the C-D-E continuum, and resources for the development process; it also bears the ultimate responsibility for the attainment of development objectives. Although the functions of government in development are residual and therefore endless, a few may be mentioned: measures for obtaining capital through domestic savings, foreign loans and grants, the procedures for allocating investment and other resources, the provision of an adequate infrastructure on the basis of which other investment (private or foreign) will be attracted, state ownership of basic industries such as communications, power, transport and steel, regulatory devices, controls and incentives to channel economic and social behaviour by individuals and groups in certain directions, etc.

The major specialised instrument of government (apart from its traditional functions of law, order and basic services) for development is the planning agency. Depending on its basic political philosophy, a state can have systems of *minimal planning*, i.e. dominance of the market economy under a few mild incentives and controls; *indicative planning*, i.e. getting voluntary co-operation from major sectoral groups towards defined targets; and *mandatory or command planning*, i.e. setting targets and conditions and allocating resources for the whole economy, requiring full conformity from all citizens. Within these types planning can be *sectoral or partial*, i.e. limited to a sector, commodity, region or activity, or *aggregative*, i.e. inclusive, overall and integrated into a national plan. The major functions of a planning agency are to evaluate an existing situation in relation to stated objectives and determine the time, sequences, resources, instruments and new strategies needed to attain them, and to establish targets in specific activities, usually in quantifiable terms. In recent years the complexities of this area of action have led to the concept of 'planning the planning'; a significant result of this idea was the introduction of evaluation procedures for policy review at certain stages of implementation, for example, the Nine Wise Men under the Alliance for Progress, and evaluation exercises of the U.N. Programmes.

3. THE MAJOR AREAS OF DEVELOPMENT

Development in any area or sector within a political society cannot be autonomous; it is dependent in direct and in complex ways on commensurate development in other areas. Finkle and Gable think that 'The multiple and interrelated transformations in all of the systems by which man organises his life and society constitute the general process of modernisation'.[14] Schumpeter indicated that 'economic development is not a phenomenon to be explained economically, . . . [but] is dragged along by the changes in the surrounding world'.[15] To mention some obvious examples: economic growth is dependent on social change involving a change in attitudes, habits and values conducive, for example, to saving, impersonal relations, achievement criteria, etc., and, of course, on adequate numbers of educated and trained personnel. Myint draws attention to the current opinion that

education was one of the 'residual' factors or qualitative
ments which accounted for economic growth.[16] Social
ment again depends on adequate resources for invest
human capital. Political development depends on reso
many essential social services and an educated and motivated
citizenry to participate in the tasks of government, which include
the provision of the conditions and resources for economic growth
and of the choices on directions of social change.

(a) ECONOMIC DEVELOPMENT

In technical terms, economic development refers to the growth
of output per capita and involves, according to Smelser: in technology, the change from simple, traditional technology to a
science-based one; in agriculture, a change from subsistence
farming to commercial production; in industry, a transition from
human and animal power to machine power; and in ecology, a
movement from rural areas to urban centres.[17]

In more general terms, the concept of economic development
means raising the levels of living of a people or peoples who are
at present living inadequate lives, through increasingly greater
investment in selected multiplier factors which will bring about
self-sustaining economic growth in their countries. The key
element is at present considered to be industrialisation, for which
the concomitant developments are the provision of infrastructure,
investment capital and policies, financial institutions and basic
government services such as public order and a legal framework.
As the economies of most less developed countries are based on
agriculture, action in this sector is considered to be the crucial
and initiating factor to set the whole development process going.
Effective action in the field of agriculture (to provide savings
and free workers for employment elsewhere) normally involves
reform of land tenure, modernisation of technology (fertilisers,
improved seed strains, machinery, etc.), the provision of credit,
marketing arrangements, etc. Recent thinking emphasises as a
further development a strategy of agro-industrial enterprises, including beneficiation, to facilitate exports and thus earn foreign
exchange with which, in turn, industrialisation could be financed.

(b) SOCIAL DEVELOPMENT

Social development involves changes in the values, attitudes, habits and institutions of traditional societies and their evolution towards more modern forms which would be appropriate for the new way of life implied in development. For example, loyalties shift from the smaller unit or group such as the tribe to the larger inclusive unit of the nation; ascription is replaced by achievement as a criterion of income or status; the solution of problems through magic or mystical methods is replaced by scientific, pragmatic procedures. This also involves significant changes in values and therefore in motivations and responses. According to Ward, the problem of leadership in this context is 'to devise conditions and motivations which will both liberate and focus an appropriate amount of popular energy, initiative and resources and at the same time minimise dysfunctional behaviour on the part of all significant elements in the population'.[18]

The major change agent which a modernising government would employ is education, beginning with the eradication of illiteracy, the provision of education on the primary, secondary and university levels and branching out to technical training, scientific research, the provisions of mass comunications, easy travel, community development, adult education, etc. The educational task is a vast one and therefore the modern approach to it is through educational planning, which lays the groundwork for a national education policy.

The other important developments in the social sector are: the provision of health services, housing, cultural amenities, a change in the status of women, protection of children, the regulation of labour and improved status for workers, human rights, etc. The most significant social measures of a negative kind, i.e. against trends which may nullify the results of development, are: the limitation of population growth and the control of narcotic drugs.

(c) POLITICAL DEVELOPMENT

It is noteworthy that in the vast literature on development, preponderant attention has been given to political development. The general fascination with this topic is probably due to the fact that whereas development in the other areas can be and is being planned, in the political field it cannot be planned. In fact, it is government which provides the authoritative planning and control for the economic and social fields, and thus becomes the ultimate source and measure for development; it thus suggests the 'primacy of politics' and the autonomous nature of the political system.

In this section we shall try to identify the dynamics of political change and of government, especially in regard to development, and then examine its development in terms of politicisation, government structures and administration.

The political system, according to Almond, is the 'legitimate, order-maintaining or transforming system in the society', and he sees political development as the acquisition of 'a new capability, in the sense of a specialised role structure and differentiated orientations, which together give a political system the possibility of responding efficiently, and more or less autonomously, to a new range of problems'.[19] Diamant thinks that although the political system also undergoes transformation, it is autonomous and independent of economic, social or other forms of change, and 'becomes the generalised problem-solver for the entire society'. Political development is a 'process by which a political system acquires an increased capacity to sustain, successfully and continuously, new types of goals and demands and the creation of new types of organisations'.[20] To Huntington, political development is 'institutionalisation of political organisations and procedures'.[21]

The consensus among most observers (except those with a strong deterministic bent) is that the political system, being autonomous, is the decisive role-player in the transformation and development process. To do this it has to undergo change itself, so as to become more effective to perform many inevitable and essential new functions produced by the development process. If government is to initiate and carry the burden of modernisation, it must itself undergo modernisation.

This change generally involves the following developments: first, an increased centralisation of power and integration of potentially disruptive elements such as groups, tribes or regions and the creation of appropriate institutions to embody this unity; second, the differentiation and specialisation of political institutions; third, increased participation by people and groups in the governmental processes; and fourth, the spontaneous formation of interest clusters and parties at the periphery of government, to articulate demands and supports to the system. To illustrate these aspects, the major elements of the political system are briefly discussed, namely, politicisation, governmental structure and public administration.

Politicisation is based on political awareness and includes political action in the identification of problems and issues, dialogue, and the organisation of groups and pressures to give effect to consensus on their solutions. People in traditional societies would therefore have to change from an attitude of political apathy to an awareness of issues and realities, as well as a perception of their own role in political and governmental processes; they would also have to include, in addition to a particularistic local, tribal or sectional interest, an interest in national issues. They would also have to accept the normal conditions typical of a democracy: pluralism, competitiveness, and the search for and uses of power. To develop such perceptions of citizenship, they would have to be convinced that reasonable conditions of liberty and equality exist so as to make their participation meaningful and satisfying. This perception should be extended to include the subtleties of democratic government, with its demands for constructive, tolerant and responsive political styles on the part of the participants. An interesting question here is whether one can train or guide political leaders to become 'democratic' politicians, or whether political training will always remain a matter of unstructured exposures and self-training through experience and perception.

A major problem confronting many of the new nations is the *integration* into a new, larger and whole polity of many different ethnic groups and tribes which have had long and proud histories of their own. Geertz points out how the conflict between 'primordial sentiments and civic politics', i.e. basic identification with 'the gross actualities of blood, race, language, locality, religion or tradition', brings about serious tensions in many new states, and that psychological identification with the larger national entity has not yet substituted parochial identifications.[22] Nation-building has therefore become a major preoccupation of many new states. Verba noted that 'the development of a clear and unambiguous sense of identity is more than a facilitating factor in the creation of a nation; it may be in some sense the major constituting factor of a new nation'.[23]

Weiner proposes five types of integration: *national integration* (in which, e.g., two strategies, that of assimilation or of 'unity-in-diversity', may be used); *territorial integration; value integration* (at least accepted procedures for the resolution of conflict); *élite–mass integration* (a closer bond between government and governed); and finally, *integrative behaviour* (habits and the capacity for political organisation).[24]

The major solutions in national integration probably lie in two areas: the psychological–cultural and the constitutional. Constitutional provisions should be flexible enough to provide, at the earlier stages of political evolution, a federal structure within which particularistic regional and ethnic groups can have a meaningful existence while developing a new loyalty to the national state. As the polity evolves, the values and priority of the latter can be emphasised, especially through a creed of nationalism, and through meaningful participation of all groups in the national government. But it should be expected that the psychological changes will involve a long period of persuasion and education.

Government structures must be appropriate and adequate to translate the demands and alternatives produced through the politicisation process into consensuses, strategies and legitimations. They should establish the basic conditions for development but also be flexible and adaptable. Spengler suggests a representative list of functions of government necessary for development: maintaining law and order and security, supporting education and public health, supporting scientific research, providing basic forms of overhead capital (for example a labour force), providing monetary controls and credit, controlling inflation, establishing financial institutions, stimulating attitudes favourable to development, influencing the uses of resources, influencing income distribution, levying taxes to encourage private capital formation, establishing an effective legal and administrative structure and establishing institutions for private and public initiative.[25] Various other lists have also been suggested; the crux of their general message would seem to be that government is the guarantor, initiator, activator and manager of development and carries an implicit and residual accountability towards its citizens to attain its objectives.

Government structures comprise two major types: first, those of the central government cluster, i.e. the chief of state, the legislature and the executive or cabinet; and second, those of the myriad operational and functional government agencies, i.e. the ministries, departments, agencies, bureaux, boards, commissions and corporations. The development process requires here a clear definition and differentiation of tasks, for example, for the authorisation of development measures, the allocation of resources, management and supervision of development, etc., for each of which designated authorities should be responsible.

The *administrative apparatus* of government plays a key role in the development process, because its many agencies and offices fulfil the technical and operational functions of development. They operate, on the one hand, on directives, authorisations and resources provided by the legislature and cabinet, and on the other, on their own interpretations and perceptions of their respective missions in the development process. In the relatively uncharted field of development, it often happens that certain functions may be neglected because no agency will accept them, while others may be duplicated by various agencies. This makes it essential to have adequate co-ordination arrangements between the agencies (either at cabinet level or through mandatory clearance procedures) which are directly concerned with carrying out development measures.

Administrative modernisation would generally involve the institutionalisation of functions through the creation of new agencies with new functions and their proper placement in the overall administrative apparatus so as to ensure differentiation and co-ordination. It also requires the necessary adaptation to changing conditions involving administrative reform and structural modifications, the expanded training of personnel, especially at the middle and the higher managerial levels, the adoption of modern techniques such as office mechanisation, programming methods, etc.

An interesting new focus of attention in this area is the rise of 'development administration', exemplified by a number of recent publications. Among these, a series of papers produced as various volumes, under the Comparative Administration Group of the American Society of Public Administration, have focused specifically on the administration of development, which some authors distinguish, not always very clearly, from development administration, although the close relationship between the two is generally acknowledged.[26] Katz, for example, defines develop ment administration as the way the government acts to fulfil its dominant role in the development process and is involved in the 'mobilisation of resources and their allocation to a great variety of development activities on a massive scale', and in this task its distinguishing feature is that it is innovative.[27] The task involves four administrative functions: decision-making, specification, communication and control; and it deals with development action which consists of six 'inputs': manpower, finances, logistics, information, participation and legitimate power.[28]

The distinction between public administration and development administration may be clarified: while the former is concerned with the normal provision of order, justice, basic services and welfare on a repetitive and routine basis, the latter, because it is bound by a time-span, specific targets and programmes *apart* from the normal public administrative activities of a state, fulfils an *ad hoc* function, which may not be repeated once the targets are attained. Development administration is therefore not only innovative, but also accelerative, i.e. to compress the time-spans in 'natural maturation'.

4. DEVELOPMENT AND INTERNATIONAL AID

It has become accepted doctrine today in national and international councils that if the less developed countries were to depend on their own resources for development they would find the task difficult if not impossible; in any case, accelerated development, without outside help, would be feasible and desirable in most cases. The obvious answer is international aid, which most developed countries are giving in various forms (bilateral, multilateral, private investment) to the total amount of about $12·8 billion, from non-communist countries alone, in 1968. Not only have they generally accepted this moral obligation, but they are being pressed by the L.D.C.s (especially through UNCTAD) to make a firm commitment to set aside 1 per cent of their G.N.P., preferably for multilateral rather than bilateral assistance. The stage is therefore set for an increase in the interest in aids if not in the volume of aid, during D.D.2.

Apart from military aid (which will be excluded in this paper), such aid falls into two broad categories: investment aid in the form of loans and grants, and technical assistance. Under bilateral aid programmes (which accounted for about 90 per cent of the flow of resources to L.D.C.s in 1967), the type of aid can vary a great deal and is based on the unique pattern of relationships between donor and recipient. Multilateral aid is differentiated as follows: investment aid is provided by the World Bank Group (sometimes by consortia of nations), and technical assistance by the U.N. and its Specialised Agencies under co-operative arrangements with the U.N. Development Programme, concentrating on pre-investment aid in the form of surveys and training. In recent years a new element, namely 'trade not aid', has been introduced by the L.D.C.s, who point out that they would be better able to finance their own development if they could have access on favourable terms to the markets of the developed countries for their products; this, if granted on a large scale, would in effect mean a third type of aid.

The special position of the United Nations as a multilateral aid organisation (and of a donor country in a bilateral relationship) is that it does not participate in the internal decision-making on development of a recipient country. But, on the other hand, its aid cannot be just a hand-out: it would naturally be interested to know, and sometimes advise on, how its aid funds are to be spent; this means that some link must be established between donor and recipient country. The key here is the development programme of the recipient country itself, in which the projects for which foreign aid from various sources is being requested are indicated in a clear functional relationship to the total development plan, thus bringing the international policy-makers to an integral view, shared with the national policy-makers, of the development of the recipient country. But these international policy-makers have, in addition, another integral view of development, which is the overall co-ordination of the aid-giving function, both on the policy level as well as on the operational level, between the various functionally diverse Specialised Agencies. The Jackson Report emphasises the importance of integrated action through a 'unified country approach' and through its proposal for a 'U.N. Development Co-operation Cycle' which gathers together in one comprehensive and integrated pattern all the interdependent processes which together constitute the development co-operation activities of the U.N. development system.[29] Habits of integrative thinking among policy-makers are thus an essential requirement for the development process.

5. THE DEVELOPMENT SITUATION IN SOUTHERN AFRICA

The Southern African region comprises nine political entities with different types of political status and political attitudes. Some of them have formulated development plans and receive foreign aid from various sources which is vastly inadequate to give a strong impetus to their development. There are also certain complementarities in the region, such as in the fields of labour, capital, technology, water resources, transport and trade, which can provide a basis for a pattern of closer co-operation on development aid, in which South Africa, with its preponderant resources of capital and skills and its industrial base, can play an important and constructive role. It could begin with a Southern African Development Co-operation Programme and for external advice and co-operation link-up with the Development Assistance Committee (D.A.C.) of the O.E.C.D. What is needed at the present stage is, first of all, a development philosophy, which will make sense for the region and be understood by its peoples, and to which the government is fully committed; second, an overall aid policy, based on constructive political assumptions (e.g. non-interference, peace and stability) and directed towards clear objectives; third, the establishment of operating instruments, for example, an Advisory Council on External Aid, an executive organisation, and procedures and policies for processing capital and technical aid and for regular evaluation, review and adjustment.

This task will require an overall and integrated approach which would involve many government departments, universities and research organisations.

6. THE INTEGRAL VIEW AND POLICY-MAKING

The need for integrative habits of thinking by the policy-maker in development derives from his rather unique task. First, he must cast the rationale for development in understandable and communicable terms, for example a document in which will be indicated objectives, policies, targets, etc. Second, he must get official approval, support and co-operation (from private as well as government organisations), and resources, for achieving the stated objectives. Third, on the operational level, he should have a strategy for the implementation including timing and sequences) of programmes, their sustained management and the necessary evaluation (comparing input and output elements), and adjustment, at appropriate points in time. Asher sees modernisation as involving 'a top-to-bottom transformation of society' and as 'at best . . . an erratic, two-step-forward, one-step-backward, one-step-sideways, movement'.[30]

The advantages of an integrated approach lie in the fact that, first, it provides a macro-approach within which the micro-elements can be seen in proper perspective (they may be sequential, constitutive, dependent, dominant or subservient, of high or low priority, etc.), which makes it necessary to look for crucial linkages which might affect development in various ways, for example, how stability may affect investment, or training productivity, etc. Second, because it is complete and includes all components of the development situation, it provides a more accurate basis for balanced programmes of development as against possible distortions resulting from a partial and therefore possibly biased point of view. Third, it provides flexibility for necessary strategic innovations, and adjustments, to attain what Katz calls 'a feedback equilibrium',[31] which is, of course, essential in the highly dynamic, often changing, and disrupted situation of development.

It is the capacity for integrative thinking which it is important to inculcate in our policy-makers on development today. Their agenda seems to increase all the time; for example, the U.N. development philosophy went through various stages and emphasised in each what was thought to be the key element in the development complex: first, all faith was centred on the economist's model of investment as the key to stimulate development activity; then on the transfer of techniques; then on the improvement of human resources and institution-building; then science and technology; then on community development (for grass-roots training in self-help and democracy); then on national planning; and, today, on the major issue of bridging the trade and exchange gap between rich and poor nations. The policy-maker should be prepared for these shifts in focus and salience, and this he can do through developing his own conceptual framework so as to include, and relate meaningfully within it, new facts and insights of the development process.

NOTES

1. Charles W. Anderson, Fred R. von der Mehden and Crawford Young, *Issues of Political Development* (Englewood Cliffs, N.J.: Prentice-Hall, 1967) p. 3.
2. Ibid., p. 9.
3. Jason L. Finkle and Richard W. Gable (eds), *Political Development and Social Change* (New York: Wiley, 1968) p. v.
4. See Max F. Millikan, 'An Introductory Essay', in Richard N. Gardner and Max F. Millikan, *The Global Partnership: International Agencies and Economic Development* (New York: Praeger, 1968).
5. Report of the Commission on International Development (Chairman: Lester B. Pearson), *Partners in Development* (London: Pall Mall Press, 1969) p. 8.
6. Quoted and explained in Finkle and Gable, op. cit., pp. 233–53.
7. Wilder Foote (ed.), *Servant of Peace: A Selection of the Speeches and Statements of Dag Hammerskjöld* (New York: Harper & Row, 1962) pp. 306–7.
8. MIT Study Group, 'The Transitional Process', in Claude E. Welch, *Political Modernisation* (Belmont, Calif.: Wadsworth, 1967) pp. 22–3.
9. Pearson Report, pp. 53–79.
10. Mary Matossian, 'Ideologies of Delayed Industrialisation: Some Tensions and Ambiguities', in Welsh, op. cit., p. 323.
11. J. A. Torres, 'The Political Ideology of Guided Democracy', in Welch, op. cit., pp. 346–63.
12. Anderson *et al*, op. cit., pp. 199 ff., 207 ff. See also p. 231 for an interesting typology of socialist systems.
13. Milton J. Esman, 'The Politics of Development Administration', in John D. Montgomery and William J. Siffin, *Approaches to Development: Politics, Administration and Change* (New York: McGraw-Hill, 1966) p. 108.
14. Finkle and Gable, op. cit., p. v.
15. Joseph A. Schumpeter, *The Theory of Economic Development* (New York: Oxford Univ. Press., 1961) p. 63.
16. H. Myint, *Economic Theory and the Underdeveloped Countries* (New York: Oxford Univ. Press., 1971) pp. 205 ff.
17. Neil J. Smelser, 'Mechanisms of Change and Adjustments to Change', in Finkle and Gable, op. cit., pp. 28–9.
18. Roy E. Ward, 'Political Modernisation and Politic Culture in Japan', in Welch, op. cit., p. 93.

19. Gabriel Almond, 'A Functional Approach to Comparative Politics', in Gabriel Almond and James S. Coleman (eds), *The Politics of the Developing Areas* (Princeton Univ. Press, 1960) p. 7; also 'A Developmental Approach to Political Systems', *World Politics*, XVII (1965) 183–214.

20. Alfred Diamant, 'The Nature of Political Development', in Finkle and Gable, op. cit., pp. 91–2.

21. Samuel P. Huntington, 'Political Development and Political Decay', in Welch, op. cit., p. 214.

22. Clifford Geertz, 'The Integrative Revolution: Primordal Sentiments and Civic Politics in the New States', in Welch, op. cit., pp. 167–88.

23. Sidney Verba, in Lucien W. Pye and Sidney Verba (eds), *Political Culture and Political Development* (Princeton Univ. Press, 1965) p. 530.

24. Myron Weiner, 'Political Integration and Political Development', in Welch, op. cit., pp. 150–66.

25. J. J. Spengler, 'Economic Development: Political Preconditions and Political Consequences', in Finkle and Gable, op. cit., pp. 261–2. Another extensive list is suggested by Milton J. Esman, in Montgomery and Siffin, op. cit., pp. 60–5.

26. Fred. W. Riggs (ed.), *Frontiers of Development Administration* (Durham, N.C.: Duke Univ. Press, 1970); Ralph Braibanti (ed.), *Political and Administrative Development* (Durham, N.C.: Duke Univ. Press, 1969); Dwight Waldo, *Temporal Dimensions of Development Administration* (Durham, N.C.: Duke Univ. Press, 1970); Edward W. Weidner (ed.), *Development Administration in Asia* (Durham, N.C.: Duke Univ. Press, 1970).

27. Saul M. Katz, 'A Systems Approach to Development Administration', in Riggs, op. cit., p. 120.

28. Ibid., pp. 117 ff.

29. *A Study of the Capacity of the United Nations Development System* New York: United Nations, 1969) Sales No. E.70/1.10, p. 25 and chap. 5.

30. Robert E. Asher, 'International Agencies and Economic Development: An Overview', in Gardner and Millikan, op. cit., p. 447.

31. Katz, in Riggs, op. cit., p. 118.

COMMENTS

Marcus Arkin and T. T. Thahane

Professor Arkin: 'The underlying merit of Professor
paper is its continual emphasis on development as   ...ulti-
disciplined concept – as an issue which not only bestrides the
continents, but which breaks down the barriers between specialist
disciplines. Economists, in their arrogance and ignorance, tend
to adopt a blinkered view of such issues – to regard "development" and "economic development" as synonymous, even
though (as Professor Arthur Kemp demonstrates in his paper
below) we economists probably know far less about the processes
of progress than the vast output of literature from our pens might
suggest. Moreover, I suspect that the same sort of criticism holds
good for the political scientists, the sociologists and many of the
other groups of specialists represented at this Conference. So the
broad interdisciplinary approach of Professor Weidner's arguments sets the appropriate tone for our deliberations.

'What struck me with equal force in Professor Weidner's paper
is the recurrence of his striking image of "spaceship planet
earth", that "bright blue ball" with its limited resources, viewed
from the vantage-point of outer space. Most of us in Southern
Africa have not experienced the exhilaration of such views;
over the last twenty years and more we have consciously deprived
ourselves of this century's most striking technique for com-
municating new ideas and fresh perspectives, and we now rank
with Afghanistan and Albania as one of the few communities
with a pre-television outlook. (That we have finally decided to
take the plunge in this direction can perhaps itself be regarded
as a symptom of development.)

'This gap in our perspectives possibly accounts for the distinction between the theory – which Professor Weidner shares with
many other scholars in this field – that development is fundamentally an equalitarian force both among nations and within a
given community, and South African experience where development to date has apparently promoted a widening of the gap
between different groups and different regions. Nor can this
simply be brushed aside with the assertion that such a possible
tendency (that is, for the development process to widen rather

than narrow gaps) "is today beside the point". In a Southern African context it is very much to the point, for that aspect of the problem will determine the nature, pattern and speed of development in this part of the world.

'Perhaps it is also a pre-television outlook which leads me to regard two other underlying features of Professor Weidner's concept of development as being a little unrealistically utopian. How, I ask myself, do we achieve the twin aims of each nation maximising its development potentialities and "at the same time" ensure "equality among nations"? Surely it would be more useful in this regard if we recognised that communities, like individuals, have markedly different aptitudes and propensities, and that to aim on a global scale at international equality is to raise false hopes and generate avoidable friction. Nor is it sufficient in this respect to suggest that humanity can no longer justify differences in standards "based upon exclusive control of particular resources"; such excluseiveness will continue at least until we have been coerced into some form of world government, and the problems of development are too urgent to await that millennium.

'Secondly, I am not altogether sure if Professor Weidner has gone far enough in trying to reconcile the selection of development goals (which he emphasises must always be done on a *national* scale) with maximising individual happiness and providing each one of us with more of the good things of life. History yields far too many examples of the state (whether in the form of some authoritarian planning commission or a charismatic leader) regarding its citizens as so many cogs in the machinery of national aggrandisement, for us not to view all schemes for development stemming from government sources as possible barriers rather than stimulants to innovation, change and an enhanced level of individual welfare.

'On the other hand, I cannot but endorse Professor Weidner's view that, in the ultimate analysis, all development depends on what is politically feasible; movement in this direction must inevitably be slowed down if the established expectations of entrenched vested interests are likely to feel threatened. It is impossible to exaggerate the importance of this consideration, for, as Wicksteed pointed out more than half a century ago, "the advance in well-being which we all desire and are all pursuing becomes an object of dread to each one of us in that particular department in which it is his business to promote it". So, experience indicates that politically influential groups will not support schemes of obvious general benefit, if these are believed to run counter to their own short-term self-interests; and again, this truism is especially appropriate to the tasks of development in Southern Africa.

'Most of us, too, will readily accept Professor Weidner's classification of development strategies, without endorsing all the details. For example, I think too much is made of the need to choose between a production or consumption strategy: the annals of economic change provide many instances of consumer industries which have served as vital sectors in the development process. Nor would I agree on the need for cohesiveness in society; for, if you mingle together all sorts of races, you may well produce something much more development-conscious than any of the stocks from which they come, as the experience of the United States tends to suggest.

'But these are minor quibbles. Much more significant for our consideration of accelerated development in Southern Africa is Professor Weidner's very wise remark on the need to establish the appropriate mix in any society between its competitive and co-operative elements. Is it not perhaps possible that one of the underlying circumstances to date retarding development in this part of spaceship planet earth has been our undue fear of competitiveness among ethnic groups and our neglect of the co-operative factors?'

Mr Thahane: 'Professor Weidner has introduced a concept of equalitarianism which presents practical difficulties at the operational level, especially if development is accepted as an equalitarian goal. Among countries the rate of development differs, mainly because initial conditions are different and natural resources vary; the size of national markets and the degree of domestic specialisation in economic transactions also differ from country to country. Geographical sizes of countries are very important in the analysis of development problems, and in assessing the speed at which equalitarianism can be achieved or approached.

'It can be argued that at the global level the concepts or principles underlying international development efforts revolve around morality and the self-interest or vested interests of nations, whether developed or developing. In fact, the main aim of international development action is not to enable the developing or less developed countries to catch up, but rather to permit them to reap some of the benefits of development.

In passing, it may be pointed out that in development we deal with man in all his dimensions: economic, political, cultural, spiritual, etc. All these aspects raise specific problems when pursuing the principle of affirmative action as referred to by Professor Weidner.

Within national borders regional goals may differ from national ones. Regional political autonomy may be pursued at the expense of a higher rate of development at the national level. Reduction of regional and cultural income disparities may act as a constraint on national and international development efforts to maximise the growth rate in gross national product.

In general, development requires a concept of man in society and in his relationship with other men. Hence the importance of empathy in development planning and of the appreciation of environmental hazards inherent in many so-called developmental activities.

Professor Weidner's concept of development as an equalitarian goal seems to find support among the new generations in the United States and Europe, with their vision of the world and man's role in it. Their vision is humanistic, and man holds the stage. It stresses candour, sincerity and plain talk, and it is remarkably equalitarian. This vision asserts man's right to self-fulfilment along the lines chosen by him, rather than dictated by some social authority. While we are grateful to Professor Weidner for bringing us into step with the times, we must never have illusions about the immediate achievement of this kind of universe. In fact, the search for a definition of a 'humanistic order, an equitable society, an ideology-free view of the world and a political order in which the state is servant rather than master' has a long way to go.

Let me make a small observation on the determination of development goals and the role of planning commissions. Statutory planning commissions were established in the Eastern European countries and later in Asia. In the former case the commissions set binding targets which have to be achieved by the whole country. Planning is very detailed and the plan relies heavily on state coercion. In Asia most commissions were created as independent agencies with certain legal powers that in some cases gave them authority similar to that of the courts. Their effectiveness was negligible, since their plans were sometimes not feasible administratively, financially or from the manpower point of view. To produce implementable plans, planning commissions should be integrated into the whole machinery of government. The activity of plan formulation should be decentralised to the lower echelons of government and should involve citizen participation in the determination of goals. If people participate in deciding development goals and priorities, they are likely to be more committed to their achievement.

The role of a planner is to submit to the policy-makers alternative plans and the implications of each alternative. His task is not to set the goals, but to advise political leaders of the alternative social time-paths, in as many dimensions as there are variables. He should scan the alternative social time-paths for a feasible set of time-paths that society could follow. The planner should generally not overrate his own importance in setting social goals.

In reading Professor Louw's paper it should be borne in mind that the so-called developed countries are themselves developing.

Generally they cannot spare their best people for service in developing countries, whose problems are much more complex and which require new, bold and imaginative approaches. One's past experience may be totally inapplicable to the environment in less developed countries.

Experience has confirmed that development involves the application of different disciplines; the farmer, for instance, views life as a whole, and he has to be helped in all aspects of life – economic, social, cultural, etc. The approach to extension work should therefore not be on a disciplinary basis, as the farmer will want to ask an extension agent about any problem facing him, whether the agent is an agronomist, a veterinary surgeon, or a specialist in any other field. Development plans should therefore take into account man and all his needs. To this end, citizen involvement is essential if these plans are not to remain simply theories on the bookshelves.

Part One

Dimensions of Development

Chapter 1
Population Factors

Some Fundamental Equations of Social Mechanics

STANISLAV ANDRESKI

The purpose of this paper is to present a few theoretical propositions about the relationships between population movements,
economic development and internal and external conflicts, which
concern some of the most general assumptions about the problems
of development.

Neither the word 'equation' nor the few mathematical symbols in the exposition should be interpreted as an indication of a
claim to superior exactitude. Having devoted an entire chapter of
a forthcoming book, *Social Sciences as Sorcery*, to castigating the
common superstition that one can attain a greater exactitude by
translating a verbal statement into a mathematical-looking formula, the author wants to stress that the equations which follow
must be regarded as very rough approximations. The only justification for the recourse to mathematical symbols is that a few
simple formulae can make the complex network of causal relations more transparent than a necessarily long verbal analysis.
In other words, rather than enhancing the exactitude, the symbols merely serve to specify succinctly the structure of causal
chains.

Underlying the scheme is the simplified conception of a human
being (analogous to the *Homo economicus* of economic theory) as
an organism producing a certain amount of energy which must
find an outlet, and which is directed by the possibilities of gratifying his desires, for which sake he needs wealth – in the wide sense
of this term as used in economic theory. This wealth he can
obtain either by producing it or by getting it from someone else.
As exchange presupposes that the buyer has produced some
goods or services which he can offer in return, we shall lump
the two activities together under the heading 'construction' –
symbolised in the equations which follow by the letter C – for the

purpose of distinguishing it from an opposite method of obtaining wealth by the use or a threat of force, without offering any goods or services in return. Let the word 'exploitation' and the letter E stand for the latter method.

Almost needless to say, these concepts are pure or ideal types which fit perfectly no concrete situation, as all real cases contain mixtures of such elements, though in very different doses. When the Romans have forced the Egyptians to supply them with corn, without giving them anything in return, or when an heir to an estate lives in a far-off city on rents collected from the cultivators whom he never sees, let alone helps, we have a clear case of exploitation. On the other hand, an assertion that a manager exploits his staff requires for its substantiation all kinds of assumptions about the just prices of their respective contributions to production, unless we employ the term 'exploitation' merely to convey our disapproval of the given pattern of remuneration.

We shall divide the total income of a group in accordance with its source, and say that it consists of the sum of income from construction and from exploitation. Employing the conventional symbols of economic theory, we can write

$$I = I_c + I_e \quad (1)$$

Without denying the existence of altruism, we can proceed on the assumption that no large group will furnish unrequited supplies without being forced, which means that exploitation involves an expenditure of energy on conflict.

From the viewpoint of the boundary of a given collectivity, conflict can be either external or internal. Waging a war or preparing for it compose the former; and we shall denote all the energies expended on such activities by the letter W. The internal conflicts can vary greatly in openness, ranging from a civil war, or a revolution, to a suppression of riots or terror – the relatively peaceful activities of the police on the one side and conspirators and propagandists on the other. Let us call all these activities 'internal struggles', and denote the energies expended on them by the letter S.

To complete the list of outlets for collective energy we must add activities which involve only the use, but neither production nor appropriation, of wealth, such as sport, feasting, courtship and copulation, games and festivities and suchlike. Let us call them hedonistic. Actually, performance of rites should also be added, but since these often include an element of feasting, let us subsume them under the same heading, and denote the sum of energy spent on this entire set of activities by the letter H.

Letting E stand for the sum of collective energy, we can write

$$E = C + W + S + H \quad (2)$$

Now let us look at how these activities mesh with the circulation of wealth. Since a booty for the victor is a loss to the defeated, the proceeds from a war can be either positive or negative. Moreover, since much wealth may be destroyed rather than grabbed, the proceeds may be negative for all the contestants. On the other hand, a defensive war can be regarded as an effort to prevent being exploited, and the gain from it (though purely notional) as equivalent to the wealth which would have been wrung by a conqueror. Internal struggles can never increase the wealth of the polity, but they can benefit the victorious factions. Even a very destructive revolution can be profitable to the new rulers; and many ruling classes have lived in luxury by operating a machine of oppression.

By definition, the hedonistic activities involve only consumption, which means that its proceeds are negative. The amount of energy expended on hedonistic activities is circumscribed by the surplus of wealth remaining after the requirements of activities which bring income have been provided for.

Using the subscripts to indicate the source, we can write the following equation:

$$I_t = I_c + I_w - I_s - I_h \quad (3)$$

To repeat, I_s and I_h are always negative. I_w may be positive or negative according to the circumstances.

Now let us consider on what does the collective energy (E) depend. Obviously in the first place on the number of units who generate it; that is, the size of the population, for which we shall write P. It is equally clear that collective energy also depends on the technology, the art of organisation and other skills, as well as on the machines and tools available to the population. To be more precise, its health is also a factor, but let us leave this factor aside in the present discussion. All these factors call for further analysis but simplifying for the sake of necessary brevity, let us lump them together under the coefficient of physical and mental tools.

Letting T stand for this coefficient, we can write:

$$E = P \times T \quad (4)$$

Substituting for E in equation (2) we can write our fundamental equation:

$$P \times T = C + W + S + H \quad (5)$$

It might be objected that equation (2) is a tautology because it must always be true once we agree to divide all human activities under these headings. This is true, but the example of Keynes's fundamental equation (which is equally tautologous) proves that even in the social sciences there can be fruitful tautologies. The test is whether the given way of classifying the phenomena yields new explanations and predictions.

The next and crucial question is what determines the shifts in the flow of energy through these outlets. This is a very complicated matter which must be approached through successive simplifications. So let us disregard the hedonistic activities and assume that there are no important internal struggles: that is, that $H = 0$ and $S = 0$. We are left with C and W; and let us consider on what may depend their relative magnitudes, that is, the ratio $C : W$.

My thesis is that, looking at broad and long-run historical trends, the distribution of energy between these outlets depends on their relative profitability. A more adequate treatment would require recourse to the concepts of marginal cost and benefit analysis, but as the first approximation let us say that the distribution of energy depends on the relative sizes of income obtainable through these outlets. Employing the previous symbols, we can write:

$$\text{When } S = 0 \quad C : W = I_c : I_w \quad (6)$$

The influence of the growth of the population on the growth of income depends on the operation of the tendency towards diminishing returns, which in turn depends on the availability of natural resources to the population in question, the progress or non-progress of technology, the art of organisation and other factors which we have grouped provisionally under the heading of physical and mental tools (T). When technology is static while fertility is unrestricted, the population tends to make full use of all the natural resources accessible to the existing technology. Under such circumstances a point of zero return on further applications of labour is approached, and the situation can only be changed by acquisition of natural resources, which normally can only take place through conquest. A war may be lost, but it is a gamble which can be won whereas an augmentation of energy devoted to construction can only bring a return not very far from o. This explains why war was ubiquitous when technology was static and fertility unrestricted, particularly when the simplicity of social structures offered little scope for exploitation and class struggles.

War is most profitable when a strong but poor nation or tribe defeats a weathy but militarily weak polity, as was the case with nomad invasions of countries of more advanced civilisation. A growth of the population which may bring into operation a tendency towards diminishing returns on labour may make war more profitable by enhancing the strength of the polity, and thereby its chances of victory – which depends on total strength, not on strength per head. International division of labour, which entails a dependence on what your enemy produces, decreases the likelihood of profits being made out of war.

The internal struggles are likely to flare when the profitability of construction as well as that of war are low. Putting it somewhat differently, we can say that the intensity of internal struggles tends to increase when the proceeds from co-operation are decreasing: that is to say, when the relationships between the various sections of the population are acquiring characteristics of a zero-sum game. These relationships can be summarised by the following equation:

$$S : (C + W) = P : (I_c + I_w) \quad (7)$$

I would claim that the simple equations presented above go quite far towards explaining the location in time and space of a wide range of historical changes such as the rise of capitalism and science, colonial expansion and decolonisation, or why pacifism has spread in industrial societies, or why underdevelopment persists in some parts of the world and not in others. Among other things the aforementioned propositions afford a more general comprehension of the politico-economic vicious and virtuous circles of underdevelopment analysed more specifically in my books, *Parasitism and Subversion: The Case of Latin America*, 3rd augmented ed. (New York: Schocken Books, 1969); *The African Predicament: A Study in Pathology of Development* (London: Michael Joseph, 1968; New York: Atherton Books, 1969); as well as of the fluctuations of conflicts studied in *Military Organisation and Society*, 2nd augmented ed. (London: Routledge and Kegan Paul; Berkeley: California Univ. Press, 1968);

and in certain chapters of *The Uses of Comparative Sociology*
(London: Weidenfeld and Nicolson, 1964; Berkeley: California
Univ. Press, 1965). Further historical data could be analysed in
the light of the foregoing propositions, but unfortunately there is
no room for this here. Furthermore, the formalised treatment can
be greatly extended by examining the interrelationships between
the variables (some of which form interesting feedback systems)
as well as by analysing some of them into their components, and
relating them to other variables not taken into account here.
However, the space here is limited, and I hope to offer a more
exhaustive exposition in book form before very long.

The Population Factor in the Economies of Southern Africa

J. L. SADIE

1. THE QUALITATIVE ASPECT

Population, as a factor in the economy, has two dimensions: a qualitative and a quantitative. Viewed quantitatively, it can be both a depressant and a stimulant. The former function is easily appreciated when numbers are considered as the divisor in the ratio national product/population, which yields the product per capita. The larger the denominator, the smaller the ratio. Population is a stimulant when its increase is a motive force evoking economic action which would not have materialised otherwise.

Which of these two opposing functions will predominate, given the supply of natural resources, depends on the quality of the population as economic material. In this regard human resources embody two factors of production: ordinary labour and entrepreneurial initiative. Of the two the latter is not only the more important but is, in fact, also the source and origin of economic growth and development. When an adequate supply or even a modicum of modern entrepreneurship obtains – with the accent on the 'modern' – the conditions engendered by a growing, and especially a rapidly growing, population will elicit a positive response in the form of new capital formation and employment, raising the economy and standards of living to new levels. These conditions include an elastic supply of labour which could mean low-efficiency wages if the free play of market forces is not interfered with; a demographically mobile and therefore potentially adaptable labour force; the economising of capital and relatively high returns to capital; a high coefficient of consumption and an expanding consumer market; a demand for residential construction and other 'demographic investments'; the realisation of the economies of scale, etc. Inadequate savings may be a constraint but not an inhibiting factor inasmuch as recourse can be had to external sources by a cadre of alert and enterprising entrepreneurs.

In the absence of such a body of persons, the above favourable conditions created by population growth will be of no consequence. They will not act as a spur to economic development. It is the dearth of modern entrepreneurs, more than anything else, which is the bane of Southern Africa, as it is of most underdeveloped societies. The primary vertical dependence between them and the other factors of production is upwards. Dependence downwards is of a second order of importance.

TABLE I.I   Population and G.N.P. in Southern Africa

Country	Population	Proportion non-indigenous (per cent)	Growth rate of population (per cent per annum)	Gross national product per capita (R)	Agricultural population density[c]
Angola	5,700,000	9	2·0	137	18
Botswana	650,000	1·4	2·2	72	2
Lesotho	960,000	0·3	1·8	62	34
Madagascar	7,010,000	1·7[a]	2·7	72	19
Malawi	4,430,000	0·5	2·4	36	263
Mauritius	860,000	72[b]	2·2	166	772
Mozambique	8,230,000	3	2·1	144	18
Rhodesia	5,310,000	5	3·5	158	74
South Africa	22,000,000	29	2·6	469	21
South West Africa	750,000	17	2·0	–	1
Swaziland	420,000	6	3·0	144	28
Zambia	4,330,000	2	2·9	262	12
Southern Africa	60,650,000	13·9	2·5		

[a] The category Malagasys have been considered indigenous even though they are descendants of waves of immigrants from Asia, Africa and Arab countries.

[b] The estimated 28 per cent descendants of slaves from Africa and Madagascar have been considered indigenous.

[c] Total population per sq. km. of agricultural land.

Sources: Africa Institute of South Africa, *Africa at a Glance*; Europa Publications, *Africa South of the Sahara*; national censuses; own estimates.

Looking at Table 1.1, we see that 86 per cent of the almost 6 million inhabitants of Southern Africa are indigenous, as qualified in the footnotes to the table relating to the special situation in Madagascar and Mauritius. The majority of them have their homes in the subsistence sector or peasant economy, even though some are periodically subjected to the influence of the money sector as a result of the migrant labour system. The circumstances ruling in these areas are anathema to the generation of a spirit of enterprise. They are traditionalist societies with a host of social, religious and cultural values and psychological traits militating against the emergence of the Schumpetarian New Men or innovators. On another occasion the author, applying McClelland's[1] psychological thesis to the South African Bantu population, made the following observation:

> Parents do not transmit to their children motivational characteristics which they themselves lack, and parents are a product of their social environment. Therefore, a cultural milieu which does not favour change can perpetuate a condition of low η achievement. The men of our underdeveloped Bantu population, through their work, do come in contact with a technologically more advanced culture whose values are orientated to achievement, but the mothers who are responsible for the generations to come remain outside the orbit of this influence, except in so far as they themselves are members of the labour force in the developed sector; and even then the influence is weak since they live in towns which form disintegrated appendices to the urban core. Under the migratory labour system even the men do not escape the shackles of tribal traditions despite their periodical subjection to the values of the developed society. Apparently, migratory labour has become a built-in custom without any liberating influence, the spells of work outside the Bantu Areas constituting no more than temporary absences regardless of the proportion of working life actually spent within the Areas.[2]

The above remarks are meant not as a denigration of their way of life, but as an interpretation of its significance for economic development.

There are, of course, considerable numbers of the indigenous population who could be called entrepreneurs, but few of them would qualify for the description of New Men or innovators, most of them being engaged in buying and selling or production which require a minimum of business acumen or industrial expertise.

It is no mere coincidence that the highest gross national products per capita are found in the Southern African countries which have the largest non-indigenous[3] population complements, and vice versa. Leaving aside Mauritius as a rather special case, the Republic of South Africa ranks first in both magnitudes, respectively R469 and 29 per cent. At the other extreme there is Malawi, which is actively seeking foreign participation, with a G.N.P. per capita of R36 and a non-indigenous population component of 0·5 per cent. Most of these non-indigenous people are products of technologically advanced cultures in which economic progress, the accumulation of wealth, high material standards of living and the willingness to accept risks to achieve these goals are important elements in the value system. Some are expatriates whose presence is the result of the establishment of branches or subsidiaries of overseas businesses.

As is to be expected, there is no perfect correlation between G.N.P. per capita and the proportions of non-indigenous population. This is due to the effect of the quality of natural resources. The discovery of a rich mineral resource in an underdeveloped country is the easiest and fastest route to modern development. Its exploitation does not require a domestic supply of enterprise, foreign companies usually being quite prepared, if not anxious, to undertake it, assuming that the host country does not at the beginning impose too onerous conditions. When the necessary investment has been made and production is running smoothly, the host country could demand an increasing participation of the local population in the higher-echelon jobs to displace expatriate or non-indigenous incumbents, thus reducing the latter's numbers to the essential minimum in the economically most strategic technical and executive posts.

The Africanisation process involved can be economically harmful when it is pushed too fast. The danger is compounded when it is coupled with nationalization, quite apart from the impact it may have on foreign investment in the future. A traditionalist society which does not appreciate the workings of a modern economy or business enterprise may regard it as an occasion for rejoicing and reduced effort and for increased wages, since the foreign concern now belongs to them. Zambia, with the second highest per capita G.N.P. among Southern African countries and a non-Bantu population component of only 2 per cent, is an example of an economy where the absence of an indigenous body of entrepreneurs has been partly compensated for by foreign investment induced by the existence of mineral resources. In the same way the economy of Botswana, with only 1.4 per cent of non-Bantu population, promises to be transformed by foreign enterprise and capital attracted by the discovery of copper and nickel.

2. THE QUANTITATIVE ASPECTS

It has been maintained that in developed countries a population of 10 to 15 million is required for the establishment of firms of optimum size to realise, with the exception of a few industries, the economies of scale. Since the per capita income is the other determinant of the size of the market, one would conclude that the required population in underdeveloped countries has to be larger. There is, however, no simple relationship between the level of G.N.P. per capita and the effective size of the market in terms of the type of industry that can be established. To be meaningful in many instances there must be a sufficient number of people whose income allows of the consumption of what might be termed 'prosperity goods'. When the average income is at or near the subsistence level there is no advantage in numbers.

The figures in Table 1.1 indicate that the populations of eleven of the twelve countries, South Africa being the only exception, are too small for the attainment of the economies of scale, the numbers ranging from 650,000 to 8,230,000, and the effect is reinforced by the low average level of national product per capita. In the case of Botswana, Lesotho, Swaziland and South West Africa this should not be an impediment inasmuch as they form a type of common market with South Africa. The inference is, of course, that the elimination of economic barriers between the states could counteract the drawback of small numbers within national boundaries.

For the rest, given the per capita level of G.N.P. and the ruling economic circumstances, the existing small sizes of the populations are not a disadvantage. This is particularly true where the richest resource is in the form of minerals whose natural markets are the developed countries. In fact, the inhabitants would in many cases have been better off if there were fewer of them, the appellation of 'underpopulated' applied to some of them notwithstanding. With the large majority of the populations dependent upon agriculture for a livelihood, numbers in their relation to the land surface area, its fertility and the manner in which it is cultivated are of prime importance. Because of the latter two factors and the fact that within each country the population is not evenly distributed over the whole of the area, the varying agricultural densities in Table 1.1 cannot serve as a measure of the relative degrees of population pressure. More vividly, perhaps, than densities, the figures in Table 1.2 portray the unfavourable ratio of man to land. They show that the productive assets at the disposal of each man are very meagre indeed.

TABLE 1.2. Agricultural land per man in hectares

	Under crop	Meadows and pastures
Madagascar	0·47	5·76
Malawi	0·34	0·11
Mauritius	0·13	0·04
Rhodesia	0·46	0·21
Zambia	0·55	8·11

Source: U.N.E.C.A., *Economic Bulletin for Africa*, vol. IX, no. 2, p. 12.

As it is, Mauritius, with the highest density, does suffer from very severe population pressure. But it does not mean that the situation in Lesotho, with a density less than one-twentieth that of Mauritius, is any better. To judge by the G.N.P. per capita it is worse. In sparsely populated Botswana many persons would have perished during the 1960s but for famine relief provided by external sources. Of Madagascar, with the second highest agricultural population density among the twelve countries of Southern Africa, it has been said: 'denudation of vast stretches of slope areas in the highlands by overgrazing and other malpractices has led to serious deterioration and to some of the worst ero-

sion to be seen anywhere in Africa'.[4] Within most of the Southern
African countries there are at least some regions where this kind
of description would apply. The existence of such 'pockets' indicates regional population pressure which could conceivably be
due to immobility and need not therefore signify a population
problem in the overall national sense.

At the same time, immobility is not economically meaningful
when there are large unused areas which can only be brought
under cultivation – via irrigation for example – by means of
very costly investment which cannot be afforded. Again, the
absence of such indicators of regional or overall pressure need not
mean non-existence, since the migrant labour system could
obviate its manifestation.

Taking all factors into consideration, including the volume of
temporary migration, absolute numbers appear to be a very real
problem in the following countries at their present stage of
development: Botswana, Lesotho, Madagascar, Malawi, Mauritius and Mozambique. In other countries the growth in numbers
constitutes at least a drag on the average standard of living.[5]

In this connection it would be interesting to inquire whether
the Toynbeean thesis, that a vigorous challenge will evoke a
change in the mode of life, is valid in Southern Africa. Positing
that the pressure of numbers on land which leads to deprivation
is such a challenge, the answer would seem to be in the negative
for the traditionalist societies. But one cannot be certain since the
migrant labour system inhibits the coming into operation of such
a vigorous challenge. The following assessment of the situation
in the South African Bantu homelands may be more generally
applicable:

Without sacrificing the security provided by the piece of land,
the inadequate yield of the latter is supplemented by wages,
which together provide the wherewithal to sustain a minimum
standard of living without changing the methods of cultivat-
ing their land, or compelling an increase in the income
generated within the tribal area. The inhabitants of our Bantu
Areas can rely on an external agent to provide them with
opportunities to fill the gap between the required necessities of
life and the product of the soil. A mentality of dependency
and low η achievement is perpetuated. It might, of course, be

argued that a gradually diminishing product per capita resulting from the pressure of population on land can, in any case,
not present a sufficiently potent challenge since it is debilitated
by the gradualness of the process and is partly resolved in a
high mortality rate which is fatalistically accepted as inevitable.[6]

3. POPULATION GROWTH

The population of Southern Africa has been growing at an
annual rate of approximately 2.5 per cent. The non-indigenous
components, particularly those of European origin, have a much
lower rate of natural increase than the indigenous, reflecting a
social, cultural and economic differential. In Angola, Mozambique and South Africa, and to a lesser extent Rhodesia, their
numbers are being strengthened by immigration from overseas.
The marginal social product of these immigrants is probably
a good deal higher than their marginal private product, swelling
as they do the ranks of the progress-oriented elements in the
population and inducing a multiplier effect with regard to the
employment of the less developed sections.

The above average of 2.5 per cent per annum encompasses
differing rates ranging from 1.8 per cent in the case of Lesotho –
for whom some estimates are, however, as high as 2.5 per cent
– to 3.5 per cent for Rhodesia. The expected future rates of
increase for eleven of the twelve countries are three to five percentage points higher than those detailed in Table 1.1. The
indigenous populations are all high-fertility communities, with
birth rates upwards of 40 per 1,000. They find themselves in the
explosive phase of the demographic cycle. This is the result of the
familiar process of declining mortality which has been linked only
very tenuously with economic advancement and has for the most
part been a function of exogenous factors. Thus we have a combination of traditionalist procreative mores and modern medical
technology.

The notable exception is Mauritius, where the birth rate
dropped from almost 50 per 1,000 in 1950 to 30 in 1967, to
reduce the growth rate from 3.6 to 2.2 per cent even though the
death rate has fallen to 8.5 per 1,000. But here the preponderant
sections of the population are not of African origin.

Taking an overall view, the economies of Southern Africa will be required to provide in future for an annual increment in the population of approximately 2·8 per cent, involving an addition of some 1·7 million persons each year. Merely to prevent average levels of living from declining, the G.N.P. has to increase by this percentage. According to figures in the background document supplied to the Conference by the Africa Institute,[7] the growth of G.N.P. in Madagascar, Mauritius and Rhodesia during the 1960s was not adequate to prevent such a decline. In Botswana the per capita G.N.P. grew by only 0·8 per cent per annum and in Lesotho by 1·2 per cent, and this only because of foreign aid in one form or another.

The implications of a 2·8 per cent increase in numbers are best illustrated by having recourse to the familiar concept of the incremental capital-output ratio. Premising a reasonable figure of 3 for this magnitude – which does seem to be more or less a minimum – an investment equal to 3 x 2·8 or 8·4 per cent of G.N.P. is required to maintain the average per capita national product. This implies an equal amount of saving. In at least five countries, viz. Botswana, Lesotho, Madagascar, Malawi and Mauritius, domestic saving has not reached this level, and the major part of their investment had to be financed from external sources. If the population growth rate were halved, so would the required savings and investment to achieve the same end. If not, and in addition a rise of say 2·5 per cent per annum in the average level of living is desired, net savings amounting to 17 per cent of G.N.P. are required. The equivalent *gross* savings percentage will be higher still. The poor countries in Southern Africa with large subsistence sectors cannot hope to attain such targets on the basis of domestic resources.

At the individual level in traditionalist Bantu societies, saving takes the form of investment in children who are to provide for their parents when they retire – which could take place at a fairly early age when the disutility of effort is high. While it does make sense to the individual parent who is not aware of alternative ways of saving, or when none such exists, it is a very costly way of providing for the years in retirement. The returns to the investment may be negative, in that the discounted value of a son's contribution to his parents' maintenance would usually be small compared with the discounted value of resources used up in the bringing-up of the child. To make sure that there will be a surviving son when the father has reached the age of 60 or 65, a couple will have to produce four to five children at the present levels of mortality.

Again, this form of saving is abortive inasmuch as the feeding, clothing and, perhaps, education of children not infrequently obviate the possibility of investing in agricultural inputs which would have raised production. When there is pressure of population on the land so that diminishing marginal returns per capita obtain, investment in children reduces the average product. The resulting malnutrition and morbidity will also diminish the quality of the children.

Moreover, in view of the major role of women in African agriculture, the frequency of pregnancies and births is a very significant factor in the amount of labour applied to cultivation. The effects of the reduced ability to participate in this, as well as in other types of economic activity, are obvious.

Thus the generation of human resources and the production of other resources are, for the most part, stark alternatives.

4. THE AGE STRUCTURE

It will be appreciated that, because of the system of migrant labour, the results of the national censuses which record the *de facto* populations cannot reflect a true picture of the actual or *de jure* populations. For this reason the age statistics have been aggregated for the whole of the Southern African region. Leaving out the non-Bantu component of the South African population, the age structure can be presented as follows:

Age	*0–14*	*15–64*	*65+*	*Total*
Percentage of population	46	50	4	100
(White population of South Africa)	(31)	(62)	(7)	(100)

With 46 per cent of the total numbers younger than 15 years, it is clear that the population is a very youthful one. This is typical of high-fertility communities. Portions of 46 and 4 per cent in the 0–14 and 65+ age groups respectively, usually described as the dependent sections of the population, reflect a dependency ratio of 100. Its significance can best be appreciated by comparing it with the age structure of the White population of South Africa, which has only 31 per cent in the youngest category and a dependency ratio of 61.

Even more serious is the fact that the indigenous population is still in the juvenescent process as the result of either an unchanged or, in some cases, a rising level of fertility and declining mortality. In the result it is subject to a demographic drag in the form of a marginal dependency burden in excess of 100.

The obverse of the above is relatively small numbers in the 15 to 64 age group which is usually regarded as the productive or potentially productive portion of the population. The implied economic disadvantage can be illustrated as follows. Other things being equal, if all those aged 15 to 64 were to be economically active, the per capita product of the youthful population with only 50 per cent in the productive ages would be 19 per cent lower than that of the older population (such as the Whites in South Africa) which has 62 per cent in the relevant age group. The difference is brought out more strikingly if we use absolute numbers and start off by assuming that only men aged 15 to 64 are members of the labour force. During the 1960s there were some 12·2 million of them in the Southern African region (exclusive of South African non-Bantu numbers). To compensate for the arrearage induced by the above difference between 50 and 61 per cent, the production of earnings of the men will have to be supplemented by those of more than 2·9 million of their women, assuming constant returns or equal wages, even while the ability of women to participate in the labour force is reduced by their high fertility. In practice, compensatory action usually takes the form of accession to the labour force at earlier ages. Since economic effort involves a disutility, any such action would represent a loss of welfare. The situation is aggravated when diminishing marginal returns obtain or female and young people's earnings are lower than men's.

On the other hand, if the relative sizes of the labour force in the youthful and demographically older populations are commensurate with the proportions in the productive age group, and the income per worker in the two is the same, the consumption coefficient of the former would be higher as a result of the expenditure required for the rearing and education of, and health services for, their children. A smaller proportion of economic resources is left for investment in productive machinery, equipment and constructions to be put at the disposal of the labour force.

One might say that expenditure on population growth subtracts from the resources available to accommodate the growth, and is thus self-defeating.

5. THE LABOUR FORCE

It might be considered that since the productive age group is small, it would ameliorate the problem of finding employment for the labour force. This does not follow. Disregarding a lower than 100 per cent labour-force participation among males, an age of entry lower than 15 and the participation of women, the group of 12·2 million males mentioned above is expanding at a rate fractionally less than 2·8 per cent per annum,[8] or by some 350,000 each year. This is twice the rate at which the labour force of the White population in South Africa is growing as a result of natural increase. To the disadvantages inhering in the age composition is thus added the drawback of a rapid increase in the numbers who have to find employment. The gravity of the problem can be gauged by the dimensions of the migrant labour system as reflected in the number of absentees or foreign-born in the various countries.[9] The following are very rough estimates of the minimum percentages of the respective labour forces (which in this case include some females as well) working away from home: Botswana 24 per cent, Lesotho 56 per cent, Malawi 22 per cent, Swaziland 25 per cent, Mozambique 25 per cent. The significance of Malawi's percentage is, however, greatly reduced when the presence of a sizeable number of Mozambique Bantu is taken into account. In Botswana itself there are 28,000 wage-earners among a work-force of 240,000, and in Lesotho, with one and a half times as many economically active, there are only 2,000. The main host countries are Rhodesia, South Africa and Zambia, which are industrially the most advanced.

In the absence of, and even concurrent with, migration as an outlet, the addition to the labour force would result in unemployment, underemployment or starvation. In Mauritius a quarter of the adult males are reported to be unemployed,[10] and in

Zambia this number has been described as large.[11] In South Africa it would be in the proximity of 100,000, less than 2 per cent of the Bantu labour force. For the rest the paucity of statistics on unemployment is understandable, since the visible type can only be significant when the money or exchange sector of the economy and the urban population have become important enough, as in the three countries mentioned above. For the most part the lack of opportunities for the accommodation of the increasing labour force resolves itself in underemployment. But to the extent that periodical non-employment may be preferred, it does not merit the description of underemployment, i.e. when, to the individual concerned, marginal disutility of effort equals marginal utility of income – whatever may be the judgement of the outsider who bases his conclusions on the low level of living.

Given the economic conditions prevailing in the countries of origin, the migrant labour system, in which some 1·5 million individuals are involved, fulfils a dire need, whatever social iniquities the moralist might discover in it. It also has the merit of permitting an adaptation of jobs to preferences – as witness the phenomenon of considerable numbers of both absentees and foreign-born or non-local population in one and the same locality. In these circumstances the youthfulness of the labour force, which implies a low average level of experience, know-how and skill, has the advantage of conducing to spatial mobility.

6. URBANISATION

Mauritius, with 50 per cent of its population in towns and cities, and South Africa with 48 per cent, are the most highly urbanised of the Southern African countries. Next in order of degree of urbanisation are Botswana (27 per cent, but around one-third in agrotowns), South West Africa (25 per cent), Zambia and Rhodesia (21 per cent), followed by Mozambique (17 per cent), Madagascar (15 per cent) and Angola (12 per cent). Lowest on the list are Swaziland (7 per cent), Malawi (5 per cent) and Lesotho (3 per cent). Compared with the industrialised areas of the world, the degree of urbanisation in Southern Africa, averaging approximately 28 per cent of the population, is still very low. But it is nevertheless a good deal higher than in the rest of Africa, Northern Africa excepted. Moreover, the urban population is increasing at a rate at least twice as fast as the rural.

While urbanisation can be considered both a function and a condition of economic development, it would appear as if the latter is not in all cases commensurate with the former. Some of the population pushed off the land as numbers increase cannot be accommodated in urban jobs, causing underemployment in rural areas to be transformed into unemployment in towns and cities. In the absence of statistics one can only record the impression that as yet the problem is less serious than in other underdeveloped parts of the world. In South Africa and Rhodesia at least, this kind of so-called 'over-urbanisation' has not occurred, partly as a result of restrictive measures. Where it does occur it is certain to be economically inefficient and subversive of social stability.

Organised urban community life demands investment in housing, streets, sewerage systems, water schemes, hospitals, schools and other public buildings, which are either not required in rural areas or can be provided at low cost, sometimes by way of mobilising the leisure time of the inhabitants. These 'demographic investments' are directly related to the rate of population growth, and their claim on economic resources reduces the amount available for investment in machinery and equipment and industrial construction required to increase the per capita amount of food, clothing and prosperity goods.

Naturally, it is not the urbanward drift but the rapid population increase which is to be blamed, given the level of development.

7. FAMILY PLANNING

The above analysis would indicate that in general Southern Africa could benefit from a reduction in the growth rate of its population. This does not exclude South Africa, the most developed country in this region. Against this, a United Nations publication reports that the governments of Madagascar, Malawi and Zambia are of the opinion that a higher rate of growth would be beneficial to their economic development.[12] At the other extreme we have Mauritius, with a firmly established family-planning programme which has probably contributed to the decline in fertility rates,[13] and Botswana, which recently initiated one. In between there is a great deal of silence or an unwillingness to regard the rapid increase in numbers as a pertinent factor in the economic ills. It can be inferred, however, that the authorities in Swaziland, South Africa and Rhodesia subscribe to the principle of a reduction in the population growth rate, the last two providing the necessary services to those individuals desirous of practising birth control. Some private organisations are also active in this field.

It seems to be difficult in Southern Africa to escape the influence of the myth of open spaces or of social inertia.

In conclusion it is, perhaps, important to stress that one's conclusion about the need for population control is not to be construed as a presumptuous attempt at pressurising countries concerned to institute family-planning programmes, whose success in traditionalist societies is, in any case, problematic. It only serves as a reminder that one cannot have your cake and eat it; that in prevailing conditions one cannot have both proliferating numbers and, at the same time, avoid unemployment, underemployment, the migrant labour system, denudation of the land, poverty and malnutrition. Even if the underlying economic forces were to change, population growth will remain an impediment to economic development in most of the Southern African countries.

NOTES

1. McClelland, 'The Achievement Motive in Economic Growth' in Novack and Lekachman (eds), *Development and Society*, p. 180.
2. J. L. Sadie, 'Economic Development Is a Way of Life', *Journal of the S. A. Association for the Advancement of Science* (Sep. 1966).
3. 'Non-indigenous' – which is certainly not an unambiguous concept – does not imply that the people involved have not been born in Southern Africa; only that the origins were elsewhere.
4. W. A. Hance, *Population, Migration and Urbanisation in Africa* (1970) p. 412.
5. It has been argued that the demographic situation in South Africa has been conducive to economic growth. See J. L. Sadie, 'Population and Economic Development in South Africa', *S.A. Journal of Economics* (Sep. 1971).

6. Sadie, 'Economic Development Is a Way of Life', loc. cit.

7. Africa Institute of South Africa, *Southern Africa at a Glance* (March 1972).

8. Determined by applying the relevant probabilities of survival to the population by age.

9. Cf. Africa Institute of South Africa, op. cit., p. 3.2.

10. Hance, op. cit., p. 413.

11. Europa Publications, *Africa South of the Sahara*, p. 892.

12. United Nations, *The World Population situation in 1970*, Population Studies No. 49 (1971) p. 71.

13. Cf. D. K. Ghansah, 'Population Policies and Programmes in Sub-Saharan Africa', in African Studies Center, Michigan State University, *Rural Africana*, no. 14 (spring 1971) p. 35.

COMMENT

B. J. Piek

Family-planning programmes have a place in the overall development programme of a country. One of the major obstacles to development is undoubtedly population growth. But there may be more serious obstacles, e.g. political obstacles, or those arising from the social structure. Too much attention is paid to the relative cost of different population programmes. It is desirable to make cost-benefit studies, using alternative assumptions, to assess the relative merits of family-planning programmes and the institution of changes in the political and social structure which contribute to economic growth.

The complementarity of family-planning programmes and changes in the economic and social structure must be stressed. As elsewhere, family-planning programmes in South Africa need to be integrated with other efforts to alter the structural factors influencing family size, such as the rural/urban distribution of population. Where family-planning schemes exist without economic planning programmes, there has been no real success in retarding population growth. Small families as a norm should be considered part of the overall plan.

Since the cost to parents of producing and rearing children may be substantially below the cost to society, particularly in rural areas, the government is obliged to take action to limit the growth of population. However, the question remains open as to how much the government should decide for the people, and how much should be left to individual decision.

The importance of research in determining the place of family-planning should also be stressed. There is a lack of knowledge of the precise nature of the significant relationships and a lack of statistics; this hinders policy-makers. The crucial variables have not been sufficiently isolated, and factual information about variables is deficient, with the result that policy is based to a large extent on guesswork. Examples are the endeavours to raise the age of marriage without knowledge of the present marriage age, and the lack of knowledge of the present number of children per family.

Chapter 2

Politics and Government:
Political Dynamics

Political Aspects of Economic Development

STEFAN T. POSSONY

Economic development means the level and the *de facto* progress of an economy as they result from the interplay of market forces, legislation, governmental policies and strategies. Societal development includes the development of the economy plus the growing complexity of the society, alterations of the psychological make-up, the distribution of skills and knowledge, as well as adjustive restructuring and expanding the capacity of political institutions. Multi-ethnicity is not an obstacle to economic progress *per se*, but it can be a delaying factor when relevant skills are unevenly divided and when the motivation for economic progress is unevenly distributed or is overpowered by the desire for traditional living.

Economic development strategy denotes a concerted effort by strong and deliberately acting forces such as governments and large corporations to reach specific major goals like industrialisation, a modernised agriculture, high levels of external trade and satisfactory living standards. Development strategy, which includes but is not limited to the economic, is a concerted effort by a government to bring about all-pervasive and fundamental changes in a society's way of life.

Economic aid, which may be used as a tool of strategy, means the granting of gifts, facilities and long-term cheap credit from government to government, with the recipients usually administering the additional resources as they see fit. The recipients may contribute matching resources, but the donor rarely receives an economic (or a political) *quid pro quo*.

The efficacy of aid is controversial. The measurement of its success depends largely on the statistics used for evaluation. In general, and save for emergency help, aid has proved most successful where it was needed least.[1] Its main drawback is that it helps the recipient to postpone indispensable reforms, involves the donor in the politics of foreign countries, delays the strengthening of self-reliance and aggravates domestic power struggles. Vasily Sergeyev, manager of the U.S.S.R's economic aid programme, summarised one lesson that was learnt: 'Economic and technical aid to the developing countries is not philanthropy. It is implemented on the basis of mutual advantage and equality. . . . It has to be well justified economically.'[2]

Such justifications are difficult to produce. Hence, more often than not, aid has been justified on political grounds. Actually, economic aid rarely buys political sympathy, let alone co-operation, and it is probably true that most of the backward countries prefer the donor of guns to the donor of butter. Still, experience has taught that any strategy which aims at strengthening political collaboration must enhance the economic interdependence between donor and recipient.

Nor is economic development strategy to be confused with centralised economic planning of the communist pattern. Naturally, economic strategy can be used both by socialists and non-socialists; and socialist economic development strategy would presumably aim at the building of socialism. This paper discusses development strategy within the parameters of the market economy.

Development strategy is often conceived in purely economic terms. The assumption is made, sometimes explicitly, that as the economy grows, it will *ipso facto* solve non-economic development problems; hence, in designing development strategy, political factors should be ignored.

This is an illusion because political conditions and objectives can never be disregarded and because all economies are necessarily tied to a political cadre and its specific action capability. Action capability depends, *inter alia*, on political leadership, the composition and will of the state population, strategic estimates and economic policies. Politics and economics are intertwined wherever the government manages economic assets, intervenes in the market, organises the labour force, controls trade, currency and credit, runs the tax system and spends (and overspends) its budget income.

Within a given political, legal and social framework the strategist may want to stimulate the market forces so that they play their customary 'spontaneous' game. But to accomplish a steep growth rate at least cost, the requisite market mechanisms may have to be created institutionally, and political hindrances preventing the functioning of the market may have to be removed. Moreover no government would permit the market mechanism to lead to results that are incompatible with the *raison d'état*. Conversely, the free market does not necessarily work with all peoples, cultures and economic motivations. The kind of rationality which is required in a market economy does not go together with magical thinking.

No state leadership is able to worry about economic matters exclusively. It also must take into account numerous non-economic problems, notably internal and external security. Therefore it may have to act in a manner not entirely rational in purely economic terms.

Economic development must predominantly be accomplished by the developing society. It cannot be transplanted; but it can be facilitated and accelerated through the transfer of know-how and resources. The strategic project must necessarily aim at helping those individuals, groups and governments who want to help themselves. To bestow help on the unwilling is a hopeless enterprise.

Economic development strategy could promote such goals as modernisation, increase and diversification of consumption, the enlargement of output, the establishment of new lines of production, the stimulation of trade, the overall enhancement of productivity, the creation of private and collective property and the sustained generation of further progress by the developing society. Economic strategy could, of course, be used for negative purposes, but that is not our present interest.

Whatever economic strategy is used, there must be a feasible economic goal. In the absence of deliberately chosen goals, strategy is restricted to day-to-day improvisations. Furthermore, since shortages of funds, materials and skilled manpower are unavoidable and requirements usually exceed capacities, an additional series of decisions must be made to determine balance or unbalance, as explained by Professor Weidner, and to select 'centres of gravity' where development is specially to be pushed.

Another major consideration is that development strategies must be applied to concrete circumstances as they exist in the real world. There are no models in this world; models are one-sided, even distorted abstractions and planning aids which must never be confused with goals or *de facto* systems. Reality means precisely that each case is *sui generis*. The strategist has no choice but to start from a *status quo* which is deeply entrenched and resistant to change. Its inevitable inertia, which is due to many traditions and taboos and which continues even during 'revolutionary' periods, limits the strategist's freedom of action. Except for non-ambitious targets that could be obtained without upsetting the *status quo*, a fundamental rearranging of conditions requires much time. In the modern era, history has supposedly been accelerated; but pre-industrial societies still move under the writ of slow change.

Acceleration or not, the continuity of history is such that in all likelihood even a successful strategy of 'social engineering' or 'modernisation' will accomplish little more, after fifty or a hundred years, than the re-creation of the old structure in a more viable and up-to-date form. Unless there are major catastrophes resulting in the elimination of states and populations, or profound changes in the environment, the rule holds that '*plus ça change, plus c'est la même chose*'.

Thus, increases in productivity will not necessarily solve but may aggravate customary social problems; and in multi-ethnic societies[3] they are utterly unlikely to eliminate the difficulties of ethnic diversity. Still, economic development remains an inescapable necessity if only because retrogression would render all problems more acute and preclude comprehensive solutions.

In other words, the developmental strategist repairs and adjusts, and perhaps improves conditions which have lasted for a long time, *but* he does not create new situations. At best, if his strategic programme be granted endurance, he plants the roots of a new epoch. However, the strategist will do well to remember that there is little constancy in politics and strategic decision-making: new governments prefer programmes that appear new, but do not in fact force great changes in habits. It is hence wise to avoid over-commitments and over-investments, as well as undue sacrifices that cannot be borne for long.

Panics about 'time running out' tend to cloud judgements. One can force specific development for some time, but one cannot force total societal development for a long time. Accordingly, the socio-economic strategist is best inspired by Talley-rand's '*surtout pas de zèle*': his should be a light hand, not a Draconian fist. This particular breed of strategist performs optimally if he injects the limited forces he can bring to bear into the natural flows of development.

THE STATUS QUO

The *status quo* is the inevitable point of departure. So what is it? Within the geopolitical region of Southern Africa, which has been defined earlier in this book, the modern, industrialised, White elements of the Republic of South Africa are economically and politically preponderant. They tend to overshadow the three smaller states bordering the Republic: Botswana, Lesotho and Swaziland. Within the Republic, the nine larger Black peoples possess their own homelands, some of which include ethnic minorities. A few African peoples, notably the Tswana, Sotho and Swazi, are divided between the Republic and the independent states.

Most African peoples are also divided between the inhabitants of the homelands and the out-migrants who are staying in the White areas. At present, about 55 per cent of the Republic's African population live outside the homelands. The Republic furthermore includes ethnic groups like the Coloureds and the Asiatics who do not possess homelands of their own. The Coloureds have historically lived in the Cape Province and most Asiatics (Indians) are domiciled in Natal.

There are in the Republic of South Africa three large nations, each numbering about four million: Europeans (or White Africans), Zulu and Xhosa. The Coloureds, Tswana, North and South Sotho number each between 1·5 and 2 million. The rest are smaller in size, though they are larger than several U.N. member-states. The complex ethnic situation in South West Africa cannot be examined here.

In addition, the South African *status quo* is characterised by the following three facts:

1. Despite advances of the native economies, the differential between advanced and undeveloped societies persists. Since growth has been uneven, the differential may have grown,

statistically speaking. However, technologies and large economic resources are available which, speaking in abstract economic terms, could be introduced into areas heretofore wedded to low-subsistence agriculture, and receiving much of their cash income from migrant labour. The progress of backward populations could thus be accelerated.

2. A substantial portion of the African population, especially the groups living outside the homelands, have been drawn into the monetary economy and are gradually adjusting to modern economic life. However, progress is still in its early phase, in the main remains restricted to skilled labour, and is in part a spillover from White affluence. Out-migration proves that the desire for economic advancement is strong and widespread. This desire is also illustrated by the growing interest in education.

3. The economic development of the homelands and the peoples themselves, as distinguished from the advancement of African individuals who are earning their livelihood in the White economy, remains uncertain. This is so in part because the entrepreneurial types cannot return without losses in earning power. However, the chief cause of retardation is that the attitudes and skills of the sedentary population need substantial development before self-perpetuating economic progress can take place. Furthermore, homeland infrastructures are as yet underdeveloped. Only in exceptional cases can the homelands be regarded as advantageous locations for new industries.

There are, of course, differences in the speed of adjustment among the several peoples. Both the slow and fast movers are subject to pressures from demographic growth and from their *de facto* involvement in the monetary economy. Modern transportation and communications as well as the attractions of modern life provide incentives for change. Nevertheless, a steep take-off, as it was observed, for example, in Japan, has not yet happened in the homelands. Such a take-off must occur if continuous large-scale out-migrations and the depopulation of the homelands are to be avoided. The open question is whether the psychological conditions are ripe for the take-off to begin.

There is no single key to economic development, but an entire host of interacting factors and forces is required, such as managerial skill, capital, credit, purchasing power, transportation, communications, markets for trading, education, etc. Psychological attitudes related to work, risk, discipline, financial responsibility, willingness to save and desire for gain must conform to the demands of a modern economy.

It is particularly difficult to transform non-initiative groups which throughout their history have stuck to magical thinking and adhered to strongly repetitive modes of behaviour. Such groups are interested in better food, ample water supplies, better housing, modern tools, improved health, and longer life, and the rest of it, but they are rarely eager to make the sacrifices that modern life demands. They may be suspicious of social innovation, they deprecate mechanised and rationalised work, they did not like the mobility and variability that economic dynamism entails, and they are attached to rural and communal living.

As long as the tribal structure is not superseded by a more advanced form of socio-political organisation, traditional attitudes may be eroding, but modern attitudes can as yet not become dominant. In particular, self-actualisers are unable to accomplish much in the old environment and tend to leave for the White cities. Out-migration, of course, means loss of quality manpower. Thus, while it provides training and initial 'accumulation', it impoverishes the homelands and reduces their development potential.

Given profitability, it is not difficult to raise capital in such a volume that considerable momentum could be generated. But the capital must be properly utilised and maintained, and the equipment must not be allowed to deteriorate. Unless profits can be realised, investment would resemble the proverbial filling of an unplugged bathtub. The rule is that capital is plentiful, provided it can be attracted by realistic hopes for gain. Yet capital for loss operations is exceedingly scarce; and who should suffer the loss? Taxes and confiscations – practices which are bound to create political trouble – cannot provide sufficient funds for sustained programmes.

Economic progress creates and deepens social cleavages. Statistics which present mathematical artefacts like per capita incomes, while ignoring non-monetised assets, understate the advances of wage earners and overstate the progress among agriculturists. In fact, the urban areas in the developing countries are the locus of economic progress. The benefits which reach the countryside are uneven and frequently minimal. As a consequence, developing countries tend to be politically restless and peasant guerrillas are recruited by urban revolutionaries.

As cities and related job opportunities grow, they naturally, pull surplus labour away from agriculture. This process remains unrelated to agricultural modernisation, which it often impedes; but it causes the emergence of psychological afflictions, such as traumas and anxieties, the loss of ethnic identity, and ideologisation. Rapid development is accompanied by inflation, the spreading of slums and crime, as well as bureaucratisation. These trends lead to instability, political radicalisation and aggravated internal power struggles, as well as 'socialism'; in brief, the process entails large wastage of resources. Still, the policies of the Republic of South Africa have proved that development need not get out of hand, and need not become a vicious circle.

The self-starters usually become active as soon as a few roads are built which allow trading, sufficient land is provided to land-starved peasants, property rights are redefined, and onerous and exploitative forms of indebtment are abolished. The examples of Vietnam and Taiwan prove the point.

The distinction between self-starting and non-initiative groups is not absolute: the non-initiative groups are simply those who have a small number of self-actualising individuals, or whose cultures restrain self-actualisation. In either case, instead of relying on bureaucratic and coercive measures, development strategy should be designed to support the self-starters in whatever number they can be found, and remove the obstacles in their path.

Successes of development should not be measured by installed horsepower, the number of electrified houses or average incomes, but by the number of big entrepreneurs and their specific incomes. Such individuals are born and they do not need conditioning. Instead they need freedom of action, credits and education.

South Africa has begun to seek out the managerial and entrepreneurial talents among the Black peoples. This operation, which is still in its infancy, constitutes a significant and imaginative innovation.

DEVELOPMENT STRATEGY

With this background in mind, what might be a promising development strategy? Strategy is a co-ordinated set of planned actions for the purpose of achieving goals. In a properly designed strategy, motives (why?), objectives (what?), timing (when?), methods (how and who?) and resources (how much?) must be clearly understood and be in tune with one another. Strategies must be tested as to feasibility and the probability of success must be realistically estimated. Alternative strategies must be prepared to allow switching whenever success becomes elusive and the probability of failure arises.

In southern Africa the motives of development strategy would include the reduction of economic differentials, the enhancement of economic self-reliance by all ethnic groups, the emergence of a regional economy which would function to the best mutual benefit of all inhabitants, the growth of the region's foreign trade, the strengthening of co-operative relations within the region and the preservation of peace, including the avoidance of intra-regional conflict which could be exploited by foreign aggressors, as well as the deterrence of foreign invasion.

Given the traditions and circumstances of the area, it is mandatory that ethnic integrity be fully preserved. Actually, development would stop as soon as any major group were to fear that its survival as a group is jeopardised. Ethnic integrity is a *conditio sine qua non* of regional development. Another prerequisite is that development, in the manner in which it is pursued, command consensus of all involved populations and arouse an urge for active and mutual participation.

In the long run the operation cannot succeed if it is pushed by only one or two groups, at great sacrifices to themselves, while other groups gladly enjoy the accruing benefits but remain unwilling or unable to assume creative roles or oppose the undertaking.

It is an illusion to think that economic progress necessarily produces peacefulness and that it will stamp out sentiments of hostility. Gratefulness does not exist in international or inter-ethnic relations. Economic development often requires unpopular decisions which are attacked by hostile propaganda. It inevitably arouses arrogance and *libido dominandi* among the most successful groups, and by itself it does not alter inter-ethnic relations: nations can be antagonistic to one another when they are rich and when they are poor. But while aggressiveness by backward groups means little, the hostility of competent groups poses real threats.

Economic development renders élite groups more capable, and by the same token more ambitious, powerful and energetic. Continuous development is dependent on, and stimulates, the growth of ethnic élites. Development is essentially the creation of active élites and prospering middle classes. Accordingly, it is not surprising that the era of industrialisation and a thousandfold expansion of international trade since the early eighteenth century has also been the era of nationalism.

The new nationalism went beyond patriotism and pride in cultural accomplishment. It insisted on national self-government and on the political separation of peoples and nations that previously were linked together in multi-national states and empires. It also insisted on the unification of partitioned groups. In some instances, modern nationalism turned imperialistic.

The nationalistic motive was so strong that multi-national structures were dissolved even when the economic and security interests of the involved populations would have dictated continued 'togetherness'. Whether national aspirations and the quest for self-government could have been reconciled through more plausible arrangements of the multi-ethnic *status quo* is an unanswerable question. But the fact is that the arrangements which did exist and which were destroyed were not optimal, and the leaders of most groups within the multi-ethnic structures persuaded their followers that separation would improve their lot.

Since optimisation in terms of equal satisfaction is unlikely, economic development and the permanent preservation of multi-ethnic states may be contradictory. Mass communications, including those that originate in hostile countries, may render such potential contradictions more acute. So would security systems that actively involve all groups within the multi-ethnic structure; yet the restricting of security functions to one or two groups also tends to weaken cohesiveness.

A multi-ethnic state may move in three different directions: it may continue to develop under the aegis of multi-ethnicity, *or* it may incline towards ethnic separation, *or* it may tend towards integration, i.e. towards a situation where ethnicity is disregarded (at least in theory) and people, mostly outside the social, personal, familial and sexual spheres, act as individuals pretending they are ethnically uniform or that their ethnicity is meaningless. There are powerful vectors towards each of these three destinations, and the strategist must needs choose one of those approaches.

Whichever direction of development is chosen, the society's entire set of economic, political and social attitudes must be modified, together with much of the underlying culture. Ways of life must be altered, preferably by an evolutionary process that avoids traumas. Such a process and the internalisation of the new attitudes take several generations, provided incentives for the change are constantly applied; and precisely because traumas would be counter-productive and dangerous, psychological revolutions should not be attempted. Withal, some attitudes will not change at all – there is psychological continuity sometimes referred to as 'national character' or 'basic personality' – and other attitudes will change in the wrong direction.

The fact is that psychological processes cannot be planned. Nor can it be predicted whether an anticipated attitudinal change will favour one or the other strategic solution. Yet it can be predicted that, except for traumatic experiences, significant attitudinal modifications affecting the majority of a given population take fifty years or more.[4] The rapidity of change may be measured by the speed of the unfolding division of labour and of urbanisation; but such measurements are partial, and since the old attitudes may be surviving in new garments, they may be misleading.

On the other hand, the question may well be asked whether we know enough about relevant attitudes and their intensity, including the attitudes of ethnic groups to one another. The answer is probably in the negative. Better knowledge of the psychological facts should permit a keener application of resources and a reduction of time requirements. But instead of trying to affect entire populations quickly, the best chance would seem to lie in the concentration on élite-building.

The creation of resources, jobs, infrastructure, industries, technology, marketing outlets and technical skills also takes considerable time. To reach suitable levels of development, about three or four doubling periods are needed which, assuming a growth rate of about 5 per cent, requires nearly sixty years.[5] Such growth presupposes an investment of 15–20 per cent of the initial G.N.P., with the yearly increments rising gradually. To do any good, these outlays must be properly utilized; and such utilisation depends on the timely emergence of new attitudes.

The practical meaning is that nation-building is a slow and uncertain business, especially if the 'one people per one territory' concept were applied and large-scale population exchange were instituted to sort out ethnic mixing. Thus, the short-run feasibility of a strategy aiming at ethnic separatism is highly questionable. There is no reason to question its long-run feasibility, but it is futile to plan a strategy for the 2020–2050 period now.

Within the context of a strategy aiming at integration, economic development *could* be comparatively rapid: for example, there would be no need for population exchange, migration control and the build-up of homelands. But the attitudinal process needed for this solution would be particularly slow. Given the correlation between development and nationalism, this solution also seems impracticable because of societal, cultural, ideological and political factors, and because it would lead to violence, the drying-up of capital, and massive losses of skilled and managerial manpower through emigration and terrorism.[6]

The difficulty with the *status quo* solution is that development would presumably continue to accelerate in the White areas and would lag in the Black homelands. If so, further large-scale out-migration tending to push ethnic distributions towards an integrationist pattern must be anticipated. By contrast, a satisfactory *status quo* solution presupposes the accelerated build-up of the homelands and a correlated shrinking of the out-migration flow. But this requirement is difficult to meet, not merely because the homelands cannot be built up at the requisite speed, but mainly because the *differential* between the levels inside and outside the homelands will remain substantial and may even grow. Hence, unless the White economy were smashed, the economic incentives for out-migration will not disappear. On the contrary, the attractions of out-settlement will become increasingly attractive.

Thus, each of the three possible roads is blocked by serious obstacles:

1. The *status quo*, if accompanied by major infusions of economic development, will hardly lead to early ethnic separation; instead it will, at least temporarily, result in additional mingling.

2. The integrationist solution is impracticable because of insoluble non-economic problems, and because it would delay and possibly arrest the economic development of the non-White peoples and jeopardise the further progress of the Whites.

3. The nationalist-separatist solution would entail economic regressions for all, especially if it were tried before development in the homelands is self-sustaining. Ethnic consolidations throughout southern Africa might be useful, but economic separations, while they could help reduce the Republic's development tasks, would probably lead to retrogression and would aggravate regional security problems. If economic growth is to be sustained – and accelerated – throughout the region, the Republic must continue to play its role as the paramount promoter of growth. Thus, the formula of 'separate development' covers ethnic self-government, ethnic self-reliance, ethnic being-by-itself, and the like, but must be recognised as a principle of political and social, not economic, organisation. *Separate ethnic development is largely predicated upon interdependent economic development.* To the extent that regional peace depends upon ethnic integrity, the inverse relation also holds true.

Economic forces push in the direction, not of 'integration', but of 'intermingling' and continuous migratory movements. By contrast, ethnic forces push in the direction of separation.

There is *no ideal solution*. This fact must be faced squarely. Fortunately the finding is by no means catastrophic. Strategists are frequently confronted by a choice between unsatisfactory courses of action. Rarely, if ever, can an ideal course of action even be imagined. The usual solution is to choose on the basis of the 'lesser evil'.

The main root of the difficulty is that *three* aims are to be pursued *simultaneously*: development, ethnic integrity and security. Some people argue that the aim of ethnic integrity should be dropped, but since 'just economic development' is not feasible, a political objective remains indispensable. An objective like 'no conflict' cannot stand by itself but requires sub-goals and implementing techniques. Moreover, if ethnic identity were left unprotected, this objective would *ipso facto* be sacrificed. Such a choice would agitate all groups that feel endangered and would incite to protracted violence.

ETHNIC INTEGRITY

The concept of ethnic integrity requires explanation and it can presumably be realised in different modes. The White group is by no means ethnically uniform, but cultural differences are minor and not divisive, and intercommunications are fairly uncomplicated. The White group may therefore be regarded as a single and endogamous South African *ethnos* whose integration is progressing steadily, on a bilingual basis, and which is quite capable of assimilating White immigrants.

Just as the European population *in Europe* consists of Swedes and Spaniards, Turks and Irish, Hungarians and Scots, so the African population is not uniform. The Bantu-speaking peoples of Southern Africa embrace four groups, of which the Nguni and Sotho are numerically large. Like Europeans, they tend to preserve their ethnic integrity in their historic settlement areas. Outside their native lands, where individuals are often ethnically isolated among 'strange' people, a tendency to intermingle can be observed.

There is no particular reason to assume that any Black African people wants to abandon its *ethnos* and merge into a large Black nation which would be formed through the interbreeding of the kindred groups. Such a development may occur in the distant future – this is pure speculation. For the time being, each of the several Black peoples is a reality. None exhibits a desire for ethnic transformation. Most or all want to advance as what they are.

The large African groups clearly possess the demographic basis of nation-building, especially since population growth continues at a good rate. However, there is out-migration of all Black peoples and out-migrants are ethnically intermingling within the Black 'race'. So far, out-migrants more or less stick to their own *ethnos*, and African townships are structured along ethnic lines. But once the out-migrants lose touch with their own people and children are born outside the homeland, ethnic ties will weaken. At that point, a Black population as an *ethnos* of its own will probably emerge and be added to the existing groups. This new *ethnos* will be largely located within the White area, and while one portion of these 'supra-ethnic' Blacks may be using specific Bantu languages which would tie them back to one or the other people, others may switch into Afrikaans or English or another advanced lingua franca. Some observers believe the process has already progressed quite far in African townships within the White areas.

Like all migrations, the out-migration in South Africa is subject to control. But within a single race ethnic integrity cannot be protected by the police, and no attempt is made to do so. Ethnic continuity depends on whether the homeland and its inhabitants are developing so that there will be a permanent reason to remain with the people into which one was born. It depends, furthermore, on whether development can be directed in such a manner that out-migration is reduced drastically and the diaspora groups *desire* to go home.

In this sense, economic development must be seen as a tool to prevent dispersal and thereby preserve ethnic integrity. Members of an ethnic group prefer to live with one another rather than with strangers. This wish may be extremely strong psychologically, but ethnic togetherness must also be economically feasible. The difficulty may very well be that as economic incentives for return migrations remain weak, spontaneous relocations to the homelands would be rare. Coercive mass transfers of population pose great hazards. Yet the continuity of out-migration does in fact threaten ethnic integrity because the elements eager for advancement are most heavily engaged in out-migration.

During the decade from 1960 to 1970 the Black African diaspora in the White areas dropped from 62·5 to 53·5 per cent, but still less than half the Black Africans live in the homelands. Although the rate of out-settlement went down, partly through enlargement of the homelands, the number of Blacks in White areas rose in absolute figures from 6·8 to 8 million. At this writing, one-third of the Republic's entire population are out-migrants.[7] It is difficult to imagine that Southern Africa will soon be divided *more geometrico* according to the 'one people per one territory' principle.

Hence ethnic intermingling is one side of the coin: Black Africans do settle in White areas, and the racial and ethnic groups maintain economic contacts. The other side is that ethnic groups who have their own psychologies, traditions, institutions, ways of life, territorial rights and self-confidence are not willing to share their lives with other peoples. If they were forced to live together in close social contact, the 'neighbours' would start fighting and would look for ways of splitting away. It is for this very reason of ethnic incompatibility that the nation-state has been recognised as the most suitable territorial concept of government, notwithstanding the fact that multi-ethnic states survive, that a number of nations are partitioned, and that the concept can rarely be applied in its pure form.

SEVEN RULES

The *first* rule of modern statecraft is that states should be ethnically as uniform as possible and that single nations living within contiguous territories should be united politically. This national principle does not exclude inter- and intra-ethnic federations.

A *second* fundamental rule of the contemporary era has been that ethnic groups must not live under foreign domination, but are entitled to self-government in a form best fitted to their circumstances.

A *third* rule has been that groups as yet incapable of running their own affairs may be administered through temporary tutelage. However, they should be assisted in transforming their traditional institutions into modern self-administrations. As the group matures it is expected to assume more and more administrative functions until fully independent self-government can be established.

The probability that not all ethnic groups will make it to the level of full independence is customarily passed over in silence. At the same time, many governments still balk at the notion that *each ethnos* has the right to 'autonomy', at a lower *or* higher level. Some governments espouse the 'melting-pot' concept. It is self-evident, however, that each people, however small or primitive, has the right of self-preservation. The realisation of this right necessitates self-administration in some form between autonomy and independence.[8]

A *fourth* rule has been that each people possesses the right of self-determination, which means that once literacy and maturity have been attained, each major change in political status should be achieved through the exercise of that right. The right does not imply that self-determining peoples must necessarily choose complete independence. Provided that international partnership arrangements are acceptable to all groups concerned, each self-determining people is entitled to select the particular relationship which it finds most suitable – limited sovereignty, independence, or federative links.

States, whether they be national or multi-national, must be in harmony with the will of the governed, that is, inhabitants must like their state and its constitution. Furthermore, governmental policies, to be succesful, must enjoy popular consent. This *fifth* rule – state and policies derive from popular consent – is just as important as the previous rules.

Consent need not be achieved through the procedures of modern mass democracy which, in order to sustain government by majority and opposition in alternation, aims at a consent–dissent constellation. Such a system is beyond the ken of developing peoples who lack issue competence and orientation. In periods of societal transformation, authoritarian modes of rule are well-nigh unavoidable. But those modes also require consent. No rule can survive long if consent is falling away; and with weak consent the best government can achieve but little. By contrast, authoritarian rule based upon consent and active popular support can be most effective.

Communal societies – Gemeinschaften – under hereditary and patriarchal regimes, and during their phase of illiteracy, consent by implication; and they change their status through revolt and war. Large and complex societies which are literate, consent explicitly through representation and voting, and after wars through treaties and their ratification. However, in its ethnic aspects legitimacy can devolve only on a government incorporating the *ethnos* of the governed group. This rule – our *sixth* – holds in multi-ethnic settings, including those where one group possesses dominant military and economic power, and hence wields the strongest political influence: in such settings legitimacy is achieved through representation by each *ethnos*. It also applies to economic development which, as a concept, a plan and a concrete execution of that plan, must be consented to by all affected groups through their legitimate and representative governments and spokesmen.

The *seventh* rule bears on continuity. It is inadvisable to 'invent' political institutions and implant them in a social and cultural soil in which they cannot take root. Political development requires institutional changes, but to be effective these must remain within the parameters of continuity.

PLANNING?

Circumstances in Southern Africa are such that the indicated core solution of the nation-state does not fit so completely as one would wish. On the one hand, multi-ethnicity is a fact of life in a far more complex and deeper sense than in most other regions of the world except, perhaps, India. On the other hand, a common trade and currency market has been in existence, whereas most of the potential nation-states are yet to be created. The comparative emptiness of Southern Africa is one of the positive factors which allows for flexible arrangements and rearrangements. Yet capital flows are unidirectional and most tax income is created within the White area. Hence the regional common market, whose preservation is a primary requisite of sustained growth, is in the nature of an economic heartland with several hinterlands. The European Common Market embraces nations who have attained more or less the same levels of economic development.

Even if it were to avoid the pitfalls of socialism, centralised economic 'planning' does not appear to be a proper method of managing common markets. Planning in the sense of *économie dirigée* involves bureaucratism and over-regulation. Granted there is a strong need to reconcile multi-ethnic interests, the danger of over-regulation is particularly acute whenever strong and costly stimulants must be applied incessantly to keep development going and accelerating. Even the most skilful planners are like boatmen in wild waters for which they have only erroneous and dated navigational charts. Hence they are bound to make mistakes which under the conditions of planning could be gigantic and must always burden the government.

Elaborate machineries of management do not handle difficult and non-repetitive situations efficiently. To make things worse, such machineries perform very slowly. By contrast, the market economy provides flexibility and adjustment mechanisms which are of particular importance in opaque social and ethnic situations.

Planning carried to the point of a bureaucratisation of the economy offers additional disadvantages:

1. The bureaucrat cannot replace the entrepreneur and his willingness to take risks.
2. Plans cannot replace initiative.
3. Since consent is based upon comprehensibility of events and planning in action remains incomprehensible, a planning system enjoys only minimal support and survives through the black (free) market it engenders.
4. The simplest system is the most promising, especially under primitive conditions.
5. Development issues are best depoliticised. If so, planning should be avoided. Instead, full trust should be placed in the interplay of market forces.

The key arguments against bureaucratic management are: (1) A plethora of regulations unavoidably leads to confusion and additional regulations. This Parkinson type of process cannot but terminate in socialism. (2) If several governments, each of them representing ethnic will, must be co-ordinated, central planning, which is autocratic rule from *one* centre, becomes impossible. Multi-centred regional planning is a conceptual monstrosity.

In brief, governmental planning must be of the limited type, and it must be aimed at stimulating the growth of the market. It is unfortunately difficult to provide a clear-cut definition dividing necessary governmental 'planning' like the building of roads and dams from unnecessary and undesirable planning like that aiming to substitute bureaucrats for entrepreneurs and managers, and that designed to build 'systems' and to alter pre-existing conditions profoundly and rapidly.

The dangerous planners are those who elaborate a blueprint

and wish to substitute it for the market – not a blueprint for a power grid, but a blueprint for a society. The task of a government that presides over the building of a multi-ethnic society is more modest: it is like that of an oarsman in a leaky boat who must get to the shore in time. If he doesn't bail, he can't make it, and if he doesn't paddle, he can't make it either. The problem is to divide his activities properly. On one paddle for three bails he won't reach land, but he may be successful on three paddles for one bail. And if the oarsman is a politically handicapped bureaucracy, it should seek help from the initiative and the resources of the market.

Within an economic region, transportation, water supply and distribution, health services and the like must be laid out on a demographic (not ethnic) basis. Currency management affects all groups. Taxation must be equitable to all individuals, classes and groups, and must not create special burdens or privileges. Education must be ethnically oriented and in some particulars should vary from group to group.

Those tasks are straightforward. But major difficulties arise with respect to the locating of industries. Such locating affects ethnic specialisation in trade and production; it influences distribution of manpower, and requires the allocation of resources on a basis of priority instead of equity. The judicious selection of individual sites is expected to alter the pattern of population movements. To some extent, this expectation is justified. But the proverbial 'flight from the land', or urbanisation, is the mass movement truly characteristic of development. Unless the homelands acquire growing cities and exciting urban life, their attraction may not suffice to lure the out-migrants back; and the locating of new industries at the homeland borders may have only limited effect. Is it feasible to build homeland cities which are psychologically competitive with existing metropolitan areas?

In any event, decisions on industrialisation and urbanisation, whether they are sound or not, are bound to arouse political dissent. If they cannot be made through the market mechanism, which would be preferable, they would be best made through multi-ethnic political concert, as distinguished from centralised or decentralised economic planning.

The main danger is that firm guidelines on the locating of

industries and of manpower, however these guidelines were arrived at, erect huge obstacles against the functioning of the market: plants and facilities that would be built under free market conditions would not be built if licensing prevails and if locations are imposed. An even more severe slowdown of progress must be expected if industrial investment is through government corporations which largely depend on budgets instead of capital markets and which keep out private firms on the grounds that these would invalidate the ethnic blueprint. If this *dirigiste* approach is tied to a naïve faith in the potential of centralised planning, the ultimate goal may still be reached, but the operation is run the hard way.

CONTIGUITY AND DISPERSAL

The notion that ultimately each ethnic group needs its own economically capable government and by the same token its own homeland is entirely valid, if only because foreign domination would be the inescapable alternative. But the related notion that the overwhelming bulk of each *ethnos* should live within its homeland appears to be more doubtful. Whether or not one likes ethnic dispersal and intermingling, this condition has had historical continuity. Yet whatever the structural-constitutional scheme of the future may be, partial ethnic dispersal does *not* preclude the development of states on the basis of the ethnic or nationality principle.

Under the monarchical principle, states were unified under one sceptre, without the state territory always being unbroken and contiguous. An ethnic group or a nation is a unit because of psychological, cultural and historical continuity dating back to a common origin, and because its members possess the will to be politically united and *'faire de grandes choses ensemble'*. Territory is an enormously important factor in nationhood, yet a nation can be completely dispersed and still remain a living political organism.

The point should not be driven too far, and as a general principle, peoples and nations are entitled to territorial property on which their life would be centred. Yet such territory need not be contiguous. Whether it is or not, national rights are vested primarily in the persons and not in the land. The fact of ethnicity is attached to the person as an attribute to his birth, even though in some situations and to a limited extent volitional factors may affect the basic ethnic personality.

Wherever one single member of group A is located, there is an element of people A; and wherever a multitude of A individuals is found, there this people has a part of its body. Thus, it appears feasible – and it is certainly necessary – to divorce the principle of ethnic integrity from the territorial principle.

Let us assume ethnic group A inhabits a historical homeland which consists of two non-contiguous territories, A_1 and A_2. In addition, there are a number of small A settlements as enclaves within other homelands, including districts in townships, a_1, a_2, a_3, ... Finally, there are scattered individuals nowhere numerous enough to establish the minimal institutions required for any measure of self-administration but who could be organised as a curia or non-territorial exclave, a_c.

Territories $A_1 + A_2 + a_1 + a_2 + a_3 + ... + a_c$ would constitute the totality of the 'homeland'. Every A individual, wherever located, would be listed as an A voter. He would vote for A candidates and be represented in the A legislative assembly. If the assembly forms the ethnic government, the individual's representation at the top level would be indirect. If the head of government were elected by popular vote, each A voter would be eligible to participate in his election. The ethnic government would administer A affairs in the homeland and in the exclaves, and it would represent the individuals on the curial list.

Something like this electoral system is coming into existence in the Republic of South Africa. The system is fully compatible with 'elite-building' and 'nation-building' within one territory as well as with the facts of compact and scattered out-settlement. It is also adaptable to the local self-administration of out-migrant groups and to multi-ethnic townships, as well as the various contingencies of ethnic redistribution.

Once ethnic governments act as authentic spokesmen and leaders of their peoples, they should be able to pursue an effective policy of 'in-gathering' the out-migrants within the homelands. Ethnic tidying-up can work only as a co-operative and inter-ethnic effort.

REGIONAL POLITICAL STRUCTURE

In the last analysis, the decisive question will be whether a suitable overall political structure can be devised to give multi-ethnicity in Southern Africa a stable and mutually satisfactory *modus vivendi*. This problem is more complicated than that confronting the European nations who, to supplement the Common Market, are looking for, but have not yet found, a suitable federative or confederative structure.

It should be remembered, however, that the movement for a European federation began in earnest only after the nationality principle was recognised and several multi-ethnic states were replaced by national states, a process that in some instances was accompanied by population exchanges. Through the vicissitudes of recent European history, regional interdependence has persisted and has been felt strongly whenever attempts were made to destroy such interdependence. At present, federation is frequently recommended to handle interdependence *explicitly* on the political level.

The European example is indeed instructive. It shows that nations are willing to enter into federative arrangements only after they gain their independence.

In Southern Africa, where there are huge differentials in the levels of development and far more profound cultural and psychological differences than in Europe, it might be foolish at this time to look for federative ties. Homelands may become independent early, they may reserve to themselves the top economic decisions, and they may be expected to collaborate closely with the Republic: still, they will for a long time remain under-developed; hence their equality will be largely of a legal nature. It would seem highly premature to worry about supra-national structures long before the processes of nation-building have been completed. No one knows how long those processes will last and what their outcome will be. It is unlikely that the final result will display much conceptual coherence. It is more probable that the several states will remain multi-ethnic and that the relations between the regional states will not always be co-operative.

Nevertheless, it is important to recognise that there is no level of societal development where political authority is absent. Joint political authority exists now which, though it is in White hands, still functions in a multi-ethnic manner.

Except for small groups below the tribal level, most Black peoples in South Africa are organised under tribal authorities, and related tribes may be run by inter-tribal councils. In some of the homelands there are emerging more advanced types of governments and legislative assemblies. These governments are regularly consulted as the spokesmen of their people, and their capabilities to understand and tackle problems of development are gradually increasing. Independence may be constitutionally promulgated, but such promulgation is merely a turning-point in the process of becoming a self-determining *ethnos*.

During the present state of history, development strategy has remained in the hands of White Africans, inevitably so, and it is executed through resources owned and controlled by Whites. Yet this does not mean that the White government can or does act unilaterally. Major decisions derive from contact, consultation and persuasion, and the tribal or post-tribal governments convey their understanding of the programme to their peoples. The minimum of political participation, without which development is not possible, clearly exists.

REGIONAL INTERDEPENDENCE

It was pointed out before that economic development cannot be separated from political strategy and psycho-political action. The tearing apart of economics from politics is a purely abstract mental exercise. Hence, as the economy develops, political problems and tasks will become increasingly important.

The concept of separate development is a rejection of colonialism, alien domination and ethnic exploitation, and it acknowledges the principle of ethnic integrity and its dynamism. The word 'separate' denotes that each people is, or ultimately will be, master of its own destiny.

But does 'separate' mean the absence of political contacts or links? Does it signify the isolation of White Africa within its region and within the world? A policy of isolation is a thoroughly impracticable concept of foreign policy and it will not become more practicable in future. The strategic inadequacies of isolation need not be laboured. It should be self-evident that a country which is heavily and necessarily engaged in foreign trade and which holds 'strategic lands' cannot go it alone.

In terms of economic development, the peoples of the region are interdependent. Consequently, factual political interdependence cannot be lacking. There is also psychological interdependence: if the psychological factors are neglected, cultural and intellectual values cannot be transmitted, development will work badly or may become counter-productive, and security will be endangered.

Interdependence must therefore be accepted as a fairly ubiquitous fact of life. At the same time, fears that interdependence must necessarily threaten ethnic integrity must be resisted. It all depends on how this fact of life is acted upon. The basic problem of ethnic integrity is that it must be preserved within the cadre, and even as an element, of interdependence. The solution of the problem rests on peacekeeping. It is also predicted on an effective political system that provides elective representation and ethnic self-government on all the levels required, plus an inter-ethnic structure which facilitates co-ordination among regional groups.

It should be recognised, however, that hostility of the dangerous kind is nearly always related to international power struggles. Hence foreign policy is involved; and foreign policy posture is dependent in part on how the regional problems of ethnic integrity and interdependence are being handled.

INTERMEDIATE PROGRESS

Suppose there are to be joint multi-ethnic institutions and their personnel is to be wholly or partially representative: it would not follow that those representatives must be elected by direct voting. To staff institutions of this type, indirect voting is preferable and almost mandatory. Among other things, indirect voting would improve personnel selection. Furthermore, the efficacy of such institutions depends on their expertise. Naturally, experts cannot be elected by popular vote; instead they must be appointed. Still, through a variety of confirmation and consent procedures, the appointees can be made representative.

As capabilities and requirements grow, development policies must necessarily be planned and implemented on a multilateral basis. This task may call for a properly formalised and institutionalised multi-ethnic or all-ethnic development council. Such a council could be composed of indirectly elected delegates from the several ethnic governments, of appointed experts, and of *ex officio* top bureaucrats and ministers of development.

The council could be advisory, but it would engage in parliamentary types of debates, committee work, the writing of committee reports and voting on recommendations. Their recommendations would be made to the top regional development authority. Disputes could be settled by an institutionalised conference of chief magistrates.

Such a council could also be constituted as an Ethnic Council whose responsibilities would include development. As the Council proves its worth, it could be authorised to draft and submit bills to the several legislatures.

It seems necessary to underpin the whole development strategy with a proper multi-ethnic foundation of education and research. For example, an inter-ethnic college could be of great help in working out the specific problems of the several groups and of the region as a whole, and it could formulate doctrines for joint development. The college could embrace special schools for each group, departments for functional problems like water supply, a school devoted to the problems of nation-building (which for the advanced students would have to be run multi-ethnically) and an inter-ethnic school dealing with interdependence, its prospectus and limitations. If there were a meeting of the minds, the development task might be greatly eased.

I want to reiterate that the strategic purpose of development can be reached only in connection with ethnic integrity and security, and that this triad of objectives is attainable only through the creation of a proper psychological atmosphere. The security problem is eminently psychological in nature; and psychological attachment to good neighbourliness and interdependence is extremely rare. Interdependence is a material fact that calls for mutual psychological comprehension and consent.

But psychological rapport cannot be created just by propaganda and persuasion. There must be a solid institutional and legal basis. For example, one can easily visualise that in a complex multi-ethnic population there would be a requirement not merely for a Bill of Rights that protects individuals, but also for a Bill of Rights and Obligations which would be addressed to ethnic groups, to races and to the several governments.

On the basis of such constitutional documents, complaints could be filed before an investigative tribunal for inter-ethnic affairs, whose findings could be given the status of recommendations.

This tribunal may be conceived as a facility available to all ethnic groups through their governments. But there is no reason why no provisions should be made for processing complaints by groups and individuals who believe their rights are being violated.

Protective arrangements must be supplemented by constructive contacts. This is perhaps the most delicate aspect of the operation, but learning, cultural advances and co-operation are impeded through isolationism, and alliances are forestalled. Isolationism is strategic self-amputation.

ACCELERATED GROWTH?

Is *accelerated* growth of the Black living standard in South Africa feasible? Since information on current growth is inadequate, the question is hard to answer. Between 1960 and 1968 the G.N.P. growth rate of South Africa was 4·4 per cent. Gross fixed capital formation, which is presumably about the same as the investment rate, stood at 29 per cent. Thus the investment/growth coefficient was about 6·5, which is neither a bad nor an outstanding performance.

Given the racial distribution, the demographic growth rates (3·8 per cent for Blacks and 2·14 per cent for the Whites) and the observable facts of Black development, the Black economic growth rate cannot really be below 4 per cent, or else visible growth creates a wrong image. Given this visible growth, even a growth rate of 5 per cent – or 2·5 times more than the pre-1960 growth rate of 2 per cent – appears low, since it translates into a per capita growth rate of 1·2 per cent. But if the Black rate were 5 per cent, the White and Coloured growth rate could not be much above 3 per cent.

It is not plausible that the Black economic growth rate is substantially above the White–Coloured rate, nor is it plausible that a 4 per cent Black rate prevails, which would correspond to a 6 per cent White rate, as the calculations suggest; for a *near-zero* Black per capita growth does not jibe with observations.

Thus the statistics indicate that the overall reported South African growth rate is too low, given the Republic's objectives, despite the fact that the investment rate seems to be quite high and should provide for an overall growth rate of 8–9 per cent. Otherwise, these basic statistics command little confidence; and the reported growth may be underestimated.

The investment/growth ratio *may* be higher in the Black than in the White economy. If it is about 7 and if the Black G.N.P. is about R1·5 billion, Black investment would have to be about R420 million – which appears to be too high.

The statistical confusion does not allow any firm answers, but if development is to be accelerated, investments (*inter alia*) will have to be increased or the investment/growth ratio will have to be improved, or both. This task is obviously difficult. So is there a policy which, to be blunt about it, results in wastage of investment? And is this wastage due to the ethnic rather than the economic locating of new industries?

Put differently, the question is as follows: Would Black growth be accelerated most rapidly by (1) maximising the overall South African growth rate, (2) investing exclusively according to economic criteria, and (3) by relying on an enlarged monetary flow into the Black economy? Or could such acceleration be achieved by directing vastly increased investment flows into the homelands and their adjacent borders?

If the second solution appears statistically convincing, the next questions arise: (1) whether the homelands are able economically to absorb a larger investment flow, (2) whether this redirection of investment flow is acceptable to the dominant groups of taxpayers and investors, and (3) whether, which is highly doubtful, such redirection conforms with the security needs of the Republic.

CONCLUSION

The foremost task of political strategy is to make psychological impact and to gain supporters for one's policy. If such policy is

reasonable and constructive, its meaning can be projecte͞
suasively – but the projection must be ventured.

Within Southern Africa, development strategy is an extremeı̗
difficult undertaking. Its success is in part dependent upon
political innovation and psychological technique, and in part
upon an attitude that rejects fear and anxiety and instead opts
for relaxed approaches. Past experience and accomplishments
allow for reasonable optimism and, if lessons have been learnt
from past mistakes, there are grounds for strong optimism. Even
if the prospects for development strategy were judged to be un-
promising, the fact is that no better alternative has yet been
proposed. The strategist must live with the problems such as
they are, and his mind must remain receptive to improvement.
If he acts constructively, he will probably advance his cause.

The secret of development strategy in South Africa is to strike
an effective *dynamic balance* between three key factors: ethnicity,
economic growth and politico-economic administration.

1. Many Americans and Europeans believe that the problem
   of South Africa would be solved satisfactorily if the ethnic
   factor were disregarded. This notion disregards the historical emphasis which virtually all modern political philosophies or ideologies – socialism, nationalism, conservatism,
   nineteenth-century European romanticism and liberalism,
   with the sole exception of American neo-Jeffersonian
   'liberalism' – have been placing on ethnicity, the national-
   ethnic principle and the right of self-determination. It also
   disregards the psycho-sociological need of man to belong
   to a kindred community wherein he feels at home and
   whose purposes he shares. The ethnic requirement cannot
   in fact be waived. It commands *higher priority* than
   economic growth.

   On the other hand, the ethnic principle can be implemented in different forms. It is argued here that ethnic
   self-government and representation are the key forms of
   implementation, while the separation of ethnic habitat,
   though highly desirable in many circumstances, is not
   always feasible: such unfeasibility neither negates the
   ethnic principle, nor does it invalidate its implementation
   through self-government and representation.

The ethnic principle does not call for isolation, let alone the cutting of contacts. It must instead be viewed as the prerequisite of *inter-ethnic co-operation*, including mutual security and common market arrangements.

2. Economic growth in Southern Africa presupposes the cultivation of economic interdependence. Accelerated development probably calls, *inter alia*, for larger and economically more efficient investments. But before final judgements can be made on this point, better information must become available.

3. The current political administration of economic growth in South Africa does not appear to maximise the contributions which a free market could make. In fact, this management seems to restrict the market unduly, on the strength of an over-interpretation of the ethnic principle; and it seems to be too highly bureaucratised, while at the same time it appears to be over-committed to centralised planning as the chief tool of solving ethnic problems.

Each of the three key factors, including political administration, is required, but the balance between them has yet to be optimised. The ethnic principle has been over-extended, to the detriment of growth and security. The use of capital seems to be frequently wasteful, with the result that the growth rates are too low and that, consequently, the processes of nation-building are slowed down. The administration of Black development appears suspicious of market forces, fails to give full rein to private initiative and overrates its proficiency at planning, as well as the potential of economic planning for the solution of ethnic problems.

Multi-ethnic problems have never been handled well. It is surprising to find that they can be handled at all, and to a high degree intelligently. Still, more perfect approaches are needed.

NOTES

1. The Marshall Plan was a project to reconstruct efficient and productive economic systems which were temporarily disarranged by war.
2. The Soviet aid programme is largely a strategic undertaking in which economic means are used to support conquest and defence. Most of the Soviet 'aid' has gone to Eastern Europe and places like Cuba and Egypt.

3. The term 'multi-ethnic society' may denote an 'integrated' single society consisting of members with different ethnicity; or it may refer to several ethnic societies which are interconnectedly living within one political unit. In the first case the ethnic groups are more or less unorganised, in the second case they are politically constituted. In both cases, multi-ethnicity is a permanently operating factor which cannot be eliminated except by expulsion or genocide of ethnic groups. The idea that multi-ethnicity would vanish through miscegenation within two or three generations is invalid, and it is hardly correct even for longer time-spans. To the extent that the mixing process works it involves the destruction of ethnic groups: demographic genocide.

4. The time requirement is three generations for European immigrants into the United States. See the data collected in Leo Srole, Thomas Langner, and Associates, *Mental Health in the Metropolis* (New York: McGraw-Hill, 1962) chaps 14–16.

5. The doubling period for a growth rate of 2 per cent is 35 years; for 1 per cent growth is 70 years.

6. I forgo discussing the type of 'integration' which is proposed as a technique to eject White Africans from their home.

7. A few illustrations from the Census of 1970 may be helpful.

(a) For example, in the area of Adelaide, Cape Province, there is only a Xhosa population. In Barkly West, there are 80 per cent Tswana, 8 per cent Xhosa, and 12 per cent Black mélange.

(b) The Black distribution in the Johannesburg area is as follows:

	%
Zulu	31
Tswana	18
Seshoeshoe	13
Xhosa	10
Sepedi	10
Shangaan	7
Swazi	4
Venda	4
North Ndebele	1
South Ndebele	0.6
Others	1.4
	100

The total Black population is 803,500.

(c) The ethnic 'purity' of the nine homelands varies from 68 per cent to 98 per cent:

Main Populations in Homelands

	%
Basotho Ba Borwa	98
Ciskei	97

Zululand	96
Transkei	95
Venda	90
Matshangana	88
Lebowa	83
Swazi	70
Tswana	68

This means that two-thirds of the homeland populations average 96 per cent of ethnic 'purity' per homeland and that five out of nine homelands approach the ideal of one-people-per-one-territory.

(d) Of the Xhosa people whose two homelands are the most advanced, 57 per cent live in these homelands, 28 per cent in Cape Province, 9 per cent in Transvaal, 4 per cent in the Orange Free State, and 2 per cent in Natal.

8. Under the pressure of Indian protests, even the U.S. Bureau of Indian Affairs has begun to espouse 'tribal solutions to tribal problems'. Harrison Loesch, Assistant Secretary to the Interior, explained:

As more tribes, more reservations in their own good time join the overall planning and development of the Indian community, the bureau will of necessity change from the management-oriented, paternalistic and authoritarian agency it has been to a service and technical assistance operation.

The Indians are supposed to get complete tribal control over education. They will be granted influence on road construction and the federal job assistance programme. 'Indian development' will be instituted in the reservations. The Indians will draft development plans to meet their own needs (*San José Mercury*, 13 January 1972).

Political Aspects
of Modernisation

DENIS WORRALL

Modernisation is a special kind of hope. Embodied within it are all the past revolutions of history and all the supreme human desires. The modernisation revolution is epic in its scale and moral in its significance. Its consequences may be frightening. Any goal that is so desperately desired creates political power, and this force may not always be used wisely or well. Whatever direction it may take, the struggle to modernise is what has given meaning to our generation. It tests our cherished institutions and our beliefs. It puts our country in the marketplace of ideas and ideologies. So compelling a force has it become that we are forced to ask new questions of our own institutions. Each country, whether modernised or modernising, stands in both judgement and fear of the results. Our own society is no exception.

David E. Apter, *The Politics of Modernisation*

I

The subject of this paper is the role of government and politics in the modernisation process in general, and in Southern Africa in particular. As such, it focuses on the capacity of different political systems to absorb technological change and promote economic development. But as modernisation also embraces political development, this paper touches on the questions of nation-building and national integration, and the role of political parties and political élites in the modernisation process. The analysis itself of the political systems of Southern Africa is performed in terms of Apter's typology of developmental political systems. The paper concludes with a cursory examination of the political configurations of Southern African regionalism and the relevance of this factor in the modernisation process.

II

Whereas definitions and descriptions of modernisation vary greatly,[1] there is little disagreement within the literature on the more important consequences of modernisation for the politics[2] of modernising societies. Huntingdon, for example, writes that modernisation has a threefold impact on politics. Firstly, it involves

> the rationalisation of authority, the replacement of a large number of traditional, religious, familial and ethnic political authorities by a single secular, national political authority. . . . Political authority involves assertion of the external sovereignty of the nation-state against transnational influences and of the national government against local and regional powers. It means national integration and the centralisation or accumulation of power in recognised national lawmaking institutions. Secondly, modernisation involves the differentiation of new political functions and the development of specialised structures to perform these functions. Areas of particular competence – legal, military, administrative, scientific – become separated from the political realm, and autonomous, specialised, but subordinate organs arise to discharge those tasks. . . . Thirdly, political modernisation involves increased participation in politics by social groups throughout the society. . . . Rationalised authority, differentiated structures, and mass participation thus distinguish modern politics from antecedent politics.[3]

And Welch writes that

> The process of modernisation has three major characteristics: (1) an increased centralisation of power in the State, coupled with the weakening of traditional sources of authority; (2) differentiation and specialisation of political institutions; (3) increased popular participation in politics and greater identification of individuals with the political system as a whole.[4]

These formulations of the consequences for politics of modernisation – seen as multi-faceted change – are based on studies of the development of modernised as well as modernising societies.

So, when Huntingdon asserts, for example, that 'The crucial institutional distinction between the two [the traditional policy and the modern policy] is thus in the organisations for structuring mass participation in politics',[5] he is referring as much to England and France before and after the emergence of political parties as to Ghana and Guinea. The historical dimension to modernisation in politics is even more explicit: Almond and Powell's discussion of the development of political systems[6] or La Palombara and Weiner's discussion of the origin of political parties.[7] However, the crucial difference between the experience of relatively modernised polities on the one hand, and modernising polities on the other, is that for the latter modernisation is a highly self-conscious process entailing choice. To the political leaders and their advisers in 'new' countries, modernisation presents itself as a series of actual problems or challenges.

With the benefit of historical hindsight and sufficient instances from which to draw meaningful generalisations, political scientists like Almond and Powell can tell us that the important stages in the political development process are *state-building, nation-building, participation* and *distribution*.[8] To political élites in 'new' countries, however, this is the stuff of actual political decisions. Moreover, while political development in Western European countries occurred in this sequence (and even then these changes were staggered over centuries), in many a new country insistent mass demands for participation in the political system and demands for the redistribution of social resources have been experienced before form has been given to the state or the problem of nation-building satisfactorily dealt with. This, of course, is the significance of the so-called 'revolution of rising expectations' – at the bottom of which lies the fact of the inter-relatedness of the modernised and modernising societies of the world. (This problem is nicely stated by Nettl.[9])

III

Not only are the leaders of new nations aware of the political consequences of modernisation, but they realise also that the structure and organisation of government, like the party system, are themselves factors, even agents, in the modernisation process. Apter conceptualises the element of choice which is involved here as follows.[10] Any political system, with 'authority' at its centre, is demarcated by the three dimensions of politics: 'a *normative* dimension involving ethical and proprietary conceptions which organise thought and action to give it meaning; a *structural* dimension, creating conditions in which alternatives are possible; and a *behavioural* dimension, representing the options in life actually identified and selected'. Thus the leaders of a new country who opt for liberal democracy, with its emphasis on accountability, will produce a political system which, *structurally*, is highly representative and which, *behaviourally*, encourages wide popular participation of individuals and groups.

Useful though this may be from an analytical point of view, the difficulty with new countries is that 'the behavioural and structural dimensions of authority do not fit together very well'. Apter illustrates the point as follows:

> Structurally, if a new nation employs the liberal formula with high accountability, a system of stalemate may result. If, on the other hand, it reduces accountability, it runs into the danger which accompanies the arbitrary and capricious use of power. Normatively, higher emphasis on social discipline could produce moral authority, but if this fails to result, abuses are likely to follow. Meanwhile, behaviour tends to be ambiguous and diffuse. There is a lack of effective socialisation in relation to norms, since no normative authority is likely to prevail. At the level of structure, with the liberal formula, competition leads to corruption – alternative behaviour becomes devious and disguised.[11]

Apter's long-term objective with this theory is 'to establish criteria for determining optimal modes of authority for different developmental stages and purposes in order to arrive at some solutions'.[12] The fact that this is a long-term objective should be underlined, for, as he admits elsewhere, 'despite the bewildering array of theories about development and, in particular, "political development", there is no general agreement with regard to terms and categories or especially strategic problems'.[13] Moreover, as political scientists, 'We are still caught by surprise by the rise and fall of governments, the failure of politics, not to speak of the effect on developing societies of those drastic alterations occurring within highly industrialised societies, the consequences of which are to create modernisation itself'.[14]

IV

The point has been stressed that modernisation for developing countries is a highly self-conscious process. Leadership in new countries perceives modernisation as a series of problems or challenges. The consolidation of the centralised institutions and decision-making processes of a modern nation-state, for example, and the development of single overriding national loyalties, are seen, in the face of the ethnic, cultural and regional cleavages of African societies, as a concrete political problem. Thus the public pronouncements of leaders like Nkrumah, Nyerere and Kaunda are peppered with exhortations to overcome the 'scourge of tribalism'.[15] Equally actual is the question of economic development. In fact, but for their hortatory overtones the speeches of some African leaders are descriptive statements of the modernisation process.[16] This awareness on the part of African leaders of modernisation as a series of problems is borne out in the relevant scholarly literature. Although many analyses of the new states of Africa assume, in Bienen's words, 'a linkage between development and integration; national integration is seen to be positively correlated with economic development',[17] where scholars have fragmented the modernisation process – in other words, where they have attempted to isolate its different problematical aspects – they have singled out national integration, economic development, and the generation of the qualified personnel needed to keep the machinery of a modern nation-state going.[18] The problem of national integration in turn has been seen in terms, to quote Bienen again, 'of ethnic heterogeneity, the lack of a shared political culture, social cleavages (rural/urban gaps, disparate levels of development within a territory, the gaps between élite and non-élite), and the difficulty in creating legitimising doctrines'.[19]

V

If modernisation (in Africa, at any rate) takes the form of concrete, specifiable problems, after roughly a decade of the 'politics of independence', it is possible to see a pattern in the political choices (used in Apter's sense) made in Africa. In most African countries the quickest way to national unity and higher living standards has been seen to lie 'through the pervasive influence, or even coercion, of a main (often single) political party under a popular and politically shrewd leader'[20] – although the increasing intrusion of the military is the striking (if not distinctive) feature of African political development in the latter half of the decade.[21]

The typical African political party is

the mass party whose organisation is designed to reach not only the constantly growing multitude of city dwellers but the rural peasantry as well. The new-style Western-educated élite, or the single charismatic leader, may in fact be the focal point of decision and action, but theory brings the mass into the decision-making process, and political prudence makes it advisable that the party have means by which it can communicate with all its constituents, which has come to mean the entire population of the country.[22]

And, of course, the typical party system in Africa is the single-party system.[23]

Some very penetrating studies have been made of one-party political systems in Africa,[24] but they have focused mainly on the origin and role of single parties as a response to the diversity which characterises most African countries, and therefore as a means of achieving national integration.[25] Few scholars, however, have tried to present the typical African political system within a modernisation context. One who has is David Apter, whose approach to modernising political systems in Africa has been found to be very helpful in the preparation of this paper.[26]

Apter's concern is the relationship between government and economics – an aspect which the two more general and familiar approaches to modernisation, the 'behavioural' and the *ad hoc* analytical approach,[27] do not do justice to. Neither of these approaches reckons with the effects (the 'needs') of governments – a consideration which is crucial, Apter maintains, in view of the fact, first, that 'new nations are not very stable entities, and, second, that their governments are rarely effectively institutionalised in relation to the society at large.'[28]

The concrete units of analysis in the alternative approach are government and society – economic development being a problem to both government and members of society. And Apter's goal is a theory which describes the interaction between government and society in regard to the challenges of modernisation, and which explains what particular characteristics or properties of one system enable it to meet these challenges more successfully than other systems. He outlines his procedure as follows:

> First, we must specify from the range of characteristics distributed among the rapidly growing number of new nations the differences in the natures of political systems. Second, we must investigate the kinds of response to the problems of technological innovation that these differing systems evoke. Some of the immediate problems are (1) whether the role of political entrepreneurship is greater or smaller; (2) the degree to which reliance will be placed on state enterprise for economic development; and (3) the extent to which talents will accumulate in the central organs of government or will become dispersed and decentralised throughout the system.[29]

Quite apart from its usefulness as an analytical tool, Apter's approach, and the typology of developing political systems which he utilises, is directly relevant to the subject and purpose of this Conference. The coincidence of interests emerges strikingly from the following passage in which he indicates the purported advantages of his approach:

> First, general technological change can be considered in relation to its effects on political organisation and on the needs and structure of governments in new nations. In addition, it enables us to indicate the role that government is likely to play in technological change, in terms of reliance on political entrepreneurship and government intervention in the economic process. By examining some of the characteristics of governments in new countries, we can provide a framework for determining the levels of development goals that decision-makers will choose, the uses and applications they will make of technology, and the terms under which they will seek and apply outside aid.[30]

VI

In terms of African experience, three models or types of developmental political systems are discernible. (The assumption underlying this is that every new country in Africa is faced with certain choices – choices, as was mentioned earlier, of a normative and structural nature – which determine the behavioural dimension of the political system and the shape of the country's governmental machinery.) These types or models are authority systems defined in terms of the relationship between government and society, and 'the critical question centres around the capacity to absorb change and generate further innovation'.[31] (Elsewhere Apter writes that 'The crucial point on which we are examining each type is whether or not it has the capacity to absorb technological change, and, in addition, to generate new political forms'.[32]) The three types are, firstly, a *mobilisation* system; second, a *reconciliation* system; and thirdly, a *modernising autocracy*. Each type has been constructed in terms of five categories: (1) patterns of legitimacy; (2) loyalty; (3) decisional autonomy; (4) distribution of authority; and (5) ideological expression.

Political systems of the *mobilisation* kind involve a radical transformation of both the institutions of government and its underlying values. Extreme examples of this system are the Soviet Union and communist China, but typical examples in Africa are Ghana and Guinea. The characteristics of mobilisation systems, measured in terms of the five categories enumerated above, are: (1) hierarchical authority; (2) total allegiance; (3) tactical flexibility; (4) unitarianism; and (5) ideological specialisation.[33]

The outstanding characteristic of political systems of the *reconciliation type* is the importance which they attach to compromise between groups sharing compatible political values. As Apter uses the term, 'a reconciliation system evolves with the formation of a simple political unit from constituent political units which do not lose their political identity on uniting'.[34] In practice, both federations (or loose confederations) and even highly organised parliamentary regimes can be of the reconciliation kind. Apter cites the United States and Nigeria 'and other federal systems' as examples of the reconciliation system, but most countries with a pluralist political culture are also likely to exhibit the characteristics of the reconciliation model. These, in terms of the five categories, are: (1) pyramidal authority; (2) multiple loyalties; (3) necessity for compromise; (4) pluralism; and (5) ideological diffuseness.[35]

In political systems of the *modernising autocracy* variety, hierarchical authority is buttressed by traditional forms of legitimacy.

Apter remarks that the crucial feature of modernising autocracies is their ability to absorb change as long as the system of authority (and legitimating base) is not undermined. The prime African example of a modernising autocracy is Ethiopia. The characteristics of this type are: (1) hierarchical authority; (2) exclusivism; (3) strategic flexibility; (4) unitarianism; and (5) neo-traditionalism.[36]

VII

The role of government in economic development varies in terms of the goals which it sets, the level of technology and available resources which can be utilised, and the measure of outside assistance which it is willing and able to receive. The types of developmental political systems which have just been elaborated are different, according to Apter, in the way they respond to these aspects of economic growth. Thus in mobilisation systems the goals figure more prominently. This is the system *par excellence* of the economic plan or programme, the goals of which are stated ambitiously, even unrealistically, thus requiring a high degree of discipline in the effort to realise them. New institutions are readily created and there is little tolerance for traditional institutions and practices which impede the processes of economic growth. Generally, mobilisation systems incline to ideologies of socialism:

> They emphasise discipline and hard work for the attainment of economic goals. This emphasis implies that economic development will restructure society so that those roles and tasks which are functional to the establishment of a modern economic order will become dominant, while older roles will be obliterated. This is why the mobilisation system places great stress on militancy and party organisation. Governmental enterprise becomes the major mechanism for economic growth. Correspondingly, high investments are made in education and social welfare, on the grounds that an efficient labour force is the *sine qua non* of economic development. Such systems need a powerful organisational nucleus which takes the major responsibility for the establishment and achievement of goals.[37]

In reconciliation systems, economic growth, like political authority itself, is more diffuse. Economic as well as political decision-making is more widely distributed through the society. There is much greater reliance on private enterprise than there is in mobilisation systems:

> Politically, the reconciliation system pays far more respect to cultural separatism and local parochialism than does the mobilisation system. Insofar as the reconciliation type is limited in its decision-making processes by the need to find some 'lowest common denominator' which will appeal to its constituent units, its progress toward goals of economic development, and the goals themselves, tend to be very moderate. The relationship between internal resources and the state of technology is closer than in the mobilisation type. In the mobilisation system, an effort is made to effect the quickest and closest approximation of the material cultures of the technologically advanced nations of the world. Goals are thus endowed with a symbolic quality which is lacking in both the reconciliation or modernising autocracy systems.[38]

To illustrate his point in this regard, Apter cites the difference in strategies adopted by India and China – both are concerned with economic growth, but India is of the reconciliation type and China the mobilisationist – and the consequences for their respective peoples.

Modernising autocracies show structural similarities with mobilisation systems, but their distinguishing feature is their 'stability within the context of rapid economic growth'.[39] Their formulation of goals is not nearly as ambitious as mobilisation systems, much less symbolic, and may not interfere with important traditional institutions. In fact, 'To be accepted, economic goals must show some positive relationship to the existing system of authority (bearing in mind here that the legitimating base of authority in modernising autocracies is of a traditional nature)'.[40]

Although, as Apter observes, the mechanisms of political and economic growth may appear very similar in the three systems, the fact is that each shows a different focus and emphasis; and as these differences are crucial, Apter is quoted at length in this regard.[41]

Modernising autocracies, in summary, reveal less dependence on control and coercion than is the case in mobilisation systems, but in comparison with reconciliation systems goals can be formulated more clearly and more effectively pursued in modernising autocracies. They tend to be highly bureaucratic and, of course, traditional values are retained.[42]

VIII

With certain reservations, Apter's conceptualisation of the modernisation process and typology of developmental political systems is (in the author's opinion) the best available theoretical approach to the questions this paper is intended to illuminate: it recommends itself as a system of analysis of the several countries of Southern Africa, with which this Conference is concerned; and it also suggests a viable basis for the formulation of a possible 'strategy of development'. However, the reservations are important and should be explained.

Apter's concern is essentially and almost exclusively with the political aspects of *economic development*. In this regard, although he appears (to a non-economist) to be correct in claiming that economic development is most effectively achieved in a political system of the mobilisation kind, he is not correct in implying (if not actually claiming) that concern for economic development is the primary reason for the emergence of mobilisation systems in African countries. As has been pointed out, the mass party in the one-party system, and the politicisation of virtually all social relations which this has generally entailed, has occurred as a response to diversity or, differently stated, as a means to national integration.

Related to the predominantly economic focus of Apter's approach is the fact that it suggests a rather circumscribed conception of modernisation. This is not a criticism of Apter – he is clearly concerned primarily with the capacity of varying political systems to absorb technological innovation and achieve economic development – but his theory does conceal the danger, particularly when applied in the context of this Conference, of other facets of modernisation – notably political development – being ignored. Thus political systems of the mobilisation type, although providing the quickest short-cut to economic development, may actually impede political development: not a few African leaders, in their preoccupation with the consolidation of power and the centralisation of authority for economic development or other purposes, tend grossly to over-simplify power relations in society as a whole. Apart from the risk of 'perpetuating the coercive, arbitrary form of political life so familiar under European rule',[43] these highly centralised political systems could prove too rigid to accommodate new power relations as the society advances.[44]

IX

Looking at the political systems of Southern Africa individually, one finds that all three of Apter's types are represented (see Table 2.1).

In terms of all but one of Apter's categories the *Lesotho* political system is of the reconciliation type. The Basotho nation is frequently described as one of the most politically conscious in Africa and, the homogeneity of its people notwithstanding, it has a particularly strong competitive party system. The exception relates to the distribution of authority, which is unitarian, probably for the reasons (1) that Lesotho is such a small country, (2) that it is much more dependent than comparable African countries on subsistence agriculture, and (3) that a very large proportion of its wage-earners work outside the country and are therefore not available for interest-group mobilisation on an effective scale. As one would expect of a reconciliation system, Lesotho relies heavily on private enterprise for its economic development.

The *Botswana* political system also corresponds to the reconciliation model. While respecting traditional institutions, and actually incorporating chiefs into the decision-making process, this is done more as a concession to the realities of the situation than for reasons of preserving them: traditional institutions would not be allowed, as in the case of a modernising autocracy, to obstruct the process of modernisation. The relative diversity of the Botswana people is reflected in the party system – the preponderance of the Botswana Democratic Party being due largely to the personal status of its leader, Sir Seretse Khama.

Although in foreign affairs Botswana, on the important issue of relations with the Republic of South Africa, has adopted a much more independent position than either Lesotho or Swaziland, the Botswana Democratic Party's ideology is described rather blandly

TABLE 2.1 Self-governing countries of Southern Africa:
types of political systems

	Mobilisation	Reconciliation	Modernising autocracy	
Botswana		×		Patterns of legitimacy
Lesotho		×		
Malagasy		×		
Malawi	×			
Mauritius		×		
Rhodesia			×	
South Africa			×	
Swaziland			×	
Zambia		×		
Botswana		×		Loyalty
Lesotho		×		
Malagasy		×		
Malawi	×			
Mauritius		×		
Rhodesia			×	
South Africa			×	
Swaziland		×		
Zambia		×		
Botswana		×		Decisional autonomy
Lesotho		×		
Malagasy		×		
Malawi			×	
Mauritius		×		
Rhodesia	×			
South Africa		×		
Swaziland	×			
Zambia		×		
Botswana		×		Distribution of authority
Lesotho	×			
Malagasy		×		
Malawi	×			
Mauritius		×		
Rhodesia			×	
South Africa		×		
Swaziland			×	
Zambia		×		
Botswana		×		Ideology
Lesotho		×		
Malagasy		×		
Malawi		×		
Mauritius		×		
Rhodesia			×	
South Africa			×	
Swaziland			×	
Zambia	×			

as a 'national philosophy'. The B.D.P.'s policy in the last general election (October 1969) was described as 'essentially modernisation at a judicious pace, thereby balancing the desire for rapid change by a cautious attitude towards economics. . . . The B.D.P. is a liberal-conservative party: liberal in its staunch opposition to racial discrimination, and in its defence of libertarianism; conservative in its belief in private enterprise.'[45] As a reconciliation system, Botswana welcomes assistance from the private sector; in fact, that country's promising industrial base has largely been laid by private enterprise, much of it South African.

With some qualifications, *Swaziland* is a modernising autocracy. The most distinctive feature of the Swazi political system is the king. Although officially a constitutional monarch and ceremonial head of state, the fact is that King Sobhuza II has very real powers in traditional as well as modernist roles. Thus he controls land under Swazi law and custom through the Swazi National Council, and he participates directly in the political recruitment function of the system: the king nominates six of the twelve Senators, and six of the thirty members of the House of Assembly. The dominant political party, the Imbokodvo National Movement, is also the 'king's' party. It swept the polls in Swaziland's last general election (1967).

The reservations mentioned earlier apply in regard to the nature of loyalty and decisional autonomy in the system. The existence of a parliamentary system and competitive party system determine that loyalty, though veering towards exclusivism, is multiple, and that decision-making is not as autonomous as in the theoretical model. While Swaziland manifests an internal solidarity and stability not evident in any other country in the region, its ability to modernise and absorb change is subordinated to the maintenance of the traditional authority system.

The *Malawi* political system is in all respects of the mobilisation type. Authority flows down from President Hastings Banda; loyalty is total and could even be personal; and authority is highly centralised both politically (Malawi has a one-party system) and administratively. The most remarkable feature of the Malawi political system is indeed the role of President Banda. Within their respective political systems, Banda's authority probably exceeds that of King Sobhuza, the only other Southern African leader who bears comparison. As a modernist in the soalled charismatic mould, Banda's decision-making autonomy is ot limited by traditional factors, although at times he has readily evived traditional institutions. (His decisions in 1969, at the time f his conflict with the High Court to extend the powers of aditional and local courts in matters involving superstition, and o give them the power to impose the death sentence, is a case in oint.)

President Banda's personality and position contribute a stra-egic flexibility to the Malawi political system which is generally bsent from mobilisation systems. His attitude towards the epublic of South Africa and Portugal is possible evidence of is. The fact that the Malawi political system does not have a oherent ideology (unlike mobilisaton systems generally) is also robably attributable to Banda's dominant leadership: the stem's values and goals are highly personalised. For this ason the question of leadership succession is more impor-ant in Malawi than it is for any other country in Southern frica.

The *Zambian* political system is essentially of the reconciliation pe. The main reasons for this are the existence of strong tribal ivisions, significant regional cleavages, a relatively good indus-ial base and a strong (by African standards) trade union move-ent. These circumstances have variously contributed to a olitical system with a vigorously competitive party system, a ecentralised system of administration and a largely pluralistic ecision-making process.

Admittedly, the trend towards one-partyism which started bout two years ago, and the recent steps taken towards this end, oupled with the removal of any serious challenger to President aunda's leadership, mark the transition to a mobilisation ystem. (The introduction in 1968 of a system of partial nationali-ation of key industries through the Industrial Development Cor-oration is another pointer in this direction.) However, it may be at Zambia's political development has gone too far to allow is; in other words, the specialisation and differentiation of roles hich forms such an important part of political modernisation, ith the emergence of a new socio-economic class, has proceeded o the point where a one-party system could lead to that 'coer-ion' which Ashford, in an earlier reference, referred to, and ossible intervention by the army.

X

The distinctive feature of Rhodesia and the Republic of Sout
Africa lies in the oligarchical nature of their political systems
meaningful decision-making is limited to the White minority b
excluding or only partially including the non-White populatio
groups[46] in the input functions of the political process.[47] Althoug
both societies are relatively developed by African standards, an
pace-setters in the modernisation process in this part of the worlc
the strong resistance of the dominant minorities in both countrie
to political change which would bring non-Whites into th
political process on equal terms suggests that, according t
Apter's typology, they are of the modernising autocracy type
'a crucial typical feature of [which] is its ability to absorb chang
as long as the system of authority is not affected'.[48] This, indeed
is the position adopted in this paper. But there are importan
differences between Rhodesia and South Africa which turn o
their respective responses to non-White political demands.

The 1961 Rhodesian constitution provided for two voters
rolls – an 'A' or Upper Roll, and a 'B' or Lower Roll. Educa
tional and property qualifications attached to both, although bot
rolls were non-racial. However, the considerable differenc
between the qualifications resulted in the 'A' Roll being domi
nated by White voters and the 'B' Roll by Blacks. 'A' Roll voter
elected fifty members of Parliament and 'B' Roll voters fifteen
(In the general election of April 1965, thirteen of the fiftee
members returned on the 'B' Roll were Black.[49])

The importance for our particular interest is the assumptio
underlying these provisions in particular and the constitution a
a whole, namely, that there is a single political system in Rhode
sia serving all its peoples, even though Black African participa
tion, as a result of their educational and socio-economic standing
was at a lower level than that of the White group. In theory
however, as Africans made economic and educational advance
they would qualify for additional votes on both rolls and the
would eventually constitute the majority of the electorate.

The assumption of a single political system serving all Rhode
sians was not in any way altered by post-U.D.I. constitutiona
developments and, specifically, the constitution which came int
force in March 1970. Although this constitution cut back on th

already limited degree of participation provided for Black Rhodesians,[50] it did not modify the principle of a single political system. The same observation applies to the conditions of the proposed British–Rhodesian settlement concluded in late 1971.[51]

Sketchy as this background discussion is, it is sufficient to show that the Rhodesian political system is of the modernising autocracy type. Where effective participation in a political system is limited to a minority in terms of the whole society, authority is likely to be hierarchical and loyalty limited. Furthermore, the political system is likely to possess a tactical, if not strategic, flexibility in decision-making. Finally, the system is buttressed ideologically in straight neo-traditionalist terms: 'keeping government in civilised hands'.

At its inception in 1910, non-Whites were afforded some measure of participation in the input functions of the South African political system.[52] The period 1910–25 in the field of race relations in South Africa was characterised by the American scholar Raymond Buell as 'one of drift, or at least piecemeal legislation'.[53] However, from the 1920s onwards two trends asserted themselves in official policy on the question of non-White participation in the political system. The first refers to their increasing exclusion down the years from participation on the political side of the system; and the second to their increasing institutional and administrative separation within the governmental functions of the system. (Hardly incidental to this is the fact that, as the demand for exclusion grew among Whites, so, correspondingly, the demand for participation became more and more vocal and persistent among Blacks.)

These processes had already reached an advanced stage when the National Party came to power in 1948. However, at a policy level the new government's goals were (1) the *total* exclusion of Africans from the dominant system, and (2) the creation of wholly distinct, *temporarily* subordinate, political systems which corresponded to a conception of South Africa as a multi-national country in *transition* to a regional system of separate nation-states.

On the level of implementation the complete exclusion of Africans from the dominant system was accomplished mainly by the following legislative enactments:

In terms of the *Bantu Authorities Act* of 1951 the advisory Natives Representative Council ceased to exist. It had last met in January 1949 when its meeting ended in deadlock as a result of Dr Verwoerd's insistence that matters of a political nature lay outside its scope.

The *Bantu Education Act* of 1953 separated Bantu education from education in general in the rule-making function of the dominant system by centralising all Native education in the Department of Native Affairs. (Later, in October 1958, the administration of the Bantu population was entrusted to two departments, namely, a Department of Bantu Administration and Development and a Department of Bantu Education.)

By means of the *Industrial Conciliation Acts* of 1956 and 1959 African interest articulation of an associational kind (trade unions) was severely restricted.

The *Promotion of Bantu Self-Government Act* of 1959 among other things provided for the removal of the three Whites in the House of Assembly and the two in the Cape Provincial Council who were elected by Cape Africans, and the removal of the four White Senators who were elected by Africans in all four provinces. This provision, therefore, finally terminated all African representation in the rule-making function of the dominant system.

The *Prohibition of Political Interference Act* of 1968, while aimed primarily at the Coloureds, excludes Africans from participating in the aggregative function of the dominant system by making their membership of essentially White political parties illegal. Apart from outlawing the 'multi-racial popular front' kind of activity, which was prevalent around 1953–6, this measure also prevents an open uniting of essentially non-White political organisations.

In addition to these specific measures, much of the security legislation of the last twenty years has been used to isolate and exclude individual Africans and their organisations from participation in the politics of the dominant system – even where the action might simply take an anomic form.

The following legislative enactments have been instrumental in creating alternative political systems which, although subordinate at present, are intended to develop to independence:

The *Bantu Authorities Act* of 1951 substituted for the Native

Representative Council (which it abolished) a system of local government which in the words of Dr Eiselen 'starts from the principle of Tribal Authorities, corresponding in great measure to the old Bantu tribal councils, whose opinion had always to be taken into account by the chiefs, and which will govern in accordance with Bantu customs as far as these can be reconciled with civilised standards'.[54]

The *Promotion of Self-Government Act* of 1959 is probably the most important legislative plank in the implementation of official policy. It 'provides for the gradual development of self-governing Bantu national units, and for direct consultation between the Government of the Union and these national units in regard to matters affecting the interests of such national units'.[55] This is the Act which sets up the hierarchy of Bantu authorities, culminating in self-government.

The *Transkei Constitution Act* of 1963 conferred a measure of self-government on the Transkei.

The significant difference in official policy after the 1940s on this crucial question of Black African political participation is that, firstly, it reflects an appreciation of the inherent explosiveness in the situation which was developing; and secondly, it recognises the necessity of creating alternative political systems to accommodate Black African political aspirations, if they were to be excluded from existing structures and processes.

Argument there may be about the extent, the desirability and the likelihood of success; but there is no doubting that the principle of sharing political power and the goals of creating new and distinct nation-state political systems is central to the political aspects of official government policy as far as the Africans are concerned. And measured in terms of its goals, namely, (1) to establish potentially self-generating political systems of the nation-state type, (2) in terms of which Black Africans within South Africa's present borders will identify, and (3) to which powers of government with respect to these peoples will be transferred, with certain important reservations (which relate more to its future) this policy of political development is working.

Moreover, largely as the result of the emergence of a new and vigorous political élite, the homeland subsystems have acquired a dynamism of their own, and Pretoria will no longer alone decide the form or the pace development is to take. Thus, in a recent paper devoted to determining the total ¦effect of all assessable factors of change in South Africa, Dr David Welsh of the University of Cape Town concluded:

> My scenario of the future is as follows:
> (a) That the internal situation in South Africa remains much as it is for the next two decades, even if the Transkei becomes a formally independent state.
> (b) That a confederal-type constellation of states emerges in South Africa, including the cluster of embryonic South West African 'states', and perhaps Botswana, Lesotho and Swaziland. The constituent states of this confederation will be 'racially dominated', that is either White or Black will be the dominant group within each state, irrespective of actual numerical proportions.
> (c) That the powers of the confederation would initially be severely circumscribed, but that subsequently confederation will become federation.
>
> It would be fruitless to examine minutely possible future constitutional arrangements in the sketch I have presented above. It falls far short of the ideal political dispensation to which I personally subscribe; but I must emphasise that I have attempted to show what I think will happen in South Africa and not what I want to happen.[56]

XII

The purpose of this discussion of the official South African response to Black African political aspirations has been to indicate the nature of the political system. Unlike Rhodesia, there is not one system, but a dominant system and several subordinate systems at different stages of political development. The dominant system is essentially of the modernising autocracy type except in regard to decisional autonomy. In this respect it is pluralistic; the process of policy formation affecting, for example, major changes in race relations is that of a reconciliation system. And herein lies one of the fundamental problems of South African politics and a matter deserving of the attention of this Conference.

As a consequence of its oligarchic base, the acceptance and implementation of a course of political development leading to national integration in a common society is highly improbable.[57] On the other hand, because it lacks the flexibility in decision-making of either a mobilisation system or a modernising auto-cracy, the South African political system seems inadequate in the face of such outstanding problems as the economic develop-ment and territorial consolidation and expansion of the home-lands; the problem of evolving acceptable formulae for Africans domiciled outside the homelands; and the problem of eliminating colour as a norm in inter-personal relations.

Of course, it may be that the stalemate noted here, although real, is theoretical, and that answers to these and the other great outstanding problems of South African society will emerge from the 'dynamics of politics'.[58]

The preceding sketch of official policy in regard to the Black African population groups, apart from throwing light on the nature of the South African political system and its capacity to modernise, brings into focus the question: What is desirable political development in a society like South Africa? In this connection, Adam points out that

> Most major studies on South Africa reflect the assumption that an essential contradiction exists between an irrational race policy and the requirements of a rationally organised expanding industrial society. . . . A race policy against industrial interests is regarded as inevitably leading to explosive conflicts, due to the interdependence of the economic system.[59]

In an important sense, this is a valid point: the main thrust of economic development is away from the officially formulated goals of political development. However, although correct in this regard, these analyses can be faulted for almost invariably assuming that the correct patterns of political development for South Africa follows modernisation patterns in other areas; and hence one returns to the question posed above: What, for example, constitutes 'national integration' in a polity like South Africa? Does it mean attempting to fuse different groups within the present boundaries of the Republic into a single nation having the same political system?[60] Or does national integration in the South African context mean recognising the more important distinctive cultural, linguistic and ethnic groups as nations, and devolving governmental and political power on a nation-state basis? And given the likelihood that one of these is the best possible course of political development, what are the intermediate steps that political modernisation should take?

These last few observations underline the need for theoretical perspectives in situations where there are possible incompatibilities between political modernisation (as distinct from the political *status quo*) and modernisation in non-political areas.

XIII

With the exception of the Republic of South Africa (including South West Africa or Namibia), which is a microcosm of the rest of the region, and where nation-building is still at an embryonic stage, it is difficult to see how the purpose of this Conference, with regard to political modernisation, can be realised in relation to individual countries. Indeed, whether it is possible for this Conference to indicate for individual countries meaningful guidelines for accelerated modernisation in non-political areas is for the economists and other social scientists present to say. No doubt, however, it will be possible for this Conference to make general recommendations applicable on a regional basis. But just as one country's capacity for modernisation depends greatly on the nature of its political system, so economic proposals involving inter-governmental proposals on a regional basis, however attractive from an economic point of view, are subject to political considerations. And the political obstacles to regional co-operation in Southern Africa are considerable.

Race is obviously a contributing factor, as is the continuance of colonialism in the form of the Portuguese territories of Angola and Mozambique. Southern Africa is furthermore an area not only of great international interest of a political, humanistic and religious nature, but an area of intense international involvement both by individual countries and by organisations like the U.N. and the O.A.U. The continued unsettlement of the Rhodesian question, the South West African issue and race relations policies in the Republic of South Africa are the main reasons for this concern. The existence of extra-territorially based nationalist movements committed to the achievement of revolutionary political change in the Portuguese territories, Rhodesia and the Republic of South Africa help in fostering the popular perception of Southern Africa as a flash-point of international conflict.

There is also the fact that political thinking in this region is characterised by radically varying conceptualisations of the nature and form of political development and, as Mr Leo Marquard recently pointed out, by certain, presently dormant, boundary problems.[61] Finally, there is the fact that nowhere in Africa are the disparities between the technologically developed and less developed societies so great as in this part of the continent.

These are obviously not circumstances in which international goodwill flourishes. So, for example, a country like Botswana, which walks a tight-rope between Black and White Africa, finds itself under constant pressure from certain quarters to be 'a Pan-African outpost'[62] within the Southern African region; and, on the other hand, it would be very surprising if South Africa, Rhodesia and the Portuguese provinces were not, to put it mildly, vexed at countries within the region which provide a haven for 'political refugees' or harbour so-called liberationist movements.

These obstacles notwithstanding, strong inter-state ties have been forged by commerce and labour, communication and transportation systems, and the various assistance schemes initiated within the private sector. Moreover, the inter-governmental achievements within the region are not inconsiderable. (The Southern African Customs Union between Botswana, Lesotho, Swaziland and the Republic of South Africa, as renewed in December 1969, springs to mind in this connection.) However, Southern Africa is nowhere near some development of the E.E.C. kind, and neither are the countries of Southern Africa about to accept the kind of federation recently proposed by Mr Leo Marquard.[63] The point in this regard is clearly made by an adviser to one of the three smaller member-governments of the Southern African Customs Union in a recent issue of *African Affairs*:

For sixty years the Southern African Customs Union was a skeletal model of a free trade area with a common external tariff. The reconstitution of the Union by the 1969 Agreement added something of substance to the bare bones. But it must be recognised that what has been added are elements of co-operation, not integration. The few integrative projects in the four countries (Oxbow in Lesotho, a possible thermal power plant in Swaziland), have been considered in isolation from the Customs Union. There is no supranational planning or advisory body comparable to the E.E.C. Commission or the East African Authority; there are no steps towards making the parties more functionally dependent on each other. Eventual political unity was at the back, at least, of everyone's mind when the Rome and Kampala treaties were signed. Nothing could have been further from the thoughts of those who signed the agreement in Pretoria in December 1969.[64]

At the centre of the problem of intra-regional co-operation in Southern Africa is the fact that the country which, both ideologically and politically, is perceived to be most out of line with the rest of the region,[65] happens also to be the 'core' country.[66]

The direction of adjustment and change within South Africa has been described, and no doubt South Africa hopes that, as its intentions regarding independent homelands become clearer and it overcomes its present credibility problem in this regard,[67] Southern Africa and the international community in general will become less chilly places. Christopher Hill of York University concludes a recent article on the extent of Botswana's independence from South Africa on this note:

> As for the original question, whether and to what extent Botswana resembles a Bantustan: clearly at present it enjoys many freedoms which are denied to a Bantustan. I believe, though, that the Bantustans may 'catch up' within the next few years, and that South Africa would be happy to allow them to do so, on the grounds that such developments would do nothing to change the existing power relations between black and white. Indeed, they might entrench them more deeply even than they are at present in the white core of the Republic, whilst assisting the consolidation of the new South African economic empire in Black Africa.[68]

South African policy and objectives are not very different in South West Africa (or Namibia). The Republic is prepared to withdraw, no doubt reluctantly, from the disputed territory. But given the strength of its position in South West Africa and the fact that South Africa's co-operation is essential whatever happens there, the Republic, not unnaturally, intends withdrawing on the most favourable conditions. Meanwhile it will press on with its diplomatic overtures elsewhere in Africa, knowing full well that it has an unchallengeable military preponderance.[69] Of course, this very broad outline of developments could be radically upset, one surmises, by events in Rhodesia and a change of mind in Lisbon.

NOTES

1. According to Welch, central to the notion of modernisation is a 'belief in rational or scientific control'. He goes on to quote Benjamin Schwartz's view that modernisation depends upon the 'systematic, sustained and purposeful application of human energies to the "rational" control of man's physical and social environment for various human purposes'. In somewhat similar terms, Robert Ward views modernisation as the movement towards modern society, characterised by 'its far-reaching abilities to control or influence the physical and social circumstances of its environment, and by a value system which is fundamentally optimistic about the desirability and consequences of this ability'. 'Political Modernisation and Political Culture in Japan', *World Politics*, xv 4 (July 1963) 570.

   In somewhat different terms, modernisation involves the spread of a 'world culture' which is based, as Lucian Pye puts it, on 'advanced technology and the spirit of science, on a rational view of life, a secular approach to social relations, a feeling for justice in public affairs, and above all else, on the acceptance in the political realm of the belief that the prime unit of the polity should be the nation-state'. Lucian Pye, *Aspects of Political Development* (Boston, 1965) p. 8.

   Other definitions have change as their focal point. Thus to Samuel Huntington, 'modernisation is a multifaceted process involving change in all areas of human thought and activity'. He goes on to quote with approval Daniel Lerner's view that modernisation is 'a process with some distinctive quality of its own, which would explain why modernity is felt as a *consistent whole* among people who live by its rules'. Samuel Huntington, *Political Order in Changing Societies* (New Haven and London, 1968) p. 32.

   Marion Levy's definition of modernisation 'hinges on the uses of inanimate sources of power and the use of tools to multiply the effect of effort. . . . A society will be considered more or less modernised to the extent that its members use inanimate sources of power and/or use tools to multiply the effects of their efforts.' ('Inanimate sources of power' Levy describes as 'any sources of power that are not produced from human or other animal energy', and a tool he defines as 'any physical device that is ordinarily separable from the body of an individual who applies it and that is used to accomplish what he would not accomplish *at all* or could not accomplish so well without it'.)

138   *Accelerated Development in Southern Africa*

According to Levy, 'The greater the ratio of inanimate to animate sources of power and the greater the multiplication of effort as the effect of the new application of tools, the greater is the degree of modernisation'. Marion Levy, *Political Modernisation and the Structure of Societies* (Princeton, 1966) p. 35.

Although a relationship between modernisation and industrialisation is generally acknowledged in most definitions, in some it is central. So, for example, David Apter writes: 'Modernisation . . . is a special case of development defined by industrialisation, but more general than the latter phenomenon.' David Apter, *Some Conceptual Approaches to the Study of Modernisation* (Englewood Cliffs, N.J., 1968) p. 334. The last point is emphasised by J. P. Nettl, who defines industrialisation simply 'as the process which involves a changeover from either agricultural *or* domestic activity to factory production on a growing scale' (p. 40); and modernisation as 'the process whereby national élites seek successfully to reduce their *atimic* status and move towards equivalence with other "well-placed" nations'. J. P. Nettl and R. Robertson, *International Systems and the Modernisation of Society* (London, 1968) pp. 56–7. Nettl and Robertson remark that this conception of modernisation draws attention 'to the dynamic relationship between the international and the domestic aspects of individual societies', and this, unquestionably, is to their merit.

Faced with the many formulations of modernisation, industrialisation and development which there are, Marion Levy's observation regarding his own definition seems appropriate, namely, that there are 'an infinite number of other possibilities for defining this concept as having a totally different referent' (p. 11).

2. 'Politics' is used here and, unless otherwise indicated, throughout this paper to include the normative, the structural and the behavioural dimensions of the political system. See Apter, op. cit., pp. 351–80.

3. Huntington, op. cit., pp. 34–5. See also Apter, op. cit., p. 336, and Apter, *The Politics of Modernisation* (Chicago, 1965) pp. 2–4; Lucian W. Pye and Sidney Verba, *Political Culture and Political Development* (Princeton, 1965) p. 13; Pye, op. cit., pp. 3–30; Joseph La Palombara and Myron Weiner, *Political Parties and Political Development* (Princeton, 1966) pp. 3–42; Gabriel Almond and G. Bingham Powell, *Comparative Politics: A Developmental Approach* (Boston, 1966) pp. 35–41.

4. Claude E. Welch, *Political Modernisation: A Reader in Comparative Political Change* (Belmont, Calif., 1967) p. 7.

5. Huntington, op. cit., p. 89.

6. Almond and Powell, op. cit., pp. 36–7.

7. La Palombara and Weiner, op. cit., pp. 3–42.

8. Almond and Powell, op. cit., p. 35.

9. ' . . . the accessibility of information and of sophisticated technological objects to societies which consume them but cannot produce them. We tend to regard the problem of technology as a national level of attainment which, once reached, is irreversible, whereas in fact the situation

is one in which technological consumption is much more readily available than the industrial-scientific base to produce it. This fact, coupled with the very uneven levels of technological capacity, is crucial in any theory of development, for it cuts right across the very idea of uniform levels of development as between one group of societies and another, and incidentally knocks away one of the main props of the relevance of the Western experience.' J. P. Nettl, 'Strategies in the Study of Political Development', in Colin Leys (ed.), *Politics and Change in Developing Countries* (Cambridge, 1969) pp. 23–4.

10. Apter, 'A Paradigm for Political Analysis', in *Some Conceptual Approaches*, pp. 351–80.

11. Ibid., p. 359.

12. Ibid., p. 361.

13. Ibid., p. 333.

14. Ibid., p. 332.

15. See, for example, Kwame Nkrumah, *I Speak of Freedom* (New York, 1961) pp. 167–8.

16. Ibid.

17. Henry Bienen, *Tanzania: Party Formation and Economic Development* (Princeton, 1967) p. 9.

18. A good example of this is W. Arthur Lewis, *Some Aspects of Economic Development* (London, 1969).

19. Bienen, loc. cit.

20. Gwendoline M. Carter (ed.), *Five African States: Studies in Diversity* (Ithaca, N.Y., 1963) p. 3.

21. On at least thirty occasions in various African countries over the past ten years the military has intervened in politics. See, in this regard, Edward Feit, 'Military Coups and Political Developments', in Marion E. Doro and Newell M. Stultz (eds), *Governing in Black Africa* (Englewood Cliffs, N.J., 1970) pp. 221–36.

22. Rupert Emerson, 'Parties and Natural Integration', in La Palombara and Weiner, op. cit., p. 274.

23. There are, of course, distinctions within the one-party systems of Africa – the broad one being between 'one-party authoritarian systems' and 'one-party pluralistic systems'. (For a discussion of this, see Emerson's chapter in La Palombara and Weiner.) There is also the rather important fact that the one-party systems of Africa lack the monolithic character generally associated with similar systems in, notably, Eastern European countries. For elaboration, see Bienen, op. cit., pp. 3–17, and Bienen, 'The Ruling Party in the African One-Party State', in Doro and Stultz, op. cit.

24. Reference here is to the work of Apter, Bienen, Coleman, Emerson, Kilson, Rosberg, Wallerstein and Zolberg.

25. See Emerson, op. cit.; Emmanuel Wallerstein, 'The Decline of the Party in Single-Party African States', in La Palombara and Weiner, op. cit.; and James S. Coleman and Carl Rosberg (eds), *Political Parties and National Integration* (Berkeley, 1964).

26. Apart from other articles, Apter's other relevant writings, for the

purpose of this paper, include *The Politics of Modernisation*; *Ideology and Discontent* (Glencoe, Ill., 1964); and *Some Conceptual Approaches to the Study of Modernisation.*

27. See Apter, *Some Conceptual Approaches*, p. 273, for an elaboration.
28. Ibid.
29. Ibid., p. 274.
30. Ibid., p. 276.
31. Ibid.
32. Ibid., p. 277.
33. Ibid.
34. Ibid., p. 278.
35. Ibid.
36. Ibid.
37. Ibid., p. 279.
38. Ibid.
39. Ibid., p. 280.
40. Ibid.
41. Ibid.
42. Ibid., p. 282.
43. Douglas F. Ashford, 'The Last Revolution: Community and Nation in Africa', in *The Annals* (Philadelphia), July 1964, p. 41.
44. Ibid., p. 40.
45. W. A. J. Macartney, 'Botswana goes to the Polls', *Africa Report* (Washington, D.C.), Dec 1969, p. 29.
46. 'Non White' is used here with reluctance, but the fact is that it is the only term which avoids the circumlocution involved in describing the different population groups which constitute the majority in both Rhodesia and South Africa.
47. See Gabriel Almond and James Coleman (eds), *The Politics of the Developing Areas* (Princeton, 1960), and Almond and Powell, op. cit. The structural-functional model is especially useful in a plural political situation.
48. Apter, *Some Conceptual Approaches*, p. 278.
49. Of interest in this regard are the comments of James Barber, *Rhodesia: The Road to Rebellion* (Oxford, 1967) pp. 74–5. He feels this constitution contained important positive breaks with the past.
50. Educational and property qualifications must still be met, but the non-racial character of the voters' rolls was abolished: the two rolls are now organized along racial lines. The number of representatives *directly* elected by 'B' Roll voters, i.e. Black voters, has been reduced from fifteen to eight. While White–Black representational parity is theoretically possible – Black representation has been pegged to their share of income-tax revenue – the new constitution effectively prevents a Black majority from emerging.
51. *Anglo-Rhodesian Relations: Proposals for a Settlement*, Presented to Parliament by the Prime Minister on 25 November 1971, Cmd R. R. 46 (1971).
52. Black Africans were on the common roll in the Cape. See, in this

regard, Denis Worrall (ed.), *South Africa: Government and Politics* (Pretoria: Van Schaik, 1971) pp. 227–30.

53. Raymond Buell, *The Native Problem in Africa* (New York, 1928) p. 131.
54. Dr W. W. M. Eiselen, 'Harmonious Multi-Community Development', *Optima* (Johannesburg) Mar 1959, p. 5.
55. From the long title of the Act (No. 46/1959).
56. Quoted in Denis Worrall, 'The Plural-State System as a Direction of Change', in Peter Randall (ed.), *Directions of Change in South African Politics* (Johannesburg: SPROCAS, 1971) p. 70.
57. Both the Liberal Party (which chose to disband with the passage of the *Prohibition of Political Interference Act* of 1968 rather than continue as an all-white political party) and the Progressive Party, both of which support change in this direction, have never demonstrated much support among the Whites for this cause. Twelve years after its establishment the Progressive Party has only one representative in Parliament (out of a total of 166) and has never polled more than 4 per cent of the total vote in the several general and provincial elections it has participated in.
58. After all, cessions of territory, population migrations and redistributions of economic resources have occurred in recent history on a scale unlikely to be even remotely approximated in South Africa.
59. Heribert Adam, *Modernising Racial Domination: The Dynamics of South African Politics* (Berkeley, 1971) p. 145.
60. For a discussion of the problem of diversity, which is relevant in this regard, see Rupert Emerson, *From Empire to Nation* (Boston, 1960) p. 335.
61. Leo Marquard, *A Federation of Southern Africa* (Cape Town, 1971) pp. 35–6.
62. This is a reference to the title of Professor Munger's pre-independence work on Bechuanaland. Edwin S. Munger, *Bechuanaland: Pan-African Outpost or Bantu Homeland?* (London, 1965).
63. Marquard, op. cit.
64. Biff Turner, 'A Fresh Start for the Southern African Customs Union', *African Affairs* (London), LXX 280 (July 1971) 275–6.
65. The most unambiguous evidence of this is the fact that all but one of the Black States of Southern Africa have assented to the Lusaka Manifesto adopted in 1969. The exception is Malawi, which reserved its position.
66. The Republic of South Africa would certainly fulfil Deutsch's requirements in this regard. See Karl Deutsch *et al.*, *Political Community and the North Atlantic Area* (Princeton, 1957) p. 138.
67. Illustration of this point abounds, but more telling than most is Sir Seretse Khama's comments in this regard during his address to the U.N. General Assembly on 24 September 1969: 'But Botswana as a thriving majority-ruled state on the borders of South Africa and Namibia will present an effective and serious challenge to the credibility of South Africa's racial policies and in particular its policy of

developing the so-called Bantu homelands and its stated goal of eventual independence for these Bantustans. It could force them to abandon the policy or attempt to make it a more immediate reality and *even face the prospect of surrendering sovereignty to genuinely independent sovereign states.* A prosperous non-racial democracy in Botswana immediately adjacent to South Africa and Namibia will add to the problems South Africa is already facing in reconciling its internal racial policies with its desire for economic growth.'

68. Christopher R. Hill, 'Independent Botswana: Myth or Reality?', *The Round Table* (London), no. 245 (Jan 1972) p. 62.
69. For a perceptive up-to-date discussion, see Louis H. Gann, 'No Hope for Violent Liberation', *Africa Report* (Washington, D.C.), Feb 1972.

COMMENTS

A. W. Stadler and D. Z. Kadzamira

Dr Stadler argued that a contradiction existed between the economic goals which Professor Possony believed desirable and the non-economic values which he considered important. The maintenance of 'ethnic integrity' was incompatible with sustained economic growth. Moreover, he offered no justification for economic development, nor any estimate of its social costs and differential benefits.

The use of the term 'nation' to describe the Zulus, Xhosas, etc., was puzzling. The existence of parochial sentiments, and the aspirations of the central government to maintain tribal structures, did not add up to a nationalist movement. The government had proscribed the only sizeable autonomous nationalist movements among Africans. The fact that a state of emergency had been in force in the Transkei since 1958 made any assertion of what autonomous opinion existed there highly speculative.

The 'ethnic groups' were not primordial groups existing in isolation from White society. Their political structure, physical location and range of economic opportunities had been shaped, constrained, limited, and had often deteriorated from contact with Whites for more than a century. It was no accident that the 'homelands' were the poorest areas in the country. There was a connection between White wealth and Black poverty. The industrial ensemble was largely based on the human resources of these areas.

Professor Possony's 'rules of statecraft' were arbitrary, contradictory and élitist. The model of politics they suggested presumed the maintenance of White control.

Mr Kadzamira questioned the validity of Professor Possony's paper outside the South African context on the grounds that, with its emphasis upon ethnic needs, it stood in direct contrast to present African efforts to erode ethnic integrity as a prerequisite to national integration.

Commenting on Dr Worrall's paper, he expressed the need to move away from the lopsided view of African politics in most of the political science literature of the last decade, which was centre-oriented and tended to ignore the role of the rural periphery in the modernisation process.*

He also questioned Dr Worrall's view that the mobilisation system was not necessarily most favourable to modernisation; he pointed out that in the post-independence period the problem facing African countries was one of political regeneration, and that in this regard the mass party fulfilled an important role.

* Mr Kadzamira subsequently pointed out that, on the basis of empirical research in Africa (e.g. *The Gold Coast in Transition*, 1955; *The Political Kingdom in Uganda*, 1967), David Apter developed his models in his *Politics of Modernisation* (1965). He had since continued to refine his conceptualisation of the process of political modernisation (as in the last chapter of his *Some Conceptual Approaches to the Study of Modernisation*, 1968), and had come up with more complex models to which Dr Worrall did not refer in his paper, such as his essay in R. T. Holt and J. E. Turner (eds), *The Methodology of Comparative Research* (1970), and his *Choice and the Politics of Allocation: A Developmental Theory* (1971).

Chapter 3

Politics and Government: Administration

The Policy of Separate Development as a Framework for Development in South Africa

W. B. VOSLOO

Concern with 'development' is probably as old as the recognition of status inequalities between societies. It can be traced back to the invention of the term *barbaros* by the ancient Greeks and to many other historical examples of contact between cultures and civilisations. But since the aftermath of the Second World War, concern with development gradually emerged as a universal priority.

CONCEPTS OF DEVELOPMENT

What constitutes development and how is it to be attained? After twenty years of universal concern with the problems of development, these vexed questions are still largely unresolved. As a result of divergent ideological commitments, socio-cultural traditions and physical conditions there is a general impasse with regard to the specification of development in terms of decisive ends and means.

During the past twenty years of concern with development, however, a number of basic considerations have changed.[1] First, the specification of development has increasingly shed its early culture-bound, ethnocentric and teleological assumptions according to which a Western-type model was both essential and inevitable.[2] Instead, an increasingly relativistic concept of development emerged, which took into account the socio-cultural values of different societies. As a result of this trend, the classification of societies in terms of a 'developed/underdeveloped' continuum has largely been discontinued. Second, there has been a growing realisation that there are different paths to development. Thus, as the linear teleology receded out of development theories, the developmental strategies, stages and styles abstracted from interpretations of Western history were discarded as blueprints for development in the new societies.[3] Instead, development action was increasingly designed in terms of the attainment of specific and identifiable goals which are self-consciously selected in accordance with particular societal assets, capabilities and cultural constraints.

These changes have important implications both for theories of development and for development action. The most important of these are that the Western model lost its hold as the *summum bonum* towards which today's developing countries have to strive, and that the means used in the process of development must be designed in terms of the requisites of each development situation. It must be pointed out, however, that the implication is not that the Western model has become irrelevant. Rather, it led to a re-conceptualisation of the Western experience in more differentiated social, economic and political terms.

GOALS OF DEVELOPMENT

Milton J. Esman's empirical surveys brought him to the conclusion that developing countries, despite individual differences, share a generalised consensus of the objectives towards which change should be directed. The joint goals of development are *nation-building* and *socio-economic progress*.[4] Agreement on the desirability of these goals is found even among political leaders who show wide variation in ideological commitment, social origins, political strategy and opportunity for success in goal attainment. Even the rank and file of the population in these countries, to the extent that they are politically motivated at all, share the belief that these paired values are proper objectives.[5]

NATION-BUILDING

Esman describes nation-building as 'the deliberate fashioning of an integrated political community within fixed geographic boundaries in which the nation-state is the dominant political institution'. The actual achievement of nationhood in most of the emerging areas is not an easy task, largely because many of the new states are artificial entities in that they are products of colonial activity rather than of a pre-existing political loyalty. Their boundaries were often drawn without proper regard to ethnic groupings, excluding people with close cultural ties and including minority groups opposed to assimilation. But whatever their prospects, the new states put a premium on establishing their nationhood, and give this priority in political action.

SOCIO-ECONOMIC PROGRESS

The related goal of socio-economic progress, although equally hard to achieve, is more tangible and measurable. It is defined by Esman as 'the sustained and widely diffused improvement in material and social welfare'. Being aware of the achievements of developed nations (both those with democratic and totalitarian orientations), the desire to triumph over poverty and to share in the benefits of an industrialised economy are powerful motivations in the new societies.

The dilemma with these goals is, however, that they set the sights for development action, but they do not specify the exact form of the machinery needed. Available information does demonstrate, however, that the special characteristics of the developing societies tend to create an expanded and emphasised role for the machinery of government. In particular, it requires a development-oriented system of public administration.

DETERMINANTS OF DEVELOPMENT IN SOUTH AFRICA

In view of its heterogeneous population structure, the differential levels of development of its various population groups and its ethnographic pattern of political development, the South African society provides a fertile ground for the study of the various dimensions of development problems. The South African situation is particularly relevant in terms of the realisation of such developmental aims as nation-building and socio-economic progress by means of a development-oriented system of public administration.

The analysis of the problems of development within the South African context is given an added complexity by the unusually intricate plural structure of the South African population; by the convoluted history of the interaction of the various groups and the nature of their settlement in the country; and by the peculiar configuration of its prevailing power structure. These factors are crucial determinants of the direction in which future developments can be expected to take place.

PLURAL POPULATION STRUCTURE

Since the early years following the settlement of European colonists in Southern Africa in 1652, the pattern of social, economic and political development has been dominated by racial and cultural factors. There are, of course, many other determinants such as the geophysical characteristics of the country, the influence of colonial powers and numerous coincidental historical events. But racial and cultural factors superseded all other factors in fashioning the peculiar multi-national structure of the South African society.

Race. The factor of race, being the most visible determinant of group affiliation, acted from the earliest encounters between 'Whites' and 'non-Whites' to distinguish differences in cultural values, economic interests and social status. These stereotyped identification patterns were constantly reinforced by military hostilities and by folk beliefs and practices. Today the collective self-definition based on race does not only apply to the White–Black relationship, but also affects the other minority groups in South Africa – the Coloureds (2 million persons of mixed race largely concentrated in the Western Cape) and the Asians (600,000 persons mostly of Indian origin largely concentrated in the coastal belt of Natal around Durban) – in their relationships with the Whites (3·8 million persons of Dutch, German, French and British heritage) on the one hand, and with the Bantu (15 million persons of Black African descent, including various ethnic entities such as the Zulu, Xhosa, Sotho, Tswana, Venda, Tsonga and Swazi) on the other. This consciousness of race is not limited to the informal sphere, but has been formalised in the occupational, religious and political structures.

Culture. The cultural factor largely reinforced social distinctions based on race and, in addition, influenced the demographic foundations of economic life in South Africa. The discre in economic status between Whites and Bantu must ii measure be attributed to the influence of cultural values o respective systems of social and economic organisation. In i of the Bantu, regard must be had to their traditional nomadic way of life, the communal land-tenure system, the diffuse obligations to the extended family, the rigid imposition of conformity, attitudes towards time and work, etc. On the part of the Whites, regard must be had to such Western-oriented cultural attributes as the emphasis on rationality, initiative and self-reliance; the self-sufficiency of the individual family unit; the emphasis on private ownership and thrift; the direct exposure to Western sources of knowledge and technology, etc. The White man was on the whole better equipped to utilise the natural resources and to build a modern diversified economy. It was therefore inevitable for the system of socio-economic stratification to coincide with racial and cultural divisions. The Whites occupy the upper stratum, the Coloureds and Indians the middle and the Bantu the lower stratum.

The cultural factor also influenced the development of ethnic group-consciousness as one of the most important ingredients of South African politics. All major population groups – Whites, Coloureds, Asians and Bantu – are subdivided into several ethnic entities each with its own language, religious affiliations and political history.

HISTORICAL PATTERN OF INTERACTION

The pattern of interaction between these groups is historically characterised by the drawing of lines in most spheres of intergroup contact. Although the various groups continued down the years to meet across territorial, economic, social and political 'frontier lines', they basically remained distinct segments of society. The *modus vivendi* based on some form of separation has, in the words of Professor Herbert Frankel, 'as a mental image and as a principle of government and legislation, survived all later policies'.[6] It has done so despite the emergence of a large measure of economic interdependence, social change and cultural diffusion over a period of many generations.

The pattern of group interaction based on separation is largely reflected in the geographical distribution of the population groups. The ethnographic map shows a number of ethnic regions dispersed across the country: a concentration of Afrikaners in the Orange Free State, the northern, eastern and western parts of Transvaal, and the rural areas of the Cape Province; a concentration of 'English' in Natal and the various metropolitan areas; a concentration of Coloureds in the Western Cape and Indians on the Natal coast around Durban; a concentration of the distinct Bantu peoples in Lesotho, Swaziland, Botswana, Pondoland, Zululand, Vendaland, Ovamboland, the Transkei and many other ethnic regions. Throughout the history of Southern Africa there has been a clustering of ethnic groups in particular regions. Certain areas, called 'homelands' or 'reserves', have traditionally been inhabited exclusively by Bantu tribes. Since the turn of the century, however, the Bantu have gradually been drawn into the White economy. Today there is no sector of the South African economy – mining, farming, trade or industry – which does not depend heavily on Bantu labour. Consequently, of the 15 million Bantu in South Africa, approximately 54 per cent work and reside outside the Bantu areas: the majority in the urban centres and the others scattered in rural areas.

POWER STRUCTURE

In the prevailing power structure, most effective forms of formal or institutional political and economic power are concentrated in the hands of the Whites. Apart from earlier historical factors, this state of affairs must be explained by the fact that since the formation of the Union in 1910 the great majority of White South Africans, whatever their political affiliations, have accepted 'White supremacy' as the basis of policy. The English-speaking section predominates in the economic sphere, but in the political sphere Afrikaner nationalism has been the strongest force for more than a century. Probably one of the oldest articulate expressions of an ethnocentric patriotic ideology in Africa, and mainly stimulated by the rivalry of the British culture for many generations, Afrikaner nationalism is resolutely indigenous and preoccupied with the needs of preserving its cultural heritage. The National Party was formed in 1914 specifically to preserve the integrity of Afrikanerdom, and to promote its philosophy of cultural differentiation. The same preoccupation with preserving Afrikaner identity, as well as the needs of protecting the

European-type White civilisation which had been built up in the course of three centuries against the danger of being swamped culturally and politically by the numerically preponderant non-Whites (particularly the emergence of a Black African move-ment), gave rise to the policy of *apartheid*.

THE POLICY OF SEPARATE DEVELOPMENT (APARTHEID)

Although policies of segregation, in some form, have dominated South African politics for many generations, the earlier policies were sporadic and pragmatic. The forces of integration were allowed to operate to some degree in many fields without much calculated planning. Particularly in the economic field, the White man's need for the benefits of non-White labour and the non-White buying power, and the non-White need for employment and the benefits of White capital and skill, produced a high degree of economic integration.

The National Party came to power in 1948 largely on the cam-paign platform of *apartheid*. In terms of this policy, the National Party government launched an elaborate programme directed towards the systematic disentanglement of the various non-White racial and ethnic groups from the social, economic and political structures of the Whites and the creation of separate opportuni-ties for the progressive self-fulfilment of each major group in accordance with its own traditions and values, and where practi-cable to develop into independent states within their own terri-tories. In the place of the present-day single South African constitutional unit, several constitutional units (even if they are not geographically contiguous) are to be established, coinciding as far as practicable with the existing major national units. The government rejects policies of integration that would lead to a majoritarian 'common society' on the grounds that it would give rise to unbearable tensions, to an intense power struggle and to chaotic conditions in which each national unit would be denied its ethical right to maintain its own identity and to manage its own affairs in its own areas.[7]

During the first decade of National Party government the implementation of its policies was characterised by a series of *segregationist* measures. It was segregationist in that the chief aim was to obtain a maximum of separation between Whites and non-Whites in all spheres of life. To obtain this general aim the following specific ancillary objectives were sought: first, the prevention of further biological integration of the races;[8] second, the removal and regulation of points of contact between the various groups;[9] and third, the total exclusion of non-Whites from the dominant political system in order to safeguard the White man's political control in the areas classified as predominantly 'White'.[10] Some of its practical manifestations are separate residential areas, separate educational facilities, separate wage scales, separate employment opportunities, separation in public transport and health facilities, separate churches and separate public amenities.

After the first decade (i.e. around 1960) the emphasis gradually shifted towards measures which were more positively *developmental* in character. It was developmental in that new and alternative opportunities were created for the non-White population groups in the social, economic and political spheres. In more concrete terms, these measures sought to achieve two basic objectives: first, the creation of separate (and temporarily subordinate) governmental institutions for the various non-White groups on both national and local government levels; and second, the launching of elaborate socio-economic development programmes. These policy objectives affect the major non-White groups – Bantu, Coloureds and Indians – in divergent ways.

DEVELOPMENT OPPORTUNITIES FOR THE BANTU

To understand the framework of development created for the Bantu (15 million) in terms of government policies, a clear distinction must be made between the Bantu in the 'homelands' and the Bantu in 'White' areas.

THE BANTU IN THE HOMELANDS

As far as the programme of homeland development is concerned, the National Party aims at the maximum concentration of the various Bantu peoples (i.e. the Zulus, the Xhosas, the Southern Sotho, the Northern Sotho, the Tswana, the Swazi, the Shangaans, the Venda, and also a number of peoples in the Territory of South West Africa, including the Ovambo, the Okavango, the

Damara, the Herero, the Bushmen and the Nama) in their respective homelands for the purposes of nation-building. The socio-economic development of the various homelands as focal points for independent nationhoods embraces the following:[11]

   (i) Political or constitutional development, i.e. the creation of political and administrative institutions needed for self-government and national independence.

  (ii) Agricultural development in view of agriculture being historically the first economic activity of the Bantu.

 (iii) Physical development of the land, including bridges, dams, towns, railways, fencing, soil preservation, etc.

 (iv) General economic development which includes mining, industries, commerce, forestry, etc.

  (v) Social development, i.e. school and university education, health services, welfare activities, etc.

 (vi) Spiritual development, including missionary work undertaken by independent churches.

(vii) Human development, i.e. the inner development of the individual in respect of dispositions and attitudes towards labour, modernisation and cultural activities.

Political institutions. Several basic laws were enacted over the past two decades in order to provide the statutory framework for the development of separate political systems in the various homelands which, although subordinate at present, are intended to lead to independence. The *Bantu Authorities Act* (1951) created a hierarchy of Bantu Authorities with local, regional and territorial jurisdictions corresponding in large measure to traditional Bantu councils and governing in accordance with Bantu customs as far as these can be reconciled with civilised standards. The *Promotion of Bantu Self-Government Act* (1959) recognised the Bantu territories as national homelands for the different ethnic groups (including those members not domiciled in the homelands) and transfers powers of self-government to the Territorial Authorities. The *Transkei Constitution Act* (1963) conferred a large measure of self-government to the Xhosa people by way of a Legislative Assembly (consisting of 64 traditional chieftains and 45 elected members), a cabinet, executive departments and other related government institutions. In 1968 and 1969 several Government Proclamations (modelled on *Proclamation R.140* of

1968) made provision for the transfer of additional executive responsibilities to the various Territorial Authorities.[12] The *Bantu Homelands Citizenship Act* (1970) confers citizenship of one or other Bantu Territorial Authority area to every Bantu in the Republic. The *Bantu Homelands Constitution Act* (1971) provides for the replacement of 'Territorial Authorities' with 'Legislative Assemblies', the establishment of executive councils and administrative agencies, the transfer of judicial functions, the regulation of financial matters, and it outlines the various stages in terms of which self-government powers are to be transferred.

The essence of this legislative programme is the utilisation of traditional and indigenous political institutions for the purposes of self-development and modernisation.

Socio-economic programmes. Programmes for the socio-economic progress of the Bantu homelands include a vast variety of activities. It takes the form of the purchase of land and the consolidation of isolated detached Bantu areas, soil-conservation works, construction of fences, road-building, dams and irrigation schemes, soil cultivation, township development, educational expansion including vocational schools and university colleges, the building of hospitals and clinics, the construction of housing schemes, etc. Of particular importance is the establishment of several development corporations, such as the Bantu Investment Corporation, the Bantu Mining Corporation and the Xhosa Development Corporation, whose purpose it is to promote and finance industrial, commercial and other economic enterprises in the Bantu homelands. Elaborate programmes have already been initiated under the auspices of these corporations.

In order to accelerate economic development in the homelands, the Minister of Bantu Administration and Development announced a new programme in 1970 entitled the 'Third Dynamic Decade'. To co-ordinate this programme, the Bantu Affairs Commission, an advisory body within the structure of the Department of Bantu Administration and Development, was reorganised to include an Economic Committee consisting of noted experts in the field of economic planning and development. The basic strategy of this committee was outlined by its chairman as the creation of a 'work and income basis' for homeland development by the establishment of economic 'growth points', not only in the border areas but particularly in the 'heartland areas'.[13] To implement this strategy the chairman envisioned an action programme which involves various steps, including:

(i) The localisation of industries in the homelands in accordance with the policy of decentralisation of industries.
(ii) The creation of economic infrastructures in the 'heartland' areas.
(iii) Housing and township development.
(iv) Canalisation and training of Bantu labourers.
(v) Rapid transport systems.
(vi) Co-operation with Territorial Authorities.

In April 1970 the managing director of the Bantu Investment Corporation announced a new five-year plan in terms of which the Corporation would spend R104 million over this period (R86 million in the Republic and R18 million in South West Africa).[14] It was further anticipated that private White entrepreneurs, acting on an 'agency' basis in the homelands, would spend an additional R20 million in establishing manufacturing concerns at selected 'growth points'. The R86 million earmarked for the Republic was to be invested as follows:

R12 million on the development of the necessary infrastructure at the growth points (initially four in number);
R31 million on the erection of 233 factories for leasing to entrepreneurs;
R22 million for the development of undertakings such as manufacturing concerns, wholesale merchandising businesses, bus services, breweries, etc.;
R6 million on the erection of business premises and housing for leasing to Bantu;
R14 million would be available for making loans to Bantu business and professional men;
R1 million for the extension of savings banks.

The total amounts allocated to the Department of Bantu Administration and Development for the year ending 31 March 1972 were:

Revenue Account	R110,390,000
Loan Account	R 87,000,000
	R197,390,000

These amounts include anticipated expenditure in 'White' areas as well as in the homelands of the Republic. They exclude expenditure by the Departments of Bantu Education, Transport, Posts and Telegraphs, and others, contributions from urban local authorities, and amounts to be spent from revenues collected in the various homelands themselves and from the South African Bantu Trust's accumulated funds.[15]

THE BANTU IN WHITE AREAS

In accordance with government policies, all Bantu persons living outside the homelands are to be identified with the national units where their forebears originated and are within the context of 'White' South Africa regarded as 'temporary sojourners' to whom property ownership and political rights are denied.

In terms of the stipulations of the *Natives (Urban Areas) Consolidation Act* (1945), as amended, and the *Bantu Affairs Administration Act* (1971), an elaborate system of local administration for the urban Bantu has been developed in the span of three decades. The central direction and control of the system rests in the Department of Bantu Administration and Development. The field activities are performed (*a*) by the Departments of Non-White Affairs established by the various local authorities (i.e. municipalities and several rural authorities such as divisional councils in the Cape, local health committees in Natal, the Transvaal Board for the Development of Peri-Urban Areas and the Orange Free State Smallholding Areas Control Board), and (*b*) by Bantu Affairs Administration Boards.

Since 1923 it has been the generally accepted practice to allow Bantu living within the jurisdictional area of a municipality some measure of participation in the administration of their own affairs by means of advisory boards. Members of these boards are partly elected and partly nominated, and 'parent' municipal councils are required to consult these councils in all matters affecting the interests of the urban Bantu. These boards are purely advisory and have no executive powers, but they may take the initiative to make recommendations and may demand that their reports be forwarded to the Minister of Bantu Administration and Development. By 1971 there were 400 of these bodies in action. In 1961, however, the government decided to phase out existing advisory boards by gradually replacing them with Urban Bantu

Councils. The object of the new system is to create representative bodies which could be vested with executive powers. In terms of the *Urban Bantu Councils Act* (1961), these bodies must consist of elected members and various defined powers may be assigned to them by municipalities, but always subject to the approval of the Minister. The main functional categories outlined in the Act include the layout of Bantu townships; the erection of buildings; the allotment of sites; the provision of sanitary, medical and health services; the removal of unlawful residents or occupants of land and buildings; the maintenance of law and order (e.g. community guards); and powers of criminal and civil jurisdiction. By 1971 a total of 23 Urban Bantu Councils had been established. At the time of writing there seems to be considerable ambivalence regarding the role these councils are destined to play – particularly whether or not they are intended to develop into full-scale municipalities for urban Bantu townships.

DEVELOPMENT OPPORTUNITIES FOR COLOUREDS AND INDIANS

The position of the Coloured (2 million) and Indian (600,000) population groups within the framework of the policy of separate development differ from those of the various Bantu peoples in that neither group has a separate 'homeland' of its own. In consequence they are apparently destined to develop 'parallel' but separately from the Whites within the geographical boundaries of the dominant political system. Over the past three decades the modes of political participation of the Coloureds and Indians have been channelled away from the White-dominated institutions into subsystems revolving around their own representative councils.

COLOUREDS

The *Coloured Persons Representative Council Act* (1964), as amended by the *Separate Representation of Voters Amendment Act* (1968), provides for the creation of a representative council consisting of 40 elected and 20 nominated members. It is authorised to legislate on such matters as finance, local government, education, social welfare and rural settlements, subject to the approval of the State President. Its executive functions are performed by a full-time Executive of five members which is assisted in its task by the Administration for Coloured Affairs under the direction of a government-appointed Commissioner for Coloured Affairs. In 1971 a total of 1,213 White public servants had been seconded to the Administration. In addition there were 18,710 Coloured persons (including teachers) on the Adminstration's staff. The Council receives an annual grant from the central government.[16] Contact between the C.R.C. and the White Parliament is maintained by way of meetings between the Prime Minister, the Minister of Coloured Affairs and other Cabinet Ministers, and the Council's Executive.

On the level of urban local government, the *Group Areas Amendment Act* (1962) provides for the development of local government institutions in three stages. The first entails 'consultative committees' with nominated members functioning under close official guidance. The second stage involves management committees with partly elected and partly nominated members exercising such powers and functions as may be conferred on it under the supervision and control of the adjacent 'parent' White municipal council. The third stage culminates in full-scale 'municipal councils' functioning as ordinary elected local authorities. The final authority in the establishment of these authorities lies with the Minister of Community Development, and his general directions are given effect by the various provincial administrations. By early 1971 there were 22 management committees and 53 consultative committees.[17] No fully-fledged, autonomous municipalities for Coloureds have as yet been established.

To implement its programme of socio-economic development for the Coloured population, the government established the Department of Coloured Affairs as a fully-fledged government department under its own Cabinet Minister in 1961. The various government services for Coloured persons which were previously distributed among numerous institutions were all brought under the auspices of one department. In 1969 most of these services were transferred to the Administration for Coloured Affairs which is now attached to the Coloured Persons Representative Council. Of special significance also is the Coloured Development Corporation which was created in 1962 to promote and finance

Coloured enterprises in the industrial, commercial and financial spheres. From the Corporation's establishment in 1962 to the end of 1970, loans had been granted to 138 entrepreneurs (in hotel, retail, manufacturing, building, furniture, transport and several other businesses) for a total amount of R3,169,779. The Corporation had itself spent R1,489,680 on establishing a property company, a supermarket, the Spes Bona Bank and a block of flats.[18]

INDIANS

The Indian population occupy a peculiar position within the framework of the South African political system. Since 1910 they have remained excluded from formal political participation and subjected to various restrictions in respect of the occupation and ownership of fixed property. Various schemes have been devised for their repatriation to India, but in 1961 they were officially accepted as a recognised part of the South African population. A Department of Indian Affairs was created to further the objectives of the policy of separate development also as far as the Indian population group is concerned.

In 1964 the *South African Indian Council* was established. It is an appointed body with advisory powers acting as a link between the Minister of Indian Affairs and the Indian community. In 1968 this council was made a statutory body with its own Executive Committee. In 1972 legislation was introduced to convert this Council to a partially elected body with expanded executive responsibilities.

The institutions created for participation by the residents of Indian group areas on the level of urban local government resemble those of the Coloureds outlined above. By early 1971 there were 7 consultative committees, 16 local affairs committees (only found in Natal) and 1 autonomous Indian town board at Verulam, Natal.[19]

ADMINISTRATIVE ASPECTS

A unique characteristic of the development situation in South Africa is the coexistence of a developed Western-oriented system of public administration which is attached to the overarching and dominant White-controlled power structure on the one hand, and several emerging administrative structures attached to the various non-White subsystems on the other. This implies the availability of a considerable *reservoir* of development aid, but the key problem is to harness the available skills in adequate quantities so that it can be applied within the developing subsystems in action programmes to accelerate economic growth, to expand social well-being and to improve public services. This problem, however, cannot be solved simply by transplanting Western organisational and managerial concepts and techniques to the new settings – partly because of the peculiar nature of the needs to be met, and also because of the distinctive features of the settings in which the new administrative systems must function.

The emerging subsystems basically need development-directed systems of public administration, that is, systems which are attuned towards change, adaptation, innovation and growth. This development-directedness must be reflected in its activities, its organisational structures and its operational style.

SCOPE OF ACTIVITIES

Apart from any ideological considerations, it must be expected that, in view of the lack of adequate private initiative, public-sector activities will have to expand. Government agencies will have to play a key role as catalytic modernising agents. In most parts of Africa governments have assumed the role of prime movers in the development process. Governments are not only expected to act as stimulators and regulators of privately initiated development, they now increasingly engage in productive activities, as entrepreneurs in agricultural and industrial development.

ORGANISATIONAL REQUISITES

The emerging non-White authorities further require administrative structures which are designed according to the needs of specific development tasks. Provision must be made for development-directed institutions such as planning agencies, development corporations and corporate public enterprises in order to stimulate the process of development. Agencies of this nature have already been created in the form of the Bantu Development Corporation, the Bantu Mining Corporation, the Coloured Development Cor-

poration and the Xhosa Development Corporation, but these
institutions function essentially as part of the (White) central
government's administrative machinery and need closer liaison
with the respective community or national authorities. It must
further be kept in mind that the organisational problems experienced in the various political subsystems are not essentially
reformist in nature because administrative structures have to be
created *de novo*. The problems of reform are primarily limited
to the administrative machinery of the dominant system. It involves the transfer of administrative functions from various
existing departments and agencies in the 'White' system to a
plethora of fledgeling agencies attached to the political subsystems. It is a matter of transforming the system of administration
based on the control of the non-White groups to new systems of
development administration for and by the non-White population
groups.

OPERATIONAL PROBLEMS

On the operational level, several important aspects require attention. Among these are planning, co-ordination, personnel training
and management development.

Planning. Planning is an essential tool for developing public
policies. But planning should not be limited to economic aspects.
It should be broadened to include non-economic dimensions to
ensure the practicability of the plans and to make the results of
development relevant to social and human development. Greater
attention should also be given to the integration of planning,
policy-making and budgeting. In this way plans can be translated
into implementable programmes and viable projects. The use of
modern budgeting systems and techniques (such as P.P.B.S.) can
make a useful contribution to increasing analytical capabilities
e.g. definition of objectives, development of criteria for measurement of results, identification of alternative means, projection of
future costs, etc.), but it requires advanced accounting and information systems. It also requires harmonisation with the
political implications of budgeting.

Co-ordination. The problem of co-ordination is given particular
prominence by the fact that a myriad of public agencies are

involved in the implementation of the policy of separate development. It involves different levels of government and the problems cut across existing political boundaries. Some of the major government departments include Bantu Administration and Development, Bantu Education, Coloured Affairs, Indian Affairs, Planning, Community Development, Treasury, Health, Social Welfare, Mining, Commerce, Industries, Justice, Police, Posts and Telegraphs, South African Railways and Harbours, etc. In addition, there are the various provincial administrations, numerous municipalities, various public corporations such as the Electricity Supply Commission, Industrial Development Corporation, Bantu Investment Corporation, Bantu Mining Corporation, Coloured Development Corporation. The functions dealt with by these agencies are interrelated and interwoven and therefore require a great deal of co-ordination. Measures must be taken to bring the various parts or units into proper relation, to ensure unity of action, to avoid contradictions and duplication of efforts, and thus to facilitate the achievement of specific objectives. There are several ways of achieving co-ordination. It may be effected through better communication and exchange of information, through formal and informal discussions, through joint co-ordinating machinery or through central planning and control.

Training. Apart from the vital question of finance, the development of self-government institutions for non-Whites depends essentially on the quality of personnel, especially those at the senior grades. Opportunities have been created for qualified Bantu to occupy administrative and professional positions in the public service establishments of the various territorial authorities for the Xhosa, Zulu, Tswana, Venda, Shangana–Tsonga, Ovambo, Herero and other units. Similarly, the opportunity has also arisen for Coloureds and Asians who have become qualified and trained to move into the many positions which will become available in the administrations of the Coloured and Indian representative councils and the numerous new local authorities. At present there are opportunities for training as secretaries, accountants, health inspectors, teachers, librarians, social workers, policemen, administrative assistants, etc., but more opportunities are required for qualification and training in technical, professional and managerial fields. At present a large number of White administrative

id technical staff are seconded to the various non-White
uthorities, but now that the goal has been set for self-government
1 the various levels of government, the training of technical,
rofessional and administrative officials has become a matter of
rgent concern. Managerial deficiencies are common at all levels
1d a key contributor to shortfalls in meeting developmental
als.

ONCLUSION

he path of implementation of the policy of separate development
strewn with obdurate obstacles: some on the level of grand
licy design and others on the level of application in specific
stances. Among the main problem areas on the level of broad
licy design are the following:

(i) arriving at equitable bases for the distribution of natural
resources and for territorial apportionment acceptable to
the principal participant groups;

(ii) making the Bantu homelands economically and politically
viable as reasonably self-contained units;

(iii) reconciling the forces of traditionalism and modernisation
which are operative in both Black and White communities;

(iv) developing feasible and equitable social, economic and
political arrangements in urban areas for sub-groups such
as the urbanised Bantu, the Coloureds and the Indians
whose aspirations are not likely to be absorbed by the
system of 'separate freedoms' on a nation-state basis;

(v) sustaining substantial support and co-operation on the
part of important segments of non-White leadership; and

(vi) mitigating active external opposition.

But apart from these wider problem areas, there are a number
more specific problems relating to the practical everyday lives
many South African non-Whites. They refer to personal hard-
ips, irritations and annoyances which are the causes of dis-
ntent. It is precisely in relation to incidents in this category –
ten referred to as 'petty *apartheid*' – that belligerent propa-
nda campaigns abroad tend to converge, that potential sources
goodwill are alienated and non-White South Africans are

antagonised. Examples of grievances or causes of discontent mos
often quoted in this regard include the following:

   (i) Differential salary scales and wages for employees doin
the same work and having the same qualifications.

  (ii) Inequities in the provision of public services such a
education, technical training, residential areas, entertair
ment, recreation and transportation.

 (iii) Officious and injudicious application of the variou
measures dealing with influx control and the ordinar
criminal code.

 (iv) Definition of permissible employment for the differei
population groups.

  (v) Injuries to personal dignity in situations of inter-person:
contact with officials and private individuals.

 (vi) The removal of long-settled people from their homes fc
the purposes of group areas planning without adequat
alternatives.

(vii) The lack of facilities and opportunities for orderly inter
personal and inter-group social contact and commun
cation.

(viii) Disruption of family life resulting from migratory labou
practices.

 (ix) The application of discriminatory measures within th
Bantu homelands.

  (x) The exercise of arbitrary discretionary powers affectin
individual freedoms such as movement, speech an
assembly and the due process of law.

It would be a distortion of facts to attribute all the allege
inequities, constraints and hardships solely to the official polic
of separate development. The Whites cannot be held responsibl
for the impediments imposed by cultural factors. In large measure
present conditions have been shaped and moulded by a variet
of historical forces. Some measures are designed to preserve ir
ternal order and to protect national independence against th
onslaught of hostile ideologies. But on the level of personal irrita
tions and annoyances, much can be done by way of improvemen
  It is important to realise that the major groups in Sout
Africa cannot be allowed to become unchanging antagonist
each fixed in frozen postures of deterrence and retaliatior

Anxieties over the preservation of group identities and interests must not be allowed to blind those in command positions to the possibilities of changing reactions, moderating attitudes and adjusting policies in order to protect the common interests of the various sub-units. Much more needs to be done by way of consultation and negotiation between leaders.

In the final analysis, it should be clear that problems of development in a plural society admit of no inflexible or final solutions. It will be the awesome task of responsible leaders in all segments of South African life to foster respect for human dignity and to protect the opportunities of individuals and groups to seek a better life and to share in the privileges, responsibilities and rewards of society.

NOTES

1. For a penetrating analysis of these changes, see J. P. Nettl, 'Strategies in the Study of Political Development', in Colin Leys (ed.), *Politics and Change in Developing Countries* (Cambridge Univ. Press, 1969) pp. 13–34; and C. A. O. van Nieuwenhuijze, *Development: A Challenge to Whom?* (The Hague: Mouton, 1969) pp. 15–142.
2. Consider, for instance, Truman's 'Point Four' in his Inaugural Address of 4 January 1949.
3. Reference must be made here to such interpretations as the 'economic priorities' outlined by W. W. Rostow (*The Stages of Economic Growth*), the 'democratic priorities' outlined by S. M. Lipset (*Political Man: The Social Bases of Politics*) and the 'bureaucratic model' of Max Weiber (as adapted by several modern writers).
4. M. J. Esman, 'The Politics of Development Administration', in J. D. Montgomery and W. J. Siffin, *Approaches to Development: Politics, Administration and Change* (New York: McGraw-Hill, 1966) pp. 59–60.
5. See Ferrel Heady, *Public Administration: A Comparative Perspective* (Englewood Cliffs, N.J.: Prentice-Hall, 1966) pp. 59–60.
6. Sir Herbert Frankel, 'The Tyranny of Economic Paternalism', *Optima* (Dec 1960) p. 3.
7. Some of the most cogent policy statements of National Party leaders include the following: speech by Dr D. F. Malan at a Party Congress in Bloemfontein on 8 November 1938; speech by Mr J. G. Strydom in the House of Assembly on 20 and 21 April 1955; speeches by Dr H. F. Verwoerd in the Senate on 3 September 1948, and in the House of Assembly on 24 January 1961; speeches by Mr B. J. Vorster in the House of Assembly on 23 September 1966 and 24 April 1971.
8. Relevant legislation includes the *Prohibition of Mixed Marriages Act* (1949), the *Immorality Act* (1950), the *Population Registration Act* (1956).

9. Relevant legislation includes the *Group Areas Act* (1950), the *Reservation of Separate Amenities Act* (1953), the *Extension of University Education Act* (1959), the *Industrial Conciliation Act* (1956).

10. See the *Separate Representation of Voters Act* (1956), the *Prohibition of Political Interference Act* (1968), the *Promotion of Bantu Self-Government Act* (1959).

11. See M. C. Botha (Minister of Bantu Administration and Development and of Bantu Education), *Multinational Development and Co-existence* (Transvaal Information Service of the National Party, 1969) p. 6.

12. These territorial administrations generally include the following departmental structure: Government Affairs and Finance, Community Affairs, Agriculture, Education, Roads and Public Works, and Justice.

13. J. A. Lombard, 'Die Staatkundige en Administratiewe Beginsels van Tuislandontwikkeling', in *Tuislandontwikkeling – 'n Program vir die Sewentigerjare* (Pretoria: SABRA, 1970) pp. 15–20.

14. *Financial Mail*, 24 Apr 1970.

15. For the brief summary of expenditure, see M. Horrell, *Survey of Race Relations, 1971* (Johannesburg: South African Institute of Race Relations, 1972) pp. 118–20.

16. The budget of the Council and its administration for 1971–2 amounted to R78,233,000. See *Estimates of Expenditure from Revenue and Loan Accounts*, R.P. 2/1971, R.P. 7/1971 and R.P. 3/1971.

17. *Hansard* 2, 12 Feb 1971, col. 144.

18. See *Hansard* 3, cols 247–8, and *Hansard* 4, cols 309–10.

19. See Horrell, op. cit., p. 150.

COMMENTS

B. S. van As, I. O. H. M. Mapena and H. W. E. Ntsanwisi

Professor van As said that the paper by Professor Vosloo concealed or partly simplified the fact that both the *apartheid* policy (or separate freedoms) and development as such originated earlier than 1948. Historically, a spontaneous tendency to segregation was evident ever since Bantu and White came into direct contact with each other in South Africa. Similarly, developmental programmes for the Bantu had also been initiated since the 1920s in South Africa.

Accepting Coleman's broad polarisation of the colonial policies in sub-Saharan Africa as either direct or indirect rule (or, in Lord Hailey's words, identification or segregation), it was evident that the present and future politico-administrative developments in the subcontinent had been and would be greatly influenced by the administrative application of these policies. These developments had been and would be affected by the obvious variations in the traditional politico-administrative situations in this region. In the formerly directly ruled, as against indirectly ruled, colonies, modern politico-administrative situations emanated earlier and were furthermore at the expense generally of the power of the traditional authorities. Post-independent trends in sub-Saharan Africa indicated nevertheless that even in formerly directly ruled colonies the traditional authorities generally had to be integrated again into the politico-administrative structures with a view to the mobilisation of the masses.

Regarding the issue of development action, Professor van As said that no aid was value-free, not even the absence of aid. Accelerated development had been variously motivated. During the late 1960s, however, the developmental programmes for recipients had generally been reappraised by the donor countries. It was furthermore conceivable that recipients regarded aid as a weapon in the Cold War, or as international bribery, or as a form of neo-colonialism or cultural imperialism. The real issue was the context of development; unless this was total, aid tended to be superficial and potentially destructive, rather than constructive.

Education and training raised the most important issue concerning development, viz. the accelerated transmission of modern knowledge and techniques. This should be rooted in and involve the people for whom it was designed; it should administratively strive to enhance the recipient's sense of his own worth. It was wrong to dictate an unqualified Westernisation to the Bantu peoples of sub-Saharan Africa; most of them were a long way off from fully internalising the Western mode of life. The inertia of centuries-old cultures was not likely to be transformed in a few decades. An entirely new pattern of living for a whole people simply could not be designed on a drawing-board or installed like a set of hydroelectric turbines. The ethos, the *ubuntu*, of the Bantu peoples had to be taken into account, and it was for them to abstract from all the operating forces what suited the people best.

This approach was also the basis of South Africa's foreign aid to other African states, which incorporated four main considerations: (*a*) the principle of non-interference in each other's internal affairs; (*b*) the notion that development aid be productive for self-help; (*c*) that this aid be supplementary to that from industrially wealthier countries; and (*d*) that aid to foreign countries be subordinate to the uplift of South Africa's own developing peoples and areas.

Mr Mapena reviewed and summarised some of the principal issues raised in the main paper and concluded with the following comments:

In South Africa use had been made of indigenous political institutions, namely the chiefs. The traditional leader had been made part of the machinery of government, so that the chiefs chosen by their people had become instruments of the central government and had come to be regarded as messengers of the White government. Thus the image of the traditional leader had suffered in the eyes of their people.

Bantu Authorities did not improve the situation and traditional leaders had not always kept abreast of developing needs. It would not be a healthy situation if all authorities followed the Transkeian constitutional pattern. More use should accordingly be made of the elective principle to recruit from the African élite, and traditional leaders could retain their dignity in a Second Chamber.

Concerning the Bantu in White areas, the official policy of concentrating the maximum number in the homelands could only be applied if the homelands were to be considerably extended. A frank discussion of this question would contribute greatly to the development of the homelands and to harmonious relations in the country.

Professor Ntsanwisi said that, while Professor Vosloo had presented a thorough study of the policy of separate development and had put the facts as they were, he had neglected the critical view in his paper. There were many influences that should be examined on the practical side of separate development. He felt that the chief ingredient lacking in the policy up to the present time was decision-making on the part of the homeland governments themselves; it was the government in Pretoria which still made the decisions. A homeland government was a government in name only, if it could not make the decisions it wanted to make. In spite of the laws on the statute book, the 'real thing', namely the decision-making power, had not yet been delivered.

Professor Ntsanwisi said that the second question he wished to refer to was that of the urban African. As far as his own homeland (Gazankulu) was concerned, it had been made clear to the South African government that urban Africans could not be received into the homeland, because no preparation had been made for them. By this he meant that there was not sufficient land to accommodate them, and there was no infrastructure worth talking about. It was well known that there was poverty, and that the homelands were reservoirs of workers who had to come to the urban areas to find the wherewithal to live.

A third matter which the Conference should consider carefully was that in the policy of separate development there tended to be separation for the sake of separation. That was one of the negative aspects of the policy, and it would be preferable if, in its application, more attention could be given to positive aspects, such as industrialisation for the people who are already in the homelands and the provision of better facilities for them. More attention to the economic viability of the homelands was needed, and an important aspect was that of finance. It was argued in many quarters that the government was spending a great deal of money on development of the homelands. While this might be true of some homelands, Professor Ntsanwisi said it was not true of his homeland. Since 1969 they had not had a budget exceeding R5 million, and he did not consider that to be a great deal of money for the development of the homeland.

He felt therefore that, instead of simply considering the historical background of the policy, some of the implications should also be studied – the pragmatic implications involved in the application of the policy. He considered that, unless a more practical, pragmatic and dynamic force was introduced into the application of the policy, the homelands themselves would not succeed. What was needed was a rethinking of the whole policy and a sincere and honest re-examination of the underlying principles.

With regard to his comment above that there was separation for the sake of separation, Professor Ntsanwisi said that one example which was disturbing was that, according to official policy, if he wished to have discussions with another homeland leader, he first had to consult the authorities in Pretoria. He felt that there should be no objection to free and direct contacts between homeland leaders.

Finally, Professor Ntsanwisi considered that there was not sufficient consultation between the South African government and the various homeland leaders. It would be helpful, for instance, if all these leaders could meet together with the government to iron out some of the difficulties which confronted them.

Executive Training for Public Administration: The Role of E.I.A.P. as a Regional Centre to Develop Executive Personnel for Latin America

ATHYR GUIMARÃES

1. INTRODUCTION

A clear need seems to exist in relation to specific training, research and documentation, as well as to teaching at postgraduate level, that is not being satisfied entirely by national centres and which could possibly be met by regional centres. A great debility is to be noticed, for instance, in the system of formation of highly qualified manpower for developing countries, especially in connection with governmental effort.

It is believed that regional centres, regarded as complementary to, rather than in substitution for, national centres, have an important contribution to offer by playing mainly a significant social and political role. Such regional centres will be justified whenever their role is clearly complementary to efforts carried on at national level. No regional centre should ever be established to perform functions already performed by national centres.

It is assumed that there are needs of a regional character that national centres are neither technically equipped for, nor politically capable of attending to. If the assumption is correct, the agency required to cope with such needs must have a scope and dimension different from those of typically national agencies. We should possibly speak of a supra-national dimension. In such cases it would be reasonable to conceive of such centres as largely autonomous agencies. They should not belong to one individual country, but equally serve all nations comprising the region. The fact that such centres are to be administratively independent from the individual countries served poses the problem of their financing. This seems to be precisely one of the most difficult aspects involved in the creation and management of regional centres. The rather diluted responsibility implied in the concept of regional centres makes it difficult to sell to beneficiary countries the idea of contributing financially. However, that those countries benefiting from such centres should contribute financially, and even technically, to their upkeep is not to de disputed. Resorting to indirect financing through already existing regional organs such as O.A.S., I.D.B. and E.C.L.A., to mention only Latin America, might be the easiest and most feasible solution.

In the case of Latin America, for example, only a regional centre can properly and systematically handle the problems related to the economic integration of the region, and the creation of a Latin American common market.

A regional centre also makes it considerably easier to conduct comparative studies of the Latin American realities because of its almost simultaneous access to official data in each country of the region. A national agency could hardly have the same easy access to official sources of information in other countries. Attempts by a national agency to collect information in another country will normally arouse suspicion and resentment. A regional centre, on the other hand, seems to have a great potential in stimulating the interchange of information and experience within the region. It may in consequence contribute to strengthening among a large proportion of the regional 'intelligentsia' an awareness of the basic similarity of their problems and the possible regional applicability of most of the typical solutions.

It also seems to be easier and far less costly to conduct studies of a multi-national character at regional centres, especially studies of integrated development projects demanding joint action on the part of various nations of the region.

On the other hand, the existence of a regional centre where regional information is collected, interpreted and systematised for reference and dissemination makes it possible to overcome the tendency to self-containment which in Latin America especially has been responsible for a marked and general ignorance of what is happening in the region. It is believed that regional centres can help to avoid the repetition of mistakes already committed by a neighbouring nation because of lack of systematised information on typical problems common to most countries of the region.

Finally, one of the most significant roles of regional centres could be that of channelling training and technical assistance so as to eliminate a few of the inconveniences of the bilateral approach. It has not proved easy to offer technical assistance within the framework of bilateral relationships without running the risk of arousing nationalistic reactions against real or imaginary cultural domestication and economic domination. Regional centres are believed to have a better chance of overcoming such resistance because of their supra-national character and the expected neutrality implied in their action.

In order to fulfil such needs as these, the Inter-American School of Public Administration was launched in 1964 as a result of an agreement between the Inter-American Development Bank and the Getulio Vargas Foundation to train managers for the public sector in Latin America.

The basic assumption which inspired the creation of the School and still orients its activities is that the Latin American public administrator is an empirical professional, in most instances unprepared to perform his duties. On the other hand, because of the marked interference of party politics in public bureaucracy, and having in mind the level of efficiency demanded to cope with the expectations created by development, the senior executive has to face extreme limitations and pressures difficult to resist in his attempt to balance political commitments and demands for fast, efficient action. The manager of the public sector therefore has to struggle between political loyalty and development, between ideology and technocracy, in addition to his insufficient technical preparation, which usually makes him the victim of bureaucratic routine.

Such an understanding of the administrative reality of Latin America has oriented the programmes offered by the School, as well as its operational methodology. The courses offered, however, try to emphasise two types of orientation:

(a) a socio-political emphasis which seeks to give the executive an awareness of his role, of the institutional limitations, the scope of his authority and his potential for accomplishment; and

(b) the technical orientation, supplying the executive with a set of systematised information about budget, organisation, project administration, personnel administration, etc., taking as examples and reference points the valid experience of Latin America, thus avoiding the application of solutions adopted in other contexts.

The School regards as a mistake the purely mechanistic conception in its double theoretical unfolding, particularly in the underdeveloped countries where the social and political conditioning of administration, and the public sector's responsibilities with regard to developmental efforts, are fundamental. Thus it seems to us that the recent theses that attribute an important role to the Latin American public executive as a fundamental element in the process of strategic decision-making point in the right direction.

The content of what we transmit adjusts itself to the philosophy which we judge to be the fundamental reality of the modern executive's function in the Latin American public sector. The processes of transmission of instrumental techniques have, for this same reason, been put on a secondary level. We emphasise the processes of transmission thought to be more adequate in favouring a broader view and sensitiveness to socio-political conditioning. Our effort is oriented more towards the direction of seminars, case studies, guided readings, visits to institutions for discussions with senior executives and, secondarily, informal lectures.

The concept of 'historical tempo' and the sense of precaution in the elaboration of administrative reform impose the incorporation of sociology of administration in the executive training curricula. This hypothesis is extremely important for E.I.A.P.'s performance criteria, and some minimum of additional elaboration is necessary.

If the meaning of reform strategy is accepted as important in the developed countries, where the technical parameter dominates because of the high rational level of these societies, it is even more important in the underdeveloped ones. In the developed countries themselves the problem of modernisation is understood as predominantly ecological, and therefore it occurs through pragmatic adaptations. Even the North American public administration seems to react very slowly to modernising solutions, whether they be initiated by the private sector or by other specific public sectors. The extraordinary repercussions of McNamara's attempt at modernisation of the Defence Ministry, which left a number of persons quite perplexed and magnetised the scientific world, was examined through different angles and provoked a great quantity of apologetic literature.[1]

It is necessary to call attention to the sociology of the phenomenon in trying to explain why an attempt to use public budgeting as a political, programming and projecting instrument, something that American experts have been recommending for years for the underdeveloped countries, appears as a problem in the American administration itself. This fact seems to strengthen the thesis of a lag between, for instance, the theoretical assimilation of the writings of Fritz Mosher or Jesse Burkhead on programme budgeting, and its practical application. The theory seems to go ahead of the facts, which, in a certain way, leads us to the necessity of thinking with greater caution about the phenomenon of modernisation – particularly in the case of underdeveloped countries, where the importation of technology is a highly problematic issue.

The existence of this kind of phenomenon seems to indicate that the School is on the right track in giving emphasis to sociology of administration or to its 'ecology'. The School feels that the formation of executives should incorporate such an approach, exactly because the administrative reforms (it is necessary to say again) are not limited to their technological parameters but incorporate political, social, economic, and cultural variables. The executive without access to this approach will most likely be unable to understand the very phenomena that involve him, nor will he be able to lead the change process that he intends at least formally to start.

Thus, executive training programmes must be substantially different from technician programmes. While these have in the man–machine relation (the mechanistic hypothesis) the fundamental ratio for the ordering of their work, the former have in the variable man–institution relation their fundamental component, and only secondarily in the variable man–man relation. This means that technician training programmes are not affected by value positions because they are essentially standardised.

Executive training, on the other hand, must necessarily incorporate an area of understanding of the reality that transcends the technological field and places itself in the universe of politics and social values.

Technical training can be cross-cultural; executive training is clearly endo-cultural. For the former, programmes such as the INSTEP in India[2] for the transfer of metallurgical technology can be organised; for the latter, a similar initiative would probably be an error and a waste.

2. PANORAMA OF THE PRESENT SITUATION

There are no data relating to Latin America for the analysis of professional formation of high-level executives. Our hypothesis, however, is that there should not be a great variation in relation to the Brazilian experience, even though in Brazil public administration teaching has been offered in a systematic and institutionalised way since the 1930s. From the 1950s a high-level institution, the Brazilian School of Public Administration (E.B.A.P.), began to operate regularly and there are at present in Brazil about thirty Schools or Institutes of Public Administration. There is no comparable panorama in other Latin American countries, where efforts along these lines are of more recent origin and have not been so intensive.

Despite this, it seems probable that our analysis of the Brazilian situation might be applicable to other Latin American countries, as far as the preparation of public-sector executives is concerned.

A rather small number of these executives have as yet had contact with regular public administration courses. The great majority come from other academic origins. Ten years ago a publication from the National Campaign for the Improvement of Postgraduate Personnel (CAPES), referring to data published by the *Mensario Estatistico Atuarial* of the I.A.P.I., indicated that 63·7 per cent of the agronomists, 53·62 per cent of the veterinarians, 21·7 per cent of the engineers, 15·2 per cent of the architects, 11·6 per cent of the chemists, 4·6 per cent of the medical doctors, 4·4 per cent of the dentists and 9 per cent of the lawyers[3] were employed in the Brazilian public administration. Assuming that this distribution is still valid, and knowing that there are now 80,000 lawyers in the country, we come to the conclusion that public administration absorbs approximately 8,000 of these professionals. That seems to be the largest group of professionals employed by the public sector. There are no specific data that indicate, with the same accuracy, the cultural background of those in command of the public hierarchy. We suspect, however, that the number of trained professionals in public administration is very low. The Inter-American School of Public Administration is at present developing a research project, of Latin American scope, that will possibly prove that point of view. For the time being we are working with hypotheses.

The number of trained executives thus being very small, our efforts to enlarge their comprehension bases for the work they have to accomplish can be justified because of the growing importance of their decisions in the process of rational and oriented change that characterises the planning effort in our societies.

From a purely legal point of view, it seems that we have already advanced in the direction of rationality. The truth, however, is different, and the socio-political dimensions of the problem are important, since our executives have not had adequate preparation for the performance of their duties. The transition of the patrimonial administration to the bureaucratic one, in the Weberian sense, making use of the law in a logical way, is not unique to Latin America. Other countries have also tried it, including European ones.

In several Latin American countries the repetition of this scheme, which Riggs named 'formalism', is known. In our country, Brazil, the constitution of 1824 already forecast admission to public employment according to the merit system. However, recent estimates indicate that the proportion of people entering public employment through competitive examination does not reach 10 per cent.

It seems evident that underdeveloped countries, particularly in Latin America, do not generate conditions that demand from the public sector an increase in rationality to face the pressure imposed by a mature industrial economy. Undoubtedly it will not be an improper exaggeration to assume that an important activator in increasing the efficiency and rationality of the public sector in developed countries, at the end of the nineteenth century, was industrialisation.

If we compare the example of Spain and Latin America, in general, with those of France and England, not to mention the United States, where training of high-level public-sector employees is already a tradition, we can notice a great difference.[4]

In France, graduates of L'École Nationale d'Administration (E.N.A.) have high status and access to outstanding positions like deputy general inspector of finance, secretary of foreign affairs, commercial attaché, etc.[5] In England the so-called 'Administrative Class', which distinguishes itself from the 'Clerical Class', is responsible for advising Ministers of State and plays an important role in formulating the economic policy of the country. The 'accusations' of technocracy, following James Burnham's scheme for future societies, have already begun to arise, mainly in France, but also in other developed countries, showing that the performance of technical functions in the modern state requires adequate training of executives and advisers in charge of specific programmes and active participation in the process of formulation of social and economic policies.

In Latin America the rapid growth in the 1960s, the vigorous beginning of heavy industry in many countries, the fast urbanisation, and demands for better standards of living on the part of the population increasingly being incorporated in the political process, caused the crisis in the traditional administration and brought new worries in respect of the so-called 'development administration'. Although the expression is still ambiguous and contested by many, it seems to make sense to talk of 'development administration' concerning Latin America.

It is at this historical moment, when pressures for dynamic action, efficiency and administrative rationality begin to be felt in our countries, that the training problem presents itself in a special way. Why? *Because it is exactly the high executives, well trained and sensitised to the new approach, who will be the most efficient instruments for change.* Sensing clearly the incapacity and lack of preparation of their subordinates, they begin to incorporate a structure of values that leads to attitudes of nonconformity as to traditionalism, or the notion of time and rhythm, and to the general lack of preparation of the group under their responsibility. Under these circumstances they become 'new Christians' of training and use their power and internal prestige to stimulate the adoption of training programmes from top to bottom.

For this reason, that is, because they are poles of power within organisations, highly trained executives have greater potential as activating elements in the change process. *Contrario sensu*, the training of less qualified groups as a priority measure, leaving for a later period the development of executives in decision-making positions, may result in a relative waste of time, as long as the groups of employees in an inferior hierarchical position do not have either the status of high executives or their capacity of persuasion. The training then runs the risk of being useless. Thus the Inter-American School of Public Administration emphasises the training of professionals who hold executive or high-level advisory positions, and orients its selection process in such a way as to attract this type of clientele for its courses.

In concluding this part of the paper, we think we are now ready to summarise our theoretical position. The E.I.A.P.'s main idea in its efforts towards executive formation is based on the examination of concrete realities in which it operates and leads to the conception of training chiefly in 'ecological' terms. Thus, for the School, executive development *is the effort to improve the efficiency of the modern executive, providing him with clear notions of managerial techniques and a broad basis for comprehension of the social, political, cultural and economic limitations of this context, trying in the same programme to expose him to the implications of his performance as inevitably exerted in the middle of an institutional power play.*

The contents of the programme are adjusted to the concept that the teaching staff has developed about the fundamental reality of the modern executive's function in the Latin American public sector. The processes of transmission of merely instrumental techniques have, for this same reason, been put on a secondary level, the emphasis being put on processes more adequate for transmitting a wider point of view and a greater sensitivity towards social and political conditioning factors. Thus, courses are run more in the way of seminars, case studies, guided readings, visits to paradigmatic institutions to allow for guided dialogue with the local executives, etc.

The priority the School gives to high executives, rather than to the lower echelons, is based exclusively on reasons of a pragmatic order. Training of medium- and low-level public employees tends to result in a relative waste of time, since those in a position of hierarchical inferiority do not have the status and capacity to persuade high-level executives. In other words, the School seeks to achieve concrete results through the 'multiplication effects' of high-level training.

Based on such a perception of the panorama of executive development in Latin America, the Inter-American School of Public Administration has stated its objectives, policies, strategies and programmes as described below.

3. THE ROLE OF THE INTER-AMERICAN SCHOOL OF PUBLIC ADMINISTRATION

In response to the demands arising out of rapid growth in Brazil in the 1930s and early 1940s, the Getulio Vargas Foundation was founded in 1944 and since that time has been concentrating its efforts on teaching and research in the social sciences, emphasising economic research and administrative rationalisation, public as well as private.

The Getulio Vargas Foundation consists of various divisions, each one having its specific function or functions, yet all being interdependent in the sense of striving for the improvement of the social sciences in Latin America as well as the provision of indispensable services to the community and to the nation as a whole.

Included along the various divisions of the Foundation are:

The Brazilian School of Public Administration (EBAP).
The São Paulo School of Business Administration (EAESP).
The Inter-American School of Public Administration
(EIAP).
The Brazilian Institute of Administration (IBRA).
The Brazilian Institute of Economics (IBRE).
The Institute for Professional Selection and Orientation
(ISOP).
The Institute for Public Law and Political Science.
The Centre for Human Resources Development
(CETHRU).
The Superior Institute for Accounting (ISEC).
The Institute for Documentation (INDOC).

Although not considered a university, the Foundation has 8,000 students enrolled in 113 academic programmes as of the beginning of the 1971 academic year, a fact which would place it ninth among Brazil's 47 universities.

Stimulated by its earlier experience in administration, the decision was made in the early 1960s to expand the Getulio Vargas Foundation's involvement, this time extending it to the rest of Latin America in response to the growing demands resulting from socio-economic development in that geographical area. In 1963, after gaining wide acceptance, especially in terms of its compatibility with the Foundation's principal objectives, negotiations were begun with the Inter-American Development Bank (I.D.B.) for the establishment of the Inter-American School of Public Administration (E.I.A.P.) with the assistance of I.D.B. funds. In collaboration with the Brazilian Ministry of Culture and Education (M.E.C.) and the Inter-American Development Bank, the first agreement was signed in 1964 and within a few months the Inter-American School of Public Administration was formally organised and physically located. The following year the first Development Administration course was offered to students from the various nations of Latin America.

Since its creation, E.I.A.P. has become increasingly involved in the area of public administration in the hemisphere, with its meaningful contribution being verified in 1969 by a five-year renewal of the earlier agreement with I.D.B. and M.E.C.

It is widely recognised that the development process involves not only purely economic activities, but also many other factors which should not be underestimated as to their importance in the process. In this respect, theorists and practitioners of development administration are becoming increasingly aware of the aggressive role that must be played by public administration and public administrators in fostering and guiding the development process.

It is on these considerations that the E.I.A.P. bases its main objectives, which are:

(a) the advanced training of Latin American public administrators, academicians and technicians so as to prepare them for a meaningful role in the developmental process;
(b) research into the many structural and functional problems of present-day public administration in Latin America, relevant to socio-economic change;

(c) provision of technical assistance to Latin American governmental entities at all levels.

Although the above listing of objectives is indicative of the School's priority ranking, the various areas will subsequently be discussed in different order, beginning with research and ending with training.

Within the School's philosophy is the idea that teaching and research are dynamically interrelated and that research activities are a continual part of each professor's responsibility. In this manner, besides attaining maximum utilisation of the teaching staff, the School hopes to give the indispensable factual support of both teaching and research to its courses.

Under the direction of a general co-ordinator and following an annual schedule, the School's research programme has two main objectives:

(i) The preparation and continual revision of the teaching material used in the various courses, including prepared texts, transcripts and/or translations of articles, basic theoretical explanation, etc.

(ii) Research into Latin American administrative problems relevant to socio-economic change, culminating in the preparation and distribution of essays and monographs on the various topics.

With respect to the second objective, one monographic series of twenty volumes has been completed and a special study series is presently in process. Lists of these series and copies of specific works are available to interested institutions and individuals, but they should be aware that all works are in Spanish and/or Portuguese.

Also included among the School's objectives is the provision of technical assistance in public administration to Latin American governmental entities at the national, regional and local levels. Such technical assistance takes the form of multilateral agreements heavily emphasising training programmes for public personnel and being carried out by Inter-American teams specialising in the particular area of assistance.

An example of such an agreement is the tripartite one between the Getulio Vargas Foundation, the Inter-American Development Bank (I.D.B.) and the government of Colombia, first signed in 1967 and presently in the process of a second two-year renewal. The main objective of this programme is the strengthening of the training function in the public service of that country.

Some of the School's special courses, especially those given outside Brazil, have been the total or part of such technical assistance programmes.

It is widely recognised that the major obstacle to the growth in Latin America of an effective and aggressive public administration is the scarcity of trained administrative personnel, especially persons capable of filling new positions emerging as a result of socio-economic expansion. Because of this scarcity and the new demands on public administration, it is vital that the means and facilities for improvement of administrative skills be made available to Latin American civil servants. Inherent in the satisfaction of this need is the provision of an atmosphere conducive to the exchange and analysis of the factors, experiences and responses to the administrative problems of the various sectors of public administration in Latin America and reflective of the realities of that geographical area.

It is towards this end that the School's courses are designed, so as to help the participants acquire or perfect the basic skills that will help them function better as executives, assistants and professors rationally analysing administrative problems and systematically searching for the best solutions. Since its creation in 1964, 910 participants from 19 Latin American nations have taken part in a total of 30 special and regular courses offered by the School.

In response to requests considered compatible with its capabilities and objectives, the School includes in its annual academic programme short courses, seminars and special activities. Examples of such special courses were two pilot programmes on public housing development given in 1968 under an agreement with Brazilian governmental agencies. In 1970 two special courses on customs value were given, one in Paraguay and the other in Venezuela, as was a special course in Brazil on transportation management. In 1971 such customs value courses were also given in Lima, Peru, and Quito, Ecuador. The initiation of such courses varies from year to year, as do the contents of the specific courses and the availability and nature of scholarships for participants.

In keeping with this philosophy, the School collaborates

directly with courses given at other institutions when so requested. Such collaboration might include the lending of professors for a specified period, the lending of curriculum consultants and the availability of the School's teaching materials. Various national and international organisations, in Brazil and in other areas, have benefited from such collaboration.

The School has been offering at its facilities in Rio de Janeiro four regular courses aimed at partial fulfilment of the objective of advanced training of Latin American public officials and academicians. These courses are:

Development Administration.
Tax Policy and Administration.
Customs Policy and Administration.
Project Management.

Although traditional lectures are a part of the regular courses at E.I.A.P., they are kept to the minimum, with preference being given to more modern techniques, including interdisciplinary seminars, group projects, group dynamics and field trips to various agencies. In this manner an attempt is made to go beyond the old process of rote memorisation to provide for a total experience of active participation, one that will hopefully stimulate the critical spirit and creative capacities of the participants.

Because of the emphasis on practical teaching techniques and also on each participant finding the right synthesis for himself and his context, the teaching at E.I.A.P. avoids instilling ideal administrative models developed in other social contexts. In contrast with this, every attempt is made to help the students find the solutions best adapted to the socio-economic realities of their own countries.

The study programme during the courses requires the full-time participation of the students, except in special cases decided at the discretion of the administration. The activities are conducted in Spanish and Portuguese and are held daily, Monday through Friday. Attendance at the planned academic programmes is obligatory.

Except for small variations from course to course, the following minimum entrance requirements must be met:

(i) Satisfactory completion of university courses leading to a degree and evidence of extensive professional experience in public administration (the university degree may be waived in cases of exceptional administrative experience).

(ii) Classification at the level of director or assistant to a director in an area relevant both to the specific course and to the development process, or as a university professor in an area related directly or indirectly to the subject-matter of the specific course.

(iii) Formal recommendation by the governmental agency or institution within which the candidate performs his professional duties, together with assurance that upon completion of the course the participant will have real possibilities of applying the newly acquired knowledge and skills.

(iv) Age not to exceed 45 years.

In the *Development Administration course*, designed for persons functioning at the decision-making or advisory level in an area relevant to the development process, and lasting six months, an attempt is made to foster an awareness of the integral and interdisciplinary nature of the development process and to motivate initiative and risk-taking in areas favourable to meaningful social change.

Although the basics of the academic area known as Development Administration are presented each year, the course's programme varies annually depending upon the evaluation of past courses, the changing needs of Latin America and varying teaching resources. For example, the seventh annual Development Administration course, given during the 1971 academic year and outlined below, provides the basics of development administration while more specifically trying to relate these to the many facets of administrative reform in developing nations. The course outline is as follows:

Theoretical Foundation.
Administrative Theory.
Sociology of Administration.
Applied Economics.
Governmental Planning.
Political Aspects of Administration.

Some technological aspects:

Research Methodology.
Human Resource Administration.

Programme Budgeting.
Project Management.
Theory and Techniques of Data Processing.
Theory and Techniques of Communication Co-ordination.

An analysis of the process of organisational change in the public sector:

Institutional Development.
The Process of Administrative Reform.
The Impact of Planning on Complex Organisations.
Current Problems of Public Administration in Latin America.
Interrelationships between the Administrative Reform Process and the Planning Process.

The *Tax Policy and Administration course*, given in collaboration with the Inter-American Development Bank's Institute for Latin American Integration (INTAL), and lasting three months, is designed for the advanced training of Latin American public administrators working in the area of taxation. The course's main objectives are:

(i) The preparation of highly specialised national teams capable of rendering technical assistance in the various countries towards the end of improvement of their respective tax systems.

(ii) An analysis of the problems characteristic of fiscal policy in the developing nations, with special emphasis on the Latin American case and the use of taxation as a fundamental instrument in the development process.

(iii) An analysis of the various Latin American tax systems, stressing the need for harmonisation of policies and the co-ordination of fiscal incentives as being prerequisites to the economic integration of Latin America.

Included in the course outline are:

An Overview of the Economic System.
The Process of Economic Development.
The Concept of Political Economy.
Economic Policy-Making and its Tools, with an Emphasis on those of Taxation.
Structural and Legal Aspects of Latin American Tax Systems.

The Various Types of Taxation and their Use in Latin America.

Tax Policies and the Economic Integration of Latin America.

The *Customs Policy and Administration courses*, also given in collaboration with the Inter-American Development Bank's Institute for Latin American Integration (INTAL), and lasting fifteen weeks, are designed for participation by Latin American customs officials functioning at the level of director or high-level adviser and thus able to influence directly or indirectly the improvement of their respective agencies upon completion of the course. The final objective is to mould craftsmen capable of responding to major challenges in the improvement and eventual integration of Latin American customs systems – craftsmen with a wider field of vision and thus capable of viewing the system as a whole, hopefully preventing future actions based solely on customs-oriented interpretations of reality. The course outline includes:

An Overview of the Economic System.
The Development Process.
The Concept of Political Economy and Related Instruments.
An Overview of International Trade.
Introduction to the Theory of International Trade.
Regulatory Instruments of International Trade.
Customs Tariff:
    Customs Nomenclature.
    Customs Rights.
    Customs Value.
Extensions and Reductions of Customs Rights.
Customs Legislation.
Special Customs Organisations (E.E.C., A.L.A.L.C., etc.).
Introduction to Macro-Administrative Analysis.
Customs Policies.

The area of *Project Management* is central to the development process. Any meaningful planning requires the effective execution of the plan, which ultimately reduces to the execution of specific projects. In Latin America the field of Project Management is in an incipient and experimental stage, to a great extent unaccompanied by the technological advances generated and developed in the more advanced nations. As a result of these facts, Project Management was singled out by I.D.B.'s Training Division and the School as one of the more vital areas of curriculum planning and the first four-month course was offered in 1968.

The course's short- and middle-range goals revolve around the preparation of technicians for the planning, programming and control of specific projects. Its long-range goals involve the consolidation and promotion of this subject area in Latin America, adapting to it the peculiarities and special requirements of that geographical area, and the development of a research programme providing for the preparation of original teaching materials. The course outline includes:

An Introduction to Project Management.
Instrumentation for Project Management:
    Data Processing.
    Cost–Benefit Analysis.
    Financial Analysis.
    Operations Research.
    PERT/C.P.M.
Techniques of Elaboration and Analysis.
Controls in Banks and Development-Oriented Institutions.
Processes of Implementation and Project Evaluation.
Integration of Specific Processes and Methodologies in Terms of the Realities of Latin America.

NOTES

1. See, for example, a series of articles in the *Public Administration Review*.
2. See K. N. Rao, 'Skilled Manpower for Continents in a Hurry', in *Public Administration Practices and Perspectives* (Washington, D.C.: Agency for International Development), vol 1 no 4 (July 1963) 8.
3. CAPES, *A Formação de Pessoal de Nível Superior e o Desenvolvimento Econômico* (Rio de Janeiro 1969), p. 17.
4. It would be just to mention that Spain, mainly after the creation of the Alcalá de Henares centre and the economic boom in the second half of the 1950s, clearly changed the behaviour of the public sector in what concerns the training of its employees. The Customs School, for example, is a living proof of this change in reference to training.
5. Cf. Henry Bourdean de Fontenay, 'La Formación de Funcionarios en la Escuela Nacional de Finanzes', *Documentación Administrativa* (Feb 1961) p. 54.

Chapter 4

Economic Factors

Dimensions of Development: An Iconoclastic View of the Economic Factors

ARTHUR KEMP

During the quarter-century since the end of the Second World War, the quantity of writing on the subject of economic development almost defies measurement. The sheer mass of literature is enormous. The general topic, of course, is not new; the classical economists – Smith, Ricardo, Senior, Mill, Marshall – were quite aware of, and concerned about, problems of economic growth and development: the wealth of nations. It is the difference in quantity, if not in quality, that makes our times unique.

As an illustration, the three-digit classification system for technical economic periodical literature currently employed by the American Economic Association contains no fewer than five sub-subclassifications devoted entirely to economic development or growth: (111) economic growth and development theory; (112) economic planning theory and policy; (121) economic development studies of less developed countries; (122) economic development studies of developed countries; (123) comparative economic development. One can only guess at the amount of pertinent material submerged in such other classifications as: (300) monetary and fiscal theory and institutions; (423) economic integration; (441) international investment and foreign aid; (442) international business; (630) industry studies; (717) land reform and land use; (721) natural resources and conservation; (811) manpower training and development; (841) population; (850) human capital – producing side; (921) consumer economics: levels and standards of living! A quick and very conservative estimate suggests that more than 15,000 articles, in whole or in major part devoted to economic growth and development, have appeared in the world's technical economic journals during the past twenty-five years – and this includes none of the books, nor the semi-technical periodicals, nor the popular press.

Few, if any, have attempted a systematic survey of the literature. This is not surprising.[1] To do so would be a lifetime's endeavour, a task so formidable that any such temptation is easily resisted. There are, nevertheless, several recurrent threads in the complex, interwoven fabric of this literature, important enough to examine briefly within the limited space of this essay. To avoid seeming to criticise particular individuals, personal credit will not be given for any particular themes, opinions or ideas. Citations will be omitted except for direct quotations or where a comment or specific source seems essential to the reader's understanding.[2] It is only fair to add that the views expressed here are probably not those of economists considered as 'experts' in the field of economic development;[3] on the other hand, *je ne suis pas seul*, as the French say. Perhaps this minority view may eventually become that of the majority. In any event, truth has seldom been ascertained by application of a majority rule.

It should be noted that, despite the space and attention devoted to phrases and concepts, to quantification or attempts to quantify economic development, there has been remarkably little in the way of systematic, structured, formal analysis. A volume labelled *Principles of Economics* or *Money and Banking* will usually contain much the same subject-matter as any other volume similarly labelled. The organisation of the materials, and the proportional content of the parts, will vary, but in easily recognisable ways; the applied economics volume also will usually be integrated into the more general analytical structure. Not so for economic development. Here anything goes; there is no accepted beginning or ending, not even hard-and-fast agreement on what constitutes economic development, less developed, underdeveloped or overdeveloped countries, let alone agreement on how, precisely, such things are to be measured. The result has been, as one might have expected, a spate of 'disputes, paradoxes and dilemmas'[4] rather than the emergence of a structured subdivision of applied economics.

In short, we do not know what we mean by economic development or economic growth. As first approximations we may accept some of the varied aggregates, such as gross (or net?) national product, expressed in nominal (or real?) terms, as totals or modified per capita, or per person employed, or per capita with added modification for varying age and sex proportions of population. Or shall we turn to per family or productive unit? Or to real disposable personal income? This last has the merit of measuring, to some extent, what the basic consumption units do choose to have instead of what their rulers permit them to have. None of them is fully satisfactory. Surely other more or less complex measures could be invented, but these would prove equally unsatisfactory, even without taking into consideration some of the measurement difficulties.

The trouble is that economic growth is a vague sort of concept: an increase in economic well-being, for which all the aggregative measures thus far concocted are at best only seriously limited approximations and, at worst, are highly misleading and irrelevant. Moreover, as with all such aggregates, they are capable of being used or misused to promote any of the particular policies the user may happen to favour.

These misgivings are increased exponentially when per capita production, income and investment estimates are computed for developed and less developed nations or regions and used for comparison. The statistical infirmities are enormous; and the diversity within the groupings is certainly as great as or greater than the diversity between. Much the same can be said about the added dimension of aggregates purporting to measure different kinds of investment – public or private, gross or net, real or nominal. There may perhaps be a single key to measuring economic development. But it is only prudent to examine critically the evidence submitted by anyone who claims he has found it.

Although we do not agree as to precisely what economic growth and development is, or how or why it occurs, almost everyone wants more of it. Like the Sunday preacher in the apocryphal Calvin Coolidge story who was 'against sin', we all want growth. The simplistic slogan of our times could well be 'Growth is Good!' Indeed, it seems that more growth is better than less, faster growth is better than slower – and this is true whether we are talking internationally or domestically. Not everyone echoes the slogan, to be sure; two quite different qualifications are raised. One is the conservationist-ecology position which seems to say: 'Growth is good – provided it does not result in any depletion of, or alteration of the balance between, any of our natural resources.'[5] The second qualification is raised by a small number of market-oriented economists, liberal in the nineteenth-century sense of that word, who are reluctant to voice a moral judgement about the goodness or badness, desirability or undesirability, of economic growth and development *per se*. This writer's sympathies and prejudices are emphatically with them. Given the opportunity to do so, people are likely to make choices leading to improved well-being, although not at any cost. If it turns out that they prefer more leisure to more goods and services, longer and poorer lives to shorter but richer ones, so be it. The almost evangelical fervour of the growth advocates may be simply a variant of the prayer for plenty – a pious hope that if only the cake can be made big enough, the unpleasant necessity of choosing among competing, and to some extent mutually incompatible, ends can somehow be avoided.

THE EMPHASIS ON CAPITAL FORMATION

The central theme in the literature of economic development (although it is being increasingly challenged), especially that dealing with less developed countries, has been to regard heavy industrial, real capital – factories, machinery, power dams, highways, etc. – as the key, indeed, causal, factor in moving from less developed to developed status. This has led in turn to an over-emphasis on the amount of that capital, on its quantity rather than its quality, on industrial instead of agricultural capital, on non-human rather than human capital, and to the calculation of such things as capital-output ratios which tend to disregard the fact that the amount of capital is of small importance apart from its form. Further, there has also been an over-emphasis on the big and the prominent forms of capital as opposed to the small and the scattered. Big dams, big factories, big industries tend to dominate the attention of the statistics-gatherers, in part, at least, because they are highly visible and obvious, and in part because monetary data are easier to obtain than non-monetary. Capital formation by heavy industry and big government almost always involves monetary expenditure, while this is less frequently true for small and scattered capital formation, particularly agricultural and human capital formation – human productive and management abilities and capacities for technological assimilation and innovation.

There is, of course, an element of truth in this en̸̸ capital formation. It is better to have more real ind̸ rather than less, other things being equal – which the̸̸ It is also true that all capital investment, in its many varieu ̸ various, human and non-human forms, is essential to any increase in productivity. But it is not true that more is always better than less; capital is not a homogeneous mass of completely substitutable units. It is a question of the adaptation of the various forms to the particular needs and circumstances, and of the costs and incentives to individuals to use their resources and their abilities in the most effective way. It seems obvious that this is a much more vital economic factor than the quantity of real industrial capital investment, although the political advantages of a different interpretation can readily be appreciated. If political leaders can convince the electorate that a high rate of real capital investment is not only desirable but essential to a rising standard of living, and that unless such decisions are entrusted to the governmental planners there will result at best economic stagnation and at worst a perpetual state of economic crisis and bankruptcy, the political power advantages are obvious.

With particular reference to less developed countries, there is a special variant of this bias towards real capital investment. In effect it is argued that there exists a vicious circle: (1) the less developed countries have such a low standard of living that they cannot save in order to accumulate real capital; (2) since they cannot accumulate investment capital, they cannot increase their productivity in order to raise their standard of living; (3) since they cannot improve their standard of living, there is no possibility of accumulating real capital from internal sources.[6] The argument is patently false. If it were true, no country would ever have developed and, indeed, no technological civilisation as we know it could have developed; we should all still be wallowing in the depths of our aboriginal poverty. Further, the very terms 'poor countries' and 'rich countries' seem to me to be ridiculous descriptions. In every country there are rich people and poor people; some people, somewhere, sometime – under much more restricted circumstances than exist anywhere in the modern world – did in fact create real capital and did increase their productivity and living standards. Difficult it may well have been; impossible it was not.

PLANNING AND ITS PERILS

One also reads in the current literature on economic development the frequent assertion, and apparently widely held belief, that a satisfactory rate of economic growth and development can be achieved only by detailed, centralised, comprehensive government planning. This is said to be true whether one is referring to less developed or developed countries, and seems to illustrate the great strength of the socialist ideology of our age. Marxist views of economic development carry this to the ultimate extreme. Theories of colonialism or imperialism insert a demonistic cause into the chain of invalid logic of the vicious circle of poverty thesis. The modified Marxist dogma is content with advising the adoption of forced domestic industrialisation, autarkic in character, and patterned somewhat after the Soviet experience. This serves, by conveniently by-passing the older Marxian dogma of the necessity of passing through a capitalist historical phase, to attract many leaders of nationalist parties to the support of international communism through the formation of common political fronts, thus furthering the ideal of communist revolution or, at least, preventing to a considerable extent the mutual and fruitful co-operation between and among people in the less developed countries and the industrialised market-oriented economies.

Then there is the similar, if more sophisticated, reasoning among some non-Marxist writers on economic development. Such is the thesis that there exists an inherent tendency for the terms of trade of the less developed countries to deteriorate, thereby intensifying and deepening international economic inequalities to the detriment of the less developed countries. To offset this, so the argument goes, the less developed countries must turn inward, they must practise protectionism (euphemistically called import substitution) by erecting multiple tariff barriers or other trade inhibitions and adopt a sort of autarkic nationalism either in each country alone or, at most, on a regional basis.[7] The end-result of accepting such reasoning is, therefore, quite similar to accepting the colonialism-imperialism doctrine except that it does not intentionally promote communist revolution. Both the Marxist and non-Marxist variants foster the aggrandisement of centralised, powerful governments, employing detailed controls over economic activities. Whether this also promotes and expands the economic well-being of the people of the countries involved is open to considerable doubt. Even if the centralisation process is promoted on a regional rather than a national basis, the effect is to strengthen and aggrandise the international bureaucrats rather than the national ones, which is perhaps somewhat preferable, but not much. Doubtless, too, it is better to promote strong, centralised, supposedly democratic and representative noncommunist regimes than to promote strong, centralised, nondemocratic, authoritarian, communist regimes. But the range of choice is less than impressive.

It may well be that we economists know less about the process of economic betterment and progress than the vast output of literature on the subject might imply. Would the degree of economic growth and development that has taken place, both in the less developed and developed countries, over the past quarter-century, have been substantially less had the spate of literature on the subject been substantially less? Surely the answer to that question is not an obvious 'yes'. Of course, the acceptance of our expertise in these matters has promoted the well-being of economists, and probably the well-being of economists favouring centralisation and control rather more than that of those favouring more liberal (in the classical sense) market solutions. Whether consciously or not, people are willing to pay rather well for the things they want to hear and to believe. And when people are willing to pay for such goods, the quantity supplied invariably increases to meet the demand.

The sustained and increasing rates of increase in economic well-being, the prolonged increases in standards of living that have thus far taken place in the world, have been the result of a fortunate, and perhaps fortuitous, convergence of many favourable conditions – political, social, ideological, institutional, cultural and technical as well as economic. These fortunate conjunctions of circumstances have been unplanned and spontaneous, frequently resulting from unforeseen and perhaps unforeseeable catalysts that might in themselves be regarded as evils – natural catastrophes, wars, religious crusades, epidemics. This judgement may, of course, be wrong, but it is not possible to be convinced by the minutes of the central planners who formulated the Renaissance, or the industrial and agricultural revolutions, let alone the committees responsible for Leonardo da Vinci, Thomas Edison, or Wilbur and Orville Wright.

Economic development does occur and will occur when people as individuals, and in their many and varied voluntary groupings, are permitted to exercise their ingenuity and to use their resources and abilities in whatever ways they see fit, with minimal exceptions designed simply to preserve and protect society from destruction. Economic development is a process of change, of trying new combinations of resources, new ways of doing things, of breaking old habits and acquiring new ideas – plus chance and good fortune. The key need is to promote flexibility, mobility, adaptability – and receptivity to change and innovation. The writer trusts that nothing said here will be interpreted as traitorous to his profession or his professional colleagues. All economists are simply splendid people, although, to be perfectly honest, some are more splendid than others. Moreover, even if we publicly confess our ignorance there will remain plenty of work for us to do. Although we are all well aware that the economic factors of production – land, labour, capital and entrepreneurship – are essential and necessary ingredients in the development process, we are much less certain of the influence the more various non-economic factors exert on the economic. Moreover, we have only begun to quantify and to qualify the various factor inputs which, we think, *may* account for the observed differences in rates of economic development between different countries and different regions. Thus far we can say little with certainty about the relative importance of the various mixes, having due regard for the limitations imposed upon us by unreliable data and non-objective data-gatherers.

HOW *NOT* TO ACHIEVE DEVELOPMENT

Let us admit that we cannot say how, precisely, to achieve an increasing rate of economic development, that we cannot be certain why it occurred when it did occur, and that the emphasis on the growth syndrome is partly a disguise for the fact that goals other than growth are involved – such as an acceptable pattern of wealth and income distribution, variable attitudes towards work and leisure, a satisfactory allocation of resources between present and future, or the desire for increased prestige and influence, to mention only a few. Let us further admit that there are an unknown number of possible trade-offs among these goals. Suppose, then, we ask not the questions we cannot answer but one we can: How can a country, or region if you prefer, *reduce* its rate of economic growth and development?

On this there is much we do know, much we can say; there follows here only a sampling of the general rules, without categorisation, classification or quantification:

1. Establish a highly effective, firmly established and well-enforced system of exchange controls with fixed rates of exchange.
2. Be sure to use all the other possible devices to provide effective protection for domestic industry, such as quotas, tariffs, licensing provisions, etc.
3. Enact or establish extensive, complicated rules concerning the formation and ownership of all businesses and business corporations, being certain to include minimal proportions of such ownership that must be in the names of nationals of the country rather than of foreigners.
4. Draw up a long list of activities in which foreigners shall not be permitted to engage.
5. Forbid businesses operating within the country from hiring more than a minimum percentage of foreign management and technical labour.
6. Establish, as publicly owned and operated monopolies, the banking system plus as many other industries as the budgetary situation will stand, giving preference to those industries having the highest costs.
7. For those industries excluded from the list in (6) above, draw up a further list, avowing that these will be nationalised and monopolised as soon as budgetary restrictions permit.
8. At irregular intervals, nationalise by expropriation some industry not covered by either (6) or (7).
9. Enact an extensive system of progressive taxation levied on both wealth and income (especially the latter), so as to penalise the most able and productive of the citizenry.

10. Outlaw all private educational undertakings and establish a wide range of other educational and welfare activities and services to be provided for the citizenry at less than market, preferably zero, prices.

11. Anticipate conflicts due to budgetary problems by exercising tight governmental control over the central bank; whenever deficit financing is needed, finance directly with the central bank, and vary the amount of such financing as much as feasible from year to year.

12. Establish a permanent incomes policy with control boards having the power to implement it by setting maximum prices and wage rates, and to specify the conditions of sale and employment.

13. Restrict, as inconsistently as feasible, both immigration and emigration, utilising for this purpose work permits, entry and exit visas and differential taxation.

14. Formulate a policy of encouragement to the formation of cartels in all industries not publicly owned and operated, with enforceable power to fix minimum prices and allocate markets.

15. Create a national board to draw up a detailed programme designed to bring about an increase in the rate of increase in the per capita gross national product.

The desired results will appear quickly. Objectives doubtless can be reached even more rapidly by adding to the list – a task the reader will surely not find too difficult. There may well be a lesson in all this.

NOTES

1. The American Economic Association's *Journal of Economic Literature* is invaluable, as is its predecessor, the *Journal of Economic Abstracts*. Stephen Enke, 'Economists and Development: Rediscovering Old Truths', *J.E.L.*, vii 4 (Dec 1969) is limited, but useful. The select bibliography, with evaluative comment, in Graham Hutton, *Politics and Economic Growth*, Occasional Paper 23 (London; Institute of Economic Affairs 1968) is especially helpful to the non-British scholar who might otherwise miss some of the pertinent, but fugitive, materials.

2. For the reader's convenience, however, there is appended a select bibliography limited to twenty books, articles or other items the writer has found particularly helpful, stimulating or provocative. The reader may decide which is which.

3. 'In more and more fields of policy nearly all the recognised "experts" are, almost by definition, persons who are in favour of the principles underlying the policy. This is indeed one of the factors which tend to make so many contemporary developments self-accelerating. The politician who, in recommending some further development of current policies, claims that "all the experts favour it" is often perfectly honest, because only those who favour the development have become experts in this institutional sense, and the uncommitted economists or lawyers who oppose it are not counted as experts.' F. A. Hayek, *The Constitution of Liberty* (Univ. of Chicago Press, 1960) p. 291.

4. The writer cannot omit a reference to an article by his teacher and long-time friend, Fritz Machlup, 'Disputes, Paradoxes and Dilemmas Concerning Economic Development', *Revista Internazionale di Scienze Economiche e Commerciali*, xiv 9 (1957), reprinted in *Essays on Economic Semantics* (Englewood Cliffs, N.J.: Prentice-Hall, 1963) pp. 269–301. The article deserves more attention than it has received thus far.

5. It is left to the reader to try to alter the statement so as to make economic sense of it – if such is possible.

6. The policy conclusion usually drawn from the argument is that the only source of capital is external rather than domestic; that private capital will not be provided under such conditions and that, therefore, the only source of real capital available is foreign economic aid on a government-to-government basis from the developed to the less developed countries. The peripheral problems of foreign economic aid are omitted, although there is much evidence that a very large part of that aid, particularly by the United States, has been more a deterrent to economic development than a help.

7. Space prevents discussion of the evidence here. The non-Marxist argument is little more wothy of reliance than the Marxist version. An excellent essay by Ramon Diaz, *The Long-Run Terms of Trade of Primary Producing Countries*, will be published shortly by the Institute of Economic Affairs, London. Excellent, too, is the concise summary in Harry G. Johnson, *The World Economy at the Crossroads* (Oxford Univ. Press, 1965) pp. 77–83. Gottfried Haberler's *Three Lectures on International Trade and International Development*, originally published by the National Bank of Egypt (1959), is now a classic and has been reprinted in R. S. Weckstein (ed.). *Expansion of World Trade and the Growth of National Economies* (New York: Harper & Row, 1968) pp. 97–136.

SELECT BIBLIOGRAPHY

Bauer, Peter T., 'Development Economics: The Spurious Consensus and its Background', in E. Streissler *et al.* (eds), *Roads to Freedom: Essays in Honour of Friedrich A. von Hayek* (London: Routledge & Kegan Paul, 1969) pp. 5–45.
Bauer, Peter T., and Yamey, Basil S., *The Economics of Underdeveloped Countries* (Cambridge Univ. Press, 1957).

Brandt, Karl, 'Economic Progress in the Developing Countries', *Modern Age*, IX 1 (winter 1964–5) 7–17.

Clark, Colin, *Growthmanship: A Study in the Mythology of Investment*, Hobart Paper 10 (London: Institute of Economic Affairs, 1961).

Denison, E. F., *Why Growth Rates Differ* (Washington, D.C.: Brookings Institution, 1968).

Frankel, S. Herbert, *The Economic Impact on Underdeveloped Countries* (Oxford Univ. Press, 1953).

Friedman, Milton, 'Foreign Economic Aid: Means and Objectives', *Yale Review* (summer 1958).

Horvath, Janos, 'Foreign Economic Aid in the *International Encyclopedia of the Social Sciences*: A Review Article', *Journal of Economic Literature*, IX 2 (June 1971).

Hutton, Graham, *Politics and Economic Growth*, Occasional Paper 23, (London: Institute of Economic Affairs, 1968).

Johnson, Harry G., 'Problems of Developing Countries', chap. 5 in his *The World Economy at the Crossroads* (Oxford Univ. Press, 1965).

Kristol, Irving, 'The Ideology of Economic Aid', *Yale Review* (summer 1957).

Meier, Gerald M., and Baldwin, Robert E., *Economic Development: Theory, History and Policy* (New York: Wiley, 1957).

Mishan, E. J., *The Costs of Economic Growth* (London: Staples Press, 1967).

Molnar, Thomas, 'Neo-Colonialism in Africa?' *Modern Age*, IX 2 (spring, 1965) 175–86.

Myrdal, Gunnar, *The Challenge of World Poverty* (New York: Wiley, 1970).

Rostow, W. W., *The Stages of Economic Growth* (Cambridge Univ. Press, 1960).

Thurn, Max, 'The Rich and the Poor Countries', *Modern Age*, VII 1 (winter 1962–3) 25–32.

Usher, Dan, *Rich and Poor Countries: A Study in Problems of Comparison of Real Income*, Eaton Paper 9 (London: Institute of Economic Affairs, 1966).

Ward, Barbara, *The Rich Nations and the Poor Nations* (New York: Norton, 1962).

Ward, Barbara, and Bauer, Peter T., *Two Views on Aid to Developing Countries*, Occasional Paper 9 (London: Institute of Economic Affairs, 1966).

Some Economic Factors for Accelerated Development in Southern Africa

MARCUS ARKIN

I

The nominal scope of this paper is both vague and vast, but two circumstances help to limit its range. The first is the formal draft programme, which allocates – quite rightly – the agricultural aspects of economic development to highly qualified specialists, and devotes a whole separate section to the external (or international) facets of the topic – the impact of foreign investment, trade and assistance. The second is the author's own ignorance of economic patterns, problems and prospects beyond South Africa itself, so that my remarks will refer mainly to the Republic rather than to the broader region of 'Southern Africa'.

Even with such limitations, however, it remains very difficult to avoid poaching in other people's preserves. Economics is possibly the least self-contained of the social sciences, and when applied to a Southern African context it overflows naturally, on the one hand, into the political arena (so that we find ourselves dealing with issues of political economy), and on the other, into the broad stream of society itself (so that at best many underlying trends are 'socio-economic' rather than purely economic). Life does not divide itself into nice little separately labelled boxes.

In short, we are concerned with people rather than with statistics. There is no dearth in this country of professional examinations of the relevant economic indicators, or of elaborate 'models' whose creators purport to be able to forecast our future rate of growth within one-tenth of 1 per cent. But these econometrical follies tend to neglect the human reality behind the statistical façade and, in view of South Africa's complex ethnic structure, such neglect can only too easily transform assessments of economic development into a string of 'Through the Looking

Glass' platitudes supported by impressive tables and graphs. The problems and limitations affecting economic development in this part of the world are not only economic in character, and their resolution is likely to be much slower and more tedious than we of the computer generation might wish.

'Economic growth' or 'accelerated economic development' are rallying cries which economists have foisted on an unsuspecting public without always explaining what they are trying to get at. We all, I think, have some hazy general notion about the implications of such terms, but they are not easy to pinpoint clearly. The main difficulty of definition arises from the multiplicity of goals and the value judgements of those responsible for trying to improve a given state of affairs. For some, then, these catch-phrases imply national economic independence and are the counterparts of political independence; for others, they denote rapid industrialisation; for still others, they suggest a balanced diversification of economic energies (sometimes coupled with further policy objectives, such as closer co-operation in regional groupings); and there are also those who would claim that these terms refer essentially to a successful transition from subsistence to market agriculture.

However, most economists would probably agree, if we said that 'economic growth' or 'accelerated economic development' presupposes a dynamic situation involving higher individual living standards – or, perhaps more accurately, that they refer to an inevitably long-term process of raising levels of productivity and widening existing or creating new employment opportunities, thereby increasing the real income per head of population.

To what extent, then, is South Africa in the process of being caught up in such a situation?

II

It is not intended here to present a chronological summary of the South African economy's growth performance over recent times – say, since the end of the Second World War. In spite of internal temporary setbacks and its vulnerability to external circumstances over which it exercises little influence, the economy, in global terms, emerged during this period as fairly mature and well balanced, and highly industrialised when compared with the rest of Africa; its infrastructure (such as transport and power facilities) also became well developed, and (again in strong contrast to most other African countries) there is a useful spread of both managers and technicians. In fact, members of the élite managerial group were addicted to placing themselves on a pedestal from which they have been known to view even their American counterparts with a certain disdain.

Such behaviour has not been without some justification: for part of this period at least, the overall annual average rate of expansion in South African secondary industry exceeded that of the United States, while during the mid-1960s the rate of gross domestic investment (or the demand for capital, if you prefer) expressed as a proportion of the South African gross national product was in the neighbourhood of 23 per cent, whereas the corresponding figure for the mature economy of the United States was only 17 per cent. To an audience largely made up of academics, it may be more meaningful to mention another significant indicator of growth: compared with some 14,000 university students in 1945, the figure now stands at over 70,000. So the last two decades have been characterised by an acceleration of the structural changes which were set in motion during and immediately after the Second World War and have witnessed the consolidation of the Republic's industrial revolution; equally significantly, they have been marked by the steady erosion of gold as the traditional base of the economy.

Conventional wisdom dies hard: less than ten years ago it was widely held, both here and abroad, that the future prosperity of the country and of manufacturing in particular depended to a large extent upon the continued profitability of the gold mines.[1] While there can be little doubt that gold served as springboard and pacesetter in the evolution of the South African economy as we know it today, a big question-mark now hangs over gold in relation to the economy's long-term growth potential. Having for so many decades thought in terms of a fixed price for gold, it is difficult for us to come to terms with one that moves up and down just like any other commodity price. But the industry itself will soon have to decide whether the price of its product is on an inevitably upward trend, as many experts believe – or whether the traditional dollar floor price is the only one to rely on with reasonable certainty in the years ahead.[2]

Hence, gold-mining could become an even riskier business than it is at present, sustaining heavy losses if forecasts of a relatively high price (some as high as $80) proved incorrect. The variables operating are numerous and unpredictable; with so much sheer guesswork involved, it would be economically unhealthy indeed to relate growth prospects too closely to the future of gold. Yet no special powers of perception are needed to prophesy that foreign trade will continue to play a prominent role in South African economic life, and if the country is to go on growing rapidly, one bottleneck which will have to be broken is the recurrent shortage of foreign exchange (which has led in recent months to such unwelcome developments as tighter import controls and devaluation). Base minerals (iron ore particularly) are likely to play an increasingly important part as foreign exchange earners once current plans to provide adequate transport facilities between remote mining districts and the ports have materialised.

Yet the most logical channel for enhancing foreign earnings would be the sale of manufactured goods to the rest of Africa, for in all territories south of the Sahara the Republic enjoys a marked locational superiority over major competitors in transport costs. The crux of the problem is not that South African firms are reluctant to take advantage of these opportunities or that they lack the raw materials; the trouble, rather, lies in the human factor, in the supply of labour and, to a lesser extent, in a shortage of investment capital.

III

Ever since Adam Smith the truism has been accepted that, other things being equal, businessmen will not actively seek outlets for their products abroad until they have saturated their home market. In South Africa today there is increasing evidence that local industry is finding it more and more difficult to meet domestic demand. Reaction in official circles has been to blame the consumer's exorbitant appetite (or, more technically, 'private-sector demand') and to clamp down on spending. This, for example, is how the Franzsen Commission views the problem:

> It would thus appear that during periods of rapid growth in South Africa there has been an inherent and increasing tendency on the part of consumption expenditure to increase too rapidly. . . . Under these circumstances a restrictive fiscal and

monetary policy would be required to retard consumption. If the authorities are not prepared to intervene strongly here, they will have to be satisfied with a lower growth rate if they desire to curb overheating and increasing price inflation.[3]

This is like blaming a pedestrian for allowing himself to be knocked down on the pavement by a heavy vehicle. Just as in such a situation we would be well advised to take a look at the driver's behaviour, so also it is folly to ignore the supply side of our productive equation, for industrialists (if not government circles) have become increasingly aware of the fact that there are insufficient workers, both skilled and unskilled, White and Black, to meet available market opportunities.

Of course, this is not a problem of overfull employment in the Keynesian sense; if it was, then the Franzsen Commission would be barking up the right tree. Instead, businessmen are unable to make effective use of a large reservoir of labour because of the continued retention of legislative prohibitions designed originally to protect the established expectations of White South Africans by limiting the economic opportunities of non-Whites. If there ever was any economic justification for such colour-bar devices, it certainly no longer exists; in fact, ironically, the retention of such measures not only hampers efforts to improve the deployment of the work-force in general, but is retarding the advancement of the great majority of White workers who (without these restrictions) would find their own positions in the labour market substantially upgraded (as a safeguard for the small minority incapable of climbing this ladder, redundancy and re-training schemes would be minor cost factors).

Under these circumstances, because there are insufficient Whites to fill all classified posts, significant changes are slowly taking place in production techniques in which skilled tasks have been split up or diluted into semi-repetitive subdivisions for which lower wages have been prescribed, so that what were once 'White' jobs are becoming increasingly common among non-Whites. But such ameliorative tendencies have been insufficient to prevent the earnings gap from steadily widening. Over the twelve years from 1958 to 1970 White money incomes on average certainly doubled, while the consumer price index rose only 30 per cent. Statistics of earnings by Africans are far from complete, but what figures are available suggest an annual increment of not much more than 5 per cent over the same period. In certain sectors the wage differential has become a yawning chasm: in mining, for example, the gap between White and Black earnings in 1936 was 10 to 1; it now stands at round about 20 to 1.

These wide disparities are, of course, partly a matter of relative scarcities in which unskilled labour (which mainly happens to be non-White) remains comparatively abundant, while skilled labour (still largely the natural preserve of those of European descent) continues in very short supply, particularly since almost 40 per cent of the White work-force is in the public or semi-public sector. But undoubtedly, too, the restrictive labour system itself has compounded these inequalities, with the upshot that the White community (comprising not more than 20 per cent of the population) is today probably in receipt of over 70 per cent of total real earnings.

It is a situation of tremendous significance to the prospects of future accelerated development. Planners are always great optimists and we must be careful not to be carried away by their infectious enthusiasm: for example, if we project their current estimate of $5\frac{1}{2}$ per cent annual growth rate for the economy over the next eighty years (which, after all, is not a very long period of economic history, though admittedly it may seem so to development programmers), and couple it with their estimate of an annual population upswing of only $2\frac{1}{2}$ per cent, we find that in eighty-four years' time a job paying R100 per month today will then be paying (at constant prices) no less than R1,250.[4] So let us be a little more realistic and assume that between now and the turn of the century average real earnings double: a White worker earning R3,000 per annum now will be earning R6,000 (again assuming constant prices) in the year 2000; similarly, his Black counterpart, now earning, say, R400 will then be getting R800 per annum. True enough, the latter's real income will have doubled; but, more significantly, the *income gap* between the two groups will have widened enormously.

At present, the majority of the population (the Africans) endure very low standards indeed when contrasted with the White level of affluence,[5] and a doubling of very little over the next generation may well make no significant difference to their relative socio-economic status. From an economic point of view, the perpetuation of low wage levels for African workers may well prevent the emergence of a mass consumer society, thereby slowing down the growth rate. From a more general viewpoint, as the relative income gap widens in this way, mounting racial friction and eventually open violence cannot be ruled out. And such a situation would not only slow down the growth rate; it could halt it altogether and perhaps even reverse it.

In short, as I see it, the fundamental question facing South Africa's economic future does not revolve around economic growth as such; instead it is likely to concern itself much more closely with the income relationship between the Whites and the African segment of the non-White majority.[6]

IV

The growing tightness of the labour market has brought to the fore another potentially unwelcome trend in the economy's long-term prospects – a possible misallocation of investment capital. Since the mid-1960s private-sector investment in commerce and financial institutions (like hotels, supermarkets and banks) has forged ahead, growing by more than 33 per cent in most years, whereas fixed investment in manufacturing has tapered off alarmingly, accompanied by a notable slowing down in the rate of growth in physical output.

Undoubtedly, labour legislation, like the Physical Planning Act, has served as a disincentive for those industrialists not prepared to switch their activities to border regions; in addition, services do not have to compete with imported goods, while consumer resistance to higher prices for such services is probably much less than resistance to the upswing of prices of manufactures.

This apparent imbalance in the recent pattern of growth must be a source of some concern to the government's economic advisers, whose projections envisage manufacturing investment growing nearly three times faster than investment in services. Rectification of this lopsided trend could take numerous forms, such as a differential rate of company tax which falls harder on the service sector or a selective employment levy on service payrolls. But those academic economists who have concerned themselves with growth models cannot as yet point with certainty to the fact that the fastest-growing economies are always those where the manufacturing sector is expanding more rapidly than any other;[7] and our own planners are by no mean infallible – they may well have misidentified the growth points, so that any forceful attempt to mould reality into some preconceived model may well retard rather than encourage accelerated development.

However, the official planners are likely to have their energies fully occupied in the foreseeable future by policies concerned with regional decentralisation.

V

Regional economics is a developing branch of the discipline highly relevant to South Africa's human problems and prospects. Such regional economic planning fits in nicely with the objective of growth (the avowed aim of all governments) as well as with the official policy of separate development.

Almost every measure adopted over the last twenty years in this field of regional planning has been motivated by an attempt to create employment opportunities not only for Africans 'endorsed out' of urban areas, but also for the natural increase of job-seekers within the tribal reserves. To date, the programme of de-urbanising African employees has worked much more effectively than the creation of fruitful job opportunities in the alternative regions. Nor is there much evidence that government policy-makers have seriously considered the costs of such policies. Although non-quantifiable factors seem to be particularly relevant in this situation, much could still be done to define the growth potential of such border regions and homelands explicitly in terms of social costs and benefits. Such a detailed cost–benefit analysis may well indicate that the expense of setting up and operating factories in decentralised areas (including, of course, the cost to the taxpayer) is lower than further growth in existing urban complexes (including social costs like traffic congestion and pollution).

At present, therefore, the gap between the objectives and achievements of planned decentralisation remain very wide indeed.[8] Even a big push towards industrial expansion in the homelands cannot for decades ahead be expected to provide employment opportunities directly for more than a very small fraction of the labour force. However, if resources were progressively diverted to border areas adjacent to the reserves, it is by no

...eans certain that in the long run the level of national economic ...rosperity would be markedly reduced.

As regards the absorption of the products of such border indus-...ies, industrial growth often generates its own demand: if large ...umbers of Bantu-speaking workers were to be given opportuni-...es of becoming fully skilled or even semi-trained and the trap-...ings of job reservation were absent from such border areas, the ...ncrease in their own purchasing power could well bring into ...eing a vast potential market for the new industries to serve.

All societies undergoing economic transformation have to ...efashion their organisation so as to gear themselves to accom-...lish what the compulsions of economic growth place before ...nem,[9] and the vital missing factor in South Africa in such plans ...or accelerated development is what development economists are ...ond of calling the 'management accumulation process' – a rather ...ebulous qualitative concept embracing all those entrepreneurial ...nergies needed to organise production, to quote Alfred Marshall ...so that a given effort may be most effective in supplying wants'.

None of our grandiose schemes to build up the tribal home-...nds and adjacent border regions can ever amount to anything ...ibstantial without the direct involvement of an energetic and ...rofit-seeking African entrepreneurial class. To date, there are ...ew signs of such a class emerging. Personal liberty and free access ...o a full range of alternative objectives are essential ingredients ...n the appearance of innovators with such qualities, but in South ...frica the potential African entrepreneur is not only confronted ...ith the inhibiting circumstances of underdevelopment;[10] he also ...as to make his way through a labyrinth of restrictive, patern-...listic regulations imposed by some remote civil-service-minded ...evelopment Corporation. It is a situation hardly designed to ...naximise those aptitudes which Schumpeter once referred to as ...the ability to perceive new opportunities that cannot be proved ...t the moment when action has to be taken, and the will-power ...dequate to break down the resistance that the social environment ...ffers to change'.[11]

This is not the appropriate place to examine the socio-economic ...nd political factors which shape and circumscribe the entre-...>reneurial function. But it should be emphasised that, as far as ...he reserves and border regions are concerned, the maximum pos-...ible development of African entrepreneurial talents seems to be pretty low down on the list of official priorities; while, as regards the major urban African locations, given the present restrictive legislative framework and its uneven application from area to area and time to time, circumstances are hardly conducive to the appearance of significant numbers with the necessary initiative and self-confidence to undertake entrepreneurial roles.[12] This wastage of scarce managerial talent must be considered as a major force retarding the pace of accelerated development.

VI

The remarks here on government policies towards the tribal area and urban Africans should not be construed as an outright condemnation of state intervention, for the role of government as *the* pacemaking instrument for economic change is no longer a matter for serious debate in underdeveloped areas.[13] In many directions, state-sponsored bodies are needed to provide services of a financial, promotional or co-ordinative nature which would not otherwise be forthcoming. In the forefront of such requirements is the provision on a far more lavish scale than hitherto of facilities to improve African educational standards, both at the general school level and in the direction of vocational and industrial training. The income gap will only begin to narrow of its own accord through raising the productivity of the non-White labour force;[14] and this in its turn can best be achieved through improved education.[15] But if this factor is to play its appropriate role in promoting accelerated development, it will entail a far higher degree of effective co-ordination and much more long-term planning than has been customary in the past.

But surely, it may well be asked, such an educational programme to raise productivity must be accompanied by a sweeping away of the restrictive labour laws? On purely economic grounds, the answer must be an unequivocal 'yes' – but then governments seldom act from economic motives alone, South African governments less so than most others. The paradox of the situation is that while it can no longer be convincingly argued that non-Whites are a threat to Whites in the labour market, some of the restrictions on their economic advance are now more severe than ever before.[16] What was once an economic fear has now become a political one. Any wholesale dismantling of the legislative colour bar is unlikely to be accomplished without the presen tightly controlled stream of Black workers flowing to the principal urban centres becoming a flood, the consequences of which (given the present electoral franchise) no government could survive.

At best, then, only some *ad hoc* tampering with the labour laws to provide a little alleviation in the short run can be expected; in the long run, those workers permitted to develop and use their skills are likely to become increasingly expensive.

This is not to imply that continued economic growth (even at an accelerated pace) and a further extension of state interference to foster separate development are by any means incompatible. In fact, since complex problems of political economy seldom resolve themselves into clear-cut patterns, neither integration nor separate development offers the ultimate answer for South Africa's future economic development. Instead, with a heterogeneous population exerting multiple pressures on resources, a state-sponsored system of effective economic co-operation may help to fuse together the more positive aspects of both integration and separate development, thereby achieving maximum growth with minimum inflation through enhancing productive capacity.

The author is aware of the highly selective nature of the topics mentioned in this assessment and that some very significant factors have been ignored altogether – such as the problem of water utilisation and the whole broad subject of conservation, the need for improvements in the financial superstructure and tax reform, the effective curbing of undesirable monopolistic tendencies, the thorny question of the extent to which government should serve as pacesetter in industrial innovation; all these and other equally important issues will impinge heavily on development trends. In the ultimate analysis, however, the only certain thing about the future is its uncertainty. Yet we are by no means entirely in the hands of fate, for undoubtedly human rather than physical factors are going to determine the pace of economic development in South Africa.

NOTES

1. See, for instance, the views of Thomas Karis in Gwendoline Carter (ed.), *Five African States: Responses to Diversity* (Ithaca, N.Y., 1963) p. 499.
2. G. Hatton, 'Gold in the South African Economy', *The Banker: South Africa Survey* (Sep 1971) pp. 51–6.

3. *Third Report of the Commission of Enquiry into Fiscal and Monetary Policy in South Africa*, para. 32.

4. See Professor S. J. Terreblanche's comments in summing up the discussion at a conference on 'Economic Development Programming in South Africa', *South African Journal of Economics* (Dec 1971) p. 404. In the case of the United States, assuming a growth rate of $4\frac{1}{2}$ per cent per annum, average family incomes in eighty years' time would have reached $250,000 a year. Norman Macrae, 'The Future of International Business', *The Economist*, 22 Jan 1972, p. vi.

5. D. E. Pursell, 'Bantu Real Wages and Employment Opportunities', *South African Journal of Economics* (June 1968).

6. For a detailed analysis of this relationshp, see A. Spandau, 'Income Distribution and Economic Growth in South Africa', D. Comm. dissertation (University of South Africa, 1971).

7. R. N. Tripathy, 'Criteria for the Selection of Investment Projects', in S. Spiegelglas and C. J. Welsh (eds), *Economic Development: Challenge and Promise* (Englewood Cliffs, N. J., 1970) pp. 65–74.

8. For a detailed interpretation of regional economic policy, see R. T. Bell, 'Industrial Location and Government Policy in South Africa', Ph.D. dissertation (Rhodes University, 1968).

9. D. K. Khatkhate, 'Management in Developing Countries', *Finance and Development* (Sep 1971) pp. 8–14.

10. These are encountered in most African countries; see, for example, P. C. Garlick, *African Traders and Economic Development in Ghana* (London, 1971).

11. J. A. Schumpeter, 'The Creative Response in Economic History', *Journal of Economic History* (Nov 1947) p. 157.

12. On this whole complex issue, a recent study merits attention: Gillian Hart, 'Some Socio-Economic Aspects of African Entrepreneurship', M.Soc.Sc. thesis (Rhodes University, 1971). In some respects, the problem is even more difficult for the Cape Coloured and South African Indian communities; see, for instance, W. M. Thomas, 'Coloured Entrepreneurship and the Economic Development of the Coloureds', paper delivered at the Abe Bailey Institute for Interracial Studies (Cape Town, Aug 1971).

13. Cf. the editors' introduction in P. Robson and D. A. Lury (eds), *The Economies of Africa* (London, 1969) pp. 32–7.

14. '. . . investment in human capital accounts for most of the impressive rise in the real earnings per worker.' T. W. Schultz, 'Investment in Human Capital', *American Economic Review* (Mar 1961) p. 1.

15. The process is cumulative: rising productivity, by pushing up the income of the family, enables children to be kept at school for a longer period. See Professor J. L. Sadie's comments in his paper 'Labour Supply in South Africa' read at the National Labour Conference sponsored by the *Financial Mail* (Cape Town, Apr 1971).

16. G. V. Doxey, 'Enforced Racial Stratification in the South African Labour Market', in H. Adam (ed.), *South Africa: Sociological Perspectives* (London, 1971) pp. 268–82.

Some Economic Aspects and Implications

P. T. BAUER

I

The author's knowledge of Southern Africa is meagre. There are, however, certain significant social and economic features of this vast diverse region, the presence of which is not disputed by people of widely different positions, which bear on any worthwhile discussions of accelerated development. The purpose of this conference can best be served by noting their significance and implications for policy.

The following are these characteristics and features: ethnic and cultural diversity within the region; comparatively recent, and still only partial, emergence of most of the population from extreme material backwardness; the large proportion of the population still engaged in production for the family or some other narrowly defined group (conventionally and conveniently termed subsistence or near-subsistence production). These characteristics are interrelated, and for most purposes of development policy have to be considered synoptically.

II

The populations of all major countries of Southern Africa are ethnically and culturally diverse. They are collections of different societies and tribes rather than nation-states or comparatively homogeneous societies. This diversity is not confined to the familiar distinctions between Europeans, Indians and Africans, but is pronounced also within these groups, notably so within the Africans.[1]

People's attitudes, aptitudes, motivations and social and political institutions are the prime determinants of economic attainment and progress. External contacts and natural resources also play a part, but their utilisation depends again on the basic determinants. Individuals and groups differ greatly in the possession of these personal and socio-cultural determinants of development, which in turn brings about pronounced and often vast differences in economic performance.

Very little is known about the causes of personal and group differences in the possession of these determinants of economic performance, nor about their likely persistence. But there is no doubt about the antiquity of some of these differences. While they are not fixed for all times (as is clear, for instance, from the phenomenon of economic decline and variations through time in the economic performance of different groups and societies), considerable differences in the presence of these determinants and in resulting economic performance are likely to persist for at least some generations in many parts of the less developed world, notably so in Southern Africa, and regardless of official policy, although the extent of these differences will be affected by it.

Experience in many parts of the world in widely different conditions suggests that within wide limits the operation of the basic determinants of economic achievement on the position of different ethnic groups is often largely unaffected by policy. Exclusion from major branches of economic activity and employment has often not obstructed the progress of the groups affected as long as they were permitted to engage in commerce and to own personal property: the political, social and economic disabilities imposed on dissenters and Jews in Britain and Europe or on the Chinese in Malaysia have not prevented their material success, and may even have stimulated it.

In a subsistence or near-subsistence economy, differences in economic aptitudes and attitudes are on the whole irrelevant and unobtrusive. The opportunities for their emergence and manifestation are limited partly by the absence of wider exchange and often also by the fear of arousing envy and resentment. Once a society emerges from the subsistence stage, personal and group differences in economic performance are apt to become prominent. Rapid change especially offers scope for differences in the readiness to perceive and exploit economic opportunities. Differences in economic attainment and progress of different and distinct groups then come to be widely noted.

III

In multi-racial societies people are especially prone to believe that the incomes of better-off persons and groups have been secured at the expense of the rest, a politically explosive notion related to the idea that the volume of economic activities and processes is somehow fixed, so that the activities of one group displace those of another. The notion that economic activity is akin to a zero-sum game in which the incomes of some are extracted from others, rather than earned from the supply of productive resources, is an old one which long antedates the writings of Marx. But its influence has been reinforced by the widespread acceptance of Marxist–Leninist ideas (which extends well beyond those who have actually read either Marx or Lenin), in which profit and property incomes represent exploitation, and service industries are unproductive.

The belief in the existence of a fixed amount of income and of economic activity has been reinforced further by certain types of state economic controls in recent decades, such as the imposition of import and exchange controls and restrictive licensing of commercial, industrial and transport enterprises, or of restrictive quotas of agricultural production. Such measures lend plausibility to the idea that certain branches of economic activity, or even total economic activity, are fixed in the aggregate, and so are the incomes to be earned from them. The presence of these ideas understandably exacerbate tension in multi-racial societies. It promotes policies of confiscation of income and wealth, which apart from obvious disincentive effects on effort, saving, investment and enterprise, also inhibit development through their effects on the political situation, as we shall see shortly.

Somewhat analogous tensions and effects derive from the operation of restrictive tendencies widespread in Africa and elsewhere in both the developed and less developed world. These restrictive tendencies derive from various distinct sources, including ethnic and tribal hostility, and more narrowly economic motives.

Reluctance to establish contact, especially close contact, with strangers or members of other ethnic or tribal groups itself derives from various motives, including physical fear, or the desire of certain individuals or groups to maintain their authority and social position, or a reluctance to dilute or jeopardise the cultural or genetic heritage of the group.

Both the motives and the effects of these types of restrictionism are frequently compounded by more specifically economic restrictionism, engendered primarily by a desire to increase the scarcity value of one's resources. As is well known, restrictive tendencies are widespread in societies in which specialisation and production for sale have made some headway, as by such measures people can increase the scarcity value of their services.[2]

Restrictionism obstructs efficient allocation of resources as well as their growth, and inhibits the movement of people and goods, the establishment of new enterprises and the expansion of efficient products. In less developed countries (L.D.C.s) especially they aggravate unemployment by obstructing the most effective deployment of the available capital and skills, as well as the growth of these resources.[3] Restrictionism also reinforces the frequency and severity of local shortages, especially of food, retards specialisation, production for the market and the growth of the economy.

These effects of restrictionism are reasonably obvious; others are less obvious, but perhaps even more important. Restrictionism is most easily aroused and administered against persons and groups readily distinguishable on ethnic, linguistic or racial grounds from the advocates of restrictions. Thus where the population is heterogeneous, the diversity often extends to differences habitually recognised by the local population, but unperceived by observers from outside. Restrictionism can thus lead to extensive fragmentation of the economy.

Restrictionism on the movement of persons and goods obstructs the spread of new ideas, methods, crops and wants and the uncoercive erosion of attitudes and customs damaging to material advance. This is true especially of restrictions on international and inter-regional movement both of people and commodities, as external contacts are often potent agents of changes in attitudes.

Advocates and beneficiaries of restrictionism often seek state support for their policies. Restrictionism was an early and often major factor in the imposition of state control of economic activity in the exchange sector in many L.D.C.s, thus promoting the recent politicisation of economic life, which has profoundly affected their political and economic history.

IV

A number of different but often interrelated factors have contributed to the politicisation of economic life which has emerged in many L.D.C.s since the Second World War, notably in Africa, where most of economic life outside subsistence agriculture has come under close state control. These relevant factors include the operation of private sectional interests; the desire of governments and of civil servants (including international civil servants) to increase their power, influence, income; the legacy of the closing years of British colonial rule in Africa, when for various reasons closely controlled economies came to be established, thereby providing the incoming governments with the ready-made framework of a politicised economy.

An especially important influence has been the belief that comprehensive planning, in the sense of actual or attempted close state control over the economy, except perhaps outside small-scale agriculture, is certainly necessary, and often even sufficient, for material progress. The idea that comprehensive planning is indispensable for material advance is of very recent origin and derives from outside the less developed world (L.D.W.), though eagerly espoused there by governments and academics who hope to benefit from it.[4]

Comprehensive planning in this sense is clearly not necessary for material advance. It was not used in the material progress of any of the now highly developed societies in North America, Western Europe or Japan, nor in the rapid advance which many L.D.C.s experienced between the closing decades of the nineteenth century, notably in South-east Asia, West Africa and Latin America. Comprehensive planning does not augment resources but only concentrates power, and thereby actually creates power, because in a market system there do not normally exist such positions of power as are created by comprehensive planning.[5]

There is no reason why the overriding of the decisions of private persons should increase the flow of income, because the resources used by the planners must come from other productive public or private uses. Even if such a policy accelerated the rise in total output, which is unlikely, this need not correspond to a rise in living standards, because under comprehensive planning the composition of output is largely unrelated to consumer demand. (This separation of output from consumer demand itself tends to retard the growth both of output and of living standards in L.D.C.s, as the prospects of improved consumption are an important incentive for improved economic performance.)

As we have already noted, close state economic controls restrict the spread of new ideas and methods, and protect habits and attitudes adverse to development. Thus these various controls obstruct that modernisaton of the mind which is a requirement of economic development.

There is a further set of reasons of the greatest importance why comprehensive planning in L.D.C.s inhibits development. The extensive state economic controls established under comprehensive planning largely politicise economic and social life, which provokes and exacerbates political tension, because it becomes all-important who has the government. The stakes in the fight for political power increase greatly and so does the intensity of struggle for it, especially, but not only, in multi-racial societies. This sequence is largely behind the bitterness of the political struggle in many parts of the L.D.W. The history of Indonesia, Malaysia, Pakistan, East Africa and Nigeria since about 1960 cannot be understood without this factor. And when political action is all-important, the energies and activities of ambitious or resourceful men are diverted from economic activity to political life (partly from choice, partly from necessity, since their economic opportunities or even survival may depend largely on political developments). The direction of the activities of able men greatly affects economic attainment and progress in any society.

Partial depoliticisation of economic life could make a major contribution to the defusing of political tension in many parts of the world, notably so in the multi-racial societies of Africa.

These observations should not be interpreted as a simplistic plea for *laissez-faire*. In L.D.C.s as elsewhere there exists a wide range of important or even essential functions which must develop under government, because part of the institutional structure within which the private sector functions does not emerge from the operation of market forces and must be established by law; and also because some of these activities yield services for which there may be a demand, but which cannot be bought and sold in the market. A list of these tasks normally includes the successful conduct of external affairs; the maintenance of law and order;

the effective management of the monetary and fiscal system; the promotion of a suitable institutional framework for the activities of individuals; the provision of basic health and education services and of basic communications; and also agricultural extension work.

This list of tasks largely exhausts the potentialities of state action in the promotion of development. These tasks are extensive and complex, and their adequate performance would fully stretch the resources of governments in L.D.C.s, including all governments of Southern Africa. Yet governments in many L.D.Cs frequently neglect even the most elementary of these functions while attempting close controls of their economies, or even occasionally contemplating coercive transformation of entire societies. They seem anxious to plan and are unable to govern.

But while the performance of these tasks is onerous and would stretch or exceed the resources available in L.D.C.s, that performance does not normally imply close control over people's lives and activities. They do not therefore politicise life and exacerbate tensions as do the main components of comprehensive planning.

V

The proximity or co-existence of different ethnic groups, notably migrants and indigenous groups, between the majority of whom there are pronounced differences in levels of economic attainment and possibly also in potential attainment, has been a prominent feature at various times in the nineteenth century in many L.D.C.s. In Southern Africa these differences are familiar and stark. But somewhat similar situations are encountered elsewhere in the L.D.W., witness the Chinese and the Malays in Malaysia, Indians and Burmese in Burma, Asians and Africans in East Africa. The history of the last hundred years in Southern Africa, as in many other parts of the continent, has not been one of stagnation, but rather of rapid and uneven change: uneven in that some groups have played a much greater part in these changes, or have been much more affected than have other groups; and also in that some institutions have been affected much more than have others. The problems, tensions and dilemmas set up by rapid and uneven change can be much more intractable than those of stagnation or near-stagnation.

The late Dr A. McPhee wrote in 1926[6] that economic change in West Africa from about 1890 to the 1920s represented the superimposition of the twentieth century A.D. on the twentieth century B.C., an observation which applied perhaps with even greater force to much of Southern Africa. In West Africa the principal agency of change was the development of cash crops for export. In Southern Africa it was the rapid development of the mining industries. The latter development and its direct results represented an even more pronounced discontinuity than did the former, with correspondingly even greater problems of adjustment.

Replacement of communal tenure of land by individual tenure (whether by individual producers, corporate bodies, co-operative societies or government departments) is one of the more important of the various complex problems presented by the rapid emergence from a subsistence economy especially in multi-racial societies. As has often been noted, communal tenure of land obstructs agricultural improvement, which may become imperative when population increases, and highly desirable when external contacts or other changes offer scope for a marketable surplus. On the other hand, rapid introduction of individual tenure, which in practice usually requires state intervention (at least in shaping the institutional structure, such as the introduction of methods for enforcing the property rights), enables people to dispossess themselves of their rights for negligible consideration, both to more alert members of their own society, and to an even larger extent to strangers more familiar with the operation of a money economy.

The operation of the market system has been tempered in many parts of Africa and Asia by varying degrees of paternalism, including the establishment of native reserves (in South-east Asia, as well as in Africa) where land transactions were severely restricted and strangers barred from acquiring land; the establishment of indirect rule designed to maintain tribal authority and custom in the administration of property; prohibition of the establishment of foreign-owned plantations; or attempts to restrict economic intercourse between members of different groups, such as effective prohibition of the operation of non-indigenous traders.

Paternalism, xenophobia, physical fear and economic restrictionism have contributed to major forms of restrictive policies in Southern Africa, the emergence, development and some implications of which are examined by Professor S. Herbert Frankel in a perceptive and penetrating study, *The Tyranny of Economic Paternalism in Africa: A Study of Frontier Mentality, 1860–1960.*[1]

Professor Frankel describes the establishment and evolution of a system of internal economic frontiers in Southern Africa (and to some extent also in Central and East Africa), drawn largely on ethnic and tribal lines restricting people's rights to move between places and occupations, and the composition of the labour force, and restricting also their access to modern forms of enterprise and ownership. This extensive replacement of market forces by government direction has extensively politicised economic life. The forces which have contributed to this system in various parts of Africa include such diverse elements as military and defence considerations; the belief that native reserves were necessary for the protection of the indigenous population; inability or unwillingness to finance public services in native areas; political fears engendered by the close presence of large numbers of non-Whites; economic restrictionism by White workers and poor Whites; and an inclination to think in abstract and aggregative terms, such as Whites and non-Whites, or European and native interest, instead of the interests, capacities and preferences of individuals and small groups.

Professor Frankel notes that the system failed to achieve its principal avowed objectives. It has obstructed agricultural improvements in the reserves by maintaining communal tenure of land and effectively forcing the more enterprising and capable people to seek employment outside tribal lands; it has increased the dependence of the modern sector of the economy of Southern Africa on a large volume of unskilled African labour; it has retarded the inflow of capital and the rise in the volume of employment, and in the real income of the White population, compared to what it would have been otherwise. It has retarded the economic improvement of the Bantu while failing to provide security to the Europeans, notably by increasing their economic dependence on a large mass of unskilled Africans and their sense of dependence on political contrivances for the maintenance of their status and security. Moreover, contrary to the objectives and expectations of the paternalistic and restrictive policies, the growth of the modern sector has brought interdependence between the different communities.

Developments elsewhere in Africa and in other L.D.C.s suggest that Professor Frankel may have been too sanguine in his expectations about the extent of the economic improvement and increased political stability which might have emerged from a more liberal policy. But his broad conclusions stand, that greater occupational and geographical mobility and freedom in the allocation of resources would materially have benefited the majority of all communities, at least over the last few decades.[8]

The relaxation of state controls is likely to diminish political tension, and the replacement of communal by individual tenure of land is necessary for substantial improvement in African agricultural methods. At present, external forces promote further politicisation of economic life in Southern Africa. Thus the worldwide influence of the view that development requires comprehensive planning is likely to influence policy in Southern Africa also. Again, the threat of external military or quasi-military reaction against some parts of Southern Africa is also apt to promote state control of economic life.

Comprehensive planning and other forms of state economic controls are especially likely to inhibit development in Southern Africa, a huge area with poor communications and with ethnically and culturally highly diverse populations, the majority of whom are subsistence or near-subsistence producers with few external economic contacts. In these conditions the effects of state controls in provoking political tension, restricting mobility, fragmenting the economy and retarding the spread of new ideas, methods, crops, and attitudes conducive to modernisation of the mind, are likely to be both pronounced and damaging.

VI

Under the communal system of land tenure of the indigenous subsistence cultivators of Southern Africa, membership of the tribe confers and confines right of access to the land; the ultimate right is vested in the tribe and its use substantially determined by the tribal and village authorities. The oft-expressed expectation has generally been disappointed that agricultural extension work and instruction would reconcile communal tenure and agricultural improvement. Whatever the abilities and attitudes of the majority of the population, under such a system the more enterprising, ambitious or able people cannot acquire holdings suitable to their methods; they cannot be sure that they will be left in possession of the land they cultivate; they cannot borrow on the security of the land which they cultivated; there is no incentive for the individual person, or family, to improve the land or to restrict the number of cattle grazing on it, as much of the benefit will accrue to others or even be nullified by them. However, although the need for the introduction of individual tenure may be both evident and urgent, it is often strongly resisted. Indeed, the more urgent the need for the change because of population growth or the emergence of new opportunities, the more emphatically tribal authorities or particular groups or individuals may resist it, as they feel that access to the land by virtue of their membership of a tribe provides their only security.

Such transformation will call for some sort of government action as otherwise the unaided attempts of the more enterprising people or groups are likely to be frustrated by those who want to maintain communal tenure.

The transformation often involves difficult and delicate choices. Delay is likely to increase the resistance to change. On the other hand, a premature policy would be useless because the advantages depend on persons able to apply new methods. Again, very rapid change often exacerbates tensions and increases the difficulties of assisting those who cannot readily adjust to rapid change.

Many newly enfranchised property-owners may, through inexperience, divest themselves of their rights, the conditions of which they do not understand adequately. This raises the question of educative restraint (to borrow a term coined by Professor Hutt), that is, of partial temporary restriction on the right to sell or mortgage property. But this in turn raises other problems, such as corresponding obstacles in the way of credit and property transactions, without which the economic benefits of individual tenure are curtailed or negated.

All these difficulties are exacerbated both by the politically highly charged atmosphere of much of Southern Africa, and by the impact of rapid and uneven change. The unwarranted belief in the compatibility of communal tenure with substantial agricultural improvement may have delayed systematic investigation of the complexities and potentialities of the introduction of individual tenure in many parts of Africa.

The introduction of individual tenure has proved relatively smooth when it accompanied the emergence of a successful cash crop suitable for cultivation by the indigenous population. In West Africa, for instance, cocoa and kola trees were often individually cultivated and subsequently individually owned, while communal tenure still prevailed in the cultivation of traditional food crops, though after a while individual tenure emerged in the cultivation of these crops too.

VII

In Southern Africa, as elsewhere, state-sponsored or subsidised industrialisation is often regarded as an appropriate prime instrument of accelerated development. Without discussing at length this well-worn theme, some points pertinent to the purpose of this Conference can be noted:

(i) The development literature makes much of the supposed educational merits of industrialisation, especially for the development of technical skills in L.D.C.s. However, in most of these countries, and notably so in sub-Saharan Africa, a prime requisite of development is not primarily the growth of technical skills, but the modernisation of the mind, notably the development of the attitudes, mores and institutions appropriate to an exchange economy. The production of cash crops and the trading activities associated with this process are usually more appropriate for this purpose than the promotion of subsidised manufacturing, because the difficulties of developing attitudes and habits appropriate to an exchange economy are not compounded or exacerbated by the difficulties of simultaneous acquisition of unfamiliar industrial techniques. And manufacturing production which emerges from these activities is generally far less costly in terms of social strain than industrialisation attempted directly from subsistence agriculture.[9] Once the production of cash crops has proceeded for some time, people get used to the ways of a money economy, which in turn promotes and facilitates the growth of viable manufacturing. Thus as it proceeds through time, the production of cash crops and the development of manufacturing are often complementary.

(ii) Another argument for sponsored industrialisation is the familiar infant-industry argument. But as is well known, the infants are notoriously slow in growing up, especially when they require such very large-scale assistance as they do in many L.D.C.s. Moreover, if the prospects of their viability are genuine, entrepreneurs could be expected to set up such establishments, if necessary with borrowed capital, which they could repay after achieving profitability.

The infant-industry argument is often linked to the suggestion that subsidised manufacturing yields substantial external economies, that is, cost reduction accruing to other activities as a result of the expansion of certain activities. Authenticated instances of genuine external economies are few. In any event, state-supported industrialisation implies the extension of subsidised activities at the expense of the contraction of the taxed activities with a loss of potential external economies yielded by these other activities. It would need to be established that the external economies yielded by the industrial activities exceed those which have been lost in other directions. No attempt appears to have been made so far to establish this condition in the context of subsidised manufacturing. Moreover, these net economies would also have to compensate for the costs resulting from the political and administrative repercussions and costs of subsidised industrialisation. These simple considerations are ignored because much of the discussion of state-sponsored industrialisation regards manufacturing output as a net addition to total income or output and ignores alternative uses of resources. This practice is an instance of economics without cost.

(iii) It is sometimes urged that the production of cash crops is inappropriate as an instrument for promoting economic advance in Africa because the production for export, even of highly successful crops such as West African cocoa and vegetable oil and oilseeds, has still not produced material

advance comparable to that of the industrial societies o
the West. This argument is an example of the unhistorica
approach to development so often encountered in the cur
rent development literature from which the time dimen
sion is often altogether omitted. Societies which only a few
decades ago were materially exceedingly backward or even
barbarous cannot be expected within a few decades to
approach the material achievements of the societies o
North America, Western Europe, Australasia or Japan
Their failure to do so is no reflection on the suitability o
production of cash crops as the instruments of materia
progress.

Manufacturing is simply a collection of activities which hav
little in common except for the fact that they represent more of a
break with people's traditional pursuits than does the produc
tion of cash crops, and thus involve the difficulty already noted o
acquiring unaccustomed techniques simultaneously with th
development of attitudes and habits appropriate to a mone
economy.[10]

If it is nevertheless intended to promote sponsored industriali
sation, three points relevant to the economic and political situa
tion in most of Southern Africa might be noted:

(i) In measuring the support extended to any branch c
manufacturing, it must be remembered that what matter
is the effective and not the nominal rate of tariff or sub
sidy, even though it is the nominal rate which is usuall
quoted. The effective rate expresses the tariff (or othe
form of subsidy) as a proportion of the value adde
domestically, while the more usually quoted nominal rat
relates the tariff to the value of the product. In measurin
the extent of effective assistance, the value of imported ra
materials and imported intermediate goods, which ar
usually duty-free or attract duty at much lower rates tha
the final product, needs to be deducted from the value c
the output. When this procedure is followed it ofte
emerges that the tariff or subsidy is far larger than appea
from the nominal rates.

(ii) If manufacturing is to be subsidised, industries catering fo
export may often be more suitable candidates for suppo

(defence considerations apart) than those producing import substitutes, because local markets are much more limited than export markets.

(iii) If imports of manufactures (or, indeed, of any other products) are to be restricted, the use of tariffs rather than of import licences has the important advantage that it does not ensure windfall profits such as accrue to the recipients of licences. In Africa price control and rationing at the ultimate consumer stage are generally ineffective, so that either the recipients of licences, or other traders between the importers and ultimate retailers, secure windfall profits. Such a situation is bound to inflate the demand for licences, lead to charges of favouritism and provoke political tension.

VIII

It will have been noted that the author's assignment was to discuss economic factors in accelerated development. What has been written above is not often examined either in economic textbooks or in the most widely canvassed literature. Yet the author believes that the factors he has examined are relevant to accelerated development.

In much of the contemporary development literature the variables chosen for discussion are not selected because of their importance as determinants of development, but on the basis of their tractability by formal quasi-mathematical methods, or because preoccupation with them may promote certain policies favoured by the discussant. Such matters as human abilities and behaviour, social institutions, customs and attitudes, and external contact are either ignored altogether or at best treated parametrically. Such treatment may perhaps be appropriate, though even this is doubtful, in the analysis of highly developed industrialised societies pervaded by the money economy. It is certainly inappropriate to the study of promotion of the development of L.D.C.s. To make matters worse, policies designed to operate on the conventional variables often, indeed perhaps generally, affect the major determinants which are ignored or treated parametically; and these repercussions may be far more important than changes in the conventional variables themselves. For instance, measures designed to increase the rate of saving or the pattern of investment often affect the volume of external contacts, the supply of incentive goods, the position and prospects of different ethnic groups and the intensity of the struggle for political power. These repercussions on the determinants of development are patently important, and yet they are bound to be ignored if the determinants themselves are not discussed.[11]

IX

The principal arguments of this paper are now summarised:

1. In Southern Africa, as elsewhere, the prime determinants of economic performance and progress are people's abilities, attitudes and social and political institutions. Different ethnic groups differ in the possession of these personal and socio-cultural determinants, but little is known about the causes of these differences, or about the likelihood of their persistence.

2. A significant characteristic of the economic and social scene in much of Southern Africa is rapid and uneven change rather than stagnation.

3. Restrictionism, derived from several distinct sources, has substantially affected economic policy in Southern Africa.

4. Close state control of economic life is much more likely to retard than to promote a rise in living standards. The notion that comprehensive planning in the sense of close state control of economic life is necessary for material progress is demonstrably unfounded and is more nearly the opposite of the truth. This notion is widely held outside Southern Africa and may come to influence policy there also.

5. Economic development requires modernisation of the mind. State controls restrict geographical and occupational mobility as well as the extent and diversity of external contacts. These implications of controls retard the erosion of attitudes and customs adverse to material progress.

6. Politicisation of economic life provokes and exacerbates political tension, especially in multi-racial societies, because it becomes extremely important who has the government. It also diverts energy and ambition from economic life to political activity.

7. In Southern Africa, as elsewhere, there is an extensive range of necessary governmental functions, adequate performance of which would stretch or exceed the human and financial resources of the governments. These tasks do not require close control of economic life and avoid its attendant adverse results.

8. There are external influences likely to promote further politicisation of economic life in Southern Africa. Accelerated development would benefit from some depoliticisation of economic life for which there may be scope both in wider issues of policy and also in more narrow specific matters.

9. Replacement of communal tenure of land, rightly recognised as a requisite of agricultural progress, raises a number of different problems and dilemmas. They might have received greater attention but for the unjustified expectations about the possibilities of agricultural improvement under communal tenure.

10. Encouragement of the cultivation of cash crops may often be more appropriate and effective for accelerated development in Southern Africa than state-sponsored or subsidised industrialisation.

NOTES

1. I shall use interchangeably the terms African and Bantu which, while not accurate, is convenient; the imprecision does not affect the argument.

2. In practice the beneficiaries often overestimate the advantage derived from restrictionism, while the rest of society is apt to ignore, or underestimate, the material damage they suffer. And even where they perceive the cost they are unable or unwilling to fight restrictionism since, extreme cases apart, each individual incident normally affects only one of the many directions in which they spend their incomes. In practice restrictionism is therefore often accepted or even supported by many people adversely affected by it.

3. These effects on employment are especially pronounced when, as is often the case, the incidence of the scarcity of cattle, land, capital and skills is geographically uneven, and these differences cannot be reduced because of the operation of restrictions.

4. In the absence of external suggestion and without external financial and administrative support, many of the controls introduced in the name of comprehensive planning could not function in many L.D.C.s, notably so in sub-Saharan Africa.

5. Power here means the capacity to restrict the choice open to other men. There are large corporations and rich men in a market system. But their resources do not confer power on them in this material sense, at any rate to nothing like the extent to which comprehensive planning confers it on politicians and civil servants.

6. *The Economic Revolution in British West Africa* (London, 1926).

7. Special supplement to *Optima* (Dec 1960). Professor Frankel has examined these matters in other publications as well, notably *The Economic Impact on Underdeveloped Societies* (Oxford, 1953). The study noted here is perhaps the most concise and convenient exposition of his views.

8. I thus broadly accept Professor Frankel's position in these matters, and that of other distinguished scholars who have written on this subject, notably Sir Arnold Plant, Professors W. H. Hutt, H. M. Robertson and D. Hobart Houghton, and Dr Sheila van der Horst. But the possibility cannot be denied that major changes in policy might have engendered fears and tensions, the results of which would have offset the possible benefits. The necessarily speculative outcome of such a change would be largely affected by the manner and circumstances of the introduction of the changes.

   It is possible that because of the greater adaptability and resourcefulness of the non-Africans, their rate of improvement and their economic position would have been even faster that that of the Bantu, even though they are less directly affected by prevalent restrictions than the Bantu. But such estimates must contain a large speculative element.

9. Several studies of the process of industrialisation in different African countries have shown that practically all successful indigenous manufacturers began their careers as traders.

10. There are many other arguments often heard in support of sponsored industrialisation. They are generally quite irrelevant to the position and prospects of Southern Africa and are therefore not examined here. I have examined most of them at some length in a recent book, *Dissent on Development* (London, 1972).

11. The development literature is much influenced by modern macro-economic models whch address themselves to problems quite different from those of long-term economic development. Their irrelevance for this purpose is clear from the explicit assumptions underlying Keynes's *General Theory*, the source of most of these models. Keynes wrote there:

    'We take as given the existing skill and quantity of available labour, the existing quality and quantity of available equipment, the existing technique, the degree of competition, the tastes and habits of the consumer, the disutility of different intensities of labour and of the activities of supervision and organisation, as well as the social structure. ... This does not mean that we assume these factors to be constant; but merely that, in this place and context, we are not considering or taking into account the effects and consequences of change in them.' (p. 245).

Economic Development
and Property Rights

SVETOZAR PEJOVICH

The idea of economic planning for development dominates both the thinking and practice of almost all underdeveloped countries today. Their leaders seem to identify the annual increment in physical output either with the rate of improvement in social welfare or, as is often the case, with the promise of its improvement in the foreseeable future. Yet it appears that the standard of living and the rate of its improvement in countries which have limited the scope of economic planning to a declaration of their aims and objectives is at least as high as in those countries which have adopted various kinds and degrees of effective administrative planning. The purpose of this paper is to develop a line of reasoning which would suggest that economic development of a community cannot be fully understood without analysis of the effects of property rights structures on the pattern of behaviour of its members.

I

Since this paper bears on a genuine, real-world problem, our discussion and evaluation must relate to the growth models actually used in various countries rather than to more sophisticated ones available in economic literature. Economic planners in most underdeveloped countries tend to fall back on the Harrod–Domar growth model or some more elaborate schemes which have evolved from it. We shall refer to all of them as the *investment only* plans. The common feature of the *investment only* plans is that they consider the saving–investment relationship as a major determinant of the rate of growth, and increase in the supply of investible funds as a major determinant of an increased rate of growth. It follows that a reduction in current consumption in favour of future consumption is a major source of larger output. It is for this reason that economic planners see nothing wrong, and in fact find it desirable, to supplement the community's voluntary savings with some forced savings whenever the people fail to save 'enough'. That the policy of extracting forced savings from the community may result either in a fall in the rate of voluntary savings out of the reduced disposable income, or in the use of private savings to create goods that yield more non-pecuniary income, is mostly ignored by economic planners.

It is not too difficult to demonstrate the advantages of forced savings, if one uses a discount rate well below the social time preference. A Soviet economist estimated, using a zero rate of interest, that to maximise a generation's lifetime consumption, the total investment fund should be increased each year by no less than 50 per cent of the increment in the value of national output.[1] A Yugoslav economist has shown some awareness of the importance of discounting the future by a positive rate of interest. However, he eliminated it through a sequence of assertions leading to *non sequitur* statements such as: 'To establish that a zero or a negative interest rate is not only a mere possibility but also a real-world phenomenon, it suffices to observe the post-war economies of those European countries where the rate of inflation was higher than the rate of interest on savings deposits'; and 'assuming that the population wishes to maximise consumption within one generation's lifetime. . . . The maximum output of consumer goods within, say, thirty years is completely determined by the technological features of the respective economies. Thus an independently determined function of the marginal disutility of saving may prove to be inconsistent and is in any case irrelevant.'[2] The economic nonsense of this argument is easy to demonstrate. Moreover, a discount rate lower than the social time preference involves not only a coercive readjustment in the community's time pattern of consumption, but a transfer of political power from the people at large to the ruling group, as well as the attenuation of one's property rights in the income from his own stock of wealth, including labour. Thus the present value of an expected stream of consumption resulting from the *voluntary* allocation of income between consumption and savings would most likely be well above the present value of expected real income from a larger (planned) output when both are discounted at a rate of interest representing the community's true time preference.[3]

II

A major reason for the failure of economic plans to fulfil planners' hopes and aspirations lies, we suggest, in their neglect to recognise that economic activity involves a double variation: variations in the quantity of inputs and variations in the 'composition' or 'quality' of inputs. The former increases future outputs by varying the allocation of inputs between current consumption and savings, investment). It is the type of variation upon which the *investment only* plans are built.

The variations in the 'composition' of inputs are independent of the problem of allocation between present and future consumption – although they may affect it. The qualitative variations change the index of significance of inputs relative to output, that is they represent a new combination of resources not heretofore evaluated by the community.

The man who injects something essentially new into the flow of economic life presents the community with a *choice* between the old and a new use of resources. He enlarges the community's set of opportunity choices. The *voluntary* acceptance of the new alternative indicates that the community considers it superior to some old ones. Otherwise the innovation would have failed. While an increase in the rate of investment contributes to future outputs via a reduction in current consumption, a successful innovation increases the community's welfare by adding to its range of choices. Moreover, the act of innovation *does not have to affect* the allocation of resources between present and future consumption.

Consider what is happening today in a number of under-developed countries. The idea of development had hit the rulers of those communities from without long before the entrepreneurial class emerged there. It has forced the leaders of these countries to 'legislate' development, thus compelling their people to accept new forms and ways of life. While it is often argued that an important advantage of planning for development is to help the community to break away from the old pattern of life, the fact remains that economic plans are promoting *changes* rather than *progress*. It is difficult to demonstrate that economic change which the people are *compelled* to accept represents the pattern of life necessarily preferred by them. It can only indicate the pattern of development which the ruling élite believe the community should prefer.

It is not too difficult to understand why modern growth theorists as well as economic planners assume the act of innovation to be an external factor which falls outside the scope of economic analysis. Innovation can hardly be planned for or predicted in advance.[4] Thus to consider innovation as an endogenous variable would render growth models indeterministic. Kuznets cautioned growth theorists from giving too much weight to their respective results and predictions. Referring to the observed relationship between patterns of change in the structure of production and income levels, he said: '. . . unless innovational changes can somehow be taken into account in the use of the cross-section data proper, use of its results may lead to erroneous inferences concerning past changes in structure in the process of growth. And the same applies, *pari passu*, to application of cross-section analysis to projections into the future.'[5]

The major difference between the effects of the quantitative and qualitative economic changes on economic growth can now be readily seen. The former leads to an increase in future outputs via a combination of voluntary and non-voluntary sacrifice of current consumption. The voluntary sacrifice of current consumption represents a desired adjustment in the community's pattern of consumption through time. The non-voluntary savings, forced savings, show what a desired adjustment of the community's pattern of consumption should be in the opinion of the ruling élite. The qualitative changes, on the other hand, increase the community's set of opportunity choices. They are brought about by the innovator, that is, a man who knowingly and willingly accepts the risk of having his 'suggestion' rejected by the community.[6] The resulting change in the innovator's wealth can therefore be treated as a reward for making the community better off.

III

If the line of reasoning presented above is basically correct, a major problem of economic development becomes the one of searching for a social organisation within which opportunities and incentives for innovating actions are maximised. This author has shown elsewhere that the flow of innovation depends on the ability of the social organisation to provide the freedom to innovate for all, the availability of economic power to innovate, and a system of sufficient incentives.[7] The relevant question is: What are the most important institutions which the community should try to strengthen in order to satisfy these three major requirements for successful economic development? Freedom to innovate means the freedom to change the allocation of resources according to the innovator's vision. Thus the freedom to innovate presupposes a contractual agreement whereby the innovator can obtain the needed resources. It follows that the conditions governing the extent of contractual agreements determine, in a round-about way, the freedom to innovate.

Consider an agreement between two parties to exchange goods or services. It must be presumed that both parties expect to be better off, that is, reach a higher indifference curve, after the contract is fulfilled. Otherwise one or both of them would refuse to enter into the contractual agreement. Since every contract means an exchange of some bundle of property rights, and since no person can transfer to another person more rights than he himself possesses, the attenuation of private property rights reduces the set of opportunity choices of the contracting parties and affects both the allocation of resources and social welfare. It follows that a reduction in the scope of private property rights must be reflected in a reduction of contractual activity. Let us mention three examples.

A minimum-wage law attenuates the worker's property rights over his own labour by forbidding him from transferring it to consumers (via an intermediary, e.g. a corporation) below a certain price. That is, the law prevents some people from entering into contractual agreements which attain for them the most preferred position. A second example should be familiar to a university professor. Assume that two departments have different ratios between secretaries and allocated space. They could both reach a higher indifference curve via exchange. They are, however, unable to enter into a mutually advantageous contract because they have property rights in neither the funds for secretarial help nor in the allocated space that they could transfer to another person. True, the administration may grant their request for exchange of several rooms for a few secretaries. But there is a world of difference between the right to enter into an act of exchange and the right to receive permission to do it. The latter suggests a reduction in the extent of contractual agreements, that is, in the scope or latitude of choices. Finally, expectations about the unwillingness of the state to defend or strengthen private property rights will make people fearful of theft of the wealth they accumulate and force them into a type of behaviour – accumulation of gold, diamonds, etc. – which reduces the scope of contractual activities.

The weakening, or expectations about the weakening, of private property rights must therefore limit the extent of contractual agreements in a community and reduce (but not necessarily eliminate) the innovator's freedom both to *acquire* and *use* resources. Some potential innovations, we may assume, would not be introduced at all. It follows that the content of prevailing property rights structures in a community is of crucial importance for its economic development, and that *private property* rights, whose basic elements are *exclusivity* of right of use of a thing and voluntary *transferability* of that right, are a powerful and possibly necessary factor for the freedom to innovate for all.

The second major requirement for creating the environment conducive for carrying out innovating activities is the availability of economic power. The innovator's freedom to enter into contractual agreements which will provide him with scarce resources is futile unless he has sufficient economic power to acquire those resources.

Schumpeter's theory of economic development is almost exclusively based on the concept of economic power. He defined economic power as a source of energy capable of disrupting the equilibrium relationships from within the system. It could be argued that the economic power of Schumpeter is merely the old concept of capital. Yet a qualitative difference between the two concepts exists. In Schumpeter's scheme, capital is not merely a medium of exchange which equalises marginal costs and utilities and moves the system towards an equilibrium. It is a major source of energy which disrupts the equilibrium relationships from within the system and becomes the engine of the qualitative economic change. The more readily is this power made available to the innovator, the easier it becomes for him to carry out his ideas and increase the community's range of choices. A well-developed banking system willing and able to extend credit appears, therefore, to be a top priority for developing countries.

The system of incentives is the third requirement for economic development. The act of innovation, being a non-routine action, entails a relatively high degree of risk and uncertainty about its outcome. To induce a person to innovate, he must be given sufficient incentives for the risk he takes. An effective way of providing the innovator with sufficient incentives is to assure him of his right to appropriate the gains from his innovation. Once again the importance of private property rights for successful economic development is strongly suggested. While this point is largely neglected by modern growth theorists, a number of economists with some practical experience in planning are becoming increasingly aware of it. A leading Yugoslav economist wrote:

> If one wants to expand and improve entrepreneurial activity, one cannot avoid the flow of entrepreneurial product of entrepreneurs, whoever they may be . . . one cannot negate the economic necessity that entrepreneurs be proprietors of their products . . . entrepreneurial activity . . . is merely a special kind of work which it is necessary to supply in adequate quantities and quality of production . . . entrepreneurial incomes can never be regarded as state or society incomes. . . . I would not be surprised, therefore, if somewhere in the future this will find its expression in giving enterprises property rights in their means of production.[8]

IV

The main results of our discussion can be summarised as follows:

1. The process of economic development includes both quantitative (substitution at the margin) and qualitative (new combination of resources) changes. The latter, that is, the act of innovation, is the true engine of economic development. Since the flow of innovation cannot be planned or ordered in advance, the most essential problem of economic development is the one of creating an environment conducive to innovating activities. Our finding is that the institutions of private property rights and bank credit are essential requirements for maximising the flow of potential innovations. The hypothesis to be tested is: the more

attenuated are property rights in capital goods, the less will the use of investible funds be directed towards enlarging the community's set of opportunity choices.

2. The *investment only* plans have frequently failed to improve the people's standard of living by a 'planned' rate because administrative interference with the social time preference presupposes a degree of attenuation of private property rights. This attenuation of private property rights leads, as we have seen, to a reduction in the content and extent of contractual activities in the community and prevents at least some potential innovators from acquiring the resources needed to add new alternatives to the existing set of opportunity choices. The result is that the benefits of an increase in physical output via non-voluntary savings are reduced.

3. Economic development requires both a positive rate of net investment and a flow of innovation. The ruling élite in underdeveloped countries should therefore bear in mind that an increase in the rate of investment via administrative measures (attenuation of private property rights) is likely to reduce the flow of innovation. And this may turn out to be a high price to pay indeed.

NOTES

1. S. Strumilin, 'Concerning the Problem of Optimum Proportions', *Planovoe Khozyaistve*, no. 6 (1962).
2. B. Horvat, *Towards a Theory of Planned Economy* (Belgrade: Yugoslav Institute of Economic Research, 1964) pp. 54–5, 196.
3. This argument is supported by Professors W. Baumol and M. Pauly in papers on the relationship between the private and social discount rates. See W. Baumol, 'On the Socal Rate of Discount', *American Economic Review*, LVIII (1968) 788–802, and M. Pauly, 'Risk and the Social Rate of Discount', ibid., LX (1970) 195–8.
4. This is true even in the case of government acting as an innovator. It is impossible for it to decide to have so many innovations next year. Someone has to have an idea first.
5. S. Kuznets, *Modern Economic Growth* (New Haven: Yale Univ. Press, 1966) p. 436.
6. This can mean a new source of supply, a new product or a more efficient way of producing goods.
7. See S. Pejovich, *The Market-Planned Economy of Yugoslavia* (Minneapolis: Univ. of Minnesota Press, 1966) chap. v.
8. A. Bajt, 'Property in Capital and in the Means of Production in Socialist Economies', *Journal of Law and Economics* (Apr 1968).

COMMENT

F. Taylor Ostrander

Mr Ostrander pointed out that all four papers were iconoclastic in challenging prevailing developmental concepts. Professor Kemp's exciting paper was full of truths. He had stressed that some people always saved and created new capital. However, Professor Kemp did not point out that inequality of income was usually a prerequisite to such capital formation. Egalitarian incomes would eliminate this source of capital formation.

Mr Ostrander agreed with Professor Kemp that huge projects such as the dams in Zambia and Ghana might not be conducive to as much growth in the right place as comparable sums spent (effectively) to improve Africa's agricultural and rural life. He added that in Zambia the fear that the government would take over 51 per cent control of an organisation as soon as it reached significant size also retarded growth.

He queried Professor Arkin's income ratio of 20 to 1 in mining incomes. Account had not been taken of non-cash incomes, and wage income which excluded food and lodging was hardly an adequate measure of *earnings*. The fringe benefits on European wages would not exceed 20 per cent if they bore the same ratio as in the United States; this was not sufficient to offset the difference between 20 to 1 and 10 to 1, which was the more accurate figure for a correct comparison of European and African wages in mining in South Africa.

Mr Ostrander drew attention to Professor Bauer's emphasis on the need for adequate economic incentives to which economic man would respond.

He agreed with Professor Pejovich that bureaucrats could not decide how much innovation there would be, nor were they effective in taking the risks of exploration for oil or minerals.

Chapter 5
Agriculture

Agriculture and Development

DON PAARLBERG

This presentation draws upon the experience of the writer's own country, the United States, in its efforts to promote agricultural development in various parts of the world. Some of the lessons Americans have learnt, or think they have learnt, may be of value in Southern Africa.

For any people of whom two-thirds or more obtain their living from the land, development must have a strong agricultural component. This seemingly obvious fact has often been missed; it is encouraging to see it recognised in the present volume.

Our generation, in the last half of the twentieth century, is witness to a conjunction of great historical events, each of which will bear brief elaboration:

First, we see an awakening of the underdeveloped nations after centuries of slumber.

Second, we see efforts by both the East and the West to assist these countries in economic advancement.

Third, we see a breakthrough in agricultural technology.

Fourth, we see fantastic growth in population numbers.

In Asia, in the Middle East, in Africa and in Latin America many people are making the discovery that life can mean more for their children than it has meant for them. Thanks to modern travel and communications, the people of many nations have become convinced that poverty, hunger and misery are not the universal lot of mankind nor a burden that they need permanently bear. Awareness has been increased, aspirations have been raised, hopes have been kindled, promises have been made. This is an outstanding fact of the twentieth century. It is a new dimension in our dealings with these people from this time forward.

Not only do the people in the less developed countries aspire to economic advancement; there is intense rivalry between the

East and the West in assisting these people to attain the goals to which they aspire. This rivalry springs from the fact that many governments in the less developed parts of the world, in their pursuit of economic betterment, hesitate between the free and the authoritarian route. These nations may ultimately be decisive in determining the shape of the world we are to live in.

The breakthrough in agricultural technology comes not from some single great discovery; it comes from bringing together the chemical, mechanical, biological and managerial advances into a new and productive relationship, so that the whole is greater than the sum of its parts.

The fourth great event, perhaps the most important of all, is the rapid increase in population numbers. The arithmetic is so familiar that it need not be repeated. In any long-range analysis this variable tends to eclipse all others.

PROBLEMS OF THE TWENTIETH CENTURY

To many of us, these four great new events seem to present enormous problems.

New areas have come into production to upset our export trade. Economic advancement has carried with it political and social upheavals which have disturbed relationships among the great powers. Seventy-one new countries have come into being since the Second World War. There are new faces at the conference table, new attitudes to comprehend, new power blocs with which to deal.

Helping these developing nations is unquestionably a problem, particularly when it brings into focus the controversy between East and West. Our overseas programmes have imposed heavy costs. Technical assistance, economic support, loans for economic development, gifts and grants add to a considerable sum, variously characterised, depending on the attitude, as 'give-away', 'foreign aid', 'mutual security' or 'economic development. . . .' The great food needs of these people, as measured in physical or nutritional terms, are in the orthodox economic sense not needs at all since they lack the means with which to buy.

The breakthrough in agricultural technology, the third of the current great events, has likewise been treated primarily as an unresolved and most vexing problem. Indeed, anyone who has had responsibility for dealing with its consequences finds it hard to consider the breakthrough in any other light. The growing stocks of surplus crops, the downward impact upon prices, the mounting costs of farm programmes, the painful adjustments required of our farm people, and the bitter legislative battles which both result from and cause these maladjustments – these are clear enough to any observer. In the less developed nations the new agricultural technology upsets the established way of doing things and requires institutional changes of enormous magnitude.

Population growth appears to tower above all other problems. Except in the well-to-do countries, growth rates are still fantastically high – so high that projections leave us either aghast or uncomprehending. For long years, concern about population growth was almost exclusively Malthusian in character, centred on the food problem. Now concern has spread to those with responsibility for protecting the environment, to those interested in preserving an acceptable measure of social order, and to those whose motives are with job opportunity and human dignity. The problem seems to be growing in both scope and magnitude. The religious, social and economic problems associated with the use and non-use of population planning seem to be tearing us apart.

Thus most people, approaching these great historical events in a conventional manner, find in them many grave and difficult problems. Looking at them from a traditional point of view leaves one bleak and baffled. This arises from the inclination to be problem-prone rather than opportunity-oriented.

What we need to do is to view these historic events from a conventional attitude, but with a fresh look. We need to see them not separately, but in relationship to one another. Let us try to bring such a picture into focus.

The awakening of the less developed nations, with the resulting revolution of rising expectations, is unavoidable. Anything that is unavoidable should be met with some attitude other than dismay. We of the more developed countries are interested in the revolution of rising expectations. We are interested from the standpoint of compassion; concern with less fortunate people is present, latent or active, in all of us. We are interested in a diplomatic sense; we wish to see the less developed nations achieve their goals through a free system, compatible with our own. We are interested from the standpoint of world peace; men with empty stomachs do not reason well together. We are concerned with respect to our economic interests; we have come to believe that a country does better in the company of nations that are prospering, just as a person does better if his customers are also well-to-do. We are coming to believe that poverty-stricken nations are not good trading partners, just as we have learnt that poor neighbours are not good customers.

To our generation is given the great privilege – and responsibility – of responding to the needs of the people whom we have awakened. In former times, before the advent of technology, productive capacity was dependent primarily upon physical strength and manual skill, in which endowments no one nation greatly exceeded another. So long as this condition generally prevailed, one nation could not achieve an average level of living dramatically above that of another. But with the advent of technology, one country can produce and utilise, per capita, perhaps a hundred times as much goods and services as another. All our experience indicates that these advances come unevenly, and new increments are more likely to come where substantial advances have already been made. By innovation and institution-building we have gradually learnt to equalise opportunities and to share gains on a broader and broader basis. But we are still in the early stages of learning to share these things across national borders, and across other boundaries, real or imaginary, imposed by history, fear or tradition. The dynamics of international relationships will not for ever tolerate a widening gap in a shrinking world. Envy, the green-eyed monster, is perhaps the greatest disturber of the peace. Ours is the opportunity to help develop the attitudes and the institutions that could avert the day that Edwin Markham feared: 'When whirlwinds of rebellion shake all shores!' We should be happy at having the capability to help solve this problem rather than deplore the awakening that creates it.

Which nations, the free or the centrally directed, have the greater capacity to help meet the growing aspirations of these people, who are overwhelmingly agricultural? It is the free nations. They have the best agricultural science, the broadest system of agricultural education, the system of government services best suited to meeting felt needs, the best comprehension of decentralised decision-making, which the people of the less developed countries generally prefer. The greatest needs and the greatest abilities of people in the less developed countries are in farming. There is kinship among farm people throughout the world. There is no better medium by which we can communicate with these people than through the thing they know best – agriculture. This is what Norman Borlaug demonstrated with his high-yielding wheat. The comparative advantage of the Western world for promoting economic growth in the less developed nations lies in agriculture. We should lead out from that advantage; in far too many cases we have allowed initiative to pass into other hands and have then responded to that initiative out of our weakness rather than out of strength.

This is a time for optimism about population numbers. Consider the facts: In much of the world, and for many centuries, the population was held in check by a limited supply of food. Now advancing agricultural technology lifts that limitation. At the same time, medical and social advances give promise of controlling population numbers. Ours is the first generation to dare think of effective population planning, the first generation to dare think in terms of food enough for all. The historian, writing perhaps fifty years from now, may well observe that it was precisely when the concern about population growth was at its greatest that we were beginning to move out from under the Malthusian shadow.

Only a problem-prone people could look at the historic events just described and come away depressed. What is needed is a balance of caution and hope, of prudence and compassion.

CONCLUSIONS FROM PRACTICAL EXPERIENCE

What follows is an outline of what appear to the writer as the proper components of the development effort – which is an effort to make the most of the opportunities described in the foregoing section. No claim is made to originality in the ideas set forth. The effort depicted is clearly discernible in the A.I.D. programme of the United States. It is evident also in the revised emphasis provided by the World Bank. The programme of work of the Food and Agriculture Organisation of the United Nations reflects, in part, the synthesis of the ideas to be described.

The great philanthropical foundations have in large measure pioneered these views, and the better-run multi-national agrobusiness firms reflect them. What is stated here has become the conventional wisdom. The fact that it has become conventional does not detract from its wisdom, though its appeal may be lessened for those who, like the men of Athens, spend their time 'in nothing else but either to tell, or to hear, some new thing'.

First, there would be recognition of the fact that development is broad rather than narrow. How so many people have come to accept 'economic' as the appropriate and sole modifier of the noun 'development' remains a mystery. Perhaps the economists were simply more aggressive, and staked out their claim earlier. Political development and social development are also important, as the agenda of this volume testifies.

Second, with respect to the economic component of development, there would be acknowledgement of agriculture's very strong role. A number of things have worked together, at least until recently, in underestimating the role of agriculture in the development process:

(i) The fact that economic development is associated with a diminishing proportion of people on the land, leading to the idea that to develop agriculture was to commit oneself to a declining sector of the economy.

(ii) The fact that agriculture is generally a low-status occupation, lacking appeal to indigenous or outside professionals.

The world food scare of the middle 1960s and the dramatic successes of the great foundations in Mexico and the Philippines served to correct this imbalance. Presently, in professional circles, agriculture approaches more closely its proper role in the allocation of developmental resources.

Agricultural economics provides an integrative effort, bringing together in efficient combination the inputs from genetics, plant nutrition, sanitation, engineering and the other subdivisions of agricultural sciences. The relationship between agricultural economics and the other agricultural sciences is not that of leader and follower; it is a symbiotic relationship. It is the equivalent of the relationship, in the medical field, of the general practitioner to a group of specialists. Without improvements in production techniques there is little that the economist can do; without knowledge of whether a thing should be changed there is limited value in changing it.

What are some of the things we Americans have learnt in twenty years of effort to help other countries develop agriculturally? The following are generalisations, personal judgements, that will receive less than unanimous agreement:

1. *Incentives seem to work.* We are fortunately moving away from the myth that people in the less developed countries fail to respond to incentives, or that their response is perverse. We do not need one body of economic theory for the developed nations and another for the less developed. We need a single body of good theory, which in general we have, plus the capacity to make applications in accordance with circumstances. Price incentives get results. Extension programmes seem to work when there is something useful to extend. Supervised credit seems to work when there are productive enterprises on which it can be used. It may not be possible for the less developed nations to *adopt* what has been learnt by their more advanced neighbours, but they can *adapt* these things.

2. *Research can be extremely useful if it is mission-oriented.* The Rockefeller research in Mexico is the pre-eminent example. There is little to be gained by sending overdeveloped scientists to underdeveloped countries. Some years ago Purdue University gave the Doctor's degree in Agronomy to a young Black South African; this young man's research consisted of tagging various plant nutrients with radioactive isotopes, thereby hoping to learn the chemical process by which plant tissues are laid down. He intended to undertake research along these lines in the new settlements of Black people being undertaken in South Africa. A more relevant need, it would appear, is for applications. Knowledge of the basic sciences is already at hand, researched by the nations that have the resources to do this expensive work, available to all at no cost.

3. *Planning can become an end in itself.* Some years ago this writer made a study of agricultural development plans and performance in twelve countries. In some countries development occurred in the absence of an overall plan, as in the United

States. In some cases it occurred in accordance with a central plan, as in the Soviet Union. In some countries planning has not yet produced significant development, as is true for several of the nations of this continent. In various other countries there is neither recognisable plan nor appreciable development. The wise commitment of resources to development is the decisive thing; with this, no plan is needed, and without it no plan is useful. If a plan leads to the appropriate commitment of resources it is helpful. Beware of the plan that takes on a life of its own!

4. *Private trade can help.* A common error is to think that agricultural development is exclusively a responsibility of government, and can occur only by government design. On the contrary, business investment, agricultural trade and private enterprise are potentially a mainspring of development. Private firms can sometimes accomplish things that public agencies, because of their political vulnerability, cannot undertake. On the other hand, government must sometimes establish the rules within which the private trade can helpfully function. Western countries that have a substantial private sector are severely limiting their agricultural development effort if they fail to make use of the dynamism and venturesomeness of the agrobusiness community.

5. *The relationship of institutions to agricultural development is exceedingly complex.* Sometimes development has occurred because an institution which blocked it has been removed. An example is the official policy in India that long held farm prices at a low level in order to benefit consumers. This has now been changed and development is taking place. Other institutions, still in effect, need changing if development is to occur; land-tenure arrangements in parts of Latin America are an example. In yet other cases the presence of an entrenched institution constitutes a rationale for timid people to postpone action. For example, some people incorrectly contend that no real effort at development can succeed until the education system is transformed so that all farmers become literate.

6. *Beware of the caretaker complex.* The caretaker complex is the feeling that we, out of our superior position, should 'take care' of other, less fortunate people. To the degree that our affluence contrasts with the poverty of others and therefore places a burden on the conscience, the problem is lessened by giving 'foreign aid'. The recipient is expected to applaud us for our

generosity and, out of gratitude, vote with us in the United Nations. To the surprise and amazement of many people, this gratitude fails to materialise. To the recipient, the caretaker motive is as transparent as a window-pane. But to the donor it is quite opaque, and he is the chief victim of the concealment. The caretaker complex is the antithesis of true development. True development works towards self-respect and self-reliance; the caretaker complex leads to a bond of dependency that neither donor nor recipient can break, and is therefore repulsive to both. Some years ago the then Secretary of Agriculture, Ezra Taft Benson, made a trip to Asia to review our food donation programmes. An old Pakistani villager said it all in one sentence: 'We want rice and we want respect, but we want respect first.' True compassion is the best motive from which to help others achieve development. Unfortunately there is not enough of it to go round. Enlightened self-interest, which is more abundant, is a legitimate and acceptable motive for economic aid. The caretaker complex, perhaps the most common motivation of all, is form without substance. The writer bases these statements on experience, having formerly had responsibility for the 'Food for Peace' programme in the United States, and now having responsibility for the agency which recruits the agricultural scientists who staff our overseas technical assistance programmes. An example of enlightened self-interest is American aid to Taiwan. Taiwan developed, and our aid was withdrawn. Taiwan and the United States now carry on mutually helpful trade. An example of the caretaker complex is the United States programme to assist the American Indians, a programme that has made these people continuously dependent on government help.

Helping people to help themselves is not a novelty. We have learnt how to do this in a number of sectors. We have helped people over periods of difficulty with our 'Food for Peace' programme, and then terminated the programme. We have helped initiate development programmes that became self-sustaining, so that we could withdraw. In other areas, where self-sustaining economic growth is a long way off, we continue to help and shall do so for many years to come. Unfortunately we have not been able to obtain the degree of public support for our international programmes that they deserve. We probably have not done as good an educational job with our own people as we should have done.

The problems of the international age in agriculture are difficult and complex. There is risk in each effort made. But the risks of failing to face up to this opportunity are far greater than those involved in considered action. Political explosions can result from a widening gap between the wealthy and the underdeveloped countries. The loss of freedom by the underdeveloped nations which insist upon economic progress and cannot find it within Western institutions – here is a risk that is grave indeed, both for them and for us. And to waste our capacity for abundant agricultural production, to make a problem out of what is in fact a great opportunity, this is a severe indictment. Every citizen senses that food is good and that abundance is a blessing rather than a burden. The problem has its moral as well as its economic and political aspects. The very possession of knowledge and the very capability of abundant production carry with them a responsibility to make these things useful.

This is truly the international age in agriculture. We have, in various ways, propelled agriculture into this age, largely as the result of unmanaged circumstances and without full consciousness of the possibilities and limitations of this course. The remarkable thing is that we have done as well as we have. Sharing the credit for such success as we have experienced are the government, the business community and the private citizen as well as a whole cadre of scientists, educators and administrators. These same persons bear responsibility for advancing us beyond the stage we now occupy.

The evidence indicates that the patterns emerging from the venture thus far make a great deal of sense. Having accumulated some years of experience in matching the capabilities of agriculture with the needs of the uncommitted and underdeveloped nations of the world, we are now reviewing and evaluating our experience to find in it those efforts which have been fruitful, to eliminate or improve those projects which have fallen short of the mark, and to evolve a conscious policy out of what has hitherto been a poorly understood though rather successful venture.

Agriculture was formerly a stagehand in the dramatic play titled 'Foreign Policy'. It is now a legitimate member of the cast.

Agriculture and
Economic Development
in Southern Africa

SIMON S. BRAND

The diversity of agro-ecological conditions and of types of agriculture practised in Southern Africa is such that one has to be
either very brave or very naïve to attempt a bird's-eye view of
the subject. In a paper of the specified length there is, however,
little scope for attempting much else, and I shall take the plunge,
leaving it to the reader to decide on the courage, naïveté or other
qualities revealed by the resulting effort. Be that as it may, I do
believe that it is not only useful but essential to consider from a
macro-economic perspective the context within which agriculture
is practised, provided this does not become a screen for avoiding
the micro-economic studies necessary to understand specific agricultural situations.[1]

I

When taking a bird's-eye view of the respective economic structures of the countries that make up the Southern African region,
one of the most striking characteristics is the prominent place
occupied by agriculture in terms of employment, contribution to
export earnings, and to a varying extent also in terms of aggregate output.[2] It is only in the Republic of South Africa, with
its highly diversified economy, and in Zambia, with its heavy
concentration on mining, that the share of agriculture in the gross
domestic product is as low as the 10 per cent range. Angola,
Mozambique and Rhodesia occupy intermediate positions, with
corresponding percentages of the order of 20 per cent, but in the
remaining countries (including the South African Bantu homelands considered as regional economies) the share of agriculture
varies from just below 30 per cent in Swaziland to nearly 50 per
cent in Botswana.

The share of agricultural products (including processed products) in total export earnings exceeds the agricultural share in G.D.P. in most of the countries in the region, Zambia being the striking exception with less than 5 per cent of its export earnings deriving from agriculture. In the Republic of South Africa over 20 per cent of export earnings still originate in agriculture, and the higher end of the scale is represented by Angola, Botswana, Lesotho, Malawi and Mozambique, with their corresponding percentages clustered around 80 per cent. As against this, agricultural products constitute a significant share of the imports of most countries in the region, South Africa once again being the clearest exception.

Of the total population defined as economically active in South Africa, those engaged in agriculture were down to below 30 per cent by 1970. In the other economies in the region, the corresponding percentages during recent years varied between 55 per cent in South West Africa and 69 per cent in Mozambique to upwards of 80 per cent in Botswana, Lesotho, Swaziland, Angola, Malawi and Zambia (if temporary absentees from the respective countries are excluded from their economically active populations).

With such high percentages of their labour forces still engaged in agriculture, it would appear that there is little likelihood that the respective countries will be able, within the foreseeable future, to achieve absolute deadlines in the numbers so engaged, even if they do succeed in reducing the percentages. As Dovring has pointed out in a classic article, it is only when the ratio of agricultural to non-agricultural employment has been reduced to a 50:50 level that an absolute decline in agricultural employment comes within reach, and then only if non-agricultural employment grows twice as fast as the total labour force.[3]

The conclusion that emerges, namely that increasing employment opportunities will have to be found in agriculture in the various countries of Southern Africa for some considerable time to come, is borne out by the prospects for employment opportunities that are apparent from such planning documents as are available for these countries. In South Africa, for example, the number of workers of all races employed in agriculture is projected to increase by 158,000 between 1969 and 1975,[4] while in Zambia, 'if massive unemployment is to be avoided, the rural

economy must absorb, on the average, additional workers numbering at least 25,000 per year, or a total of 250,000' during the
1970s.[5] In Lesotho the employment target set by the First Five-
Year Development Plan is expected to absorb less than three-
quarters of the increase in the male labour force,[6] in Swaziland
'the majority of the labour force will continue to depend on agriculture for their livelihood',[7] and in Botswana it is stated that 'for
the next decade, and longer, even with the maximum possible
diversification of the economy, agriculture will remain the most
important source of domestic income and employment'.[8]

This conclusion stands in sharp contrast to oft-made statements
that agricultural development in various parts of Southern Africa,
in particular in the tribal or peasant sector, will have to be preceded by an absolute reduction in agricultural employment. It is
not, however, contrary to the experience in many other less
developed parts of the world, where unemployment has become a
major social problem for reasons which were recently summed up
as follows in a survey of experiences with and prospects for the
creation of employment through agrarian reform in various
countries:

> The more dynamic sectors of the developing economies, for
> example, industry, transport and the 'modern service' sector,
> which have been favoured by development planners have cer-
> tainly increased their share of G.D.P. significantly, but have
> failed to increase their proportion of the labour force in a like
> manner. The agricultural sector with its limited growth rate
> has had to absorb a large share of the newcomers to the labour
> force, while the traditional service sector has been forced to
> take up the difference. Most indicators show that the situation
> is likely to deteriorate further unless: (1) the growth rates of
> the L.D.C.s are dramatically increased; (2) rural–urban migra-
> tion is considerably reduced (implying the creation of a larger
> number of jobs in agriculture and other rural pursuits); and/or
> (3) some 'new' alternative approach is developed.[9]

Since the first condition mentioned in this quotation could only
be met through G.D.P. growth rates which, given the prevailing
labour–output ratios in the 'dynamic' sectors, are extremely
unlikely to be achieved by most of the economies in question, it is
again obvious that agriculture will have to bear a dispropor-

tionate burden in creating employment opportunities. Although the non-agricultural sectors can be expected to carry a relatively greater share of this burden in at least some of the economies in Southern Africa than elsewhere, it would still appear to be essential that the need for creating the maximum employment opportunities in agriculture should be clearly recognised in the planning of agricultural development in the region.

II

Having noted the important place that agriculture still occupies in the various economies of Southern Africa, and in particular the employment aspect of its overall sectoral role, a second striking characteristic of agriculture in the region, with important implications for development, is its dual character. This dualism consists generally therein that in clearly demarcated parts of the various countries, White farmers operate commercial farms on a relatively large scale of operation, employing wage labour on a regular basis, and applying relatively modern techniques of production, whereas in the remaining farming areas agriculture is practised on a predominantly subsistence basis by tribal families on small plots, and with low-productive technology.

Generally speaking, the growth in agricultural output recorded in the region has been concentrated in the sector operated by White farmers, and there is even a fairly close correlation between the weight of the White-operated farming sector in the economy and the ability of the country to feed its population. In South Africa, for example, production (value added) in the tribal or traditional agricultural sector represented only some 5 per cent of agricultural production in the country as a whole around 1950, and it has been estimated that, while total agricultural production (real value added) in South Africa as a whole increased at average annual rates of roughly 4 per cent between 1950 and 1960, that part of it which originated in tribal agriculture remained virtually stagnant. Similarly, it was estimated fairly recently that the value of agricultural output by tribal farmers in Rhodesia was only about one-third of that produced by Whites,[10] and, while the predominance of the White-operated farming sector is nowhere else near the same order in relation to total (including subsistence) agricultural output as in these two countries, it does tend to dominate production for the market.

Thus in Zambia the 'line-of-rail' commercial farming sector, operated by less than a thousand White farmers, was responsible for 70 per cent of the 'gross value of output on non-African farms plus sales of African grown crops' in 1964; in Malawi the relatively small number of White-operated estates and plantations, while occupying less than 2 per cent of the total land area of the country, were responsible for over one-third of the value of agricultural exports in 1967; in Swaziland, tribal farmers contribute almost a negligible proportion of agricultural exports; and, with the exception of Lesotho, similar conditions obtain in the other countries in the region as well.[11]

To avoid an erroneous conclusion that a completely watertight distinction can be drawn between a commercialised White-operated agriculture on the one hand, and a purely subsistence-oriented tribal agriculture on the other, it should be emphasised that some degree of commercialisation of tribal agriculture, or of aspects thereof, is fairly common throughout Southern Africa. Moreover, since some degree of commercialisation would appear to be a prerequisite to raising the productivity of tribal agriculture, such instances of spontaneous commercialisation as have occurred merit close study. It so happens that the respective directions in which commercialisation has occurred in different situations in Southern Africa appear to suggest a useful hypothesis concerning the conditions that influence the commercialisation of tribal agriculture in the region. To begin with, it would appear that in those tribal agricultural economies where cultivable land is scarce relative to population, such as Botswana, Lesotho, Swaziland and most of the South African Bantu homelands, entry into the cash economy has proceeded mainly through the selling of livestock and livestock products, rather than through the selling of traditional subsistence crops or a shift of resources from subsistence production to the production of cash crops. In contrast, tribal farming in economies such as that of Mozambique, which appears to enjoy a rather more favourable land–population ratio, is characterised by a pattern consisting of subsistence farming significantly supplemented by the cultivation of one or more cash crops and the gathering of cashew nuts and copra – to the extent that the contribution to the value of all commercial crops was as high as 35 per cent in 1967, and still higher in earlier years.[12]

The hypothesis suggested by this pattern is that the factors which condition the commercialisation of tribal agriculture in Southern Africa are similar to those which, according to Myint, influenced the spectacular expansion of peasant export production in some parts of West Africa and South-east Asia. These were, on the one hand, the improvement of transport and communications systems and the establishment of commercial channels linking the peasant to world markets, and on the other, the ready availability of surplus resources above what was required to meet basic subsistence needs.[13] As in the instances cited by Myint, production for cash sales appears to have been readily entered into where this could be done without having to draw resources away from subsistence production. The dimensions assumed by the institution of migratory labour in any event suggest that the constraints on the commercialisation of tribal agriculture must not in the first place be sought in a lack of responsiveness to cash incentives. Similarly, the fact that, despite the important social functions involved in the ownership of livestock in these societies, the selling of livestock and livestock products has been one of the most general avenues of commercialisation in the region, would seem to suggest that tribal customs are not as inflexible a barrier to the commercialisation of tribal agriculture as is sometimes averred. The fact that in most of the tribal agricultural economies in Southern Africa commercial production has not expanded at rates comparable with those achieved in some West African countries must then, if the above analogy to Myint's hypothesis holds, be ascribed largely to the fact that the margin of other than human resources (especially of land) available to tribal farmers above subsistence needs has generally been much narrower in Southern than in West Africa. This would suggest that, to the extent that this margin can be widened by supplementing, and/or substituting for, the limiting resources, opportunities for the commercialisation of tribal agriculture will not only be opened up, but are likely to be met by positive responses from tribal farmers.

The remainder of this paper will be concerned, on the one hand, with a categorisation of the ways and means through which such opportunities for commercialisation of tribal farming in Southern Africa can be or are being opened up, and tribal farmers persuaded and enabled not only to utilise such opportunities, as they can be expected to do, but to utilise them in such ways as to introduce technological development into tribal agriculture as a continuing process. On the other hand, attention will be given to ways in which attainment of the employment objectives implicit in the conclusion of the previous section may be affected by the different possible approaches to the development of tribal agriculture.

The development problems of the already commercialised, or White-operated, farming sectors in the various countries, which have been dealt with in detail elsewhere,[14] and which are in many respects similar to the adjustment problems of agriculture in economically advanced countries, will be alluded to here only where necessary to shed light on the issues concerning tribal agriculture.

III

The required widening of the margin of non-human resources available in excess of basic subsistence needs, and with it the expansion of opportunities for the productive employment of labour in agriculture, can basically be approached in two ways.[15] First, attention can be given to resources already committed to agriculture, but either underutilised or inefficiently allocated. Second, the possibilities can be explored of increasing the amount of resources committed to agriculture.

Many parts of the less developed world are characterised by striking inequalities in the size distribution of agricultural land between holders, and in many instances an inverse relationship can be demonstrated between the size of holdings, on the one hand, and both labour input and agricultural output per unit of land on the other. Where this is the case, a programme of land redistribution, supported by a complementary package of measures of the kinds to be discussed below, can be expected to raise both total agricultural output and agricultural employment opportunities without adding to the total area of land used for agricultural purposes. From descriptions of the principles underlying the traditional allocation of tribal land in various parts of Southern Africa, one would assume that glaring inequalities in the distribution of tribal land are not commonly found in the region. In the case of Lesotho, for example, the size of holdings varied from below 4 to over 40 acres in 1960, but it would appear that this was to some extent related to regional variations in agro-economic conditions, and in any event holdings of 15 acres and larger constituted only 3·8 per cent of the total number of holdings. Moreover, there appears to have been no definite relationship between size of holdings and per acre yields of the main crops, while the per capita acreage actually decreased fairly sharply with increasing size of holding.[16] In such circumstances there would appear to be little scope for land redistribution, and little prospect for significant benefits in terms of either agricultural output or employment to be derived from such redistribution as could be effected.

The situation in Lesotho in this respect might not be representative of tribal areas in Southern Africa as a whole. It can be accepted, however, that in those countries where the White-operated farming sector assumes a relatively important place, not only in terms of production but also of landholding, the possibilities for land redistribution would, if only in purely physical terms, appear much more dramatic, if they encompassed not merely a redistribution between existing tribal holdings, but also the transformation of some relatively large-scale White-operated holdings into smaller, peasant-type holdings. This would apply in particular to South Africa, where the tribal farming sector in 1960 occupied only some 13 per cent of total farmland, or 17 per cent of total cultivated farmland, and in Rhodesia, where it disposes of some 53 per cent of total farmland.[17] To a lesser extent it would also apply to countries such as Swaziland, Botswana, Zambia and the Portuguese territories, but much less to Malawi, and not at all, of course, to Lesotho.

In South Africa such a process of redistribution has indeed been taking place through purchases of land to be added to the Bantu homelands in terms of the Native Lands Act of 1913 and the Native Trust and Lands Act of 1936. But the quantitative effect of this process, in terms of the overall distribution of land between the two agricultural sectors, has been modest, and will remain so within the prevailing policy framework. Elsewhere in the region, too, even where the particular political constraints on such a process that operate in South Africa do not apply, policies aimed at the markedly skew distribution of land between the White-operated and tribal farming sectors appear to have been remarkably moderate, even tentative. Thus in Botswana's

National Development Plan the explicitly mentioned objectives of tenurial reform are limited to the modernisation of tribal tenure and the development of some form of individual title for presently undeveloped State Lands; in a recent official Zambian publication on manpower planning, commercial agriculture, that is, mainly White-operated, large-sized farms, is included in the 'industrial' sector of the economy and not considered any further in discussion of rural manpower problems; and even in the case of Swaziland, where the acquisition of more land for tribal farming is mentioned among the top priorities of agricultural policy, the statement of this priority is accompanied by an assurance that the government is committed to the development of agriculture on title deed as well as Swazi Nation land.[18]

Quite apart from the political aspects, there are sound economic reasons for reacting warily to suggestions for the large-scale redistribution of land from the 'modern' to the tribal agricultural sectors in the region. Unlike the Latin American and Asian instances cited by Sternberg in support of his statement that 'size of holding and the value of output per unit of arable and agricultural land . . . are almost everywhere inversely correlated',[19] land is generally utilised much more productively in the White-operated than in the tribal agricultures of Southern Africa. By way of example, the average gross output per unit of farmland area operated by Whites in South Africa was estimated some years ago to have been more than four times that in tribal farming, and this difference is likely to be even wider today, despite the fact that the tribal areas include a higher proportion of high-potential farming land.[20] Unless it can be ensured that productivity would be maintained on redistributed land, the transfer of significant areas of land from the modern to the tribal agricultural sectors could seriously affect agricultural production in the region.

If, whether for political or economic reasons, it is accepted that such land redistribution is unlikely to supplement the resources available to tribal agriculture significantly in the foreseeable future, there remain other, potentially more mobile resources, the redistribution of which could result simultaneously in the maintenance of productivity in White-operated agriculture, the raising of productivity in tribal agriculture, and increased employment of labour in both. The single resource in respect of which this is most evidently the case is capital.

With reference to South Africa, I have argued elsewhere that during this century the White-operated farming sector has been a beneficiary of a substantial net flow of funds from other sectors of the economy in various forms, of which specialised credit institutions catering for the farming community on specially favourable terms are but one type of example.[21] Similar arrangements have favoured the commercial farming sectors in several of the other countries in the region as well, and the overall effect of such arrangements cannot have been other than to lower the cost at which farmers in the favoured sectors could gain access to capital. In combination with notions of efficiency derived from observation of agricultural practices in economically advanced countries, such as the United States, this has almost certainly resulted in higher capital–labour ratios being employed in these modern agricultural sectors than are economically appropriate, given the relatively elastic supplies of labour generally available in the region. This is reflected in a steadily rising ratio of real capital stock per worker of all races observed for the modern agricultural sector of South Africa since the end of the First World War, and in the fact that employment of labour in this sector appears to have reached a maximum at around 1960, and may even have declined somewhat since then, despite a continuing absolute increase in total agricultural employment.[22] If this diagnosis is accepted, it would follow that if some of the funds at present flowing towards the modern agricultural sector could be diverted towards development applications in tribal agriculture or other productive uses, agricultural output in the modern sector could well be maintained, and its employment-creation potential significantly enhanced, through the substitution of labour for capital in operations where this is technically feasible – provided, of course, that access to such additional labour is not prevented administratively. While I am fairly convinced of the overall applicability of this argument to South Africa, I can only speculate that it may also have some relevance to some of the other economies in the region.

Such a reallocation of capital funds towards the tribal farming sector could, of course, be an important way in which to increase the flow of various kinds of specific resources, each of which will be briefly discussed below, into tribal agriculture, thus widening the margin of resources over subsistence needs. This would apply to current inputs such as seed, fertilisers and pesticides, and to such items of investment as improved livestock, transport and storage facilities and irrigation works. It would also apply to such crucially important specific resources as extension services and training and research facilities, although in these instances a competitive relationship between the two agricultural sectors is perhaps more likely to arise.

The flow of those various kinds of specific resources into tribal agriculture could, of course, also be increased by raising the overall flow of resources, in particular of finance, into agriculture, instead of merely reallocating resources already being committed to agriculture. In South Africa, and conceivably also in one or two of the other economies in which the White-operated farming sector has occupied both a prominent and a favoured position, there would appear to be little justification for such an increased flow of funds into agriculture, and the emphasis should be on reallocation, as argued above. In the least developed economies in the region, on the other hand, the very size of the agricultural relative to other sectors of the economy severely constrains the possibilities of channelling a greater share of development funds into agriculture, while such foreign finance as becomes available tends to concentrate on mining developments. In a few countries, in particular Malawi and Lesotho, the share of development funds allocated to agriculture is already remarkably high, presumably reflecting a dearth of alternative development potentials. The emphasis in such instances must, therefore, of necessity be on increasing the availability of agricultural land.

Steps in this direction are already being taken in several of the countries in the region. In Botswana, for example, a preliminary agro-ecological map has been prepared and is being upgraded, the object being to identify areas of highest agricultural potential, and planning is in progress to bring large tracts of undeveloped State Lands into use, *inter alia* through a borehole-drilling programme; and in Mozambique the settlement of sparsely occupied regions appears to be an important element of agricultural development policy.[23]

Some such efforts at increasing the amount of agricultural land are aimed at dryland farming, but many involve irrigation schemes. Thus in Lesotho detailed plans are to be drawn up during the present planning period for 1,800 ha to be brought under irrigation, and an Irrigation Research Unit was to be established in the Ministry of Agriculture; in the tribal areas of Rhodesia both smaller and larger irrigation schemes were said recently to have contributed significantly to the apparent increase in total agricultural production during the 1960s, and plans were in hand for further major schemes; in the South African Bantu homelands 9,700 ha of irrigation land had been developed by 1969, which was said to represent only 37 per cent of the potential area suitable for irrigation in these areas; and in Botswana the apparent potential of the Okavango delta has excited the imaginations of many.[24] It is essential, however, to realise very clearly that irrigation projects can be a very expensive way of creating employment opportunities, and that before scarce resources are committed to such projects, the prospective benefits in terms of output and employment creation should be carefully weighed against alternative applications of such resources.

In sum, then, there would appear to be at least some potential in most of the countries of Southern Africa to widen the above-subsistence margin of non-human resources available to tribal agriculture, and thus to open up opportunities for commercialisation, and to increase employment opportunities in agriculture in general, by redistributing or reallocating certain resources already committed to agriculture, and/or by expanding the non-human resource base of agriculture. The actual dimensions of these potentials can, however, best be determined by intensive study in specific localities. As far as this paper is concerned, it remains to have a brief look at some of the specific kinds of measures that would be required to support the overall resource adjustments, so as to ensure that the fullest possible advantage will be taken from the opportunities thus opened up.

IV

Factors conditioning agricultural productivity and change can conveniently be classified into external factors, 'determined by government measures and other outside influences, that affect the nature of the production possibilities available to farmers, and the extent to which they have the knowledge, desire and command over resources to act upon the opportunities that exist', and proximate or farm-level factors that 'depend on the decisions and performance of individual farm operators'.[25]

As regards the last-mentioned set of factors, tribal agriculture in Southern Africa, as compared with the White-operated farming sectors, is generally characterised by a low level of managerial development and a prevailing subsistence philosophy, reflected in such derived characteristics as an absence of diversification of agricultural activities according to comparative advantage, little use of purchased inputs, a limited stock of capital often inefficiently allocated between livestock and other, more productive forms of capital, and, finally, a low level of output per unit of input.[26]

These farm-level characteristics are to a large extent conditioned by the external factors defined above, and attention will now be turned to these. In the limited space available it will, of course, only be possible to skim over the surface.

In studying the historical development of these external conditioning factors, one is struck by the extent to which the provision of agricultural extension, education, research, marketing and input provision services was all biased in favour of the White-operated farming sectors throughout the subcontinent, with only token measures typically taken in respect of tribal agriculture, usually by a separate division or sub-department. With the coming of political independence to former colonial areas, however, there has been a shift in emphasis towards tribal agriculture.

In respect of *agricultural education*, the past decade and a half has seen a significant increase in both the number and variety of institutions, and in the output of such institutions. The emphasis in this respect appears to be on schools or colleges of agriculture, providing diploma or certificate training for lower- and middle-level extension personnel, and on farmers' training centres or institutes, providing short courses for farmers. But in some instances agricultural education is extended up to university level, as with the establishment of an agricultural faculty at Fort Hare University near the Transkei, and the Swaziland Agricultural College and University Centre.

Extension services for tribal farmers in Southern Africa tended at first to concentrate, sometimes with a degree of compulsion involved, on land reclamation and conservation, but despite a general shortage of experienced and adequately trained field personnel, the emphasis appears to be shifting towards improvement of agricultural practices. The techniques used in extension programmes vary widely. In the Transkei and other South

African Bantu homelands, for example, reliance appears to be mainly on field lectures and demonstrations, supplemented by the use of the press and radio and the running of demonstration plots. Elsewhere, as in Botswana, Malawi and Rhodesia, the idea of selecting pupil farmers who are then encouraged and assisted to qualify eventually as master farmers, and who serve as demonstration nuclei from which development influences can spread to other farmers, has been used with some effect, although recently some doubt appears to have arisen as to whether this allows for the most economic use of scarce extension personnel.[27]

Agricultural research was especially affected by the differential approach towards the two agricultural sectors commonly adopted in Southern Africa. The situation is typified by the following quotation from the report of a select committee appointed in Nyasaland at the time of Federation:

> It would appear from the evidence that in the event of non-African agriculture becoming the responsibility of the Federal Government, it is the desire of the non-African farming community that the Federal Government should exercise its powers to assume responsibility for all fundamental and basic research, while the Territorial Government would carry out any necessary localised research.[28]

The effect of such differentiation in research was generally a severe neglect of localised research pertaining to tribal agriculture, rationalised in terms of the avoidance of duplication. That there are sound reasons for leaving much basic agricultural research to be carried out elsewhere cannot be denied, but it must be emphasised that intensive localised research of an applied nature is an essential element in any agricultural development programme. While localised research programmes into aspects of tribal agriculture are reported from several countries in the region, research in progress tends to be limited to seed and fertiliser trials, and it is only in some instances that concerted research efforts aimed at a much wider set of problems appear to be in progress. These must include not only research on dryland, irrigation and animal husbandry practices, but also on farm management and the development of farm machinery and implements appropriate to local socio-economic conditions.

In the *marketing* of farm produce, tribal farmers in Southern

Africa have traditionally had access to various official marketing channels which gave them some assurance of stable prices, but which, because these channels were most often established in the first place with the interests of White farmers in mind, seldom took account of the special circumstances of tribal farmers. Where such marketing channels are already in existence, as with the agricultural marketing board system in South Africa, and where they are accessible to tribal farmers, there would appear to be little reason to establish alternative marketing channels. Instead, efforts could be concentrated on supplementing such channels through the provision of services for which a special need is apparent among tribal farmers. Examples of what is intended are the provision of bulk storage facilities, grading assistance, market information and transport facilities.

Similarly, where official marketing channels have not yet been established, much can be done to serve the interests of tribal farmers simply by providing services supplementing existing private commercial channels, a good example being the government-sponsored collective shearing-sheds in the Transkei and Lesotho, where trained classers are available to assist in the preparation of the clip, and bulk lots are made up for dispatch to wool-brokers. It is not difficult to find in the farming literature the world over all kinds of disparaging remarks about private traders and the many ways in which they exploit the farmers, and these are often followed up by attempts to eliminate private traders, usually by the creation of statutory marketing bodies. It is as well to keep in mind, however, that these traders perform certain essential functions which alternative institutions, such as government marketing boards, are not necessarily in a position to perform more efficiently. As Williams remarks on the situation in Lesotho:

> A general trader is a person of many talents. He must (a) organise finance and the transport of produce and merchandise, (b) grade wool, mohair, cattle and crops, and (c) be familiar with the economics of business management, especially in pricing and bookkeeping. These talents are rarely found among the Basotho.[29]

The process of eliminating weaknesses in present marketing systems presents one kind of opportunity for the formation of *co-operative societies* among tribal farmers, which has shown quite impressive growth in most of the countries in the region during the post-Second World War period.[30] Generally speaking, it would appear that the soundest developments in this field have indeed occurred where co-operatives have acted as links in the marketing chain for agricultural products, usually as agents for principals higher up in the marketing chain. Thrift and credit, or savings and loan, associations are another form of co-operative that appears to be flourishing in terms of numbers, while in several countries co-operative societies also act as distribution points for purchased agricultural inputs, such as seed, fertilisers, pesticides, and in some instances farm implements and machinery. With few exceptions the countries in the region have adopted legislation for regulating the activities of co-operatives, but the situation as reported in Botswana's National Development Plan applies in most of the countries, viz. that while the administrative agencies created in terms of such legislation are well able to cope with the purely legal supervision over societies, training requirements cannot be met adequately. In the light of the resulting general scarcity of suitably trained and experienced personnel to run co-operative societies, it would seem advisable at this stage to limit carefully the functions that the societies are expected to perform.

The extension of *credit* to tribal farmers for the purchase of current inputs and certain items of capital equipment is an essential element in bringing about the kind of agricultural transformation that is required. However, the difficulties in doing this within the framework of traditional land tenure are considerable. Although specialised credit institutions serving agriculture used to be limited to the commercialised, large-scale farming sectors, attempts have more recently been made in several of the countries in the region to create access to credit for tribal farmers. The difficulties that are in general experienced are well summarised in a study of an experimental credit scheme set up in Botswana in 1965, financed by charitable contributions.[31] The main difficulties identified were the high cost of servicing loans, due to the small size of the average loan; the high risk factor, due to low and variable crop yields; the low level and illiquid nature of collateral security, due in part to the traditional system of land tenure; and a relatively high and increasing level of outstanding loans, due in part to unfamiliarity with the concept of credit, and in part to the narrow margin above subsistence needs available for interest on and repayment of loans. Attempts at and suggestions for overcoming some of these difficulties included limiting the loan facilities to participants in Pupil Farmers' Schemes or to individuals on larger holdings; the use of extension and demonstration personnel, co-operative officials and tribal secretaries to assess loan applications, oversee the use of loans granted and assist in the recovery of loans; and the involving of co-operative societies as collective borrowers and/or as agents for debt recovery. Obviously most of these suggestions are open to serious objections in that they tend either to prejudice the primary functions of the personnel involved or overtax their administrative abilities, or they militate against socio-economic objectives such as, in the case of Botswana, an even distribution of economic opportunities. Although there is some prospect that economies of scale may eventually reduce the costs per unit of lending, it must probably be accepted that 'the criterion of narrowly commercial recoupment of costs is not a proper one to apply at this stage' to credit schemes of this nature.[32]

Perhaps the most important conditioning factor of all, viz. *land tenure*, can only be mentioned here very briefly. In discussions of tribal agricultural development in Southern Africa, the traditional system of land tenure is invariably cited as a factor inhibiting change in both crop and livestock farming. Agricultural policies in most of the countries in the region include suggestions for tenurial reform. In Botswana, for example, the emphasis is to be on the modernisation of tribal tenure, with individuals or groups of individuals to be granted conditional grazing and watering rights over defined areas, while in the large areas of undeveloped State Land outside the traditional areas, some form of individual title is contemplated.[33] In Lesotho, although the compatibility of the traditional tenure system with rapid expansion of agricultural productivity has been officially questioned, actual efforts towards reform have been described as 'piecemeal and largely ineffective' in the face of resistance from the chieftainship.[34] In the Portuguese territories various settlement patterns are being introduced on irrigation schemes and other settlement areas; in Malawi, policy is aimed at individualisation of land use; and in the South African homelands and the Rhodesian

Tribal Trust Lands the emphasis is on adjustments in land-use patterns and rules of land allocation within the framework of an evolving traditional tenure system.[35] Whatever the individual variations in policy, there appears to be a general acceptance that a wholesale switch towards individual freehold tenure is not the panacea it has sometimes been held out to be, and that reforms introduced into tribal tenure systems should be supported by the creation of alternative institutions to take over various functions, such as social security, traditionally provided in terms of the tenure system.

An issue that is very closely related to the tenure question is that of *farm size*, and the supposed need to increase the average size of holdings as a prerequisite to the introduction of modern technology into tribal farming is often an important element in arguments for tenurial reform. The available evidence is not, however, unambiguously in favour of this supposition. Williams, for example, presents evidence that does not indicate any observable increasing returns to farm size in Lesotho,[36] and although his evidence cannot be regarded as conclusive, since similar low-level technologies were applied in all his size groups, his conclusion is supported by evidence from other parts of the world. Particularly relevant is the conclusion in a recent survey of the literature that 'the economic advantage of enlarging the size of farm seems to be primarily related to the relative price of labour and capital, and the effects of the capital inputs on output.[37] In the light of the labour-surplus situation projected for Southern Africa earlier in this paper and the mixed results with mechanisation of tribal agriculture in various parts of the region, this conclusion places a question-mark behind arguments for increasing farm size that rely on the supposed advantages of mechanisation.

There may well be other types of technological change sensitive to farm size, and essential to sustained increases in the productivity of tribal agriculture in some localities. A case in point may be the introduction of rotational crop and grazing systems which can only be planned for areas several times the size of the average tribal holding. Where this applies, the required scale of operations could be attained by the formation of large-scale company farms or plantations, as with the so-called 'project crops', Phormium tenax and tea, in some of the South African Bantu homelands.

From the viewpoint of maximising the labour input in agriculture, involving the local people in a greater diversity of roles and avoiding outright conflicts with traditional systems of land tenure, some form of communal or co-operative farming system would be a more attractive alternative way to realise potential economies of farm size. An interesting proposal in this direction, based on the tribal family or kinship group, was recently suggested as part of a development plan for agriculture in Fingoland, in the Transkei.[38] Despite its interesting possibilities, this proposal, like similar ones elsewhere, does not succeed in clarifying several crucial aspects of the working of such a system in practice, in particular the reconciliation between group interests, individual contributions and individual incentives.

V

This paper began with a brief bird's-eye view of the present functional role of agriculture in the economies of Southern Africa, which pointed to the conclusion that agriculture will in the foreseeable future have to continue to make a positive contribution to the creation of employment opportunities in the region. It went on to point out the dualistic framework within which agriculture functions in the region, and within this framework to present a qualitative appraisal of the potentials for reallocating and supplementing the non-human resources applied in agriculture, with a view to opening up possibilities for commercialisation of tribal agriculture by widening the above-subsistence margin of production, and to increasing the capacity of agriculture as a whole to provide productive employment opportunities for labour. It concluded with a very selective look at some of the specific ways in which resources allocated to tribal agriculture can be or are being applied to bring about required changes in the pattern and productivity of tribal farming in the region. It is not the kind of paper out of which firm conclusions emerge, but if at least one conclusion must be drawn, it would be that overviews of this nature can be no more than a starting-point for identifying the kinds of micro-research at a local level that are an essential prerequisite to rational policies for agricultural development.

NOTES

1. The reader must in fairness be warned that I shall use the opportunity to get some mileage out of my doctoral dissertation, which has been quietly gathering dust since it was written several years ago. Cf. 'The Contributions of Agriculture to the Economic Development of South Africa since 1910', unpublished D.Sc.Agric. dissertation (University of Pretoria, 1969).

2. The following, impressionistic summary of the statistical picture is mainly based on S. S. Brand, 'Problems of Agricultural Development in Southern Africa, with Particular Reference to the Role of Tribal Agriculture', *South African Journal of African Affairs*, 1 (1971) 74–92. However, where inconsistencies are apparent between the main statistical magnitudes reported in various sources, the data available in the fact sheet prepared for this Conference by the Africa Institute were used as a guide (Africa Institute of South Africa, *Southern Africa at a Glance*, 1972).

3. F. Dovring, 'The Share of Agriculture in a Growing Population', *Monthly Bulletin of Agricultural Economics and Statistics*, VIII (1) (Aug–Sept 1959) 1–11.

4. South Africa, Department of Planning, *Economic Development Programme for the Republic of South Africa, 1970–1975* (Pretoria: Government Printer, n.d.).

5. Zambia, Development Division, Office of the Vice-President, *Zambian Manpower* (Lusaka: Government Printer, 1969) p. 86.

6. Lesotho, Central Planning and Development Office, *First Five-year Development Plan, 1970/71–1974/75* (Maseru, 1970) p. 30.

7. Swaziland, *Post-Independence Development Plan* (Mbabane, 1969) p. 23.

8. Botswana, *National Development Plan, 1970–75* (Gaborone: Government Printer, 1970) p. 27.

9. M. J. Sternberg, 'Agrarian Reform and Employment: Potential and Problems', *International Labour Review*, CIII (5) (May 1971) 453–76, on p. 454. The 'new' approach which the author had in mind emphasises the reduction in the size of the workforce and redistribution of income.

10. Cf. Brand, 'The Contributions of Agriculture', pp. 226–30. More recently, agricultural production in South Africa as a whole has been growing at average annual rates of 4·7 per cent, but separate estimates for tribal agriculture are not available. Cf. *Economic Development Programme*, p. 52. The estimate for Rhodesia was taken from A. F. Hunt, 'Progress with Agricultural Development in the Tribal Trust Areas of Rhodesia', *Agrekon*, IX (1) (Jan 1970) 59–63, on p. 60.

11. Zambia, *Agriculture Production in Zambia, 1964* (Lusaka: Central Statistical Office, 1965); H. Dequin, *Agricultural Development in Malawi* (München: IFO-Institut für Wirtschaftsforschung, 1969) pp. 29, 198; G. M. E. Leistner and P. Smit, *Swaziland: Resources and Development* (Pretoria: Africa Institute of South Africa, 1968) chap. ix.

12. E. Missiaen, *Mozambique's Agricultural Economy in Brief* (United States Department of Agriculture, Economic Research Service, ERS-Foreign 249, Feb 1969) pp. 5–6. For the typical situation obtaining in the other group of countries mentioned, cf. J. C. Williams, 'Problems and Prospects of the Economic Development of Agriculture in Lesotho', unpublished D.Phil. dissertation (University of Natal, 1970) chap. 3.

13. H. Myint, *The Economics of the Developing Countries* (London: Hutchinson University Library, 1965) pp. 41 f.

14. Cf. J. A. Groenewald, 'The Position of South African Agriculture: A Diagnosis', *Agrekon*, x (1) (Jan 1971) 12–26.

15. Sternberg, op. cit., pp. 462–8.

16. Williams, op. cit., pp. 120, 123, 125.

17. Brand, 'The Contributions of Agriculture', p. 229; Hunt, op. cit., p. 60.

18. Botswana, op. cit., p. 29; Zambia, *Zambian Manpower*, p. 1; Swaziland, op. cit., p. 28. In Malawi, too, White land rights are guaranteed although it is government policy to buy out such land for resettlement with Malawians. Cf. Dequin, op. cit., p. 94.

19. Sternberg, op. cit., pp. 462–3.

20. Brand, 'The Contributions of Agriculture', pp. 213–14.

21. Ibid., pp. 148 f.

22. Ibid., pp. 235–40. Cf. also Groenewald, op. cit., pp. 15–16.

23. Botswana, loc. cit.; A. R. Figuiera, 'Brief Notes on Agrarian Settlement in Mozambique', *Agrekon*, ix (1) (Jan 1970) 74–6.

24. Lesotho, op. cit., p. 70; Hunt, op. cit., p. 60; J. J. S. Weidemann and D. J. G. Smith, 'Economic Planning of Farming Units in Certain South African Bantu Areas', *Agrekon*, ix (1) (Jan 1970) 35–49, on p. 36.

25. B. F. Johnston and S. T. Nielsen, 'Agricultural and Structural Transformation in a Developing Economy', *Economic Development and Cultural Change*, xiv (3) (Apr 1966) 279–301, on p. 288.

26. Cf. Brand, 'The Contributions of Agriculture', pp. 203–26, for a detailed comparison of the two argricultural sectors in South Africa.

27. These rather impressionistic accounts of agricultural education and extension, as with those on other external factors below, are based mainly on information appearing in the various country sources already referred to above. Cf., in addition, *Transkei Department of Agriculture and Forestry, Annual Report 1969–70* (mimeographed) pp. 6–8, 10.

28. Nyasaland, *Report of the Select Committee Appointed on the 8th February, 1957, to consider the Effects of non-African agriculture being included in the Concurrent Legislative List*, p. 2.

29. Williams, op. cit., p. 200.

30. For a brief survey, cf. Margaret Digby, *Agricultural Co-operation in the Commonwealth* (Oxford: Basil Blackwell, 1970). Cf. also the various country sources already cited.

31. A. Harrison, *Agricultural Credit in Botswana* (University of Reading, Department of Agricultural Economics, Development Studies No. 4, Dec 1967). Cf. also Williams, op. cit., pp. 169–81.

32. Harrison, op. cit., p. 3.

33. Botswana, op. cit., p. 29.
34. Lesotho, op. cit., p. 56; Williams, op. cit., pp. 137 f.
35. Missiaen, op. cit., p. 7; Dequin, op. cit., p. 120; J. S. Murray, 'Social Factors in the Development of Agriculture in the Bantu Areas with Special Reference to Land Tenure Systems, *Agrekon*, IX (1) (Jan 1970) 29–34; A. J. B. Hughes, 'Tribal Land Tenure an Obstacle to Progress? Special Reference to the Tribal Trust Land of Rhodesia', *South African Journal of African Affairs*, 1 (1971) 56–73.
36. Williams, op. cit., pp. 123–4.
37. K. G. Bachman and R. P. Christensen, 'The Economics of Farm Size', in H. M. Southworth and B. F. Johnston (eds), *Agricultural Development and Economic Growth* (Ithaca, N.Y.: Cornell Univ. Press, 1967) pp. 234–57.
38. H. J. Geyer, Fingoland – 'n Studie in Landboupotensiaal', unpublished D.Sc.Agric. dissertation (University of Pretoria, 1971) pp. 296–306.

A Decade of Agricultural Development in Tanzania and Kenya

HANS RUTHENBERG

Between 1965 and 1970, available estimates indicate that agricultural production in Tanzania and Kenya, measured in constant prices, increased by rates of 3·6 and 4·7 per cent respectively (see Table 5.1). Many schemes failed and many more succeeded,

TABLE 5.1 Some indicators of agricultural growth in East Africa

	G.D.P. per capita 1964	of which: Agriculture	Growth rates of agricultural production (constant prices 1964 base)	
	($U.S.)	(%)	1956–60 to 1961–5	1965–70[a]
Ethiopia	41	70	1·9	2·7
Tanzania	62	54	2·9	3·6
Kenya	87	41	4·6	4·7
Uganda	97	54	3·1	1·5
Malagasy	101	46	2·5	3·7

[a] Preliminary figures for 1970.

Sources: F. Stoces, 'Agricultural Production, Productivity and Investments in the Development Plans of East African Countries', *Agricultural Economics Bulletin for Africa* (F.A.O.), no. 11 (May 1969); U.S.D.A., *The Agricultural Situation in Africa and West Asia* (Washington, 1971).

but particular and overall development targets were not fully attained. The record is nevertheless remarkable if compared

(a) with other African countries;

(b) with the expectations of many observers in the early 1960s; and

(c) with the problems of independence and Africanisation.

Comparatively high growth rates were achieved despite the fact that the conditions for agricultural production were by no means particularly favourable. Neither country is richly endowed with natural resources. The high-potential areas in Kenya are mostly overcrowded and most of the land in Tanzania is either marginal or expensive to develop. Furthermore, the internal markets are rather limited; development had to be export-oriented in spite of unfavourable world markets. The price of sisal in 1968, for instance, was half that of 1963. Finally, both countries experienced a massive exodus of skill with outgoing Europeans and Asians. The large-farm economy, the main industry in Kenya and an important one in Tanzania, was seriously affected by political changes.

The fair success in spite of the odds is certainly to some degree due to development aid. More important were some technical innovations such as hybrid maize, rust-resistant wheat varieties, etc. But the decisive fact was the economic activity of a great number of African farmers. Their efforts indeed carried the economic growth of both countries. This, however, took place under very different policies. Both countries are therefore considered separately before some general conclusions are drawn.

AGRICULTURAL DEVELOPMENT IN TANZANIA

Tanzania's agricultural development in the early 1960s made a promising start which more than offset the decline in the sisal industry. The market sales of the principal cash crops, which are more reliable than estimates about total production, indicate the increase in supplies (see Table 5.2). Production grew in spite of the fact that many public ventures yielded only low returns.

Various types of settlement were carried out. Most conspicuous and rather expensive was the move for 'villagisation', i.e. for capital-demanding settlements on newly claimed land. Only a few of these schemes survived and even fewer showed reasonable results. Mechanised block farming in the cotton-growing areas ended after a few years with heavy losses, and the remaining tractors were sold to individuals.

Certain other measures were more effective:

(i) Expansion in sugar and tea was mainly the result of plantation investments.

(ii) Land suitable for wheat could be ploughed because the independent government was no longer tied to land-tenure rights claimed by herdsmen during the colonial period.

(iii) The government promoted and expanded some large state farming, particularly in ranching.

These measures were helpful but carried little weight in the overall picture. Most of the expansion was represented by additional supplies of cotton, coffee, cashew nuts and tobacco. These commodities originated from smallholdings which received very little support indeed. Smallholders in the tropics are often assumed to be lethargic, to prefer subsistence farming to cash cropping, and to react inversely, that is, to supply less in an improved market. Tanzania's figures indicate that these assumptions cannot be generalised. Smallholders reacted normally and in some cases with amazing speed. What were the reasons for this? In the attempt to identify the important factors, the following situations deserve emphasis:

1. The colonial agricultural administration in Tanzania in the early 1950s wasted much time in trying to prevent erosion and to promote subsistence farming. The result was negligible or outright negative. During the late 1950s the emphasis was changed. The agricultural officers and their

TABLE 5.2 Market supply of principal cash crops in Tanzania in 'ooo metric tons

	Sisal	Cotton (lint)	Coffee (clean)	Cashew nuts	Sugar	Tea	Tobacco	Wheat
1960–2								
average	206	34	24	46	32	4	3[a]	12
1966	221	78	51	82	70	7	5	33
1967	217	70	40	75	71	7	8	29
1968	194	51	51	115	81	8	7	24
1969	206	70	45	123	91	9	12	29
1970[b]	n.a.	81	54	n.a.	98	9	12	30

[a] Average 1961–5.   [b] Preliminary figures.

Source: United Republic of Tanzania, *Annual Plan 1970–71*, Table 32, p. 21; F.A.O., *Production Yearbook, 1970*.

instructors were expected to push cash cropping by 'persistent persuasion' and by organising inputs and markets. The approach of offering incentives obviously worked. A sizeable group within the farming community, particularly in coffee- and cotton-growing areas, became more and more money-conscious.

2. This tendency was helped by independence. It was Nyerere's basic idea that the cultural change which he expected to occur with independence, which obviously took place and which pronounced itself in high expectations by almost everybody, should be guided into additional cropping. TANU, equipped with the power of a political administration, was expected to be the driving force behind this. And indeed, the number of activities at the village level were numerous. Even in remote villages some kind of scheme and planning was going on. Most of the efforts led to nothing tangible or lasting. Communal gardens were established and soon neglected. Marginal land was cleared and soon reoccupied by bush. Sisal was planted far away from processing factories, etc. But it can be conjectured that the great number of events, coupled with the high expectations of the time, created an economic climate in which more and more smallholders became active, changed their valuations of leisure, risks and income, and joined the growing group of small cash-cropping rural entrepreneurs.

The pragmatic socialism of the early 1960s was apparently no hindrance to smallholder development. Socialisation in trade, industries and the large-farm sector were above all interpreted as Africanisation. Smallholders considered their command over their land and cattle as absolutely secure. Under conditions like these, the political mobilisation at the grass-roots level which was actually carried out in wide parts of Tanzania increased the number of petty 'capitalists'.

This led to a growing differentiation between areas and within the rural community. Those with somewhat more land and/or those with more drive than the others discovered their chances in more cash cropping by employing seasonal labour. Smallholder development proved to be far removed from the idea of activating the rural collectivity. Roughly one-third of the total number of farmers supply most of the cash crops, and this third is receiving roughly two-thirds of the total income.

These tendencies were unexpected and are obviously against the objectives of Nyerere's political thinking. The original idea of establishing a socialist society by socialising the urban sector and the large-farm economy first and by absorbing a relatively shrinking small-farm sector proved to be inapplicable and was discarded. *Ujamaa*, a summarising word for all kinds of communal activities, which should finally lead to communal working and living, became the key word for rural development in the late 1960s.

The first and decisive move in this direction was the introduction of obligatory co-operative trade for all major crops, including food crops. This move took place in the early 1960s. The move for co-operative production gained momentum in the late 1960s. The support for individual smallholder production via extension and loans more or less ceased. All government and TANU personnel are expected to push *ujamaa*. *Ujamaa* villages receive higher prices for their produce than individual producers, and various kinds of material supports are extended to them.

The move for *Ujamaa* is clearly meeting many difficulties:

1. Obligatory co-operative trade tends to develop heavy overheads and high trading margins. The rural scene experienced the change from a low-cost trading system run by Asian traders to a high-cost trading system run by functionaries.

2. Participation in *ujamaa* is expected to be voluntary and people in densely populated areas, where most of the cash cropping occurs, show little enthusiasm in joining. The number of existing *ujamaa* villages was small up to 1971 and the degree of communal action low in most cases.

3. Most *ujamaa* villages are in newly settled areas or in areas where shifting cultivation used to be practised, i.e. their economic weight is not high.

4. There seems to be a growing number of technical, managerial and organisational problems.

It can be assumed that the move to obligatory co-operative trade and the resulting reduction in prices to the producer have already acted as a brake to the promising start in production development.

It remains to be seen whether *ujamaa* and its economics of scale is offering long-term advantages to the national economy. In the short term it is likely to reduce incentives and to make agricultural development more expensive. By pursuing the *ujamaa* policy the government of Tanzania indicates that this step towards a strongly egalitarian rural society is considered to be better than increased rural supplies and incomes now. Tanzania is thus pursuing a policy which is the exact opposite of the general '*enrichissez-vous*' which is the driving force behind developments in Kenya.

AGRICULTURAL DEVELOPMENT IN KENYA

The conditions for agricultural development in independent Kenya were and still are very different from those in Tanzania, where most of the additional supplies came from extended plantings on marginal soils in a tropical savanna climate. The more important agricultural zones of Kenya show a temperate highland climate. Here we had the 'White Highlands' stretching over 7 million acres, including a highly developed plantation economy, wide ranching areas and an important mixed farming sector. The 'White Highlands' were surrounded by traditional subsistence areas.

The big change to this dualistic society came with the Mau Mau uprising. The response of the colonial administration to this challenge was positive and had far-reaching consequences. The Swynnerton Plan brought private ownership of land and cash cropping into the reserves. Both aspects caught on like wildfire and yielded truly astonishing results. Smallholders entered in a large scale into the production of coffee, tea, pyrethrum and dairying. Their contribution to market sales increased from about 20 per cent in 1954 to 40 per cent in 1964 and, with the land transfer by settlement, to more than 50 per cent in 1970. Political independence came when this movement was in full swing.

Two objectives stood in the foreground:

(a) Sustaining high rates of growth in production; and
(b) Africanisation of the rural economy, particularly that of the former 'White Highlands'.

Both objectives were achieved without major frictions. Agricultural production increased at high rates, although less rapidly in the late 1960s than in the earlier part of the decade (see Table 5.3). The main instruments were the following:

TABLE 5.3   Development of production for sale in Kenya
('ooo metric tons)

	Coffee	Tea	Sisal	Pyrethrum	Cotton (seed)	Maize	Rice	Wheat	Milk	Cattle ('ooo head)
1960	24	14	64	1·1	11	170	11	128	n.a.	155
1961	28	13	63	1·4	9	156	14	109	n.a.	175
1962	50	16	60	1·3	5	152	15	84	n.a.	182
1963	40	18	71	–	9	210	13	110	n.a.	162
1964	41	20	67	–	11	136	13	135	n.a.	156
1965	39	19	64	1·2	11	104	14	172	n.a.	183
1966	57	21	64	1·3	14	134	17	128	260	187
1967	48	23	57	1·3	13	249	16	162	247	216
1968	40	29	52	1·5	14	353	19	216	262	194
1969	52	36	50	1·3	17	280	23	242	234	190
1970	58	41	44	n.a.	14	206	29	205	259	n.a.

Source: *Kenya Statistical Digest*, IX 3 (Sep. 1971), Table 19 (Statistical Abstracts, Ministry of Planning, Nairobi).

Agricultural administration and extension. The efficiency of the agricultural administration is a serious problem in almost all tropical countries and Kenya offers no exception to the rule. But the guidelines of work given to the administration during the last years of the colonial administration are still widely applied. The services rendered to the smallholders are still greater in volume and more effective in approach than in most other African countries.

Tea developments. Extension according to the principle of 'persistent persuasion' and 'take it or leave it' was supplemented by contract farming for special crops. Most important is the case of supervised tea production, organised by the Kenya Tea Development Authority. This approach works remarkably well and is popular with the growers.

Irrigation developments. Most noteworthy is Kenya's approach to irrigation development. The National Irrigation

Board owns or buys the land and organises settlements under 'close supervision'. Irrigation settlers have to follow rules about good husbandry. Husbandry practices are prescribed and supervised and those settlers who do not follow them are evicted. Table 5.4 demonstrates the effectiveness of this approach.

TABLE 5.4   Irrigation development in Kenya

	1965–6	1969–70	1970–1
Area cropped (ha)	3,323	5,716	6,605
of which:			
Rice at Mwea-Tebere	2,593	3,788	4,311
Number of plotholders in all five schemes	2,163	3,369	3,807
Gross value of produce (£K'ooo)	435	785	815
Average rice yield at Mwea-Tebere	5·6	6·1	5·7
Average cotton (seed) yield at Tana (t/ha)	1·2	2·1	2·3

Source: National Irrigation Board, *Annual Report 1970–1* (Nairobi).

SETTLEMENT IN THE FORMER 'WHITE HIGHLANDS'

Settlement in the former 'White Highlands' was a political and social necessity. More than a million acres were distributed to about 33,000 families in the mid-1960s. Most observers at the time feared serious economic losses. Meanwhile, it seems evident that settlement brought net gains to the economy. Settlement areas are still facing many problems:

(i) Things do not look as tidy as they used to be in the days of large farms. Husbandry is often poor, houses decay and erosion spreads.

(ii) Loan repayment is unsatisfactory: in 1967–8 repayments reached about 50 per cent of the dues, and since then their level has been even lower. Debts accumulate.

(iii) Entrepreneurial skill and capital have moved from the ex-reserves to settlement areas, and this has affected production development in the ex-reserves.

But the economic advantages clearly outweigh the disadvantages:

(i) The change in the man/land ratio due to the settling of numerous people on relatively small holdings of 15 to 50 acres led to a very noticeable increase in farming intensity. Much more land is cultivated and more cattle are kept per unit of grazing. The gross return per unit of land is much higher than before settlement and in African large farms, while there is a reduction in purchased inputs. Extended areas changed from extensive grazing to intensive mixed cropping with maize, dairy cattle and milk, and the value added per acre increased many times.

(ii) Settlers employ many more people than large farms.

(iii) Settlement developed entrepreneurial attitudes among a sizeable proportion of the settlers. The tendency to keep dairy cattle may be taken as an indication. The dairy industry is now mainly a smallholder affair and production levels have been maintained or even increased.

(iv) Observation of the people in the settlement areas suggests that subsistence food consumption increased significantly. There is little doubt that the transfer of dairying from large farms to small farms led to much more home consumption of milk and thus to a better protein supply for rural families.

One could, of course, argue that the continuation of the European large-farm economy would have led to even higher rates of growth, but this is not a relevant question. The 'White Highlands' had to be Africanised and settlement seems to be a better choice than African large farms. What we find now is a firmly established peasantry. A noticeable indicator for this is the quality of fencing. Fences in the settlement areas seem to be what the enclosures were for England's agriculture. Fences have become a symbol of attachment to the newly acquired land.

AFRICAN LARGE FARMS

Much more problematic than the settlement seems to be the transfer of large farms to African individuals or groups. Roughly two-thirds of the remaining mixed farming areas are owned and managed by African buyers, who received generous loans from the Land Bank. The performance of these farms is a rather mixed one. About a third of these farms are run according to standards. Kenya now has a sizeable group of Africans who are in a position to manage large farms, as well as remaining European farmers.

The performance of another third, however, is very poor indeed and offers little hope for economic production. The performance of the Agricultural Development Corporation, a state-owned body, which owns and manages, partly with African staff, a sizeable number of farms in the Highlands, is much better. It should not be overlooked, however, that there are still many European farmers in Kenya. They farm roughly a third of the mixed farming areas and most of the plantations and ranches. Their developments and performances clearly show the usefulness of a gradual approach in Africanisation.

Summarising, it can certainly be said that the listed instruments were adequate to the situations and the objectives. Kenya's agricultural development in the last decade is one of the few success stories in African development and it is mainly the activity of the smallholders which is responsible for it. A development path is pursued which offers much scope for further improvement. It should not be overlooked, however, that serious problems remain:

1. Kenya's agricultural development has been very expensive. There is the problem of inertia. Agricultural services have to become much more efficient in terms of input–output relations.

2. The success in rural development seems to have led to a drastic reduction of infant mortality. Population in Kenya is reported to be growing at rates of 3.5 per cent per annum. Unemployment is already a serious problem and might reach unmanageable proportions.

3. Income disparities in Kenya are high. The high windfall gains of Africanisation went to those few individuals who were educated when independence came or who owned some starting capital. In the run for the land some individuals showed a most fortunate hand indeed. Discontent is high, particularly among the students and the numerous unemployed school-leavers. Today's Kenya seems to be socially and politically more stable than at any other time during the last decade. The widespread improvement in rural welfare is obvious. But social unrest, fed by pronounced income disparities, could show up at any time.

4. Kenya may be at the beginning of a more difficult phase of its agricultural development. External markets offer increasing difficulties and the internal market remains rather limited. Further agricultural development will largely depend on the rate of urbanisation and industrialisation. Kenya, however, is too small an economic unit for internal industrialisation.

SOME HYPOTHESES DERIVED FROM THE AGRICULTURAL DEVELOPMENT IN TANZANIA AND KENYA

In trying to generalise the experience of Tanzania and Kenya for other areas in Africa, south of the Sahara, the following hypotheses may be proposed:

1. Rural development, based on cash cropping, is likely to reduce infant mortality to such a high degree that a net gain per capita can only be sustained provided the push is a very powerful one. The danger of stagnation on a higher level or a fall back to a low-level equilibrium is very high indeed. Agricultural development must therefore be accompanied by rapid urbanisation and by family planning.

2. The success or failure of agricultural development policies does not primarily depend on a few capital-demanding schemes but on the activation of a great number of smallholders.

3. Some large-scale farming is useful under almost all conditions, but smallholder farming is generally more economic in national terms, provided inputs, innovations and markets are supplied. The competitiveness of the smallholders is based on their low opportunity costs for labour and capital, their preference for in-farm investments, provided these are rewarding, and their desire for cash. The money-consciousness in Kenya is certainly exceptionally high. But information from Tanzania, Uganda and elsewhere seems to indicate that the smallholder's interest in the cash economy can be aroused by soundly conceived and executed schemes.

4. Smallholder development is not to be confounded with the mobilisation of some rural collectivity. The rural society is not homogeneous. Farmers differ as to their drive, objectives and resources. The economics of smallholder schemes depend on a proper approach to those who may become interested, and they rarely comprise more than 30 to 50 per cent of the total number of farmers.

5. The African farmer has close ties to the land. The change from tribal ownership to individual ownership is a powerful incentive for rural development.

6. Political changes which are strongly propagated and deeply felt (Mau Mau in Kenya and independence in Tanzania) seem to be connected with rising expectations which can elicit additional efforts. The performance of smallholders is the better the more they are expected to perform.

7. Smallholder expansion depends on supplementary services which are not needed by large farms and which have to be supplied by governments. Most of the stagnation in agriculture and most of the failures in project development are not due to 'irrational' farmers but to administrative ineffectiveness or the choice of unsuitable measures for the given problem.

It is not useful to emphasise any one device. It is better to work with a strategy of smallholder development which employs various instruments. The more important ones seem to be the following:

1. Innovations, like new seeds, mineral fertiliser or new crops, should be spread by agricultural extension services which work on the principle of 'take it or leave it'. The Ministries of Agriculture face increasing difficulties in organising these services within their administration. Autonomous agencies are probably better choice.

2. Special crops or demanding activities like dairying are often suited to contract farming as developed by the Kenya Tea Development Authority. Nobody is pressed into participation, but those who want to earn cash have to follow husbandry rules.

3. Wherever high investments per unit of land are undertaken, as in irrigation development, and where settlers are

attached to the land, production should be organised according to the principles of 'production under close supervision'.

4. Company farming is the best choice wherever large farms are more economic than smallholders, and these companies may be state-owned wherever private large-scale farming is politically not feasible. Group or co-operative large farms are facing many managerial difficulties and are not competitive.

The establishment of a dualistic rural society is an effective method for agricultural growth in the initial stages of development. The large-farm sector introduces innovations, infrastructure and markets more efficiently than any administration. Its performance is furthermore likely to act as a challenge for the great number of smallholders. Large farms lose, however, in relative advantage with increasing cultural change within the small-farm community. If – as in Kenya – the dualistic society is discarded and people in crowded reserves gain access to developed land, then the initiative of the smallholders may be very powerful indeed. If, however, the dualistic society is continued indefinitely, then smallholder areas are likely to turn into subsistence living and labour-supplying districts, with the danger of becoming rural slums.

BIBLIOGRAPHY

Blume, H., *Organisational Aspects of Agro-Industrial Development Agencies* (München: Afrika-Studien Nr. 58 des IFO-Institutes, 1971).
Giglioli, E. G., 'Staff Organisation and Tenant Discipline on an Irrigated Land Settlement', *East African Agricultural and Forestry Journal*, no. 3 (1965).
Golkowsky, R., *Bewässerungslandwirtschaft in Kenya, Darstellung grundsätzlicher Zusammenhänge am Beispiel des Mwea Irrigation Settlement* (München: Afrika-Studien Nr. 39 des IFO-Institutes, 1969).
Heyer, J. U., *An Investigation of the Limits on Peasant Agricultural Production: Case Studies from Machakos and Kericho Districts of Kenya* (University College, Nairobi, 1965).
Ruthenberg, H., *Agricultural Development in Tanganyika* (Berlin: Afrika-Studien Nr. 2 des IFO-Institutes, 1964).
Ruthenberg, H., *African Agricultural Production Development Policy in Kenya, 1952–1965* (Berlin: Afrika-Studien Nr. 10 des IFO-Institutes, 1966).

Ruthenberg, H., 'Zusammenhänge zwischen Produktion und Markt in der Landwirtschaft der Entwicklungsländer, dargestellt an Beobachtungen in Ostafrika', in *Landwirtschaftliche Markforschung in Deutschland* (München, 1967).

Ruthenberg, H., 'Some Characteristics of Smallholder Farming in Tanzania', in H. Ruthenberg (ed.), *Smallholder Farming and Smallholder Development in Tanzania* (München: Afrika-Studien Nr. 24 des IFO-Institutes, 1968).

Scheffler, W., 'Tobacco Schemes in the Central Region: Production under Close Supervision', in Ruthenberg (1968).

COMMENTS

L. L. Sebe and S. B. Ngcobo

Mr Sebe said that it was clear from the papers that in the broad field of development in Southern Africa agriculture must for the foreseeable future receive priority attention. Other aspects of development were important, but the economy of emergent Africa would depend on agriculture for many years to come.

While there had been a breakthrough in agricultural technology which had made increased food production possible, there had at the same time been a fantastic growth in population. Thus in Kenya the success in rural development based on cash cropping had led to a population explosion, as Professor Ruthenberg had indicated. There was a need, therefore, to be more outspoken on the subject of family planning. More information was needed among the illiterate peoples who suffered most from overpopulation.

It was of interest to note that experience in Kenya indicated that, while some large-scale farming was useful, smallholder farming was generally more economic in national terms. It was also important to note from Professor Ruthenberg's paper that the smallholder's interest in the cash economy could be aroused by soundly conceived and executed schemes. The smallholder had a great role to play in African agriculture, and incentives, extension programmes and supervised credit had to be geared to his needs. These subjects should have received greater attention in the papers presented.

Mr Sebe referred to what had been described as the caretaker complex, which, he said, could also be described as a patron complex, in view of the patronising attitudes of the caretaker. This complex was probably disappearing, but it was good that Professor Paarlberg should have mentioned it. The people of Africa were not unmindful of the help received from those who wished them well. But a patronising attitude had not always engendered a grateful response.

He wished to comment briefly on the questions of irrigation, tractor ploughing and co-operatives, which had been mentioned in the papers, but not extensively. There were great opportunities in these three fields for accelerated agricultural development and spectacular increases in production. Kenya's approach to irrigation development, as referred to in Professor Ruthenberg's paper, was of special interest, because, while there was so much potential in irrigation, so few irrigation projects were an unqualified success. Proper selection of settlers and discipline seemed to be essential for success.

Mechanised agriculture was a subject of great interest to African peasant farmers, but government-sponsored projects in this connection in many African countries had not been very successful, as indicated in Professor Ruthenberg's paper. This was unfortunate, and it was hoped that the answers to the problems involved could be found.

Mr Sebe pointed out that the question of co-operatives had received scant attention in the papers presented. This might mean that there was some disillusionment regarding co-operatives. Production depended to a large extent on agricultural credit facilities being available, as well as on marketing organisations. He felt that co-operatives could supply both, and he asked therefore whether they should not rate high in an accelerated development programme. Referring to the *ujamaa* movement, he said that he hoped the obligatory co-operative trade and the reduction in producer prices involved in that movement would not sound the death knell for the co-operative movement generally in Africa.

Professor Ngcobo questioned whether the situation was indeed as rosy as depicted in Professor Paarlberg's paper. In this connection he drew attention to the following points:

(a) The possibility of increasing prosperity was remote for many African countries, particularly since many Africans dismissed fears of overpopulation as a 'neo-colonial myth', and consequently, where demographic growth exceeded the growth rate of the economy, employment opportunities were reduced.

(b) While agricultural technology had indeed developed remarkably in the United States, parallel developments had not occurred in capital-poor countries. The inhibiting factors had to be borne in mind.

(c) Attempts by the United States aid programmes to transfer this new technology to other countries had certainly made no significant impact on Southern Africa, except in White agricultural areas.

(d) While Eastern and Western countries certainly competed in aid, recipient countries were influenced much less by the type of rule in the donor countries than by the form of aid and the conditions attached to aid (project versus programme loans, tied versus untied aid, interest-bearing versus interest-free loans). To some extent many countries receiving aid had thus to undergo an agonising process of decision.

In agreement with Professor Paarlberg, he noted that African farmers did respond to price and wage incentives, given the right incentives (this was a point common to all three papers), and that assistance from the private sector in developing subsistence agriculture was essential. In Rhodesia, for instance, it was now recognised that government agencies were not adequate to initiate, supervise and control programmes, but required private assistance. This aspect was still in the experimental stage.

On Professor Ruthenberg's paper, Professor Ngcobo said that the value of this empirical research was enhanced by the fact that it had been carried out in Kenya and Tanzania, two countries in the forefront of the argument about the relative priority of agricultural or industrial development. He doubted Professor Ruthenberg's assertion that individual land tenure was the most successful incentive for agricultural progress; in Lesotho the World Bank was recently shown a most successful agricultural scheme based on consolidating individual farms on a voluntary basis, the resulting farm being worked jointly, not as a co-operative, but under overall supervision. He was surprised to hear of the success of African smallholdings on the Kenyan 'White Highlands'. This development in Kenya's agriculture was in contrast to that in Zambia where a more or less similar take-over of White cultivated lands had also taken place.*

* After the initial setback to agricultural production in formerly White cultivated lands along Zambia's line of rail, steps have been taken to step up production. Firstly, the government of Zambia has itself taken over the derelict White farms for ranching and crop production. Secondly, the Anglo-American Corporation has embarked on a big farming venture by buying up a large block of farms with a view to increasing production. This is an illustration of the complementary efforts of the state and private enterprise. [Footnote subsequently submitted by Professor Ngcobo.]

Professor Ngcobo commended Professor Brand's paper as more relevant to African agricultural problems in South Africa itself than in other areas. He pointed out that the problem of trying to commercialise tribal farming areas was being faced by Rhodesia and South Africa. As far as South Africa was concerned, it had been clear from the Tomlinson Commission's report many years ago that difficulties in estimating the economic size of farms in different types of areas were severe, as also were the problems of uprooting and unemployment necessitated by the introduction of economic farming units. The income that African peasant farmers could make with better land use and farming methods was a useful guideline.

Chapter 6
Social, Cultural and Religious Factors

Some Aspects of African Society Influencing Development

ANNA F. STEYN

1. INTRODUCTION

When looking at the process of accelerated development in general, it becomes clear that the development of the economic sector of society is a high-priority objective of every modernising society and has been accordingly emphasised in the discussions at this Conference. Economic development, however, is not an isolated process and is accompanied by considerable changes in the social structure of the societies in which it is taking place. As a matter of fact, changes in social structure are not only a corollary of economic development, but certain changes in the structure of traditional society are essential if viable economic growth is to be effected and maintained.

Sociologists refer to these processes of social change necessary for economic development as the process of modernisation, as Lerner (in Miner, 1969, p. 21) states very aptly: 'Modernisation . . . is the social process of which development is the economic component. If economic development produces "rising output per head", then modernisation produces the societal environment in which rising productivity is effectively incorporated.'

Modernisation can therefore, in accordance with Moore (1963), p. 89), be briefly described as an all-embracing process where total transformation of traditional societies is effected, leading to the behavioural patterns and societal environment in which rising productivity and sustained economic growth are effectively incorporated and maintained.

As far as economic growth is concerned, one could state in broad and general terms that it entails a movement away from subsistence living towards commercial production of commodities (Moore, 1965). To bring about this commercial production of commodities it is essential that the technology of traditional society be changed from the prevailing simple techniques of production to a technology based on the application of scientific knowledge and the fabrication of raw materials into products by primarily mechanical means dependent on inanimate sources of power, thus leading to the process of industrialisation. In fact industrialisation appears to be a major and essential requirement for substantial economic growth.

The social structure sustaining industrialisation and economic growth entails the following:

(a) DIFFERENTIATION OF ECONOMIC ACTIVITIES

The structure of traditional society is characterised by the fact that it is structurally undifferentiated. The economic sector centring around subsistence farming is not differentiated from other activities of life and is deeply embedded in the extended kinship system. Production as well as other supplementary industry is located within the extended kinship units, and division of labour is slight, mainly between the sexes. Exchange and consumption is also determined by and deeply embedded in the normative structure of the kinship group and village life.

In contrast with this structurally undifferentiated nature of traditional society, the societies with advanced economic development are characterised by a high degree of structural differentiation, which entails the development of structures and organisations providing in a specialised way for the functional exigencies of society.

For economic development to take place it is imperative that in the first instance structural differentiation should take place with regard to economic activities. This differentiation of economic activities is actually a threefold process, and entails the following (Cilliers, 1969, p. 6):

(i) The development of labour as a differentiated function in the sense that a clear-cut difference develops between work and the other life activities of a person.

(ii) The development of a system of differentiated organisations within which the economic activities can be performed independently of the kinship system. This requires the rationalisation of organisation and the creation of concrete systems of action and decision-making designed for the attainment of specific and limited goals (Moore, 1965, p. 23).

(iii) Differentiation within the labour function itself in the sense of the development of specialised work roles through an increase in the division of labour. This increase in division of labour brings about an increased demand for skilled labour as well as highly trained professionals. One type of occupational role which is of special importance in the process of economic growth is that of the entrepreneur. This type of innovative leadership is emphasised as being of critical importance as a change agent in the process of economic development. Entrepreneurship does not appear automatically – it is the product of a large number of complex forces. It is noteworthy that one of the peculiar features of many traditional peasant and tribal societies is that their kinship–community–religious complex of institutions offers serious obstacles to the effective appearance of entrepreneurs.

(b) URBANISATION

The development of a differentiated, skilled industrial and professional labour force has an important impact on the ecological arrangements of society, in that it leads to a movement away from agricultural centres to urban centres. One could, in fact, state without hesitation that the formation of population concentration centres has decided advantages for economic development. Unfortunately, this population shift and ecological redistribution does not always proceed smoothly, with the result that strains can develop at quite a number of points which could easily lead to serious social disturbances. One of the gravest problems which could, and in fact does, arise in this migration to the city is caused whenever and wherever urban populations increase faster than employment opportunities and facilities such as housing, water supplies and sewerage. Such an inundation of great urban centres by people who have no work there – leading to a rootless mass of urban unemployed – can easily lead to a very explosive situation. Lerner (Miner, 1969, p. 24) says in this connection:

The point that must be stressed in referring to this suffering mass of humanity displaced from the rural areas to the filthy peripheries of the great cities, is that few of them experience the 'transition' from agricultural to urban-industrial labour. They languish on the urban periphery without entering into any productive relationship with its industrial operations. . . . These are the displaced persons, the D.P.s, of the developmental process as it now typically occurs in most of the world, a human flotsam and jetsam that has been displaced from traditional agricultural life without being incorporated into modern industrial life.

(c) AGRICULTURE

The process of structural differentiation of economic activities does not only lead to the development of an industrial and professional labour force within the urban centres, but also affects the development of the subsistence agricultural sector. Industry and a differentiated labour force employ persons whose labour is not applied directly to the land, and this is only possible with an agricultural system capable of producing a surplus of food, unless elaborate international trade is involved.

Industrialisation therefore involves on the one hand the transfer of many workers from food production into manufacturing and services, but on the other hand requires a complete reorganisation of the agricultural subsistence sector which actually involves very deep and thoroughgoing changes. The crucial change to be brought about is that subsistence agriculture must be changed from a traditional way of life with a characteristic social organisation into a specific occupation with emphasis on production for a market economy. This most often involves the following two aspects, viz. (i) increasing functional differentiation within the agricultural undertaking with concomitant specialisation and role specification, and (ii) the beginning of an increasing variety of organisations directed to attending to the needs and interests of agriculture. These, however, also require the willingness to co-operate with these organisations on the part of farmers.

(d) MOTIVATION

Although the differentiation of economic activities in general and the development of a sufficiently differentiated skilled labour force in particular is of the utmost importance for economic development, this differentiation alone will not suffice to bring about economic development. Another very important aspect which has to be taken into consideration is the motivation of the workers who have to participate in this differentiated labour force. Economic development will only take place if the development of a sufficiently differentiated and skilled labour force goes hand in hand with the development of an adequately motivated and committed labour force in the agricultural as well as in the industrial sectors.

As far as the agricultural sector is concerned, it can be pointed out that the changing of agriculture, which is in traditional society a basic way of life, into a specialised occupation, is one of the most difficult aspects of modernisation, because the existing motivations and commitments are deeply rooted in the organisation of a religiously entrenched traditional society.

As far as the skilled and professional occupations are concerned it is often found that the prospective workers are neither strongly motivated to undergo the technical and specialised training for highly skilled and professional work, nor are they heavily committed to the new pursuits expected of them in industrial society.

This is indeed a grave problem in the process of occupational differentiation and eventual economic development. The main problem in this connection is that the worker is committed to a specific value system in traditional society which to a large extent determines and motivates his economic activities. For the worker to become an adequately motivated and committed worker in a specialised labour force would entail the acceptance of and becoming committed to a completely new value system. This is perhaps the most difficult aspect of modernisation to accomplish, because deeply engrained values change very slowly, and this very often involves a change in basic personality structure.

To summarise these personality changes briefly, one could say that in contrast with traditional man who shows a passive and fatalistic orientation towards his environment and to life's difficulties as a result of his value system, which is entrenched in the traditional religious system, modern man is one who believes that man can learn to dominate his environment to a substantial degree, in order to advance his own purposes and goals, rather than being dominated entirely by that environment (Inkeles, in Weiner, 1966, p. 143).

Some of the most important value orientations to be inculcated in man to make economic development possible, are: (i) an achievement orientation in contrast with the ascription orientation of traditional man; (ii) a strong commitment to mobility through which resources are freed from traditional bonds and restraints, so that one could use them in the most appropriate and effective and rational way to reach one's economic ends (Moore, 1965); and (iii) a belief in economic rationality with a problem-solving, innovative orientation on the basis of universalistic principles.

(*e*) INFLUENCE ON THE OTHER SECTORS OF SOCIETY

The process of differentiation of economic activities, together with the change in basic value orientation which is necessary for economic development, has an important influence on all the other sectors of society and in fact necessitates change in most of these other sectors:

1. *Stratification.* One of the most important features of traditional society that has to be changed for economic development to take place is that of the ascribed status system where primacy is given to kinship position. The values of the traditional status system are directly adversative to those necessary for economic development, that is, achievement, mobility and rationality. The status system will in principle have to be changed to an open stratification system, where status is primarily based on achievement.

2. *Kinship.* The extended kinship system is also affected in so far as removing the economic activities from the kinship nexus means that the family will lose some of its previous functions, becoming a more specialised agency. The family thus ceases to be an economic unit of production and the activities within the family become more concentrated on emotional gratification and socialisation. As a result, structural isolation of the nuclear family takes place, making kinship relations permissive rather than obligatory.

   Because social and geographical mobility is much easier to attain in the structurally isolated nuclear family than in the extended kinship system, the development of the nuclear family facilitates economic development.

3. *Education.* The differentiation and specialisation in the labour function, demanding various levels of technical skills and professionalisation, lead to a strong emphasis on schools and other agencies of education, thus facilitating the structural differentiation of the educational system.

In addition to the task of training for new skills to meet the demands of the differentiated labour force, the educational system has the task of reshaping values. As Moore (1965, p. 90) points out, the task of education in this connection is to encourage a rational problem-solving habit of mind rather than an unquestioning acceptance or explanation in terms of non-rational categories. The aim of modernised child-rearing must be to produce highly educated, self-directed, flexible and resourceful men and women, who seem to be best suited to the modern requirements of individual mobility in a continuously changing system.

4. *Change in religion.* The development of any new value system in a society will have some effect on the existent value system of that society – relating to it in some ways and changing it in other ways. The development of a system of rational economic values also affects traditional religion in that these values of rationality in the other institutional spheres are no longer legitimated by religious beliefs. In so far as such rationalities replace religious sanctions in these spheres, secularisation occurs.

The secularisation of religious values does not mean, however, that religious values become obsolete. All life's problems could not be handled through rational considerations alone, and some form of religious orientation survives even in highly secularised societies (Moore, 1965).

In a modern society it is often found that a process of differentiation takes place in the sphere of values and that religion, ideology and science develop adjacently and unconnected to each other.

Considering the importance of a sustaining social structure in economic development, it is clear that, when planning for economic development, the social structure of the particular region or population group should be taken into consideration and a detailed analysis made of those aspects of the social structure which could lead to the failure of the developmental programme and of those which could contribute to its successful application. Developmental programmes should thus also entail planning for bringing about favourable social conditions or utilising existing social conditions for the acceptance of the programme.

2. ASPECTS OF AFRICAN SOCIETY

When surveying the various population groups in South Africa, the population growth rates of these various groups, as well as their economic position in the South African economy, one is struck by the necessity as well as the urgency of modernisation and accelerated development for some of them.

The economy of South Africa could be described as a *dualistic economy* in the sense that it is an economic system in which a modernised industrial economy and a subsistence economy, characterised by a traditional and primitive agriculture, low income and lack of capital and technical abilities, exist and function side by side.

When taking into consideration that it is especially the economic life of the African section of the population which is mainly on a subsistence and/or low income level; that this section is characterised by a lack of technical skill; that the Africans form the largest proportion of the total population of South Africa (1960 census: 68·3 per cent) with an extremely high population growth rate, it is obvious that the modernisation and economic development of this population group should be a matter of very high priority.

In this paper the focus will therefore be directed to the problem of the modernisation of the African population group. The structure of present-day African society will be analysed with an attempt to indicate, on the one hand, those aspects in the social structure and social life of the Africans which could facilitate and promote the process of modernisation, and on the other hand, also to discuss those aspects in their social set-up which are obstacles in the way of their modernisation.

Unfortunately very little research has been done in the field of sociology or any related discipline with specifically this type of analysis in mind, i.e. an assessment of the social structure of present-day African society in terms of the degree of modernisation and an evaluation of their evolving behavioural patterns in terms of the way these facilitate or obstruct their development.

For the purpose of this paper I shall have to rely to a large extent on a number of unrelated studies in various disciplines in which different aspects of the social structure of present-day African society are analysed. An attempt will be made to interpret the results of this research in terms of the conceptual scheme with regard to modernisation which was set out in the introductory part of this paper.

When studying the structure of present-day African society, one is immediately struck by its considerable complexity. The structure of this society no longer represents what could be typified as a traditional social system. Seeing that social changes in varying degree have already taken place, one is confronted with a number of different groupings with complex patterns of social behaviour at various stages of modernisation, and it is actually extremely difficult to piece together diverse findings of researchers to get an overall picture of African society in its various stages of development within South Africa. To get an overall picture of African society, a procedure which suggests itself is to divide the population broadly into groups at various stages of development and then to look at each of these groups separately.

From an ecological point of view the African population can be divided into three such groups, namely the Africans living in the so-called homelands (approximately 40 per cent of the population), the Africans living on the farms of the Whites where they are employed as farm labourers (29·4 per cent), and the Africans living in the urban areas, comprising approximately 31·6 per cent of the total African population. Of those living in the cities two separate groups can be distinguished, namely the migratory labourers who have no permanent residence in the urban areas, and the urbanised Africans who have a permanent residence there and who look on the city as their real home.

For the purpose of this paper, the Africans working on the farms of the Whites will not be taken into consideration and the analysis will be limited to some of the behavioural patterns of the Africans living in the homelands, the migratory labourer and the Africans with permanent residence in the cities.

(a) THE AFRICANS IN THE HOMELANDS

The first population group of interest here is the group engaged in agriculture, who constitute the majority of economically active persons in the homelands (an estimated 916,000 persons in 1960). In the Transkei, for example, it was calculated that for 1960 more or less 84.5 per cent of the working males found a means of livelihood in the agricultural sector (Stadler, 1967, p. 170).

The agriculture in the communal Bantu tribal areas is mainly on a traditional subsistence level with concomitant soil neglect, erosion, poverty of soil and decrease in production which has led to a condition of economic stagnation.

It is, for example, interesting to note that although the gross geographic product of the homelands doubled over the period from 1936 to 1960, that of the Republic increased sixfold, with the result that the share of the homelands in the gross domestic product of South Africa decreased from 6 per cent in 1936 to 2.3 per cent in 1959–60 (Smit, 1969, p. 26). In 1969–70 the gross geographic product of the economically active persons in the homelands was about R160 million, which represented less than 2 per cent of the gross domestic product of the Republic of South Africa.

This is disproportionally low if one takes into consideration that large parts of the homelands are situated in the most fertile and productive parts of the country. It is calculated, on the basis of rainfall and climate, that 100 morgen of land in the homelands have on the average the potential of 147 morgen of land in the White areas (Grobler, 1970, p. 3). The calculated production potential of about R617 per morgen in these areas has, however, never been realised, and statistics show that in 1961 the actual production was only a third of this potential.

The development and modernisation of the agricultural sector of the homelands have become an urgent necessity, because the total economic development of an area is only possible when the agricultural output is in harmony with the physical resources, climate and soil. If the agricultural potential of the homelands is not realised, it could be detrimental for the total economy of the country (Grobler, 1970, p. 4).

Except for the purchase of land and reclamation of soil, no plan of development and no development principles were devised in the first half of this century. It was only as late as 1952 that a purposeful and positive overhead policy was formulated, and a commission of enquiry was appointed to investigate the possibilities for the social and economic development of these areas.

In an attempt to realise the overhead plan for agricultural development, the government has taken positive steps in developing an infrastructure and the natural resources which could promote agricultural development. Thus, for example, 25,521 miles of road had been built, 619 bridges, 4,707 dams, 7,400 boreholes had been sunk and about 23,500 morgen had been put under irrigation up to 1965.

Although the government could do a great deal to assist agricultural development by drawing up plans and creating circumstances and physical environments conducive to development, it is in the last instance the extent to which the individuals in the population can be reached, and will accept all the innovations and be motivated to change their way of living, which will determine the final success of plans for agricultural development.

In order to reach the individuals, an extensive scheme of agricultural extension services has been developed, and the extension officers working with the Africans are themselves Africans, who have undergone intensive training at one of a number of agricultural training centres to qualify them for this work.

The questions which interest us here from a sociological point of view are the extent to which these development plans and programmes have been applied successfully; whether the agricultural population has accepted the innovations and improvements brought to them by the agricultural programmes; and which sociological factors have played a role in the acceptance or rejection of these plans.

When one considers the relative decrease in the share of the homelands in the gross domestic product, it seems as if little progress has been made in this connection. The gross domestic product, however, does not tell us much about the human factor in agricultural development, the degree to which people have accepted or rejected innovations, and the reasons for it.

Unfortunately, studies evaluating and analysing the success of agricultural programmes in South Africa are extremely limited in number and scope, and in making an assessment of the situation I have had to be guided by a few unrelated studies which were conducted among limited numbers of the African population. Apart from that, only one of these was in the field of sociology, where a thorough sociological analysis was made of the failures and successes of two developmental programmes in Lesotho (Wallman, 1969). The other two studies were in the field of agricultural science (Weideman, 1969; Lilley, 1967), in which attempts were made to assess the social and cultural factors playing a role in the acceptance of innovations.

The overall picture one gets from these studies is a negative one, pointing to the fact that there is a large degree of resistance, unwillingness and direct opposition to development programmes. From the discussion in these studies it is clear that the resistance and opposition to these changes can be attributed to a large extent to the traditional way of thinking and to behavioural patterns which are so deeply engrained in the Africans that they find it completely impossible to accept innovation, especially if these innovations are incompatible with the traditional cultural patterns.

Unfortunately there are quite a few aspects of modernised agricultural production methods which are not compatible with the basic cultural values and social organisation, thus forming major barriers to overcome if accelerated development is to take place. The following aspects of the traditional culture and social organisation contribute to the rejection of innovation and agricultural development:

Firstly, agriculture is for the African a way of life and is intimately bound up with the rest of his culture, a culture which is tenaciously ensnared in the belief and perpetual fear of supernatural forces. Lilley (1967) points out in this connection that the behaviour of the Amansimakwe is determined by a perpetual fear of spirits, sorcerers and evil-doers, who, they believe, command power over the elements and material things. Their only safeguard against this evil is their absolute adherence to customs.

This trait has become so engrained that to this very day rationality may be found to succumb to custom. As a result of this they rely on magic and appeal to their spiritual ancestors rather than on science to overcome their difficulties. This state of affairs is rather general among the rural African, and impedes development greatly.

A second very important factor hindering the process of development is the nature of their social organisation and institutional life. Apart from the fact that agriculture is strongly embedded in the traditional religion, it is also very strongly embedded in their basic social organisation and extended kinship system. The livestock and cattle of the African male, for example, are closely tied up with his social ranking and the cohesiveness of family ties.

Furthermore, the African agronomy must be regarded as a communal or semi-communal effort rather than an individual one, and it ties in very closely with the pattern of authority in the community. Fundamentally this is the position to this day. The individual is merely a member of a group and his behaviour is determined by group norms on a prescriptive basis, rather than by personal drive or initiative. There are no rewards for sons who show initiative in the economic field: such persons could, on the contrary, easily be accused of witchcraft. Under these circumstances it is of course very difficult to show any initiative or change in the direction of modernisation, and where a person takes initiative he is sanctioned and strong group pressures are brought to bear on him to enforce conformity.

The system of land tenure is a third obstacle to agricultural development. The traditional Bantu see land tenure as the fundamental right of a community member to participate in a reasonable share of the community's land and the natural resources thereof. A person therefore does not 'own' the land in the true sense of the word, but the right to till the land is bestowed on him as long as he needs it. This right is hereditary through the male line. Pastures are used communally for the grazing of cattle and for obtaining other necessities.

Furthermore, the soil is looked upon as the home of the ancestral spirits, who play an active and important role in the daily life of the African. In this system of land tenure, land is not at all alienable or transferable and it does not provide for the commercialisaton of land and land rights. It further leads to fragmentation and subdivision of land, which in itself adversely influences agricultural production in the long run.

A change in the system of land tenure therefore seems to be required to enable the Bantu to move in the direction of modernisation. This, however, is a difficult problem as the whole system, apart from the fact that it is deeply embedded in their religion, also gives a feeling of security to the African.

Although the resistance to the acceptance of the agricultural programmes can largely be attributed to the existing values and social organisation of the rural Bantu, these factors are not the only ones playing a role in the failure of agricultural development.

Such failure could also be due to the wrong application of administrative techniques and a wrong line of action on the part of the extension officers in their approach to the rural people. Wallman, in her work *Take out Hunger*, makes an excellent analysis of the mistakes which were made in the administration of two developmental programmes in Lesotho, in that important traditions were not taken into consideration, and in that the plan of action was based on false assumptions as to the nature of the people. The results were mistakes in the approach to the people to be reached and a breakdown in communication.

These problems confronting the staff of a developmental programme need not be insurmountable. This is illustrated by the fact that one of the projects discussed by Wallman (Farmech mechanisation scheme) became successful after a change of administration and a change of procedure had been effected. There has in fact been a growing awareness during the past two decades of the human factor in the successful application of agricultural development programmes. To illustrate this point, it can be pointed out that apart from basic courses in agronomy and animal husbandry, the training of extension officers also includes courses in administration and planning of extension work, where a great deal of attention is paid to the role of cultural factors in human behaviour and factors influencing the acceptance of innovations.

From the facts presented above one could easily come to the conclusion that the reaction to the agricultural programmes in question had been totally negative, with little prospect for modernisation and development of the rural population in the homelands – let alone accelerated development. In studying the available material, however, one comes across indications that these development programmes have not been totally without effect.

In the first instance, it can be pointed out that although not accepted in their totality, some aspects of agricultural innovations have been accepted. The diversity of summer crops, for example, has been accepted to a statistically significant level, as shown in a study by Board (1964, p. 48).

Secondly, Weideman (1969, p. 215) also points out that there is a section of the Bantu community, be it ever so small, who are striving for betterment. They are the 'dissenters' and the 'Samurai' who are working within the communities and propagating the development programmes. They are to a large extent the professional people like teachers, clerks and extension officers through whom change could be effected in the long run.

Another category of people who are breaking away from the traditional way of life and have become motivated to accept the idea of producing a surplus and moving into the money economy (and thus to accept some of the basic principles of development) are those people who were given a chance to break away from the traditional pattern of farming within the context of the kinship group. These are the farmers on the irrigation schemes, where, as Weideman points out, an average of 95 per cent of the farmers preferred to stay on. This high percentage, according to him, shows that development as planned by the government on these irrigation schemes coincides with the wishes, needs and abilities of the farmers, and that they have accepted the development plans despite the restrictions placed on them by the traditional kinship groupings.

Apart from the slight though positive signs of acceptance of innovations, the question that really interests us here from the sociological point of view is whether any changes have taken place with regard to the social structure and value system of the rural African, which could in due course facilitate accelerated development. It has already been pointed out that the rejection of the innovations was due to a great extent to the value system and existing social structure and social processes. This could easily give the impression that no changes have taken place in the social structure, which would not be quite correct.

It must be pointed out that the great majority of the African population of South Africa – urban as well as rural – has had some contact or other with the cultural system of the Western world, and in actual fact very few groups could be found, even in the remotest regions, who have not been influenced by this contact in one way or another. As a matter of fact, quite a number of changes have taken place which leave the social structure more susceptible to the possibilities of development. In pointing out a few of these changes, it must, however, be borne in mind that these did not take place among all parts of the population to an equal extent, and that some groups within the population are more positively oriented towards change than are others.

One result of this cultural contact has been that structural differentiation has taken place to some extent, in that education and religion (especially Christianity) have been differentiated from the extended kinship system and are given recognition as separate social structures with positive social functions in the homelands.

The reactions of the African to this cultural contact in general, and to the development of these differentiated structures in particular, have shown great variation. One study in which these differences are clearly shown is that of Mayer (1971a). He shows (p. 23) that two distinct groups can be identified among the rural Xhosa, namely the 'Reds' and the 'Schools', each with their own distinct way of life and value system, and both being mutually exclusive reference groups.

The ways of life of these groups are to a great extent determined by their willingness to accept the Western influence. The Red Xhosa are the conservative people who still prefer the traditional ways of life, and refuse to be influenced by the cultural contacts they are having with the Whites, looking down on the so-called School section of the population. The School people, on the other hand, are the products of missionary activity and schooling (p. 4), holding up Christianity, literacy and other Western ways as ideals, in their turn looking down on the uncivilised ways of the Reds.

As far as schooling as a differentiated structure is concerned, Mayer points out (p. 27) that it would be wrong to typify the Reds as illiterate and the Schools as educated. The difference between them in this respect lies more in their attitude towards schooling. The Reds are in essence opposed to education and keep their children's schooling strictly limited. They make concessions by sending one or two children to school, because it is useful to have a literate person around the house. The majority of the children in the Red group, however, never go to school. The Schools, on the other hand, have a much more positive attitude towards education – an attitude of 'the higher the better'. For them it is a matter of prestige and a way of life to attend school.

This pronounced cleavage between the Reds and the Schools is not found among the Africans in all the homelands. Pauw, for example (1960, p. 7), did not find this sharp division and he states in this connection:

> The school is an institution fully accepted and desired by all in Taung. Although many children do not attend school, one is not aware of any cleavages between 'school people' and those who do not send their children to school, as has been observed in other areas. On the whole there would be little difference between the way of life in the homes of those who go to school and those who do not. Most households have, or have had, connexions with the schools.

A positive orientation to formal education is an important factor which could be conducive to development and which could be utilised constructively for accelerated development. The acceptance of schools and Christianity among large sections of the African population is not the only change to have taken place which in the long run could be conducive to development.

As far as religion is concerned, the same difference is found as was found in the case of formal education. For the Red section the pagan religion with its ancestor cult is still centrally important, while the School people are predominantly Christianised (Mayer, 1971*a*, p. 29). The implications of religion for development will be discussed at the end of this paper where religion for the total population, rural as well as urban, will be examined.

Although the basic social organisation of the people in agriculture centres mainly around the kinship group in which primary social control is still very effective, and although people still abide by the principle of the traditional patriarchal ideals (Mayer, 1971*a*, p. 23), quite a great deal of change is also taking place in this sector of society. Kinship is slowly becoming less important than it used to be and there is an increasing breakdown in such customs as those related to mate selection, sexual relations and strength of kinship ties (Mayer, 1971a, p. 37; Pauw, 1960, p. 5; Ralushai, pp. 6, 29). This breakdown in norms and consequent breakdown in control could be advantageous for development in the sense that people will be more readily allowed to accept innovations which could lead to accelerated development in the rural areas. On the other hand, when changes are too rapid a situation of anomie might develop which could be detrimental to change.

One last important change that is taking place in the rural social organisation, which might be important for accelerated development, is that the rural population have become much more money-conscious and have actually started to move in the direction of a money economy. Money has become important to them, not only in providing for everyday necessities, but also in providing for some of their needs concerning basic traditional activities. This money-consciousness unfortunately is not tied up with improved farm practices conducive to development in the sense that farming is defined as an occupation which produces for markets on a profit basis, and through which the required money is obtained.

The way in which the rural people provide for their money needs and thus tie in with the money economy is through a system of migratory labour in which the wages earned in the urban areas are used to provide for their needs in the traditional set-up. Labour migration contributes greatly to a rise in the income of homelands. Smit (1969, p. 26) points out in this connection that the per capita gross geographic product of the homeland population in 1959–60 was approximately R25, but when the wages of migratory labourers are added, this figure rises to R53.

It is important to note the way in which migratory labour as a social system has been incorporated in the traditional social system. It is to a large extent expected of the young men to go to the cities to earn some money. If a young man does not do so, he is not socially acceptable (Ralushai, pp. 11–14; Reader, 1961, p. 59). Going to work in the city is even tied up with initiation, and Reader (1961, p. 58) says in this connection: 'Johannesburg is the city to which young Bantu go almost ritually to "change clothes" after circumcision. Its strange big-city ways symbolise the dramatic change from adolescence to manhood, and the money and "know-how" with which the worker returns are a tangible sign of his new status.'

The next question to be considered is, thus, how the phenomenon of migrant labour influences development.

(b) THE MIGRATORY LABOURER

During the 1960 census it was found that apart from the Africans who were in actual fact present in the homelands, a further estimated 651,000 persons who actually regarded the homelands as their normal home were temporarily absent from these. Of these, 594,000 were males, representing 11·9 per cent of all African males in the Republic, and more than 25 per cent of all males regarding the homelands as their permanent residence. These people are the migrant labourers, working on a temporary basis outside the homelands. It has been found that they quite often stay for many years in town without making the city their permanent and final place of residence. It is interesting to note that the highest rate of temporary absence from the homeland is to be found in the age group 25–29 years, and that this rate decreases progressively in the higher age groups. This decrease is especially marked after the age of 40. This means that a major portion of the African men are away from the homelands during their most productive years. It also implies that though they might work for quite a number of years in the city, a large number of them return permanently to the homelands when they reach a more advanced age.

The needs motivating the African to take up work in the urban areas are still to a large degree defined by their traditional culture and traditional way of life, and, as was pointed out in the previous section, migratory labour has even taken on a positive social function within the traditional social structure and in this way is to some extent integrated in the traditional social system.

Through this system of migratory labour the individual worker is nevertheless placed in a completely new environment, which in most areas is an urban one in which he is confronted by a differentiated labour market. The question arises whether contacts and the urban way of life have an influence on the migratory labourers, leading to a change in values and behavioural patterns which could lead to modernisation in the long run.

It is common knowledge that the process of urbanisation is looked upon as of prime importance for modernisation. Leistner (1970, p. 44) says in this connection:

> The following is the gist of what the writer learned from a senior agronomist whom he met in December 1968. This man ... argued that a fundamental change in peasants' outlook comes about only when their environment is changed. His own dealings with German farmers have led him to believe that all extension work, advisory services, demonstrations, etc., is more or less love's labour lost for as long as those at which these efforts are directed are not directly touched by urban and industrial living conditions.

According to this view, migratory labour, in as far as it is directed towards urban areas, should contribute a great deal in facilitating development. Research results show, however, that this is not unequivocally the case, and that the Africans react in varying ways to the urban environment. Some of them even attempt to exclude the influence of the city environment and new way of life deliberately and consciously from their behavioural patterns.

Mayer (1971a) came to some important conclusions with regard to the reactions of the migrant Xhosa to the urban environment. His findings might not be representative of the process of urbanisation among all the ethnic groups in South Africa, but evidence from other studies suggests that the same tendencies shown by the Xhosa are also present among some of the other ethnic groups, and Mitchell (in Holleman *et al.*, 1964, p. 40) says in this connection: 'The sort of closed networks Professor Mayer describes for his incapsulated migrants are probably to be found in all towns.' The findings of Mayer could therefore have implications in a much wider context.

This study by Mayer shows very clearly that a high proportion of the Xhosa going to East London never become urbanised. This is not necessarily due to the fact that their stay in town is short. On the contrary, they often remain country-rooted[1] through long years of almost continuous residence in town and after a whole working life spent in East London such a person will go 'home' to his own place.

In isolating the factors which make for different patterns of rootedness, it became clear that the division of 'red' and 'school' played an extremely important role in the extent to which the Xhosa became town-rooted or not, and that especially among the Reds the so-called home-boy groups play a very important role in the conservation of the traditional way of life. From the social organisation and social networks of the Red migrants in town, it appears that the Reds wish to remain bound by traditional structures and are guided by the principles of keeping the country relations intact, of avoiding new ties, especially with non-Red people, and of showing solidarity with the rest of the 'home-people' in town.

These networks seem to be very close-knit and to consist for an individual Red of people who are all related to him or bound to him by personal ties, often existing since boyhood, and exerting strong social control to keep him to the traditional way of life, thus *incapsulating* him within the home-boy group. Mayer (1971*a*, p. 133) says in this connection: 'The master plan of incapsulation, then, means that the highest value is put on roles either belonging to the country home or derived from the country home. The incapsulated migrant must, at the same time, play certain roles in town at large, but those which take him outside the circle of his *amakhaya* and his Red mates are performed mainly in a passive spirit, without positive ambition.'

These closely knit networks of the home-rooted Africans, incapsulating them in the traditional way of life and ruling out the possibility of change, can lay serious obstacles in the way of development. If one considers Mayer's estimate that about one-third to a half of the *whole* male population of East London is Red, one can fully appreciate the seriousness of this obstacle to modernisation.

The situation is, however, different as far as the 'School' migrants are concerned, and it is found that their social organisation in town seems to reflect a willingness to accept diversified new ideas and structures. In the School migrant's choice of associates he does not emphasise the paramountcy of home ties as such and he tends to build up new networks in town which have little connection with the old network in the country. This whole situation results in a more open type of network which allows for the choosing of different individuals or sets of friends for his different purposes, thus leading to great diversity, which carries within itself its own dynamics of change in the migrant situation and which could facilitate modernisation in the long run.

Adaption to work. The nature and influence of social networks constitute but one of the aspects of the migrant situation affecting modernisation. One other very important aspect which is of prime importance for development is the adaptation of the worker to the new work situation. In this connection two questions arise, namely in the first instance the selection and training of the worker for industrial work, and secondly the motivation of the worker to become a committed industrial worker.

The first question, namely that of the placement and training of the workers in such a way as to provide the optimum productivity, considering the fact of their low educational level and lack of technical skills, is of great importance for accelerated development. One method of placement of the totally unskilled and often illiterate worker would be a procedure of trial and error. This procedure, however, has disadvantages in that low production may be unduly prolonged, because of transfer or even dismissal of the person if placed wrongly. Poor placement may thus also lead to a higher turnover rate as well as to impaired human relations which could in the long run affect productivity adversely. More accurate selection and better placement, on the other hand, could lead to job satisfaction with subsequent reduction in labour turnover and absenteeism and reduction of accidents, and in this way loss of time and production can be avoided.

This problem of placement of the worker with no skills and a low degree of literacy has been rather acute in various branches of industry and mining in South Africa, and a great deal of research has been done to find a solution for this problem. Special mention must be made of the tremendous contribution of the National Institute for Personnel Research in this respect.

After making a thorough study of all the jobs performed by Africans – skilled and unskilled – the N.I.P.R. team developed batteries of tests (which were recently revised) for the selection of workers and leaders. These tests have been used successfully by an increasing number of gold mines, and lately the bigger industries in South Africa have also started using them. On the whole these tests facilitate the placement of workers and consequently produce an early adaptation to the job.

In most of the industries, and especially in the mining industry, the workers, after having been selected, undergo intensive training before they start work. A great deal of research has also gone into developing successful training programmes for the various industries. This training adds to the cost aspect of production but contributes greatly to closing the gap between the level of ability and the skilled level of the job, leading to maximum productivity with the labour resources at hand.

In this way the research done in the field of selection and training and the work done in this connection within the mines and major industries contribute tremendously to accelerated development and the development of a differentiated labour force. Selection and training of the worker is an expensive process, and if there should be a high labour turnover, it could mean a great loss to the concerns which invested in it. A stable and committed labour force is therefore of great importance not only for the industries concerned, but also for the problem of accelerated development in general. This brings us to the second question in connection with the problem of adaptation of the migrant labourers to the work situation, and that is whether and to what extent they have become a committed labour force.

Although some research has been done on the motivation and commitment of the migrant African worker, this field is still virtually unexplored. Available research on this topic shows that not all the Africans react similarly to the urban work situation and become equally committed industrial workers. One factor influencing the nature of the commitment of the migrant worker, especially the traditionally oriented worker, is that of the social networks to which he belongs. Mayer (1971a, pp. 133, 142–6), for example, shows that the process of incapsulation influences commitment to industrial work adversely, in that the Red man incapsulated by his home-boy group does not really become a deeply committed worker in the industrial economy – his basic attitude being that he must learn to keep a job, but he need not value the job as highly as he values his homestead. In spite of this lack of commitment the Red man has certain characteristics which help him to be a successful employee, while the School man, in spite of his superior education, may actually be at a disadvantage in comparison with the Red man.

Basically the Reds are against frequent changing of jobs,

regarding it as undignified and unmanly, and believe that it might lead to displeasing the spirits. This attitude leads, according to Mayer, to a high degree of work stability among the Reds. In spite of this work stability among the Reds, however, which actually could promote the development of a modernised orientation, one still finds that their positive economic ambitions remain formulated in terms of the rural system. Mayer (1971a, p. 146) says in this connection: 'The participation in the large scale economy as a worker, is after all the simultaneous discharge of a more valued rural role, as provider.' This phenomenon of the migrant worker who remains essentially part of a subsistence economy, with his work in the city subsidiary to this, is rather widespread among migrant labourers.

Not all research results, though, point to a pattern of work stability of the traditionally oriented migrant worker. Research done by Glass (in Holleman *et al.*, 1964, p. 66) shows that apart from the fact that this group of workers is not committed to the work situation, they do not show a pattern of work stability either. This pattern of work instability together with non-commitment as found by Glass could be even more detrimental to accelerated development than the pattern of work stability and non-commitment as found by Mayer.

Glass and Mayer also differ with regard to their conclusions on the influence of migratory labour on the traditional way of life at the rural end. According to Mayer, the attitude of the migrant labourers leads to the fact that no far-reaching changes in economic outlook are induced at the rural end. As far as the Red migrant is concerned he does not appear significantly more money-minded nor does he conduct his homestead affairs in a more businesslike way. It seems as if their aspirations continue to run along the conventional lines. The occasional ex-migrants who have developed some business acumen, or a more rational approach to farming, are but isolated cases. Seen this way, the traditionally oriented African workers who remain committed to the subsistence economy and to their traditional way of life do not contribute much to the process of development. Glass (in Holleman *et al.*, 1964, p. 83), on the contrary, is more optimistic about the possibilities of development entailed by this situation. She points out that in spite of the fact that the African migrant workers do not change their fundamental attitude towards their traditional way of life, they still acquire new habits, new attitudes and insights, new skills, and develop new material wants. In the process of receiving recognition for their own capacities and achievements, and by being held responsible for their own actions, they discover the idea of individuality. These changes lead to the fact that even though they revert to their old ways when back in the traditional environment, a dualism has been established in the sense that they also find it possible to shift freely from one set of attitudes to the other. Looking at migratory labour and especially at those migrants who remain traditionally oriented from this angle, it seems that although they return to traditional ways, some underlying changes have taken place which could be interpreted as a positive factor in the process of development in the long run. Research results, however, are inconclusive in this respect.

As has been pointed out earlier in the discussion, not all migrants are incapsulated by traditionally oriented groups, and quite a considerable percentage of them do eventually succeed in breaking away from the traditional environment and become gradually more urban-oriented.

In research done on the motivation of the industrial worker, no differences are apparent between the permanent residents of the cities and the migrants who have moved in the direction of an urban-oriented way of life (Holleman *et al.*, 1964, p. 65). The motivation and commitments of the city-oriented migrant or ex-migrant will therefore be examined in the next section on the urban Africans.

Considering the aspects treated above, this section on migratory labour(ers) can be concluded by saying that a system of migratory labour which to a large extent leads to the formation of traditionally oriented groups incapsulating the labourer, at least retards the possibility of change and can be a serious obstacle in the way of development. The rural migrant coming to work in the city to earn money for fulfilling traditional obligations at his rural home might be a satisfactory compromise between the traditional and modern system during the first stages of development, but this does not provide a final solution, because for accelerated development a skilled, committed labour force is needed.

One alternative which could serve as a solution for this problem is the development of decentralised industrial areas and growth points adjacent to or inside homelands, which is at the moment a high-priority objective in South Africa, and which could also be seen as an attempt to solve the problem of the internationally recognised problem of over-concentration of population in fast-growing industrial centres. In these urban industrial areas the problem of migratory labour could perhaps be eliminated, which could lead to a more permanent and more stable and committed labour force in the long run. These areas are, however, of recent development and very little research has been completed which could give an insight into the nature of social structures and processes developing in them, and the way in which these structures relate to development.

Some contract research done by the N.I.P.R. in a few industrial concerns situated in the border areas points to the fact that there were no particular problems with regard to absenteeism or labour turnover among the Africans, and that a stable labour force was developing within these industries. In fact the labour turnover and absenteeism rate were higher in industries in an urban area studied by them at that time. To interpret these findings is rather difficult, and much more research is needed before one can come to final conclusions in this connection.

One last factor which could be mentioned in this connection is that these border industries and the industrial development of the homelands could be of great value in the general economic development of the homelands. It is already a well-known fact that the immediate spheres of influence of highly industrialised and commercialised metropolitan areas experience a relatively high rate of economic growth in an area of expansion. In this way the developing border industrial centres could through their radiating influence contribute directly to the economic growth of the homelands in the hinterland.

(c) THE URBANISED BANTU

Apart from the two previously discussed population groups, that is, the rural Africans in the homelands and the African migratory labourers, there is a third population group which should be considered as far as the problem of accelerated development is concerned. This group is composed of those Africans who are to an increasing extent becoming an urbanised group. In 1936 only 17·3 per cent of the Africans were living in urban areas, while 31·6 per cent were living in urban areas during the 1960 census, and it can be expected that the figures for the 1970 census will show an even higher percentage. Although a large proportion of the urban Africans still have ties with the rural homelands, the major proportion of them regard the city as their place of permanent residence and have to some extent become integrated with the new way of life as demanded by urban surroundings. An indication of this tendency is given by Glass, who applied an urban–rural scale to a section of the population in an urban township and came to the conclusion that 35 per cent were completely urban, 42 per cent had urban preferences, 29 per cent were uncommitted or rurally oriented and 10 per cent completely rural (in Holleman *et al.*, 1964, p. 63).

As the town-rooted African – to use Mayer's terminology – is not a negligible minority of the total African population, the degree to which this group has moved in the direction of modernisation is of prime importance for accelerated development. The main question to be answered in connection with this permanent urban population with a basically urban orientation and preference is whether changes have taken place in their basic social structure, leading to behavioural patterns which could facilitate accelerated development.

Structural differentiation. When making a study of the urban African society, it is quite clear that in the process of contact with a developed industrial economy, and adaptation to a dynamic urban way of life, the structure of African society has undergone significant changes.

One of the most important of these is the fact that a structurally differentiated society is evolving, which is one of the necessary requirements, from a sociological point of view, for economic development. The Africans in the city have completely moved away from a subsistence agricultural economy to a money economy based on work done in the economic sector differentiated from the primary kinship system. This differentiated economic system did not evolve from within the African community itself, but was actually effected by the fact that the Africans moved into and had to adapt themselves to an already developed economy in the urban areas. The fact that this differentiation has taken place, however, is in principle important for economic development.

Apart from this differentiation of labour from the kinship system, economic development also requires differentiation within the labour function itself in the sense of development of specialised skilled and professional work roles and an increase in division of labour. When looking at this differentiation of the labour function itself, it is clear that there are factors which could retard economic development. According to the 1960 census figures, the occupational distribution of the male African population was as shown in Table 6.1.

TABLE 6.1 Occupational distribution of male African population, 1960

	%	
1. Professional, technical and related	0·753	(23,000)
2. Administrative, executive and management worker	0·18	(5,458)
3. Clerical worker	0·6	(18,276)
4. Sales worker	0·84	(25,572)
5. Agricultural worker	42·02	(1,282,300)
6. Transport and communication	2·07	(63,174)
7. Services, sport and recreation	7·07	(215,989)
8. Craftsman, production worker	2·4	(73,000)
9. Labourer	37·9	(1,156,097)

A breakdown of this last category in terms of industrial grouping shows:

	%
Mining	43·46
Industry	21·91
Construction work	12·63
Commerce	8·19
Transport	4·47
Services	4·92

Looking at these figures, it is clear that to some extent diversification has already taken place and that a small percentage of the African population has moved into skilled and professional work categories. It is, however, noticeable that, apart from the agricultural workers, the largest percentage of the workers, viz. 37·9 per cent fall within the category of labourers.

The shortage of skilled workers and a surplus of unskilled workers is one of the main problems confronting a developing society, and it is clear that this is a problem the urban African labour force has to contend with. The selection and training of the unskilled worker needs special attention and, as has been pointed out in the section on the migratory labourer, pioneering research has been done in this connection.

These tests and training programmes were not solely constructed for use among the migratory labourer, but have found wide application in a number of industries and have been adapted to the needs of particular industries. This research thus contributed a great deal to the upgrading of the unskilled worker and to closing the gap between the level of ability and the skilled level of the job.

The contribution made by this type of basic research could be looked upon as absolutely indispensable for development, especially in a period of transition. In the long run, however, it will not suffice in promoting accelerated development, and the need for higher education will, to an increasing extent, become a matter of urgency. The situation with regard to the role of higher education in development will, however, be discussed in the next chapter, although it is very relevant at this stage. An important aspect which could be pointed out in this context is that education for skilled and professional work should go hand in hand with the provision of sufficient job opportunities at the high-skill levels. Otherwise it could lead to strain and dissatisfaction which could have a detrimental influence on economic development.

Apart from the selection and training for industrial work, the motivation and commitment of the African to industrial work is also of prime importance for accelerated development. During the past two decades important research has been undertaken by the N.I.P.R.[2] in this connection. Although this field of study is extremely wide and complex and a number of methodological problems still remain to be solved, the results nevertheless enable one to determine a few important trends with regard to the nature of motivation and commitment of the urban African industrial worker.

Some of the trends which seem to emerge and which could be of great significance for development are the following (Vorster, 1970, p. 62):

1. Turnover rates and absenteeism rates of the African worker are found to be highly comparable with those in highly industrialised communities.

2. As far as attitudes are concerned, the African worker requires substantially the same satisfactions and the same attention as the comparable categories of labourers in Britain and the United States (Glass, in Holleman *et al.*, 1964, p. 66). Basically, thus, the motivation and positive attitudes and aspirations of the African industrial worker are determined by his working conditions, wages, good supervision, the work burden and sympathetic management (Vorster, 1970, pp. 60, 61).

   If, therefore, the work conditions are favourable, the motivation and commitment of the African worker are positive and compare well with other Western groups. Management in mines and industries is becoming increasingly aware of this fact, and is to an increasing extent attending to the problem of creating favourable working conditions for the African labourer. The research done by the N.I.P.R. on a contract basis for several industries could, for example, be taken as an indication of their concern in this connection. This interest on the part of management in the motivation of the African worker, and the research done in this connection, can in the long run contribute greatly to the development of a committed labour force and thus to accelerated development.

3. Whereas the first two trends could be interpreted positively in terms of development, this is not the case as far as career aspirations are concerned. Vorster (1970, pp. 60, 61) points out in this connection that the African industrial worker does not seem to be at a stage where he thinks in terms of a career, neither when first taking a job, nor when changing jobs. He says in this connection: 'There seemed to be no strong desire on their own behalf for occupational advancement. Even in the middle-class group the need for "self-actualisation" was not expressed in personal terms.'

Although this positive career orientation, which is highly desirable for economic development, is largely absent as far as the African industrial worker is concerned, one finds a more positive attitude towards occupational advancement as far as their aspirations for their children are concerned. The research results in this connection show that the great majority of the tribal-oriented migrant workers, the urban working class and the urban middle class wanted their children to enjoy secondary education and achieve professional qualifications (Vorster, 1970, p. 61). Whether this could be realised at this stage of development is an open question, but at least the attitudes are favourable for occupational advancement.

Social stratification. Apart from these slow processes of differentiation and diversification within the economic sector, other changes are also taking place within the urban African society. On the one hand, these changes are a result of changes within the economic sector, but on the other, these changes are necessary if economic growth is to be maintained in the urban areas.

An area where social changes are highly desirable if a diversified economy with motivation on an achievement basis and with concomitant occupational aspirations is to develop, is the status system of traditional society. This status system, based on ascription with primacy of kinship position, is directly adversative to the systemic needs of mobility, rationality and achievement of a developed economy. The status system will in principle have to be changed to an open stratification system where status is primarily based on achievement.

The questions arising in this context are, then, whether changes in the stratification structure have taken place, and if so in what direction. One should also try to determine whether these changes would be positive for economic development or not.

When examining the nature of the developing social status system within the urban areas, the answer to the first question is in the affirmative. Quite a number of changes have taken place with regard to the status system and there is a movement away from the ascriptive–kinship type of social stratification. What exactly the stratification system will finally be like is difficult to say at this stage because we are clearly, in this context, confronted with a situation of transition which is still very fluid. Added to this is the fact that there is a dearth of research in this field, and that the research that has been done is inconclusive with regard to the total stratification system within the urban areas. There are, however, indications that the status system developing in the African urban society is typically that of class differentiation based on the principle of achievement and more specifically educational and occupational achievement (Hall, 1967).

In her study of urban social class, Hall distinguished two classes on the basis of occupational achievement, viz. a middle class and a working class. Brandel-Syrier, however, in her study of social mobility in an African community on the Reef (1971), points out that a distinction between only two classes in urban African society reflects more the European national point of view. From the African national point of view much finer distinctions could be made, and even more distinctions could be made from the African local point of view. These different classes are not necessarily comparable with the European social class structure. The term 'middle class', for example, has no meaning in terms of association and social interaction with the European middle class, and it is not meant to have such a meaning (Brandel-Syrier, p. 28). Because of these problems of comparison she prefers the term *élite*, and in her use of this term she refers exclusively to social position in the prestige structure of a particular social structure.

Brandel-Syrier finds in her study specific changes in the African society which have been producing and supporting an élite group together with a certain amount of status anxiety. This élite group, however, has not as yet developed a clearly defined status, nor do they have a traditionally recognised status.

The creation of a new status system is a slow and painstaking process. In Reeftown, too, the élite group is slow in evolving, and has to overcome a great number of obstacles in the process. Brandel-Syrier (p. 61) comments as follows:

But for the educated and well to do who desired to distinguish themselves from the ordinary Reeftowners by more Western patterns of social intercourse and hospitality it was difficult to find new bases for personal relationships and for the creation of an integrated and life-enhancing social existence. While individually the people seemed to be emerging rapidly from previous habits, beliefs and values, socially the rise of new ways of social interaction and the formation of new group loyalties were painfully slow.

In Reeftown the most important factor in achieving status was found to be that of education, while income was far less important. As far as occupations are concerned, however, the same non-commitment and lack of personal involvement to specific careers, which was pointed out by Vorster, was found, in this study as well.

In spite of this non-commitment to a specific career, the striving to reach the top still remained. The continuous changing of careers Brandel-Syrier partly ascribes to a lack of knowledge of what was involved in a specific profession and a lack of experience concerning the requirements of the modern world.

The developing élite group is composed of a relatively small percentage of the community. A high percentage of African men have a slight education and do unskilled and semi-skilled work, and consequently fall within the lower strata. In spite of the small numbers of the élite, however, they were widely known and talked about and in general recognised as the social leaders by the other residents of the township. They were in fact conspicuous by virtue of the functional significance of their jobs and their spare-time activities (Brandel-Syrier, p. 97).

This awareness of class and the important functions of the upper class found in Reeftown were also found in other studies, for example in Kuper's (1965) study, executed in Durban. One new development among the Reeftown élite group, was, however, threatening to diminish the wide acceptance of this group. This development was the rise of a social exclusiveness and aloofness which led to the shirking of social responsibility by the top people. This development is completely contrary to important values and convictions of the community, thus leading to antagonism from sections within the community.

An attempt to make generalisations as to the nature of the evolving social stratification system of the urban Africans on the basis of one or two studies could be very misleading, and a great deal of research is still needed in this field. It seems, however, that one could tentatively conclude that the traditional status system is undergoing a decisive change in urban African society. It is perhaps too early to say that a clearly defined status system has evolved, as the situation is still very fluid. There are, however, indications that the urban African society is moving in the direction of a hierarchically structured class society with status based on the principle of achievement.

The status system as manifested at present in Reeftown contains some aspects which could be detrimental to development, for example the non-commitment of the élite to specific professions, and antagonisms developing towards the élite because of an evolving pattern of social exclusiveness and aloofness. On the whole, however, the changes in the status system could be interpreted positively with a view to economic development, as the achievement aspirations manifested are in keeping with the structural requirements for economic development.

Family life. One other aspect of traditional social structure which has been affected in the urban environment is that of the kinship system. The contact with Western values, the influence of the urban environment and the incorporation of the Bantu labour force into a differentiated economic structure contributed to the rapid disintegration of the extended kinship system and concomitant social organisation, resulting in a number of important developments with regard to the family.

The structure of blood lineages and wider kinship groupings which in tribal life had played an important role in the creation and maintenance of organised community life have in the cities either disappeared or to a great extent lost their function. Not only the consanguinal groups but also other important primary groups, such as the tribal initiation schools, regiments and age groups, have disappeared as a result of this shift to urban areas. Where initiation schools are still held in the urban areas, they no longer have the same function as in the tribal areas. With the disappearance of these primary groupings, important social control measures have also lapsed.

This disintegration of the wider kinship system is accompanied by a change and disappearance of customs and norms with regard to family life. When reading the numerous research reports in this connection, one can easily come to the conclusion that one is confronted with a situation in which anomie prevails. In spite of this first impression of anomie, however, certain tendencies of the direction in which the pattern of family life is developing can be recognised.

One important tendency among the urbanised Bantu is that the family is increasingly tending to become more and more structurally isolated from the wider kinship system. Empirical research has, however, shown that in the process of change, various factors are influencing the family and giving it a complexion different from the pure nuclear family. The family types listed in Table 6.2 have been found by Pauw (1963) in his study of East London – as well as by other research workers in various urban areas throughout the country.

TABLE 6.2   Structure of Bantu households in East London

Family type	*Number of households*
Man, woman, child	23
Man, woman, child and other members	12
Multigenerational (male head)	12
Multigenerational and other members	6
Woman, children	8
Woman, children and other members	9
Multigenerational (female head)	18
Multigenerational and other members (female head)	3
Other: Male head	11
Female head	7
Total	109

As has been pointed out earlier, the family type facilitating sustained economic growth to the largest extent seems to be the nuclear family. From the above sample and from other research findings, it is clear that this family type is developing in urban society, but constitutes at present only a small proportion (20 per cent) of the various categories of families to be found. Whether there is an increase in the frequency of the nuclear family is difficult to say because of a lack of comparative studies.

The characteristics of some of the other family types to be found in the urban areas have certain implications for modernisation and economic development. One of these characteristics is the presence of additional members in the family, either third-generation members or the presence of lodgers, or other kin as lodgers. Altogether 58 per cent of the families in the East London sample included additional members.

The phenomenon of additional members in the family – either kin or lodgers – could be interpreted as the continued existence of the kinship group and extended family. This interpretation of extended kinship groups is in my view, however, too wide. When one has a closer look at the additional members in the family, no clear-cut and consistent pattern of the way in which these groups are composed is apparent. It is also clear that a great many of the norms regulating behaviour in the wider kinship system have become obsolete or are no longer seen as obligatory. In addition, primary control no longer effectively enforces these traditional behavioural patterns.

Even if these additional members within the urban family could not be interpreted as the continued existence of the extended kinship system in the city, it still shows the residual importance of kinship ties. These remainders of the kinship system have important positive functions for a large proportion of the Africans in urban society. Living together in large groups of kinsmen seems to meet a sociability need as well as providing emotional security. For the newcomer the kin also seem to serve as a link and as a starting-point in the city for eventually forming their own networks within the wider community. In this way the kin networks in urban society assist people, and especially rural people, to adapt to city life. Apart from this emotional security, material security is also provided within the urban family, in the sense that no unemployed person, no aged person and no orphans will be left completely destitute, but will be taken care of by the family.

This tendency of the urban African family to take in and care for the destitute could, however, in the long run be detrimental for economic development in so far as it encourages undue dependence, which puts a heavy economic burden on the employed in the home and could thus impede economic advancement of the individual family.

Another important tendency to be observed in the urban African family is the high percentage of the families with a female head (approximately 60 per cent). These families are mostly established through the birth of illegitimate children. Research findings on the whole show an extremely high illegitimacy birth rate.

This high incidence of illegitimate children within the family is mainly due to the breakdown of the sexual behaviour code and to the changing function of *lobola* (bride's price), which has actually become dysfunctional within the urban African society. If one takes into consideration that the illegitimate children very often grow up in a state of poverty with little or no supervision and with few of life's chances, it could lead to a state of affairs which could, in the long run, adversely affect economic development.

It is, however, not only the illegitimate children who seem to suffer as far as care and control is concerned, but also children coming from unbroken homes. This problem arises from the fact that in traditional society the children were taken care of and disciplined not only by the parents but by any number of adults living within the kinship grouping. Thus the responsibility of child-rearing in the traditional kinship unit was shared with the other adults in the unit. Contrary to tribal life, in the city where the kinship system is disintegrating the child's own parents are solely responsible for discipline, and they cannot depend on the support of the wider kin group in this respect. The parents, however, have not yet succeeded in taking over this responsibility in full, and without the support of the wider kin group lose control over the children.

Apart from this problem, other factors also contribute to the loss of control over children. One of these is the difference in schooling between parents and children in a large number of cases. Most of the parents have had no schooling, while most of the children attend school for a few years at least, where they come into contact with the Western value system. Consequently the generations draw apart and children do not attach much value to their parents' guidance because they consider them to be ignorant.

This loss of control over the younger generation leads to the fact that the children are neither socialised in the traditional system nor socialised to participate in a more modernised industrial system. Consequently a great deal of juvenile delinquency and vagrancy is found among the youth. The result is actually a loss of valuable human material that cannot contribute much to economic development, but rather puts an obstacle in the way of accelerated development.

Much more attention should perhaps be given to the development of community services for the family and youth to counteract these disorganising tendencies.

Voluntary associations. Taken as a whole, it seems that the African urban society is becoming increasingly structurally differentiated. Apart from the structures described thus far, other formal structures have also developed and taken root in urban African society, providing for a great many needs and fulfilling the demands of an urbanised society with a money economy. Most of these formal structures – and I think here specifically of education, formal church groups, and legal and administrative organisations – were derived from the White society with which they have been in contact, and have actually developed with the help of the White sector of society.

One of the main problems to be found in the urban areas is that these new structures which have emerged have not as yet been able to fill the vacuum that was left by the disintegration of the kinship system. Thus some needs are left unsatisfied, and inadequate social control measures are provided.

It is, however, interesting to note that within the ranks of the Africans themselves a new type of grouping, which could be referred to as voluntary associations, has started to develop in a spontaneous attempt to fill the gap caused by the disintegration of the kinship groupings. These groupings are to a certain extent rather individualistic and not cohesive enough to serve as a foundation for a stable social order, but they nevertheless provide for important needs which would otherwise have been neglected, and they also furnish certain important social control measures.

Quite a great deal of research has been conducted into the development of voluntary organisations of the urban Bantu. A great variety of organisations, on various levels and in different sectors of African society, have developed, viz. in respect of religious, leisure-time, social welfare, mutual aid and special interests. There might be a great deal of difference between the various groupings with regard to size, degree of formal organisation, duration of life and development of a set of formal norms and formal sanctions. But basically they develop spontaneously and provide for certain needs of the urban African population.

The most important needs they seem to provide for are the following:

1. Mutual aid and financial and social security. With the disintegration of the wider kinship system it is not possible to provide for these needs of the kin on a wider basis. In the isolated nuclear family where the father, providing for his family's needs, has a very low income, it is not always financially possible to look after other kinsfolk, and a great deal of financial insecurity prevails in the urban areas. It is interesting to note that some of the very first voluntary associations which arose in the urban areas were the savings and mutual aid societies, referred to as *stokfel*, which enable each member to have at his disposal a large sum of money in rotation. Although their savings are not used for investment and therefore do not contribute much to capital formation, it shows a certain consciousness of and orientation towards a diversified economy.

2. Adjustment to the impersonality of urban life and the prevention of social isolation. Especially with the breakdown of the close-knit kinship system, social isolation could easily occur, and voluntary association provides in this instance for a fundamental need of sociability.

3. Exercise of social control over its members. Control measures are observable in all these groups, although their effectiveness as control mechanisms could easily be questioned. The most powerful social sanctions in these groups were observed where the interaction of the members is primary interaction.

The relevance to modernisation of this development of voluntary associations among the urbanised Africans is that voluntary association seems to be an important component of the structure of an urban industrial society. The extent to which voluntary associations have developed among the urbanised Africans can be an indication of the extent to which they have moved in the direction of a structurally differentiated population, thus complying with some of the structural conditions for economic development.

Apart, however, from being a positive step in the direction of modernisation, voluntary association also provides the individual with necesary experience in fulfilling new obligations and new types of roles. Voluntary associations develop in part as a response to the need for role differentiation, to the need for developing a new structure of roles and statuses in a confused situation. In these associations the African learns the principles of conduct in a universalistic, differentiated category of roles in an achievement-oriented society. Thus, while helping to create new groups to which the individual in the city could belong, and which could provide for important needs, the association also teaches new values, which could be invaluable in the process of modernisation.

(d) RELIGION

Thus far our attention has mainly been focused on the changes taking place in the social structure of the urban African and on factors leading to structural differentiation which could in the end facilitate economic development. The structural changes as such, are, however, not sufficient to bring about the desired development, and it is of great importance that the value system of traditional society should also change.

As the values of a particular society are closely tied up with the religion of that society, in that religion legitimates the values, it is obvious that a change in religion could be imperative if the traditional religion and value system are of such a nature as not to allow for change and acceptance of innovation, and if it results in a passive and fatalistic approach to problems confronting man. This decisive role that religion could play, not only in economic development, but in the total development of a society, is amply illustrated by Max Weber's monumental *Gesammelte Aufsätze zur Religionsoziologie*, and especially the now famous essay, *Protestant Ethics and the Spirit of Capitalism.*

It is therefore imperative that the religious and value system of a particular society should be taken into account in a discussion of accelerated development. In this connection, two questions should be considered. The one concerns the nature of the traditional religious system and whether there are elements in this system which could be obstacles to accelerated development. The second question is whether changes have taken place in the religious system and whether these changes could facilitate development.

It is well known that the religious systems of traditional society constitute a serious problem with regard to development. The traditional religious system of the Africans is no exception to this rule, as has already been pointed out in our discussion on the problems encountered in the development of the agricultural sector. The ancestor cult of the Africans, as well as the belief in witchcraft, magic and supernatural forces, leads to strict social control measures in case of deviance from tradition and on the whole to a passive and fatalistic attitude which is not conducive to change, let alone to accelerated development.

In spite of the fact that traditional religion is extremely difficult to change, a number of forces have acted upon African society which in the long run did result in changes in this field. One of the factors influencing the traditional religion of the Africans and contributing to changes in this respect is the contact with the Christian religion and the missionary effort in rural as well as urban areas for the past 150 years. Another factor is the process of urbanisation itself where a breakdown in kinship systems has taken place accompanied by a loss of social control in an environment which is not conducive to pagan ritual.

Official statistics, as a matter of fact, show an increase in the percentage of the population who have been christianised, as can be seen from Table 6.3.

The extent to which the African population has been christian-

TABLE 6.3   Religious affiliation of South African Bantu: percentage distribution 1951 and 1960

	1951	1960
Bantu Separatist churches	18·6	21·2
Methodist	12·2	12·1
Anglican	6·8	6·9
Roman Catholic	5·4	6·9
Other Christian	1·3	5·2
Lutheran	4·8	5·0
Nederduits Gereformeerd	3·5	4·8
Presbyterian	2·0	1·9
Congregational	1·4	1·2
Apostolic Faith Mission	1·7	1·1
Baptist	0·9	0·9
Seventh-Day Adventist	0·3	0·2
Nederduits Hervormd	0·2	0·2
Gereformeerd	0·1	0·2
Other unspecified	40·6	32·0

ised differs, of course, in different geographical areas, as well as in the rural and urban areas. Mayer (1971*b*, p. 181) points out that around East London the population of the rural reserves is evenly divided between Christian and pagan, but in East London itself at least two-thirds of the population of over 50,000 have claimed affiliation to a Christian church.

According to Durand (1970, p. 69) between 40 and 45 per cent of the population of Port Elizabeth have some ties with a Christian church or sect, 13 per cent or less were self-declared Red Xhosa, while a further 45 per cent could not be described either as Red Xhosa or as Christian. This group had only one common characteristic, viz. some degree of Westernisation together with a high degree of disinterestedness in religion, be it Red Xhosa or Christian.

Although statistics could be quite valuable in giving an approximation of a specific situation, it does not in the least give an indication of the complex dynamics involved in this whole process of change and of the reciprocal influence of Christianity and paganism on each other. Because of these reciprocal influences it is not always possible to dichotomise the population into pagan and Christian or even to add a third category of irreligious.

Pauw (1960), for example, shows in his study of religion in a Tswana chiefdom that paganism is to some extent on the wane, in the sense that a great deal of the pagan ritual has disappeared and that traditional rites and beliefs are frequently confused. He says in this connection (p. 39): 'Moreover, I have the impression that Christian belief and practice have penetrated even to all pagans to such extent that it seems doubtful whether one is justified in referring to them as pagans.'

On the other hand, remnants of paganism are still found under a proportion of the people who have official connections with the church, although, according to Pauw, a substantial core of church people have no connection with paganism. Furthermore, he points out that the structure and organisation of the churches have been influenced by traditional patterns of social structure and organisation, and that in some instances elements of pagan ritual and belief have found their way into church ritual and belief.

Pauw's description of the degree of Christianisation of the Africans in Taung leaves a more positive impression than Durand's view on the degree of Christianisation in Port Elizabeth. While

Pauw's middle group has ties with the church together with lean-
ings to paganism, Durand's middle group shows more signs of
having neither, and one gets the impression that in Durand's
study a higher degree of secularisation, both with regard to
paganism and Christianity, is found. It must, however, be taken
into consideration that Pauw's study took place in a rural area,
and Durand's in an urban area. The reason for discussing both
is not for the sake of comparison, but rather to point out that it
is extremely difficult to generalise in this field and that various
degrees of Christianisation and paganism with various degrees of
reciprocal influence may be found in different parts of the
country.

In spite of a difference in the findings as to the extent to which
Christianisation has taken place, there is one aspect in connection
with the religious beliefs of the Africans on which there is general
agreement. This is the fact that, in spite of the waning of paganism and of ancestor cults, and in spite of the secularisation among
the Africans in the urban areas, both the Africans in the rural
areas and those in the urban areas cling to a large extent to belief
in magic and witchcraft. Pauw (1960, p. 212) says in this connection:

> Apart from the general waning of paganism as illustrated by
> the fact that some pagan ritual has already become completely
> obsolete and some people have abandoned paganism alto-
> gether, the most important fact about it is that different aspects
> of the traditional system of magico-religious beliefs and activi-
> ties are not receding in equal proportion. The ancestor cult has
> largely disintegrated but traditional magic tends to *persist* to a
> considerable degree.

This also seems to be the case in the urban areas. Durand
(1970, p. 160) also points out that although Africans, under the
influence of city life, might have discarded their belief in ancestral
spirits to a certain extent, they still cling tenaciously to a philosophy of life in which magic and witchcraft play a dominant role.
Tied up with this belief in magic is also a changed attitude
towards the role of the ancestral spirits. Instead of being a protective force, the forefather spirits seem to be associated with the
world of incalculable forces and misfortune which must be
exorcised through magical actions, instead of being reconciled

through sacrifice. Even the Christianised section of the population does not seem to be free of this belief in magic. On the whole it could be stated that the greatest resistance to change with respect to the traditional religion seems to be experienced in connection with this belief in magic.

The religious beliefs of Africans have far-reaching implications for modernisation and accelerated development. Although much more research is needed in this field, scattered research findings suggest a positive correlation between the acceptance of Christianity and modernisation and development. The Benghu sect, for example, endorses values which could facilitate development. As far as these values are concerned, Mayer (1971 *b*, p. 184) points out that the Benghu endorse typical urban middle class values, with emphasis on thrift, neatness, education, working skills and generally raising the social status, all of which are values which could facilitate development.

Research findings also suggest that the African people themselves to a large extent endorse the idea that the acceptance of Christianity leads to and implies modernisation. In his discussion of the problem of secularisation among the urban African with a Christian background, Durand (1970) points out that one is struck by the fact that Christianity was only an intermediary phase – an interlude – in their existence, in the sense that they tried to enter the Western way of life by way of the Christian religion. The acceptance of Christianity in fact leads involuntarily to a more Western way of life, a fact which is increasingly realised by the Xhosa themselves. Durand further points out that the word *Ubukristu* (Christianity) has in Port Elizabeth a rather comprehensive meaning, including some sort of a tie to a Christian church, to economic and social advancement, social norms with regard to correct behaviour and the maintenance of certain outward moral norms.

In considering this modernising effect of Christianisation on the African population, one could perhaps state in broad and general terms that the more the Africans move away from their traditional religion and become Christianised, the more likely it will be that they will move in the direction of modernisation.

The most serious obstacle in this connection is the degree to which the Africans still cling to a belief in magic and witchcraft. This belief in magic runs counter to the basic value orientation of a rational problem-solving approach to situations, and the belief that can master the environment – a belief which is absolutely essential for development.

How to overcome this belief in magic, or perhaps more important, how to utilise this belief in magic for development, poses a formidable problem in the modernisation of the African population. Pauw (1960, p. 217) points out that knowledge of the existence of scientific techniques does not suffice to dispel the belief in magic, and that only if real insight is gained into the principles of causality could one hope for a rejection of magic, and he says in this connection: 'It may be relatively easy to educate isolated individuals to an understanding of such processes, but to attain this for a society as a whole seems to be a tedious task.'

One last aspect of the influence of religion on development which I should like to point out very briefly is the way in which the Separatistic or African independent churches might have implications for accelerated development. These churches do not have links with any of the White churches, and are distinguished in some instances by emotionalism and a mixture of traditional and Christian symbolism and belief. There is also in some instances a very close tie between these churches and politics.

The phenomenon of the development of the Separatist churches is not limited to South Africa only, but has made its appearance in large sections of the African continent. In South Africa there is an ever-increasing number of these churches. Sundkler (1961), in his very well-known study, *Bantu Prophets in South Africa*, points out that in 1913 there were some 30 of these churches, in 1948 the number had risen to 800, and in 1960 to 2,200. An increasing number of Africans are also becoming members of these churches, as can be seen from the official statistics on p. 339 above. The rapid multiplication of these churches is, however, due to a fission within the churches themselves. It is also interesting to note that the development and incidence of these churches vary between the different parts of the country. According to Mayer (1971b, p. 182), for example, there is not much evidence of activity by these churches in the Transkei. Among the Tlhaping, again, some of these churches are found (Pauw, 1960), but in their activities they differ to some extent from those found in Zululand. In Zululand as well as on the Rand there is a preponderance of these churches.

Sundkler distinguished mainly between two types of these churches in South Africa, namely the Ethiopians and the Zionists. In an analysis of the types and dynamics of the African religious movements, Fernandez (1964) gave an interesting interpretation of the way in which the Zionist and Ethiopian churches in South Africa could possibly influence development. According to him, the African churches can be divided into four categories on the basis of a traditional-acculturation axis and an expressive-instrumental axis. The Zionist churches have a very strong traditional-expressive orientation in that they turn back to tradition, thus interpreting the Christian message in terms of the traditional religious heritage – a situation which could be detrimental for development. The Ethiopian churches, on the contrary, have a much more active orientation, which could be more conducive to modernisation, than that of the Zionist churches. According to Fernandez (1964, p. 535), their orientation is an acculturated-instrumental one, in that they continue on the one hand to adhere closely in religious belief and ceremony to that of the parent organisation, while on the other hand they make fairly pragmatic attempts to compensate for problematic situations in a realistic and goal-minded fashion.

3. FINAL REMARKS

In concluding this paper there are two more remarks to be made:

1. In an attempt to construct a picture of the changing social structure of African society from the viewpoint of evaluating the degree of modernisation attained and the degree to which it could sustain a viable developing economy, one is struck by the scarcity of systematic and comprehensive research in this field in South Africa.

2. From the existing research findings it would appear that the traditional value system and social structure of the Africans seem to lay serious obstacles in the way of development. Changes in this respect seem to be most difficult to attain in the rural areas where the Africans remain within the traditional kinship system and are involved with traditional agricultural activities. Changes are more readily

effected in the urban areas where the African is forced to adapt to an urban way of life and to move into a differentiated economic structure. Even then, changes do not take place easily and are accompanied by a certain degree of anomie. This anomie need not be completely dysfunctional, as it is an indication that people have been prised loose from their traditional way of life and in a sense are free to adapt themselves to a social structure and value system sustaining viable economic development. At this stage of our knowledge, however, some of the developed structures could be used more efficiently for development and more attention could be paid to deliberately planning and introducing structures in the urban areas to counteract the imbalances and anomie which are detrimental to accelerated development.

NOTES

1. According to Mayer (1971*a*, p. 5), the country-rooted are those who are *in* the location but not *of* it. They are staying in town but regard themselves as having their real homes or roots in the country. Looking at it from the viewpoint of the network of social relations, the country-rooted migrant continues to lay the main emphasis on people in the country and on his relatedness to them, even if he can only keep up these relations *in absentia*. The town-rooted are those whose homes and roots are in the city and there only, and they mainly emphasise people and relations in town. Country-born people can become town-rooted, too, by deciding to stay on permanently and becoming incorporated in the town community.
2. Apart from a number of contract research reports, the following could be mentioned: C.S.I.R. Special Report No. PERS 124, *Motivational Patterns of a Rural and an Urban Group of Adult Male Vandas*; C.S.I.R. Special Report No. PERS 154, *Motivation among a Rural and an Urban Employed Group of Adult Pedi Males*.

BIBLIOGRAPHY

Adendorff, J., 'Aspekte van Ekonomiese Ontwikkeling van die Bantoevolke: Ontwikkeling binne die Tuislande', *Journal of Racial Affairs*, XVIII 2 (1967) 65–71.
Annual Report of the Department of Bantu Administration and Development, 1966–1967.

Banghart, P. D., 'The Effects of Migrant Labour on the Social Structure of the Bantu Homeland', in *Migrant Labour and Church Involvement* (Missiological Institute, Umpumulo).

Board, C., 'The Rehabilitation Programme in the Bantu Areas and its Effect on the Agricultural Practices and Rural Life of the Bantu in the Eastern Cape', *South African Journal of Economics*, XXXII (1964) 36–52.

Brandel-Syrier, M., *Reeftown Elite: A Study of Social Mobility in a Modern African Community on the Reef* (London: Routledge & Kegan Paul, 1971.

Breese, G., *Urbanisation in Newly Developing Countries* (Englewood Cliffs, N.J.: Prentice-Hall, 1966).

Carr, W. J. P., 'Cultural Change in Soweto', unpublished (Johannesburg Dept. of Bantu Affairs).

Cilliers, S. P., 'Maatskaplike Vraagstukke en Beplanning', unpublished paper read at a national conference on Welfare Planning, Pretoria, 24 June 1969.

Durand, J. J. F., *Swart Man, Stad en Toekoms* (Cape Town: Tafelberg, 1970).

Fernandez, J. W., 'African Religious Movements – Types', *Journal of Modern African Studies*, II (Dec 1964) 513–30.

Fortes, M., and Dieterlen, G., *African Systems of Thought* (London: Oxford Univ. Press, 1965).

Grobler, J. H., 'Die Landboupotensiaal van die Bantoetuislande', *Journal of Racial Affairs*, XXI 1 (1970) 3–10.

Hall, S. K., 'The Manifestations and Perception of Social Class among an Urban African Group', paper read at 'Focus on Cities' conference (July 1967).

Hamburger, H., 'Zur Förderung der tierischen Erzeugung bei Entwicklungsvölkern im Südlichen Afrika, *Mitteilungen für Tierhaltung*, Heft Nr. 125–70, Pamphlet, no date.

Hattingh, D. S. and Hugo, M. L., 'Tendense, van Bantoeverstedeliking in Suid-Afrika 1960–1970', *Journal of Racial Affairs*, XXII 4 (1971) 124–30.

Holleman, J. F., *et al.*, *Problems of Transition* (Pietermaritzburg: Natal Univ. Press, 1964).

Hoselitz, B. I., and Moore, W. E., *Industrialisation and Society* (The Hague: Mouton, for UNESCO, 1966).

Kuper, L., *An African Bourgeoisie: Race, Class and Politics in South Africa* (New Haven: Yale Univ. Press, 1965).

Leistner, G. M. E., 'Economic and Social Aspects of Physical Control over Rural–Urban Population Movements', *Journal of Racial Affairs*, XIX 3 (1968) 3–19.

Leistner, G. M. E., 'Some Thoughts on Bantu Development', *Journal of Racial Affairs*, XXI 2 (1970) 41–51.

Lilley, H. W. L., 'Characteristics and Motivational Orientations of the Amanzimakwe Land-Occupiers of Location 4B', M. Agric. (Inst. Agrar) thesis (University of Pretoria, 1967).

Mayer, P., *Townsmen or Tribesmen* (Cape Town: Oxford Univ. Press, 1971*a*).

Mayer, P., 'Religion and Control in a South African Township', in Heribert Adam (ed.), *South Africa: Sociological Perspectives* (London: Oxford Univ. Press, 1971*b*).

Miner, H., *The City in Modern Africa* (London: Praeger, 1969).

Moore, W. E., *Social Change* (Englewood Cliffs, N.J.: Prentice-Hall, 1963).

Moore, W. E., *The Impact of Industry* (Englewood Cliffs, N.J.: Prentice-Hall, 1965).

Pauw, B. A., *Religion in a Tswana Chiefdom* (London: Oxford Univ. Press, 1960).

Pauw, B. A., *The Second Generation: A Study of the Family among Urbanised Bantu in East London* (Cape Town: Oxford Univ. Press, 1963).

Population Census, 6 Sep 1960, vol. III: *Religion.*

Population Census, 6 Sep 1960, vol. VIII, no. 1: *Income, Occupation, Industry Division, and Identity of Employer.*

Ralushai, V., 'Some Aspects of Social Change in Vendaland' (unpublished).

Reader, D. H., *The Black Man's Portion* (Cape Town: Oxford Univ. Press, 1961).

Smit, P., 'Die Ontwikkeling van die Bantoetuislande: Probleme en Vooruitsigte', opening paper read at the four-yearly congress of the Society for the Teaching of Geography (Potchefstroom, 1969).

Stadler, J. J., 'Nywerheidsontwikkeling in die Bantoetuislande: Die Behoefte aan Nywerheidsontwikkeling', *Journal of Racial Affairs*, XVIII 4 (1967) 165–83.

Steyn, Anna F., *Die Bantoe in die Stad: Die Bantoegesin* (Pretoria: SABRA, 1966).

Sundkler, B. G. M., *Bantu Prophets in South Africa*, 2nd ed. (London: Oxford Univ. Press, 1961).

Vorster, D., 'The Ambitions of African Workers', *Management* (Nov 1970) pp. 60–2.

Wallman, Sandra, *Take out Hunger: Two Case Studies of Rural Development in Basutoland*, London School of Economics Monographs on Social Anthropology No. 39 (London: Athlone Press, 1969).

Weideman, J. J. S., 'Die Ekonomie van Ontwikkelingsbeleid in die Suid-Afrikaanse Agtergeblewe Gebiede met spesiale verwysing na Bantoebesproeiing', unpublished D.Com. dissertation (University of Pretoria, 1969).

Weiner, M. (ed.), *Modernisation* (New York: Basic Books, 1966).

Yamane, T., and Nonoyama, H., 'Isolation of the Nuclear Family and Kinship Organisation in Japan: A Hypothetical Approach to the Relationships between the Family and Society', *Journal of Marriage and the Family*, XXIX 4 (Nov 1967) 783–96.

Social, Cultural and Religious Factors in Changing African Societies

D. M. NTUSI

INTRODUCTION

The old saying that Africa always has something new to show comes to the mind of the author as he seeks to make a contribution to a discussion of accelerated development in Southern Africa. This discussion, in which he has been asked to participate, concerns how best to speed up all the planned programmes, projects, schemes and procedures for development that are found in so many forms in the trends and processes of culture change and in the modernisation of life of African societies in this region of Africa and elsewhere. As an African the author feels affected in a profound way, because he is at the same time the subject under discussion and a participant in that discussion.

In considering human development, a subdivision of the subject into watertight compartments is not really possible. This is, however, being done to some extent at this Conference for convenience in discussing the subject. This paper will therefore attempt to focus on the social, cultural and religious factors in the process of change and development.

BACKGROUND

In the days prior to contact between the African societies and the outside foreign human groups – be they missionaries or traders – indigenous cultures had their own distinctive characteristics which, essentially speaking, had much in common.

1. The African society had a definite social system of its own, which was stable in the narrow sense that change was very slow and in fact unconscious, because the elders and rulers, who alone

held strong opinions about change, guarded against deviation from the accepted custom. Their families and communities upheld their judgement. The fact that the elders and councillors were invariably tried and experienced men, loyal to the chief and dedicated to the welfare of the people, was a sure guarantee against a faulty and unworkable social organisation. Corruption and bribery, double-dealing and selfish acts were easy to detect and remove from their communal life.

It is necessary to note that whoever became a chief's councillor attained that position only by merit and popular approval. It is a matter of special interest now that the functions of chief's councillor compare in some respects with those of the modern Ministers of State in the older-established countries and in the new African states. However, it must also be remembered that in the then simple governments military *coups d'état* were almost unthinkable, because the circumstances and conditions of life in pre-contact times differed considerably from those of our era.

2. The early aboriginal society lived a life of illiteracy, and whatever form of education existed was handed down from father to son and from mother to daughter. The book was an unknown commodity. History tells us that on the age-beaten walls of one ancient school built in Mesopotamia in the days of Hammurabi about 2100 B.C. there was written these words: 'He who shall excel at tablet writing, shall shine like the sun.' In those times, as now, Southern Africa had many a man who regarded education as a source of power, beauty and prestige. This rather materialistic attitude must still assail many of our educated youth even today: it appeals; it captures the imagination of a young person fresh from college; emotion is aroused; it promises to give him immediate satisfaction and power. But, needless to say, the young African states certainly require a strong corps of faithful, dedicated workers and citizens, in order to ensure real lasting progress. Today education seeks to prepare scholars for service in such a way that they render the greatest amount of satisfaction to their fellow-men and the state. To this remark can be added a strangely novel idea, that of constructive dissatisfaction: let education infuse in the scholar a kind of drive and dissatisfaction that will make him never rest until he has freed others from the ills and wrongs of his time.

3. Custom observed a sort of division of labour, which required that all the boring, routine household chores be done by women. In practice they acted as hewers of firewood and drawers of water, nursed the babies of the nation, cooked food and hoed weeds in the fields. The males guaranteed protection and security for the family. 'Medicine men' and soldiers came from their ranks. They organised hunting sorties to provide the necessary meat. Unfortunately, despite the changed times which have come to Southern Africa, the simple African people have never really freed themselves from this kind of discriminating mentality. Today, in many a humble backward family group, some of the semi-sophisticated males are either at a loose end for the greater part of the day and form an undefined company of irresponsible 'nice-timers', or alternatively disappear into the urban areas to find themselves a pleasant type of occupation.

The illiterate or semi-literate males are not in a much better position, as they sooner or later join the migrant labour force and thus come to spend their better years of robust health in movement between their families at home and the labour centres. Who, then, should remain behind in the 'homeland' to see to the agricultural work which should be in the hands of healthy, intelligent people, if justice is to be done to it? It is not possible to elaborate on this matter here; suffice it to say that a social research scientist should find this field of migrant labour one of great fascination, for in it he would wade through a fertile matrix of varying levels of literacy and cultural development, human frustration and broken homes, corruption and bribery, the methods of recruitment and procurement of travel permits, the functioning of labour bureaux, the demand for and supply of labour, the labourers' aptitudes and anxieties, scales and use of wages, elements of human gangsterism and also the effects of recruitment of labourers on their families, on health, on the varying standards of agriculture and on the communities in general. One is strongly persuaded to believe that the evolution of an underdeveloped area or territory will always tie in with the question of the supply of labour. Development will not be effective until the question of labour has been solved satisfactorily. If the living standards of African people are to be raised in the coming years, an improvement must be made here. This is like a piece of human drama requiring to be unravelled.

A word may now be said about the position assigned to women in present-day African societies. With the growing expansion of education as a modernising factor, and with the increasing appreciation of their valuable service in the building-up of the family, in the church and in education, restrictions against their employment are being relaxed. Thus female teachers may now rise to become principals of small and large primary, secondary and teacher-training schools – and even Ministers of State. On the average they are known for thorough work wherever they are employed, and, with their finer sense of beauty, sincerity, responsibility and leadership, they should indeed play a very important role in the development of the country.

4. At the earlier stage the communities lived from hand to mouth, and they produced mainly to satisfy their family needs. Their goals showed very little foresight, and organised marketing was unheard of in their life. The people were given to a traditional type of economy, the subsistence economy. Production for purposes of profit-making was almost taboo. Tradition and law went hand in hand, and there was no thought of making supply exceed demand and thus of producing surpluses. In this same spirit they attached very little importance to time as indicated by seconds, minutes and hours. They measured their wealth in cattle which, by modern standards, were worth little and belonged to no breed. A cow or bullock slaughtered for a marriage or sacrificial feast was according to their way of life, put to a far more worthy purpose than if offered for sale, because 'money is the root of all evil'. The slaughtering of a beast in this fashion was also an attempt to make possible a reunion between the living and the dead, and to appease the shades, a most essential element in pagan religion. Such a static attitude must tend to close all gates to modern advancement.

THE CHANGING SOCIETY

The above background depicts traditional societies faced with the forces of change and fighting a losing battle before the rising tide of irresistible forward movement resulting from schemes of educational, technological, industrial, political and religious developments everywhere in our cash-oriented Africa.

This movement has been marked by effective schemes born of careful planning and an efficient machinery of administration. Laws and regulations were made for the control of land tenure on government-owned land, of the drift of rural communities to urban areas, and of the movement and residence of work-seekers in White-owned and urban areas. The process of industrialisation affects all.

At the same time, education and the Gospel always working side by side, have been formidable factors in the promotion of advancement, and their effect on the culture and life of simple societies has from very early times been very definite and directed by well-trained and understanding men and associations of people from the more modern countries.

The following observations may now be made:

(a) BORROWING OF CULTURE TRAITS

We know that on the whole a simple society borrows culture traits, practices and ideas, such as folk legends, musical tunes, dress styles, kitchen utensils, modern perfumes, recipes, games, science nomenclature and so on, because it is unable to reproduce them by itself and therefore becomes aware of the inadequacy of its own culture heritage. Thus its own inventory of possessions must be enlarged and enriched. This explains how many educational, agricultural and technological practices have been adopted wholly or in modified form by traditional societies in Southern Africa. On the other hand, a simple society may in some cases resist borrowing from a complex society, for the reason of its conservatism or its suspicion of foreign ideas, especially in cases where it either distrusts members of the complex society or is not favourably impressed by the attitudes and approach of the culture-bringers.

Under these circumstances there is a great need for those in positions of authority and influence, perhaps as chiefs or government officers, to be men of integrity, if they are to succeed in transmitting to simple societies new ideas relating to national schemes of development. This holds true within the family, in the school, in the church, in the state and at all levels of human activity. Any state service or system of administration that is not free from bribery and corruption, from frivolity and favour, does irreparable harm.

(*b*) RELIGION AND PRACTICE

The church has made an invaluable contribution towards improving the lot of simple societies; its powerful hand has reached every corner of Africa. Indeed, it has been revolutionary in its approach and a 'force compelling change in society for nearly two thousand years', preaching not only man's salvation but also fellowship and harmony, service and loyalty, attributes which imply co-operation and interdependence, harmony and human welfare together with 'sweeter manners, purer laws'. Down the ages the role of the church has always been to give leadership and, as an auxiliary body, to initiate new programmes of service for education, care of the sick and disabled, the aged and the destitute, as well as to establish new institutions and welfare associations. But simple societies have always known God (uQamata/uNkulunkulu/Modimo) through their ancestral spirits as the intermediaries, and that He acts as the Creator and Giver of all things such as rain, good harvests, good health, success and prosperity, while catastrophes like illness, accidents, drought and floods are attributed to evil spirits or evil-doers like ooThikoloshe (a river dwarf), iiMpundulu (an evil lightning-bird), witches and witch-doctors. It is for this reason that the clergy and other influential well-placed men should be upright and give good leadership, because otherwise they and their congregations, 'being let go', may 'go back to their own company' and revert to old-time heathenish practices in the same way as some sophisticated Christian individuals here and there are known to do in the hours of darkness! If there ever was a time and place for governmental officials and for all those highly placed in administration or leadership to do nothing short of their very best, it is now in Africa.

It has been pointed out by Vincent van der Westhuizen[1] that more than half of the 14 million Bantu people in South Africa can be called Christians, although among them there are some 4,000 denominations or sects. Some of these have combined Christian and pagan beliefs, including elements of ancestral worship.

Of late there has been born a new brand of theology, known as black theology. It is perhaps too early yet to say with precision what this type of theology is. However, if it is a rallying-point for the Black people versus the White people, then it is neither religion nor theology, but a form of nationalism, a doctrine which in turn may give rise to division between one national group and another; as such it would be Africa's counterpart of the U.S. Black Power movement, and sow seeds of dissension between group and group.

(*c*) RESISTANCE TO CHANGE

The traditional society may resist change for the following reasons:

(i) The conservatism of its members may be so strong that a change is opposed for no other reason than that it is new, and that it may even bring a calamity to its accepters and make them look different from the many whose social approval protects and gives them security within the society.

(ii) The ignorance and fear of the unknown may also be a stumbling-block, lest the shades should be angered by the change.

(iii) If the complex society from which culture traits and new ideas are borrowed does not enjoy the full confidence of the borrowing society for one reason or another, borrowing is difficult to effect.

(*d*) KINSHIP

A kinship group comes into being when the normal family, the extended family, the members of the clan and others closely associated with these groups live together on communal ground under one head or more belonging to the same group. The head may be a headman, a sub-chief, a chief, a senior chief or the Paramount Chief.

Kinship within the traditional society takes priority in community development. Blood relatives tend to support one another in all that they do together. The rules of life are largely dictated by custom which tends to make decisions binding on each member of the group. Group pressure forbids dissent. The prevailing ethos stresses the male sex and age, and so decisions are made for the whole clan by the senior or Paramount Chief.

New ideas or government schemes must be accepted first by

the senior men, and endorsed by the Paramount Chief. Then a report is given to the whole clan by the senior men in the families.

(e) LAND TENURE

The system of land allotment requires that the interested party, usually a married male, should approach the chief with his request to be given a site and a piece of arable land. The chief, if satisfied, recommends the request to the administration (the magistrate) for approval. Thereafter the applicant has a certificate issued to him for the allotment. The recipient pays a land and service tax each year, and non-payment may cause forfeiture.

The man now has the full status of a citizen and may attend local meetings at the tribal court (Great Place) and express his opinions freely on all subjects tabled.

(f) WORK-SEEKERS: MIGRATION TO LABOUR CENTRES

This group is a large one consisting of a variety of people: urban labourers, urban dwellers, casual workers, farm labourers and miners. They all migrate from the rural communities to centres where work is available. Usually they are required to obtain official permits from their district magistrates beforehand. The farming and mining areas have special agents to contact the prospective labourers for recruitment.

The recruited male labourers usually stay away from their families for three to nine months, during which time the mothers, assisted by blood relatives or neighbours, look after the families, the home and also see to the ploughing of the lands. Though assisted in this way, the mother finds this work very onerous, especially when there is illness among the children, or when the bigger boys become too difficult to manage as the traditional society draws them away into the ranks of the large social group. This is a most important fact, because the children brought up in this atmosphere are very likely to suffer and to have their future marred. They may even grow into gangsters or become maladjusted to their society. Furthermore, the arable lands do not receive proper attention, and if this continues, then the simple society will continue to have poor crop returns from its fields and the standard of agriculture will continue to be at a low level.

What has been said of the farm and mine labourers above, holds true for those male urban labourers who work in the cities for several months each year, and then return home for a rest or 'on holiday', as they often describe the few days, weeks or months they spend with the family at home.

Then there are those labourers who are engaged in continuous employment for ten years or more, and who regard themselves as permanent town-dwellers. They live in the townships with their families. In this class of labourers the father and mother usually work by day while the older children go to school, leaving the little toddlers in the care of 'somebody' about the house. Here again the children are brought up without the parents' supervision during the day.

However, the picture painted above has a brighter side: there is in all the large cities a truly urbanised section of the African population. This section has its parents employed mostly in such professional jobs as teachers, lecturers, professors, doctors, clerks, journalists, radio announcers, lawyers, technologists and librarians. Their families live decently and the children are well brought up. It is perhaps from this emergent section of the people that an African middle class must come. This class is also beginning to appear on the scene in rural communities, but to a lesser degree than in the cities, and it is a class that is going to be a powerful anchor in the implementation of very many development programmes.

With regard to the labour drawn from a rural environment, it could be described as unstable and uncertain, and therefore not easy to organise; it also does not readily lend itself to selection and special training for specific jobs.

The unstable nature of such urban labourers must also affect the nature and composition of an urban population: the labourer is 'on and off', as he must continually move between the city and his rural family. This double type of life must have an adverse effect on African businesses run in municipal areas. A section of a businessman's customers must, as a result, remain temporary, especially in the smaller townships.

Casual labourers are engaged in temporary jobs and constitute a very unstable class of workers.

African labourers seek work in the cities because they desire cash and material wealth which is readily available there. Some of the younger people migrate to town also for adventure, new experiences, wanderlust, the evasion of 'home' duties or community obligations, a more attractive standard of living and for the White man's good things of life, like modern clothing, bio-scope shows, radio music, travel by bus or train. In the city the standard of living of migrants, especially on the Copperbelt, is above tribal standards in every way, and offers many amenities and chances to learn new skills and pick up new ideas and tech-niques. Some of these men decide after several years' experience of urban life to give up the rural community and live in town for the rest of their lives. And then, if they should be married men, what of their families!

The life of an African labourer is becoming urbanised and industrialised every day that he remains in town, and this is a fact that must be accepted. Urbanisation and industrialisation must no longer be regarded as unholy and disruptive forces on traditional cultures, but as 'powerful generators of social change'. Rural life and urban life must be taken as part and parcel of one social system, in the same way as migrant labour and money economy go hand in hand in the life of the people.

CONCLUSION

As the kinship system and social structures of simple societies are becoming broken down, it is most heartening to see an ever-growing number of bodies such as welfare organisations, youth movements, self-help projects, church and health councils and special schools for disabled children established everywhere to fill the place vacated by the old order. Indeed, this line of develop-ment must be welcomed as a sane approach to this vexed question we have under discussion.

NOTE

1. *South African Panorama* (Sep 1971) p. 43.

Cultural Discrepancies and Social Change: Studies of Developmental Processes in German and Indian Villages

GERHARD WURZBACHER, SIEGFRIED SCHÖNHERR AND BADAL SEN GUPTA

CONCEPTIONS OF SOCIO-CULTURAL DISCREPANCIES AND THEIR THEORETICAL BASIS

In politics as well as in research on development, conceptions of socio-cultural discrepancies frequently form the basis for the choice and application of measures as well as for scientific explanation or prognosis of processes of change. We usually find that normative conceptions of economic, political, social, educational, hygienic or other cultural goals are critically compared with different actual situations. Accordingly, measures are conceived and applied in order to diminish or abolish these discrepancies between goals and reality, and, mostly on the basis of experiences gained in developed societies, corresponding expectations are combined with the measures applied.

In most cases such comparisons of normative and factual levels are based on rather vague or simplified conceptions of the very complex field of different factors relevant to such a developmental process. Likewise, the different stages of such a process are either ignored or not sufficiently taken into account. It is not surprising, therefore, that numerous measures of development fail to achieve the intended goal.

As the authors were seeking a more detailed insight into the interdependence between cultural discrepancies and social change, their theoretical approach as well as their comparative application to German and Indian village studies might be of value to developmental theory and politics in Southern Africa too. The authors were looking for a theory which helps to:

(a) clarify the different stages of such a developmental process; and

(b) explain more clearly the interdependence between the individual and the social structure in such a process.

The social sciences abound with theories for the description and explanation of socio-cultural discrepancies:

1. Theories on discrepancies between components of cultural systems range from Durkheim's and Weber's statement concerning the greater resistance of religious and other systems of orientation to change, or Ogburn's 'cultural lag', to Parson's and Merton's disintegrations and dysfunctions against functional imperatives or prerequisites, Schelsky's discrepancy between the public and the private sphere or Srinivas's (1967) coincidence and counter-trends of modernisation and Sanskritisation.

2. Theories on discrepant role expectations, causing intra- as well as inter-role conflicts, from Linton's and G. Mead's first role conceptions to Gross's empirically examined theory of role conflict.

3. Theories on conflicts between groups and group interests, from Marx to Sorel, Simmel, Coser or Dahrendorf.

4. More psychological oriented theories on cognitive and evaluative dissonances, from Freud's conflict between ego, superego and id, or Dewey's conception of conflict, to Festinger's or Zollschan, Perucci and Willer's exigencies, dissonances and conflicts.

THE SELECTION OF ZOLLSCHAN, PERUCCI AND WILLER'S THEORY AND ITS REVISED APPLICATION

Usually only one of the above-mentioned theoretical conceptions is applied in empirical studies on socio-cultural discrepancies and change. Rarely do we find the attempt to combine the structural aspect of society with interpretation and articulation by the individuals involved. In this regard, Zollschan, Perucci and Willer's *Explorations in Social Change* seems most helpful. They combine the approach of cultural discrepancies with that of individual and social conflict as factors of structural changes in society. Furthermore, they distinguish the following interdependent stages of individual and structural change: exigency, articulation, action and institutionalisation:

1. 'An *exigency* is experienced as a discrepancy (for a person) between a consciously or unconsciously desired or expected state of affairs and an actual situation' (*Explorations in Social Change*, 1964, p. 89). In a following chapter Zollschan and Willer explain the stage of exigency in detail and with greater orientation to social change: 'An exigency is a feeling of unease in the person and the occurrence of unrest in a collectivity stemming from a differential between the person's definition of the relevant social situation as it is and as it should be. Typically an exigency as such is on a pre-verbal level.'

2. The next step is *articulation* of the exigency. It implies 'the recognition . . . of the existence and nature of the exigency and postulation of goals for its removal, prevention, or amelioration. Once articulated, the nebulous exigency condenses into more or less stable configurations which we shall call needs; in the absence of articulation only free-floating discomfort may be experienced' (ibid., p. 90).

3. The next step in this theoretical scheme is *action* 'as loco-motion toward postulated or unconscious goals'. In a later chapter Zollschan and Willer elaborate some of the social details of this action towards change. A latent interest group is turned into a manifest interest group and that into an organised group. It is 'organised to undertake collective action in support of interests common to the group' (ibid., p. 134).

4. The resulting stage is *institutionalisation*. It 'may be defined as a process consisting of changes in established patterns of interaction' (ibid., p. 91).

This conception starts with the exigencies and needs of the individual, who is the agent for translating social and cultura structures into action. Social change occurs by changing individual attitudes and behaviour.

Although Zollschan *et al.* also take into consideration groups and institutions in which the changed attitudes and behaviour become manifest as structural elements, the bias of over-emphasising the role of the individual as a factor of change could occur, whereas the structural factors of society could be neglected. It therefore seems preferable to add to the above-quoted theory of social change some aspects of the theories on diffusion and adoption of cultural elements as well as of socialisation. At every step of change we shall therefore ask the question: which persons or groups in the population under study felt an exigency and translated it into articulation, then into action, and finally into institutions, and which people were the early, which the late adopters of the changed attitudes and behaviour, and which were non-adoptors? From here we are better led on to the social and cultural structures as socialisation factors influencing these different individual attitudes and actions. It should thus become possible to distinguish factors of change within the individuals from those in the social subsystems (for example in the German and Indian villages) and those of the greater society. Only by bearing in mind the context of these different socio-cultural structures shall we be able to evaluate the more psychological aspect of exigencies and their recognition and articulation against the structural factors of socio-cultural changes.

This essay examines the usefulness of this revised and complemented theory by applying it to the results of a study on social change in 45 German villages and hamlets which were parts of one administrative community from early industrialism in the nineteenth century to the end of the Second World War, and which one of the authors investigated in 1952 (Wurzbacher and Pflaum-Mayntz, 1954, 1960). Our findings on this intense and long German process of social change will then be compared with those of an investigation of two South Indian villages. Being a follow-up study of an investigation by T. S. Epstein fifteen years ago, this Indian research provided us with a fairly differentiated insight into the changes of certain factors and into the interdependence of these factors over a period of forty years. The data are most exact within the period from 1954 to 1970 (Schönherr, 1972).

APPLICATION TO SOME RESULTS OF A STUDY ON GERMAN VILLAGES

The German villages that were studied changed in the course of 150 years from rather isolated and economically almost self-sufficient communities of small farmers to well-differentiated communities of commuters, highly interrelated economically, politically and culturally with the larger society. When we ask with Zollschan which factors led to recognition and articulation of exigencies of change, we find a primary role played by the influence of the state on the rural population. In the first half of the nineteenth century, social and residential mobility of individuals, including the right to marry, was set free by state legislation. A great increase of the population resulted from these reforms and was further supported by state measures of medical hygiene. The new liberty and the population pressure led to emigration or to commuting into industrialised areas. Thus a growing part of the rural population came to know new groups and persons of reference which made possible imitation, identification and critical comparison of their rural standards of life with urban ones. Such contacts were increased by the introduction of compulsory school education and the enlargement of military service as well as by government construction of roads and railways. Furthermore, the self-administering community found itself under continuous state influence and the recipient of frequent requests to promote the forming of various associations to further economic and social development. The communal administration had to report regularly to the higher level of state administration on the results achieved and the situation and problems of its population. The teacher, as a government official, held another key position in transmitting to the population public policies intended to stimulate development.

With growing contact to the cities and to industry, these state initiatives were supported or adopted in the course of critical and innovative activities of individual inhabitants, who had been working or living for extended periods in cities and had returned to their rural communities. Following urban models they founded numerous associations with political, cultural or economic goals. Our research on leading people of such associations from their beginning up to the time after the Second World War showed the importance of increased mobility and of numerous urban contacts as factors in the recognition of exigencies. Almost all these people had either come from outside the village or had lived and worked outside for a longer period or had received a higher education. They had thus enjoyed the opportunity to compare (a condition for 'articulation') urban experiences and models against their rural ones. This enabled them to articulate their critical attitude towards the situation in the villages, to explain it to the others, and to transform latent interest groups into organised group activities and into new institutions.

These contacts with the wider society and the resulting new socialisation processes and the consequent diversification of jobs changed the basic value orientation by which the people were accustomed to ranking each other. In a protracted process, landownership lost prestige, while the competing values of secondary-school education, professional education and, later, of institutionalised social security and finally of leisure time and leisure means increased as indices of esteem and ranking. Thus various value dissonances arose which led to faster changes in all rural structures by way of critical articulation and action.

The process of competition between the values of landownership, modern education and occupational achievement was accompanied by a growth in influence of the representatives of new professions and jobs on the political structures of the society on the different regional levels as well as on the village level. In the villages the bigger farmers retained for a long time the leading role in public functions, in village council, church council, associations and the like. Only the increasing democratisation of the wider society after the revolution of 1918 enlarged the influence of representatives of non-agrarian professions and jobs at the village level. The development of political democracy and of economic diversification was not synchronous. They were interdependent but not correlative; they are interrelated by numerous intervening variables belonging specifically to the cultural and subcultural sphere (Wurzbacher and Pflaum-Mayntz, 1954, 1960).

Our studies on the process of change in the villages lead to the conclusion (which seems important not only for a theory of social change but for the politics of socio-cultural development as well) that officials of the higher state level were the first to be motivated by conceptions of discrepancy. Guided by the economic, political and social goals in the larger society, they considered the situation of the rural society as unsatisfactory. They transformed their exigencies into public criticism, programmes, laws and other such action. Compared with such government actions from outside, the possibilities open to rural subgroups and individual village-dwellers were rather small; moreover the individual in a highly integrated village has always been strongly exposed to social control. Without support from outside factors his free space for innovations – his chance to change anything – has usually been too limited.

Alongside the higher state officials the next group of agents and adopters of change were the state officials in the local administration and the schoolteacher. The third group included those village inhabitants who had come into longer and more intense contacts with the larger society – through higher education, through military service, through their work or as members of modern associations. After the primary initiative of the state officials and the states measures for a better infrastructure had enabled this group to come into broader and closer contact with industry and with urban life, its members became autonomous agents of new experiences of discrepancy and dissonances which led to role conflicts and to innovations in their individual attitudes and behaviour. Through them, a greater amount of new values, habits and material goods of the industrial society diffused into the rural subculture and increased the variety of attitudes and structures of behaviour as well as individual mobility, choices, and chances to introduce and adopt innovations.

The relationship of the various subgroups of the villages and their specific influence on the population of the village, however, were not markedly changed until a considerable number of inhabitants had been activated and organised in voluntary public associations engaged in co-operative, economic, religious, political or leisure activities. As new centres of social activity in the villages, these associations became institutionally linked with their organisational structures on a national and sometimes on an international level. The experiences and connections of these national or international bodies reinforced the status and influence of their rural branches. Thus realising institutionalised leadership and an electoral procedure, these local associations fulfil the function of stimulating socially active people to take over a formal leadership position and to be trained in the forms and skills of public activity. This meant more possibilities for social change in rural communities, because individual criticism of rural structures could be articulated and translated into action within them with greater social competence and public effect. The associations brought about changes of local power structures and in other cases made them receptive to innovations, which could therefore be attributed to the members and especially the leaders of these organisations.

Being organised local centres of public activity, at the same time the associations brought wider opportunities to the rural population and its subcultures to have their interests represented on the higher organisational level of the larger society. The organisations of farmers and rural co-operatives were examples of such an influence exercised on the state and the economy of the German society during the nineteenth and twentieth centuries until the present (Freifrau v. Schrötter, 1971). This example demonstrated that these new organisations, taken over from urban and industrial value standards, acted in an ambivalent way: besides their modernising effects they can also contribute to conservatism in some cultural fields.

Summing up, we find that development progresses not always in an integrated or parallel manner but often in contrary directions with disintegrative consequences. With respect to sociological theory and methodology, this means a warning not to over-emphasize the integrative and homogeneous character of a larger society and of its social and cultural subsystems. (This happens frequently when simplifying categories are used to characterise certain societies, for instance when confronting industrial with agrarian, developed with underdeveloped, and socialist with bourgeois or capitalist societies.)

Another frequent source of methodological inadequacy is the tendency of the social scientist to take only the individual on the one hand and the larger society on the other into consideration, without paying attention to the numerous subgroups and subcultures as intermediate factors with their influential intervening and interpreting effects.

APPLICATION TO SOME RESULTS OF A STUDY ON INDIAN VILLAGES

(a) EPSTEIN'S FINDINGS ON CULTURAL INCOMPATIBILITY

T. S. Epstein (1962) carried out her research in two South Indian villages from 1954 to 1956. Both villages are situated in the same region and have a similar cultural background. Nevertheless, there were conspicuous differences of social change. Epstein maintained that the rapid change in one of the villages correlated with a remarkable occupational diversification of a part of the inhabitants. In the other village a strong economic development on the basis of agriculture was to be found, but there was almost no social change or occupational diversification among the inhabitants. Epstein explained the change in the first village by the hypothesis that, as a result of occupational diversification, members of the social system had adopted new roles and relations in the economic field which were incompatible with the traditional rural role system. Such new roles and relations had destroyed, for instance, some traditional patterns of income distribution and consequently the structure of income. This had changed the structure of economic power.

The change had provoked conflicts with the hereditary power structures of the Indian villages. The conflicts having been solved in favour of new holders of economic power, the social system had adjusted to the new economic roles and relations, with which it had become compatible again.

Epstein derived her hypothesis from the following empirical facts. The introduction of an irrigation system in the Mandya region (state of Mysore) and the construction of a big sugar plant in the 1930s had brought different effects on the two investigated villages, Wangala and Dalena. (Both villages are situated between 7 and 10 km from the town of Mandya, Mysore.) The Wangala fields now could be irrigated and the farmers could grow 'cash crops' – especially sugar cane which was very much wanted by the sugar plant; thus, their income increased considerably. This development was unilinear (the agrarian work was continued merely on another level) and to a high degree compatible with traditional economic as well as with political and cultural relations. Discrepancies or tensions with traditional subsystems of the village were scarce or non-existent.

The fields of Dalena, on the other hand, could not be irrigated from the new channel because they were situated on a higher part of the region. Not being able to grow 'cash crops', many villagers turned their economic activities away from their village. They grasped other occupational opportunities which were offered to them in the rapidly developing region of Mandya. By taking over new economic jobs they promoted an economic development in Dalena which was not unilinear but rather multifarious. By occupational diversification many economic relations were changed and became incompatible with the old social and political relationships. Open conflicts caused a change in the leadership structure of the village.

In her explanation, Epstein chooses as her starting-point those discrepancies which she understands as incompatibilities of sub-systems – the economic and the political (operationalised as formalised democratic leadership) – within the whole village system. She states only the fact of the discrepancy and does not inquire further to find out explicitly how these cultural discrepancies are experienced and interpreted by the various villagers and what further actions follow, until a change of social structures takes place.

At this point we shall try to examine and continue her explanation with the help of the above-discussed and revised theory of Zollschan *et al.* The new relations with the town, combined with occupational diversification, brought new knowledge of other groups, of other values and norms to villagers which led to critical comparisons with the traditional village values and norms. This may have started with a diffuse feeling of dissatisfaction – exigency – first with the economic, then with the social and political structure. Such needs and interests may be articulated by reference to those new groups and new opinion-leaders considered as models which may, for example, reject the principle of hereditary leadership, and demand instead the principle of achievement for recruiting leaders. The next step, then, that of articulation, will mean the transposition of exigency into socially relevant attitudes and behaviour. Epstein describes how factions are formed within the dominant farmer caste in the village, and how they struggle for political and religious dominance in caste and village. Institutionalisation takes place when the new leader is acknowledged by his fellow-villagers (e.g. is accepted as ordinary member in the village council).

Yet by applying only the theoretical conception of Zollschan *et al.*, some relevant questions remain unanswered. We have to ask, how does it happen that one individual is able to turn exigency into articulation, action, and even into socio-cultural change by institutionalisation, and others are not; and furthermore, that the same population in one period of time or in one dimension of culture turns to change and in another stays conservative?

In our follow-up study of the two South Indian villages in 1969–70, we found that in spite of a continuing integration of the villagers into the regional economic and administrative system, the political system of the villagers has changed only partially. The traditional local leaders still supervise and keep stable the basic ingredients of the traditional system, as for instance the rigid caste structure with its strict norms of endogamy, and rigorous discrimination against the Untouchables. They still recklessly enforce the claim of one caste to dominate in all public spheres, and to select leaders according to hereditary regulations. Thus, it is not only empirically but theoretically important to find out why the change begun in 1954–6 did not continue, but decreased or even stopped altogether.

Ogburn's theory of 'cultural lag' could explain why structural discrepancies between the economic and the political subsystems lead to different modes and speeds of change. The political change stated by Epstein had indeed followed the substantial change of the economic system with a remarkable time-lag. The plausible assumption that the change had reached a point of stagnation because the discrepancies between both systems had been abolished by the time of Epstein's investigation is unsatisfactory. In fact, the rapid continuing economic development of the industrial town of Mandya and of the agriculture in the region near that town promoted a growing occupational mobility which is objectively incompatible with the rigid caste structure of the village. We believe that these open questions could be at least partly answered by applying the role theory and especially its conceptions of social control and its sanctions. An example from the investigated villages may illustrate our argument.

1. As our starting-point, let us take the position of a member of the Dhobi caste (the caste of washermen and women) in the village of Dalena. The members of the farmer caste

expect a Dhobi, whose caste is considered inferior to that of the farmers, to perform certain rituals on certain occasions – this behaviour demonstrated his willingness to fulfil the villager's role expectations. His role behaviour is socially institutionalised by traditionally fixed rituals and in addition subjectively controlled by internalised religious values (Dharma) of the participants. In the case of positive role fufilment the rewards consist of social and psychic equilibrium; in the negative case of deviant behaviour, in disruption of the Jajmani relations by the farmers (hereditary formalised economic relations between families of different castes regulating service and gratification) and, as an extremely severe sanction, it is believed that an additional punishment takes place after death. If these attitudes dominate, we can state that the Dhobi will behave in accordance with role expectation.

2. The Dhobi has secured employment in a governmental administration in the town nearby. His position has changed by a new – an urban – role sector being added to the old ones. In the urban enterprise new role partners exhibit new role expectations with new forms of control, e.g. rewards and sanctions. The Dhobi is expected to act according to the organisational and not the ritual hierarchies. Furthermore, other urban influences tend to reduce his internalised and religiously reinforced village and caste superegos. If his family can live on his earnings in the enterprise he may after some time not feel obliged any more to recognise his ritual subordination in the village. Thus, his role structure in the town has become incompatible with that in the village.

3. The solution of the incompatibility. The Dhobi, as incumbent of this enlarged role field, now experiences intra- as well as inter-role conflicts in relation to his town and his village role partners. He develops new needs concerning his farmer partners, e.g. he no longer expects to be discriminated against as subordinate. The farmers stick to their traditional expectations. The Dhobi and the farmers put sanctions into effect against each other: the Dhobi by refusing certain ritual symbols of service and subordination, and the farmers by interrupting the Jajmani relationship. In our ideal-type reflection we have put aside numerous other

kinds of sanction which are applied in such cases of conflict within a densely interwoven primary-group structure of Indian castes and villages.

The above-mentioned sanction of breaking off traditional relations does not trouble the Dhobi too much because he and his household live on the earnings of his employment in town. Therefore the farmers cannot enforce behaviour in accordance with their expectations as they could before. The new occupation has greatly improved the Dhobi's position with regard to sanctions by the villagers. Thus we find that some structures of the social system of the village have changed and sooner or later the farmers will have to adjust their expectations to this new situation.

To sum up, when applying the role theory we can explain incompatibility as a situation in which role incumbents and their partners are defining their role in a different way. In addition, role theory allows still further explanations of possible effects of incompatibility. By our example we demonstrated that only under certain conditions will economic change produce change in ritual status and in other socio-cultural structures. Under different conditions of sanctions, cultural incompatibility may produce a permanent state of conflict (that means a permanent state of action without institutionalisation), or the specific incompatibility may be abolished by forcing the Dhobi, through very severe sanctions, to submit to the expectations of the traditional social system. That means regression from action to articulation or even to the vague state of exigency – a rather frequent alternative. Impediments to change are thus explained by a behaviouristic approach. We are now able to differentiate Epstein's hypothesis in the following manner. Occupational diversification leads to socio-cultural incompatibilities under the condition of role conflicts between the members of the social system (special case of incompatibility), and it leads to change in the social system if the influence of social control on the part of the traditional role incumbents decreases.

(*b*) INCOMPATIBILITIES AND CHANGES IN THE FIELD OF
     GENERATIVE BEHAVIOUR

When we consider, as another example, the generative behaviour of the population of the two villages, and their attitude towards family planning, we find cultural discrepancies likewise as factors of social change. They become most evident when we compare the macro-system of the state with the micro-system of the village. Similarly to the above-described German villages and to the economic development of the Indian villages, we find state officials to be the dominant innovators and promoters of socio-cultural change. The special structure of macro-systems and their legally defined functions of responsibility and order demand more rational analysis, prognosis, planning and regulation of social conditions. Obviously, the state officials are the first who pass through Zollschan's phases of recognition and articulation of exigencies, typical of which are the discrepancies between the generative behaviour of the rural population and the economic resources and plans for development.

Since 1951 every new Five-Year Plan has shown an increasing recognition of the problems of Indian overpopulation. In the last plan the problems of population explosion, their impact on social and economic development, and consequently the programme of family planning were given urgent priority. Whereas a certain tendency towards stabilisation of population development is visible in urban areas, the problem is still tremendously urgent in rural areas, where 82 per cent of the Indian population are living, according to the last census (Ghosh, 1970, p. 176; *Family Planning Programme, Report for 1962*, p. 14; Dandekar and Dandekar, 1953, pp. 115–87; Sovani, 1952, *passim*). The rural population is therefore the prime target group aimed at by all measures to promote the idea of family planning. Accordingly, it is emphasised: 'The message of family planning should be carried to the door of the illiterate masses living in the subsistence sector of our economy. The Gram-Sevak (social worker in a community), the pilot of Community Development, can be trained to perform some effective work in this direction. The Indian overpopulation problem should be considered as the main offshoot of the semi-stagnant nature of the agriculture-dominated subsistence sector of our economy' (Ghosh, 1970, p. 178; also *Family Planning Programme, 1962–63*, pp. 88–9). 'The extension network of Community Development will be harnessed for programmes of nationwide priority and coverage like . . . family planning' (*Fourth Five-Year Plan: A Draft Outline*, 1968, p. 47). And with special concern to the family-planning programme the Indian

Ministry of Health declares: 'It can and should be assigned to develop the family planning activities in a community development block area in association with the C.D. Organisation and Panchayati Raj institutions. . . . It is obvious that the villages should be reached urgently' (*Family Planning Programme, Report 1962–1963*). Meanwhile, the family-planning programme has become an integral part of the Community Development Organisation. Clinics for family planning have been installed with far-reaching organisational competences and facilities in all development blocks. They certify, at least on the part of the government, the decided willingness for action.

A second group experiencing exigencies and responding with articulations and actions in the field of family planning were the representatives of the state on the rural local level. Their function was quite similar to that observed on the part of officials in the process of village modernisation in Germany. So far, the rural population itself has accepted the ideas of family planning to a rather modest extent. Twenty years after its articulation by the government the statistics in Table 6.4 show how diffusion spread in the two villages of our research.

TABLE 6.4   Attitudes towards family planning in Wangala and Dalena[a]

Categories of attitudes	Villages									
	Wangala				Dalena				Total	
	Women %		Men %		Women %		Men %			%
Very negative	9	12·5	13	18·1	8	13·8	9	15·5	39	15·0
Negative	15	20·8	18	25·0	8	13·8	11	19·0	52	20·0
Ambivalent	28	38·9	25	34·7	25	43·1	24	41·4	102	39·2
Positive	20	27·8	16	22·2	17	29·3	14	24·1	67	25·8
Very positive	–	–	–	–	–	–	–	–	–	–
Total	72	100·0	72	100·0	58	100·0	58	100·0	260	100·0

[a] Results of a random sample of 305 of the married couples, females 18–40 years, males 21–55 years old.
Source: Sen Gupta (1972).

If we ask to what degree the changed attitudes have been transformed into new patterns of behaviour, we find the number of adopters even smaller. In both villages only 18 out of 413 couples have applied contraceptive means or methods (according to information from the board for Family Planning Authority of the Mandya District). These data indicate that only a minor part of the population agrees with the conception of government and scientists on discrepancies of economic resources and generative behaviour, and that only a tiny minority act according to this conception. Here again we observe that different components of the development process can go along in integrated as well as in disintegrated, even contrary, ways. In this regard, the macro-system of the state can differ substantially from regional, cultural or religious subsystems in direction, intensity and intercorrelation of change.

We have already found such discrepancies when investigating the early industrial development of German villages; in the Indian society they are much more salient because of the strong influence of traditional subsystems, such as caste and religion. It nevertheless seems probable that in the long run, factors similar to those of the development of the German rural society will succeed in changing the situation of rural India too. We can refer to them as factors of rationality, secularisation, education, mobility and openness. In the course of our research in India we tried to consider a multitude of components of these basic factors and their correlation with the capability to recognise, articulate and evaluate the population problem as it is represented through the attitude towards family planning. The results as shown in Table 6.5 partly support the theoretical conclusions drawn from the research on German villages; partly they indicate a far more limited capability to interpret and adopt innovations in the Indian villages at the present level of development.

These results, of course, call for some limiting specification of the same kind we used when discussing the impact of occupational diversification. The above-mentioned factors for a system becoming open to change are at the same time always counteracted by conservative factors which tend to keep the system stable and which are nearly always accompanied by particularly severe social control, especially in small rural structures. They can influence the individual member of a group in such a manner that on different occasions he might behave in a very different and even contradictory way. Such conservative factors may also be found on higher levels of the interacting systems and subsystems. Special

TABLE 6.5. Correlation between selected independent variables and the attitude towards family planning among the married male population in Wangala and Dalena

($N = 130$)

Independent variables	Dependent variable: positive attitude towards family planning
1. Rationality	0·41*
2. Secularism	0·36*
3. Education	0·32*
4. Extension contact	0·29*
5. Modernity	0·29*
6. Community participation	0·27*
7. Extension knowledge	0·25*
8. Radio exposure	0·24*
9. Age	−0·23*
10. Change programme contact	0·19*
11. Social status	0·18†
12. Aspiration level for children's occupation	0·17†

*Significance level = 0·01.
†Significance level = 0·05.
Source: Sen Gupta (1972).

groups of a society like some higher castes in India may take over modernisation programmes, adopt better educational opportunities, etc., and by this strengthen their own influence and predominance against all innovative and equalising tendencies of other groups within the greater society.

Despite these counter-trends and limitations, we consider our general hypothesis on the interdependence between the openness of a society and the capability of its members to recognise cultural discrepancies, to evaluate and articulate them and to translate them into socio-cultural development to be relevant to development in general. In addition, we maintain that the developmental interrelation of the larger socio-cultural system, the regional and the village systems might be similar in Africa to that found in German and Indian society. That is:

1. Rural structures on a subsistence level allow only very limited chances for personal as well as for structural change. Therefore, larger national and even international systems

with their superior intellectual and material resources have to influence them from outside if development is to occur.

2. This influence must be communicated to the regional and village structure by representatives of these larger authorities. They serve as indispensable innovative models and as new opinion-leaders besides and against traditional authorities.

3. In addition, there is need for new economic, cultural and political institutions which gain competence for public activity and development and which select and train active personalities for leadership on the basis of individual initiative and achievement.

4. These factors could systematically be organised to work together on the village, regional and state level to stimulate and support economic as well as cultural entrepreneurship by educational, financial and organisational means, as has, for example, been started by the Brigades and the Co-operatives in Botswana, or even more so by the 'Small Entrepreneurs' Development Corporation (SEDCO) in Swaziland.

5. The application of these different measures unavoidably produces cultural discrepancies and personal conflicts. To recognise, articulate and translate them into action is a fundamental task of all those engaged in developmental processes.

BIBLIOGRAPHY

Barnett, E., *Innovation: The Basis of Cultural Change* (New York, 1953).
Dandekar, V. M., and Dandekar, K., *Survey of Fertility and Mortality in Poona District* (Poona, 1953).
Epstein, T. S., *Economic Development and Social Change in South India* (Manchester, 1962).
Ghosh, A., *Indian Economy: Its Nature and Problems* (Calcutta, 1970).
Government of India, *The First Five-Year-Plan: A Draft Outline* (New Delhi, 1951).
Government of India, *The First Five-Year-Plan* (New Delhi, 1951).
Government of India, *The Second Five-Year-Plan* (New Delhi, 1956).
Government of India, *The Third Five-Year-Plan* (New Delhi, 1961).
Government of India, *The Fourth Five-Year-Plan: A Draft Outline* (New Delhi, 1968).

Hagen, E. E., *On the Theory of Social Change* (Homewood, Ill., 1962).

Kiefer, K., *Die Diffusion von Neuerungen: Kultursoziologsche und kommunikationswissenschaftliche Aspekte der agraroziologischen Diffusionsforschung* (Tübingen, 1967).

Lionberger, H., *Adoption of New Ideas and Practices* (Iowa, 1960).

Pflaum-Mayntz, R., in Wurzbacher, G. (Hrsg.), *Das Dorf im Spannungsfeld industrieller Entwicklung* (Stuttgart, 1954, 1960).

Raina, B. L. (ed.) *Family Planning Programme, Report for 1962–63* (New Delhi, 1963).

Rogers, E. M., *Diffusion of Innovations* (New York and London, 1962).

Rüschemeyer, P., 'Partielle Modernisierung', in Zapf, W., *Theorien des sozialen Wandels* (Köln-Berlin, 1970, 2. Aufl).

Schönherr, S., *Berufliche Diversifikation und Führungsmodernisierung im ländlichen Indien – Follow-up-Untersuchung von zwei Dörfern in Süd-Indien, 1954–56 und 1969–70* (Saarbrücken, 1972).

Sen Gupta, B., *Hemmende und fördernde Fatoren der Ergebnisse der Diffusion und Adoption der Innovationen 'lokale Selbstverwaltung', 'Genossenschaft' und 'Familienplanung'* (Diss. Erlangen-Nürnberg, 1972).

Schrötter, G. Frfr. von, 'Agrarorganisation und sozialer Wandel (dargestellt am Beispiel Schleswig-Holsteins', in Rüegg und Neuloh, *Zur soziologischen Theorie und Analyse des 19. Jahrhunderts* (Göttingen, 1971).

Sovani, N. V., *The Problem of Fertility Control in India: Cultural Factors and Development of Policy, Approaches to Problems of High Fertility in Agrarian Societies* (Papers presented at the 1951 Annual Conference of the Milbank Memorial Fund, New York, 1952).

Srinivas, M. N., *Social Change in Modern India* (Berkeley, 1967).

Wurzbacher, G. (Hrsg.), *Das Dorf im Spannungsfeld industrieller Entwicklung* (Stuttgart, 1954, 1960).

Wurzbacher, G., 'Bevölkerungsumschichtung und Führungsauslese in der ländlichen Gesellschaft', in *Die neue Gesellschaft*, 3. Jg., 3. Heft, 1956.

Wurzbacher, G., 'Die öffentliche freie Vereinigung als Faktor soziokulturellen, insbesondere emanzipatorischen Wandels im 19. Jahrhundert', in Rüegg und Neuloh, *Zur soziologischen Theorie und Analyse des 19. Jahrhunderts* (Göttingen, 1971).

Zollschan, G. K., and Hirsch, W., *Introduction to Explorations in Social Change* (New York, 1964).

Zollschan, G. K., and Perucci, R., 'Social Stability and Social Process: An Initial Presentation of Relevant Categories', in *Explorations in Social Change*, a.a.O.

Zollschan, G. K., and Willer, D., 'Prolegomenon to a Theory of Revolutions' in *Explorations in Social Change*, a.a.O.

Urbanisation and National Development: A Probable Case

ARCH DOTSON

I

CONDITIONS AND TRENDS

Rapid, and rising, urbanisation now characterises world development. But this is not a simple condition. While the overall pattern is plain and persistent, its specific features vary considerably.

Davis's critical distinction must be applied. As a comparative demographic matter, urbanisation is relative. That is to say, it involves an internal relationship – the proportion of total population concentrated in urban settlements. 'Since total population is composed of both the urban population and the rural, however, the "population rural" is a function of both of them.'[1] Viewed this way, it may be seen that parts of the world are not only, and obviously, urbanised disproportionately, but also are urbanising at quite unequal rates. The developed nations of the world are urbanising at slower rates than the underdeveloped ones. Indeed, advanced urbanisation can be seen to be finite, bounded. A termination can be anticipated when urban and non-urban population change has slowed to the same rate, or both populations remain stationary. Developing countries have far to go to reach such an equilibrium. Not only are their total populations now increasing faster, but so also are their urban ratios. 'Contemporary underdeveloped populations have been growing since 1940 more than twice as fast as industrialised populations, and their increase far exceeds the growth of the latter at the peak of their expansion.'[2] High rates of urbanisation are, especially, Third World phenomena.

But while valid statistically, the calculation obscures much of the function of urbanisation and, as will be noted later, the problem. It is not merely a higher proportion of urban population that gives rise to the issue, but scale changes and ultimately absolute increases themselves. Magnitude, not ratio alone, is the matter.

VISIONS OF APOCALYPSE

Nowhere have these trends been celebrated. On the contrary, they have raised universally, if not uniformly, alarums.

Popular journalism and the media in the advanced countries have decried the 'deteriorating cities', 'the urban garrison', the 'sick, sick cities', etc. The penitential effects elsewhere have also been reported. For the *New Yorker*, Ved Mehta described the nightmares of the 'City of Dreadful Night' – Calcutta. Among them:

> Streets packed with milling, barefoot people and inquisitive half-naked children, old cows, and stray dogs. *Pukka*, or permanent houses, made of brick and cement, but mouldy and decaying. Maze of spidery alleys, gullies, and footpaths leading away from the street. Ordure, rotting garbage, and mud underfoot.[3]

Disease; starvation; alienation; anomie; violence – personal and political; and so on and on. One of the popular topics for television documentaries 'as a public service' has become the world's urban crisis, and its frightening aspects.

The anxiety is shared by professionals concerned directly with urbanisation. At conference after conference, at every level, under national, bilateral and international auspices – at Hong Kong, New York, Nagoya, Stockholm, Bangkok, The Hague, Pittsburgh, Tokyo – fear and gloom are expressed. The notable P.C.U.G. Conference in Honolulu in 1967, with its large delegation of Asian officials and planners, estimated that urbanisation 'poses "great threats" '; causes developing nations to 'sink deeper into the mire of social and environmental deterioration'; produces 'disorderliness' and 'mounting unrest' in which 'the very framework of social stability on which a nation's economic development depends can be destroyed'.[4]

Consultants sent to developing areas have joined (and no doubt considerably abetted) the dire predictions, as illustrated by the recent Metcalf and Eddy warning:

. . . certain Asian cities, unhinged from the industrialisation that caused Western urbanisation, are growing at dangerously fast rates. The year 2000 population projection of 14 million for the Bombay area is closely paralleled by projections of 12 million for Bangkok and 14,500,000 for Manila for the same year. Growth of this magnitude may cause serious economic and political difficulties for the nations involved. The provision of urban infrastructure and employment to accommodate the population polarisation that this urban centralisation will bring may preclude significant overall economic growth for Asian nations.[5]

Scholarly literature has also been dominated by foreboding. Sovani's critical cautions have gone largely unheeded.[6] When demographers, geographers, the new urbanologists and other social scientists confront the implications of their data, frights and shocks of over-, premature, excessive urbanisation – perhaps 'tyrannopolis' – are the outcome.

The ultimate scholarly alarum has been raised by McGee.[7] The two-thirds of the world which is underdeveloped is experiencing 'pseudo-urbanisation'. This is unlike the West where 'the growing cities gradually absorbed an increasing proportion of the total population until the majority . . . was living in cities and an "urbanised society" had come into being'. Absorption was possible because while 'the industrial revolution brought about the increasing concentration of people in cities, it also introduced the technical improvements which made possible increased productivity in agriculture and allowed the rural population to shift to cities'.[8] But the developing countries cannot follow this path, because urban areas cannot absorb new population, because they cannot industrialise; and they cannot industrialise because of their colonial economic legacies, and because of their disadvantage in world markets dominated by the already industrialised nations. 'Cities grow, despite their failure to industrialise, not because of industrialisation, as they did in Western countries.'[9] A 'wasteland' will develop.

The McGeevian argument incorporates old doctrine, but indicates a neo-orthodoxy. Following Bogle's example, the Senior Adviser on Regional Development of the United Nations and former Director of the U.N. Centre for Housing, Building and

Planning has recently accepted the didactic:

> The nineteenth-century industrial revolution in Europe and
> North America ... proceeded at a relatively moderate pace.
> In the main, the market mechanism regulated economic
> growth. As cities expanded a new social structure emerged
> gradually.... People and factories were settling in the
> developed areas of the most advanced nations and world trade
> favoured their industries. Now the rush to the capitals and
> metropolises of Africa, Asia and Latin America is most inten-
> sive, massive and rapid in countries whose natural resources
> remain underdeveloped and their man-made counterparts –
> the economic and technological resources and skills – are in-
> sufficient. Now the terms of trade are highly adverse to the
> developing nations....[10]

Others have pressed the explanation, adding usually the predictions of extending squalor and mounting social and political
tension.

From all quarters, the dominant response to urbanisation has
been growing desperation and dread. An almost prophetic question spreads: how shall we be delivered?

THE BASIC ISSUE, AND OTHERS

That anguished question begs a prior question, and raises a subsequent one. The prior question is: do we in fact require
deliverance? No one can deny that the conditions which give rise
to the apocalyptic visions are there – conspicuous and evidently
urgent. Are they inevitably associated with urbanisation? Have
they been interpreted correctly; and do they tend towards a wasteland? At the more general level, the issue is: what is the relationship between urbanisation and national development?

The subsequent question is one of method. If we need in some
way to affect the relationship between urbanisation and national
development, how shall it be done? The answer here seems clear.
Without some new revelation, it will have to be done through
public policy. Only the state, through political authority, can
command the resources required.

The cardinal orientations are: (1) do nothing; (2) try to stop
urbanisation; (3) try to increase it; (4) attempt to manage urbanisation. To date, overall choices have been confined almost en-

tirely to options (1) and (2). In relation to the first, 'do nothing', this is not to say that public policy has not had an effect on urbanisation. National, provincial and local budgets contain large components, often buried in sectoral categories, devoted to urban services and projects, and urbanising outlays. But it is to say that little *policy* is to be found, in the sense of deliberate efforts by governments to alter the patterns or characteristics of urbanisation. It seems clear also that international and bilateral assistance agencies have been equally unaware, and unintentional, about the effects of their intervention. Banks that lend money for roads, bridges, steel mills, airports, dams and water systems, for example, have been conspicuously oblivious of their urbanising consequences. It required a special project recently to get even crude and partial estimates of the expenditures of the United States Agency for International Development for urban development.[11]

II

The search turns first to conventional wisdom and its potential contribution to explanation. As noted in the preceding section, much of that wisdom is of the apocalyptic variety. This interpretation must be evaluated, and since it incorporates most of the lesser alarums, the ultimate statement may conveniently be utilised.

THE 'WASTELAND THESIS' EVALUATED

The sources of the wasteland thesis are, purportedly, historical and functional. When one asks, why is the urbanisation that is sweeping over the Third World 'pseudo', the answer is found in several assumptions and inferences. Comparatively, this urbanisation departs from a model – taken as a norm. That model is Western, in which urbanisation (a) proceeded more slowly; (b) was associated with rising industrialisation; (c) allowed social adjustment gradually; and (d) was accompanied by advantages in international trade.

This is not, in fact, an accurate representation of the Western experience. As Sovani has pointed out, in answering Davis's and Golder's earlier alarum of 'over-urbanisation', the record is by no means uniform, either as among countries or over time:

For example, when in 1895 the degree of urbanisation in

Sweden was comparable to that of Asia today (8·2 per cent in cities of 100,000 or more), the proportion of the labour force in non-agricultural occupations there was less than 45 per cent. Even in 1970, though urbanisation had increased slightly to 9·3 per cent, this proportion was only 51 per cent. Conversely, in Switzerland, though the proportion of the labour force in non-agricultural occupations was 60 per cent in 1888, there was no city with a population of 100,000 or more in the entire country at that time. In fact, if we logically pursue the analysis based on this norm, the whole of South and Central America would have to be classified as over-urbanised, and, for this matter the whole of Africa and so too the world![12]

The urbanisation/industrialisation ratio has not, then, been consistent. A few countries only – notably Britain, France and the United States – furnish the paradigm. Wide disparities still exist between industrialisation/urbanisation ratios in developed countries. The wastelanders look to the West for their example – but the East, notably Japan, and on a different scale Australia, Taiwan and Singapore, supply alternative models. The urbanisation experience of each also differs, and differs historically from that of Europe and North America. Trade disadvantage and late starts apparently have not precluded urbanisation and rapid national development. Tensions and revolutions seem no more impending there than, say, in the United States. Adaptability, surely, is a very elastic social attribute.

The analysis has other obvious defects. The state of technology is profoundly different today from the period of rapid Western urbanisation. The precious 'surpluses' required to release men from the production of food and fibre may now be accumulated easier and faster, despite population increases. Jakobson and Ved Prakash, drawing on Fourastie's suggestive analysis, have urged that 'technological progress – being fastest in secondary sector activities – affects not only the various cost variables, but importantly the job generation potential and human resource requirements within the sector itself'.[13] If industrialisation be taken as the indispensable requirement for true urbanisation, then the advanced nations are now entering a period of rapid de-urbanisation!

The proof is unsound methodologically. How does pseudo-urbanisation, explicitly defined, somewhere, lead to the results predicted? Empirical evidence and data are conspicuously lacking. Nor has the problem of dependency been confronted. If the wrong kind of urbanisation can produce a wasteland and impair national development then the latter is depicted as a dependent variable. But as industrialisation occurs, urbanisation can proceed, as will national development. Industrialisation must therefore occur first. But few industries can be established without a complex physical infrastructure – energy, transport, roads, public services – the necessary skilled and unskilled labour, access to capital, the advantages of complementarities, externalities, etc., all of which imply concentration. In short, all require urbanisation.

The logic locks. The developing countries cannot have national development without urbanisation; but they cannot have urbanisation without national development. And the independent variable is industrialisation, a condition which is in fact dependent and which has been presumed incorrectly to have characterised a model. Detectable, of course, is the classical problem of redundancy. Without explicit specifications of urbanisation and national development, the argument slips easily into an equation in which pseudo-urbanisation becomes simply not-national-development.

Of incidental importance has been the tendency of all alarmists to concentrate on the all too apparent 'problems' created by urbanisation. Crowding, crime, unemployment, etc., are indeed more conspicuous when concentrated than when spread over rural landscapes. Costs are also more easily perceived than benefits; and short-range considerations displace those more distant.

While the analysis could be extended and each of the alarums considered at its own level and in its own context, the same basic interpretative deficiencies would be disclosed: failure to adopt an appropriate perspective, the omission of benefits, the fallacy of composition, the absence of a developmental standard, and so on.

A CONCLUSION AND SOME COUNTER-INDICATIONS

The wasteland thesis, and its associated alarums, are not systematically founded: they do not correctly predict an urban apocalypse. Their explanations are improbable. It seems that McGee and Malthus were both wrong!

Social scientists must, then, begin to search for more systematic explanations. Actually, a great deal of probable evidence is at hand, some statistical, but most functional. By the latter is meant simply empirical and experimental information and data about urbanisation and development, their conditions and processes. The tendencies, behaviour and interdependencies of many of their elements are fairly well documented. (The literature in the several aspects of this documentation is so extensive that no effort will be made to review it here.)

Of primary importance is a consistent relationship which the wastelanders had to discount in order to reach their conclusion. The fact is that urbanisation (as measured by concentration of population) and national development (as measured by output factors) are associated positively. Whatever the sectoral mixes involved, this pattern holds in the nineteenth and twentieth centuries alike. Of course, this is an aggregate test; but at the very least it would signify that the conditions which yield higher gross products are positively related to urbanisation. At no time, anywhere, have significant improvements in productivity or material well-being been achieved through non-urban forms.

There is, as well, a great and growing body of record which shows how urbanisation allows the things to be done that are required to increase productivity, raise standards of living and achieve national development targets. Industrialisation has been mentioned. Parallel capacities are formed through the concentration of capital, task specialisation, the efficient use of space, support for specialised facilities, and so on. The regional 'drain' theory has been discredited; and in fact it has suggested that cities should become larger, not smaller, and urbanisation more concentrated. The point of diminishing returns has not been demonstrated.

In the psycho-social realm, studies of migration and migrants build up evidence that the pains of displacement, the breaking of ties with land and village, the disintegration of the family – the costs so often cited – are offset by pride in new skills, sophistication and independence. Administrative theory extensively supports propositions indicating that urbanisation enhances social capacity to create and function effectively in large, complex organisations. Such organisations are, of course, required to provide more efficient and higher levels of public service, to industrialise, build infrastructure and employ public policy to secure political goals.

These, and other enlarging *corpora* of evidence, are quite contrary to the alarum traditions. Further, they tend to be basic, and are empirical and existential. They do not attempt to deal with the essence of either urbanisation or national development, but rather with their properties, processes and interactions. The tendencies of these evidences show considerable convergence and mutual reinforcement.

III

While the 'wasteland thesis' has not been proved and seems improbable, and certain aggregate and functional evidence suggests a contrary relationship, it remains to express these indications as a general hypothesis, and to test that hypothesis.

Such was the purpose of a collaborative research project conducted in three South-east Asian countries during the past two years.[14] The cases investigated were the Philippines, Thailand and Malaysia. The findings from the first two are now substantially complete, and will be reported here.

THE BASIC METHODOLOGY[15]

In its most parsimonious form, the contrary hypothesis would be: urbanisation yields national development. So formulated, national development would be depicted as the dependent variable. Other factors may intermediate; but the analysis controls for urbanisation and examines developmental 'responses'. The linkages between these intervening variables and urbanisation are considered closer than to national development. Association would suggest a direction of dependency, which would be strengthened by sequential or cross-lagged associations.

The methodological problems of empirical research in social science are well known to its practitioners. Experimental techniques are seriously confined. Statistical analyses, supplemented by functional tests, have to substitute for experiments for most complex problems. The research necessarily adopted this latter approach. Of course, every methodology incorporates the limitations of its component assumptions and tools – for example, that the relationships involved are linear.

Reduced to its basic elements, the procedure required that,

initially, the hypothesis be expressed in testable propositions – as follows:

> (a) the more urbanised the unit of observation (town, municipality, city, tesaban, province, etc.), the higher the level of its development;
>
> (b) increases in levels of urbanisation should be positively associated with increases in levels of development; and
>
> (c) increases in national levels of urbanisation should be positively associated with increases in levels of national development.

Definitions, measures and observations of each of the variables were required. Whereas population concentration was used in the Philippines, differences in available data made it necessary to employ a more complex definition of urbanisation in the Thai research. Slightly different indicators of development had to be adopted in each case. Other analytic techniques varied. Nor could exactly the same time-periods be used for all observations. All the data were generated and processed by political units and are therefore 'official' – with all the implicit deficiences as to accuracy, completeness and consistency. None of these variations, however, can be considered to affect fundamentally the indications of the relationships analysed.[16]

As noted, the formulation allowed for intervening variables. Early in the research it seemed that a cluster of items, which was termed 'administrative capacity' and defined as the ability to engage in complex co-operation, indeed mediated between the primary factors. These relationships were tested in both cases.

The units of observation in the Philippines were 37 cities for at least two points in time, and 55 provinces for at least two points in time; in Thailand, 22 tesabans (cities) for at least two points in time.

FINDINGS FROM THE PHILIPPINES

The urbanisation measure produced 8 out of a possible 16 correlations with the dimensions of cities assessed (for this purpose, a 0·33 correlation was taken as the cutoff point of significance for an $n = 37$). To test administrative capacity, three governmental and political indicators were employed. For all measures there were strong correlations with urbanisation. Not only are these correlations strong and positive, but they increase over time with the 1960 level of urbanisation: 1957, 0.56; 1960, 0.65; and 1962–3, 0.85. The increase in the strength of the correlation might be grounds for making a case for a plausible causal relationship. What the last two correlations mean is that the level of urbanisation in 1960 not only predicts administrative capacity in 1960, but predicts even better capacity in 1962–3. This brief time difference, however, should not be considered decisive. With respect to change in administrative capacity 1956–60, a four-year period, nothing can be said. This last measure of capacity, however, is based entirely on changes in property taxation. Although one image of the big city is that of a more politicised and mobilised electorate, this did not hold for the Philippine cities in the study.

The relationship between urbanisation and industrial-commercial activities produced a mixed pattern. In terms of both the size of the (industrial-commercial) enterprises, and the economic significance of the city in the province (city salience), there was no correlation. This means that the size of the industrial enterprises and the general economic importance of the city, relative to other areas in the province, have nothing to do with the urbanisation level of the city. If we examine another infrastructure measure, road development, again we find no correlation. The correlation, however, between urbanisation and the concentration of industrial, service and commercial activities, of all sizes, is strongly positive: 0.53. (The second dimension of this is a weak but insignificant correlation: 0.30.) This relationship, perhaps more than others, suggests the linkage between urbanisation and administrative capacity, for it implies the range of structures within which people interact and co-operate. The more urbanised the city, the greater the number (and presumably the wider the distribution) of such structures – not only enterprises of great scale. It is the sheer number, per capita, of such structures that is positively associated with concentration. In other words, taking the definition of urbanisation literally, the greater the concentration of the population, the greater the concentration of industrial, service and commercial enterprises of all sizes.

The correlations support a generalisation that the greater the urbanisation, the greater the educational attainment of the population (first factor: 0.56). There is, however, no relationship between the urbanisation level and educational change; but all the indicators of change refer to public rather than private education. More urbanised cities are better able to provide educational facilities (or have provided them) than less urbanised cities.

The correlation of urbanisation with the quality of the amenities, as they were measured, was negligible.

In sum, then, the highly urbanised cities in the Philippines, in contrast to the less urbanised ones, (a) have more manufacturing and service establishments for their population; (b) have a population that has higher educational attainment and with more educational facilities; and (c) have governments that raise more revenues and spend more for public purposes. More urbanised cities, however, cannot be distinguished from less urbanised ones by the politicisation of their population or by the size of their economic enterprises.

FINDINGS FROM PHILIPPINE PROVINCE DATA

Although the data on Philippine provinces were not as comprehensive as those on cities, they reflect somewhat better some of the dimensions of development, and extend over a longer period. In many cases the information was too discreet to be used as general indicators across several provinces. In certain instances, such data were summated into an overall indication, such as 'cost of facilities'.

Urbanisation correlates significantly with 8 of the 15 dimensions examined (a 0·273 correlation was used as a significance cutoff for $n = 54$ and 0·34 for $n = 35$). It is striking that the measures of urbanisation for 1960 and 1969, although expressing nearly a decade of urbanisation, produced no differences in relationships. The relationship between the urbanisation and developmental dimensions remains constant, regardless of the changes in the level of urbanisation of the province.

The correlations between urbanisation and industrial activity are, as might be expected, very high and consistent for the two time-periods. The correlations remain high, even though there are several cases of missing data for the years 1956 and 1962.

The availability of electrical energy, utilities and developmental loans is also associated with the more urbanised provinces. The correlation between these variables and urbanisation in 1960 is 0·39, and in 1969, 0·44. On the other hand, there is no similar correlation between urbanisation and governmental input into cost of roads, bridges, waterworks, etc. Indeed, outlays for roads are clearly rural rather than urban investments, with correlations of − 0·51 in 1960, − 0·50 in 1969, and − 0·31 for roads and urbanisation in 1968. But in education and housing the relationship reverts. The correlation between urbanisation and education in 1960 is 0·32; and between 1954 and 1960 the correlation between urbanisation and education change is 0·29. But the conventional view that the more rural the province, the more likely there will be both high birth and death rates, does not hold for the Philippines. Finally, there is one strong and clear relationship between the kinds of amenities available and urbanisation – housing. The correlation between urbanisation levels, both for 1960 and 1969, and the quality of the housing is 0·51 and 0·55 respectively.

As would be expected, there is a positive correlation between communications and urbanisation, but not as strong as might be anticipated. The correlation is not significant for 1960; but it is significant (0·34) for the urbanisation level in 1968, a change that might suggest a dynamic relationship between increasing communication and increasing level of urbanisation.

Generally, then, even though differences within provinces might exceed differences among them, and even though urban populations may be quite concentrated in particular areas of provinces, the conventional measures of development at the provincial level are strongly related to the level of urbanisation. These correlations, especially if some data errors are taken into account, are very high – so high, in fact, that it is inconceivable that a province would have modern economic growth without growth in urbanisation. Despite the urbanisation–industrialisation nexus, more urbanised provinces do not appear to have achieved economic growth at the cost of critical items in the standard of living of the population.

FINDINGS FROM THE THAI TESABAN DATA[17]

The Thai research, utilising a somewhat different methodology as reported earlier, yielded the following findings concerning the relationship of urbanisation and development:

1. Comparison of the urbanisation and development indices for 1960 and 1966 revealed that towns that were high on

urbanisation tended also to be high on development, and towns low on urbanisation tended also to be low on development.

2. When the comparison is made across time, there is a general tendency for changes in urbanisation to correspond with changes in level of development.

3. A six-variable correlation matrix was constructed containing the indicators: development score of 1960; development score of 1966; actual urbanisation score of 1960; standard urbanisation score; actual urbanisation score of 1966; and standard urbanisation score of 1966. The findings from the matrix were:

   (*a*) the correlation between urbanisation and development in 1960 was 0·71;
   (*b*) the correlation between urbanisation and development in 1966 was 0·66;
   (*c*) the correlation between urbanisation in 1960 and development in 1966 was 0·64.

(In this analysis, 0·40 was taken as the cutoff point of significance for $n = 22$.) These findings indicate the positive relationship between urbanisation and development.

When the connection between urbanisation and administrative capacity was tested, the analysis yielded parallel results. That is, cities high on the urbanisation index tended to be high on the level of administrative capacity. Those with increasing urbanisation had higher performance scores than those with decreasing urbanisation. A 2×3 dimensional analysis clearly revealed the tendencies, as no town that was low on urbanisation was high in administrative capacity, and conversely. When the mean score of administrative capacity was computed for each group of tesabans divided according to high, medium and low levels of urbanisation, the mean administrative capacity score for the high urbanisation group was 67·24; for the medium urbanisation group, 49·45; and for the low urbanisation group, 31·89.

The aggregate historical relationship between urbanisation and national development was noted earlier. Contrary to the predictions of the wastelanders, the same trend is asserting itself within the Third World. Those countries in East and South-east Asia experiencing the most rapid urbanisation, e.g. Japan, South

Korea, Taiwan, Singapore, are also realising the highest rates of national development. While urbanisation was rising in the Philippines and Thailand over the periods of the analysis reported above, so also was productivity, as reported in official national economic analysis and in development plans.[18] Longer time-spans may in future reflect yet more clearly the apparent tendencies. Similar examples are emerging elsewhere; and no contrary case can be adduced.

The hypothesis that urbanisation yields national development seems probable, therefore. That is to say, the urbanisation that is instanced by the cases of the Philippines and Thailand is neither 'pseudo' nor unproductive, but genuine and accelerative. This does not argue that urbanisation is the prime or an exclusive condition, but, instead, a central and essential one. It would appear that the connection is mediated, saliently, through the generation of higher levels of capacity for complex patterns of social interaction and co-operation.

IV

Inasmuch as the considerations in this volume focus on 'accelerated' – and presumably the matter of accelerating – development in Southern Africa, several lessons would appear to be suggested by these estimates. That the forces of urbanisation can be affected deliberately only through public policy is axiomatic. In view of their widespread failures, negative courses are dysfunctional – or futile. The only reasonable option is to attempt to manage urbanisation. This requires, basically, working with, not against, its powerful forces. Efforts must be directed towards the manipulation of urbanisation attributes in relation to national development targets and goals.

Several instrumental features of this task may be anticipated. The need for more and better data concerning the processes of urbanisation and development is abundantly clear; and this information can only be developed publicly. National economic planning must be recast to reflect spaces and places, as well as aggregate sectors, and must project the urban/non-urban structures for developmental goals to be pursued. One of the devices for this new articulation will undoubtedly be a national urban budget. Inter-governmental activities affecting urbanisation must within essential limits be controlled and co-ordinated, as must intervention by external assistance agencies. Urban planning, as it has been preached and practised for many years, must either be subordinated to the purposes of national development, or adopt them.

Once the positive tendencies of urbanisation are appreciated, a wide way is open for optimising choices and constructive experiment.

NOTES

1. Kingsley Davis, 'The Urbanisation of the Human Population', *Scientific American* (Sep 1965) p. 41.
2. Ibid., p. 49.
3. Ved Mehta, 'City of Dreadful Night', *New Yorker*, 21 Mar 1970.
4. A Conference Report, 'The New Urban Debate' (Agency for International Development, Feb 1968). *passim.*
5. James E. Bogle, 'The Coming Urban Crisis in Asia' (Mar 1971) p. 111, published by Ministry of Public Works, Republic of Vietnam, and A.I.D., Contract AID-VN-86.
6. N. V. Sovani, 'The Analysis of "Over-Urbanisation"', *Economic Development and Cultural Change* (Jan 1964).
7. T. G. McGee, *The South East Asian City* (London: Bell, 1969).
8. Ibid., p. 16.
9. Ibid., p. 19.
10. Ernest Weissman, 'Introduction' to Aprodicio A. Laquian (ed.), *Rural–Urban Migrants and Metropolitan Development* (Toronto: Intermet, 1971) p. 1.
11. 'A Summary Report of A.I.D. Technical Assistance for Urban Development: A Study of Agency Experience, 1949–1970', Bureau for Technical Assistance, Urban Development Staff, 25 June 1971.
12. Sovani, op. cit., p. 117.
13. Leo Jakobson, and Ved Prakash, *Urbanisation and National Development* (Beverley Hills, Calif.: Sage, 1971) p. 25.
14. This interdisciplinary project was conducted under the auspices of the Southeast Asia Development Advisory Group, funded by the Asia Society through a grant by the United States Agency for International Development. The principal investigators were Professors Norton Ginsburg, University of Chicago; Milton Kaplan, State University of New York, Buffalo; Henry Teune, University of Pennsylvania; and the present author. The results reported here draw primarily upon the investigations of the public administration unit, one of three central research groups.
15. This approach to measurement, the evaluation of factors and the statistical evaluation of the findings for the Philippines were developed by Professor Teune.
16. Both studies relied considerably on techniques of item and factor analysis.

17. The Thai research was conducted by Mr Pramote Nakornthab for his doctoral dissertation in the field of Government at Cornell University. The findings reported here are from the examination draft of that dissertation, 'Urbanisation and National Development: A Study of Thailand's Local Urban Government'. A final copy will be submitted in March 1972.

18. U.N. demographic and economic data are particularly unhelpful for the comparisons involved here because of the cutoff points employed for urbanisation.

COMMENT

D. H. Reader

Professor Reader prefaced his commentary with a few remarks about the sociology of modernisation. The word was in danger of acquiring so many general meanings that it could become almost as useless as that 'dirty' word *detribalisation*.

The study of modernisation in sociology had tended to focus around two major problem areas. The first, with which he associated the paper of Professor Dotson, was the identification of the major structural and socio-demographic characteristics of modern societies. The second, in Eisenstadt's words, was 'the *identification* of the modern society as one which has to adapt itself to continuously changing demands, to absorb them in terms of policy-making and to assure its own continuity in the face of repeated new demands and new forms of political organisation'. This covered the social, cultural and religious dimensions of development which formed the subject of the remaining papers of this session.

Since urbanisation was frequently used as one operational index of development or modernisation, Professor Reader confessed to some puzzlement over the struggle which Professor Dotson, in a generally excellent paper, had between urbanisation and national development. If modernisation was a constructed typology within which national development fell, and urbanisation was an acknowledged index of modernisation, then there seemed little point in asking questions about which were the dependent and independent variables. Indeed, all too often in entering the industrialisation–Westernisation–urbanisation spiral, the choice of an independent variable was an arbitrary one, depending on which index was seized upon first, and what the hypotheses were. The exemplification of the association between urbanisation and national development in the Philippine case study, however, was interesting and convincing. It would have been most valuable if Professor Dotson had indicated in detail the sub-indices which he was using for urbanisation besides population concentration.

In spite of some 'prophets of doom' present at the Conference,

Professor Dotson was right to overturn what he called the 'waste-land thesis'. He applied it to the Third World, but it might be applied to the *whole* world. This was not to say that the population control called for by Professor Sadie and Professor Andreski previously was unjustified. Surely ours was the first generation which had dared to approach the ethics of population control, and the problem needed to be met. But there were signs in some of the most developed countries that birth rates, when optimal crowding and modernity were passed, might perhaps become self-regulating.

On Professor Steyn's paper, Professor Reader said that she had performed a signal service in assembling under the heading of modernisation, as she defined it, the meagre and scattered data for Southern Africa. She was naturally very concerned about motivating a peasant population which seemed to share a number of rural traditional characteristics found probably in peasant populations everywhere. Professor Reader shared her concern, but not her pessimism, and had two points to make. One was the thesis of Ester Boserup, that technical advisers often seemed to take it for granted that peasant cultivators had a preference for regular employment instead of the full country life which it was known they enjoyed; and that they were willing to give up seasonal leisure in exchange for a very modest compensation in additional output. Instead of unreasoning obstinacy or indolence, it might be sound economic reasoning which induced a community to refuse to abandon fire and axe, when they were offered plough cultivation.

The second point arose from his experience at an International Seminar on Agricultural Change at Reading University about two years previously. There they examined about seventy case studies in agricultural development from all over the world. Most of these cases had been unsuccessful, especially those where the innovating agency belonged to a different culture from the developing population. But it was specially noticeable that the one or two successful ones had been those where the inno-vating authority had initially adopted a highly authoritarian stance: specifying the crops to be planted, the times of ferti-lising, weeding and reaping, and the amount of labour to be used; and withdrawing these controls one by one as the people came to see and take over the advantages of the scheme for themselves. It seemed that the characteristics of development schemes could change historically as the scheme unfolded and developed, and that stereotyped development typologies would not do.

From researches in Rhodesia, Professor Reader was highly dubious about the detailed relationship of education and religion to modernisation. It was common cause that the nineteenth-century-type education with which we were still beset gave a poor basis for those needing a technological education. For Rhodesian Tribal Trust Land farmers it was found that *women*, who were very important in agriculture, had negative attitudes towards fertiliser and manure, conservation and extension, if they had less than *one* year's schooling. Men showed no improvement in their crop yields until they had achieved *four* years of education; but beyond that, more men in any case migrated. Religion was not a significant factor for either sex, unless the church was a *prescriptive* one (e.g. Seventh-Day Adventist, laying down tithing and agricultural practices) *and* the person was a regular church-goer.

Finally, Professor Reader mentioned the papers of Professor Wurzbacher and Mr Ntusi. The first paper, apart from its interesting theory of social change, showed how in a village development situation social change could be introduced through a descending hierarchy of 'prime movers'; and that the *process* towards modernisation was not smooth, continuous, or even unidirectional. Mr Ntusi in a very wise paper had defined the base of the traditional typology, and shown in traditional terms the disruptive effects of urbanisation upon it.

Summarising what he had said, Professor Reader gave five *negative* propositions for examination in future research:

1. It does not necessarily follow from prevailing socio-demographic trends that the world is due to crowd itself or waste itself out of existence.
2. Economic criteria are not necessary *and* sufficient determinants of modernisation in all its forms.
3. The motivation of rural peasants need not involve irrationality, and may be activated by unexpectedly authoritarian means.
4. Sustained education need not be a primary determinant of

willingness for agricultural change; it may be a matter of bare literacy.

5. The African rural male may not always wish to earn his living entirely from the soil or from town; he may have reached a judicious mix of his own choice.

Chapter 7
Education and Training

Education Workshop

EXPLANATORY NOTE

EDUCATION WORKSHOP: EXPLANATORY NOTE

On the day before the main Conference, a Workshop was held for a limited number of participants. The theme was 'Education and Training for Development', and this was discussed under three heads:

1. Basic considerations on which a system of education and training for accelerated development should be planned.
2. Identification of the major problems involved in planning education for development (with special reference to evidence contained in questionnaires completed beforehand by Education Ministries in Southern Africa).
3. Practical ways and means to realise the most important objectives identified by the Workshop.

Professor Franklin Parker's keynote address to the Workshop and a brief report on the findings of the Workshop, presented to the main Conference by Professors Parker and W. M. Kgware, are reproduced below.

A full report on the proceedings of the Workshop, as well as statistical data and other basic information contained in the replies to the questionnaires submitted to Ministries of Education in the countries of Southern Africa, will be published in a separate volume, *Education for Development in Southern Africa*, edited by David Hirschmann and Brian Rose.

Educational Strategies for Accelerating Development in Southern Africa*

FRANKLIN PARKER

EDUCATIONAL CRISIS

Just over four years ago the important International Conference on the World Crisis in Education was held in Williamsburg, Virginia. That an education crisis existed was amply documented and its ramifications were analysed and discussed. In our present context we need to explore the dimensions of that crisis under conditions peculiar to Southern Africa. Then, hopefully, we may try to find some solutions. At least five major educational problems comprising that crisis can be identified.

RISING DEMAND, LIMITED RESOURCES

The heart of the educational crisis lies in the widening imbalances or gaps between school systems and their socio-economic environments. One such gap is between educational demand and supply. A population that suddenly gets more education wants even more. A bright African youth of illiterate parents who learns to read wants to finish primary school and to enter secondary school. He in turn will want more schooling for his children. Educational expansion in one generation increases the educational demand in the next generation. One dramatic example is in the United States where, between 1900 and 1967, the population increased two and a half times while secondary-school enrolments increased from 12 per cent to 90 per cent of the age group and higher education from 4 per cent to 44 per cent of the age group. Democratic

* Professor Parker presented this paper as the keynote address to the Education Workshop, held in conjunction with the Conference.

aspirations, parental demand, population growth, better health, longer lives, family migration from rural to urban areas – all have contributed to a rising educational demand which strains limited resources. Unfortunately, the thin spread of limited resources to more and more students results in reduced quality and increased numbers of drop-outs and repeaters.

The crisis of demand and supply from which a solution is needed is that of rising enrolments and lowered quality. The ideal is an education system expanding in numbers and quality at all levels. Such a system should provide sufficient skills at ever-improving quality levels to attain high employment and a rising gross national product. Strategies to attain this ideal require a balance of educational inputs to accomplish desired educational outputs; that is, a planned systems analysis approach that is somewhat like a physician's concern with balancing total bodily health. Thus, a first problem to be solved is this gap between demand and supply.

LESS INCOME, HIGHER COST

A second problem to be solved is the gap between income and costs. Education budgets, which have recently risen steadily, have now levelled off because of other pressing national needs. Since poor countries have a growing proportion of younger people, a proportionately smaller working population must support those not working. In the battle of the budget, education cannot get an expanding share of the national economic pie in the face of inflation and the higher salaries needed to hold good teachers and administrators and to hire new ones in competition from industry and business.

Education is a rising-cost enterprise, needing more money each year to accomplish the same results as in the previous year, and of course needing substantially more to meet increased enrolments. The lack of money as a root of the educational crisis requires strategies that will find new money sources, relate educational expansion to economic growth and improve educational efficiency and productivity. Thus, the second problem to be solved is this gap between income and costs.

MOUNTING SCHOOL OUTPUT, RELATIVELY FEWER JOBS

A third problem is an imbalance between school output and jobs.

A poor country with less labour mobility and job absorbability needs a close match between school output and available jobs. This imbalance has affected rich countries too, as in France in May 1968 when anxious university students, mainly in the social sciences, worried that their numbers exceeded jobs, helped touch off the revolt that almost toppled President De Gaulle.

Poor countries tend to produce an imbalance of needed skills: too many graduates in the classics, arts and law, and not enough in health, agriculture, mathematics and science. A proper school mix would reflect the fact that the urban and industrial sector houses and employs about 25 per cent of the people, and that the rural and agrarian plus the small-town and small-industry sectors employ and house three-fourths of the people. The latter is where development must be accelerated and where the transition to modernity must take place. Rather than educate youth to escape to the urban areas where jobs are scarce and frustration high, the schools need somehow to attract, equip and challenge young people to improve and modernise the rural areas.

Imbalance in skill levels is costly and inefficient when professionals perform work that para-professionals should do. Unemployment and underemployment, long accepted as inevitable in static and traditional societies are now becoming unacceptable and even intolerable. Unemployed school-leavers in their loud clamour and swift anger have overthrown governments before. Thus, the third problem to be solved is the imbalance between school output and jobs.

NEW TIMES, OLD CONTENT

A fourth problem, a qualitative one, is the lag in course content and teaching methods at a time of rapidly advancing frontiers of knowledge. Critics hold that much of what is taught is irrelevant to current personal and national needs and hardly suitable for tomorrow. Old teaching methods designed for yesterday's intellectual élite do not fit today's heterogeneous students who have a wide range of abilities, motivations and career aspirations. A student today needs guidance to select a more effective individualised fit from the expanded curriculum. But traditional courses and teaching methods continue. This built-in resistance to change is expressed in the quip that it is easier to move a graveyard than to change a curriculum. Thus, the fourth problem is to assure the continued relevance of educational content and methods.

FORMAL V. INFORMAL EDUCATION

A fifth problem is the imbalance between the formal school system and out-of-school training and opportunities. Informal education – lifelong education is a better term – has a vital role to play in poor nations, whether in updating the skills of those already educated or in bringing literacy to the masses deprived of formal schooling. Lifelong education, a key need for rural transformation, needs to be organised, administered, financed and motivated. Lifelong education can involve national youth service, literacy campaigns and the work of women, girls and the elderly in rural improvement. Thus, the fifth problem to be solved is the gap between formal and informal education.

LATE START IN AFRICA

These five problems of rising demand, high cost, job shortages, old content and poor methods, and the need for lifelong education, weigh heavily on Africa, which has only lately come to grips with its lack in education and development. Independent African states, which have increased from 3 to over 40 in the last twenty years, were late starters in development. Their hopeful mood in the 1960s, expressed in the slogan 'Seek first the political kingdom and all else will be added', is giving way in the 1970s to a serious facing-up to the need to overcome their poor economic condition.

Independent African states, among the world's poorest, include 19 of the world's 21 least developed countries. In 1967, 86 per cent of the African people earned an average of under \$160 per person and 55 per cent earned under \$80 per person. Unequal income distribution between urban and rural people and between wage-earners and subsistence farmers make conditions even worse for the majority. By one account, at present growth rates Africa would need 200 years to reach the present levels of the industrial states. By then, of course, the developed countries will have pulled far ahead and again widened the gap.

DEVELOPMENT OBSTACLES

Obvious major obstacles to African development include a lack of road, rail and air transport; meagre communications, housing and health facilities; the predominance of subsistence farming, which employs two-thirds of the people; illiteracy of over 80 per cent of the adults; unemployment and underutilisation of human resources. At the same time there are such problems as a shortage of trained manpower; too many small local markets in a continent of too many small states; reliance on a few major food and mineral exports whose prices fluctuate on the world market; low personal income, even for that one-fifth of the working population who earn cash wages; scarce investment capital; inadequate knowledge of and poor exploitative possibilities for natural resources; piecemeal rather than organised planning; and rapid population explosion.

SCHOOL EXPANSION

Despite obstacles, Africa's new leaders, many of them former teachers, believe in education as a vital catalyst for modernisation and have had to promise it to gain political support. Their drive to advance African education resulted in a continent-wide UNESCO education conference held in Addis Ababa, Ethiopia, in 1961. The estimate then was that 80 per cent to 85 per cent of Africans over age 15 were illiterate, nearly double the world average; that fewer than half of middle Africa's 25 million school-age children would complete primary school; fewer than 3 out of every 100 would enter secondary school; and fewer than 2 out of every 1,000 would receive any higher education. These educational targets were set for 1980: primary education free to all, 20 per cent of these to enter secondary schools and about 2 per cent of these to enter higher education. In these twenty years education expenditures were expected to rise from $450 million (1960) to $2·2 billion (1980). African countries accepted periodic growth targets and were encouraged to align their economic priorities for increased investments in education.

Another UNESCO conference in Nairobi, Kenya, assessed

educational growth between 1960 and 1965. It showed that primary-school enrolment, which was 36 per cent of the relevant age group in 1960, reached 44 per cent in 1965, or 3 per cent below the 47 per cent target for 1965 (1·1 million pupils short of target). Secondary-school enrolment, which was 3 per cent of the relevant age group in 1960, reached just under 5 per cent in 1965, or more than 1 per cent below the 1965 target of 6 per cent (272,000 pupils short of target). Only in higher education was the Addis Ababa target slightly overfilled: the enrolment of 0·02 per cent of the relevant age group in 1960 reached 0·05 per cent in 1965, or 0·01 per cent above the Addis Ababa target. Another target called for a 5 per cent annual increase in primary-school enrolment, but the average annual increase from 1960 to 1965 was 1·8 per cent. The result is growing illiteracy. On the basis of 1960–5 trends, and assuming that at least four years of education are needed for literacy, it was estimated that 3,816,000 Africans or 71 per cent (as against 54 per cent forecast earlier) of those at age 6 in 1960 would be adult illiterates at age 15, and 4,160,000 Africans or 69 per cent of those at age 6 in 1965 would be adult illiterates when they reach age 15. Nor were Addis Ababa targets reached in the number of trained primary- and secondary-school teachers, although substantial gains were made.

This first Africa-wide assessment showed that the mere expansion of school systems, when not designed to sustain planned stages of economic development, does not solve but compounds education problems.

EDUCATION AND ECONOMIC GROWTH

Economist Frederick Harbison of Princeton University, who served on the Nigerian Education Commission headed by Sir Eric Ashby in the late 1950s, stressed the key role of manpower training in the economic development of low-income countries. The Ashby Commission report projected Nigeria's manpower needs to 1980 and set comparable goals for the educational system.

In a developed country like the United States, education has been a factor in economic growth. In the early 1960s economist Edward F. Denison attributed 23 per cent of the economic growth of the United States between 1929 and 1957 to education and an additional 18 per cent of the economic growth during these same years to advances in knowledge. These figures have been confirmed by economist Theodore W. Schultz. In a later study, Denison claimed that between 1955 and 1962 one-fifth of the increase in U.S. national income per person employed was a result of workers' higher educational levels. He added that for that same period advances in knowledge, coming mainly from higher education, added another one-fourth to the increase in national income per person employed. These studies suggest that schooling and advances in knowledge are both sources of economic growth for all countries and that, unlike limited natural resources, they are man-made resources which can be continually improved.

What strategies, then, can make education serve better a people's material welfare?

STRATEGIES

The suggested and interrelated education and development strategies that follow may be obvious to national planners but are presented here for consideration as to their relevance to Southern Africa.

SETTING EDUCATIONAL OBJECTIVES

School systems by their very organisation and financing have built-in objectives, aims and goals. But benefit can be derived from stating objectives explicitly, reviewing them regularly, and restating them frequently in the light of changes in the school system and in the society it serves. The hope is that when objectives are under continual and careful review, they may be improved for continual renewal of efficiency, innovation and service to society. All important elements of the society have their part to play in setting educational objectives, with the chief responsibility being on those officials chosen to carry out the mandates of the people.

NATIONAL PLANNING

By one account, three-fourths of African countries have some form of development plan. Planning departments are frequently separate from but at top levels co-ordinate the efforts of the ministries of agriculture, education, economics, industry, social welfare, youth services and others. Here growth rates are set and the objectives and programmes of supporting ministries are corre-lated with these growth rates. Essential aspects of planning in-clude better co-ordination of all resources, stress on innovation or changes calculated to achieve improvements, and a clear order of priorities. Critics say that in most national plans the allocation of resources shows an exaggerated priority for industry and rela-tive neglect of agriculture. Yet it is agricultural development in bare subsistence countries which can most practically aid eco-nomic growth and hold down urban migration and unemploy-ment. Where non-existent, national planning should be begun under trained personnel as an essential part of any strategy for development. It is necessary in setting goals, co-ordinating efforts and ordering priorities.

REGIONAL PLANNING

Regional co-operation that mutually benefits participating coun-tries and the region as a whole is widely practised and exists in Southern Africa for customs and trade purposes. Much good could be gained if such co-operation were enlarged to its best operating limits to accomplish such things as advantageous ex-change of goods and common use of appropriate services and communications facilities; co-operative buying, storage, processing and distribution of agricultural and other products; and joint planning by experts in various fields, including education. Econo-mies would result from eliminating duplicate facilities and, on the other hand, needed facilities can be introduced to serve local and regional needs.

In the education sphere, incentives might result from the exchange of students, teachers and administrators and the posting of personnel to needed areas; the creation of university extension centres, adult education centres and curriculum experiment centres to advance materials and methods in such subjects as languages, mathematics, science, the social studies, language arts and particularly vocational education. Regional planning might bring better co-ordination of the size, scope and contribution of educational systems with already existing rural and urban growth centres, thereby strengthening these growth centres in a proper balance of industry, agriculture and supporting infrastructures. A model for the educational part of such regional planning centres already exists in UNESCO's regional centres around the world. But the idea could be improved upon if in Southern Africa the richer and poorer countries could co-ordinate their efforts in balanced total planning for national gain and regional progress.

Once co-ordinated regional planning is begun it would undoubtedly lead to adoption of national planning in those countries in the region without such programmes. It would also strengthen existing national planning programmes. Such a regional approach would more likely attract and probably more efficiently use loans and aid from such international organisations as UNESCO, the United Nations Development Programme fund and the World Bank. Certain population, education and other strategies also lend themselves more readily to a regional approach.

FAMILY PLANNING

Of the two major forces behind rising school enrolments, one is the social and political demand for education and the second is population growth. It was estimated in 1970 that the proportion of total population under age 15 was 27 per cent in developed countries and 41 per cent in developing countries. This heavier concentration of school-age children in poorer countries illustrates the need for information on family planning. Such planning and information exists nationally, of course, in some Southern African countries, but it would likely have greater impact, produce better research and arouse more public attention if organised on a regional basis.

EASING ALIENATION

Western education to some degree alienates the recipient from his traditional society. Development and the changes thus brought about alienate the schooled from the unschooled. What can be done to ease the shock of alienation? In school the problem might be reduced by including in the curriculum units on understanding cultural change and appreciation for cultural heritage. For the out-of-school and the unschooled, mass media can revive pride in, and community clubs as ethnic centres can offer direct participation in, the people's culture in dance, song, legend, stories and humour. Such community culture centres may not only ease alienation but may also provide a bridge to modern industrial and urban life.

THE UNSCHOOLED AND LITTLE SCHOOLED

Although universal primary education is the goal in the 1980s, there is still a long way to go in the current decade. The 50 per cent or so of school-age children in Southern Africa who never go to school or who drop out in the first few years before literacy takes root comprise the bulk of the labour force. Put another way, in East Africa about 70 per cent of new entrants into the work-force have either no primary education or have never finished their primary education. The proportion is probably similar in Southern Africa. Most of these will be in the labour force in the year 2000 as unskilled, illiterate subsistence farmers or as unskilled, underemployed urban dwellers. If anything is to be done for this unschooled and little schooled group, a variety of programmes wil be needed: literacy centres, training centres, on-the-job training and special mass-media programmes. Also pre-school enrichment education for the culturally handicapped, community centre programmes, vocational programmes for drop-outs, school leaving equivalency tests for over-age learners, easy entry to evening school for late bloomers, and a host of other extra-chance avenues will be needed for those hitherto cut off from such opportunity. The lifting of this large labouring group to more acceptable stages on the educational ladder is essential for national and regional economic and social progress.

MASTER TEACHERS

An effective and creative teaching force is a keystone of national and regional progress, while the problem of creating one is the bane of poorer countries. The field of education and particularly teacher education is still in a handicraft stage compared with the revolutions that have modernised industry, medicine, transportation and communication. Today's teacher is trained for yesterday's schools in yesterday's world and his professional growth is problematical, especially in the isolation of a village school. Education systems will hardly be modernised until teacher education is made more intellectual, more challenging and more rewarding.

One way is to add a Master Teacher Academy concept to existing teacher-training schemes. The most talented teachers and administrators can be selected for high-level courses leading to career advancement at salaries comparable with those of other professions. Too long have too many poor teachers driven out the few good teachers. We need to reverse the process so that growing numbers of master teachers, trained, advanced and paid as professionals, will take the place of poor teachers.

CONCLUSION

There is no simple solution, no easy way out of the dilemma except through the whole cluster of parts that make up development planning – including money, systems analysis, reform, co-operation, efficiency, enthusiasm, clearly defined goals, and determination to accomplish these goals. Development can be accelerated, but it requires local support, national planning and regional co-ordination. The key may lie in *esprit de corps*, a spirit of pride, an overwhelming drive to pull oneself, one's country and one's region out of the past and into modern times. In the last analysis, it is concerned and dedicated people such as are convened here who must find ways to set in motion a people's determination to move forward in peace and dignity towards the common good.

BIBLIOGRAPHICAL NOTE

The working document discussed at the October 1967 Williamsburg, Virginia, conference was Philip H. Coombs, *The World Educational Crisis: A Systems Analysis* (New York: Oxford Univ. Press, 1968), which has an excellent annotated guide to further study. Conference papers are in George Z. F. Bereday (ed.), *Essays on World Education: The Crisis of Supply and Demand* (New York: Oxford Univ. Press, 1969). Mr Coombs directed UNESCO's International Institute for Educational Planning, Paris, whose growing list of studies, particularly on East and West Africa, is essential reading on the topic. The Virginia conference led in part to the UNESCO-sponsored International Education Year 1970, in which connection the following useful conference papers were issued: *Proceedings of the First World Congress of Comparative Education Societies on the Role and Rationale for Educational Aid to Developing Countries during International Education Year* (Ottawa: World Council for Comparative Education, Aug 1970).

Educational shortcomings in developing countries are discussed object-ively in John W. Hanson and Cole S. Brembeck (eds), *Education and the Development of Nations* (New York: Holt, Rinehart & Winston, 1966). The Addis Ababa and Nairobi UNESCO conferences are reviewed in context in Richard Greenough, *Africa Prospect: Progress in Education* (Paris: UNESCO, 1966).

For education's relation to economic growth, see Edward F. Denison, *The Sources of Economic Growth in the United States and the Alterna-tives before us*, Supplementary Paper No. 13 (New York: Committee for Economic Development, 1962); Edward F. Denison and Jean-Pierre Poullier, *Why Growth Rates Differ: Postwar Experience in Nine Western Countries* (Washington, D.C.: Brookings Institution, 1967); and Theodore W. Schultz, *The Economic Value of Education* (New York: Columbia Univ. Press, 1963).

Invaluable is Lester Pearson *et al.*, *Partners in Development: Report of the Commission on International Development* (New York: Praeger, 1969), and Pearson's speech on his report before the Columbia University Confer-ence on International Development, February 1970, in *Ceres* (F.A.O. Re-view), III 2 (Mar–Apr 1970) 21–5. See also the World Bank's *Education Sector Working Paper* (New York: World Bank, Sep 1971).

Report of the Education Workshop

presented by
W. M. KGWARE AND FRANKLIN PARKER

A. BASIC CONSIDERATIONS IN PLANNING

1. It is recognised that education is an integral part of development.

2. This education must be both rooted in the culture of the people and must equip the children for a place in the modern world. Put another way, this education must both enrich the quality of life and also equip people for making a living.

3. Thus, educational progress must reflect the hard facts of economic life in its financial support and in its phased growth.

B. MAJOR PROBLEMS IN PLANNING

1. CURRICULUM CONTENT

Can primary education be heavily academic when most youths do not finish the course? A well-rounded curriculum in the primary years can best serve both those forced out of school into the world of work, and also those who can continue at school.

2. RISING ENROLMENTS

The factors behind rising enrolments are well known: population explosion, the social and political demands for schooling, rising expectations (the more benefits one gets, the more one wants for himself and his children), and other factors. Malawi, for example, can enrol only 35 per cent of its primary school-age children. What shall be done with 65 per cent who are unschooled and/or little schooled? Despite the cry of no money, a case can be made for universal and compulsory primary education in phased steps, i.e. four years, five years, six years and then seven years.

3. RURAL BIAS

How can the inevitable pull of the towns be overcome, when rural life and livelihood are facts of life for the majority?

It is often pointed out that agricultural education for rural retention of youths falls short of expectations. We believe that the whole curriculum can be pervaded by the enhancement of rural life. This need not be done *in* agriculture and crafts but *through* them. It is recognised that satisfying rural employment is essential for rural retention of youths.

4. MASTER TEACHERS

How is it possible to reverse the pattern of teacher shortage, low esteem for teachers, and teachers leaving for better-paid jobs in other fields? How can the best candidates be selected for teaching, efficiently trained, competitively paid and continually improved and upgraded? Beyond money – and increased pay is an essential part of any profession – we feel that the community that respects teachers and offers high status to teachers will attract and retain good teachers.

5. FINANCE

Education is costly, but how can the needed share for planned development be secured in competition with the many other demands that are made on the treasury? If indeed education is an investment in people and in national economic development, then wise government leaders backed by informed public opinion must find and allocate more adequate funds. Private industry, perhaps encouraged by tax rebates, might enlarge on existing or initiate new job training and support lifelong education. International aid for education can also be encouraged.

6. MEDIUM OF INSTRUCTION

Instruction from the earliest primary year in the mother tongue is essential for cultural security. The changeover to a world language should then come at whatever stage research indicates.

C. STRATEGIES

I. PLANNING

An educational component of planning already exists in most countries of Southern Africa and should be instituted where it does not exist.

2. OBJECTIVES

We recommend the setting of educational objectives and their continual reformulation by educational authorities, with due regard to community concerns.

3. LIFELONG EDUCATION

A prime strategy must be lifelong education (informal or adult education), i.e. to find mechanisms to provide literacy for the illiterate, skills for the unskilled, updating performance, and encouraging upward mobility to the deprived.

4. COMMUNITY INTEREST

Community involvement, such as parent–teacher associations, is essential to an atmosphere of acceptance of better schools and better teachers.

5. MASTER TEACHERS

A first consideration for accelerating development and for the production of master teachers should be through intensive and ongoing in-service programmes.

6. PRE-SCHOOL EDUCATION

As soon as practicable, following attainment of universal and compulsory primary education, we feel that the pre-school opportunities should be considered.

7. HEALTH AND NUTRITION

Cost aside, it is universally recognised that health services and nutrition are essential.

8. REGIONAL CO-OPERATION

Wherever it does not hinder national educational planning, we suggest that regional avenues of co-operation should be explored.

Chapter 8

Planning for Development

Requirements for Effective Development Planning

BRUNO KNALL

There is general agreement in the developing countries that accelerated and continuous growth cannot be achieved so long as blind confidence is placed in the spontaneous and self-regulating forces of *laissez-faire* liberalism. Problems which need to be solved in these countries are so numerous that an adequate and efficient policy of economic and social development can be pursued only on the basis of comprehensive development planning. There are, of course, developing countries which can be considered as showcases of development without the benefit of a formal development plan (but guided by co-ordinated action through budget and specific governmental policies), while other countries with plans have failed to reach even modest targets of development. It may be possible to do without a formal plan, but it is not possible to avoid taking decisions in the socio-economic field and analysing their future implications. It is my contention that for achieving accelerated growth in developing countries, integrated development planning is a necessary condition, though not a sufficient one.

In spite of the fact that by now almost all developing countries have some sort of a plan and therefore can learn from the planning experiences of other countries, few make effective use of this experience. Notwithstanding their structural differences, it is rather astonishing to see that many developing countries encounter the same planning problems but make more or less the same mistakes.[1] The shortcomings of many planning efforts and their lack of success were due partly to the fact that they reflected the wishful thinking of political decision-makers, and partly to lack of experience in formulating and carrying out development plans.

In writing a paper on development planning, a professional development planner is tempted to indulge in technicalities involving growth models, simultaneous equations, input–output analysis and linear programming, as well as implementation and evaluation techniques and procedures. This temptation can be resisted, since a considerable literature on development planning methods and techniques has accumulated during the last two decades. Consequently, the purpose of this paper is not to describe the available techniques for plan formulation, implementation and evaluation, but rather to emphasise the criteria which should be satisfied for realistic and effective development planning. The approach chosen here is deliberately a normative one.

The distinction made between 'plan' and 'planning' is more than a question of semantics. The best-conceived plan is bound to fail if it is badly implemented. All too often it is overlooked that *integrated development planning* has to be understood as an interdependent, interdisciplinary and continuous process which involves five consecutive stages of work:

1. Diagnosis or information stage.
2. Determination of development strategies and of general objectives.
3. Formulation of the plan, i.e. development programming *sensu stricto*.
4. Implementation of the plan.
5. *Ex post* evaluation of the plan.

The details of these stages are outlined in Table 8.1 opposite.

The stages can only be distinguished conceptually, because none of them constitutes an autonomous phase in comprehensive development planning. Keeping this in mind, we shall proceed stage by stage and list the most important criteria that development planning must satisfy. Some of the criteria may sound platitudinous; but it is striking how the planning process in many developing countries disregards these criteria in practice.

1. DIAGNOSIS OR INFORMATION STAGE

A far-sighted development policy presupposes the possession of factual statistical information and insight into interrelated factors in the development process. Work in this phase is not, however, limited to a mere stocktaking of data relating to resource inventory and social and economic structures of the past and present,

TABLE 8.1   Working stages of integrated development planning: functions and operating institutions

Phase	Functions and operations	Institutions
1. Diagnosis or information stage	1.1 Collection of socio-economic data (including opinion-polling)	Data collection points (local, regional) Central Statistical Office (= C.S.O.) Research Institutes (= R.I.) Local self-government organisations
	1.2 Survey of the state of the economy (inventory)	C.S.O. R.I.
	1.3 Analysis of historical and present trends	Planning Bureau's (= P.B.) Perspective Planning Division R.I.
	1.4 Appraisal of development potentialities	P.B. Perspective Planning Division National Development Council (= N.D.C.)
2. Determination of development strategies and general objectives	2.1 Determination of development strategies	Government and Parliament N.D.C.
	2.2 Formulation of general socio-economic development objectives	N.D.C. P.B.
3. Development programming: elaboration of the medium-term development plan and of annual plans	3.1 Macro-economic programming	P.B. Economic Programming Division R.I.
	3.2 Sectoral programming	Ministries concerned (planning units) P.B. panels and working groups
	3.3 Regional planning	P.B. Regional Division Regional planning agencies
	3.4 Project formulation	Ministries Consulting firms Regional planning agencies P.B.
	3.5 Co-ordination of the various programming levels (3.1 to 3.4) and consistency tests	P.B. meetings N.D.C. Ministries (planning units)
	3.6 First considerations on and determination of development policies	P.B. and regional planning agencies N.D.C. Government
4. Plan implementation	4.1 Initiation of development policy measures to achieve the plan targets	Government Ministries P.B.
	4.2 Controlled implementation of development projects and programmes	Ministries Regional planning agencies Public-sector undertakings Extension services District, block and village-level officials
	4.3 Continuous progress appraisal	Evaluation agency (= E.A.) Public-sector undertakings Local self-government organisations

but has to include the diagnosis of factors that might hinder or promote development.

(*a*) The most important criterion that this stage must satisfy can be termed the criterion of *statistical availability*. Unfortunately this requirement is not always fulfilled, and planning without hard facts is still widespread.[2] However, the lack of directly available statistics should not be over-emphasised, nor should it lead to resignation. Often data are in existence but they have been poorly used, if at all. What is really lacking in this instance is, on the one hand, statistical material that has been specially prepared for economic and social development programming, and on the other hand, so-called 'organised information', that is to say, a constant and institutionalised flow of information at regular intervals, from the various source units (e.g. customs points, village and district councils, production units, etc.) to the corresponding statistical collection points at the regional and national levels.

(*b*) The qualitative counterpart of (quantitative) statistical availability is the criterion of *accuracy*, which means that data should reflect reality. Since many developing countries cannot wait until statistics are gathered in line with the criteria of availability and accuracy, other courses have to be taken. One of these consists of using synthetic data, that is, taking statistics from a developing country with economic and social structure similar enough to be judged comparable to the country for which data are lacking. Careful analysis of earlier data for more advanced countries can sometimes give valuable hints. Even if the synthetic statistics are duly adapted, the undertaking is still risky. Another method often applied to fill statistical gaps is the use of techniques like weighting, interpolation, extrapolation of the results of random samples, etc. The approximate data thus gained have been significantly called 'reasoned or educated guesses' or 'guesstimates', because they indicate only a very approximate order of magnitude. But in development planning it is better to have estimated values to work from than no statistical data at all.

(*c*) A further important criterion of the diagnosis phase concerns the assessment and analysis of *human development potential*. Opinion-polling can and must be carried out in developing countries, firstly to establish in which fields of human activity and behaviour resistance to development exists, and secondly to recognise the real needs and wishes of the population. This kind of investigation in particular – which extends partly into the realms of sociology, psychology and cultural anthropology – has been almost entirely neglected in development planning up to now.

(*d*) Last but not least, there is the criterion of *adequacy of statistical data* for planning. It is of the greatest importance that information-collecting and processing should take place in such a way that it corresponds directly to the demands of the programming and implementation stages and that it can be used in the decision-making process. This criterion works in two directions: the aforementioned planning stages can provide useful indications as to what kind of statistical data are most needed.

2. DETERMINATION OF DEVELOPMENT STRATEGIES AND OF GENERAL OBJECTIVES

The stage of information-collecting and diagnosis is a necessary but not by itself sufficient condition for integrated development planning; it serves merely as a starting-point for further working phases.

(*a*) Every development plan is based, implicitly or explicitly, on certain general concepts or images of the future society to be achieved. Among these are ideas about the political system, such as the kind of constitution to be chosen and the extent to which the state will participate in the development process. Realistic planning should therefore satisfy the criterion of *compatibility between the political system and development strategies.* A development plan although technically perfect, would still be doomed to failure if it clashed with prevalent ethical, political and societal concepts. Decisions about the political system are in the exclusive domain of the politicians, not to be influenced by the development planners. It cannot be the latter's task to suggest to the politician a definite form of constitution, e.g. the pursuance of a mixed economy or a socialist or communist political system. But it is obvious that the planning process has to be closely related to the strategy of the political system which it is to serve.

(*b*) In contrast to the political choice just mentioned, development planners can certainly help with their specialist opinion in designing development strategies which are largely (although not entirely) neutral as far as the political system is concerned. It is a question of crucial strategic choices concerning development policies, with the help of which the scope and nature of the future economic and social development are determined in broad, though not quantifiable, terms. Since the determination of strategies is not only an economic art but also an exercise in political compromise, the accepted strategies may differ from country to country:

Balanced or unbalanced growth.
Diversification of the economy or specialisation.
Pre-eminence of a leading sector.
Export promotion or production for the domestic market (import substitution).
Productive or social investment.
Achieving and maintaining balance-of-payments equilibrium.
More equal distribution of income between individuals and regions.
Mobilisation of domestic capital.
Creation of employment possibilities.
Modernisation of administration, etc.

Nothing general can be said about the criteria that are applied in the final choice of specific development strategies. They must be decided upon separately for each individual case. Since not all the strategies mentioned here are mutually compatible, it is imperative that the very general criterion of *consistency* should apply. This means not only the avoidance of conflicts between the accepted strategies themselves, but also a harmonious accord of strategies with the planned economic and social development.

(c) The development strategies selected form the basis for the choice of general objectives which serve as the foundation of the susbsequent programming phase. Since developing countries have varying resources at their disposal and the development strategy is also influenced by various other premises, the objectives for separate developing countries are not always the same. However, if one examines from this viewpoint the large number of development plans already in existence, one is struck by the fact of how strongly they resemble one another in objectives. In almost all development plans the attempt is made, for example, to increase income per head, the saving ratio, industrial and agricultural production, and so on. In this conceptual phase of development policy it is not a question of quantitative but merely of qualitative formulation of objectives. Quantitative targets are important, of course, but what matters in the first place is policy: deliberate choice of the direction in which society wants to move in conformity with the chosen strategy. To illustrate these three basic terms, let us suppose that on the basis of the analytical diagnosis, the decision-makers of a developing country decide on the *development strategy* of furthering the *formation of capital* in the next development plan. This development strategy takes on a concrete stature in the choice of the appropriate *development objective*, that is to say, the *increase of the saving ratio*. But in this way a decision is only taken on 'what to do'. To operationalise this objective, development planners deal with 'how much', i.e. they have to calculate a specific numerical *target*, for instance a *saving ratio of x per cent*. The exact setting of this quantitative target belongs to the subsequent stages of programming and implementation, in which the question 'how' is answered, that is, which *developmental means* (or policy measures) are suitable and necessary for the achievement of this target? All these considerations lead to the important criterion of *logical sequence in decision-making* which, by nature, applies not only to this stage of work but also to programming and implementation. Although this criterion implies a sequential pattern (development strategy $\longrightarrow$ objective $\longrightarrow$ target and means), feedbacks are not only possible but necessary. It is vital for this 'decision chain' that no link should be omitted.

(*d*) Finally, there is the criterion of *partnership between decision-makers and development planners*. A close co-operation between these two groups is indispensable. If the objectives were to be determined solely by development planners, the plan might well indeed be fully consistent in economic terms of national accounting. But the planners might miss important societal and other non-economic realities.[3] Conversely, the decision-makers can formulate their development strategy more competently and realistically if the planning technicians give them the expert advice they need to estimate the consequences of their decisions, at least in broad terms. This criterion stresses, therefore, the importance of the give-and-take relationship between planners and decision-makers already at this early planning stage, in which strategies and objectives are determined. As we shall see, this criterion leads to the programming stage, where this problem of co-operation is taken up again.

3. DEVELOPMENT PROGRAMMING: FORMULATION OF THE PLAN

On the basis of the previous stages of work, the development planners now possess the factual information necessary for drawing up the development plan. The task consists mainly in projecting the targets and probable development trends of the various sectors and of the overall economy. By balancing what is desired as goals against what seems practicable, the attempt is made with the help of programming techniques to project an optimum growth path. In order to be realistic, development programming should satisfy the following criteria:

(*a*) Every development plan must, in the first place, satisfy the criterion of *comprehensiveness*. This means that the programming work should embrace the national economy in its entirety. A two-sector model, for example, which only takes into account agriculture and industry, would not be comprehensive because it fails to consider sectors important for economic development such as foreign trade, transport and services. It would also not be comprehensive if it were to include all the above-mentioned sectors of purely economic activity without, however, explicitly taking up the social sector in the development model. It is not without a certain irony that comprehensive, integrated development plans are most indispensable for precisely those countries for which they are most difficult to draw up, because the statistics and trained personnel necessary for them are mostly lacking. In fact, 'comprehensiveness' is very costly and demanding in terms of time and effort spent, as well as in terms of know-how and administrative organisational machinery. Despite these limitations, the programmers must try to construct their development model as broadly and extensively as the abilities of those taking part in the programming will permit.

The more comprehensive the plan, the more dependent it is on private-sector performance – at least in market (or mixed) econo-mies. To satisfy this criterion, the plan should include explicit reference to the activities of the private sector and to the specific governmental measures which will induce the private sector to behave in conformity with the objectives of planned development.

(*b*) One of the most important prerequisites is the criterion of *flexibility*. Many unpleasant surprises in development planning stem from the fact that the plan is rigidly formulated and also supposed to be carried out to the letter. This attitude is questionable for the obvious reason that every development plan is based on a weak foundation of information with qualitative deficiencies. This is where the criterion of flexibility makes its appearance and demands that in development programming certain qualitatively and/or quantitatively expressed margins of error be left for critical sectors or macro-economic categories. What is meant here is the provision of a 'built-in flexibility'. A few examples may illustrate this point. In projecting foreign trade, development planners are well advised to estimate export figures on the conservative (low) side while import targets should be projected rather liberally. In projecting agricultural production targets it makes no sense to set over-ambitious goals; it is more realistic to take into account the possibility of a poor harvest (the diagnosis stage should provide information about this eventually). It is also not advisable to plan budgets without contingencies.

(*c*) The demand for flexibility leads to the further criterion of *continuity*. In order to guarantee that planning is a continuous operation and to permit continuous harmonisation of the plan with the realities, it has been suggested that gliding or rolling plans be drawn up. For example, a five-year plan is not merely reworked every five years, but programming work is carried out every year. In practice this would be so designed that at the end of the first year of this medium-term plan a new plan would be worked out, that is to say, an extra year would be tacked onto the original five-year plan. This continual development programming would have the advantage (admittedly obtained at the cost of considerably more work) that at the end of each five-year period the experience gathered in the meantime can be taken into account in the revisions and thereby new developments can be foreseen with greater flexibility.

Besides 'rolling', continuity in development programming has two further aspects. Decision-makers should formulate a long-term development strategy, i.e. a perspective of the general direction in which the economy is likely to move in the long run. The criterion of continuity makes it necessary that the medium-term plan be fitted into the perspective plan. The other aspect concerns the indispensable breaking-down of the medium-term plan into operative short-term (annual) plans. In both plan formulation and implementation there is a perennial conflict between short-, medium- and long-term plans, due mainly to different time-horizons which depend on the specific problems to be solved.

(*d*) Effective development programming requires that the criterion of *adequacy of development models* must be satisfied; excessively sophisticated models unrelated to real conditions must be avoided. Development models differ not only with regard to the degree of complexity and the calculation techniques employed, but also regarding the type, amount and quality of statistical data required. (Especially in African countries, planning technique is subject to limitations of data which make systematic data improvement imperative.) As for programming techniques, one can distinguish between single projections, such as trend extrapolations and regression analysis, and systems projections, i.e. formalised models, showing functional relationships between desired objectives and the policy instruments that are proposed to achieve them. Systems projections include Tinbergen-type 'fixed-target policy models', and Leontief-type models (input–output projections), as well as rather complicated mathematical (linear and non-linear) programming models which, in contrast to the other two types of models, are optimising 'flexible-target decision models'. Sometimes, even by using mathematics, the only way to solve a problem is to apply the trial-and-error method.

The decision as to which of these methods or models is considered adequate depends on several factors: (1) stage of planning that the developing country has already reached; (2) quantity and quality of available data; (3) ability of the development planner to handle programming techniques. It should be made clear, however, that the use of programming techniques and development models in planning cannot be a substitute for common sense and responsibility.

(*e*) Another prerequisite of good development programming is the criterion of *consistency*. It requires, in very general terms, that supply and demand of all factors involved in the development process should coincide, i.e. the physical and financial resources required must not exceed available supplies. Plans that are too ambitious (e.g. with an exaggeratedly high growth rate, without having the necessary human and physical resources) do not satisfy the criterion of consistency, because in the course of the planning period supply and demand would necessarily be divergent. Furthermore, consistency means that in programming, macro-economic, sectoral and regional projections must be co-ordinated and harmonised. Only in this way can probable incompatibilities between the different projection levels be eliminated.

This criterion does not, however, refer only to consistency in the sense just mentioned, but also holds good for the formal construction of the programming model itself. Since these models reflect the country's development policy, they have to identify not only the various development targets but also the policy instruments to be used in their pursuance. If the number of instrument (or policy) variables equals the number of target variables, the model is called 'determined' and a solution is possible. If, however, the number of instruments the government is willing and/or capable to apply is smaller than the number of target variables, the model is over-determined and the 'solution' is inconsistent. A consistent model can only be obtained when the number of instrument variables is raised and/or that of the target variables lowered. Finally, where the development model is under-determined (i.e. if more instruments than targets are available), a corresponding number of alternatives, the so-called degrees of freedom, can be chosen. In the cases of a consistent solution the development path may represent the optimum efficiency, but this is not necessarily so, becaused fixed-target models do not possess a criterion of optimum efficiency. Macro-economic models of the Tinbergen type can therefore solve the consistency problem, i.e. they can ensure the absence of contradiction between instruments and targets in development policy. What they cannot do is offer the optimum alternative of action (the efficiency criterion will be mentioned under (*h*) below).

(*f*) The criterion of *complementarity* belongs properly to the consistency criterion, but is singled out here because of its importance. It applies not only to programmes but specifically to projects, and it is satisfied if complementarities among projects are taken into account. Developing countries offer many examples of lack of co-ordination between projects, in spite of the fact that technically they depend on each other: for example, the neglect of import quotas for spare parts to maintain imported capital goods; another typical case is the neglect of complementarity between a development project (e.g. school or hospital buildings) and its current expenditures (mainly for personnel).

(*g*) The criterion of *realistic target specification* sounds trivial, but many development plans have neglected it. The criterion implies that the targets and subtargets must be fully specified both in physical (real) and financial (monetary) terms. This renders possible a detailed breakdown of the targets and, later on, the identification of the responsibilities of the major implementation agencies for the realisation of specific targets. This criterion also implies that the quantitative targets should be stated in current and capital terms, although it is not always easy to distinguish sharply between current and development outlays. The word 'realistic' means that targets must be formulated so they can be attained if suitable policy measures are taken in the implementation stage.

(*h*) In elaborating the plan, development programmers strive to realise the targets with a minimum of effort and costs. This raises the question of *efficiency criteria* that the programming stage must satisfy in order to guarantee an efficient allocation of resources, in view of the planned targets. The nature of these criteria depends on whether they deal with the micro- or macro-level. To the micro-level belong the so-called investment criteria, which are methods of appraising projects according to their attractiveness to the country's development (project identification and selection by using cost–benefit analysis, linear programming, etc.).

On the macro-level there exists the method of linear and non-linear programming by which it is possible to determine mathematically an optimal allocation of resources for the whole economy under specified constraints. While this method corresponds to the criterion of optimum efficiency, it is still in an experimental stage as far as macro-planning is concerned.

(*j*) The criterion of *co-operation* refers in a very general sense to the necessary co-operation between development planner and all who participate in the elaboration of the plan. The greater this co-operation, the better the formulation and implementation of the plan. On the one hand, this co-operation is indispensable between the planning bureau and experts outside the bureau for the many technical programming tasks.[4] On the other hand, this criterion also refers to the co-operation already hinted at between development planners and the decision-makers. Very often the draft plan worked out by development programmers becomes the official development plan after it has been accepted by the political decision-makers (government and parliament). But there is a danger that the politicians may accept the draft without reservation – because they lack the necessary expert knowledge and/or because they are mesmerised by sophisticated development models. If such is the case – and it is unfortunately a frequent occurrence in planning practice – the programming phase no longer assists the making of a decision but the decision is rather anticipated, that is to say, *de facto* usurped by the plan-technocrats. The only possible way of guaranteeing necessary communication between develement programmers and decision-makers during the whole programming phase lies in the intensification of a two-way learning process. The decision-makers have to get to know the instrumental planning techniques better than they have done up to now, so that they are in a position at least to estimate the dimensions of the probable consequences of their decisions on development policy (thinking in implications). The development planners, on the other hand, should increase their awareness of the responsibility they assume in drafting the plan. They need to know much more about institutional and societal problems, as well as development strategies and political realities.

Conventionally, development programmers are supposed to make impartial projections of targets, assisting in the decision-making process but not actually making the decisions. There is, however, little merit in the distinction between 'value-free' planning and 'value-loaded' decision-making. If development planners (not the caricature of 'plan-technocrats' who live in an ivory tower and know nothing but sophisticated econometric models) think of implications and understand the real systemic interactions of society, it is difficult to see why normative considerations should not be introduced in the setting of targets. It is essential, however, that the planners state explicitly the base of their judgement. Development planners are thus not limited to the formulation of optimal targets and means, but they are also in a position to search for and reflect on development purposes and goals.

All this, of course, presupposes a much more intensive dialogue and a great deal of mutual understanding between the development planners and the (leading) politicians.

(*k*) Finally, there is the criterion of *commitment* which must be satisfied not only in the programming stage but also in that of plan implementation. This criterion is so overwhelmingly important that sustained governmental and political commitment must be rated as a *sine qua non* for accelerated development. The prevalence of pseudo-planning in many developing countries is perhaps as much due to the planner's lack of realism and/or competence as it is the result of the politicians' inability or unwillingness to commit themselves to structural reforms and other development strategies required by the plan. This lack of commitment of national and local authorities is prejudicial to planning, because it prevents the formation of the psychological climate of readiness needed for mobilising wide popular support.

4. IMPLEMENTATION OF THE DEVELOPMENT PLAN

However excellent the development plan elaborated during the previous programming phase might be in terms of technico-economic conception and inner consistency, its targets must remain wishful thinking as long as the corresponding implementation measures in the field of development policy are not taken. Thus the execution of a plan should not be viewed as a separate working stage after the plan document is drawn up, but has to be closely integrated into the planning process itself and especially related to the formulation of the plan. There is no doubt that the implementation stage is one of the most (if not the most) difficult stage of development planning. Programming (i.e. formulating and blueprinting the plan) can be done by relatively few experts possibly with the help of foreign advisers. The implementation process on the other hand involves the people of the developing country and numerous governmental agencies. While programming is at times a glamourous conceptual exercise consisting of devising and manipulating more or less sophisticated programming models, in the implementation stage decision-makers are faced with recalcitrant reality; the necessary (sometimes unpleasant) decisions are not always easy to make and even more difficult to carry through. Against this background it can be stated that in general the 'implementability' of a development plan is assured if the following criteria are met:

(a) An important criterion is that the proposed *plan activities* (at national, regional, sectoral and project level), by means of which the plan targets are to be achieved, must be *fully specified*. This requires the classification according to whether the principal responsibility of execution will be assigned to the public or the private sector. If the activities are to be carried out by the public agencies, then it is essential for efficient implementation to include managerial considerations and requirements in budgeting.[5]

(b) A corollary of the preceding criterion is the *time-phasing of the plan activities*. This means that during the implementation stage the executive units should follow the time-phased indication for allocation of physical, financial and human resources. The neglect of the sequential aspects and temporal interdependencies of development programmes or projects has all too often delayed and/or impaired the successful implementation of these activities. This timing criterion shows how inseparably intertwined the stages of plan formulation and implementation are. In order to make more extensive use of the time dimension, special operation techniques of network analysis such as PERT, C.P.M., etc. should and can be applied in development planning.[6]

(c) The criterion of *conformity of ends and means* requires that the selection of development policy instruments should be closely geared to the attainment of the proposed targets.[7] It is not possible in this short paper to evolve a single comprehensive operational criterion of conformity which can be applied to all conceivable types of development policies, because they are far too many. Functionally these policy measures (referred to in economics as 'instruments') consist of incentives, disincentives and restrictions both in the field of general economic policy and in the more specialised fields of fiscal, price and credit policies, savings and investment policies, foreign trade and exchange policies, manpower and educational policies, regional policy, etc. A particular policy has to be formulated and implemented with due consideration to the given *ad hoc* situation of a specific developing country. Here the experience, political realism and intuitive feeling of development planners and decision-makers play an important role, as the adequate selection of measures and their successful implementation depend upon them. It should be added, however, that the selection and use of these policies has all too often been influenced by existing vested interests rather than by the internal logic of development planning. Finally, this criterion requires that foreign aid be fully and consistently integrated into the framework of development policies.

This necessarily incomplete list of policy measures is given only to indicate the complexity involved. There is no need to mention here the unavoidable difficulties caused by the interaction of these policies.[8] This leads to another important criterion:

(*d*) The criterion of *compatibility of development policies*, being a corollary of criterion (*c*), is fulfilled when the implementation of one policy is in harmony or at least reconcilable with the others and when their direct effects are complementary rather than contradictory. As yet, no development plan fully conforms to the criterion of compatibility, although attempts in this direction are discernible in quite a few of the latest development plans. The main problem lies in the difficulty of projecting not only the direct but also the indirect (i.e. the secondary, tertiary, etc.) effects. Even if it is possible to predict the response to a particular policy measure (this knowledge is still rather sketchy), there is uncertainty about the suitable policy mix, i.e. the effect of a policy instrument and its relationship with other instruments. The combined impact of all policy instruments depends not only on the intensity with which they are used, but depends also on their nature. Finally, consistency in the use of policy measures depends on effectiveness of administration. The more economic development depends on private-sector performance, the greater the need for compatibility in the use of policy measures. Many official policy measures will affect only the private sector, the range of which may extend from large private corporations and small enterprises all the way through to illiterate farmers. The authorities have at their disposal a panoply of instruments for providing incentives and disincentives in order to influence behaviour and decisions in the private sector. The difficulty, however, that in practice seems incapable of general solution has been to achieve (1) compatibility between these policy instruments, and (2) consistency between the policy measures applicable to the private sector and those affecting the public sector.

(e) The criterion of *flexibility* is met when the planning and operating authorities do not adhere rigidly to the development targets and policies, but are flexible enough to adjust to unforeseen contingencies and changing needs with respect to targets, policy measures, composition or timing. Sometimes plan targets cannot be attained for reasons that have little to do with planning itself, but a great deal with unpredictable events (poor harvest, drop in world prices, political upheaval, deterioration in international relations, etc.). Necessary and desirable corrections should be made on an *ad hoc* basis. These alterations and adjustments must be incorporated into the successive annual plans and annual budgets. The (ordinary and investment) budget is of particular importance: almost everything the government does is directly reflected in the budget; furthermore, the budget is an excellent means of co-ordinating short-term and medium-term policies and of putting into force the necessary plan modifications. Thus, annual plans and budgets provide an excellent opportunity to update the medium-term development plan. This built-in flexibility is such a major condition of success in plan implementation that it merits far greater attention than it has received in the past.[9]

Apart from the above criteria, which deal with the implementation measures exclusively, a second set of criteria which are more institutional in character needs to be listed.

(f) It is obvious that effective plan implementation can take place only if the very general criterion of *institutional operationality* is also kept in view. In the narrow sense, this criterion requires that the central planning bureau be endowed with capable personnel,[10] and be organised functionally and institutionally in such a way as to make the timely performance of development tasks possible. It furthermore requires as close an integration of planning and budgeting as possible, because usually the two functions are carried out by separate institutions, and consequently by different groups of persons with different motivations and skills. In a broader sense, this criterion requires an efficient public administration as well as properly operating private organisations involved in the implementation of policies and targets which the planning process calls for. The desire for development must therefore be accompanied by the willingness to improve the administrative apparatus.[11]

(g) An important institutional aspect of the planning machinery is dealt with by the criterion of *authority delegation*. Since development policies and activities cannot be performed by a single omniscient super-organisation, these functions have to be delegated hierarchically in terms of functions or geographical responsibility. The decision how and what to centralise or decentralise in the implementation process should not be based on political or ideological arguments, but must be determined from the viewpoint of effectiveness. In general, however, one can say that 'excessive centralisation may in the end put the brake on the development process, whereas too much decentralisation may result in loss of guidance, if not total chaos'.[12]

Therefore, the decision cannot be a question of *either* centralisation *or* decentralisation, because *both* forms of organisation are needed. Although the 'adequate' relationship between these two opposite aspects of authority delegation depends ultimately on the degree of economic development, the economic structure (e.g. the proportion between public and private sectors) and political determinants, it would be a good policy (even for public programmes) to decentralise the implementation function whenever possible from the national to the state level, the provincial and the local level. It is self-evident that the criterion of authority delegation implies the detailed specification of the task which the lower units should perform. It is only when the lower execution unit is missing or not functioning properly that the higher unit should assume responsibility.

(h) The criterion of *information* is met when there is sufficient, adequate and intelligible information (and not only in a one-way direction) between the different units involved in the implementation of plan activities, viz. the planning bureau and, on the other hand, the public sector (ministries, public corporations, research institutes, etc.), as well as the private sector (enterprises, consulting firms, professional organisations, trade unions, etc.). The kind of information and institutionalised or informal communication channels required naturally depends on the specific development policy and activity. The effectiveness and success of this feedback process of communication depends to a great extent on the simplicity and clarity with which the plan document explains the content of different stages in the implementation process. Information implies also the need for identifying the responsibilities of all those who participate in plan implementation: public agencies, communities and individuals. For purposes of effective communication the technical terminology of the policies should be expressed in a generally intelligible language.

(*j*) The information required in the above criterion of communication is a necessary but not a sufficient condition for effective plan implementation. The criterion of *active participation* must also be fulfilled. The successful implementation of a plan cannot be the responsibility of the thin upper crust of esoteric technocrats only; instead it should call for active participation and adequate performance, not only of the public agencies, but also of the private elements of the society, such as individuals (producers and consumers), productive and commercial organisations (both regional and local), co-operatives, trade unions, etc. How to mobilise public participation cannot be stated in general terms, for no two developing countries have the same traditions, culture and mentality. Active, as opposed to mere verbal, participation will be forthcoming only if the plan reflects the will and desire of the great majority. At the same time, people should be informed about the efforts and sacrifices that will be indispensable for the plan's success. Without this 'critical minimum effort' any plan will remain a paper document.

(*k*) Realistic and efficient plan implementation must satisfy the criterion of *operational co-ordination*. The central planning bureau seems to be the appropriate organisation where the progress in implementation is registered and where corrective measures can be initiated. In order to do so, the planning bureau must have the necessary institutional power and the prestige to reconcile the various conflicting situations, problems and interests that arise in implementation, so as to assure effective co-ordination.[13] This co-ordination at the highest level is all the more important because the implementation of the plan is done at the sectoral and the project levels by the special ministries concerned, the public corporations and, of course, the private sector. The task of co-ordination by the central planning bureau would be considerably easier if the planning units located within ministries and public and private corporations maintained constant and continuous contact with the planning bureau. As to the argument sometimes brought forward that the function of plan formulation is incompatible with the executive function of controlling and co-ordinating plan implementation, it is the author's conviction that for the sake of effectiveness these functions should not be completely separated from one another. This, of course, does not mean that the central planning bureau can or should carry out directly *all* the activities related to plan implementation, because in practice these are delegated to the operating ministries and public enterprises, not to mention the private activities which can be influenced only indirectly by the government's planning bureau. An all-powerful 'planning and implementation agency' which does everything would simply duplicate the ministries' work by creating unnecessary conflicts. (Besides, if an agency could be given such power, the political pluralism in a society with a mixed economy would have virtually disappeared.) The author's contention in this matter is that the central planning agency should co-ordinate development activities. As for its power, the crux is really the extent to which the Prime Minister or President is committed to support this agency and to enforce the discipline of the plan.

5. EVALUATION OF THE DEVELOPMENT PLAN

The formulation and implementation of a plan is no end in itself, but simply a means of fostering development and improving the standard of living of the population. Therefore, the essential question arises, to what extent has planning contributed to the promotion of economic and social development? The purpose of the evaluation stage is to give a scientific and objective answer to this question by continuously reviewing the plan performance. This stage in the planning process is of utmost importance because only critical evaluation makes it possible to judge whether the development plan was well conceived and to determine and possibly quantify the economic and social changes the plan has brought about. The feedback function of evaluation from the standpoint of planners and decision-makers is to diagnose failures, to determine their direct and indirect causes in order to avoid as far as possible the same mistakes in the future. Whereas considerable literature has accumulated on techniques and methods of plan formulation, and to a lesser degree on plan implementation, evaluation has unfortunately received little attention hitherto. This is probably the decisive reason why a scientifically based, comprehensive method of plan evaluation is still lacking. Another reason is its interdisciplinary character. To be effective, evaluation of development planning requires the observance of the following criteria:

(*a*) It is obvious (although not common practice) that the evaluation work should meet the criterion of *objectivity*. This entails an important institutional aspect. It has been argued on the one hand that no special agency should be created for the evaluation task, which should be left to the planning bureau, because the non-initiated are supposedly not in a position to analyse and pass judgement on the very complex, interdependent problems of programming and implementation. On the other hand, it has been maintained that institutionalised evaluation, outside the central planning agency, is imperative because, human nature being what it is, planners may not always be capable of taking a fully objective view of their own failures. As a compromise and a feasible solution it is suggested here that evaluation may be left in the hands of a permanent body which should be integrated into the existing planning agency, while at the same time enjoying a certain degree of autonomy.[14]

(*b*) The criterion of *periodicity* implies that evaluation of the planned development activities should be carried out not only after the termination of the plan (i.e. every four or five years) but also during the planning period, e.g. on a quarterly, semi-annual or annual basis; the periodicity depends of course on the nature of activity (projects, programmes, overall performance). Only then will it be possible to take appropriate corrective measures for the next planning period.

(*c*) In order to measure development progress objectively, the evaluation criteria must be relevant to the plan targets. This basic requirement of effective evaluation is the criterion of *target conformity*. The targets should not be too vague and general in character. The more precise and accurate the formulation of the development goals and the plan targets are, the more exactly and realistically the evaluation criteria can be specified, so that suitable measuring instruments can be selected or devised. In practice, however, it is sometimes conceivable to follow the procedure of successive approximations when targets are too complex and/or too generally formulated. In these cases the targets can be broken down into subtargets in relation to which the results can be measured. Very closely related to this criterion is another one which stems from the well-known *ends-means* issue of economic policy. It is imperative to evaluate not only the plan targets themselves, but also the various development policies in order to ascertain whether they were appropriate to realise the chosen targets. Checking the adequacy of policy prescriptions in the evaluation stage is a test of the fulfilment of the criterion of conformity between ends and means.

(*d*) As the purpose of measurement in evaluation is to eliminate subjectivity in judgement, the *measuring instruments* should have the following two qualities. The principle of *validity* requires agreement between the measuring instrument and the chosen evaluation criterion. In some cases, the criterion and the method of measurement are so closely related that the measuring instrument registers accurately the object's state or performance vis-à-vis the criterion to which it relates.[15] More often than not the selected criterion has no appropriate measure, so that the measuring instrument applied can only measure performance indirectly.[16] Thus objective measurement is more difficult in the field of sociology than in the field of economics, for the simple reason that human behaviour is very often a subjective phenomenon. However, if quantitative measurement and evaluation are not feasible one should still not refrain from making a qualitative evaluation. The other required quality is known as *reliability*, which requires that the measuring instrument should be dependable, i.e. it must give the same results each time the same object or activity is measured.

(*e*) In evaluating development programmes and projects, the criterion of *efficiency and effectiveness* should, whenever possible, be taken into consideration. This means that projects should be preferred which show a minimum cost for a given output, or alternatively, those with a maximum output for a given cost. In order to perform a cost-benefit or cost-effectiveness analysis, the measurement in money terms of costs and of anticipated results should be possible. In the case of techno-economic programmes and projects this is relatively easy to apply, but it is difficult when applied to activities classified as 'social investment'. Unfortunately it has not yet been possible to evolve an operationally feasible technique to evaluate the profitability of social projects.

(*f*) During the process of economic development, situations occasionally arise where change or progress takes place not as a result of the plan, but because of other causes and influences, which are independent of the development plan itself. However welcome this may be, difficulties arise in evaluating such non-plan causes and influences. Here the criterion of *imputation* is important, by which plan evaluators come to know to what extent the development plan has been responsible for the noted changes. There is not too much difficulty in evaluating economic and technical progress, because this is measurable. The difficulty arises when the social programmes and projects and/or administrative processes are to be evaluated and measured. Such an evaluation can be done by using the method of comparing the control group with the experimental group. The latter is represented by the population that is directly affected by the social programme, and the control group is represented by the population that is not exposed to the programme. By way of correlating the results obtained with both groups, the changes caused by the development programme can be verified in quantitative or, if that is not possible, in qualitative terms. Care should be taken that both groups are homogeneous in nature (the matching principle). Furthermore, the same criteria and measuring instruments should be used for both groups.

(*g*) Experience has shown that the criterion of *comprehensiveness* has not yet been considered in evaluation. Evaluation work has been rather restricted to social programmes and to specific economic and community development projects. In spite of their usefulness, progress reports, published more or less regularly by planning agencies in several developing countries, do not meet the criterion of comprehensiveness, because they mainly answer 'what?' and 'how?' A genuine and comprehensive evaluation of plan performance should reveal both the internal relationship as well as the direct and indirect causes and consequences of the observed changes. Therefore, more important than merely asking 'what?' and 'how much?' is to analyse the causal factors and to ask 'why?' What is therefore needed is to give up the misleading distinction between economic and non-economic factors, as it does not represent a distinction between relevant and irrelevant factors. The complexity of a causal analysis emphasises its necessity and shows clearly that comprehensive evaluation of the development planning process is interdisciplinary in character.

(*h*) Finally, two special aspects of the evaluation stage which are essentially qualitative in character should be mentioned. The fact that development planning is no end in itself but a means to improve the standard of living makes it obligatory to incorporate *opinion polls* as a constitutive element of the evaluation work. This will enable the planners and policy-makers to determine how far the development plan and its implementation are compatible with the actual needs and aspirations of the people. In particular, opinion polls can give important clues regarding the scope and location of needed projects and programmes, as well as locate idle human resources and determine where the people could participate more actively in development.

The second aspect refers to the *efficiency of the institutions* that directly or indirectly participate in the implementation process. Proper evaluation should be in a position to establish whether these institutions have been able to meet the organisational requirements of development planning successfully, and also whether the initial impulses of development have been sustained. In practice, such questions arise as: Was the implementing institution provided with dynamic people and sufficient financial resources, and what are the results obtained? Are the schools, roads and canals built voluntarily by the villagers and taken over by the village authorities properly maintained? Experience in developing countries has shown that it is not sufficient to establish development projects if effective follow-up is not ensured. Many good projects have failed after successful beginnings, because of the absence of follow-up measures. These measures should by no means be disregarded as being 'only' organisational, since all too often development projects failed owing to insufficient attention to organisational matters. Such failures have led not only to the misallocation of physical and human capital, but also – and this is more aggravating – have discouraged those who have participated from making a new attempt.

6. RESEARCH ON UNSOLVED QUESTIONS IN DEVELOPMENT PLANNING

The shortcomings of the planning process do nothing to reduce the need for integrated development planning. They indicate, however, the most desirable directions for research in the field. No comprehensive catalogue of research needs will be provided here, as they have been tried frequently elsewhere.[17] What is intended here is to single out very briefly a few important problems still unsolved in development planning.

Among the unsolved questions is that of a spatial dimension which must be taken into account in addition to overall and sectoral considerations. How to do this and when, i.e. whether the regional programming stage should precede or follow the sectoral stage, or even follow the project stage, is still unsettled.

The adequacy of a particular development model for a particular developing country is another unsolved question. Under this very broad theme a multitude of research topics can be conceived, all of which pertain to the future improvement of development programming techniques, such as dynamic and stochastic programming methods, making linear and non-linear programming operational for development planning, use of systems analysis in development planning (systemic planning), etc.

As for the decision-making process, there are many unsolved questions, in particular with regard to improving its rationality and to the feedback process between people's need and decision-making. Furthermore, intensive research is required to avoid incompatibilities in development strategies and policies.

Further research is also needed on the whole complex of relationships between human behaviour and socio-economic development, and especially on the interrelationships between social and economic variables and their integration into the planning process. There is still insufficient knowledge about the mechanisms that can ensure an active participation and adequate performance of the masses of the people.

Last but not least, the need for research with regard to a genuine and operationalised interdisciplinary method must be emphasised. Integrated development planning is, by its very nature, an interdisciplinary process which involves many fields of knowledge. This makes a mere multidisciplinary approach insufficient, because it does not take into account the many interdependent and indivisible problems of development planning. Therefore the plea is made here to reinforce research efforts in this neglected field.[18] Even the most modest progress in forging scholarly co-operation will contribute towards increasing the foundation of knowledge of interdisciplinary co-operation.

NOTES

1. Some examples of failures and successes in development planning are listed in Albert Waterston (assisted by C. J. Martin, A. T. Schumacher, F. A. Steuber), *Development Planning: Lessons of Experience* (Baltimore, 1965).
2. See the interesting remarks by Wolfgang F. Stolper, *Planning without Facts: Lessons in Resource Allocation from Nigeria's Development* (Cambridge, Mass., 1966) pp. 6–16.
3. African plans especially are, in their majority, born of independence, thus having a marked political significance.
4. India is among the few developing countries in whch working groups and panels of qualified people support the planning commission in its programming activities with expert advice. In these panels, representatives of the planning commission and the ministerial planning units as well as experts of the private sector and members of specialist institutes and universities confer together and contribute to the solution of specific programming problems.
5. What is meant here is the necessity of a more extensive use of programme and performance budgeting in plan implementation. 'In programme budgeting, the principal emphasis is on a budget classification in which functions, programmes and their subdivisions are established for each agency, and these are related to accurate and meaningful financial data. Performance budgeting involves the development of more refined management tools, such as unit costs, work measurement, and performance standards. Of course, the measurement of work, both in a physical and financial sense, presumes an already formulated set of work units which can be derived only when programmes and their subdivisions are first established. In this sense, performance budgeting is an all-inclusive concept embodying programme formulation as well as measurement of the performance of work in the accomplishment of programme objectives.' United Nations, *A Manual for Programme and Performance Budgeting* (New York, 1965) p. 3. For an improved version of the P.P.B.S. (planning–programming–budgeting system), see A. J. Catanese and A. W. Steiss, *Systemic Planning: Theory and Application* (Lexington, Mass., 1970) pp. 67–96.

6. There is a growing literature on PERT (programme evaluation and review technique) and C.P.M. (critical path method). A particularly interesting application of these techniques, especially to the 'implementation gap', is given in a paper by Max F. Millikan, 'Comments on Methods for Reporting and Evaluating Progress under Plan Implementation: Addendum', United Nations, Committee for Development Planning, Second Session, Santiago de Chile, E/AC.54/L.18/Add. 1, 24 Mar 1967.

7. This criterion is similar to the one listed above under (*a*). However, here we are not concerned with *plan activities* but with the important question whether a particular development policy is adequately formulated and then operationalised in the form of specific measures (or 'instruments'), so that the planned targets can be attained.

8. The difficulties are primarily due to the fact that by formulating a development policy one has to keep in mind many constraints and boundary conditions which often make it necessary to envisage supplementary policy measures. This means, for example, that the behaviour of the various economic units has to be influenced in such a way that with the aid of these modifications the plan targets can be realised. A high savings/investment ratio, for example, cannot be achieved unless adequate incentives and motivation are provided to the private and the public-sector units of the economy, which is basically a function of an appropriate allocation policy, fiscal and monetary policy.

9. It is sometimes argued that changes in plan targets or development policies during plan implementation would result in the population of a country losing its confidence in the development plan. Therefore, according to this argument, it would be better to maintain the original form and contents of the plan or, if inevitable corrections have to be made, they should not be publicised, lest the confidence of the people be affected. I believe this is a most unfortunate and irresponsible attitude because it favours the development of a 'plan myth', thus leading to a situation where the people develop the fatalistic belief that the mere existence of a plan would automatically force economic progress without any efforts to be made. The publishing of plan amendments would have the advantage of frankly explaining to the people why certain targets could not be realised and at the same time convey an idea of the necessary efforts.

10. 'Capable' is to be understood not only in terms of know-how (economic, technical, etc.), but also implies the general understanding of the nature of development problems and sound sense of intuition and common sense.

11. As further obstacles to an efficient plan implementation in some developing countries, mention should be made of the bureaucratisation and corruption in the public administration as well as the political instability.

12. *Economic Bulletin for Asia and the Far East*, XVII 3 (Dec 1966) 42.

13. The mere organisational structure or form of the planning bureau is not that important, but it is essential that it meets the above criterion.

For co-ordination to be effective at the highest level, the planning bureau should be given a very high status, i.e. it should preferably be established within the Prime Minister's or the President's secretariat. 'The status and location of the planning agency are, in fact, not merely an administrative question but are indicative of the importance attached, at the highest political level, to development planning.' United Nations, *World Economic Survey, 1966, part* 1: 'Implementation of Development Plans: Problems and Experience' (New York, 1967) p. 10.

14. For certain tasks it is certainly possible to visualise one and the same person in the planning and implementation agencies. This compromise might be necessary anyway in many developing countries in order to overcome the shortage of trained personnel.

15. For instance, rice production, per capita income, ability to sign one's name, etc.

16. In a community development project, for instance, the criterion for measuring an increase in agricultural production per acre could be through measuring the increases in the use of fertilisers and agricultural machinery. However, this is not an unambiguous and objective measurement, since the primary causes for these increases may be found elsewhere, as for instance in adult education teaching the farmers how to attain more and better results.

17. It is interesting to note that some years ago three books were published devoted entirely to basic and applied research needs on developing countries in general and on planning in particular. It would be interesting to investigate how many research topics have been taken up since, the rest being still unsolved. See *Development of the Emerging Countries: An Agenda for Research* (Washington, D.C.: Brookings Institution 1962); I.E.D.E.S., 'Vers un plan international de recherches prioritaires concernant les pays sous-développés', *Tiers Monde* (Paris), II 5 (1961) 41–103; Bertram M. Gross (ed.), *Action under Planning: The Guidance of Economic Development* (New York, London, Sydney, Toronto, 1967), pp. 264–80.

18. Principles, methods and problems of interdisciplinary co-operation are treated in a forthcoming article by Bruno Knall, 'Interdisciplinary Co-operation in Development Research', *Law and State* (Tubingen: Institute for Scientific Co-operation), V (1972).

Planning for Development

T. T. THAHANE

INTRODUCTION

The topic 'Planning for Development' is so general that it makes rigorous analysis difficult if not impossible, especially in the context of the Conference theme: 'Accelerated Development in Southern Africa'. Analysis is complicated because Southern Africa is not a homogeneous economic or ecological region. It consists of political, economic, social and administrative areas which are at different stages of development and which enjoy different standards of living and degrees of autonomy. Short- and medium-term goals and means for achieving them will generally vary in accordance with the initial conditions in each region; adopted planning techniques will vary according to the different economic structures and the statistical data available for each regional economy.

The scope of the topic may, however, be an advantage, since it may enable discussion of the process and problems of development planning from the most general premises down to the more specific cases within Southern Africa. This approach will be adopted in the present paper. Part I will attempt to define the task and meaning of planning for development and analyse the nature of the planning problems. There will be a cursory examination of material and human resources, including land, in the context of underdeveloped countries. Part II will deal with the problems of target-setting in Southern Africa. In Part III a few selected issues relevant to the development of Lesotho, and the planning approach which the government has adopted, will be examined.

I

The concept of planning for development is, strictly speaking, relevant or applicable to those countries or economies which have been described in the literature of economic development as 'underdeveloped'. A few remarks will be made later about the criteria of underdevelopment and some characteristic features of such economies. At this stage, it is important to emphasise that underdeveloped countries are those that have not fully developed one or more of their natural or human resources. In this wider sense, underdevelopment would cover countries such as Canada, Australia, Lesotho, etc.

Why is it necessary to plan the development of underdeveloped countries, rather than leave them to *laissez-faire* automatism which has proved its value in Western Europe and America? There are two main arguments that could be advanced in connection with the question. The first is that the *laissez-faire* mechanism is short-sighted and cannot always transmit accurate information to both producers and consumers about the expected state of affairs in the future. It is efficient and effective in the short run, where structural changes in the economy are not involved. Once structural transformation of production is contemplated, careful planning becomes necessary.

The second argument relates to the distortions in the price mechanism, which arise from the presence of monopolistic and monopsonistic tendencies in both the product and factor markets. These distortions are largely attributable to activities of the giant international corporations whose budgets exceed by far the gross national products of many developing countries, especially those of Africa. The acquisition of monopoly power is part of the contemporary economic process, and the essence of monopoly is control over the terms of sale of the products and control over the terms of purchase of the inputs. In addition to monopoly and monopsony practices, price mechanism is further distorted by factor immobilities. Taking labour as an example, people do not often emigrate to different countries or regions in response to wage differentials. For historical and cultural reasons they may prefer to remain in their own place. Even where the government has subsidised their movement and resettlement in the new area, a reverse flow may develop after a while. This was the case in some rural resettlement schemes in Newfoundland.

From the long-term point of view, the essence of planning consists in reshaping the economic structure in such a way that self-sustaining growth can be achieved. The concept of self-sustaining growth implies, first of all, the internal generation of domestic (public and private) savings in such a way as to maintain a steady growth rate. The second aspect of the concept relates to the transformation of the structure of production. Transformation further implies the development of the capacity of an economy to apply innovations and to adapt to changing situations. This capacity is closely tied to the political, social and attitudinal processes that underlie the process of economic growth and structural change.

Structural transformation also implies an increase in the number of market transactions and the forging of linkages between the various parts of domestic production structure in the national economy. The development of interdependencies in production through the formation of backward and forward linkages is the end-product of economic policy in underdeveloped countries. This will generally be achieved by a change in the composition of imports away from consumer goods towards intermediate products – together with the elimination of dualism in the national economy.

It is clear from the above that the *laissez-faire* price mechanism cannot cope with long-term problems of economic development and structural transformation. This shortcoming should not, however, lead to a total rejection of the mechanism, but rather focus on its control and manipulation through careful planning and use of economic incentives. The success with development planning depends *inter alia* on the stage of development reached by each country, the quality of public administration, the degree of development of the private sector and the availability of statistical data. The effectiveness of economic incentives, on the other hand, depends on the ability of various channels of communication – from committees to mass media – to transmit the information and respond to it accurately. To cite but one example, tax concessions for new industries are of no use unless they have been clearly communicated and understood by the investors, and unless the latter use them in their investment planning decisions.

NATURE OF THE PLANNING PROBLEM

What, then, is the task of development planning in underdeveloped or less developed countries? Simply stated, development planning involves the mobilisation and organisation of scarce resources for the purposes of achieving predetermined socio-economic objectives. Of course, the objectives may be determined by political or security considerations. But having accepted the goals, the task of development planning is to decide on the relative emphasis to be placed on the various targets and the means for attaining them. The assignment of priorities (to use the economists' jargon) is a dynamic process which can only be defined with reference to time or the planning period.

Since many textbooks and articles have been written on the methodology and techniques of planning and the setting of priorities, these will not be discussed in the present paper. It is sufficient to note that there are many models which have been devised to assist policy-makers in deciding development priorities.

As a general observation, it can be pointed out that for development planning to succeed, it must proceed from a careful and thorough analysis of the initial socio-economic, political, institutional and legal conditions in each country. Such an analysis must include an evaluation of the classical factors of production, such as land, labour and capital. From this, realistic economic and social targets can be set, and modified accordingly when circumstances change.

EVALUATION OF THE FACTORS OF PRODUCTION

Let us now look briefly at the problems of less developed countries. Underdeveloped countries face serious problems with respect to development of land, labour and capital accumulation. Although some countries, such as Zambia, Canada or Australia, have a relative abundance of land, to make it usable requires an investment of capital in drainage, forest clearance and levelling. These activities involve heavy expenditures of capital inputs relative to other factors. Hence land can only be regarded as concealed capital which is potentially useful.

Another factor in scarce supply in the underdeveloped countries is labour. This may sound paradoxical, since it is often assumed that underdeveloped economies have a surplus of cheap labour. An unskilled and malnourished body with a pair of hands and feet is useless in many production activities. To convert such a factor into labour requires heavy investment in health programmes, education and training over long periods of time. Only after these capital investments have been made can we have a factor of production called labour. Education and health programmes are fundamental to the conversion of labour into a useful human capital. Only in this peculiar sense can both education and health expenditures be regarded as fully developmental.

It is clear from these observations that the scarcity of skilled labour and of usable land both boil down to the relative scarcity of capital investment. This means that the nature of the development problem and the strategy for each country will therefore be determined by the missing factors. Hence there can be no general formulae to guide economists in their efforts to solve the problems of underdeveloped economies. Each country has to devise its plan and programme in accordance with its initial conditions. Development plans, their targets and policy instruments are indigenous to each country and are not transplantable from country to country.

II

Development planning is a process of organising national economic and social effort for the promotion or achievement of clearly defined national development goals. Critical in this process is target-setting and specification of the policy instruments to be used to achieve the goals. The goals can be regional or national. A problem which economic planners generally have to face is the determination of regions and their goals. Once regions and their targets have been defined, they have to be reconciled with national goals. More often than not, these may be inconsistent.

Among some of the approaches or criteria used to determine regions, the following may be mentioned:

(a) *Homogeneity criterion.* This criterion considers a region to be a continuous space with respect to one or more economic variables, natural or human resources. The level of income, population, literacy or some other variable could be used to define a region. It may be useful to point out that the homogeneity criterion implies a minimisation of dispersion of differences in a particular variable; hence a region is that continuous space that satisfies minimum dispersion.

(b) *Nodality or polarisation criterion.* According to this criterion a region consists of spatial economic units which trade hierarchically with higher economic centres. This approach relates largely to centres of production and consumption such as cities and villages. The strength of the linkages between the centre and the periphery vary in accordance with distance, size and the degree of economic diversification.

(c) *Programming or policy-oriented criterion.* This criterion defines a region in terms of administrative and political cohesion which is necessary for bringing policy decisions into fruition. Here political considerations predominate.

Given the above criteria, it is difficult to see how Southern Africa could be defined as a cohesive region. The only common denominator seems to be geographical – the region consists of all countries in the southern tip of the African continent. Within this definition there are numerous other groupings, especially political, which can be identified and which differ considerably in their goals and aspirations.

The different socio-political systems in Southern Africa make the setting of regional targets difficult. For example, the desires of Botswana, Lesotho, Swaziland and Zambia to maximise the growth rates of their respective national incomes could act as a constraint to the maximisation of the growth rate of South Africa's national income. Similarly, the goal of reducing the income disparities of these countries may not be consistent with income maximisation for the region as a whole.

The above comments have been made simply to indicate that a number of analytical and practical problems would have to be resolved in order to set mutually acceptable goals or targets for Southern Africa. This is particularly important if we recognise the differences in political outlooks and philosophies of the countries which constitute Southern Africa. For example, Botswana's and Lesotho's major objectives are to be self-reliant and less dependent on other countries for employment and incomes. For South Africa's rapid mining development these countries' dependence may be critical.

A further complication arises from finding a suitable framework for the formulation of regional goals, which would be consistent with the maximisation of the standards of living of the various peoples within the region. Such a framework, if it could be defined, should also specify the policy instruments to be used and the authority which will use them for the achievement of agreed regional goals.

III

Let us now turn to a few special problems relating to Lesotho, a small enclave country contiguous to the advanced economy of the Republic of South Africa. Lesotho, together with Botswana and Swaziland, enjoys a customs and monetary union with South Africa. This arrangement has both advantages and disadvantages. An advantage arises from the easy access of Lesotho products to the South African market and the need not to worry about the external value of its currency. The biggest disadvantage arises from the fact that through polarisation of development it is difficult to attract industries into Lesotho where supporting institutions and infrastructure are lacking. Industry prefers to go where the infrastructure, communications and other services are already abundant and where it can internalise the external economies created in such a setting. In addition, the small industries being started in Lesotho have to compete for the market with long-established ones. While the customs agreement provides for protection of infant industries in these countries, it will be rather difficult to apply such a protection device.

Another disadvantage arises from the fact that advanced South African financial institutions such as building societies, insurance companies and commercial banks tend to syphon savings from the other countries and invest them in South Africa where opportunities have already been identified and resources mapped.

A characteristic feature of underdevelopment in Lesotho relates to an abundance of unskilled labour and shortage of other factors. A fundamental problem is to create human and material capital in sufficient quantities to initiate and support the self-sustaining process of development. Capital is scarce in the sense discussed above. All this boils down to the problem of converting the unskilled labour into a useful productive human resource.

The importance of human capital or skilled manpower in the process of development has been illustrated historically by Germany. During the Second World War its material capital was destroyed, but through the know-how of its people who survived the war, Germany has become a strong economic giant. Switzerland and Israel are examples of countries without much natural resources; but through the skills of their people they are now advanced and enjoy high standards of living.

The recognition of the relative importance of human capital underlies the priority which the government of Lesotho attaches to education and health, even at the expense of short-term income considerations. In fact, the government's First Five-Year Development Plan states:

> The attainment of the development targets for the Five Year period, as well as for the long-run objectives of socio-economic transformations of the country, depends on the capability of the Basotho people to execute the development programmes. This can be secured only with education and training, which will provide in appropriate quantities and quality the skills required for economic development.
>
> A country's population can indeed be its greatest asset or its worst liability, depending on the state of its education and training. Lesotho, a country poorly endowed with natural resources, has to rely heavily for its economic advancement on the development of its human resources and the formation of human capital. Promoting education and training as a means of creating skills and attitudes must therefore be a focal point in Lesotho's development strategy.

Closely related to education and training is the government's goal for the improvement of the health and nutritional condition of the population. Again to quote: 'Although such an improvement is an end in itself, it is also a prerequisite for economic development as essential as education and training, since healthy and properly trained workers are also more efficient.'

Thus, of the total capital programme of R28·8 million, education and health have been allocated 17 per cent. This reflects the priority attached to the development of social infrastructure, in order to create the preconditions for a sustained long-term development process.

Following a careful appraisal of its limited natural resources and heavy exports of able-bodied men to the Republic of South Africa, Lesotho has set a modest goal of concentrating its efforts on absorbing the annual labour force increment of about 6,000 people in the country. Those who are already working in South

Africa (approximately 120,000 men) will be left to continue to earn incomes there. But through education and training an increasing percentage of young people will be retained in Lesotho. The implication of this is a high participation rate by youth in development efforts and local employment.

The emigration of able-bodied men into South Africa is a serious obstacle to Lesotho's internal domestic development which is shouldered by women, children and old men. The latter spend their useful life out of Lesotho and return when they are old and become a social liability to the country, since they have no old-age benefits. The lack of social security schemes in the mines causes hardships to returned miners who cannot be recruited again. Another economic cost to Lesotho results from the fact that these men do not perform any skilled jobs in the mines and farms which they could use at home upon their return. Other costs and benefits of the migratory labour system have been fully analysed in the government's Five-Year Plan. The system is inextricably tied up with the country's external economic dependence.

The export of labour from Lesotho has been used as a rationale for accepting development planning as a method of co-ordinating and integrating government policies. After carefully analysing the benefits of migratory labour and proximity to an advanced economy, the Prime Minister commented as follows:

> However, the abovementioned effects, important as they are, should not obscure the fundamental fact that Lesotho is becoming a reservoir of unskilled, cheap labour for South Africa, with little hope of creating an indigenous base for economic development. This situation will not change radically as a result of a spontaneous process. Change must be brought about by deliberate well-planned action, which will end stagnation and initiate a process of gradual expansion of the domestic base. . . .
>
> The alternative to planned development would simply be to surrender the economic future of the country to exogenous and entirely uncontrollable forces which have so far been inimical to the promotion of domestic sources of income and employment.

As a result of this conviction, the machinery for planning has been established throughout the civil service. It consists of the

Central Planning and Development Office which is directly under the Prime Minister, Departmental Planning Units in the executive ministries, and District Development Committees which provide for consultation with people at the grass-roots level. These committees include representatives of villagers, chiefs and other economic and social interest groups. The government believes that people know better what their problems are and how they could be overcome, even though their priorities may be slightly unclear. Thus, citizen participation is a focal point of Lesotho's planning process.

PLAN IMPLEMENTATION AND EVALUATION

Economic and social development is a trial-and-error process. This is because it involves reshaping the economic, social and administrative structures of a country, quite often without adequate information and experience from similar operations.

Every effort should of course be made to minimise mistakes and to ensure realisation of planned objectives. At the same time, however, it is most essential to be able to learn from experience, i.e. to draw the right lessons from failures or successes, and thus continuously to improve the development performance through applying appropriate corrective action.

This presupposes the existence of a machinery which would ensure:

(a) timely collection of information on the progress of plan implementation;

(b) evaluation of such progress, and decision-making about the kind of corrective action required; and

(c) effective transmissions of decisions to responsible operative units.

This machinery establishes a closed circuit or a feedback cycle between planning and implementation. The nature of this cycle is clearly show in Fig. 8.1.

It can be seen that implementation (I) depends on planning (P) – which includes overall, sectoral, regional and project planning – and the administrative machinery for implementation (A). This is described by the relations P–I and A–I. If progress on I is adequately reported (In), evaluation (E) becomes possible and appropriate decisions for corrective action can be taken when such action is required (relation E–I). At the same time, however, evaluation may also draw attention to the need of improving planning itself, the administrative machinery or the information system (S) (relations E–P, E–A, E–S, respectively). Thus, the arrows from E indicate feeding back instructions for remedial action in order to improve implementation, planning, the administrative machinery or the information system. The whole process could be seen as a four-loop feedback system which is triggered by deviations between performance and expectations. Loop I–In–E–I shows how performance on implementation is improved through evaluation. Loops A–I–In–E–A and S–In–E–S describe similar relations between implementation on the one hand and the administrative machinery or the information system on the other. This is therefore a central system aiming, on the one hand, at reducing disparity between planning and implementation, and on the other hand, at continuously increasing the realism and flexibility of planning itself, and making the machinery for plan implementation more efficient.

FIG. 8.1

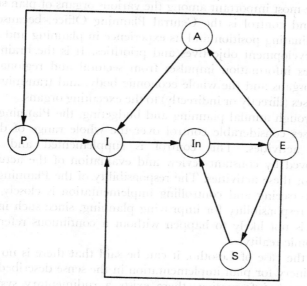

P = Planning; A = Administrative machinery for plan implementation; I = Implimentation; In = Information; E = Evaluation; S = Information System.

Plan revisions may become necessary because of inadequacy of data, over-ambitious or too modest development targets, or unforeseen events which may call for reconsideration of objectives and reordering of priorities. Administrative handicaps may also point to the need for developing the administrative machinery for plan implementation to be commensurate with development objectives.

The progress of ongoing development activities must therefore be kept under constant review and scrutiny, so that the responsible authorities can distinguish between good and poor performance, draw appropriate conclusions, and transmit back timely decisions for remedial action.

There can be no serious talk of development administration without this two-way response-and-control system between planners and executors. This is the only way to make sure that the responsible agencies for implementation move in the right direction and also that sufficient information is obtained to modify initial hypotheses or establish suitable objectives more firmly.

The most important among the various organs of plan supervision and control is the Central Planning Office, because of its co-ordinating position and its experience in planning and analysing development objectives and priorities. It is the brain which receives information impulses from sectoral and regional planning organs and the whole economic body, and transmits action impulses (directly or indirectly) to the executing organs.

Through annual planning and budgeting, the Planning Office exercises considerable control over the whole range of development activities. This control is supplemented and further improved by constant review and evaluation of the actual progress of these activities. The responsibility of the Planning Office for overseeing and controlling implementation is closely related to its responsibility for improving planning, since such improvement is not likely to happen without a continuous reference to economic reality.

In the case of Lesotho, it can be said that there is no control machinery for plan implementation in the sense described above. As regards information, there exists a rudimentary system for reporting progress on projects both to Cabinet and the Planning Office. There are no arrangements for processing and appraising these reports, and consequently haphazard instructions for corrective action are transmitted to the executing agencies. Great improvements are needed in the three main areas of plan implementation and control machinery, i.e. in the collection of information, the evaluation of progress and the transmission of instructions for remedial action.

CONCLUSION

Because of the wide nature of the topic, an attempt has been made above to give notes on various aspects relating to development planning. Reference has also been made to Lesotho, which is known best to the writer, but this could not be subjected to critical analysis. Similarly, passing references have been made to the difficulties which would be encountered in trying to plan for the development of Southern Africa as a whole. The best approach is for the various organisations and agencies engaged in development studies to co-operate and exchange research materials. Such co-operation could only be institutionalised at a very late stage.

Background to Planning the Development of Bantu Homelands in South Africa

JAN A. LOMBARD

1. INTRODUCTION

For the purposes of a discussion of development planning, the main features of the South African economy may be characterised as follows:

1. Capitalism is the dominating form of enterprise, while market structures range from fairly workable competition to monopolies.

2. Government direct participation in the production of goods and non-public services is significant, but is in principle confined to the basic services such as transport, water, power and telecommunications plus some basic manufacturing in steel, fuel and allied chemical products. The public corporations managing these enterprises, however, adopt an attitude to marginal costs which can hardly be distinguished from the practices in private enterprise. A possible exception in certain circumstances is the behaviour of the publicly owned Industrial Development Corporation.

3. The major policy decisions, with incisive effects on the character of the South African economy, were the formation of a South African customs union between the Transvaal, the Cape Province, Natal and the Orange Free State in 1910, the protection of domestic industry against foreign competition in 1925, the establishment of ISCOR in 1928 and of SASOL in 1950. For the rest, economic policy has attempted no more than marginal correction of the patterns of expansion dictated by the decisions of private enterprise.

4. Broadly speaking, the geographical distribution of economic activity used to play little part in the thinking of both private enterprise and public policy. South Africa was in practice treated by both as a *quasi-homogeneous region* with maximum freedom of location and an assumed maximum mobility of factors of production except land.[1]

5. Owing to the geographical immobility of harbour facilities and gold ore deposits, an extremely high degree of geographical concentration arose mainly around Johannesburg, the Cape Peninsula and Durban–Pinetown. The traditional areas of the Bantu remained unproductive dormitories of these peoples, participating in the economic development of South Africa only in a biological sense, i.e. to produce the unskilled labour used, and sometimes trained, by employers in the few islands of rapid economic growth.

6. As the idea of creating viable processes of economic growth within the Bantu homelands became an expressed collective aim of the South African community through its central government since the early 1950s, and as fairly determined efforts were made to implement these decisions, it became clear that the goals aimed at could not be achieved without significant government interference in the economic processes of the South African economy. That interference of this order cannot succeed without considerable forward planning is obvious. At least four major obstacles to effective planning, however, presented themselves:

  (i) the fundamental opposition of private enterprise against state interference, comprehensive planning and physical restrictions on managerial decisions;

  (ii) the weakness of the existing planning machinery in the public administration in handling an economic reconstruction of these dimensions;

  (iii) a large measure of uncertainty among the public and the members of their government, not only about the road to reconstruction, but its specific priority in the aggregate of collective aims charged to the government; and

  (iv) an unclear pattern of Bantu leadership and a neglect among identified leaders of the issues involved in the economic development of their homelands.

2. PLANNING IN A MARKET ECONOMY

The economic homegeneity of South Africa assumed in much of this country's economic policy was, of course, an illusion, as the events of recent years are rapidly proving. Since the economic theory of development and the model of 'dualism' became a matter of interest since the Second World War, South African economists frequently stressed the dualism of the South African economy, but the policy implications of such a model were not worked out or followed up in practice. In addition, very few South African economists were prepared to devote much thought to the ways in which the economic viability of the Bantu areas could be achieved.[2] Significant exceptions are the Holloway[3] and Tomlinson[4] Reports.

As far as national accounting figures may be relied upon, the value added to the basic resources of the country ($\pm$R11,000 million at current prices) is overwhelmingly produced through market processes located in the activity islands mentioned above. With these processes go most of the derived demand for labour and the income productivity of labour.

Although it is conceivable that entirely original economic processes for the creation of gainful employment opportunities may be established in the Bantu homelands, their practical significance in achieving, on their own, the settlement aims proposed in the Tomlinson Report and accepted by the government in the late 1950s can be seriously questioned. The major road to the desired reconstruction in the short and medium terms seems to be the regional deflection of the economic growth potential of the sub-continent to these underdeveloped dormitories of labour.[5]

Without, therefore, detracting from the long-term value of the internal reconstruction of the currently dominant pattern of activity in the homelands, namely agriculture, the short- and medium-term generation of activity in the homelands will largely have to derive from the 'spreading out'[6] of the South African market economy into these areas – that is, *if* the numerical targets of employment and settlement are to be anything like the population figures entertained by the South African government in 1956 in its reaction to the Tomlinson Report.

The Tomlinson Report, which fired a great deal of public

enthusiasm and discussion, also brought about important definitions of public policy, *inter alia* in the White Paper following the
Report.[7] Of particular importance was the relevant address in
Parliament by the then Minister of Native Affairs, Dr H. F. Verwoerd, who became Prime Minister of South Africa two years
later.

Dr Verwoerd, on behalf of the government, did not disagree
with the Commission on goals. The major goal was to accomplish
a regional redistribution of economic activity in South Africa, so
that about 9 or 10 million Bantu expected to be born during the
half-century up to the year 2000 should settle in their own areas
rather than in or around the concentrations of White communities in the Republic.

Secondly, both the government and the Commission desired
that the areas should remain the exclusive domain of the Bantu.
The government took the view that private White enterprises
(important and large ones) would not contribute towards this
goal. The majority Report of the Tomlinson Commission hoped
that such industries contributing to employment in the areas
would eventually revert to Bantu control. It is important to note,
however, that Dr Verwoerd considered this difference to be one
'about *method* and not about *goals*'. In his view, the methods
suggested by the Commission would defeat their own ends, and
the government accordingly rejected the idea of White industrial
development within the Bantu areas.

Thus the Minister accepted an idea put forward by a minority
of the Commission, namely to promote the location of White
industrialists *near* (but not in) the Bantu areas, the so-called
'border areas'. This decentralisation programme was to represent
the maximum that the existing White market economy of South
Africa could directly contribute to employment and growth in the
homelands, without seriously disrupting the socio-political road
to separate development.

According to the economic advice available to the Minister in
1956, 100,000 people employed in industry could directly support
500,000 people (at five persons per family) while a further multiplication of income *sufficient to support 2·5 million people would
be generated indirectly*. On these figures the government was convinced that on the basis of sound location of industry in the
vicinity of Bantu areas, it would indeed be possible to settle the

number of residents in these areas necessary for the safety[8] of South Africa generally.

Since Dr Verwoerd presented this model of (*a*) internally self-generated innovation and growth within the several areas at their own pace, plus (*b*) White industrial location just outside their borders, and (*c*) Bantu townships just within the border to accommodate the Bantu labour force, sixteen years have elapsed. During these sixteen years decision-makers, administrators, private enterprise and planners have had plenty of opportunity to gain practical knowledge of processes which were more or less theoretically discussed in 1956, particularly with regard to the African as a socio-political decision-maker, and with regard to the socio-economic effects of border area development. The experience of these years suggests that Dr Verwoerd was too pessimistic about the political ability of African states to avoid indirect colonialisation of their domain through the power of foreign private enterprise within their borders, and too optimistic about the influence of the border area programme on the indirect generation of economic development within the homelands.

It has to be recognised, however, that as long as the central government of South Africa remains constitutionally responsible for the matter of foreign entry and property acquisition in the Bantu homelands, it would be politically quite unethical to promote a situation which might be rejected by future Bantu governments, even if the South African government should undertake to compensate investors for damages following nationalisation. A reasonable adjustment during the interim (i.e. until the Bantu authorities take these responsibilities upon themselves) was to allow White enterprise and capital to enter the homelands on an agency basis.[9]

With regard to the decentralisation of industry to the so-called border areas, it would be wrong to minimise the technical successes already achieved, particularly at Rosslyn near Pretoria, but from the point of view of politico-economic effectiveness, the ten-year-old programme has given rise to some rather questionable trends. Owing to a very limited outlook on the costs and benefits of the programme, government planning has led to a concentration of attention on the most accessible and consequently cheapest growth point at Rosslyn near Pretoria, subsequently at points near Durban (the Durban district itself being classified as a 'border area') and East London. Further efforts are mainly concentrated at Brits, about 50 km from Johannesburg and Pretoria; Rustenburg, also along the railway line running west along the Tswana border from Pretoria to Mafeking; Ladysmith in Natal on the main communication artery from Johannesburg to Durban; and Richard's Bay, the new main all-purpose harbour arising on the north coast of Natal.

This short-term direct-cost-dominated strategy has led to (a) the establishment of peculiar types of growth poles along the western and south-eastern railway line and in the main urban concentration of the Ciskei, near East London; and (b) an over-concentration on the employment needs of Tswanaland and Zululand, with very serious shortfalls in the Transkei in the south, and Lebowa and Mashangana* in the north of South Africa.

In Pretoria, Durban and East London the township development for border industries merged into the *resettlement* of Bantu out of the old Bantu 'locations' of these cities to their own towns within their respective homeland borders. Consequently, very substantial concentrations of urban Bantu arose in Garankua, Umlazi and Mdanzini respectively. Unfortunately these large Bantu towns, the major potential growth poles of their respective hinterlands have thus far remained satellites of their economically much further advanced 'White' poles. Instead of giving rise to multiplier effects on further domestic employment in the homelands, as Dr Verwoerd expected they would do, incomes from labour are, for the most part, 'leaking back' to the established poles of activity. A further consequence of this satellite situation is the confluence of people from the interior of the homelands to these border towns, in order to come into working distance of Pretoria, Durban and East London. In so far as neither East London, Durban, Port Elizabeth nor Richard's Bay will suffer from restrictions on the number of Bantu which may be employed in their industries – as distinct from the Witwatersrand – much of the latter growth potential will move to these centres, which also happen to benefit from a renewed policy emphasis on industrial export promotion. One may therefore confidently expect a very strong migration of Bantu to the Bantu township nearest to, *but also most closely drawn into the polarising economic orbit of*, these centres. In short, the trend is towards strong Bantu urban

* Renamed Gazankulu since this was written.

concentrations near White poles of economic activity, with little or no multiplied spread (or backward linkage) into the homelands.

The second problem is that the direct-cost-dominated policies of the authorities led to a distribution of industrial employment to the economically cheapest, instead of the demographically most urgent, Bantu areas. Consequently, such a shortage of labour has arisen in eastern Tswanaland, for example, that the serious surpluses of workers available in its eastern neighbour, Lebowa, are moving in at a very rapid pace. In the major city of the Ciskei the number of Transkei immigrants is exceeding that of the local population.

It would appear, therefore, that the *economic* basis for the development of all the Bantu homelands is not in practice emerging along the regional lines nor at the growth pace hoped for by Dr Verwoerd – at least not from the point of view of *numbers of people* gainfully employed. The contention so far in this paper has been that the market economy in whose power it is to decide upon the location of industry and the employment of people in South Africa has not operated in the socio-politically desired directions. It has indeed not acquired any serious propensity to do so, because the collectively desired regional distribution and size of economic activity does not harmonise with the private quest for maximum profit.

The question is whether the situation could be satisfactorily improved by planning. To work out the answer to this question, even in terms of economic analysis only, we should have to agree on the meaning of 'satisfactorily' in the present context, and we should have to agree on the political scope of state interference that may be required.

It can be said that economic progress in the development of any particular homeland, or any country for that matter, is achieved when the rate of increase in the number of gainful employment opportunities in the country begins to exceed the rate of increase in the local population of the territory.[10] The progress may begin to be regarded as 'satisfactory' only if such positive differential between the growth of employment and that of the local population is generated from the resources of the territory's peoples themselves, whether these people happen to find themselves inside or outside the area. For the purpose of this definition, 'resources' include merchandise imports acquired through trade, capital imports acquired through interest or dividend-bearing foreign investment, and remittances to the area by its people gainfully employed elsewhere. In terms of this definition, Tswanaland* and the Ciskei are probably making economic progress, while Zululand and Vendaland are not losing ground. A country like Lesotho has not been viable during most of the twentieth century, nor has the Transkei, nor the homeland now called Lebowa. These territories have not been able to generate gainful employment opportunities at a rate commensurate with the natural rate of increase of their local population.

For several statistical and other reasons it is not yet possible to determine whether the economy of Tswanaland is really making 'satisfactory progress' as defined above (and even if it is doing so, its polarisation peculiarities remain a problem). But whatever the actual descriptive position of each economy may be at present, it is suggested that acceptance of some definition of satisfactory economic progress, such as has been proposed above, would provide the necessary point of departure for the investigation of the possibilities of success through planning.

What political scope for state interference is available for planning some strategy towards satisfactory economic progress in the homelands? Three roads to the necessary economic reconstruction of South Africa may be considered in principle:

(a) If the market economy has a sufficiently competitive structure, and decisions, are made on price and cost differentials, some scope exists to harmonise private and collective aims through the traditional methods of taxing socially undesirable ones. For maximum effectiveness, the incidence of both taxes and subsidies should be perfectly clear to the decision-makers in the private sector. In the planning of such an indirect policy system, private decisions remain the responsibility of private enterprise, the public sector being responsible for moving towards the goal, without raising the average cost structure beyond the requirement of other public goals such as the promotion of exports or the avoidance of domestic inflation.

The present system of subsidies provided for the decentralisation of industry remains unsatisfactory despite the investigations of an interdepartmental committee under the chairmanship of

* Named Boputhatswana since this was written.

the Economic Adviser to the Prime Minister and a White Paper setting out the government's reaction to it. The subsidies, as well as the construction of basic services at certain border areas discussed above, was, and still seems to be, guided by the principle that the total costs should be held down to an *absolute* minimum almost regardless of the regional distribution of employment opportunities, hence a continued emphasis on growth points nearest to the existing centres of White concentrations. But it is unfortunately simply not possible for the Treasury to establish a *balanced pattern of trade* between communities prevented from migrating to each other, on the basis of lowest *absolute* costs. The principle which should have guided the policy is that, *given* the socially *desired* regional distribution of employment opportunities, the various types of industries should have been lured to the various homelands in the desired proportions at the lowest *comparative* costs, in so far as it was practically feasible to do so. *Lowest comparative rather than lowest absolute costs determine the most beneficial pattern of trade between communities prevented from migrating to each other.*

If, as seems likely, the Republic's government is unable to apply the principle of lowest comparative costs, the only other alternative short of emigration from areas like the Transkei and Lebowa would be for the authorities of the areas themselves to introduce the principle through independent *local* subsidy systems, with each area subsidising domestic location of export activities to the extent of its employment needs. It should be realised that an economy with an independent currency system, e.g. Malawi, could and did achieve exactly the same effect through the devaluation of its external exchange rate. Since such a measure of regional independence in manipulating regional cost differences might introduce serious uncertainties into the South African market, a great deal of inter-authority co-ordination would be necessary on the lines of a mini-International Monetary Fund!

(*b*) Another approach would be a system of direct physical boundaries on the freedom of private enterprise. The co-ordinated planning and execution of such a system is more complicated than the system of indirect policy under (*a*), where policy calculations are made directly on prices and costs. A system of direct restrictions must rely on complicated calculations of indirect effects on managerial decisions. To the layman a direct restriction seems absolutely clear and consequently attractive. Indirect effects seem immaterial, as long as the direct boundary is not overstepped. Such an outlook may be sensible in the case of one single goal and one single restriction. As soon as more goals and restrictions exist, the planning and administrative machinery becomes very problematic. It is, moreover, very difficult to use the system to achieve positive goals. The most sensible use of this approach seems to be to use direct restrictions as a system of 'back-stops', if the indirect policies under (a) above fail to have the desired effects. Thus most permit systems (whether it be for foreign exchange, Bantu labour or the right to sell alcoholic beverages) work more smoothly if the incentive to obtain the permit is reduced by charging a price for the licence commensurate with its social or economic disadvantages to society.

(c) The third approach would be a system of direct government participation in economic processes, undertaking the activities which private enterprise regards as 'unprofitable' on the basis of *private* costs and benefits. Basically, such an approach provides considerable scope, provided (i) the public corporations are efficiently staffed, and (ii) the democratic style of the country upon which private enterprise usually rests its 'organised case' allows such procedures.

The possibilities of indirect policy (see (a) above) should not be minimised. Although the size of the domestic economy in South Africa is still rather small and the distribution of economic power still too skew to realise effective competition price-wise, one should not overlook the factor of overseas interest in direct investment in South Africa. These overseas firms, being internationally footloose in any case, will approach the location decision very largely in terms of the profit differentials (after taxes and subsidies) in the various alternative location points. Staff inertia could also be more easily overcome by large firms which are used to transferring staff to less attractive locations for limited periods.

In addition to the three roads to reconstruction mentioned above, there is a fourth programme which seems to be a necessary supplement to any of the former three, namely the development of attractive social and physical infrastructures in the desired geographical directions. This is the policy area in which good forward planning is most necessary. Mistaken decisions on, say, growth point X might result in a white elephant or, worse, wrongly placed polarisation of activity. It makes fewer resources over time to amortise the capital costs of a failure than to neutralise the recurrent effects of an ill-conceived success.

3. THE PLANNING ADMINISTRATION

In view of the history of economic policy in South Africa, the allegation that the existing planning machinery in the public administration falls short of requirements is no accusation. The South African public and its administration have no tradition of continuous planning for collective economic goals far removed from trends and patterns caused by the automatic operation of the market mechanism. The problem might, however, be solved by attracting the right kind of expertise and determination into the administration, at whatever remuneration proves necessary to do so. There can be no doubt that the incidence of planning costs on total project costs is very small. The most effective use of consultants should be carefully considered.

This paper has not endeavoured formally to define the well-known stages of dynamic or iterative planning, because they are so well known. But it may be useful at this stage to distinguish between the conceptual work of translating politically or socially conceived aims into technically manageable target and instrument variables, on the one hand, and the purely technical job of working out the critical functional relationships between targets and instruments on the other hand. Only the translation job must be done by South African experts who know their local situation. Much of the technical work can be placed in the hands of outside technicians with worldwide experience in their own functional specialities. This is as true of construction as it is of agriculture, or even health and education, if the situations really demand such steps.

One must, of course, take care not to isolate the planning process (as a form of capital formation) from the process of execution (as the current inputs and outputs), for practice has shown that such a gulf simply results in the gradual or even total depreciation of the value of the planning work. Planning, if not geared to the main shaft of administrative decision-making, soon becomes an absolute burden on the system. If, however, it is properly geared to current decision-making, its effectiveness is increased at a geometric, but almost costless, rate. This statement is true of planning in the most standardised public functions such as, for example, monetary policy, but it is especially relevant in the case of development planning where we have to operate on the basis of largely unique situation, imperfect knowledge, low percentages of successful experiences and no acknowledged 'general theory'. Consequently a very important characteristic of good development planning is the improvement of the process through learning by experience – the feedback from the executives to the planners of data on progress.

In the case of homeland development, we have seen a very rapid process of administrative and even political decentralisation from Pretoria to the several homeland capitals and the shifting of the emphasis from pure administration to development administration. The details are dealt with in another paper read at the Conference, but the process has very important implications for effective planning, both advantageous and disadvantageous. The advantages of administrative decentralisation are largely socio-political and long-term. In the fields of education and agriculture they may be more immediate, but in the field of commerce, construction and industry the value of decentralised decision-making becomes more problematic and the outcome depends more on practice than on principle.

Decentralised planning, while having all the advantages of regional motivation, regional knowledge and regional authority, obviously calls for entirely new systems of inter-regional communication and co-ordination, particularly in those fields where communication is not merely enlightening, but positively necessary for practical success. Where regional activities are mutually neutral, e.g. in attracting footloose industries from the Republic, or producing tomatoes for export to the Republic's markets, or where regional activities may significantly complement one another, as in the development of a transport system through the northern homelands of Vendaland, Lebowa and Mashangana, co-ordinated planning has important advantages over 'going it alone'. In these cases of competition and complementarity, many economists, abstracting from the socio-political reasons for nationalism, tend to favour centralisation of planning. On the other hand, if nationalism has the positive social values in the real world ascribed to it by history, the idea of centralised planning will have to be replaced by the idea of international co-operation as a third alternative between isolation on the one hand, and integration on the other hand. In practice this would mean that the several autonomous administrations in the various homelands (and in the other African areas in the Southern African economic union) would have to be so strengthened to enable them not only to interpret local aspirations into economically operational variables, but also to communicate and co-ordinate with their counterparts in the Republic on the same technical and terminological level. They must understand and use the same technical language and the same analytical techniques. In the author's experience, the broad operational importance of these two, ostensibly simple, matters can hardly be over-emphasised.

4. THE DETERMINATION OF PRIORITIES

Analysis, and therefore plannng, of the most efficient way in which to achieve a set of goals is economically impossible when the relative order of values of these goals is indeterminate or keeps changing within the period of decision-making. Inasmuch as most projects involved in the development of the homelands have a gestation period of at least two and often three or more years, annual changes in the relative priority accorded to this goal within the set of collective aims of the Republic's government may not merely result in inefficiency within individual projects such as the establishment of Bantu townships, but may cause more widespread damage through the frustration of the entire spirit of forward planning as such.

The problem is accentuated by the traditional reliance of the territorial development programmes on funds provided by the South African Parliament to the South African Bantu Trust Fund (established in 1936). Until recent years the income of Bantu authorities from their own sources was of negligible importance. During the 1960s, however, the improvements in the political status of territorial authorities were accompanied by serious efforts to improve the position. In 1972–3 about one-quarter of the funds spent by these authorities will be financed from their own resources, including their respective shares in the revenue from the direct taxation of the Bantu (which is separated from the direct taxation of non-Bantu in South Africa). Thus about three-quarters of the fiscal income of the various homeland administrations is still voted by the South African Parliament from the Consolidated Revenue Fund, although the largest proportion of the allocation will be statutory in 1972–3. As time passes, however, the 'additional grant' over and above the statutory amount will necessarily increase (as it did in the case of the Transkei). The larger this amount, the more the financing of the development process reverts back to a reliance on annual decisions by the South African Parliament which, seen from the point of view of development needs, may change arbitrarily.

It should be made clear that the 'statutory grant' is not in fact a straightforward gift from White to Black South Africa. At present only the direct taxation of the Bantu is separately identified and channelled to the revenue funds of the respective Bantu homelands administrations. Indirect taxation paid by Bantu is still an unidentified part of the total of indirect taxes flowing into the Consolidated Revenue Fund of the central government.[11] (In the case of Swaziland, Lesotho and Botswana, a percentage of customs excise and sales-tax revenue is transferred to them in terms of a customs union agreement.[12]) In so far as such public revenues paid by Bantu cannot be identified and transferred to the Bantu authorities directly, the formula for the calculation of the statutory grant could be amended to increase commensurately with increases in Bantu purchasing power and increases in the level of indirect taxes. At the same time, the idea may be considered of financing the remaining annual shortfall between estimated expenditure on the one hand, and own income plus statutory grants (as reformulated) on the other hand, by low or zero interest loans rather than 'additional grants'.

Whatever fiscal arrangement may turn out to be fair to the Bantu authorities, it seems highly desirable for serious development planning that the matter be extricated from the normally rather muddled priority determination in the budgetary processes of the central government. Good planning, it might be added, does not require an amplitude of finance in relation to targets. On the contrary, staff responsible for the allocation of physical and manpower resources find that a closely designed budget protects planning against the possibility that political authorities with the assistance of the budget office may unexpectedly find scope to introduce entirely unplanned projects into the programme between one budget and the next.

5. BANTU LEADERSHIP

Few schools of experience could do more for the development of responsible government and a planning outlook than fiscal administration. Not until one has the power and the responsibility to allocate scarce financial resources among competing social ends, does one graduate from a position as the object of the decision of others to the position as subject of one's own destiny. By the same token, the planning of homeland development cannot properly 'take off' until the aims and policies for these territories emerge realistically from the minds of the Bantu leaders themselves after having struggled with the problem of population pressure on scarce resources.

The space is not available here to enter into a thorough discussion of planning within the organisation of Bantu leadership in their own public affairs. The evolution of Bantu systems of government in South Africa since the beginning of the century displays an interesting dynamism. The early emphasis on the strengthening of the tribal basis of government in the 1920s, for example, swung towards the idea of homogeneity and integration in the Natives' Representative Council for a short period between 1936 and 1950, after which development returned to an emphasis on traditional forms of government adapted to modern constitutional concepts. The most recent step is, of course, the Bantu Homeland Constitution Act of 1971, which provides for separate legislative assemblies and executive councils or cabinets for each Bantu nation.

It would be fitting to conclude with a very free restatement of the development philosophy of Dr W. W. M. Eiselen who, beside Dr Verwoerd, is generally regarded as the architect of the idea of separate development for the Bantu nations in South Africa.[13]

In the concepts of our Western society, a state of autonomy of a person or an enterprise is closely associated with economic and financial autonomy, more or less as defined above under the discussion of the definition of 'economic progress'. In Bantu society, autonomy is acquired at a much later stage, that is, after a man takes a wife, begets children and maintains his family in a hut complex of his own.

Although these norms are still respected with regard to persons and enterprises, they have been largely abandoned after the Second World War with regard to the erstwhile colonies in Africa and elsewhere. To them, political independence has been granted irrespective of their ability to manage their public administration and finance from their own resources – the gap being filled by development aid. The original conditions, namely that the donor country should be satisfied as to the effective end-use of such aid, have also been considerably watered down or removed, because they smacked of neo-colonialism.

Economic autonomy of many of these newly independent states therefore consists in full control over their public expenditures irrespective of the sources from which these expenditures are financed. This situation, whether desirable or not, has been created because the colonial powers felt themselves obliged to declare these colonies free and of age. Since they could not, with the best will in the world, force the economies involved into self-generating growth in a short time, the colonial powers gave them what they could – sovereign independence with an attractive but unpractical democratic constitution. In the case of the Bantu homelands in South Africa, their development has been guided by principles peculiar to the Bantu culture – from tribal authorities to regional authorities, territorial authorities and eventually parliamentary self-government. The intention was that the Bantu national units should receive administrative skill and economic experience *pari passu* with political development, so that self-government would be founded on a stable economic structure. In the climate created by the 'head over heels' political emancipation elsewhere of communities less developed than the South African Bantu, this time-sequence had to be abandoned, because doubts would arise about the good faith of the South African government.

The problem which now has to be faced is how to restore the balance as rapidly as possible, by making up the administrative and economic leeway behind the headstart allowed in the political sphere. Dr Eiselen did not specify *who* should take the lead in making up this leeway, but it seems almost axiomatic that it should increasingly come from the Bantu political leaders, lest a new gulf open up between the locally inspired political system on the one hand, and an economic and administrative system controlled by White political leaders on the other hand.

This paper may be criticised for a lack of interest in the analysis of the administrative and economic problems encountered within the homelands (apart from other deficiencies the paper probably has). The reply to such criticism is that we are often perhaps too keen to tell the Bantu people and their leaders what mistakes they are making – in our Western eyes – with regard to their *internal social framework*. According to many anthropologists we are in the process not only making ourselves ridiculous, but, when successful in our restricted aims, we are rather blindly splitting atoms in a socially very sensitive matrix, with very harmful and defeating wider effects on the community.

On the other hand, the fact of serious population pressure on scarce resources cannot be ignored, and new institutions to perform economically effective functions are imperative. The most stable means of having the necessary social change brought about would be to graft these institutional ideas on to existing institutions which have the root system suitable to the social soil from which it must draw its nourishment. This grafting operation could best be done by the domestic leaders of the Bantu peoples themselves. Even if they encounter social upheaval in the process the consequences will probably be better handled by these leaders than by Whites who do not understand the deeper elements of the social dynamics of the Bantu.

Consequently the major contribution of the non-Bantu socio-economic system, within which the homelands are to advance to viability, seems to be the identification and introduction of the *external framework* within which this can happen.

CONCLUSION

Development planning in South Africa may be approached from three points of view about the socio-political basis of its economy: firstly, as one, quasi-homogeneous region; secondly, as a collection of politically arbitrary nodal zones arranged around a few outstanding growth poles; or thirdly, as a collection of autonomous planning regions. No effective planning machinery can, however, be designed to accommodate all three conceptions about the nature of the system at the same time.

Despite sincere hopes by the younger generations of South Africa that conceptual issues would have been solved by the time they have to manage the subcontinent, basic doubts seem to be continuing unabated. The integrationists are insisting that planning regions, in the sense of autonomous Bantu homelands, are proving economically too difficult. The separate developers say integration is socially too dangerous. There is no established school of politically arbitrary regional growth-pointers, but this seems to be the historical outcome of the clash between the other two extremes.

The economic problems of establishing autonomous Bantu states in South Africa are indeed formidable, but is long as they have not deteriorated into dilemmas, practical planning could greatly assist in overcoming them. It should be clearly recognised, however, that the difficult political ideas can only be achieved within a framework of minimum preconceived political boundary conditions on detailed methods of planning. Secondly, and of greater importance, this road to reconstruction requires as a necessary, but not a sufficient, condition for success the emergence of clear conventions as to a number of basic issues. These basic conventions would have to deal with at least the following five isues:

1. The geographical areas of the several homelands.
2. Public finance.
3. Legislative and administrative autonomy.
4. The maximum limits of labour migration.
5. The minimum freedom of merchandise exports to the Republic and capital inflows into the territories.

NOTES

1. In law, the mobility of Bantu labour into White areas was subject to various control measures since the earliest days of White settlement in South Africa.
2. e.g. most of the papers read at meetings and national conferences of the South African Economic Society deal with problems of the quasi-homogeneous economy of South Africa.

3. *Report of the Native Economic Commission 1930–32*, U.G.22 (1932).

4. *Report of the Commission for the Socio-Economic Development of the Bantu Areas within the Union of South Africa*, U.G.61 (1955).

5. The implications of this view for foreign investment in the territories is further elaborated in section (*b*) below (p. 468).

6. The 'spread effects' referred to above in the technical jargon of regional economics are the opposite of the so-called 'polarisation effects' of a market economy. In the latter case, activity within the nodal zones of the growth poles tends to migrate *out of* the hinterland to the poles. Labour migration is an example.

7. *White Paper F.1956*: 'Memorandum: Besluite deur die Regering oor aanbevelings van die kommissie van die sosio-ekonomiese ontwikkeling van die Bantoegebiede binne die Unie van Suid-Afrika'.

8. The term 'safety' was used by the Minister.

9. The Promotion of the Economic Development of Bantu Homelands Act, 1968.

10. There may obviously be numerous qualifications necessary to avoid spurious academic interpretations of such a 'rule of thumb'.

11. A further argument is sometimes made out that the Bantu in the Republic contribute more to the national product than the total of their wages, implying that the difference may be a further basis for special fiscal redistribution of public revenue. This argument cannot, however, be sustained on purely economic principles.

12. See Government Notice R.3914 of 12 Dec 1969. The formula is contained in Art. 14 of the agreement.

13. W. W. M. Eiselen, 'Die Ontwikkeling van die Bantoevolkseenhede na Selfstandigheid', in J. A. Lombard (ed.), *Die Ekonomiese Politiek van Suid-Afrika*, Cape Town: (H.A.U.M., 1967).

COMMENT

Jan F. Beekman

Profesor Beekman began by suggesting that, although the theme of the Conference was Southern Africa, the lack of data pertaining to some areas, and mainly to the Portuguese territories, hampered discussions of development planning in the Southern African region.

Regarding Professor Knall's paper, he pointed out that while it was both an admirable and a concise summary of the theory of development planning, he felt that it placed too much emphasis upon economic rather than social development, i.e. social planning *per se* and the by-products of social planning. He also pointed out that Professor Knall's paper tended to suggest that the roles of those involved in development planning were clear-cut; this was not necessarily so.

Turning to the sources of developmental aid, Professor Beekman mentioned his preference for multilateral vis-à-vis bilateral aid, especially since the latter was often affected by political considerations or by psychological factors in terms of which planners tended to orient their programmes in the direction of the expected reactions of financial donors.

He endorsed the speakers' emphasis on the importance of elements of continuity and flexibility in development planning, and explicitly suggested that long-term plans be recurrently revised in terms of new realities, on the one hand, and that plans be established for a period slightly longer than government tenure, if possible, on the other. The latter would tend to bind succeeding governments and thus preserve some continuity over periods of governmental change.

Concluding with reference to the centralisation–decentralisation problem, Professor Beekman pointed out that resolution of this problem was related in the ultimate instance to the size of the country with which development planning was concerned.

Chapter 9

Special Development Problems of Multi-Ethnic Societies

Development Problems of Multi-Ethnic Societies

KURT GLASER

ETHNIC PLURALISM AND DEVELOPMENT

In so far as multi-ethnicity determines the framework for development, the problems it raises are not special or unusual but almost universal in Africa. The typical African state contains a number of self-identifying ethnic groups of various sizes. Clifford Geertz, who has constructed a typology of ethnic patterns, classifies most of Africa in the category of 'ethnic fragmentation'.[1]

Specific problems traceable to ethnic pluralism, as they affect political, economic and social development, fall mainly into two categories. The first consists of problems connected with designing and building a political structure that can mobilise and harmonise the political-social integrators of divergent groups. The term 'integrator' is used here to mean a 'criterion of nationality' in the sense established by Eugen Lemberg in his classical study of nationalism: a factor in which an ethnic group visualises its own identity and differentiates itself from other groups. The repertoire of possible integrators includes race, actual or mythical lineage, religion and cultural tradition, identification with a landscape or region, loyalty to a monarch, dynasty or state, and any of a spectrum of political ideologies. As Lemberg has shown, integrators are interchangeable and may appear in an infinite variety of combinations.[2] Within a state or region, however, prima facie conflict may occur between the integrators and goals of various groups.

The second category of problems derives from tensions provoked or aggravated by differences in levels of development attained by ethnic or social groups within the system. Such tensions, if unresolved, may strain the political system to the point where progress is blocked, or disrupted altogether. Frequently, the group enjoying the highest material and cultural level exercises a measure of hegemony over the others. But sometimes the contrary is the case, as in Bohemia under Czechoslovakia and in Nigeria after the coup of July 1966. In both countries, tensions led to political collapse followed by campaigns of violence and brutality against the more advanced ethnic groups.

A viable political structure must have adequate capacity for conflict resolution. This means that it cannot, over the long run, reflect the model of plural society developed by J. S. Furnivall, in which a single dominant group determines policy and the other groups are mere objects of that policy.[3] Instead, a viable political system encompassing two or more nations or ethnic groups must be based on the model of a forum or exchange containing interacting bargainers. In the bargaining process, each party sacrifices part of his maximum goals to obtain the greatest feasible goal-fulfilment. The bargainers do not necessarily start out from equal positions, but it is essential that each party perceive itself and be perceived by the others as an active agent, capable of and responsible for determining its own destiny. While critics have applied the Furnivall model to Southern Africa in the past, it seems evident that inter-ethnic relationships are today moving towards a pattern of multilateral bargaining.

ETHNIC NATIONALISM AND DEVELOPMENT IN WESTERN AND CENTRAL EUROPE

The history of Central Europe may throw some light on the problems of multi-ethnic societies in Africa, since it abounds with examples of both good and bad management of inter-ethnic relations. Austria–Hungary, in particular, was a testing-ground for political theories and ideologies.

The viability of social micro-structure in the clan, village, neighbourhood or urban complex depends on its ability to mobilise, co-ordinate and control basic human drives such as the needs for food, shelter, sex, love and self-perpetuation. Analogously, the viability of a politico-social macro-structure encompassing diverse ethnic elements depends on its ability to mobilise, harmonise and control the integrators of ethnic communities: the complex of factors that adds up to tribalism or nationalism as the case may be. This feeling of belonging is like fire: its warmth draws people together and its light illumines our modes of self-expression. But like fire, it can be immensely destructive when out of control. Millions have perished in the conflagrations nationalism and tribalism have ignited.

The political and economic development of Europe, and hence of modern nationalism, began in the West and moved slowly eastwards across the continent. The first modern nation-states were Spain, France and England. These states were territorial in concept, and assembled through the processes of dynastic politics – such as war, marriage and diplomatic horse-trading. Ethnic-linguistic identification seemed unimportant; French remained the court language of England for almost three centuries after the Norman invasion – that is, until the Hundred Years War kindled the first flames of French and English nationalism.

The strong monarchs of Spain, France and England created ethnic-linguistic nations by centralising the educational systems and making their courts centres of national culture. This policy worked where speech throughout the region belonged to the same linguistic family derived from Latin or Anglo-Saxon as the case might be, but not where different linguistic roots were involved, as in the Basque lands, Brittany and Wales. The rise of ethnic-linguistic nations in Italy, Germany and elsewhere in Central Europe came later and was not the result of dynastic policy but rather a spontaneous response to Western European nationalism. In both cases the rise of ethnic-linguistic nations was accompanied by the rise of the bourgeoisie as a motor of economic and later of political activity.

With the rise of the bourgeoisie, language became a political actor it had not been before. The aristocracy was international in its social contacts, cultural tradition and outlook. It was generally multilingual, and considered language a means of communication rather than a criterion of identity. The Low German patriot William of Orange wrote and thought in French; when stabbed by an assassin he spoke his dying words in that language. The bourgeoisie, however, was narrowly nationalist and usually monolingual: for them, language was the main criterion of identity and speakers of other tongues were 'foreigners'.

The Habsburg rulers of Austria, whose approach to statesmanship was aristocratic, never attempted to form an ethnic-linguistic

'Austrian nation', for which they saw no need. The Empire possessed a multi-ethnic political élite in the nobility, the army, and the civil servants of the Josephine school. German was used as a language of communication, but there was no conscious attempt to impose German culture on the other nationalities. Linguistic integration of the Habsburg Empire would hardly have been feasible in any case, since its territory encompassed four disparate linguistic families: Germanic, Slavic, Romance and Finno-Ugric.

Within the Austrian Empire, as elsewhere in Europe east of the Rhine, linguistic-ethnic nations defined themselves and became aware of their distinctive characteristics and traditions without regard to political boundaries. Bourgeois nationalists began to demand not only cultural but also political expression, the extreme cases being the demand for sovereign ethnic-linguistic states.

The rise of nationalism was accompanied by upward socio-economic mobility, reflecting a rising G.N.P. The latter was made possible by the large-area, geographically specialised economy that existed in the German *Zollverein* and later in the Empire, and by the economic unification of the Habsburg lands, a process completed in 1851. In Bismarck's Germany the goal of nationalism was achieved in unification of the Reich, a development that consolidated the large-area economy. But in Danubian Europe extreme nationalism threatened economic fragmentation; dogmatic adherents of absolute ethnic sovereignty were prepared to sacrifice precisely those economic forces that had nurtured and sustained their nationalism. The problem of survival for Austria thus became how to find a formula whereby ethnic nationalism and national self-expression could be accommodated within the territorial state.

THE DOWNFALL OF AUSTRIA–HUNGARY: CAUSES AND EFFECTS

The Habsburg Empire did not die of economic causes. Throughout its final decades it enjoyed rapid and consistent growth. Furthermore, its experience showed that in a multi-ethnic large-area economy, even with disparate levels of development to start with, the long-range trend under free-market conditions is towards equalisation: that growth is *comparatively* faster in the less developed areas.[4] These differentials in the level of development did, however, inject a certain element of class struggle into inter-ethnic relations within the Empire.

In discussing political development, it is necessary to distinguish clearly between the Austrian and Hungarian halves of the monarchy after 1867. Austria proper, extending in an arc around Hungary from the Italian provinces to multi-ethnic Galicia and Bukovina, was divided into Crown Lands. These all had diets with broad legislative powers: most government activity was performed by civil servants of the Crown Lands or subordinate authorities. These Lands, however, did not correspond to ethnic groups. They could never have been shifted to eliminate minorities because of the intricate interlocking and overlapping of peoples.

The Austrian Basic Law of 1867 guaranteed the right of each nationality to its cultural development and the use in government of all 'regionally customary languages.' This arrangement afforded substantial autonomy to the ethnic groups that enjoyed majorities in particular Crown Lands. But these were not always scrupulous about the rights of others: the Poles in Galicia tried to polonise the Ukrainians, while the Czechs and Germans in Bohemia indulged in a *Kulturkampf* about the use and teaching of languages in schools. The Cabinet in Vienna, which always contained members from various ethnic groups, sought to moderate the zeal of nationalists in the Crown Lands – sometimes successfully, sometimes not. Most importantly, however, the concept of Austria remained that of a territorial state and in no sense the exclusive preserve of a privileged *Staatsvolk*. (The word *Staatsvolk*, for which an English equivalent is lacking, means that ethnic nation that considers itself the proprietor of a national state, a role denied to other national groups within the state.)

The situation was entirely different in Hungary. After the Equalisation of 1867 granted internal autonomy to the kingdom of St Stephen, the Magyars established a centralised ethnic-linguistic state with themselves as *Staatsvolk*. They refused autonomy to non-Magyar ethnic groups, and introduced educational magyarisation: ethnic groups could have their own primary schools, but secondary and higher education were conducted only in Magyar. It is hardly necessary to explain further why Hungary not Austria, became the politically unstable part of the Empire.

In Austria, loyalty to one's ethnic nationality was compatible with loyalty to the inclusive territorial state. Austria recognised its nationalities as components and its government tried, as best it could, to assure their national existence and to mediate quarrels. In Hungary, however, the non-Magyars were systematically denied the existential security that is basic to the life of any nationality or ethnic group.

There were many proposals for constitutional reform. Most revolved around the idea of reorganising both parts of the Empire into a federation of nationalities.[5] The most original proposal was that advanced by the Social Democrat Karl Renner at his party's Austria-wide congress at Brno in 1899. Renner, a young jurist who was to serve many years later as President of the Republic of Austria, took account of the fact that the Empire's nationalities were not settled in compact blacks, but scattered and intermingled. He therefore invented the concept of 'personal autonomy'; each ethnic group would have a National Corporation to administer its schools and cultural institutions and welfare programmes. The Corporations would be given proportionate shares of taxes, and each would serve the members of its group, wherever they might live. Combined with the territorial autonomy of Crown Lands following national settlement areas as closely as possible, Renner's plan involved what might be called 'two-track federalism'. A partial but successful trial of the idea was begun in Moravia in 1905; the outbreak of the First World War prevented its further extension.

After the break-up of the Empire in 1918, the leaders of the successor nations proceeded to organise ethnic-linguistic states over the heads of their subject minorities. Although Masaryk's foreign minister Dr Beneš promised that the new Czechoslovakia would be 'like Switzerland', Czech nationalists created a centralised and basically monolingual government: all civil servants who could not speak and write Czech were dismissed from their posts. The situation was much the same in Poland, Romania and Yugoslavia. The typical incidents of the inter-war period include:

(a) The shooting to death of the Croat leader Radić and his brother on the floor of the Yugoslav Parliament.

(b) Polish expeditions that burned Ukrainian schools, libraries and co-operatives and manhandled or murdered their custodians.

(c) The famous 'musical session' of the Czechoslovak Parliament, which broke up in disorder to the tune of three national anthems plus the 'Internationale'.

The economic growth of the pre-war years was brought to an abrupt halt by the 'Balkanisation' of Danubian Europe. Both industrial and farm production were retrograde in most of the area throughout the 1920s and even more so during the world depression.[6] Political history between the wars was that of the breakdown of constitutional government in one country after another in Central Europe and finally the temporary disappearance of Czechoslovakia altogether.

After the Second World War, Czechoslovakia 'solved' its nationality problem by expelling $3\frac{1}{2}$ million Sudeten Germans from their historic homeland. Under Tito's guidance, Yugoslavia adopted a pseudo-federalism modelled after that of the Soviet Union. While the Belgrade government has recently granted the regions and nationalities a certain autonomy, it seems probable that fear of Russian invasion is the principal integrator that holds Yugoslavia together today. Most of the Croats supported a separate republic during the war, and there is indication that they would not remain in a state dominated by the Serbs of their free choice. As of this point in time, most of the former Austro-Hungarian Empire is governed by a series of communist regimes established between 1945 and 1948.

The following conclusions can be drawn from Central European experience:

(a) A large-area economy, such as exists in a federation or common market, is far more conducive to rapid growth than a series of small economies behind high tariff walls.

(b) Disparities between states of cultural development and living standards are not an immediate economic problem, since there is a natural trend towards equalisation. But they do present a political problem because people are inclined to regard such differences, at close range, as prima facie evidence of injustice.

(c) It is therefore necessary to design a political structure that reduces friction by providing legal personality and functional autonomy for each natonality or self-defined ethnic group, so that each perceives itself as responsible for its own welfare. Each group should, so far as total resources permit, be assured that the direction and rate of its progress depend on itself, not on someone else.

(d) Fragmentation of a large region into uncoordinated national territories is not the solution. It voids the benefits gained by specialisation within a diversified area. Furthermore, a region filled with small and feeble states invites the intrusion and domination of great powers.

ETHNIC NATIONALISM AND DEVELOPMENT IN OTHER AREAS

Before considering the effects of multi-ethnicity on development beyond the continent of Europe, it is necessary to raise a point of political theory. Early Western political scientists, including Hobbes, Locke and Rousseau, had accepted as a 'nation' the people living under a particular government. The proper function of the state was to promote the prosperity and freedom of all its subjects, regardless of descent, culture or language. This rationalist concept of the nation, which still prevails in Western Europe and the United States, knows only two political categories: the state and the individual. Substructures, such as the family, the church, linguistic groups and classes, are relegated to a subordinate 'private' sphere; the state is expected to be neutral in dealing with conflicting 'private' interests. While the latter may generate 'inputs' into the political system, they are not a legitimate part of that system. Rousseau, it will be recollected, inveighed against 'partial societies' in his *Social Contract*.

The rationalist concept of the nation found its dialectical antithesis in the romantic concept of the *Volk* as proclaimed by Johann Gottfried Herder, which achieved general acceptance in Central Europe through the linguistic-cultural revivals of the early nineteenth century. Herder's *Volk* is defined as a spontaneous group linked by primordial ties such as actual or supposed descent, language, culture and tradition.[7] Personality is shaped through membership in the group and partakes of its 'collective subconscious' and its 'archetypes' (C. G. Jung). In the Herder model, substructure plays a vital role in the political process: the individual is related to the state not as a free-floating atom but as a member of a tribal group to which he owes his entire being. The preservation and adaptation of traditions thus becomes a major function of the state. Of the two models, the Herder concept of the *Volk*, which can be applied to smaller as well as larger ethnic groups, seems more applicable to the African situation than the rationalist notion.

The one thing that should *never* be done is to mix the two models. Where a nation that has defined itself under the Herder model of the *Volk* invokes the rationalist concept of the territorial state and its citizenship, it is then likely to employ the supposedly neutral state as a vehicle for its particular interests. In Europe such a policy has led to political disintegration and ultimately to war.

As this writer has shown elsewhere, Americans on the whole have not understood the consequences of the difference between territorial and ethnic-linguistic nations. While American political scientists have recognised the ethnic concept in dealing with Europe, they tend to employ the rationalist territorial idea in prescribing medicine for Africans. Claude E. Welch, Jr, for instance, defines modernisation as:

1. An increased centralisation of power in the state, coupled with the weakening of traditional sources of authority.
2. The differentiation and specialisation of political institutions.
3. Increased popular participation in politics, and greater identification of individuals with the political system as a whole.

Tribal chiefs, petty princes, and religious and ethnic authorities, he adds, are supplanted by the single secular state. While Welch does not expect traditional social structures to disappear, he wants them downgraded and depoliticised. Tradition may be utilised where it happens to favour modernisation, but, he says, 'modernisation requires fundamental changes in cultural values, patterns of authority, [and] consensus'.[8]

Edward Shils deals rather harshly with what he calls the 'particularism' of ethnic communities:

> ... the constituent societies on which the new states rest are, taken separately, not civil societies, and, taken together, they certainly do not form a single civil society. ... They lack the affirmative attitude toward rules, persons, and actions that is necessary for consensus. They are constellations of kinship groups, castes, tribes, feudalities – even smaller territorial societies –but they are not civil societies. The sense of identity is rudimentary, even where it exists. The sense of membership in a nation-wide society and the disposition to accept the legitimacy of the government, its personnel, and its law are not great. Society-wide institutions, other than the state, are scant in the societies we are discussing.[9]

William A. Gamson, addressing himself to the American situation, claims that for pluralist institutions to 'operate properly', there should be a network of cross-cutting solidarities. Each person should belong to several overlapping and articulate groups, a situation that would dilute the power of ethnic organisations.[10] Robert A. Dahl, in his book on *Polyarchy* (which turns out to be a fancy name for liberal democracy with mass participation), observes that ethnic conflicts may be among those that a competitive political system cannot manage, particularly where a large group feels its existence or way of life threatened. Subcultural pluralism, he says, strains tolerance and mutual understanding. Conditions are best for 'polyarchy' if there is little such pluralism, but if the level of pluralism is high, then 'polyarchy' is most viable if

(a) no ethnic group is a majority;

(b) none is regional; and

(c) none is indefinitely out of government.

Furthermore, the groups should exchange mutual guarantees.[11]

Dahl states correctly that opponents in a conflict will not tolerate one another if one believes this will lead to his own destruction or severe suffering. But he stops short of the conclusions that his well-presented analysis suggests. These are:

(a) Parliamentary democracy on the one-man-one-vote principle, or even with qualified suffrage, may not be a suitable form for the overall governance of a region containing many disparate ethnic-linguistic nations.

(b) The most effective way to guarantee the existence and way of life of a nation or ethnic group is to build it into the political system, providing it with legal personality and institutions through which it can translate goals into policy – in other words, determine its own destiny in co-operation with other groups.

How has the rationalist model of the nation, which dictates modernisation through the political emasculation of ethnic traditions and authorities, fared outside Central Europe? The example that first comes to mind is Northern Ireland, in which Catholics as well as Protestants enjoy democratic representation at Westminster and in the (currently suspended) regional parliament. The struggle is evidently more national than religious, since Catholics enjoy full freedom in England. While we cannot stop to analyse its causes in detail, it would appear that several dysfunctional factors, any one or two of which could have been resolved by the political system, combined to trigger a disintegrative process. The solution will have to be structural, but cannot exist of merely transferring the Six Counties to the Republic of Ireland; that would only enlarge the problem.

Two states where the rationalist model of parliamentary government was applied at the end of colonial rule are Guyana and Trinidad–Tobago.[12] Guyana has a slight Indian majority and an African minority; Trinidad has a heavy African majority and a smaller Indian minority.

In both countries the Indians tend to be merchants and farmers, while Africans are more likely to be industrial workers. Business below the level of the foreign firms that control oil, sugar, banking and large-scale trade, is mainly in the hands of Indians. Africans do not get jobs in these firms, not because they are Black, but because they do not belong to the family. The upper income group among the Africans consists mostly of Creoles – defined in these countries as persons of African or partly African lineage who have embraced European culture. The Creoles dominate the public service of both countries, since it had been colonial policy to keep the Indians 'down on the farm' producing sugar. The two groups tend to segregate themselves residentially, though this is not required by law. The main political parties of both countries are racially oriented: Guyana politicians have openly sanctioned the slogan 'Vote Your Race!'

From 1953 to 1963 Guyana was governed by the Marxist Cheddi Jagan's People's Progressive Party. Under Jagan, the government spent the largest part of its development budget on agriculture and rural water supplies and very little on industry. After a period of severe race riots, the People's National Congress headed by the Afro-Guyanese Forbes Burnham came to power in 1964 with some Indian support that has since evaporated. The Burnham government reversed development priorities; it spent the largest sums on transport and public works and relatively little on agriculture.

In Trinidad, which had a gross domestic product of U.S.$690 per capita in 1967 as compared with U.S.$284 in Guyana, the mainly Creole National People's Movement led by Dr Eric Williams has governed since independence. The largest opposition group is the Indian-dominated Democratic Labour Party. Since the Indians are only 35 per cent of the population, the D.L.P. is trying to form a trans-racial coalition, especially with the Creoles on the smaller island, Tobago, who feel themselves neglected by the Port-of-Spain government. The motive is evidently a desire to share in power rather than a specific sense of grievance, since the Williams economic policies tend to favour Indian business and farming rather than African wage workers.

The Indians in both countries have recently founded cultural organisations, which resist the tendency of the mass media to promote Creolisation and which attempt to maintain a specific Indian identity. Both countries also have extensive African cultural manifestations, which are openly political in tone. The process of cultural polarisation is making the balance uneasy in both countries, so that maintenance of racial peace depends on the day-to-day good judgement of political leaders in the absence of institutionalised shock-absorbers. It is evident that the Indians of Trinidad and both groups in Guyana cannot really feel secure within a political structure that treats racial and cultural differences as non-existent and provides no mutual guarantees among ethnic groups.

Our final example of the rational-territorial concept of the nation in practice, Nigeria, was expected by many to be the model for British-inspired constitutional development in Africa. It was large enough, with a sufficient variety of climates and natural resources, to support a diversified modern economy. It was recognised, of course, that Nigeria contained several large tribes or tribal nations and many smaller ones totalling 250 in all – and that traditional, cultural and religious differences might act as centrifugal forces. People believed, however, that balance could be secured by making Nigeria a federal state with self-governing regions corresponding roughly to the habitats of the largest tribes: the Hausa, the Yoruba and the Ibo. American public administration experts also asserted that the British-trained administrative and military élite would hold the country together despite unfavourable factors.[13] Such optimists did not consider that, in addition to the normal infighting caused by career competition among bureaucrats, the administration in a country with weak parliamentary institutions becomes an arena where major policy issues are fought out.[14]

Of the major tribal nations in Nigeria, the Hausa–Fulani number about 8·5 million and the Yoruba and Ibo about 5 million each – together slightly less than two-fifths of the country's total population of 52·8 million.[15] The significant fact for our purposes, however, is the sharp disparity in the exposure to Western education and technology enjoyed by the South Nigerians, the Ibos in particular, as contrasted with the peoples in the North. The British colonial administration had left the Moslem North very much to its own devices, governing through the traditional emirates with a loose kind of indirect rule. During the last few decades of the Protectorate the British undertook some modernisation of the traditional royal bureaucracy, which provided part of the personnel for the new Federal civil service.[16] But otherwise modernisation proceeded at a leisurely pace: most of the population continued their traditional pursuits of handicraft, simple farming and cattle-raising.

The peoples of South Nigeria – divided into the Eastern, Western and, later, Mid-West Regions – were in far more frequent contact with Europeans throughout the colonial period. A large number attended missionary schools, as suggested by the fact that 50 per cent of the population in the Eastern and 30 per cent in the Western Region are Christian as compared with only 3 per cent in the Northern Region.[17] The Ibo, whose culture was open and competitive, were particularly subject to the changes that Deutsch sums up in compiling his index of social mobilisation.[18] Being badly overcrowded in the Eastern Region, they migrated to cities all over Nigeria, where their better schooling helped them rise rapidly in business. Ibo soon dominated trade in the North, which led to Hausa resentment and occasional massacres. Contact with other ethnic groups fused local tribal loyalties into an Ibo nationalism.[19] The Ibos seemed quite ready to project this nationalism up to the level of all-Nigerian patriotism. But their efforts to do so were misunderstood by other ethnic groups as a grasping for Ibo hegemony over the whole of Nigeria.

Our frame of reference does not permit examining the coups and political manoeuvres that preceded the 30 May 1967 decision of the Eastern Region to secede from Nigeria and form the sovereign state of Biafra.[20] The salient fact is that a series of events, including the wholesale killing of Ibo officers and soldiers during the coup of 29 July 1966, and the subsequent massacres of Ibo civilians, provoked the *belief* that the Gowon government was engaged in a deliberate attempt to exterminate the Ibo as a people. The Federal authorities did nothing to correct this impression. They provided £300,000 relief money for 300,000 refugees who had fled the North leaving all their possessions: exactly £1 per refugee.[21]

To sum up, the Ibo felt deprived of the existential security that every nation or ethnic group must have when it takes part in a larger political community. By existential security is meant the certainty of playing a constructive role in the larger polity, of enjoying self-government in the homeland and the protection of law throughout the larger area, of a fair share of common resources, and the right to make or share in making all decisions affecting the vital interests of the nation or ethnic group. This is the essential minimum for stable symbiosis of divergent ethnic groups and thus the basic political platform for development of a multi-ethnic society.

MULTI-ETHNICITY AND DEVELOPMENT IN SOUTHERN AFRICA

While we are not here engaged in economic analysis as such, a few basic data are desirable as a point of departure for our concluding discussion of structural problems. The aggregates for Africa as a whole are significant, because social structures in Southern Africa resemble those elsewhere on the continent, and because there are people who would impose on Southern Africa political systems such as prevail further north.

To begin with, Africa has 12 per cent of the world's population but produces only 3 per cent of the world's gross national product.[22] Outside South Africa, the African per capita G.N.P. is U.S.$130, as compared with $135 for the Near East and South Asia, $150 for East Asia excluding Japan, $425 for Latin America and $2,600 for Western Europe and North America. For Southern Africa, including South Africa, South West Africa, Botswana, Lesotho, and Swaziland, the per capita G.N.P. for all ethnic groups together was $633 in 1968. The G.N.P. growth chart for Africa outside the Republic shows a total increase of about 36 per cent, or 13 per cent per capita, between 1960 and 1968. Figures are slightly higher when South Africa is included.

The statistics of food production are more disturbing, however. Excluding South Africa, the figures show an absolute increase of 24 per cent from 1958 to 1969. But in view of population growth, this meant a drop of about 5 per cent in per capita food production.

That the stagnation reflected in these figures is not the result of lack of resources has been pointed out by the late Arnold Rivkin, Adviser on African Development for the World Bank. 'The African independence syndrome', he wrote, 'has been characterised by the presence of many, perhaps in some instances all, of the major factors often identified as crucial, followed by a longer or shorter time interval during which the factors have been consumed, dissipated, or utilised without apparent result, leading to stagnation, frustration, and even retrogression.' Most African states, Rivkin comments, are still confronted with the same basic tasks they faced on their independence days: state-building, nation-building, economy-building, technological revolution and social restructuring.[23]

There are alternative theories about the cause of this deficiency in development. Henry L. Bretton, for instance, attributes it to the persistence of neo-colonialism. African countries, he feels, are doomed to indefinite satellite status and will not progress as long as the great powers give priority to weapons systems and space exploration rather than to development in Africa.[24] Bretton's argument will of course be very comforting to the African politician who is looking for an external scapegoat to blame for the lack of progress.

Rivkin, however, points out that Africa has received substantial financial and technical aid from the West and the communist bloc; there has been much planning and considerable investment but little growth. It can be inferred that merely stepping up aid input would not accelerate development very much. The problem, he observes, lies in quite a different area: in the lack of political institutions capable of creating the preconditions for development.

Rivkin's thesis that the key to economic and social progress is to be found in the areas of political structure and institutions is supported by an analysis of processes taking place in some African states under the name of 'nation-building' or 'integration'. We have already noted the medicine prescribed by British and American professors, and it seems fair to say that much African policy is a feedback of Anglo-American political science.

Anglo-Saxon political theory, as we have seen, accepts the rationalist-territorial concept of the nation and looks on ethnic and linguistic particularism as a disturbing and reactionary element. Recently, however, Black militants in America have charged that 'integration' often means enforcing the particularist standards of the Anglo-Saxon; their objective is autonomy for a Black community, although its political form remains somewhat vague.[25] Despite this Black heresy, which White liberals excuse as an understandable reaction to persecution, the prevailing American opinion is that cultural pluralism is an unmitigated evil. Multi-ethnicity may sometimes arise through historical accident, but the approved policy is to combat it with aggressive assimilation.

A standard American judgement about ethnicity in Africa is reflected in the collection *Pluralism in Africa*, containing papers given at a conference of the University of California, Los Angeles, African Studies Center.[26] The book centres on a model derived by M. G. Smith from J. S. Furnivall. It defines a plural society as one in which a culturally distinct minority *necessarily* wields exclusive political power while other groups are deliberately kept leaderless and disorganised.[27] This model excludes the functioning of a plural society through the interaction of group leaders chosen by traditional authority patterns. It admits progress only in the direction of territorial integration. It does not visualise the possibility that a multi-ethnic society, without becoming less plural, may evolve towards a pattern of bargaining and co-operation based on mutual interests. (Such interaction and bargaining *is* visualised in the essay on Zululand by Max Gluckman, who rejects the Furnivall–Smith model.)

American writers on political modernisation tend to see the task in Africa as that of creating European-type nations to match the territories left by the Berlin Conference of 1885. That such modernisers are prepared to force or persuade the Africans to accept the necessity of a basic reorientation of personality is evident in the proposals of Clifford Geertz, who observes that people in multi-ethnic states 'tend to regard the immediate, concrete, and to them inherently meaningful sorting implicit in such "natural" diversity as the substantial content of their individuality'. Such identification, he adds, conflicts with organisation in a larger, modern political system. Categorising the lifting of what he calls 'primordial' ties to the level of political supremacy as 'pathological', Geertz calls for their 'domestication', that is, for 'divesting them of their legitimising force with respect to governmental authority'.[28] Geertz points out correctly that a dominant tribe or ethnic group may use the apparatus of a unitary state to attain particularist goals at the expense of others. It does not occur to him, however, to question the wisdom of superimposing a unitary state on a multi-ethnic society.

This leads us back to our basic problem of designing a political structure that will mobilise and harmonise the integrating forces in multi-ethnic African communities. Under the label of democracy, Anglo-American political science has offered the European model of a unitary state – a model that has already proved defective in the multi-ethnic areas of Central Europe. This model does not fit African personality or African society. As Rivkin has shown, it leads to the distortions of the one-party state and military dictatorship: to antagonistic coalitions of 'ins' and 'outs'. Where coercion is used to impose uniformity on the plural, disparate population of African states, sterility, stagnation and collapse are the inevitable results.[29]

Modernisation should begin by strengthening, not diluting, the natural cohesive forces of African society. These forces are rooted in African tribal structure, tradition and religion. As John S. Mbiti shows in his book, *African Religions and Philosophies*, Africans do not merely profess their religion; they *live* it. It is this religion, the societal aspects of which are little affected by conversion to Christianity, that links the individual with his clan and tribe, his ancestors and his children, and shapes his total personality.[30] This tradition, this total pattern of existence, is the foundation of authority for Africans. As a political force, and as a basis for modernisation, such a living tradition is far more effective than any vague European civic virtue borrowed from Rousseau or Saint-Simon.

The workable model for political development in Africa is therefore one that is consciously pluralist. Its function should be to preserve and strengthen traditional societies as constituent elements in a larger regional system. Such pluralism has its own moral imperative, and that is that each ethnic group recognise the right of each other to existential security: the right to shape its own policy and to develop in the direction of its own collective aspirations.

The ultimate political and economic relations among the peoples of Southern Africa will no doubt be shaped over the long run through processes of negotiation and experimentation. That the emerging pattern will be one of balance of political forces, bargaining and co-operation is dictated by the fact that the peoples need each other and need the fruits of cross-cultural co-operation.

NOTES

1. Clifford Geertz, 'The Integrative Revolution: Primordial Sentiments and Civic Politics in the New States', in Clifford Geertz (ed.), *Old Societies and New States: The Quest for Modernity in Asia and Africa* (Glencoe. Ill.: Free Press, 1963) pp. 105–57, at p. 118; reprinted in Claude E. Welch, Jr, *Political Modernisation: A Reader in Comparative Political Change*, 2nd ed. (Belmont, Calif.: Wadsworth, 1971) pp. 197–218, at p. 206.
2. Eugen Lemberg, *Nationalismus*, 2 vols (Hamburg: Rowohlts Deutsche Enzyklopädie, 1964) II 34–54.
3. J. S. Furnivall, *Colonial Policy and Practice* (Cambridge Univ. Press, 1948) pp. 304–12.

4. Frederick Hertz, *The Economic Problem of the Danubian States* (London: Gollancz, 1947) pp. 40–51.
5. For a critical account of the major developments in Austro-Hungarian constitutional history, see Wenzel Jaksch, *Europe's Road to Potsdam* (New York: Praeger, 1963) part 1.
6. Hertz, op. cit., pp. 123–37.
7. Lemberg, op. cit., 1 120 ff.
8. Claude E. Welch, Jr, 'The Comparative Study of Political Modernisation', Introduction to his *Political Modernisation*, pp. 7, 12–13.
9. Edward Shils, 'On the Comparative Study of New States', in Geertz, op. cit., p. 22; reprinted in Welch, op. cit., pp. 9–10.
10. William A. Gamson, 'Stable Unrepresentation in American Society', *American Behavioral Scientist*, no. 12 (Nov–Dec 1969).
11. Robert A. Dahl, *Polyarchy: Participation and Opposition* (New Haven: Yale Univ. Press, 1971) pp. 105–23, 203.
12. Most of the information about Guyana and Trinidad and Tobago (shortened to Trinidad here) is taken from Barbara and Victor C. Ferkiss, 'Race and Politics in Trinidad and Guyana', *World Affairs*, CXXXIV 1 (summer 1971) 5–23.
13. J. Donald Kingsley, 'Nigeria', in Joseph La Palombara (ed.), *Bureaucracy and Political Development* (Princeton Univ. Press, 1963) pp. 301–317.
14. S. N. Eisenstadt, 'Bureaucracy and Political Development', in Nimrod Raphaeli (ed.), *Readings in Comparative Administration* (Boston, 1967) pp. 199–268, esp. p. 224.
15. Figures on tribal nations from *Plural Societies* (The Hague), 1 1 (1970) 18, and II 1 (1971) 45. Figure for Nigeria from Agency for International Development, *Africa: Economic Growth Trends* (Washington, D.C., 1970) Table 1, p. 14.
16. Anthony H. M. Kirk-Greene, 'The Merit Principle in an African Bureaucracy: Northern Nigeria', in Arnold Rivkin (ed.), *Nations by Design: Institution-Building in Africa* (Garden City, N.Y.: Doubleday, 1968) pp. 253–332.
17. From table in *Plural Societies* (The Hague), 1 1 (1970) 33.
18. Karl W. Deutsch, 'Social Mobilisation and Political Development', in Welch, op. cit., pp. 153–76.
19. Charles W. Anderson, Fred R. von der Mehden and Crawford Young, *Issues of Political Development* (Englewood Cliffs, N.J.: Prentice-Hall, 1967) pp. 34–7.
20. A balanced account, critical of both the Federal government and the Biafran leadership, will be found in Raph Uwechue, *Reflections on the Nigerian Civil War* (New York: Africana Publishing Corporation, 1971).
21. Ibid., pp. 43–7.
22. The statistics quoted here are taken from Agency for International Development, op. cit.
23. Arnold Rivkin, 'The Role of Institution-Building in Africa', in Rivkin, op. cit., pp. 5–6.

24. Henry L. Bretton, *Patron–Client Relations: Middle Africa and the Powers*, 24-page 'module' (New York: General Learning Press, 1971) *passim*.
25. Thus, Stokely Carmichael and Charles V. Hamilton, in *Black Power* (New York: Random House, 1967) *passim*.
26. Leo Kuper and M. G. Smith (eds), *Pluralism in Africa* (Berkeley and Los Angeles: Univ. of California Press, 1969, 1971).
27. M. G. Smith, 'Institutional and Political Conditions of Pluralism', in Kuper and Smith, op. cit., pp. 27–65, esp. p. 33.
28. Clifford Geertz, in Geertz (ed.), op. cit., p. 128.
29. Rivkin, loc. cit., pp. 16–23.
30. John S. Mbiti, *African Religions and Philosophies* (Garden City, N.Y.: Doubleday, 1970) *passim.*, esp. chaps 1, 5, 10 and 19.

Political Stability and Economic Development

THEODORE L. SHAY

INTRODUCTION

At a minimum, this volume and the Conference that gave rise to it have served to indicate the complexity of development and the interrelationship of the multiple factors that are involved. Even if we are unable here to delineate a comprehensive blueprint for accelerated development, we shall at least have set forth more clearly the factors involved and have shared insights into the preconditions and perhaps the priorities for effective future action.

This essay will deal briefly with some of the relationships that link political stability and economic development. Obviously the two factors are closely interrelated. The approach is that noted by two American authors who state: 'There is, of course, a rich literature on what might generally be called the economic basis of politics. But our attention is attracted to the opposite problem – the political basis of economic development.'[1] The thesis advanced here is that political stability is a necessary, though not a sufficient, condition for economic development. This is not meant to relegate other important factors, such as available investment capital, skilled manpower, accessible resources, creative entrepreneurship, to a status of less importance than political stability. It is rather to identify and examine the dimensions of the political factor as one of such importance that the other elements are rendered insufficient for economic development, if the factor of political stability is lacking.

The first subthesis is that healthy political stability is dependent upon a sense of national identity and national unity. In addition, the legitimate function of participation in the political process is a natural outgrowth of a sense of national identity and unity, and a contributing factor to the healthy stability of the system. Political stability may be achieved in a police state, national unity may be fostered by totalitarian controls imposed by the state on all associations and individuals within it and on all channels of communication, and economic development may be facilitated by creating a command economy, as in the Soviet Union. But such coerced unity and regimented stability are 'unhealthy' by the standards of our value system, and the assumption that the people of Southern Africa are not interested in following the Soviet model of stability and development is one easily made.

The nation-state has emerged from the break-up of the great imperial states as the almost universal twentieth-century political unit. However, many of the new states are independent political entities that still lack a sense of national unity. In other words, many new states, and many new states in Africa especially, are still intensively involved in 'nation-building' even though they have achieved political sovereignty. This produces a simultaneous demand for both nation-building and for economic development which inhibits the potential for accelerated development. This process is described by Charles W. Anderson with reference to Latin America, but also with obvious application to Africa:

> The objectives of economic development and nation-building are closely interdependent. Nation-building implies that a people will come to feel that a most relevant human community, a primary arena for human relationship and intercourse, will come to exist in that area circumscribed by the jurisdictional boundaries of the state. Economic development ... implies that the nation itself will contain most of the institutions and processes necessary for sustained economic growth. When the state moves to 'convert' economic performances in alternative economic systems, ... it simultaneously seeks to enhance the significance of a nation as a relevant human community.[2]

Historically, the most important element in the creation of national unity has been a sense of national identity based primarily on a common language. Few of the nation-states existing prior to the Second World War lacked a common language, most notably Belgium and Switzerland and the then Union of South

Africa. Also of importance were such factors as a shared sense of history and tradition, a common social culture, a common material culture and common racial origins. As a general rule, the more of these elements that were present, the more easily a sense of national unity was achieved. It was only in the era after the Second World War that a great many new states gained their political independence, but lacked many of the bases for national unity. Undoubtedly the most striking example of this was the creation of the new state of Pakistan, based on the shared religious system of Islam but lacking a common language, common culture and common race and being divided by a thousand miles of Indian territory. The exigencies of nation-building and comprehensive economic planning, the necessity for the allocation of resources, and feelings of regional dominance and resource misappropriation frustrated development and eventually destroyed whatever sense of national unity existed. To many observers the only wonder is that Pakistan, divided East and West, survived for twenty-four years.

In a number of other new states which lack a sense of national unity, political stability is often tenuous and *coups d'état* and rebellions, abortive and successful, secessionist demands and restive minorities, political repression by dominant groups and even civil wars, are almost characteristic of the state system of our times. The existence of multi-racial, multi-linguistic, multi-cultural states, not the product of natural evolution but rather the result of the withdrawal of colonial powers, leaving behind administrative areas suddenly become sovereign, has created an environment in which nation-building is immensely difficult and thus contributed to massive political instability.

In many states where nation-building has had to proceed without a sense of national identity, various devices have been employed. In some cases it involves an elaborate use of symbols of unity without very much substance of unity. In some cases it proceeds only through constant manipulation of crisis situations, especially crises involving real or pretended foreign dangers, as witness Sukarno's 'confrontation' policy with the Dutch over West Irian, and with Malaysia over northern Borneo. At times it takes place through increasing governmental repression exercised by majority groups over dissident minorities. And, most often, it depends upon a series of kinds of compromises and accommodations that maintain a tenuous semblance of unity. As John H. Kautsky has written:

> Indian nationalism is not an attempt to unite all people speaking Indian, Nigerian nationalism is not an attempt to unite all people speaking Nigerian, for there are no such languages. If anything, it is the policy of governments of countries such as these to consolidate people speaking different languages into a so-called nation, and thus to take actions which, like those of the late Austro-Hungary monarchy, were regarded as anti-nationalist in the European context.[3]

The second subthesis is that not only is a sense of national unity a necessary condition for healthy political stability, but it is also a necessary condition for the mobilisation of the people to their own economic betterment. A sense of national community, a sense of national purpose, a sense of national endeavour is greatly enhanced if those factors of language, tradition, culture and race are held in common. This psychological dimension of economic development is well indicated by Rajni Kothari, writing about the Indian situation, when he says:

> The important point is that the nation and the society that economists assume as given to them to develop have yet to come into being. Development is as much a process of building a nation as to raise levels of living of some or all segments of the people. Mobilising and involving masses of people in the productive process is not simply a function of the accumulation-and-saving construct but involves such imponderables as incentives, involvement, morale, motivation, participation, and articulation of demands.[4]

The psychological dimension of development involves the willing acceptance of the necessities of mobilisation. Development demands personal sacrifices, increased productivity and lowered or at least restrained popular consumption, and the capacity to accept deferment of expectations until the system can provide a higher standard of living without distorting developmental priorities.

The cost of modes of mobilisation other than willing acceptance based on a sense of national endeavour are prohibitively high. We cannot easily calculate the costs involved in mobilisation through repression and possible consequent reactions such as armed resistance and civil war. It is possible to measure the cost of the attempted Biafran secession in terms of lives lost, homes, businesses and resources destroyed, material expended, and even, perhaps, establish a figure for the development potential irrevocably retarded. We can measure the costs of physical reconstruction, but the psychological scars will remain uncalculated long after the buildings are rebuilt and the crops replanted.

The interrelation of economic development, political stability and a sense of national unity and endeavour might well be examined in two brief case studies. First, the example of India, which lacked many of the necessary elements for national unity and political stability, and secondly, Japan, which lacked many of the material elements for economic development but possessed to an exceptional degree those factors contributing to national unity.

THE INDIAN MODEL

The most striking example of the multi-racial, multi-linguistic, multi-cultural democratic state struggling to achieve accelerated economic development is, of course, India. In 1947, when India and Pakistan became sovereign states and the princely states were integrated, a federation of twenty-seven heterogeneous states became the Indian Union. The original intention was to retain the internal structure of twenty-seven states, many of them multi-lingual, in an effort to avoid linguistic and communal subnationalist tendencies. A special committee appointed by Prime Minister Nehru confirmed that, if India were to be reorganised into linguistic states, '[it] would unmistakably retard the process of consolidation [and] let loose, while we are still in a formative stage, forces of disruption and disintegration'.[5]

But the problem of linguistic subnationalism did not disappear. In 1953, after the fast-unto-death of one of Gandhi's old followers in South India, the new Telegu-speaking state of Andhra was carved largely out of the old state of Madras. The floodgates of linguistic reorganisation were opened. By 1956 the internal map of India was redrawn to create fourteen linguistic states and six territories. But this did not solve the problem, because two of the most sensitive areas, the Punjab and Bombay State, were not originally reorganised on a linguistic basis. And after considerable bloodshed over the critical question of the fate of Bombay City, these states were divided. The creation of linguistic states proved to be more divisive than unifying and encouraged the sentiments such as 'I am a Gujarati', or 'I am a Bengali', or 'I am a Maratha', rather than the sense of national unity expressed in the statement 'We are Indians'.

The language issue not only fragmented the federal structure of India, but in another dimension created many disturbances in 1956. The Indian constitution of 1950 provided that after fifteen years a single official Indian language should be adopted. But there is no single language spoken by a majority of the Indian people; and in 1965, when it appeared that government policy was about to force Hindi upon the entire population as the official language, serious disturbances broke out in many non-Hindi-speaking areas. The government was forced to compromise by retaining English in the national government and by not forcing Hindi upon the reluctant population.

Religious diversity and its cultural correlates have also contributed to the political instability of India. Most notable have been the recurrent outbreaks of rioting between Hindus and Moslems which have occurred in many areas of the country. The Sikh population of the Punjab struggled non-violently for years, with some leaders threatening violence, to achieve the partitioning of the state of the Punjab into a predominantly Hindu and a predominantly Sikh political entity. This objective was finally achieved, further fragmenting the subdivisions of the subcontinent.

Caste and communal differences have grown since independence, and the examples of caste demands on the government and communal antagonisms tearing at the thin fabric of national unity are too well known to need documentation here. Nehru called communal fragmentation India's greatest domestic problem.

Racial as well as cultural differences have entered into prolonged and sometimes violent demands for redress. The example of the Naga people of Assam engaging in guerrilla warfare to advance their demands for the creation of a Nagaland state, and in southern India the case of Dravidian restiveness which produced an active secessionist movement demanding the creation of a fully independent Dravidistan nation-state, are most drama-tic. The success of the D.M.K. party in becoming a major political force in southern India has for the time being quieted the demands for complete secession. However, the possibility remains real.

Regional rivalries have had many debilitating influences, not the least of which are those which have had negative impact on plans for economic development. One example cited by William McCord is:

> In 1957, to take one instance, Assam (one of the least developed of Indian regions) benefited from the discovery of oil reserves. The central government faced the decision whether to build a refinery in Assam or in another area. On rational eco-nomic grounds, they chose a region where trained workers, power, and transportation were readily available. Assamese politicians let out a wail of affronted 'nationalism'. 'Every drop of oil in Assam is as sacred as a drop of blood of every Assamese', one member of Parliament proclaimed. 'We can-not allow it to be sucked by others.'[6] Because of political pres-sures, the government eventually made the economic sacrifice of establishing an expensive refinery in Assam.[7]

Finally, India may have contributed to its own future dismem-berment by assisting the people of East Bengal (Bangladesh) in seceding from Pakistan and creating an independent Bengali state. For the people of the Indian state of West Bengal are Bengalis by language, by race and by culture, and it is not unlikely to specu-late that the pull of 'Maha-Bangladesh' may become irresistible to the Indians of West Bengal. As McCord wrote: 'The internal nationalistic sentiments *within* India boil over into combats that are sadly reminiscent of European history.'[8]

Throughout its brief independent history, India has struggled mightily to increase her economic viability. The planned five-year development schemes, the highly centralised mobilisation of capi-tal and resources, the massive infusions of foreign aid and the toil of her hundreds of millions have little more than kept pace with the mounting population and the escalating demands on the economic system.

Many factors in addition to political instability and tendencies towards national disunity have contributed to the problems of

India's economic development. But the psychological elements must not be overlooked. In order to achieve popular mobilisation the Indian government has had to encourage the 'revolution of rising expectations', and though economic progress has been made, it is becoming increasingly apparent that the expectations are not being met. The frustrations inherent in national mobilisation are not offset by a sense of common endeavour. India's First Five-Year Plan was modestly successful, being devoted primarily to agriculture. But India's subsequent plans, addressed to the demands of industrialisation, have consumed the bulk of her scarce resources and produced a neglect of agriculture. Yet 80 per cent of her people live in rural areas, and when agricultural planning became fragmentary, the people became understandably frustrated. They became increasingly unresponsive to the exhortations of the planners. Rajni Kothari has summed it up in writing: 'The gap between expectations and realisation was filled by pious declarations, a continuous flow of new ideas which were never implemented, and a snobbish attitude on the part of the planners and the administrators who shifted the blame to the low motivation of the farmers and the rural people.'[9]

Not only is economic growth impaired, but also at every major crisis the spectre of recurrent political instability is apparent. As an Indian author has written: 'India's domestic situation can be seen to have reached the stage at which general discontent among the people is approaching a dangerous level.'[10]

THE JAPANESE MODEL

Let us now briefly examine the example of Japan in its formative first fifty years of modern economic development. The contrast with India is readily apparent, for Japan is the best example of rapid development within an optimum environment of national unity and political stability.

It was only one hundred years ago that Japan emerged from the isolation of the Tokugawa period and began the process of modernisation. Few observers would have been encouraged by the objective conditions confronting the new Meiji government. Japan lacked an industrial base even equivalent to that of Western Europe in the 1790s. She lacked sufficient natural resources to undertake major industrialisation, and only 16 per cent of the total land area of the Japanese islands was arable. Though there was some capital accumulation in private hands, it was insufficient to the tasks demanded, and the level of technical skills available in the population was very limited. On the plus side, Japan had a well-developed sense of national unity and a stable government after the Meiji restoration. As Ambassador Reischauer has noted: 'Japan entered its great revolutionary period a unified, centralised nation, unravaged by any prolonged period of political disruption.'[11]

With these conditions prevailing, it was easy to mobilise the people to the great national endeavour. The Japanese peasants were long accustomed to hard work, and, when called upon to increase production, they did. The application of fertilisers and new farming techniques, the cultivation of new products for the growing urban market, and intensive labour permitted Japanese food production to double. In the critical decade 1878–87 the total national product of Japan increased more than 40 per cent and continued at this rate for the next forty years. The government took the lead in stimulating industrialisation and in financing the economic infrastructure. The basic railroad system was built by the government, which also established model factories producing silk and cotton textiles, cement, soap and other products, and then permitted private entrepreneurs to take control and operate the new industries. The government made exceptional investments in a modern education system so as to develop a reservoir of technically skilled manpower.

The only way in which the government could raise the necessary funds was to tax the peasantry. While agricultural production mounted, ever-increasing taxation held down the peasants' consumption. Yet the peasants supported this programme because the men of the Meiji were able to provide a psychological framework in which to create a spirit of common national endeavour. Policies that in another context would have been resisted as exploitative were accepted by the people as necessary contributors to national mobilisation.

Light cottage industries, widely decentralised, were encouraged. Many peasants became involved in industrial production without having to leave their villages, and the shock of rapid urban growth was to a considerable degree avoided. Every effort was made to integrate the new productive processes into the traditional life-style. As McCord has written:

> The Japanese policy, therefore, demonstrated for the first time in history that 'labour-intensive' light industry could serve as the vehicle for economic advance. . . . While the Meiji desired the human resources to staff their expanding industries, they did not by any means wish to disband traditional society. In fact, they deliberately tried to cement the ties which linked a person to his family, his community, his traditional values, and to the Meiji emperor.[12]

The emphasis on reinforcing and adapting traditional values was psychologically imperative and contributed incalculably to the success of the process.

The environment of political stability and the highly developed sense of national commitment are components essential to an understanding of the successful economic development of modern Japan. Viewed objectively, in terms of available resources, capital and other economic indicators, Japan did not stand a good chance in 1872 of becoming the third greatest industrial nation in the world one hundred years later.

NOTES

1. R. T. Holt and John E. Turner, *The Political Basis of Economic Development* (Princeton, N.J.: Van Nostrand, 1966) p. 40.
2. Charles W. Anderson, *Politics and Economic Change in Latin America* (Princeton, N.J.: Van Nostrand, 1967) p. 48.
3. John H. Kautsky, *The Political Consequences of Modernisation* (New York: Wiley, 1972) p. 56.
4. Rajni Kothari, *Politics in India* (Boston: Little, Brown, 1970) p. 13.
5. Quoted in Joan V. Bondurant, *Regionalism versus Provincialism: A Study in Problems of Indian National Unity*, Indian Press Digests, Monograph Series No. 4 (Berkeley: Univ. of California Press, 1958) p. 29.
6. *Bhoodan*, 3 July 1957, p. 4.
7. William McCord, *The Springtime of Freedom* (New York: Oxford Univ. Press, 1965) p. 174.
8. Ibid.
9. Kothari, op. cit., p. 145.
10. B. R. Shenoy, 'And Still the People Wept', *Far Eastern Economic Review*, LXVI (Oct 1969) 18.
11. E. R. Reischauer, *Japan Past and Present* (Tokyo: Tuttle, 1964) p. 117.
12. McCord, op. cit., pp. 62–3.

COMMENTS

F. J. van Wyk, C. J. Jooste, N. J. Rhoodie and B. I. Dladla

Mr van Wyk commented on Professor Glaser's paper in the light of the South African situation and experience. He said that South Africa was at present committed to what Professor Glaser described as the romantic concept of the *Volk*, rather than the rationalist concept. The South African government had been committed to this concept more or less since 1948 in its policy of establishing homelands for various Black ethnic groups. The government was, however, not at present thinking of separate homelands for the 2 million Coloured people and the 750,000 Indian or Asian people. Nor was the government thinking in terms of separate homelands for the approximately 2 million Afrikaners, the $1\frac{1}{2}$ million English South Africans and the other smaller national groups, such as Portuguese, Germans, Jews and so on.

In its efforts to implement this homeland policy the government was encountering many very real and practical problems. Mr van Wyk mentioned briefly some of these:

1. Since 1948 the Black population in what are called 'White' areas had increased enormously. According to the 1970 census, South Africa had 15 million Blacks. Slightly more than 8 million were in the so-called 'White' areas, and slightly less than 7 million in the homelands. Of the 8 million in the 'White' areas, about $4\frac{1}{2}$ million were in the urban areas and $3\frac{1}{2}$ million in the rural areas, mainly the White farms. (Johannesburg, a 'White' city, consisted of about 400,000 Whites and 1 million Blacks. About 200,000 Blacks came daily from Soweto to work in 'White' Johannesburg.)

2. 'Non-Whites' constituted about 80 per cent of the Republic's labour force.

3. The present division of land, with 13 per cent for Black homelands and 78 per cent for 'White' areas, constituted a major possible future source of tension. 13 per cent of the land might not be inadequate if there were intensive use of the land as in Israel. But there were the unfortunate psycho-

logical effects of such a division, and already some of the homeland leaders were demanding more land.

4. Another very real problem was the consolidation of the present 'patchy' homeland areas.

5. Another possible point of tension was the distribution of the country's wealth. Would the Whites be prepared to invest a significant and adequate share of this wealth in the homelands, and would they be prepared at least to finance essential infrastructures in the homelands? Furthermore, would the Blacks regard whatever was given for these purposes as sufficient?

6. If sovereign independence was given to the homelands, the people of Southern Africa would have to sort out the problems which would inevitably arise, e.g. in trade, in the possible establishment of separate armies, in negotiation with foreign powers, etc.

Mr van Wyk maintained that the government's policy would in any case take a very long time to be implemented, and he questioned whether there was the time available. In the process he considered that the area could become one of great tension. Black 'awareness' was gathering momentum and there were indications that Africans, Indians and Coloured people were moving towards one another in reaction to what they considered White 'oppression'.

Prior to 1948 there had been a movement away from ethnic identities among the Blacks in urban areas. But since 1948 there had been new emphasis on ethnic differences, with separate residential zones, separate schools and other separate institutions being created for the different Black ethnic groups. He felt that this all involved deliberate attempts to reverse trends towards unity, perhaps in order to prove the correctness of the thesis as propounded by Professor Glaser.

Dr Jooste said he was in agreement with the main argument of Professor Glaser's paper, but he would like to elaborate on two of the major points raised in the paper:

1. *The greater part of Africa is an area of ethnic fragmentation*
This was a valid observation which must form the basis of an analysis of the socio-political upheavals and the economic stagnation of the post-Second World War period.

Colonial rulers had left Africa at a time when population growth tended to exceed economic growth, and when increasing problems of socio-political tension were beginning to manifest themselves.

Basic to the solution of these problems was the building of a viable political structure, which could only be achieved if proper recognition was given to ethnic identification, i.e. to the concept of a 'people' or 'nation' or *Volkstaat*. This was a formidable requirement, because it would involve a fundamentally new approach to nation-building. It would require a reorientation on the basis of Professor Glaser's formula that each 'nation or ethnic group' must be enabled 'to see itself and to be seen by others as . . . capable of and responsible for determining its own destiny'.

African nations had been brought up on a concept of the state by which the major emphasis was placed on the territory and little emphasis on ethnic-linguistic solidarity. The acceptance of a new concept would be a cumbersome process, as it would also involve a readjustment of territorial boundaries and of political organisation. However, Dr Jooste considered it to be the only satisfactory long-term procedure. If the aim was accelerated development or just development, the political power structure must be right – right in the sense that the continued existence of the ethnic group could be safeguarded. Otherwise the energies and resources would be used up on political power struggles and social strife before goal-directed efforts in the economic field could get under way.

2. *Professor Glaser's model for political development in Africa*

It had to be consciously pluralist in character, according to Professor Glaser. Its function should be to preserve and strengthen traditional societies as constituent elements in a larger regional system. The moral basis for such pluralism was that each ethnic group should recognise the right of every other to shape its own policy and to develop in the direction of its own collective aspirations.

A nation or ethnic group could only exercise this right effectively if it controlled its own state exclusively. Professor Glaser's reference to a nation's capability and responsibility for determining its own destiny could not satisfy, if it excluded the possibility of developing towards separate statehood, i.e. towards full political sovereignty.

A viable political system could not encompass two nations. This would be in conflict with the experience in Western and Central Europe and elsewhere, as well as with the requirements of existential security.

Professor Glaser's advice that one should never mix two models should be heeded. Wherever a nation had tried to organise itself on the *Volkstaat* concept and to invoke rationalist-territorial ideas of the state and of citizenship at the same time, this has led to disintegration and ultimately to war. The evidence advanced in the paper would seem to favour the *Volkstaat* model for Africa. It could be added that, if this model was to work in Southern Africa, it should be applied consistently and on the explicit understanding that ultimate sovereign independence of the peoples concerned was not excluded when it was said that a nation's responsibility to determine its own destiny was recognised.

Professor Rhoodie said that the main problem of the Republic of South Africa was not caused by the differential social treatment and unequal civil rights of the local non-White groups, but by the *political* tensions and strains caused by a progressively ecalating level of political aspirations among the non-White sociological minorities involved. Consequently, one main question would in the foreseeable future dominate the minds of the White establishment, namely: how can the Whites accommodate these minorities in the central decision-making institutions of the state?

South Africans who favoured a local commonwealth or confederation geared to the needs of disparate ethnic groups, interacting within a common geo-political system, might have much to learn from the Austro-Hungarian model. For instance, much could be learnt about accommodating ethnic minorities on the basis of *ethno-national autonomy* coupled with *supra-national participation in national decision-making*.

The one-man-one-vote principle was no cure-all for the frustrations generated by the political aspirations of minorities. In South Africa it would certainly not be the open-sesame to the golden millennium. South Africa's socio-political structure, particularly the political subordination of its ethnic minorities, embodied a system of historical realities. These realities would largely determine the political accommodation that would gradually evolve from the cross-ethnic bargaining and experimentation that the dominant White nation would necessarily have to initiate in order to meet the demands created by the forces of history.

Professor Rhoodie said that he was absolutely convinced that many of South Africa's development problems would become less onerous if a workable and realistic system of political accommodation could be implemented – through a process of institutional evolution (*a*) guaranteeing the ethnic minorities a share in the national decision-making – a share commensurate with their *real* bargaining power and level of development; and (*b*) guaranteeing the integrity and socio-cultural identity of each participant ethnic group. This two-tier system (based on institutionally reconciling *ethno-nationality* with *supra-nationality*) was to his mind the only political solution that satisfied the basic requirements of cross-ethnic accommodation. Institutionally this accommodation would require the creation of a supra-communal power system.

At the level of national decision-making, a permanent retention and entrenchment of the present gap between the political 'haves' and 'have nots' could easily become a vortex sucking South Africa into the horrors of revolution. He granted that the Bantu homelands did constitute safety-valves in their capacities as embryonic ethno-national states, but even should they one day become excised from the Republic of South Africa to settle in their own separate orbits of development, the Republic would still be left with a national population embracing a dominant White nation and several non-White minorities. Would these minorities always remain statisfied with a system based on communal autonomy, but with no provision for negotiated participation in national decision-making?

Mr Dladla asked whether Professor Glaser honestly believed that ethnic grouping would be to the benefit of the people of South Africa, when Professor Glaser's own country, the United States, was composed of people originally belonging to various ethnic groupings? He referred to the Afrikaner nation as one which had not existed three hundred years ago and which was composed of people of several different origins, such as Dutch, German, French, etc. They were a good example to the Africans, because, if the way the Afrikaners built their nation could be followed, he felt the Africans in South Africa could also reach their goal of one nation.

Mr Dladla also raised the question as to whether the different ethnic groups in South Africa would agree to separation, if consulted in a referendum. His belief was that this separation was 'being rammed down our throats by our superiors' who controlled the whole political set-up in South Africa. He felt that, if necessary, the Africans would rather prefer South Africa being separated into only two parts, that of White and Black, because the Blacks considered themselves as nothing less than Africans, whatever names they were called by the Whites. Furthermore, they considered themselves as a Black African nation residing in the southern end of Africa.

DISCUSSION

This brief summary gives the main points raised in the discussion which followed the above comments on the two papers. The summary is based on the Rapporteurs' report circulated at the Conference.

Professor L. Fourie pointed out that there were also economic problems involved, such as that of deflationary unemployment. In the homelands one could not reduce unemployment by increasing effective demand. Whereas fictional unemployment would not be serious in Western capitalist countries, in the homelands it was a serious problem for economic development. The solution lay in the field of politics.

Mr R. F. Margo criticised Professor Glaser's emotive use of the key concept of 'political-social integrators'. Emotive formulations could serve political but not scientific functions. Any adequate articulation of the concept must be highly complex and could not ground Professor Glaser's simplistic conclusions about 'the African personality'. The exclusion of non-'ethnic' integrators, such as economic activity, was arbitrary and unrelated to the logic of the key concept. Urbanisation was affecting 'traditional' identity elements of both Afrikaners and Blacks, and outsiders had no more right in the latter case than in the former to interfere in this process. Yet in many cases, especially in urban areas, the

White government was forcing 'ethnic' separation on Blacks against their will. This ethnic policy purported to be the opposite of colonialism, but as applied was nothing less than the colonialistic tactic of 'divide and rule'.

Mr A. Erwin said that, in regard to KwaZulu, it would be very hard for Professor Glaser's suggestion to be carried out, since a large number of Zulus would still have to go to White industries for work, and KwaZulu's tax base would remain small, resulting in its political decisions continuing to be affected by decisions taken in South Africa.

Professor J. H. Coetzee said that ethnic groups were not based on rational concepts. They were not metaphysical, nor were they non-existent. They were emotional but a reality, and in the emotions lay their explosive power. It was submitted that present attempts at African unity were only temporary expedients until the moment of victory, when fragmentation would result.

Mr T. T. Thahane commented that there were some contradictions in the South African system. Even with common cultures Ireland had its problems. It was questioned whether there was an appreciation of the costs involved in making the homelands viable, and whether White and Black South Africans understood each other.

Professor Shay, in reply, stated that his paper had simply been a warning from an outsider that multi-ethnic states did not succeed. The critics of government policy did not offer any viable alternative.

As to Bantu working in urban areas after independence had been granted to the homelands, their situation might be analogous to that of various foreign nationals who worked as migrant labourers in Germany and who did not claim political participation.

Professor Glaser, in reply, expressed the view that the price of separate development had to be paid, and the cost would be the lesser of any alternative. This would require giving free rein to the equalising effect of an economy operating in a free market.

With regard to the definition of national groups, this would have to be settled ultimately by self-determination of the group concerned. Sovereignty could be divided, he said, and the nearest model was the European Economic Community in which there could be multiple loyalties.

Part Two

Development and International Co-operation

Part Two

Development and
International Co-operation

Chapter 10

International Trade
and Investment

International Trade and Investment: the Case of Swaziland

SISHAYI S. NXUMALO

On a world map, or even on a fairly large-scale map of Southern Africa, Swaziland appears as a tiny speck. But several hours would be needed to give a detailed analysis of the country's resources and its economic potential.

Apart from the munificence of its resources, Swaziland has a special position in the context of accessibility to multi-national markets. While benefiting from the open gateways to the vast markets in Southern Africa, as a result of its membership of the Southern African Common Customs Area, it also enjoys uninhibited trading relationships with the remainder of the countries on the African continent, and indeed with countries in all the five continents of the world. Nor do these facts alone constitute the sum of Swaziland's beneficial situation. Certificates of Swaziland origin carry with them the rights to 'Commonwealth Preference' and 'most-favoured-nation' tariff concessions which are a considerable inducement to overseas buyers to seek their sources of supply in Swaziland.

There are, of course, other countries which have similarly beneficial situations, but have these benefits aborted by poor communications or by excessive internal transportation costs due to the enormous distances which goods and commodities have to travel between the producing locations and the ports of shipment or distribution points. In Swaziland this nullification of its advantageous situation does not occur. The rail link to Lourenço Marques and the excellent cargo-handling and frequent shipping opportunities to all parts of the world provide an easy outlet and ingress for exports and imports to and from overseas countries. Excellent roads and an efficient road/rail service direct to the heart of the major marketing points of the Southern African

Common Customs Area ensure that goods and commodities reach those markets cheaply and swiftly.

Again, there are other countries which sit astride the paths of international trade and which can only benefit by serving as entrepôt centres, because of their deficiencies of indigenous resources. This is not the case in Swaziland, which has a broad spectrum of resource availability. The variety of climatic and geoponic conditions makes the growing of almost any species of crop feasible and viable. While traditional agriculture is still focused mainly upon maize-growing, this sector now comprises only about one-third of the agricultural activity of the country. The most important cash crops produced by the modern agricultural sector are sugar, rice, citrus fruits, cotton and tobacco, but the diversification into higher-income and exotic crops is taking place rapidly, and the earnings from exports of pineapples, avocado pears, fresh vegetables, grenadillas and such other produce are by no means insignificant.

Animal husbandry has always been one of the main preoccupations in Swaziland, and livestock production remains an important feature of the economy of Swaziland. A considerable measure of modernisation has taken place in this sector as a result of selective cross-breeding, the establishment of large-scale ranching operations and cattle holding-grounds.

Almost the first impression one gets of Swaziland, especially when entering by air or by the northern and north-eastern border gates, is of the vastness of Swaziland's forests and timber resources. It was only very recently that Swaziland lost the title of possessing the largest man-made forest in the world, and when the new forestry extensions are completed Swaziland will again be able to claim this 'blue riband'.

Completely comprehensive data upon the mineral resources of Swaziland are not yet published, but the range of minerals available is considerable and the potentials for exploitation are enormous. In the forefront of the catalogue of minerals are iron ore and asbestos, which are already being efficiently exploited. Both bituminous coal and anthracite are mined, although there is room for much-expanded activity according to the most recent geological assessments of these resources. Lead, barytes, high-purity kaolin, silica and ball clays are a few of the other minerals which are already being exploited to a lesser extent.

The scenic beauty of Swaziland cannot be ignored in any tabling of natural resources. Certainly it cannot be omitted in any discussion of international trade and investment, because the tourist trade which it engenders contributes to no mean extent to Swaziland's currency earnings, and considerable opportunities still exist for lucrative investments in the tourist facilities sector.

Last, but certainly not least, there are Swaziland's human resources. While Swaziland does not have any great mass of unemployed, which could be a factor disruptive of political and economic stability, there has not yet been any instance, nor is a possible occurrence foreseen, of any industrial, commercial or agricultural development being restrained by non-availability of sufficient numbers of workers.

These are the main resources of Swaziland. Although it is not claimed that they have been exploited to the full, they are by no means latent. Based upon these resources, Swaziland has a rapidly expanding manufacturing and commercial sector. Because the indigenous market is comparatively small, by reason of the low population level, it is a corollary that manufacturing and trading enterprises established in Swaziland must be aligned to international trade.

Swaziland has always been aware of the danger, which other developing countries have encountered, of remaining as a supply base of raw materials for the processing and manufacturing industries in the more developed countries. To remain so incurs the penalty of having to accept the dictates of the more developed countries as to what proportion of resources can be disposed of and as to what prices must be accepted. Swaziland has therefore adopted a three-pronged approach to the economic development of the country. Firstly, secondary industries have been encouraged to process the agricultural and mineral resources, in order that these resources should be acceptable over the widest possible international market area and also to provide materials upon which tertiary industries can be based.

Secondly, stimulants have been provided and an 'open door' attitude established for investors, both from within and from outside Swaziland, who are prepared to take advantage of our unique marketing position and our array of resources so as to convert the output of our secondary industries into fully manufactured goods, giving to our resources the maximum added value and providing our citizens with skilled employment opportunities. Thirdly, the marketing activities have been spread over a very wide front, so that foreign trade is not dominated by any one major trading partner, and so that this trade is not prone to fluctuations due to economic regressions in a particular country or global area.

Added to these factors is the parallel and balanced development of all our resource sectors. Approximately 30 per cent of the gross national product originates from agriculture and forestry and the secondary industries associated therewith. About 10 per cent of the G.N.P. arises from mining and mineral exploitation. Another 15 per cent arises from tertiary manufactory activities, and the remaining 45 per cent is accounted for by service enterprises, such as the distributive and construction trades, communications and tourist services.

Based upon the agricultural and forestry resources, Swaziland has major industrial undertakings in the form of sugar-milling, wood-pulp production, timber sawmills, cotton-ginning, meat-processing, maize- and rice-milling and citrus fruits packing and processing. Tertiary manufacturing, based on the secondary conversion of agricultural and forestry resources, includes fruit-canning, builder's joinery and furniture manufacturing, canned meat production, telephone and electricity pole impregnation, confectionery production and brewing.

The development of processing and manufacturing activities based upon Swaziland's mining and minerals resources is not so far advanced as is the case with the agriculture and forestry resources. This is largely because the magnitude of industries based upon minerals and mining resources is such that a number of years of research is required to establish the proper setting and environmental conditions which are necessary to ensure that the massive investments are most secure and capable of the maximum yield. But Swaziland is coming very close to the initiation of a large-scale iron-ore beneficiation plant which could in turn make iron-smelting and steel production feasible. The final stages have now been entered leading to the establishment of a heavy-output thermal power station.

There are other industries which have grown up in Swaziland, not so much because of the resource availability as because they are needed to meet the demands of the resource-based industries, or because Swaziland provides them with an advantageous location for serving outside markets. These are too numerous to catalogue completely, but they include the production of ready-made garments, packaging containers, cement, constructional steelwork and engineering supplies.

The extent to which we have succeeded so far in the third aspect of the three-pronged approach towards development mentioned above is evident from the fact that, in addition to maintain trading relationships with the other three countries in the Southern African Common Customs Area, trade agreements have been signed with Uganda, Tanzania, Kenya, Zambia and Malawi, and agreements of a similar nature are being negotiated with a number of other countries. The day is probably not far off when Swaziland will finalise arrangements for association with the East African Community and the European Economic Community.

In addition to the trade engendered by our membership of the Southern African customs union and by the trade agreements with other countries on the African continent, there is a significant amount of export trade with the United Kingdom, Japan, the United States, Canada, West Germany and elsewhere. There is often an assumption that Swaziland is very largely dependent upon its partners in the Southern African Customs Area for market outlets for its products. This is in fact a very wrong assumption. Only 15 per cent of our exports are in this direction, and 85 per cent – or more than R50 million worth – of Swaziland's export trade is with countries overseas. On the imports side the statistics show total purchases amounting to about R40 million, with 95 per cent of these imports arriving from the Republic of South Africa. This percentage is misleading, in that a fairly high proportion of these imports originate from other countries, but they pass through South African ports and the South African distributive system prior to reaching Swaziland.

There may be other countries with equal resource availabilities; there may be countries which have similar accessibility to multi-national markets; there may indeed be other countries which are as fortunate as Swaziland in providing both advantages. But, unlike so many other countries, the opportunities for investors to profit from these factors have by no means been exhausted. Traditionally the selection of the best projects might have been considered to be the prerogative of British investors. However, Swaziland's re-emergence as an independent nation brought first the slackening of colonial ties. Then, more recently, British preoccupation with joining the European Common Market has tended further to leave investment opportunities in Swaziland more easily available to investors from elsewhere.

Swaziland is not beset by the tribal dissensions which have plagued many other developing countries during the years following the attainment of independence. Nor has there been any wave of xenophobia leading to the nationalisation of non-Swazi investments and the haphazard expulsion of expatriate technical and managerial personnel. Naturally, there is concern to see Swazi citizens in higher-level management and technical occupations, but there is no intention of forcing acceptance of unqualified persons into such jobs. Investors are instead being helped with the training of the local personnel needed to fill such positions.

In addition to the political stability which Swaziland enjoys and which is mandatory for a healthy investment climate, the country is far removed from the areas of world conflict. In its development efforts there is considerable support from international and bilateral technical assistance services. The wealth of information and data compiled by the experts of the various agencies of the U.N. Development Programme, which have made surveys of Swaziland's resources and prospects, as well as feasibility and viability studies relating to specific investment opportunities, is available to investors who are thus not only saved the heavy preliminary research costs, but are also enabled to get their projects moving at a much earlier date.

Swaziland favours regional economic development. This means, in particular, that available markets should not be divided by the establishment of enterprises in direct competition with enterprises which already exist in other countries within the same region, and which already serve the market demands of that region adequately. There should be a greater measure of consultation between countries, so that there will be a minimum of overlapping in new industrial project developments and a maximisation of investment capital utilisation.

While the declaration of governmental policies is a necessity to ensure that investors' interests are sensibly secure, investors often require more tangible demonstration of the validity of these policies. Approximately two years ago the Small Enterprises Development Co. Ltd (SEDCO) was founded to give practical aid for the establishment of industrial, commercial and service industries wholly or mainly owned and managed by Swaziland citizens. There was a need to demonstrate to non-Swazi investors that the country's own citizens were capable of management. Furthermore, it was realised that potential large-scale investors needed to ensure that their projects would not be fraught with problems due to the lack of ancillary producers of their minor needs, or the absence of repair and maintenance services. SEDCO has already helped to establish nearly 100 small enterprises in the manufacturing and service industries sectors; it already operates three specialised industrial estates; and it has grown to the stage of employing more than 100 persons. Although many of the small enterprises were established with less than R1,000 in capital, there is at least one example of a so-called small industry where the capital investment is nearly R250,000.

Another organisation which has been set up to extend a hand of welcome and friendship to non-Swazi investors is the National Industrial Development Corporation (N.I.D.C.S.). It has a majority government holding, but it also has substantial support from the private capital market. Although N.I.D.C.S. commenced its activities only six months ago (September 1971), it has already participated in the establishment of eight new factories, and it is confident of being able to assist another 15–20 medium- and large-scale business ventures before the end of 1972, in conjunction with investors from outside Swaziland.

As indicated above, it is impossible to give more than the barest outline of Swaziland's potential and intentions for investment and international trade development. There is much more which could be told about the present very healthy state of Swaziland's economy and its enormous future prospects. However, it is hoped that this is sufficient to show that in Swaziland the policies and intentions are very clearly directed to ensure that the resources are developed to the full.

While the focus of attention may be on the creation of a greater level of industrial activity, in order to serve Swaziland's needs for an enhanced measure of modern-sector development, the outlook is by no means wholly introspective. Constant attention has been paid to international attitudes towards investments

in the developing countries, and there is awareness of the reper-
cussive effects upon the country of the changing motives of both
public and private investors in the international scene.

In the late 1950s and early 1960s there was a considerable
amount of investment by the developed countries in the newly
emergent and less wealthy countries of Asia, Africa and Latin
America. This was inspired by a sense of moral obligation on the
part of the more affluent nations towards those nations which had
formerly been their colonies and dependants. Unfortunately this
investment, which was often quite incorrectly called 'aid', was
made without any sensible reference to the actual needs of the
recipient country. In consequence the resources of the recipient
countries were depleted rather than enhanced, and the only
beneficiaries were the investors themselves. The gap between the
economic affluence of the developed countries and the economic
poverty of the lesser advanced countries was thus further aggravated.

Over the past seven or eight years there has been a swing
towards investments by the European nations and the United
States in the developing countries on a more rational basis, and
the situation has shown a marked improvement. Furthermore,
Japan has joined the coterie of overseas investors seeking and
finding investment opportunities in lesser developed countries.
Investors in the United States, the European countries and, to
some extent, Japan are now being persuaded to seek out investment opportunities in the developing countries for a number of
reasons. Firstly, the shortages of manpower within their own
countries, combined with the ever-increasing demands from their
workers for higher remuneration, make it sensible for them to
utilise the superfluities of cheaper labour in the developing countries. Secondly, the unrest among their indigenous labour forces
and the possibilities of strikes and recessions make it economically
unsafe and unwise to concentrate total production in one area
only. Diversification of investments over a number of countries is
a buffer against any complete shutdown. Thirdly, the rapidly
growing buying power within the developing countries makes it
feasible and viable to establish industries in trade countries instead
of, as before, supplying these markets from abroad. Fourthly, the
higher shipping freight charges and other shipping problems, such
as the closure of the Suez Canal, have added to the attraction of

industrial investment in the developing countries which are accessible to markets formerly served by shipments from Europe, America and Japan. Finally, many European and American investors are becoming so plagued by the activities of environmentalists, who secure bans upon new industrial developments because of their potential in adding to pollution problems, that those investors are seeking venues for their projects where they are less harassed in this direction.

This move towards a much greater level of international investment co-partnership cannot be other than to the good of the whole world. The investment, on sound business grounds rather than for reasons of transient charity or moral obligations, by investors of those countries which have an abundance of capital resources and high technical skills, must tend towards a lessening of the distinction between 'haves' and 'have nots' among the nations of the world. As this happens, the envies and jealousies of the lesser developed nations will diminish, and as industrialisation grows in the developing countries the great masses of unemployed and underemployed will start to disappear. As these things happen, peace in our time becomes that much more secure, and the world becomes a happier place for all of us wherever we may be situated.

Botswana Nickel–Copper: A Case Study in Private Investment's Contribution to Economic Development

F. TAYLOR OSTRANDER

On 7 March 1972, at a legal 'closing ceremony' in Gaborone, the capital of Botswana, the Selebi–Pikwe mining project was formally launched, together with its related infrastructure of electric power, water supply, township, roads, rail connection, etc.

The closing ceremony in Gaborone was a grandiose legal exercise on a multi-national scale. There were lawyers from three continents reflecting six different systems of law; there were lawyers and other officials from the lending agencies of four governments, lawyers and other officials of the Botswana government and of a variety of new Botswana public authorities, lawyers and other representatives of a major overseas metal company, two major multi-national mining finance companies and several smaller mining or investment companies; the interests of about 50,000 smaller investors in the financial communities of New York, London and Johannesburg were also represented. Altogether sixty-five men sat down in Gaborone to sign or act upon the forty-three interrelated legal agreements that became effective simultaneously at 12.15 on 7 March.

Anyone who has been to Gaborone can imagine the logistical problems of transporting this assembly of lawyers, company directors and government officials – and their papers and documents – to that tiny town, and housing them there. What is less obvious, but of even greater wonder, was the complexity of the arrangements represented by those forty-three interrelated legal documents.

Behind all this activity lay four years of involved negotiation of the terms of the deal and its financing, against a background of metallurgical and economic feasibility study, and behind that lay another twelve years during which the basic concession agreement was negotiated, nine successive annual exploration programmes were pursued and, finally, minerals successfully discovered.

Sir Ronald L. Prain, the chairman of the Botswana companies that are undertaking this mineral development, said at the banquet after the closing ceremony:

> By any reckoning this is an historic occasion. It marks the culmination of sixteen years of discussion, scientific endeavour, negotiation and the creation of an international financial structure which can have few, if any, parallels in complexity and scope. It marks the beginning of a mining enterprise which will have a profound effect on the economy of this nation and its place among the developing countries of Africa.

The Selebi–Pikwe mining enterprise is one of the major recent instances of private capital undertaking the risk of large-scale mineral development in a less developed country. The scale of this project is large by any standards – for the less developed or the developed world. Botswana is certainly one of the poorest and least developed of all the countries of Africa, or indeed of the whole developing world, with a national income of about $100 (R75) per capita in 1969.

Before the production of refined nickel and copper begins in early 1974, a total investment will have to be made of about R160 million. This figure does not include the investment that the writer's company, American Metal Climax Inc. (AMAX), will make in the United States in providing refining capacity to produce the refined nickel and copper from the matte shipped from the project's smelter in Pikwe.

When we consider that Botswana's gross domestic product in 1969 was only about R48 million, one can appreciate the impact that this single project is destined to have on the economy of a country that despite its size (about that of France) has a population of only some 625,000 persons. Indeed, only some 100,000 Batswana are gainfully employed as wage-earners, and nearly two-thirds of these work outside Botswana in the mines, industry and services of South Africa. In 1970 Botswana's total exports of goods were only R16 million, and the major part of that was meat and livestock products, the principal products of Botswana's predominantly pastoral economy.

When AMAX first began to be interested in this project, we had a very different concept of its potential size, though we were no less conscious of its potential impact on the Botswana economy. In a speech in New York in November 1967, AMAX's chairman said:

> . . . investment invariably has a leveraged impact on the economy of the country in which it is made and the less developed the country, the greater the leverage which results. For example, a $20 million raw material project in Botswana would have a major, indeed a revolutionary, effect on the tempo of development in that country.

Today that $20 million (R14 million) has grown to $205 million (R160 million). Its impact on the economy of Botswana and the prospects for economic development will be immensely greater than we then anticipated.

This essay will briefly describe the project, its financing and scope, and add a touch of history. It will then discuss more fully its probable development impact on Botswana, its relationship to the regional economy of Southern Africa and a few related matters.

Two private companies registered in Botswana are involved: Bamangwato Concessions Ltd., and Botswana R.S.T. Ltd. We refer to them as B.C.L. and B.R.S.T. B.C.L. was the company formed back in 1959 to conduct exploration in the entire 45,000 sq.-mile territory of the Bamangwato tribe. This was under the terms of a ten-year exclusive prospecting concession negotiated between the tribe and Rhodesian Selection Trust (later named Roan Selection Trust), called R.S.T., which was then a major copper producer in Northern Rhodesia (later Zambia). In this negotiation the Bamangwato Tribal Authority was represented by the late Chief Tshekedi Khama, then regent of the tribe and uncle of the then recently deposed hereditary chief, Seretse Khama.

Largely because of the interest of the British Commonwealth Relations Office in ensuring the essential fairness of the concession terms being granted by the Tribal Authority, and the interest of the British Parliament, these negotiations extended over a period of three years, from 1956 to 1959.

Tragically, Tshekedi Khama died at about the time of the signature of the concession agreement on 2 June 1959. Other members of the Tribal Authority, including Seretse Khama, signed for the tribe, and Sir Ronald Prain signed for R.S.T.

The relationship between Sir Ronald Prain and his associates and Tshekedi Khama and his associates was from the beginning one of mutual respect and trust. While there may have been differences in the amount of prior experience at this type of negotiation, the two sides met as man to man in honest discussion. This has been true of our relationship with the Batswana ever since. Fortunately, as businessmen and mining executives, lawyers and economists, we had neither the time nor the inclination to enter into elaborate analyses of the differentiations between our separate 'élitisms', or to make the elaborate probings of personal relationships and animosities so beloved by sociologists. It always seemed apparent to our side that the Batswana had essentially the same incentives and goals as we, and used the same essential techniques of discourse and negotiation. As Sir Ronald Prain put it at the banquet in March 1972, 'both sides were inspired by a common purpose in Africa'.

To return to the Selebi–Pikwe nickel–copper project, it is not necessary to describe the intervening years of exploration, or the four years spent searching for means of financing its development, ensuring markets for its products, and negotiating the underlying tax agreements, master agreement, loan agreements, etc. It is enough to say that geochemical anomalies indicating nickel–copper mineralisation were found at Selebi in late 1963 and at Pike in 1965. In February 1967 – less than six months after Botswana's independence – B.C.L. was able to announce publicly that some 30 million tons of nickel–copper ore had been found. It took five years from then to complete the financing, marketing and all other arrangements for the project.

When production begins in 1974 it will have been eleven years from the first mineral indication, fifteen years from the beginning of exploration and eighteen years from the first discussions with Tshekedi Khama. This is a not unusual time-scope for modern mineral development – a point that needs underlining in any discussion of the pace and financing of modern mineral development and its role in the less developed countries.

By early 1968 about R2 million had been spent on exploration.

By the end of 1970, after more adequate defining of the extent of the Selebi– Pikwe ore bodies and bringing ore reserves up to 43 million tons of proven and probable ore, and making the necessary metallurgical and feasibility studies, R7 million had been spent – risked, that is – in this entirely preparatory work. By the time of the closing ceremony about R35 million had already been spent on construction of the mine and plant and other pre-production expenses. This sum had been put at risk by the company and its major shareholders without any sure knowledge that the deal and its financing would be successfully consummated. As indicated above, by the time the project is completed and production is fully under way, when the first sales are made and income finally begins to be realised in 1974, the shareholders will have put their money at risk over an extended period of years and supported a total project outlay of R107 million.

Until the project is successfully operating, this entire sum will be at risk by the private shareholders, including the many small investors to the extent of the cost of their shares, and the two major corporate shareholders to the extent of their equity investment, *plus* their nearly R90 million of completion guarantees to the lenders. Completion guarantees mean that until the project is fully completed and operating satisfactorily, the major guaranteeing shareholders are obligated to the lenders for the entire amount advanced; after such completion, the lenders must look to the project itself for their security.

This is what is meant by risk-taking, and it is this kind of risk-taking by private capital and private investors which authenticates the profits that one hopes will flow from the project over the twenty-three years of its currently estimated life.

There is no need for a full description of the changes in the corporate ownership of the two private companies over the years and of the intricate corporate reorganisation that was carried out earlier this year. Only a few points need be mentioned for our purposes: Botswana R.S.T. Ltd was formed in mid-1967 to hold R.S.T.'s interest in the new discoveries announced earlier that year (R.S.T. was then a Zambian company). In April 1968 Botswana R.S.T. raised $6 million (R4·3 million) capital by a rights issue offered to R.S.T. shareholders. AMAX has for many years had a 43·3 per cent interest in R.S.T. shares, and by subscribing to our rights in this issue AMAX became equal partner with R.S.T., each owning 30 per cent of Botswana R.S.T.; thousands of small outside investors, mostly R.S.T. shareholders, then came to own 40 per cent of Botswana R.S.T. Although it is a complication, one other point requires mention: Botswana R.S.T. owned 61 per cent of Bamangwato Concessions Ltd, and three other corporate investors who had participated in the early exploration held the balance of 39 per cent. These were Mineral Separation Ltd (23 per cent), Anglo-American Corporation of S.A. Ltd (11 per cent) and International Nickel Company (5 per cent). INCO's small interest, by the way, was subsequently purchased by Anglo-American.

Now, with the successful launching of the Selebi–Pikwe project in March 1972, Botswana R.S.T. plans a second rights issue to raise nearly R20 million of further equity capital from its shareholders. After this rights issue, and taking into account the rather complex corporate reorganisation carried out in January of this year, which became effective on 7 March, Botswana R.S.T. will then be owned 30 per cent each by AMAX and by Anglo-American,the latter jointly with its associated company in England, Charter Consolidated Ltd, and certain of their affiliated and associated companies; and 40 per cent by the investing public, including Mineral Separation's residual 6 per cent interest. AMAX and Anglo-American with its associates as the two major shareholders will share 50:50 in the huge completion guarantees undertaken to the lenders.

The reorganised B.C.L. is now owned 85 per cent by Botswana R.S.T., and the remainder is the Botswana government's free 15 per cent ownership of the Selebi–Pikwe project as provided for in the original concession agreement of 1959, these shares having been issued on 7 March when B.C.L. formally reconstituted itself in a mining company and received a mining lease from the government.

The writer and his colleagues at AMAX have particularly welcomed our new association with Anglo-American and we greatly appreciate both the spirit and the high technical skills that Anglo-American brings to this project.

Finally, it seems best to resist the temptation to describe the successive ordeals that were faced by all the participants during the past three or four years of negotiations, the setbacks and the recurrent dangers of a possible collapse of the entire deal. H. E.

the President of Botswana, Sir Seretse Khama, at the closing ceremony banquet referred to this aspect of the project as having been 'something of a cliff-hanger . . . it had us sitting on the edge of our chairs at times'. We at AMAX, and our associates at Anglo-American, became almost accustomed to sitting on the edge of our chairs. We had large outlays of money and years of future profits at stake. The Botswana government had at stake the king-pin of their entire developmental hopes and prospects.

The last of these perils of delay or collapse occurred only three or four working days before the closing ceremony, after lawyers had begun to assemble in Johannesburg and Gaborone to exchange and authenticate their documents. Botswana's Vice-President, who is also Minister of Finance and Development, rushed to Bonn, as did also various representatives of AMAX, and with only one working day and one weekend before the closing they managed to settle what had seemed to the major German lenders and the West German government as an insuperable obstacle – though it was only another of the myriad of legalisms that has to be dealt with in a project of this size and complexity.

Let me now describe the Selebi–Pikwe mining enterprise as it will look in two or three years, when it is finally in full operation.

It will include the mine at Pikwe and an ore body at nearby Selebi awaiting further development in 1979. On the basis of present knowledge, the ore reserves will be sufficient for twenty-three years' production, until 1996, at an annual production rate of 2 million tons of ore. After crushing, grinding and concentrating, this ore will be treated in the huge new smelter at Pikwe which will be one of the largest and most complex industrial installations on this continent, where 45,000 tons per year of a nickel–copper matte and about 125,000 tons per year of by-product elemental sulphur will be produced. This matte will then be shipped to the AMAX refinery on the Mississippi river below New Orleans, where it will be toll refined (that is, treated without passing into our ownership). The resulting refined nickel and copper, some 15,000 to 17,000 metric tons per annum *of each*, will then be shipped back to West Germany, where for the first fifteen years of production a large metal firm, Metallgesellschaft, will sell, backed by AMAX, about 55 per cent of the nickel and all the copper. The remaining nickel will be sold in West Germany for the account of B.C.L. itself. The sulphur will be marketed in South Africa; already about two-thirds of the sulphur is under long-term contract to Triomf Fertiliser (Pty) Ltd, in South Africa.

Loan finance for the private mining enterprise will come from two principal sources. Approximately R52 million will be loaned by an investment bank owned by the West German government and an associated consortium of German commercial banks, 90 per cent of this loan being insured against political risks by the Bonn government. This loan is to be repaid in the ten years after 1977, and the effective interest rate will be $9\frac{3}{4}$ per cent. Obviously, this major finance from official sources in West Germany is related to the fact that B.C.L.'s entire output of metals will be available to the West German economy for a period of fifteen years.

The remainder of the principal loan finance to the private enterprise will be a R13·5 million loan from the Industrial Development Corporation of South Africa, also an official investment bank of the Republic of South Africa. This loan is repayable in ten years after 1974 and is at the gratifying interest rate of $6\frac{1}{2}$ per cent. This loan will be insured by another agency of the Republic, the C.G.I.C., which insures export credits. Until this loan is effective upon completion of the project, Union Acceptances Ltd, a South African merchant bank affiliated with Anglo-American, will provide the bridging finance. Again, as in the West German case, there was a reason for this loan: it was extended on condition that the South African content of capital goods, works and services provided to B.C.L. on the insured contract totals at least R13·5 million.

Of course, in addition to these major loans, Botswana R.S.T.'s primary risk of R36 million is taken by its shareholders, and particularly by AMAX and Anglo-American as described above. These two major shareholders are also to provide such additional funds above present cost estimates as may be needed to bring the project to completion and successful operation.

Infrastructure for the Selebi–Pikwe project costing R53·5 million for the electric power, water, township, roads, etc., 'is to be provided by the Government of Botswana' – as the press releases state. This is, indeed, the way the project has been arranged, but it seems essential to point out in this case study on the role of private investment in development that practically none of the capital being loaned to the Botswana government for the purpose of constructing this infrastructure would have been made available to it, if it were not for the existence of the private mining enterprise.

In addition, the mining enterprise (B.C.L.) has undertaken long-term 'take or pay' contracts for power, water, etc., which will provide the means of servicing the loans made to the government. B.C.L. will be obligated to pay the total amount of these charges for power, water and township services for the entire life of the mine, even if the mine should not come into successful operation. Without this undertaking from the private side, the Botswana government could not have borrowed this money either in the case of the 'hard loan' finance, the World Bank's R24 million loan, or in the case of the 'soft loan' finance, the Canadian and United States governments' fifty- and forty-year loans of R22.5 million and R4.9 million, respectively, at little or no interest. Finally, in the case of the World Bank loan, AMAX and Anglo-American, and Metallgesellschaft for the first fifteen years, have had to guarantee the World Bank to repay the loan over its full term of twenty-three years.

It is understood that usually the World Bank prefers to extend loans providing infrastructure for private industrial projects directly to the private company. Such loans would also be guaranteed, of course, by the host government in accordance with the World Bank's basic charter. In the Botswana case and in at least one other case, the Boké aluminium project in Guinea, the World Bank has been prepared to waive its usual procedure and to make its loans in support of a private mineral enterprise to the government, but only when guaranteed by both the government and the private enterprise.

The Botswana government put great emphasis on being responsible for the Shashi power, water and township, even though their size, scope and purpose were tailored almost solely to the Selebi–Pikwe mining project. This is because the government hopes that this industrial development in the Shashi area will lead the way to, and provide a base for, additional development there. The new Power and Water and Township Authorities will be functioning and ready to take on additional business.

Before going on to the basic economic development implications of the Selebi–Pikwe and Shashi projects, one or two further comments are appropriate. It has become an axiom of U.S.

government and international development agencies that projects involving investment from several national sources are to be preferred to projects having a single national source of finance. Bradford Mills, president of the U.S. Overseas Private Investment Corporation (O.P.I.C.) that insures U.S. investments in developing countries against political risks, recently stated that O.P.I.C.'s policy on natural resource ventures is to 'insist upon multi-national participation'. 'We'll insure the American portion', he said. (Incidentally, O.P.I.C. has approved insurance on the investment being made in B.R.S.T., by AMAX and by the public U.S. investors.) The Selebi–Pikwe enterprise certainly meets this test. It has few parallels in multi-national complexity.

One must wonder, though, whether the added complications, the need to adapt to differing legal systems, the multiplicity of parties to the negotiation, even the added travel costs to multiple centres of negotiation, etc., do not add an unduly heavy cost, particularly in the case of small countries. One would hesitate to compute this 'added cost of multiplicity of parties' in the Selebi–Pikwe project as a percentage of a normal year's recurrent budget of Botswana!

On the other hand, there are advantages and protections in this 'multi-ethnic' origin of investment capital, be it loan or equity. The finger of nationalistic anger or political animosity is not as apt to be pointed in several directions at once, as it is at a single-nationality investor. An action of discrimination or even expropriation is less likely to occur when it would damage a country's credit-worthiness in a number of countries at once. The assurance given by multi-national sources of finance is only one of the protections for the outside investor that has been built into the structure of the Selebi–Pikwe deal.

It is generally believed that the participation of the World Bank in a project makes the project far less vulnerable to arbitrary action than if only private investors are involved. There seems good reason to accept this point, especially when a borrowing government has agreed, as Botswana has, to submit any major disputes with the investor to arbitration by the new World Bank-sponsored International Centre for the Settlement of Investment Disputes (I.C.S.I.D.). Any serious contravention of such arbitration, or any unjustified tampering with the underlying security of the World Bank loan, would certainly jeopardise a government's access to further World Bank credit. The importance of this 'sanction' is emphasised in the recent action of the U.S. Congress requiring the U.S. member of the World Bank Board (whose vote is weighted by the proportion of U.S. participation to total World Bank resources) to vote against any further loans to any country that has expropriated U.S. property without making prompt and adequate compensation.

It would be hard to conceive of a major new private project being negotiated against a less favourable world background than the Botswana project. The past five years have seen a worldwide wave of nationalisations of foreign-owned mining enterprises. There was the nationalisation of the Zaïre copper industry, the required 51 per cent sale of the Zambian copper industry to the government – although both these different cases worked out in the end with an accepted compromise between the former owners and the governments. Then there were the flagrant cases of expropriation in Bolivia, Peru and Chile, and some elsewhere. All these developments did not enhance the investment climate in which B.R.S.T.–B.C.L. and the Botswana government sought major new finance. At the same time, the world capital markets went through several waves of unprecedented capital stringency, and as a result interest rates rose to levels seldom previously known. That the Botswana nickel–copper project could be financed at all in the face of these external conditions is a tribute to perseverance and to an unusual degree of concern for a successful outcome on the part of all the participants.

It will be noted that the basic loan finance for the private mining enterprise comes from the official agencies of the German and South African governments, each of which had specific reasons for making these loans. It may also be noted that the interest rates charged, even the $9\frac{3}{4}$ per cent on the German loan, are essentially sub-economic rates of interest; they are not what private investment banks would have charged this project, in its situation, in recent market conditions and in the light of related developments in other natural resource enterprises.

Now let us try to assess the impact of the Selebi–Pikwe project on Botswana's future economic development. Here we enter the realm of forecasting the results of metal prices, market conditions, costs, labour relations, natural and political events – and great caution must be exercised. We can estimate with some assurance that the nickel, copper and sulphur produced by B.C.L. will at present metal prices have a total sales value of approximately R50 million in a full year. If nothing changes, gross sales revenue over the twenty-three-year life of the mine would be just over R1,000 million!

Botswana's total exports in 1970 amounted to some R16 million, already a new record. We can roughly estimate that Selebi–Pikwe matte, not yet carrying the full sales value of the finished metals, may increase Botswana's exports by about two and a half times their present level.

The Botswana government's direct return from Selebi–Pikwe will consist of a mineral royalty of 7·5 per cent of gross profit, a 40 per cent corporate income tax of residual gross profits, fixed under Botswana law for twenty-five years from the time production begins, and, finally, the dividend received by the government on its 15 per cent equity ownership of B.C.L. for which it made no outlay.

It is not appropriate at this time to estimate what gross profits on a mining project like the Selebi–Pikwe project will be after taking into account operating expenses, interest and other charges. This would be the source from which royalty, income tax and dividends would be paid and, of course, the loan principal repaid.

In the case of De Beers' large but low-grade new diamond mine at Orapa, which began production in 1971, it has been announced that the project's gross profits will be shared roughly 50:50 between the Botswana government and the shareholders. Possibly a similar ratio may be expected over the life of the Selebi–Pikwe project.

Under the British-inspired system of recapturing all capital expenditure before income tax becomes fully payable, the full tax return to the Botswana government may not begin for nearly ten years. Government's 15 per cent share of net profits will be higher in the earlier stages, but net profits will be used to repay debt during the early years. The Botswana National Development Plan for 1970–5 estimates that the tax and royalty return to the budget from mining might rise to about R8–R10 million per year after 1980, but will be only about R3.5 million in 1974–1975. (These figures include revenues from De Beers' diamond mine at Orapa.) This would represent about 20 per cent of estimated recurrent revenue and expenditure for the 1971–2 fiscal year, excluding British budgetary support. One thing that appears certain is that even the first year of rising revenues from mining will enable Botswana to end its dependence on British government grants and loans, and to achieve budgetary self-sufficiency.

An important immediate impact will flow from customs revenues under the revised customs union agreement, especially during the construction years, owing to heavy imports of mining equipment. Revenue transfers under the customs union agreement attributed to the Selebi–Pikwe and Shashi projects alone are estimated at R17·5 million during the four years 1971–2 to 1974–5. After construction, the customs revenue impact of the project is estimated to fall back to an annual rate of R1·5 million.

Indirect effects of the project will of course be much greater than the direct effects, and will begin to influence revenues and the economy even during the construction period. Indeed, the impact of the construction on the Botswana economy will be major. Already there are 50 per cent more men at work constructing the project than the anticipated normal employment of nearly 2,000 after operations begin. It is anticipated that the secondary and 'ripple' effects of the project will add another 3,000 or so jobs by 1980. This may well represent a significant underestimation of the profound effects which the Selebi–Pikwe project will have on employment in Botswana.

It is estimated that Botswana's gross domestic product, as computed for 1968–9, would have increased by 50 per cent if Selebi–Pikwe had been in operation in that year. This measures direct impact only, and it would not be diffcult to estimate that G.D.P. in 1974–5 will be influenced to a similar degree by the total impact of the project.

The Shashi electric power station is to be fired with Botswana coal and waste heat from the B.C.L. flash-smelting and sulphur-recovery process. The use of Botswana coal will be one immediate development consequence of the Selebi–Pikwe project, for Botswana coal deposits have never before been opened or utilised. An affiliate of Anglo-American will open a coal mine at Moropule, about 65 miles from the project. The cost of this coal will be greater, because of the small scale of the operation and quality factors, than the cost of imported coal that would be available from existing higher-grade coal mines outside its borders. In addition, the power station is being constructed on a scale that is more than ample for the needs of the Selebi–Pikwe project. There will be 60 MW of installed capacity, including 25 per cent stand-by equipment.

As a result of using Botswana coal and providing this extra capacity for potential future industrial or mining growth in the area, the cost of power to B.C.L. will be significantly higher than otherwise. In fact, B.C.L. will pay nearly double the cost of power to the mining industry in the Copperbelt in Zambia. A part of this extra cost could be considered as a form of developmental tax on B.C.L. for the benefit of Botswana's general economic development.

In employment policy Botswana's long-run aim is to provide for full localised employment as early as practicable. B.C.L. has agreed with the government to seek to achieve full localisation by 1990, and meanwhile to conduct training programmes and reduce the relatively low degree of present expatriate employment to the extent possible.

It is well known that Botswana is closely integrated with the broader regional economy of South Africa and also Rhodesia and Mozambique. In addition to the common currency unit, the importance of the revised customs union agreement has been noted above. Transport links to the outside world, supplies of modern equipment, technical skills and services, an outlet for its products and for its surplus labour, are all factors in this regional economy pattern. The Selebi–Pikwe project reflects all of these: its matte will be transported to the coast via Rhodesia and Mozambique or South Africa; a considerable portion of the mining equipment and most of the construction services will be obtained in South Africa, which will also provide a market outlet for the by-product sulphur output; B.C.L. will particularly benefit from what has been described as, in effect, a single regional market for technically skilled manpower and specialised services. On the other hand, the rapidly accelerating Botswana economic development resulting from the Selebi–Pikwe and Shashi development will also exert an upward pull on economic activity in the Southern African region as a whole. The project will of course also greatly increase Botswana's economic links with the outside world, especially in North America and Europe.

There has been a great deal of discussion in development

economics in recent years of the so-called 'enclave' aspect of foreign private investment in large mineral projects in less developed countries. It has been argued that these enclaves are virtually isolated from significant economic impact on the local economies. Those who have seen the Copperbelt mining industry transform Northern Rhodesia and Zambia during the past forty years, or who consider the wide developmental impact which revenues derived from the copper industry are having today in Zambia, know that this is a false argument, often originating in a doctrinaire dislike of such private investment. Recently the United Nations Secretariat has begun to take a more realistic line and has officially acknowledged that investment in mining in a less developed country can be a prime engine of economic development.

As Sir Ronald Prain said in his statement at the banquet in Gaborone in March 1972, 'history is full of instances of a mining industry revolutionising the prospects for a country in far quicker time than can be achieved by any other type of industry'. He stated his belief that Botswana will prove to be a classic case of this and that the Selebi–Pikwe project would increase employment, gross national product, exports and balance of payments, 'to a greater extent in percentage terms than in comparable mining industry in any other developing country I know'.

But we must also heed the concluding remarks of H. E. President Khama at the banquet celebrating the opening, as well as the 'closing', of the Selebi–Pikwe and Shashi projects. He said: '. . . let none of us underestimate the magnitude of the social and political challenge which we face. All of us are familiar with the problems – economic, social and political – that can be created by a dual economy, by islands of industry and urbanisation in a largely agricultural and pastoral environment.' 'We are devising policies', he said, 'to tackle these problems.' Finally, referring to the need for mutual understanding in the development of this new mining community, he said: 'We are faced with a challenge and an opportunity – an opportunity to demonstrate that people of different racial and cultural backgrounds can work together and live together in harmony.'

That is certainly our goal, as we on the side of the mining enterprise proceed into the completion and operation of this project.

COMMENT

Arthur Kemp

Professor Kemp expressed his appreciation of the value of these two concrete and complex illustrations of the themes of the Conference, and noted the complementarity of the papers. Clearly, Mr Nxumalo's paper constituted a sincere invitation to potential investors to open discussions and negotiations which might lead to subsequent investment in Swaziland. But, Professor Kemp noted, potential investors who were about to enter into such negotiations should not suppose that these were likely to be either simple, short-lived or inexpensive. Indeed, Mr Ostrander's paper supplied the details of the effort, the day-to-day triumphs and disappointments, the infinity of problems both large and small, the exasperation – all of which were apparently unavoidable and necessary prerequisites not only to the discussions and negotiations, but also, in extended and expensive form, to the successful completion of the specific investment project itself. Even this was not the end, but the beginning; for no project could be successful unless it was regarded as such by the investors themselves.

Professor Kemp referred specifically to that part of Mr Ostrander's paper in which he described the multiplicity of interest rates on the various funds employed in the Selebi–Pikwe project. In Professor Kemp's opinion, this provided supporting empirical evidence of the decidedly imperfect market for capital funds employed in such projects, and also suggested that both the capital-importing country and the investors would greatly benefit from improved institutional, legal and economic arrangements leading to freer and broader capital markets.

Chapter 11

The Forms of Development Assistance

Some Aspects of the Role of Private Financial Institutions in Economic Development

W. H. BEATTY

This essay will identify some types of private financial institutions engaged in development finance and will discuss their functions.

First, a bit of history. A Senator by the name of Edge from the state of New Jersey in the writer's country, the United States of America, introduced legislation in 1919 which has been amended subsequently from time to time to permit commercial banks which are members of the Federal Reserve System to establish two kinds of wholly-owned subsidiaries for the purpose of making equity investments in enterprise abroad – one type in non-banking enterprise and the other in banking. Many of the important international banking institutions in the United States, some on the Eastern seaboard, generally centred around New York, some centred around Chicago, and those in the Far West centred around San Francisco and Los Angeles, have availed themselves of this permissive legislation and the related regulations of the various regulatory authorities by doing the following:

(a) establishing international investment corporations; or
(b) overseas banking corporations; or
(c) both.

The international investment corporations are capitalised and organised to take equity positions in and make loans to industrial and agricultural projects; and the overseas banking corporations are capitalised and organised to own shares in foreign commercial banking institutions.

Today, one or more American international banking institutions are identified and have a presence directly or indirectly in all of French-speaking Africa and in all of English-speaking Africa south of the Sahara, through either an international investment corporation or a commercial banking corporation or both. This includes the Republic of South Africa, Botswana, Lesotho and Swaziland. The development of these kinds of presences by American institutions in Africa has taken place largely since the Second World War and was accelerated during the proliferation of independence that took place largely in the 1960s. The operations of these corporations have made significant contributions to economic development in a number of countries in developing Black Africa. They can be expected to continue to do so increasingly in the future.

Here are some examples of the kinds of projects that have been sponsored or co-sponsored and invested in, including long-term capital lending, by a number of international investment corporations of American commercial banks:

1. Hotel, iron-ore mining and pelletising, and a national development corporation in the Republic of Liberia.
2. A national development bank in the Republic of the Ivory Coast.
3. In the Federation of Nigeria, a textile mill, a national development bank and a timber–plywood operation.
4. In Kenya, a complex of lodges for tourists on game-viewing and photographic safaris.

Some of these enterprises have been spectacularly successful, some have been only modestly successful, some are marginal so far and one has to date not been successful owing to the effects of a civil war. But even the latter is being reconstituted with good prospects. The criteria applied for success in the above context are earnings, profitability and dividends accruing to the shareholders.

From the standpoint of some other criteria, all the projects have been successful in that:

1. They have provided employment and have accomplished the effective training of Africans in a whole range of technical and managerial skills.
2. They have fulfilled a need for the country in general and for the community in particular where the project is located.

For example, a modern hotel in the capital city of a developing country is virtually a prerequisite for those elements of economic development depending upon foreign investment and trade.

The elements and ingredients that form the basis for these projects run along the following lines:

(a) The American overseas investment corporation takes a substantial equity in the enterprise, frequently tied in with a long-term loan.

(b) A technically competent operating partner who is also a substantial equity investor is a key factor. It is important that this partner have a stake in the success of the enterprise.

(c) A local partner or partners from government entities or from the private sector in the host country. For example, in some instances a national or regional development corporation or a national development bank is the vehicle for providing local equity participation.

(d) Frequently, the International Finance Corporation of the World Bank joins the enterprise as a shareholder; also, frequently, the facilities of the Export-Import Bank of Washington are called upon to finance the U.S. capital-goods content of the project.

(e) There have been occasions when the overseas development corporations of British banks operating in Africa have participated with American-sponsored projects in providing at least a portion of the longer-term capital loan requirements.

Most successful projects have been done without hard-and-fast requirements for percentages of stock ownership. The important element is that there be a meeting of the minds at the beginning as to who does what – who manages and who controls. Under these circumstances, a minority shareholder can in fact functionally not only manage but control the enterprise. For most overseas investment corporations it is a doctrine that the majority shareholder in an enterprise should not be a government or government entity.

One of the important things is that the sponsoring financial institution be represented on the board and in management where their financial skills and financial managerial know-how and counselling can be fully brought to bear upon the day-to-day running of the enterprise. Another important requirement is that there be complete rapport, co-operation, mutual understanding and mutual respect between all parties involved – that government gives its blessing and creates an appropriate climate in which the enterprise operates.

There have been a number of industrial projects in recent years in Africa and other places in the developing world where the above ingredients have produced a profitable enterprise to the stockholders, where debt has been retired in an orderly manner, where employment has been provided, successful training of local people has been accomplished and where the product produced has wide acceptance and growing demand in the community, and in some instances abroad, in which case foreign exchange earnings have been generated.

It is the philosophy of several overseas investment corporations that in such enterprises the shares in foreign hands are eventually to be sold to local private interests – this to provide by example what benefits can be derived by permitting the private sector to make a contribution to economic development. It is believed that this is a worth-while and constructive type of activity that enhances the trade, financial, economic, cultural and social relationships between the host country and the nations of the various investing, lending, and operating and managerial participants on a mutually profitable and beneficial basis, with emphasis on mutuality.

The multi-national character of some of these enterprises should be stressed. In the case of the Liberian Development Corporation, for example, there are involved:

1. Four U.S. commercial banks through their overseas investment corporations.
2. A German development organisation.
3. An indigenous Liberian commercial bank; and
4. The Liberian government.

In the case of the Ivory Coast Development Bank, you have:

1. Several U.S. commercial banks through their overseas investment corporations.

2. Several French commercial banks.
3. One U.S. commercial bank through its affiliation with a French commercial bank which has a branch system in every French-speaking country.
4. A U.S. investment bank.
5. A French investment bank.
6. The Ivory Coast government.
7. A line of credit available under certain circumstances from the foreign aid programme of the United States.
8. The general manager, in the beginning, being a Western European specialist in financing overseas projects. The present general manager is an Ivorian.

In the case of a textile mill in Nigeria, the participants are:

1. A Swiss-Italian technical partner whose manager is from Greece.
2. An overseas investment corporation of a U.S. commercial bank.
3. A Nigerian regional government development corporation.
4. A British commercial bank, which provides local financing.
5. Recently, a significant portion of the shares was offered in the markets in Lagos after eight years of operation.

The development corporations of British overseas banks have already been mentioned. The history of these corporations since the end of the Second World War is filled with examples of effective direct development finance in Africa. One British bank's overseas development corporation has financed 1,300 projects over a twenty-year period. Some 28 per cent of its commitments have been in industrial projects, 15 per cent in agriculture and forestry, 18 per cent in commerce, 20 per cent in building developments and 19 per cent in public works.

Broadly speaking, the overseas development corporations of British banks do not take equity, confining themselves generally to lending to the enterprise at tenors between around three years to twelve years. I believe their charters do not preclude the equity route and in the future they may make use of this feature.

Another important private-sector institution is SIFIDA. This organisation, the Société Internationale Financière pour les

Investissements et les Développements en Afrique, is a multi-national finance company for the shareholders from fourteen different countries in the industrialised world. They come from Western Europe, from the United States and Canada, from Japan and Australia. Some sixty of these shareholders are banking and finance houses, while the remainder are industrial and commercial undertakings. SIFIDA was established last year with its head office in Geneva. It has a paid-in capital to date of about $25 million equivalent.

The purpose of SIFIDA is to identify, evaluate, promote and finance viable projects in the industrial and 'agro-business' sectors of the economies of any or all of the independent and developing states of Africa. It will have a strong nucleus of consultants capable of injecting business acumen and methods into this task; and it will be well placed, through its many shareholders all over the world, to bring in specialised consultants to assist as and when necessary. It will have the wherewithal to provide equity capital for a project, to act as a catalyst for further equity subscriptions and for loan finance. Again, through its shareholders in the first instance, it will be favourably placed to find the necessary management and technical expertise to ensure the success of a project, wherever this is lacking locally. In accomplishing its aims, it will also draw upon the resources of institutions in the public sector such as the Commonwealth Development Corporation, the International Finance Corporation of the World Bank group and the African Development Bank.

This emphasis on the multi-national concept weakens any tendency towards one nation's domination of a country or region. We do not believe it is in the best interests of our African friends or in the best interests of the long-term well-being of these enterprises for them to be monopolised by one nationality. We believe that an open-door policy on new capital investment in Africa is one that will contribute most to effective development. We do not believe in exclusive spheres of influence. This is not to deny the beneficial and good aspects coming from the implications of historic ties with the metropole and the special relationships that exist between the United States and certain West African states as an example.

Another example is the special ties between the Republic of South Africa and Botswana, Lesotho, Malawi and Swaziland.

The maintenance of these special ties on a completely mutually profitable and satisfactory basis will certainly contribute to stability, growth and economic development in an atmosphere of peaceful evolution, but it is desirable that these relationships be diversified to include other nationalities.

CONCLUSION

As can be seen, there are a great many financial institutions capitalised and organised to engage in development finance. These institutions in the aggregate command substantial resources.

There is no lack of money for development finance. The writer's experience in travelling over the African continent during the years has been that any viable industrial or agricultural project has no difficulty in obtaining finance. A going concern with a satisfactory record of performance has no difficulty in getting finance for a feasible expansion programme, for example, from a commercial bank. In this connection, it should be emphasised that a significant amount of development finance is done by the commercial banks in the form of loans (sometimes up to three years), overdrafts and letter-of-credit facilities.

While there is no actual shortage of money for development, the shortage is in talented promoters of integrity, entrepreneurs, organisers and managers. There also seems to be a shortage of corporations willing to do some pioneering in Africa. Perhaps when these companies have saturated the more immediately lucrative areas of Western Europe and North America with their resources, economic necessity will induce them to do some things in developing Africa.

When that time comes, there will have been in place for some time modern, sophisticated and very successful industrial enterprises in some relatively primitive environments. The newcomers can have the benefit of learning the histories of these enterprises and the ingredients that made them successful by consulting their friendly bankers.

Co-operation for Development in Southern Africa

G. M. E. LEISTNER

1. INTRODUCTION

For South Africa the Third World does not – reassuringly – lie across the ocean, on the other side of the globe. It is right here, within and immediately beyond our borders. Hence, for South Africa, the development of economically less advanced groups and peoples is more than an interesting field of study for academic theoreticians; more than a touchstone of human brotherliness; more than a far-sighted strategy to secure the markets of tomorrow; more than a slogan of political oratory.

South Africa clearly has a vital interest in promoting the economic and general well-being not only of the less developed peoples and groups within its borders, but also of the other countries and territories of Southern Africa.[1] Since South Africa's position differs in many important respects from that of other Western countries, it is no wonder that it shows little interest in issues such as the percentage of G.D.P. to be devoted to 'aid', multilateral versus bilateral aid, or the tying of aid. Development aid in the South African context is not primarily the financial flows shown in O.E.C.D. and U.N. statistics. Far more important is the fact that a dynamic and broadly based industrial economy has been created in South Africa and is fast transforming the peoples and the environment of Southern Africa.

The present paper serves to illustrate this point. More specifically it indicates that the functioning of South Africa's modern economy promotes and helps to sustain development in neighbouring countries through ordinary commercial relations such as private investment, tourism, trade, labour movements and the sharing of technical know-how. Special emphasis is being laid on the last-mentioned aspect. It will become apparent that South Africa also provides development assistance in the conventional meaning. However, important though that assistance may be for all concerned, its contribution to development is secondary to that of the stimuli emanating from the sustained growth of the South African economy. In the present paper no attempt is made to distinguish neatly between these two basic ways of promoting development.

2. SOUTH AFRICA'S APPROACH TO INTRA-REGIONAL ECONOMIC CO-OPERATION

OFFICIAL APPROACH

Much is being made at present of South Africa's so-called 'outward policy' in Africa, as if it represented a radical departure from earlier policies. In fact, South African governments have for a long time acknowledged this country's sincere interest in the well-being of other African countries and territories. Thus in April 1959 the then Minister of External Affairs, Mr Eric Louw, stated that 'South Africa has a vested and also a sympathetic interest in the continent of which we have for more than 300 years formed a part'.[2] In the same context, Mr Louw referred to the late Prime Minister, Mr J. G. Strijdom, who had officially expressed 'the wish for friendly relations and co-operation between South Africa and the non-White states in regard to matters of common concern'.[3] Six years later, in 1965, the Minister of Mines and of Planning, Mr J. F. W. Haak, re-emphasised the government's goodwill towards other African countries, 'and more particularly towards their progress towards economic viability'.[4] His concluding words clearly foreshadow later events:

The development of our continent should never be seen statically. Where economic co-operation for one reason or another is not possible today, it may be so tomorrow, or in the years to come. Whatever our present differences, we have a common interest in the promotion of the well-being of our peoples, and the increase in their standards of living. Closer economic co-operation can serve the attainment of our common goal.[5]

Briefly, the aims and principles guiding South Africa's policy in respect of development aid are as follows:

(i) Non-interference in each other's internal affairs.

(ii) South Africa seeks to promote economic development in neighbouring states primarily by encouraging trade and other commercial relations, whereas aid in the conventional meaning comes second.

(iii) Assistance must be requested expressly and for specific projects.

(iv) South Africa's development aid must be productive and help the recipients to help themselves.

(v) The main stress lies on technical rather than financial aid, and on loans rather than grants.

(vi) South African aid is seen as supplementary to that provided by the economically stronger Western countries and by international organisations.

(vii) Aid to neighbouring countries must not be at the expense of the emergent Bantu states and of other important developments within the Republic's borders.[6]

When South African leaders speak of this country's responsibility towards neighbouring countries, these must not be lightly dismissed as empty words because such responsibility is inseparable from White South Africans' claim to a right of existence in this continent. Enlightened self-interest alone demands that South Africa assist its less developed neighbours to become more prosperous. As the present Minister of External Affairs, Dr Hilgard Muller, put it some time ago:

> We do not only lay claim to our right of continued existence in Africa – we also accept the concomitant responsibilities. Our whole Africa policy must therefore constantly be viewed in the light of our responsibility towards ourselves as a nation of Africa and towards our fellow nations on this continent. . . . We willingly co-operate in this task . . . [of] the development of this subcontinent . . . in the interests not only of the other nations on the continent, but also of our own.[7]

NON-OFFICIAL ATTITUDES

Naturally, the insight and the policy goals outlined above are not shared by all South Africans. However, it would be difficult to find any prominent leader in political, business or academic life who is not essentially in agreement with official policies concerning co-operation with neighbouring states. In one of seven widely publicised interviews with business leaders published by an Afrikaans Sunday paper, Dr Anton Rupert, head of the Rembrandt group, used the simple phrase which has since been endlessly repeated: 'If they [i.e. the Black people] do not eat, we [the Whites] do not sleep.'[8] None the less, relatively little is being done by the press and official bodies to bring home to the man in the street, and on the veld, the implications of South Africa's unique position on the Black continent.

In the following outline, the main emphasis falls on co-operation in respect of technical and related matters, while trade, private investment, labour migration, joint infrastructural ventures and financial aid must be dealt with even more summarily for reasons of space.

3. TECHNICAL AND SCIENTIFIC CO-OPERATION

Notwithstanding local differences, the countries of Southern Africa have much in common with regard to features such as geology, climate, soil, fauna, flora, parasites, insect and other pests, human and animal diseases, nutritional problems, population factors and economic structures. Close co-operation in finding solutions for common problems, in avoiding duplication of research efforts and in sharing experiences is dictated by reason, if not by necessity. Thus, as early as 1908, delegates from the various countries of British Southern Africa as far north as Northern Rhodesia, as well as German South West Africa and Portuguese Mozambique, came together in Durban to discuss the combating of locust swarms – for plagues do not respect international boundaries. In that same year the famous Onderstepoort Veterinary Research Laboratory was founded which was to play a vital role in elucidating and solving many animal diseases of Africa.

On the whole, however, there was little co-operation, and in 1929, during a speech at Oxford, General Smuts appealed for a joint approach to Africa's problems, to end the waste of effort, talents and funds which would inevitably continue as long as the administering powers in Africa persisted in their efforts to find separate and different solutions to common problems. As a direct result of this speech, Lord Hailey and his team of co-operators undertook a survey of Africa. His *African Survey*, as well as the related studies, *Science in Africa*, by Professor S. H. Frankel, a South African, which were published in 1938, all stressed the desirability of closer co-operation between scientists in Africa.

These publications, the experience of the Second World War and a number of international conferences led to the formation of the Scientific Council for Africa South of the Sahara (C.S.A.)[9] in 1949, and of the Commission for Technical Co-operation in Africa South of the Sahara (C.C.T.A.)[10] in 1950. The story of C.C.T.A.–C.S.A. from 1950 to 1965, when it was merged into the Organisation of African Unity, is now history. But it has to be referred to here in order to demonstrate that South Africa is serious in declaring its willingness and its ability to contribute towards progress in Africa, scientifically and otherwise. The following passages from a recent study on the C.C.T.A. by Dr Isebill Gruhn of the University of California substantiate the point:

> White South Africa and Rhodesia had considerable experience and interest in dealing with the technical and scientific problems of the African continent. Their experts provided the backbone of most C.S.A./C.C.T.A.-sponsored conferences, giving no indication of political motivation, and many of them were on the permanent staff. The official stance of South Africa was to emphasise the non-political, scientific approach. But newly independent African countries found her presence intolerable. . . .[11] From the technical point of view, the departure [in 1962] of the many high-calibre South African scientists was a serious blow. (South Africa's contribution to C.C.T.A. had been considerable; . . .)[12]

We can now turn to those forms of co-operation that are still functioning today.

SARCCUS

The Southern African Regional Commission for the Conservation and Utilisation of the Soil (SARCCUS) was established in 1950 in pursuance of recommendations made by a conference held at

Goma in the former Belgian Congo two years earlier.[13] The broad objective of the Commission is 'to promote closer technical co-operation among the territories comprising the Southern African Region in all matters relating to the control and prevention of soil erosion and the conservation, protection, improvement and rational utilisation of the soil, the vegetation and the sources and resources of water supply in the countries concerned'.[14] The members at present are Angola, Botswana, Lesotho, Malawi, Mozambique, South Africa and South West Africa, Rhodesia, São Tomé and Principe, and Swaziland.

According to its first Secretary-General, Dr J. C. Ross, the *modus operandi* of SARCCUS has proved to be highly satisfactory and effective – so much so that this organisation is today widely regarded as one of the most successful of the various bodies that have been created from time to time to promote interterritorial co-operation in Africa at the technical level. Its activities have given a powerful stimulus to co-operation in Southern Africa in the field of land use and the conservation of agricultural resources, and have produced results of considerable significance to agricultural development in the region.

The Commission's working procedures and the principles evolved over the years would warrant detailed examination, but only the following can be mentioned here. SARCCUS concerns itself primarily with matters of policy rather than with the technical details of the matters that come before it, and for this reason the delegates attending meetings are professional officers of high seniority and wide experience. They are men concerned with the direction of policy in their own countries and competent to speak with authority on behalf of their governments. Meetings are regarded as gatherings of territorial representatives rather than of individuals. The papers presented by delegations invariably take the form of reports representing the views of the respective governments, not of individuals. SARCCUS functions as an action body and not as a mere discussion group. The participant officials are expected to do everything in their power to ensure that their governments implement the recommendations of meetings.

SARCCUS functions primarily by way of ten standing committees which meet annually and comprise the following: (1) Soil Science; (2) Animal Health; (3) Animal Production; (4) Plant

Production; (5) Plant Protection; (6) Forestry; (7) Hydrology; (8) Conservation and Land-Use Planning; (9) Nature Conservation, Wildlife Utilisation and Management; and (10) Education and Extension. In addition, there are specialist subcommittees which report back to the respective standing committees on a wide diversity of matters such as seed production; quelea control; phytosanitary control; agrometeorology and climatology; fisheries conservation, utilisation and management; and international co-operation in the management of elephant populations.

From the beginning, the Commission's permanent secretariat has been located at Pretoria. The two Secretaries-General who served between 1953 and 1970 were very senior and capable officials of the South African Department of Agriculture, and so is the present one. South Africa has always borne a substantial share of the costs of SARCCUS.

In a recent article, the second Secretary-General speaks of 'The good fellowship that SARCCUS has managed, over the years to foster amongst the representatives of all its member territories',[15] and one can only endorse his view that this has 'engendered a suitable climate for further intensified and expanded co-operation . . . in Southern Africa'.[16] These words and conclusion hold true for many of the other forms of co-operation discussed below.

THE ONDERSTEPOORT VETERINARY RESEARCH INSTITUTE

From the earliest days, animal diseases such as anthrax, rinderpest, botulism, bluetongue and trypanosomiasis have hindered the growth of commercial agriculture. Only after these scourges had been either eradicated or brought under control could the important cattle and sheep industries of South Africa and neighbouring countries begin to flourish. Even today, constant watchfulness is essential, and the outbreaks of foot-and-mouth disease in South West Africa, Botswana and Swaziland during the 1960s were illustrative of the disasters ever threatening animal husbandry in Africa. South African veterinary and other scientists have done pathbreaking work in elucidating the animal diseases of Africa and developing counter-measures. So great is the international fame of the Onderstepoort Institute that on occasion Pretoria has been referred to as 'a small town near Onderstepoort'.

As part of the control measures, Onderstepoort annually produces more than 100 million doses of vaccine against 28 different diseases. The vaccines are made available to any other country in Africa and the rest of the world on request. In 1969–70, for instance, well over 7 million doses of vaccine and other biological substances were thus supplied, including 1·25 million doses to Malawi (6 different vaccines), 3·02 million to Rhodesia (17 vaccines), 1·81 million to Zambia (9 vaccines), about 315,000 doses of 20 different vaccines to Botswana, and smaller quantities to Angola, Mozambique, Zaïre, Lesotho and Swaziland.[17]

The Institute can give valuable guidance and assistance in the diagnosis of and research on viral, protozoal and bacterial diseases. Officers of the South African veterinary field services have on many occasions been sent to neighbouring countries to help in diagnosing and combating outbreaks of diseases, and have helped in various ways to protect the health of their stock.

Onderstepoort has played a leading role in the establishment (in 1952) and functioning of the Inter-African Bureau for Epizootic Diseases (I.B.E.D.)[18] in Kenya, which was intended to be a permanent centre for the interchange, co-ordination and dissemination of technical information on all aspects of animal diseases in Africa. When South Africa had to withdraw from the C.C.T.A. in 1962, its participation in the Bureau also came to an end. However, Onderstepoort is an active member of the Office International des Épizooties (O.I.E.), of which most African countries are members, and they therefore still benefit from the Institute's work. The O.I.E. has proclaimed Onderstepoort as World Reference Centre for horse-sickness and bluetongue.

OTHER OFFICIAL CO-OPERATION IN AGRICULTURAL MATTERS

For many years South Africa has actively participated in the work of the Inter-territorial Foot and Mouth Disease Advisory Committee. The other members are Malawi, Rhodesia, Lesotho, Botswana, Swaziland, Mozambique and Angola. The Committee meets regularly in one of the member countries. Its work has led to timely and efficient handling of stock diseases throughout the region. Outbreaks of foot-and-mouth disease have been effectively localised by international co-operation. In 1965, for instance, South Africa sent 111 veterinary and other officials to Swaziland to help contain a serious outbreak, and 67 officials again in 1969–70. Even though the Committee is separate from

SARCCUS, close liaison exists. South Africa is at present establishing a Foot-and-Mouth Disease Research Institute.

South Africa co-operates closely with Rhodesia and Mozambique in combating the tsetse fly in its north-eastern regions, and with Angola and Botswana in the Caprivi complex. Similarly, joint action is being taken together with neighbouring states in respect of red-billed finches and red locusts, whenever necessary. The International Red Locust Control Service was officially terminated on 31 December 1970, because Zambia and Tanzania – the main breeding areas – as well as Uganda, Zaïre, Rwanda and Burundi felt they could no longer co-operate with the 'White South'. Yet, ironically these countries asked South Africa not to withdraw its aeroplanes, equipment and experts.[19]

The multifarious ways in which South African agricultural experts assist may be illustrated by outlining official contacts (and their subject-matter) in 1969–70:[20] Botswana (finches), Lesotho (staff requirements of the agricultural department; lectures and demonstrations on grazing management; weevils infesting grain in storage), Malawi (mites), Mozambique (lectures on veterinary surgery), Rhodesia (red spider) and Swaziland (foot-and-mouth disease; imports and exports of animals and animal products; finches).

ASSISTANCE BY THE SOUTH AFRICAN WOOL BOARD

South Africa is one of the world's major producers of merino wool, and the industry readily shares with neighbouring countries the results of its extensive and sophisticated research concerning breeding of sheep and classing of wool. Special reference may be made to the South African Wool Board's assistance to Lesotho, whose annual wool clip of approximately 4·5 million kg is the principal export. Apart from an annual grant of R8,000 to promote the wool industry (demonstrations, lectures, purchase of merino rams, etc.), Lesotho was also assisted by the secondment, for two years, of a South African merino expert. He did extension work, conducted courses on breeding and wool classing, advised on the buying of merino rams, and generally helped to improve the quality and quantity of Lesotho's clip. Further, the Wool Board conducts courses of one or two months' duration at the Quthing stud farm, and contributes R1,000 a year to finance the costs of travel and accommodation on the trip that rounds off these courses, that is, a visit to the wool auctions, woollen mills and research institutions at Port Elizabeth.

A scheme of major importance is the establishment by the South African Wool Board of a 1,300-ha stud farm at Mokhotlong in north-eastern Lesotho. Under the supervision of the manager provided by the Board, the open grazing area of the high Drakensberg mountains has been transformed into a model farm comprising twenty camps with five strategically situated sheep-yards and numerous watering-points; housing for the manager, visitors and workers; shearing, grading and storage sheds. There are eleven blocs of farming land where lucerne and winter cereals are grown as supplementary animal feed especially for the winter. No fewer than 500 stud ewes and 13 rams have been purchased. R171,000 has been provided by the Wool Board over the five-year period ending June 1972. At the Lesotho government's request, the Board will manage the farm for one further year and has budgeted about R26,000 for the purpose. A Mosotho sheep and wool officer is being trained to take over the management. The Lesotho authorities are to establish an agricultural training centre nearby which will make use of the farm as far as sheep and wool are concerned. At the opening ceremony of the latter, early in 1971, the chairman of the South African Wool Board aptly remarked: 'The humble but remunerative merino has brought us closer together and we shall give you whatever guidance we can in a spirit of helpfulness and good neighbourliness.'[21]

THE SOUTH AFRICAN COUNCIL FOR SCIENTIFIC AND INDUSTRIAL RESEARCH (C.S.I.R.)

Looking at South Africa today, with its highly diversified manufacturing sector and its even more sophisticated financial and distribution sector, one is apt to forget that less than four decades have passed since the first ingots were poured by ISCOR, our national iron and steel industry, and that really noteworthy industrial development began only about twenty-five years ago. The basic technological and scientific knowledge on which the truly phenomenal growth of the recent past has rested, had to a large extent to be imported from abroad. However, it had to be adapted and developed further to suit South African conditions. In 1945, as a matter of major national importance, and under the guidance of some of the country's foremost scientists, the C.S.I.R. was established so as to enable South Africa to hold its own in the technological sphere and to cope with the expected rapid development of the post-war years.

With its enormous range of activities and the high levels of scientific achievement, the C.S.I.R. is unique in Africa and compares with the best of similar organisations overseas. Only a few examples can be quoted to illustrate the manifold direct and indirect benefits derived by neighbouring countries from the work of the C.S.I.R.'s numerous specialised research institutes. The National Food Research Institute is contributing significantly towards health and hence poductivity in Southern Africa by studies on the handling, processing and utilisation of foods, and by investigating means to improve and augment food supplies by technological development and application. A recent major achievement is the development of a cheap yet highly nutritive and concentrated food additive known as P.V.M. (= proteins, vitamins and minerals) which serves to eliminate the deficiencies caused by a one-sided diet of maize or other grain food. At the price of a mere $2\frac{1}{2}$ cents per day, infants and children up to six years of age can now be fed properly. For older children and adults the daily needs go up to 5 cents per day.

The National Institute for Personnel Research (N.I.P.R.) answered 48 inquiries in 1967–8 from Zambia, Swaziland, Lesotho, Rhodesia, Botswana, Zaïre, Malawi, Tanzania, Ghana and Senegal, as well as from overseas countries. In the same year 12 persons in Botswana and several in Lesotho were trained in the administration of the Spiral Nines test; 5 were trained in the administration of the G.A.B. (General Adaptability Battery) in Swaziland. In Botswana 75 trainees at the Agricultural College were tested; and in Lesotho 84 candidates were selected for agricultural training.[22] In 1970–1 similar help was given, and in one country[23] more than 5,000 answer sheets to an intelligence test, developed by the N.I.P.R., were scored for the Department of Education in order to screen scholars seeking entry to secondary school.

The National Mechanical Engineering Research Institute, among many other tasks, is active in the field of rock mechanics in order to improve efficiency and safety in mining. Industries in neighbouring countries make use of the relevant services which comprise consultation, the testing of rock properties and measurement of rock stress. Extensive use is being made by mines in Rhodesia, Zambia and other neighbouring states of the Institute's facilities for the routine testing of steel-wire ropes. In 1969 the C.S.I.R.'s Technical Services assisted the Gatooma Research Station in Rhodesia with the repair and re-calibration of instruments used in the standardisation of cotton. Nine sugar mills in Swaziland, Rhodesia, Malawi and Mozambique are associated members of the Sugar Milling Research Institute, in the financing and research work of which the C.S.I.R. is closely involved.

Apart from the many practical direct contributions such as these to the economic and social well-being of nearby countries, the results of the C.S.I.R.'s research are shared with these countries through numerous conferences, symposia, personal visits, lectures and publications. The results of the C.S.I.R.'s research concerning road construction, building, timber, leather, paint, water, fishing, human health and a host of other subjects are equally applicable to neighbouring countries, and are readily available, thus saving them the cost of duplicating research.

THE SOUTH AFRICAN BUREAU OF STANDARDS (S.A.B.S.)

The Bureau's range of activities is as impressive as that of its sister organisation, the C.S.I.R. However, even if the S.A.B.S. is dealt with more briefly here, this is not a reflection on its importance for neighbouring countries. It is now generally understood that a well-developed system of industrial standards is indispensable for industrial growth and maintenance. The S.A.B.S., with its more than 600 scientists and technicians, and its modern laboratories, has significantly contributed towards the quality of South Africa's output of processed and manufactured goods, and this has promoted employment opportunities by rendering the country's products more competitive on external as well as local markets. The Bureau is an active and respected member of the International Organisation for Standardisation (I.S.O.) and is responsible for the Southern African secretariat of the international Secretariat of Standard Reference Materials.

As the Bureau's specifications are specifically designed for Southern African conditions, it is only logical that wide and increasing use is being made thereof in neighbouring countries.

Apart from drawing up specifications on request for individual countries, the Bureau also provides a wide range of other services. Products ranging from canned foodstuffs to safety helmets are being tested. Regular inspections are carried out for some countries. In the case of Malawi and Mauritius, for instance, these services are now in their thirteenth and fifteenth years respectively. Assistance is always readily provided when requested, and S.A.B.S. experts have on many occasions travelled to countries throughout Southern Africa to advise on the introduction and application of standards or the establishment of standards organisations.

CO-OPERATION IN RESPECT OF WATER RESOURCES

Whereas many parts of Southern Africa have a superabundance of water, others are either dry or are rapidly reaching full utilisation of local and surrounding supplies.

Angola is the source of the bulk of the surface run-off reaching South West Africa via the Kunene and the Okavango, of the water reaching Botswana via the Okavango and Kwando, and of a large portion of the Zambezi flow reaching Rhodesia and Mozambique. The latter territory receives run-off from Angola, Rhodesia, Malawi, South Africa, Botswana and Swaziland.[24] Under circumstances such as these co-operation is a matter of course. The effects of changed land use on water supplies; sediment transportation and deposition, with particular reference to its effect on the useful life of storage works; flood hydrology; pollution by industrial effluents: these are but a few of the more obvious aspects where inter-territorial study and action are taking place.

Apart from the SARCCUS Standing Committee on Hydrology, there are inter-governmental conferences on rivers of common interest. Meetings at a technical level have taken place in 1967, 1969 and 1972, with representatives from Swaziland and Mozambique, concerning the Komati, Usutu and Pongola. Similar discussions are being held with Botswana and Angola, in respect of the Okavango, Kwito and Kwando, and with Angola in respect of the Kunene. The more spectacular inter-territorial water and power schemes are listed in section 6 below.

4. CO-OPERATION IN RESPECT OF DIVERSE SERVICES

ARRANGEMENTS CONCERNING MIGRATORY LABOUR

South Africa is the only country in Southern Africa which is able gainfully to employ a substantial portion of its domestic labour force. In addition it provides employment for approximately 600,000 workers from neighbouring and also more distant African countries.[25] Apart from these countries' general interest in the well-being of their citizens working in South Africa, they are naturally anxious that the greatest possible portion of these migrants' cash earnings should be available to promote development at home in the form of savings deposits and as tax payments. Whereas arrangements have existed for a long time, whereby workers recruited for South African mines can voluntarily remit earnings either as deferred pay or as immediate support for their dependants, more formal agreements have been concluded with Mozambique and Malawi. These ensure that remittances are channelled through specified institutions, and – in the case of Malawians – provide for taxes to be deducted by employers and transferred to the Malawian government. Both agreements make it obligatory for a certain portion of wages to be retained for specified periods of time.[26]

BUILDING AND CONSTRUCTION

The fact that they are physically close to each other and share similar climatic and other physical conditions entails distinct advantages both for South Africa and for its neighbours in many spheres. In building and construction it means that South Africa's neighbours benefit from the research into materials and methods of construction being conducted in this country. Furthermore, they can obtain the services of South African engineers, architects and construction firms more readily and more cheaply than those of overseas ones who rarely have the same intimate knowledge of local problems. The significance, and notably the cost aspect, of this is easily overlooked. The benefits for South Africa, financially and in terms of goodwill, are more readily appreciated.

Examples of major construction works, where South African firms have successfully tendered against strong international competition, are the Swaziland railway (completed in 1964) and the rail link from Mpinde in Malawi to Nova Freixo in Mozambique (completed in 1970). Large South African firms, i.e. Anglo-American, L.T.A. Ltd and Vecor, are playing a leading role in the construction of the Cabora Bassa project in Mozambique.

HOTELS AND TOURISM

If in earlier days trade followed the flag, it now follows the tourist. Once attractive tourist facilities start drawing businessmen and financially potent visitors to hitherto little-known parts, new avenues for paid employment open up, the sale of handicraft and new patterns of consumption are promoted, and commerce generally is stimulated. Beyond that, familiarity with local conditions, especially if there is the added attraction of congenial accommodation and a pleasant environment, generally encourages the investigation of investment opportunities. In this respect, South African commercial interests have already benefited neighbouring countries.

In recent years large South African hotel groups have begun to explore the appreciable tourist potential of these countries, particularly the islands off the east coast of Southern Africa. Highly profitable hotels and casinos have been established in Swaziland and Lesotho, while another is currently being built at a cost of R2·1 million in Botswana. A five-star hotel is to be opened in 1973 at Nossi Bé, the holiday island off the west coast of Madagascar, and a 120-room hotel and casino is to be built at Majunga in Madagascar by another South African group. Plans are being actively pursued for new ventures in Mauritius, the Seychelles and elsewhere by hotel groups which already operate some of the largest hotels in Rhodesia, Mozambique and South Africa itself.

An interesting development is the proposed Southern African Regional Tourism Council (SARTOC), the main objective of which is to promote and develop tourism through regional co-operation. According to press reports,[27] South Africa, Malawi and Portugal have already signed the articles of agreement, but there must be four members before SARTOC can be officially established, and it is not yet functioning.

The privately financed South African Wildlife Foundation, of which Dr Anton Rupert is chairman, promotes the tourist potential of neighbouring countries by assisting them with the establishment or improvement of nature reserves. It helped to expand appreciably Swaziland's only significant game sanctuary, Mlilwane. Botswana and Malawi each received R17,000 to buy equipment urgently needed to give proper access to, and control over, game reserves. The Foundation was instrumental in giving Lesotho its first national park, Sehlabathebe. 56 white rhino were reintroduced in game reserves in Mozambique, and a large number of black rhino were relocated in Rhodesia to save them from extinction.[28]

5. TRADE AND RELATED MATTERS

An expanding volume of two-way trade between the more and the less developed countries is, of course, one of the principal means of promoting the development of the latter. South Africa's exports to other African states have steadily risen from R196.3 million in 1966 to R263.9 million in 1970, whereas imports from the rest of Africa during the same period fluctuated between R111 million and R141.3 million and amounted to R131.2 million in 1970. These figures reflect the fact that South Africa can offer machinery, building materials, agrochemicals, pharmaceuticals, etc., at competitive prices, whereas, on the whole, the primary products that other African countries can supply are competitive with, rather than supplementary to, the output of South Africa's own primary industries. This pattern clearly militates against the formation of a Southern African trading bloc. This topic cannot be pursued here, although brief reference will be made to the customs and currency union comprising South Africa, Botswana, Lesotho and Swaziland (for brevity, the latter three are referred to as 'B.L.S.').

The union between these four countries dated from colonial days (1910), but what is relevant here is that the first revision of the customs arrangement was negotiated *after* B.L.S. had attained independence, and that they declared themselves highly satisfied with the new terms agreed on in 1969. In contrast to the earlier agreement, the present one provides for a detailed set of administrative rules and provisions for consultation on problems which may arise. This mechanism should ensure that all contracting parties are able to protect their individual interests, and is, in particular, to the advantage of B.L.S. because they now have an effective say in matters concerning the agreement.[29]

Among the major benefits for B.L.S. is their greatly increased share of the area's total customs, excise and sales-tax revenue. Whereas they could expect a joint share of R6·4 million for 1969–70 under the old agreement, they actually received R22·7 million under the new formula. South Africa's share of the total pool consequently fell from about 98·69 per cent under the old agreement to 96·45 per cent in 1969–70. Thus the 1969 agreement is another indication of South Africa's readiness to promote the economic well-being of its less developed neighbours.

This readiness was also proved in another, entirely different context when the South African Minister of Finance, Dr N. Diederichs, was the only representative of the more highly developed countries who pleaded on behalf of developing countries, when the 1971 meeting of World Bank and I.M.F. governors discussed the international currency crisis.[30]

Lastly, attention is drawn to the fact that B.L.S. are marketing their wool, mohair, meat, butter, wattle, cotton and citrus through the respective South African marketing boards, and benefit from the orderly market conditions and more particularly the stable prices brought about by these boards. These countries have ready access to South African capital markets and, owing to their membership of the rand currency area, they are spared the balance-of-payments problems that beset many other less developed countries.

6. CO-OPERATION IN RESPECT OF INFRASTRUCTURE

WATER AND POWER

As indicated above (end of section 3), large parts of Southern Africa are poorly endowed with natural water supplies, and the availability of water is a major consideration in deciding upon the exploitation of rich mineral deposits or the establishment of industries. In South West Africa and Botswana, with their large desert areas, this is a particularly pressing issue, but it is also a major consideration for the future growth of South Africa's industrial heartland, the Pretoria–Witwatersrand–Vereeniging region. By the turn of the century, South Africa, it is estimated, will need two and a half times as much water as at present.

Significantly large additional supplies can be obtained only from rivers which South Africa shares with other countries, or even from beyond its borders. The Lesotho Highlands Water Development Project could supply 100,000 million gallons (455 million cubic metres) to the Vaal Dam annually. There have even been serious proposals to take water from the Okavango to the Witwatersrand, a distance of approximately 1,600 km.

Work is at present under way on the first stages of a water- and power-supply scheme on the Kunene. In terms of an agreement signed between South Africa and Portugal in 1969, up to 6 cumecs (cubic metres per second) can initially be drawn from the Kunene and taken across the border into Ovambo. The 160-MW hydroelectric scheme on the Kunene, including dams at Gove and at Calueque, was expected to cost over R45 million for the first phase, not counting the transmission system estimated at over R10 million. The first phase has been provisionally scheduled for completion in 1975, and a second phase, involving an additional R25 million to double the generating capacity, has been envisaged for completion ten years later.

The capital cost of providing the additional water which, it is estimated, will be required by the whole of South West Africa by the year 2000, will be about R2,667 million, including about R800 million for the territory's non-White homelands alone. Practically all this water will have to be obtained from the northern rivers, the Kunene and the Okavango.

The R352 million Cabora Bassa Dam, currently being constructed by an international consortium on the Zambezi in Mozambique, is the best known hydroelectric scheme in which South Africa is associated with neighbouring countries. The ZAMCO consortium comprises major South African companies, and in December 1969 the Industrial Development Corporation of South Africa Ltd (I.D.C.) granted a R20 million credit, the largest single export credit extended by the I.D.C. up to that time, to the Portuguese government for certain aspects of the Cabora Bassa project.

This project will initially have a capacity of 1,200 MW (twice as much as Kariba), and this will ultimately be raised to 4,000 MW (as compared with the Aswan High Dam's 2,200 MW). Cabora Bassa is to deliver a firm supply of 680 MW to South Africa annually from 1975, 1,070 MW from 1977, and 1,470

MW from 1979. South Africa will take the power at 0·3 cents per unit for 80 per cent of the firm supply. A lower tariff will apply if electricity in excess of the firm supply is purchased. Barring 'very exceptional circumstances', the tariffs are to remain unchanged for twenty years. By the time capital costs have been largely redeemed, the basic tariff of 0.3 cents will be reduced to between 0·2 and 0·175 cents per unit. The large initial capacity of the power scheme and hence the low unit costs would have been inconceivable if South Africa had not undertaken to purchase a substantial portion of the electricity generated, because for the time being Mozambique's own little-developed economy will require only a fraction of the total. Cabora Bassa power will account for about 8 per cent of South Africa's total power consumption, but, on account of South African participation, Mozambique – and perhaps Malawi at a later stage – will be able to obtain power at prices that will be among the lowest in the world.

By the end of 1972 the power-supply system of Swaziland is to be linked to that of South Africa, allowing Swaziland to draw any shortfall in power requirements from across the border. Swaziland is currently investigating the possibility of building a 1,500-MW power station, which will cost an estimated R170 million to R200 million, in the vicinity of its large low-grade coal deposits at Mpaka. If South Africa purchases a large portion of this power, it could mean annual earnings of R30 million for Swaziland; otherwise the scheme will have to be scaled down to Swaziland's needs. There is also the possibility that a major thermal power station may be erected on the Palapye coalfields in Botswana.

A huge Southern African power-grid network is gradually coming into existence, extending from Cape Town in the south to Zaïre in the north. Even today, power is being supplied to Lesotho by South Africa's Electricity Supply Commission, while Zambia imports power from Zaïre and in turn is expected to sell large quantities to Rhodesia once further generators come into operation at its Kafue Gorge project, probably later this year. Power is being sold by Rhodesia to Mozambique.[31]

TRANSPORT AND COMMUNICATIONS

In Southern Africa, as in other less developed regions, the network of transport and communications established in the colonial era was oriented towards the nearest port, whence agricultural and mineral raw materials were exported to the metropolitan country. Much still needs to be done to facilitate intra-regional (and also intra-territorial) rail and road transportation.

In the foreseeable future, though, it will be possible to travel on a good tarmac road from Beira in Mozambique to Cape Town and thence to Windhoek and to Luanda (Angola). The road from Blantyre (Malawi) to Salisbury is being greatly improved with the help of South African and Portuguese funds. New – or improved – road links, with which South Africa is not directly concerned, are those between Francistown (Botswana) to Kazungula on the border to Zambia; between Malawi and Zambia; and between Luanda and the Katanga province of Zaïre. Rhodesia is establishing a direct rail connection between Rutenga and Beit Bridge (South Africa). Reference has already been made to the Mpinde–Nova Freixo rail link, financed by an R11 million South African credit, that gives Malawi another outlet to the sea (at Nacala).

All telecommunication services between Botswana, Lesotho and Swaziland and the rest of the world are routed via South African channels.

The ever-closer economic links between Southern African countries are responsible for a continuously increasing volume of intra-regional air traffic. South African Airways is at present operating numerous services in partnership with the national airlines of Lesotho, Swaziland, Malawi, Mozambique, Rhodesia, the Malagasy Republic and Mauritius. Passengers, mail and cargo are conveyed by these services which are regulated by various pooling agreements that have proved highly satisfactory for all partners.[32]

7. HEALTH, EDUCATION, SECONDMENT OF PERSONNEL, ETC.

HEALTH

In the medical field South Africa's neighbours benefit from the work of the South African Institute for Medical Research, the five medical schools, the facilities for specialised medical treatment, the blood-transfusion services and the well-organised channels for the distribution of medicaments. Vaccines and serums are readily available to meet the specific needs arising in Southern Africa and elsewhere in Africa. South African scientists have been and still are performing pioneering work in combating kwashiorkor, sleeping sickness, malaria, bilharzia, typhus, poliomyelitis, silicosis, syphilis and many other diseases and afflictions. Whenever a serious threat of epidemic is suspected in nearby countries, South African medical specialists and technicians are often on the spot within hours. Obviously this help is no less in the interest of South Africa as of the neighbouring country. There are, however, examples of help where no such common interest exists.

In Lesotho there is only one medical doctor to every 23,300 of the population (as against 1 to 1,950 in South Africa – 1967 figures). Hence it was a most welcome gesture when many of South Africa's foremost surgeons and doctors offered their services free of charge. The Lesotho government urgently requested Dr Anton Rupert to find a way in which these services could be utilised. The result was a medical shuttle service between Maseru and Johannesburg, Pretoria, Durban, Cape Town and other cities, with travel and accommodation expenses met by the Rupert organisation. Leading surgeons, anaesthetists, physicians, ear, nose and throat specialists, ophthalmologists, gynaecologists, orthopaedic and plastic surgeons, as well as nurses, give up their weekends and work extra-long hours operating and treating Basotho patients.

Since 3 February 1968, when the first team flew to Maseru, until quite recently, 258 volunteer specialists had already made 101 visits, performed 1,667 operations and given 4,243 consultations, accompanied by 267 theatre sisters. Not one patient has died under operation in what the *Christchurch Times* of 11 February 1972 has called 'the biggest voluntary specialised service of its kind in the world'.

Similarly, Mr Harry Oppenheimer of the Anglo-American Corporation sponsors fortnightly trips by groups of outstanding medical specialists who render unpaid weekend services in the Mbabane and Hlatikulu hospitals in Swaziland. In the two and a half years to the end of 1971 these doctors had seen about 10,000 patients and performed approximately 2,000 operations. The magnanimity of the specialists has encouraged hundreds of medical students to do voluntary work in hospitals in B.L.S., Malawi and South African Bantu areas during their vacations; the Rembrandt organisation contributes towards the expenses of those from Stellenbosch. The South African government, as well as commercial firms and charitable organisations, has donated appreciable quantities of equipment, medicines, surgical dressings, blood supplies, etc.

An important feature of the medical shuttle services is the experience gained by Basotho and Swazi doctors and theatre personnel by working with top people of their profession.

EDUCATION AND TRAINING

Much use is being made of South Africa's educational and training facilities by people from neighbouring countries. In February 1972, for instance, 40 auxiliary and 7 general nurses from Rhodesia, as well as 9 auxiliary and 8 general nurses from Lesotho, were in training at the Baragwanath Bantu Hospital in Johannesburg. These had come on their own, but a number of Malawian radiographers have been trained there at the request of their government. Of the 25,444 students enrolled with the University of South Africa (UNISA) in 1971, 846 were living in other African countries and were distributed as follows: Rhodesia 538, B.L.S. 176, Zambia 49, Mozambique 43, Malawi 30, Angola 7, rest of Africa 3.

The National Development and Management Foundation of South Africa (N.D.M.F.), the membership of which includes virtually all the country's important business undertakings, has as one of its basic objectives 'To extend management development activities to neighbouring territories, in order to promote the national growth and prosperity of these territories'. A special committee to determine priorities and co-ordinate efforts in this regard was set up early in 1970 under the chairmanship of the N.D.M.F.'s president, Dr Anton Rupert. Of the priorities examined, two have been incorporated in special projects. The first concerns training and the transference of management skills to emergent African peoples. Courses to teach these skills to businessmen and government officials in B.L.S. and other neighbouring centres are provided, for instance on the basic economics of retailing and on the principles and practice of supervision. In Swaziland this has been extended by the mounting of courses on subjects ranging from financial planning to the setting-up and management of a wage board. Lecturers of high standing in South Africa's academic and/or business world are enlisted. The second part of the N.D.M.F.'s project for assistance entails the secondment of experienced executive and other personnel to development projects.

SECONDMENT OF PERSONNEL

In February this year it was reported in the local press that during the past three years South Africa had seconded 53 public servants to neighbouring countries for temporary service in a professional, technical or administrative capacity. Their distribution was given as follows: Lesotho 26, Malawi 22, Swaziland 3, Mozambique 1 and Botswana 1.[33] By mid-February this year the distribution of officials then on secondment from the various departments was as follows: *Swaziland* – Inland Revenue 1, Agricultural Technical Services 1, Customs and Excise 1; *Malawi* – Post Office technicians 5, S.A. Police dog-trainer 1; *Lesotho* – Health 1, Justice 8, Agricultural Technical Services 2, Customs and Excise 1, Information 1, Post Office 2, Water Affairs 1, Agricultural Economics and Marketing 1, Community Development 1, Town Clerk 1.[34] This total of 28 officials on secondment may not look impressive, but these officials are filling important posts. Besides, taking into account the serious shortage of personnel throughout the public service, the absence of these men means a real sacrifice.

The best known and the most successful instance of secondment by South Africa's private business sector is that of Mr Wynand van Graan who held an executive post with the Rembrandt Group's Canadian partners until he became head of the Lesotho National Development Corporation (L.N.D.C.) in August 1967. When van Graan arrived, there was very little industry – half a mile of railway, two miles of tarred road, no barber, not even a typewriter mechanic. The following light industries and services have since been set up by the L.N.D.C. with the participation of outside investors: a stone-crushing plant; a candle factory; a tyre-retreading establishment; a milling company; a furniture factory; a fertiliser mixing and bagging plant; an assembly plant for tractors and agricultural equipment; a weaving factory; a block of flats; an office block; a training and service centre for motor mechanics and technicians; a 250-room hotel; Lesotho Airways; a diamond-cutting works; a clothing factory; the manufacture of electric lights and fittings; two potteries; and a jewellery-making factory. All the ventures initiated have been successful because they were tailored to meet the specific needs and opportunities of Lesotho – instead of trying to adapt the country to certain industries.

In addition, the L.N.D.C. has the following industries and services under construction or in a final stage of negotiation: a shopping centre; a shoe factory; a ladies' shoe workshop and a plant to make leather handbags; a glassworks; a toy factory; a building corporation; and a factory for the hand-printing of materials. L.N.D.C. projects, since the inception of the Corporation about four years ago, have brought direct foreign investment to Lesotho of over R10 million. Through its own commercial activities the L.N.D.C. now has an income of over R400,000 a year, all of which is reinvested in Lesotho. A great deal is being done to promote tourism. What makes van Graan's achievements even more remarkable is the fact that, apart from two secretaries, he is assisted by only two other people, viz. the general manager and an accountant.

ADVISORY SERVICES

Numerous services provided by South African organisations have already been referred to above. Special mention may, however, be made of the free technical advisory service provided to Lesotho by the South African Institute of Civil Engineers (S.A.I.C.E.). This service can draw on the expertise of S.A.I.C.E.'s 4,000 members as well as of other engineers and scientists in South Africa. Among the ten projects receiving attention in the second half of 1971 were an international airport at Maseru and a road across the country ending at or near the Sani Pass. According to the president of S.A.I.C.E., 'it was difficult for the state engineers in Lesotho to provide the right solution [for the latter scheme], as they were very short-staffed. . . . Many were expatriates on a two-year contract who could not be fully aware of the facilities available in South Africa.'[35]

OTHER FORMS OF DEVELOPMENT ASSISTANCE

It is not possible even to list all the diverse ways in which South

Africa directly or indirectly promotes development to neighbouring countries. However, the efforts of the South African Voluntary Service (S.A.V.S..), a students' organisation, deserve to be mentioned. Established in 1967, and with branches on the campuses of the Universities of the Witwatersrand, Cape Town, Rhodes and Natal (Pietermaritzburg and Durban), the S.A.V.S.'s 'overall objectives are to involve men and women in voluntary work for the underprivileged in underdeveloped areas of Southern Africa'. During their vacations and over weekends, these students erect clinics, schools and fences, lay pipelines, teach, etc. Going out in groups of from four to thirty volunteers, they work together with the local people in whom they seek to encourage the development of a spirit of self-help and self-reliance. The Johannesburg branch alone had completed forty projects up to the end of 1971, partly in South Africa and partly in B.L.S., including remote places such as Maun and hamlets in the high mountains of Lesotho. The work is supported by donations from business firms and private individuals.[36]

8. FINANCIAL ASSISTANCE

THE ECONOMIC CO-OPERATION PROMOTION LOAN FUND

This fund was created in 1968 with an initial contribution of R5 million from the surplus of the 1967–8 fiscal year, and is administered by the Secretary for Foreign Affairs. The Fund receives *inter alia* amounts that used to be paid to the World Health Organisation, the International Labour Office, the Food and Agriculture Organisation, as well as other bodies and funds of the United Nations. The aims for which these organisations were set up are thus still being served by South Africa, although it is no longer a member of all of them. During each of the financial years 1969–70 and 1970–1 a further amount of R5 million was allocated. On 31 March 1971 loans totalling R5·31 million had been granted, while the capital available for lending amounted to R10·51 million.[37] A R2·3 million loan has been made from this fund to the Malagasy Republic to improve the infrastructure on the island of Nossi Bé, in conjunction with the tourist hotel being established by South African interests there. The R8 million loan granted in 1968 for the building of Malawi's new capital of Lilongwe appears to have been financed from a different source.

COSTS IN CONNECTION WITH TECHNICAL AID

During 1970–1 and 1969–70, approximately R700,000 was met annually from the Foreign Affairs vote. Details are as shown in Table 11.1

TABLE 11.1. Foreign Affairs vote, 1969–70 and 1970–1

	1969–70	*1970–1*
(*a*) Secondment of South African government personnel and other persons for service with foreign governments	R249,206	R289,852
(*b*) Various visits to and from foreign countries for purposes of training, advice, consultations, preliminary investigations in connection with proposed projects, postgraduate study in South Africa, etc.	R19,062	R20,875
(*c*) Economic, agricultural and indirect financial assistance to foreign countries	R396,485	R354,560
(*d*) Various other projects	R31,674	R46,058
Total[38]	R696,427	R711,345

As regards item (*c*), it may be pointed out that it includes the subsidy ($\pm$ R250,000) which the South African government annually pays on maize and maize products sold to B.L.S. The subsidy was claimed from these countries until 1968–9, but has been charged to the Foreign Affairs vote since, and the amounts in question can be used by these countries to finance agricultural projects.[39]

EXPORT CREDITS

The Industrial Development Corporation of South Africa (I.D.C.) plays a major role in promoting investment in neighbouring countries by providing export credit facilities to South African firms. Two types of export credit are available for the post-delivery financing of export contracts, these being suppliers' credit and financial credit facilities respectively. As Table 11.2 shows, these facilities are particularly significant in respect of exports to African countries.

TABLE 11.2. Value of I.D.C. export credits

Country	As at 30 June 1969	As at 30 June 1971
	(R million)	*(R million)*
Botswana	0·25 ⎫	
Lesotho	– ⎬	21·8
Swaziland	– ⎭	
Rhodesia	40	49
Malawi	26	15
Angola	3·5	1·5
Mozambique	24	68
Malagasy Republic	–	2·2
Overseas	20	42·7
Total	R113·75	R200·2

Source: G. M. E. Leistner, 'South Africa's Economic Interests in Africa', *South African Journal of African Studies*, ii (1972) 41.

Note: The I.D.C. undertakes to provide credit to South African exporters while negotiations between exporter and importer are under way and prior to the submission of tenders. Hence figures such as those shown above change from month to month, e.g. because negotiations are called off and no contract is concluded, or because the tender is not accepted.

The first credit granted by the I.D.C. was in respect of a R4 million contract for the supply and installation of a pipeline at Luanda. A credit of R11 million was granted to the South African firm that built the new rail link between Mpinde in Malawi and Nova Freixo in Mozambique. A R2·5 million sugar mill in Malawi was equally assisted by an I.D.C. credit. I.D.C. financing plays a major role in the Cabora Bassa project (cf. Section 6 above).

THE CORPORATION FOR ECONOMIC DEVELOPMENT OF
EQUATORIAL AND SOUTHERN AFRICA (EDESA)

In 1970 the Societé Internationale Financière pour les Investissements et le Développement en Afrique (SIFIDA) was formed by a number of Western-incorporated bodies with the aim of promoting private investment as a means of contributing towards the development of Africa. SIFIDA will be mainly concerned with North, East, West and Central Africa, and a similiar organisation (EDESA) is being set up to provide primarily for the improvement of living standards of the Black peoples of

Southern Africa through the acceleration of economic development. The National Development and Management Foundation of South Africa is acting as the catalyst in the formation of EDESA.

9. CONCLUSION

The foregoing can convey only a very incomplete picture of the manifold ways in which co-operation between South Africa and its neighbours is promoting development throughout the region. Even so, it is indicative of the innumerable intra-regional bonds that are being strengthened through humdrum commercial dealings, through co-operation in combating locusts and finches, through joint water and power schemes, through dealing with common problems in respect of natural resources, labour, transport, tourism, and so forth.

These bonds are promoting better mutual appreciation and understanding of the various countries' problems and attitudes. Practical needs have already led to various more or less formal regional organisations and arrangements. One can appreciate the political problems besetting the road towards yet closer regional co-operation, and it would be unrealistic at present to envisage a regional organisation with executive functions. However, the goal of optimum growth throughout the region demands a central body to pinpoint and study those problems that affect Southern Africa as a whole, and to serve as a clearing-house for technical and economic information.

NOTES

1. Cf. G. M. E. Leistner, 'South Africa's Economic Interests in Africa', *South African Journal of African Studies* (Pretoria), II (1972) 321–46.
2. E. H. Louw, 'The Union and the Emergent States of Africa: Opening Address', *Journal for Racial Affairs* (Stellenbosch), X 4 (July 1959) 110.
3. Ibid.
4. J. F. W. Haak, quoted in *Africa Institute Bulletin* (Pretoria), III 6 (June 1965) 134.
5. Ibid.
6. Cf. G. M. E. Leistner, *South Africa's Development Aid to African States*, Occasional Paper No. 28 (Pretoria: Africa Institute of South Africa, 1970) p. 5.

7. H. Muller, *South Africa: An African-Rooted Nation* (speech by Dr H. Muller, Minister of Foreign Affairs of the Republic of South Africa, during a dinner given by the Africa Institute of South Africa, Pretoria, 25 June 1968), Occasional Paper No. 5 (Pretoria: Africa Institute of South Africa, 1968) pp. 3–4.

8. Interview with W. van Heerden, reported in *Dagbreek en Sondagnuus* (Johannesburg), 30 Oct 1966.

9. Conseil Scientifique pour l'Afrique au sud du Sahara.

10. Commission de Coopération Technique en Afrique au sud du Sahara.

11. I. V. Gruhn, 'The Commission for Technical Co-operation in Africa, 1950–65', *Journal of Modern African Studies* (London), IX 3 (October 1971) 462.

12. Ibid., p. 463.

13. Of the four regional committees into which sub-Saharan Africa was divided at the Goma Conference – Western, Central, Eastern and Southern – only SARCCUS has survived the early 1960s.

14. See D. M. Joubert, 'SARCCUS', in *The Use and Protection of Natural Resources in Southern Africa* (Johannesburg: South African Institute of International Affairs, 1973) appendix I.

15. E. D. Adler, 'Inter-territorial Technical Co-operation in Southern Africa, with Special Reference to SARCCUS', *South African Journal of Science*, LXVII (1971) 144.

16. Ibid.

17. Cf. B. C. Jansen, 'The Onderstepoort Veterinary Research Institute in relation to Animal Diseases in Southern Africa', *South African Journal of African Affairs*, II (1972) 50. Also Republic of South Africa, Department of Agricultural Technical Services, *Annual Report 1969–70*, R.P.22 (1971) pp. 188–91.

18. The name was changed to Inter-African Bureau of Animal Health (I.B.A.H.) in 1960.

19. Report in *Beeld* (Johannesburg), 19 July 1970.

20. Department of Agricultural Technical Services, op. cit., pp. 238–9.

21. *Bantu* (Department of Information, Pretoria), XVIII 4 (Apr 1971) 9.

22. Particulars taken from the N.I.P.R.'s *Annual Report 1967–1968*, pp. 1 and 31.

23. Probably Botswana; cf. Leistner, *South Africa's Development Aid*, p. 26.

24. SARCCUS, *Regional Symposium on Water for Progress*, Lourenço Marques, Mozambique, 9–12 Feb 1970 (Pretoria: Government Printer, 1970) para. 2.1.

25. Cf. Table 3.2 of *Southern Africa at a Glance*, briefing paper compiled by the Africa Institute of South Africa for this Conference. Also G. M. E. Leistner, 'Foreign Bantu Workers in South Africa: Their Present Position in the Economy', *South African Journal of Economics*, XXXV 1 (Mar 1967) 30–56.

26. For details about the formal provisions governing these arrangements, see W. J. Breytenbach, *Vreemde Bantoewerkers in Suid-Afrika en Rhodesië*, Mededelinge Nr. 17 (Pretoria: Afrika-Instituut van Suid-

Afrika, 1970). (An English version of this publication is currently being prepared). Although no treaties such as those with Malawi and Mozambique have been concluded with Botswana, that country's legislation compels recruits for the mines to make arrangements for deferred pay and regular remittances to dependants.

27. *The Star* (Johannesburg), 1 and 13 July 1971.
28. Cf. brochure, *The S.A. Wildlife Foundation: Bulletin on Southern Africa 1968–1970* (n.p, n.d.) pp. 9, 10, 13, 16.
29. Cf. E. J. van der Merwe, 'The Customs Union Agreement between Botswana, Lesotho, Swaziland and the Republic of South Africa', *South African Journal of African Affairs*, II (1971) 64–75, on p. 72.
30. I.B.R.D./I.F.C./I.D.A.–I.M.F., Boards of Governors, 1971 Annual Meetings, Washington D.C., Press Release No 16, 28 Sep 1971.
31. For further particulars, see H. J. van Eck, 'A Central Scheme for the Supply of Electric Power in Southern Africa', *Tegnikon* (Suid-Afrikaanse Akademie vir Wetenskap en Kuns, Pretoria), special edition (Mar 1967) pp. 37–48; also the Mar 1971 issue of the *South African Journal of Science*, LXVII 3, containing papers read at a symposium on 'Water for Progress'.
32. More details will be found in the annual reports of the General Manager of the South African Railways and Harbours.
33. *Rand Daily Mail* (Johannesburg), 26 Feb 1972.
34. Information obtained from the Secretary for Foreign Affairs, Pretoria.
35. See report in *Business South Africa* (Johannesburg), Sep 1971, p. 36.
36. The annual reports, entitled *Achievements*, provide detailed accounts of the various projects and also critical appraisals of the various 'work camps'.
37. See Republic of South Africa, Controller and Auditor-General, *Report on the Appropriation Accounts and Miscellaneous Accounts and the Finance Statements, 1970–71*, vol. III R.P.65 (Pretoria: Government Printer, 1971) pp. 551–2.
38. Ibid., vol. II, R.P.64 (1971) p. 219; *1969–70 Report*, vol. II, R.P.51 (1970) p. 220.
39. See Republic of South Africa, *House of Assembly Debates*, 18 Feb 1970, cols 1331–4.

BIBLIOGRAPHY

Breytenbach, W. J., *Vreemde Bantoewerkers in Suid-Afrika en Rhodesië: Reëlings in Verband met Werwing en Indiensneming*, Communication No. 17 (1970).
Clark, W. M., 'In Science and Technology South Africa Has Made a Great Contribution to the African Continent', *Africa* (Johannesburg), 11 (1965) 41–8.
Cowen, D. V., 'Towards a Common Market in Southern Africa', *Optima* (Johannesburg), XVII 2 (1967) 43–51.

Cronjé, F. C. J., 'Can a Free Trade Association be Created in Southern Africa?', *Optima*, xv 3 (1965) 113–19.

Eklund, S. O., 'A Highway System for Southern Africa', *Road International* (Geneva), no. 77 (1970) pp. 9–11, 13–15, 18.

Financial Gazette (Johannesburg), supplement on South African Common Market, 28 Apr 1967.

Green, L. P., and Fair, T. J. D., *Development in Africa* (Johannesburg: Witwatersrand Univ. Press, 1962).

Gruhn, I. V., 'The Commission for Technical Co-operation in Africa, 1950–65', *Journal of Modern African Studies* (London), ix 3 (1971) 459–69.

Landell-Mills, P. M., 'The 1969 Southern African Customs Union Agreement', *Journal of Modern African Studies*, ix 2 (1971) 263–81.

Leistner, G. M. E., 'Foreign Bantu Workers in South Africa: Their Present Position in the Economy', *South African Journal of Economics* (Johannesburg), xxxv 1 (1967) 30–56.

——, *Aid to Africa*, Communication No. 3* (1966).

——, *Die Republiek en hulp aan ander Afrika-State*, Occasional Paper No. 11* (1967).

——, *Können wir Afrika helfen?*, Occasional Paper No. 12* (1967).

——, *Perspektiven der wirtschaftlichen und politischen Zusammenarbeit im Südlichen Afrika*, Occasional Paper No. 12* (1968).

——, in P. Smit, *Botswana: Resources and Development*, Communication No. 13* (1970) chap. vi.

——, *South Africa's Development Aid to African States*, Occasional Paper No. 28* (1970).

——, and Smit, P., *Swaziland: Resources and Development*, Communication No. 8* (1969) chap. vi and *passim*.

Lombard, J. A., 'Economic Co-operation in Southern Africa', *Tegnikon* (Pretoria), special issue (Mar 1967) pp. 18–25.

——, Stadler J. J., and van der Merwe, P. J., *The Concept of Economic Co-operation in Southern Africa* (Pretoria: Econburo, 1968).

Muller, H., *South Africa: An African-Rooted Nation* (speech by Dr H. Muller, Minister of Foreign Affairs of the Republic of South Africa, during a dinner given by the Africa Institute of South Africa, Pretoria, 25 June 1968), Occasional Paper No. 5* (1968).

Robson, P., 'Economic Integration in Southern Africa', *Journal of Modern African Studies*, v 4 (1967) 469–90.

Sadie, J. L., 'An Economic Commission for Southern Africa', *South Africa International* (Johannesburg), 14 (Apr 1971) 167–75.

Smit, P., 'Co-operation in Southern Africa on Water and Power', *Africa Institute Bulletin* (Pretoria), v 10 (1967) 289–97.

——, and van der Merwe, E. J., 'Economic Co-operation in Southern Africa', *Journal of Geography* (Stellenbosch), iii 3 (1968). (Also available from the Africa Institute of South Africa as Occasional Paper No. 3.)

South Africa, Minister of Planning, 'South Africa Policy Statement: Aid and Economic Co-operation', *Africa Institute Bulletin*, iii 6 (1965) 128–34.*

South Africa, Information Service, *Union's Role in Co-operation South of the Sahara*, Fact Paper No. 81 (Pretoria, 1960).
South Africa, Department of Information, *Friendly Aid*, Fact Paper (Pretoria, 1967).
South African Journal of Science (Johannesburg), symposium on 'Water for Progress', LXVII 3 (1971).
Spence, J. E., 'The New States of Southern Africa', *Journal of Modern African Studies*, V 4 (1967) 541–55.
van Eck, H. J., 'A Central Scheme for the Supply of Electric Power in Southern Africa', *Tegnikon* (Mar 1967) pp. 37–42.
Ward, M., 'Economic Independence for Lesotho?', *Journal of Modern African Studies*, V 3 (1967) 355–68.

* Sources marked with an asterisk (*) are publications of the Africa Institute of South Africa, P.O. Box 630, Pretoria.

COMMENT

J. J. Stadler

Professor Stadler suggested that development aid could be classified under two headings: (*a*) financial aid and (*b*) technical assistance. The former supplemented limited local savings and the formation of real capital, whereas the latter supplemented technical expertise where this was restricted.

These aspects had been well covered in the two papers, which had also emphasised the importance of creating the institutional framework conducive to development through ordinary trade. This constituted the answer to the plea of developing countries for trade rather than aid.

Professor Stadler said that he wished to lay stress upon two aspects mentioned throughout the Conference: (*a*) economic development was a multi-dimensional process, and (*b*) it dealt with man himself. These aspects had to be reflected in the method of granting aid. There must be a diversified programme of both financial and technical assistance based on the needs of the people of the recipient country. It was necessary to accord priority to the requirements of the recipient country rather than to those of the donor. Thus, Professor Leistner had appropriately felt that assistance should be requested and not based upon charity, and that loans were preferable to grants. The principle involved required that the initiative emanated from the recipients themselves.

Chapter 12

Policies and Interests of the User and Donor Countries

The Donor–Recipient Relationship and Development: Some Lessons from the Iranian Experience

NORMAN JACOBS

This paper will attempt to provide *one* possible explanation for an admittedly complex problem, namely the often strained relationship which exists between the correlative partners, usually termed donor and recipient, in international development programmes. This interpretation will reflect both the author's academic specialisation – bias if you will – as a comparative institutional sociologist with an area focus on Asia, and his experiences as a rural community development adviser for the United States International Co-operation Administration (the donor) at a field post in Fars Province, Iran, from 1959 to 1961. In trying to understand the sources of his difficulties with Iranian provincial officials in particular (the recipient) attending the effort to implement the Iranian community development programme at the operational level, the author probed both his own previous experiences and training and the insight of others, Asian and non-Asian, theoretical and empirical, moving back, step by step, from the actual work situation to increasingly theoretical and abstract levels of interpretation. This paper will present that intellectual exercise in brief. Only, in accord with the ritualistic demands of scientific explanation, the discussion will begin with the most abstract and move successively towards concrete reality.[1]

I

In the present context, the donor is a derivative of European culture, and therefore, for better or worse, has been influenced by the ways of thinking and the historical experience of that culture.

Though one must never minimise the often tremendous variations in specifics within European thought, yet that thought does appear to share a common approach, albeit often implicitly, in its interpretation of non-European culture as far as two key tenets are concerned, namely positivism and social evolution. Although these two precepts are theoretically discreet in the sense that one can be used independently of the other, they are usually integrated in most European development analyses, and this will be assumed in the present discussions.

Very briefly, the doctrine of social evolution[2] may be considered a method to describe a society's relative position vis-à-vis any other society, and to assess its prospects for productive social change – both with reference to an assumed common global pattern of social development in definitely defined stages of maturation. The content of those stages and the process of maturation have already been determined through the earlier effort of various contributors to catalogue the universal developmental characteristics of Society (with a capital S), and subsequently to rate and rank the world's societies on a universal, unilinear scale in terms of conformity to those expectations. Accepted wthout question is that, in spite of cultural diversity and the possible play of the historically unique – that is, those accidents of history which can and do make a difference – all societies are heading in a similar (or unilinear) course, passing through similar basic changes in their social fabric termed their typological stages of social evolution, no matter how diverse their specific paths and no matter how devious those paths may appear superficially to the untrained observer. Also assumed is that a necessary linkage exists among the various characteristics of any society. Of special interest is that a society's material and non-material characteristics will be identically interpreted and evaluated, and then ranked in the evolutionary scale. Since it is the European who is doing the correlating and evaluating, it is – not surprisingly – the content of European society which has served as the standard against which the characteristics of all non-European societies are rated and ranked, in terms of their difference from European norms.

Positivism offers a method to describe and a means to transform the existing social environment, primarily through the agent of empirical science. For it is assumed that science not only provides man with an accurate knowledge of the universe in all fields, including the non-material, so that man *can* make the most reasonable and productive choices to master his environment, but it also demonstrates that man is *obligated* to master that environment. For once exposed to the possibility and probability of improving his material and non-material well-being, who dares deliberately to be irrational and not serve his best interests? One might say that positivism provided both the moral imperative and what appeared to be a practical means to ensure the success of social evolution by moving all societies most efficaciously towards what came to be viewed as a universal, inevitable and desirable goal; to wit, the achievement of every society's full potential as exemplified by the most advanced societies.[3]

The feasibility of applying the abstractions of both social evolution and positivism is predicated on the conviction that the concrete, historical social experience of Europe, interpreted as a transition from a 'pre-modern' feudal society to a 'modern' industrial society, can and should be reproduced universally. One of the key assumptions of that conviction is that all pre-modern societies in their 'highest stage of evolution' are feudal.[4] Feudal societies, like any other general type, vary in concrete specifics, but have the following common characteristics:

1. The primary social unit consists of an organised group of warriors, one of whom is the superior (termed 'lord') with whom all the others (termed 'vassals') are bound by personal ties, which usually but not always are rewarded with land tenure or profit (termed 'fiefs'). This unit must be constantly defended against political and economic unrest.

2. Land is the economic foundation of the society. Few individuals actually own land. Most have only relative but reciprocal rights, privileges and obligations in graded descending steps of a hierarchy from the socially superior lord to the many socially inferior vassals. The workers of the land (termed 'peasants') are outside the warriors' feudal relationships, but are subject to the military protection of the warriors.

3. If the warriors also claim public political power, the fief rights correspond to political authority and land possession corresponds to social status.

Two major observations. First, the feudal concepts of rights, privileges and obligations were formally defined in feudal contracts and law. These rules helped to convert the pyramidal feudal hierarchy into a social organisation which some observers have suggested was a rational bureaucracy in embryo. These rules and organisation survived the downfall of feudal society and became, in the European view, one cornerstone of the post-feudal modern society. Second, the transition from feudal to modern society in Europe was accompanied by replacement of the military with the civilian, especially the industrial innovator, in the key social role, and replacement of the feudal ethos and social organisation, based on rigid class distinctions, status honour and fixed laws and distinctions termed 'tradition', with a more rational, pragmatic allocation of the society's resources, human and material, in the interest of maximising the society's potential, termed 'modernity'. To the positivist-evolutionist, the emerging industrial ethos and social organisation came to be viewed as the primary benchmark against which to evaluate the overall worth of a society. For all *non*-industrial societies, which in evolutionary terms could but be designated as *pre*-industrial societies – feudal, traditional and underdeveloped – were viewed as the not very attractive polar opposites to industrial, modern societies. The implicit positivist moral imperative dictated that the sooner these non-industrial societies were converted to industrial societies, the better.

II

The non-European societies share neither an indigenous positivist-evolutionary philosophy nor a feudal past as it has been defined, save perhaps for the once noticeable exception of feudal Japan which is significant, but beyond the scope of the present discussion.[5] What these societies do share in common is much harder to determine. This essay will therefore restrict its remarks to one geographical area, Asia, and in particular to one society, Iran, in the belief and hope that the observations will be of value because they might illuminate what happens when European ethos and social practice confront non-European ethos and social practice in the development context.[6]

To the Iranian, as to other Asians, the legitimate social order above all else is a moral order, established in accord with precepts attributed to some eternal moral force. In this social order a minority of individuals judged to be superior morally to their fellow-men have both the legitimate right and the sole responsibility to define, enforce and exercise the decision and prerogatives associated with the society's fundamental rules. By acknowledging the superiority of the moral men, the society's vast majority are entitled to services, termed 'benefices', from their moral superiors. These services are offered not as a right but as a patronal privilege of grace, and hence may be withdrawn at will without review by the moral inferiors.

Most typically, the men of morality are organised into a political élite, a civil administrative bureaucracy, in alliance with or coincident with the society's priesthood. Although primarily politicians, the members of the élite strive to monopolise decision-making in all spheres of social life, on the assumption that, as the society's exclusive specialists in morality, they are simultaneously generalists in the moral aspects of whatever is essential to the establishment and maintenance of the legitimate social order. Morality is also constant over time. Hence it is difficult to conceive that any situation could arise which would seriously challenge the right of the moral élite to monopolise primary decision-making in the society. Rather, the élite is supposed to accommodate itself to any new specific roles and functions which might arise in the society. The only concession is that the ranks of the élite may periodically be purged of its misfits, solely a self-inflicted punishment. For this symbolic act is a moral judgement, and only the moral élite can judge morality. At worst, if the élite is beyond moral redemption, then a novel élite may have to be sanctioned, since above all else the moral foundations of the social order must be preserved if that social order is to be accepted as legitimate.

Concrete examples of these general principles may be found in moral-élitist administrative principles and procedures. For one, primacy is assigned to maintaining good human relations among human beings, which is often as concrete as one can be as to what moral connotes in the development context. Thus, manipulative roles are emphasised over task-specific and non-political roles. (In comparing this system with feudalism it is worth noting that, under this principle, civil roles are emphasised over military roles, even in what appear to be military regimes.[7]) And although moral decisions are generalised decisions, they are individual judgements. For although an individual is supposed to refer to some arbitrary constant standard defined as moral, formal restraints on his ability to make those decisions of grace in the interest of institutionalising and protecting morality in the society cannot be tolerated. Consequently, impersonal formal law, stable rules, certainty and calculability may all very well be obstacles to an individual moralist's ability to create morality according to his assessment of the moral imperatives of the particular situation. Further, those occupations which might establish the primacy of non-moral or amoral standards and goals in the society to the detriment of the primacy of moral standards and goals are viewed with great suspicion. For example, economic actors and actions must be subordinated to moral-political values either by integrating economic action into the moral-political orbit or by supervising objective profit-seeking activities, all in the name of moral profit. This does *not* imply that Asian moralism is other-worldly and indifferent to economic activity. Quite the contrary, it is argued that without moral goals and guidance, economic activity cannot succeed in crass material terms. For without that guidance, economic action will degenerate into individual, short-term material advantage and the economic war of all against all, destroying good human relations as unrealistic greed overtakes the prudent use of economic resources.

Finally, although morality is a generalised, seemingly abstract and rather vaguely defined system of rules for individual judgement, nevertheless its adherents maintain that it is a system which must be learnt. Whether this is so because of the choice of decision-making or supervisory roles by the moral élite, or whether the moral élite has been able to monopolise these roles because of an initial concern for literary accomplishment, or both, cannot be definitely determined. In any case, even though morality is to be found more readily among the members of the élite than the non-élite, it is a literate virtue, such that the moral man can but be a learned man, and a learned man is assumed to have busied himself with mastery of the general principles of morality as defined in the literate cultural heritage of that élite. For this reason, the defence of a society's cultural tradition has become synonymous with defence of morality, and vice versa, and defence of the moral culture has implied defence of the integrity of élitism (if not of the specific élite in power), and vice versa.

III

With very few exceptions the non-European political élite is willing, even eager, to accept the European's material blessings. For there is little or nothing in the indigenous moral value system to encourage the members of the élite to reject improvement in economic well-being, at least for themselves, *provided* the means by which that well-being is achieved does not run counter to the moral imperatives of the social order just described.[8] This apparent tolerance towards non-indigenous materialism has inadvertently generated not a cornucopia of material bliss but an intellectual can of worms. For it has raised the vital question as to whether the material well-being of Europe can be accepted, adapted and locally integrated without at the same time accepting those non-material aspects of European culture and society which arose concurrently with European material development. The members of the ruling élite have perceptively realised on the one hand that their ability to maintain the primacy of their roles and their moral standards in the society have more recently come to depend directly on their ability successfully to meet the challenge of material improvement, if for no other reason than that material prosperity is required for maintaining the political integrity of their society in the international community of nations, which not unimportantly coincides with their continued existence as a viable élite. Yet, on the other hand, the élite has discovered that the qualitatively different European definition of the goals of the social order and the means by which to achieve those goals will bring into question the vital moral-élitist role in society. Hence for the élite the choice might have to be: is it worth saving the nation if its élite runs the risk of sacrificing morality, not to speak of itself, in the process?

But this is not the only dilemma facing the élite. For, to recall, not only have its members identified the society's national integrity with their own political integrity, but they have also associated the society's cultural integrity, as they define that culture, with their own personal integrity. Yet if the European material prosperity is accepted as superior to local economic ways, is the culture of the European also superior, or at the least worthy of serious consideration? And if that culture is taken seriously, will this not create a negative image of the moral élite, not only within but, perhaps more dangerously, without the charmed circle of the élite? And even if the members of the élite are somehow able to maintain élite integrity and the right to rule and define the perimeters of the culture, what within the confines of European culture do they define as locally relevant? Will not such acceptance adversely affect national pride and self-respect as well as personal psychological security?

For all these reasons, for those non-Europeans who first confronted Europe, the not surprising reaction was to hold the cultural line so far as possible and to sanction acceptance of European ways only reluctantly and as a phased, step-by-step retreat from initial outright rejection, to acceptance of the material and rejection of the non-material, to acceptance of the non-material in so far as the élite felt it was not incompatible with its own definition of the non-material, to acceptance of the non-material in form but the indigenous in spirit, to acceptance of the non-material in spirit to revive, or 'modernise', the indigenous (usually termed 'old wine in new bottles') and, finally, to selective acceptance of the non-material in substance; as, for example, acceptance in those areas most closely associated with economic action and political nation-building in the hopes that this would not erode the existing patterns of interpersonal relations and the moral-religious system. Latecomers on the scene of international confrontation, for no other reason than that the prior steps had already proven ineffective, have moved directly to the last stage, that is, to acceptance or rejection of European goals and practices in the light of local goals and practices deemed irreducibly vital to national integrity by particular local élites.

Not surprisingly, then, how wisely these supposedly irreducible cultural and social norms are chosen – that is, whether or not they are truly vital to national integrity, and irreducible or not, if in retaining these values and norms the development effort is jeopardised, and with it the survival chances of the élite, not to speak of the nation – is the crux of the development problem to many non-European élites. Complicating matters is the fact that, although there is usually general agreement that *total* acceptance of an alien culture and social presuppositions will compromise a nation and the self-appointed élite defenders beyond redemption, there is no consensus as to what or how wisely to select from among the many possibilities that Europe offers. Although usually a particular political ideology, often imported into the local situation, may seem to be the ultimate judge of what is accepted and what is rejected, ideology is much too European and hence too simplistic, as locals find themselves liberal, or modern, on some issues and conservative, or traditional, on others, as judged by European standards. Rather, many influences come to bear upon individual decisions, not the least being local loyalties.

Many decisions are essentially defensive and negative reactions to Europe, most especially the glorification of perhaps a not very viable past, in which an ill-defined and incoherent alternative to the European development proposals is the best that can be offered. Consequently, without an obviously attractive alternative to grasp, many in the local élite have come to ask, in private if not in public, if the material attributes of Europe are attractive, are not the non-material aspects of European culture equally of value? The indigenous, because it is so deeply rooted in any culture, is *a priori* held tenaciously. But is such defensiveness legitimate and, perhaps more to the point, feasible, in the face of the local society's obvious needs? And yet, for all the reasons explored earlier, in those societies in which non-material considerations loom so large – and this is certainly true in the morally oriented societies of which Iran is one member – this is not a question so quickly or easily answered by the local élite, in spite of the obvious consequences of not being modern and developed in European terms. It is in truth the moral élitist nightmare – the primary present-day dilemma.

Up to this point, the discussion has only too typically been addressing itself to the élitist perspective of the development process. Lost in almost all discussions between local élites and foreign and domestic academics is the alternative response of the inarticulate overwhelming majority of the population, which, regardless of the decisions by fiat on high, can very well determine the success or failure of development programmes. It is on this, the operational level, that donor–recipient relations must often be translated into reality. Here, often in spite of conventional wisdom to the contrary, perhaps paradoxically, there is much less resistance to European-inspired innovation, especially but not exclusively material innovation, regardless of the obvious lack of familiarity with European ways and ethos as compared to the ruling élite. Especially is this true among the supposedly unsophisticated peasantry. In fact, to the élite it is this very lack of sophistication that is to some extent at the root of this dilemma. For it is unawareness of the effects of uninhibited, uncritical acceptance of non-indigenous techniques and goals which can compromise the integrity of a nation, its culture, and coincidently of the élite itself. At various times the élite has believed that the naïve man in the village and in the street was consciously or not in league with the European, requiring élitist control over both to maintain the moral *status quo*. From the outsider's point of view, an alternative explanation of the non-élite's indifference to accepting the élitist interpretation of what is best for the society may be found in the the fact that after living the way they have and being told it is justified morally as well as legitimately for so long, the non-élitists may very well have decided that they cannot afford the luxury of maintaining the *status quo* conception of a society when offered a viable alternative providing at least more material and psychological security, concerns which the élite, either out of self- or other interest (or both), slight. Herein lies a revolutionary potential, not only in the conventional sense but also in the context of challenging the moral-élitist concept of society, a state of affairs of which the local élite is very much aware, thus further intensifying existing élitist ideological and psychological insecurities concerning the development challenge.

IV

The European donor's counter-reaction to the local élite-recipient's reaction to the donor's offer has been that the recipient is at best a malingerer, is at least a devious dissimulator, and is most typically an incompetent who might or might not measure up to standard in time.[9] Especially when the recipient affirms that at least he shares the material goals of development with the European, the donor is either confused or is disbelieving. For, armed or entrapped with his view of development as but one aspect of an inevitable, universal process of positivist evolutionary maturation, the donor finds it hard to understand, let alone tolerate, those who seem wilfully to be standing in the way of history. In positivist thinking, allowing a man the opportunity to serve his objective best interests, which in the European context has implied the primacy of maximising one's economic potential, can only lead to a rational maximisation of that potential. If a man does not maximise, then either the donor or recipient has somehow misunderstood or misapplied the iron law of rational maximisation; or in positivist terminology the distortions of ignorance and error have somehow occurred. Since in these terms there cannot be any alternative reasonable explanation for failure to accept and implement development goals, the donor views his role as primarily educative, either in conveying innovative techniques to the unenlightened or in overcoming resistance to innovation. In positivist, universal-unilinear terms, resistance can only be visualised as doing things and believing things in the same old, unproductive, pre-enlightened way, instead of responding pragmatically to the needs of the new social order; or, as the developers put it, being traditional instead of being modern.

Since the donor is convinced that the process of transition from the traditional to the modern is universal and unilinear, then at least the essential aspects of that process in European society can serve as benchmarks for the development process in non-European societies. Also asumed out of the same conviction is that the functions associated with the European forms must have the same functions in the non-European context, subject only to the distortions of ignorance and error noted previously. These potential distortions are expected in a so-called transitional period in which a lag relationship exists between the initial adoption of the form and the ultimate, inevitable adoption of the respective European function, while the recipient is adjusting his traditional techniques and ethos to modern demands. The donor considers that his essential role is to help narrow the time-span of that lag period. Since, once again, developmental change is considered a unilinear, universal process, the donor views lag as the result of some malfunction in the social processes rather than as a clash between two qualitatively different social systems. Hence he believes the situation may be altered by employing the techniques which Europe has developed to deal with social dislocations in its own environment, especially the manipulative communications media to create favourable reactions to mass distribution of commodities and ideas on the aggregate level, and trustful face-to-face relations with work associates on the interpersonal level. The donor has been reinforced in his convictions by the often favourable response to his efforts, especially, it is worth repeating, outside the élite orbit where he has practised close face-to-face working relationships, in spite of the fact that the audience is less sophisticated in European ways and is supposed to be more committed to traditional ways of doing things.

V

The Iranian development endeavour in particular has been irritated by donor–recipient misunderstandings and frustrations. We wish to suggest that many of these tensions are a consequence of those differing historical backgrounds, goals and assumptions of social order and change between donor and recipient which have been the substance of the discussions to this point. This supposition is not intended to slight either of the more popular symbolic-cultural or human relations explanations of the development literature. But it does suggest that these explanations are not sufficient.

Space and time preclude even attempting to list donor–recipient issues, let alone comment on them.[10] Rather, some typical examples illustrating the themes of the paper follow.

1. *The macroscopic administrative level.* The donor has strongly suggested that his often massive grants-in-aid be allocated in accord with European public administrative procedures. To accomplish this goal, the donor has invested a great deal of time and effort expounding on the virtues of, and the material benefits to be derived from, mastering his organisational flowcharts and putting into practice an administrative system of defined rights, privileges, obligations and standard operational procedures. The Iranians have accepted the charts and the formal structure of European organisation in good grace, and have demonstrated that they are as facile as the donor in learning and using the appropriate administrative argot. Nevertheless, the formal system has never functioned according to the donor's expectations. Decision-making has not been clear-cut, nor has it corresponded to the specifications of the charts. Rather, one might say that the Iranians are using an alternative system requiring a chart radically different from the nominal one.

To be specific the channels of command and responsibility are non-pyramidal, that is, not necessarily vertically hierarchical or transitive. Authority below the top level is deconcentrated rather than decentralised. Little or no horizontal co-ordination exists. Technical roles are downgraded in relation to administrative roles regardless of individual, relative ranks in the formal hierarchy. Finally, decision-making is personal, idiosyncratic, dependent on cliques and cliental loyalty, and beyond the review of objective standards of rationality and efficiency when measured against the formal system. Not surprisingly, the donor has interpreted these discrepancies primarily in his own administrative terms, namely, as a conflict between staff and line and as the looseness of fit between formal and informal structures – that is, as managerial problems which are assumed to be typical of all administrative systems. Ignored is that *both* staff and line in Iran operate under similar principles and procedures, and that these principles and procedures have rarely if ever in Iranian history – and bureaucratic administration is very old in all Asian societies, to recall – been articulated with any formally defined administrative structure in the European sense, and therefore cannot necessarily be considered, as the European has explained out of his experience, to be either distortions or modifications in the interest of improving efficiency by accommodating personal human abilities and needs to formal administrative requirements. Rather, the discrepancy between formal administration and informal function may be a consequence of the circumstance that the Iranian is striving to accommodate the novel European formal administration to cherished moral-élitist administrative procedures and goals. The donor considers that the Iranian must qualitatively realign his goals and procedures to fit the European administrative model. The Iranian is convinced conversely because, since the issue is administrative, no alteration is required in that the control and manipulation of human beings are involved.

The Iranian has also argued on pragmatic grounds that in order to get the lethargic bureaucratic apparatus to move more efficiently, it has been essential to use tried and tested procedures, and in this sense the Iranian was more rational and more realistic than the donor who was unaware of or unwilling to accept the local political culture (preferred translation: Iranian moral-élitist presuppositions). And it can be cited, for example, that operations can grind to a halt if the senior patron cannot hold the loyalty of his followers by dispensing tangible political or economic favours (benefices in moral-élitist terms, to recall). Which perhaps provides one possible explanation for the range of efficiency and 'progress' in individual development projects, especially why some enterprises work so well and others do not without any apparent difference on European standards in complexity of task or staff training. For some enterprises may serve as benefices to reward the faithful, while others, for any number of reasons (e.g. because they are crucial for foreign exchange or national defence) are immune.[11]

2. *Iranian interpersonal relations.* In European eyes, community development (or C.D.) implies viable, face-to-face small-group, self- generative initiative and productive activity. To the donor, therefore, C.D. represents a prime means to mobilise the non-European passive predominant majority to contribute to, and develop a positive attitude towards, its own and its society's welfare and future by participating in community-initiated and organised self-help uplift projects. The Iranian élite is certainly interested in the possibility of increasing the material bounty of the society through C.D., especially since this programme offers an opportunity to do so with minimal effort and risk on its part. But it is suspicious of creating autonomous, productive groups outside the élite circle. Hence, at worst C.D. is ignored or changed into a programme in which the community groups do the work and the élite receives the political and economic credit by sponsoring, reviewing or partially funding and technically guiding individual projects. At best there is a compromise in which the élite lead, educate and discipline the community organisations during the period of élite tutelage, until at the élite's initiative the populace at large will be considered ready to assume the full burden of its development responsibilities.

In this interpretation of C.D., the selection of tasks to perform and the training and organising into groups of those who will carry out the tasks lies outside the community groups themselves. In other words, no distinction is made between those who may very well be privy to the technical knowledge necessary effectively to carry out development tasks, and those who may be best able to determine their own needs and work capacities. For, in moral-élitist terms, non-élite initiative in formulating and solving potentially significant social problems often cannot be tolerated no matter what the economic potential benefit, lest this compromise the moral-élitist foundation of the social order.

3. *Interpersonal relations between donor and recipient on the operations level, especially the relationship between the foreign resident adviser and the local counterpart representing the recipient.* To the European donor, the resident adviser is his representative on the spot, a technical expert who facilitates the success of the donor's project in whatever capacity he can be effective. For that is the role of an adviser in modern European society. To the Iranian recipient the technical adviser is a non-administrative specialist, and hence a modern-day craftsman who serves the interests of, and at the initiative of, the moral administrator. For that is the role of the technical adviser in that society. Hence it is soon obvious to the European adviser that, contrary to the positivist-evolutionary theory, the transmission of technical knowledge and techniques may be the least of his development problems, if it even is a problem at all. In fact, the adviser often finds that his local counterpart is far more learned than he is, not only with respect to specialised knowledge itself, but also with respect to the practical application of that knowledge under unusual, that is, non-European conditions. But, at the least, the adviser realises that knowledge is relatively easy to implant, and those whom it is ultimately to reach are eager to receive it once its utility has been satisfactorily demonstrated, which may not be difficult. And certainly, the underprivileged in Iranian society, as suggested previously, cannot afford the luxury of slighting their precarious material welfare in favour of their alleged anti-positivist, traditional prejudices.

It is suggested rather, that the advisory problem is rooted in the conscious or unconscious fear of the recipient, as a moral-élite administrator, of the effects of the adviser's knowledge on cherished moral-élitist goals and procedures, no matter how attractive that knowledge may be in objective, development terms. Imprisoned by the positivist-evolutionary view that knowledge has its own intrinsic power to convert sceptics, the adviser can only see the difficulty in terms of some managerial, human relations problem. Hence the adviser believes that, if he can somehow gain his counterpart's confidence and friendship, he will be able to convert the recipient to the adviser's rational and hence desirable point of view. Such is the material out of which the legend of the Ugly American has been created.[12] The recipient is not above using the legend for his own purposes, especially to avoid one of the major dilemmas of the development process, namely, how to retain the essentials of moral-élitism, while simultaneously transforming the society at least to the extent that it can survive in the face of the unavoidable confrontation with European ideas and procedures.

In sum, Iranian development has been an uneasy compromise, one of doing whatever is possible productively, but within the range of established élitist presuppositions. A great deal can be accomplished, as attested by Iranian material progress these past decades. Yet logically and on the face of the same evidence, such accomplishment has its limits. Therefore it is worth while to make a logical distinction between maximising a society's potential using the latest available rational and productive techniques (or means), but within selected, vitally maintained institutional presuppositions and goals – such as moral-élitist political values – and maximising a potential which includes a critical review of, and if necessary an alteration in, those presuppositions and goals. The present author has termed these two attitudes towards social change, respectively, modernisation and development.[13] In this terminology, Iranian experience is better interpreted as modernisation rather than development. One hastens to add that it must be the Iranian's choice as to whether he wishes his society to be developed or only modernised, and that choice cannot be made on the basis of non-indigenous, especially European, ultimate goals and values. But it seems evident that as long as the difference between these two contrasting views of social change persists unappreciated by donor and recipient alike, tensions between them will persist.

VI

The present discussion cannot be closed without taking into account the recent non-European élite's intellectual and spiritual attack against the European vision of man. This onslaught has been equalled in ferocity and aided by the European's own cultural soul-searching at this very moment when the non-European is regaining the cultural confidence and pride he held before his unwelcomed confrontation with Europe.[14]

First, the non-European is attacking positivism and unilinear-universal evolution. On the one hand he is opting for a spiritual, subjective and intuitive approach to the study and evaluation of man, and he has challenged the right of any but an indigenous member to define and evaluate the content of any culture or society. In this attitude the non-European shares an almost universal disenchantment with positivism and with the belief that the European has truly succeeded once and for all in determining and mastering the means to understand and achieve man's perfectibility. On the other hand, the non-European has gone on the offensive, not only in rejecting European goals as his own, but in loudly proclaiming that his own goals are superior to the European's. The non-European particularly has attacked the idea that maximising a society's material prosperity is a legimate criterion for evaluating the worth of a society, and even that material maximisation is a goal compatible with the best interests of a society's integrity or perhaps survival. Evidence from the European's recent experience with pollution problems and industrial social tensions seems to offer substantive demonstration for these charges.

In attempting to place these serious charges against development theory and methods in perspective, it may be worth considering the following. First, in most instances these are the charges of an élite which, because it is a society's privileged class, is already reasonably secure materially and otherwise, and hence can afford the luxury of slighting these concerns. Merely because the European has over-emphasised the material aspects of development, in some cases to the detriment of human life, is no logical reason to ignore the material, especially when the non-élite, which constitutes the vast majority in most non-European societies, is almost by definition suffering from various degrees of material deprivation and insecurity. At the least it is worth while to consider the majority's feelings in this matter, since past experience suggests that the majority does not necessarily share the élite's disdain or ambiguity towards the majority's material betterment. And on the other hand, it is worth considering that an answer to the naïveness of positivism does not lie in intuition, any more than the answer to European cultural domination and arrogance lies in non-European cultural defensiveness and chauvinism. The valid and necessary search of the non-European for cultural integrity and pride need not and should not encourage cultural xenophobia which will preclude choosing realistically and without fantasy what could very well be of value in other cultures.

In sum, the world undoubtedly needs a new version of what is productive change and how to achieve it. For too long, although they have differed on details as sketched in this essay, both donor and recipient have assumed that change is economic and national rather than social and individual. As the more recently emerging societies come to the fore in the international community, they too will face the challenge of productive change, or development as it is usually termed. Most especially, as we now have learnt, this implies making choices and establishing realistic goals and priorities in terms of *human* happiness variously defined. Fortunately these societies have the lessons of the past, especially the illusions, delusions and frustrations of donor–recipient relations, to serve as a guide. This may not resolve or even lessen the difficulties which lie ahead, but it can be hoped that such experience will help to avoid the mistakes and misconceptions of the past – which is all the past can hope to provide. As has often been said, 'Those who refuse to learn from the mistakes of history, are destined to repeat them'.

NOTES

1. Further discussions and case details on many of the specific observations of the present paper may be found in N. Jacobs, *The Sociology of Development: Iran as an Asian Case Study*, Praeger Special Studies in International Economics and Development (New York, 1966).

2. Though the jargon of social evolution seems to approximate that of biological evolution, and it is commonly assumed that the former is an offspring of the latter, more recent scholarship has demonstrated that in fact the concepts of social evolution predate those of biological evolution, and hence do not depend on biology for their existence. See, for example, J. W. Burrow, *Evolution and Society: A Study in Victorian Social Theory* (Cambridge, 1970), and L. Schneider, *The Scottish Moralists on Human Nature and Society* (Chicago, 1967).

3. For a prime mover in the field of positivism and evolution, one who has had a profound effect on the thinking of many outside European culture often in local translation, see the works of Herbert Spencer, especially

his *Synthetic Philosophy*. Of particular interest to the sociologist are his three volumes, *Principles of Sociology* (London, many editions).

4. This description follows the suggestions of the Japanese institutional historian, Kanichi Asakawa; see his *Land and Society in Medieval Japan* (Tokyo, 1965), esp. pp. 22–4. His views have influenced a number of non-Japanese feudal specialists; see, for example, R. Coulbourn, *Feudalism in History* (Princeton, 1956).

5. Japan is significant because up to this point it is the only non-Western society to develop and appears to be one of the most dynamic societies, if not the most, in the world. A torrent of literature has appeared in the attempt to explain why this is so. The present author's early views may be found in his *Origin of Modern Capitalism and Eastern Asia* (Hong Kong Univ. Press, 1958). He is now preparing a revised study tentatively entitled *Feudalism, Patrimonialism and Japanese Development*.

6. This argument follows the lead of the sociologist Max Weber and his concept of patrimonialism. See especially the *Theory of Social and Economic Organisation*, trans. by Henderson and T. Parsons (New York, 1947) pp. 346–54, 373–82, and his monographs, *The Religion of China* (Glencoe, Ill., 1951) and *The Religion of India* (Glencoe, 1958). See also N. Jacobs, 'Max Weber: The Theory of Asian Society and the Study of Thailand', *Sociological Quarterly* (Columbia, Mo.), XII (autmun 1971) 525–30, and for a general discussion in relation to Iran specifically, Jacobs, *The Sociology of Development*, chap. 10.

7. See, for example, J. Johnson (ed.), *The Role of the Military in Underdeveloped Countries* (Princeton, 1962).

8. Materials on Iranian élitist reaction to the development challenge are scarce indeed. A number are cited in Jacobs, *The Sociology of Development*. See especially L. Binder, *Iran: Political Development in a Changing Society* (Berkeley, 1962), for a view contrary to that of the present author. For reactions in other (Asian) societies, especially on the critical differing reactions of Japan and China, cf. K. Pyle, *The New Generation in Meiji Japan* (Stanford, 1968) and Mary Wright, *The Last Strand of Chinese Conservatism* (Stanford, 1957).

9. For a systematic review of various myths of development, see Jacobs, *The Sociology of Development*, chap. 11.

10. Further details on the cases selected for discussion in this section and other cases are found in Jacobs, *The Sociology of Development*. Similar and other problems in another society reviewed from the same vantage-points are discussed in N. Jacobs, *Modernisation without Development: Thailand as an Asian Case Study*, Praeger Special Series (New York, 1971).

11. The writer has presented a case study on this theme in 'Economic Rationality and Social Development: An Iranian Case Study', *Studies in Comparative International Development* (Social Science Institute, Washington University, St Louis, Mo.), II 9 (1966).

12. W. Lederer and E. Burdick, *The Ugly American* (New York, 1958). For some comments on the book in terms of development theory, see Jacobs, *The Sociology of Development*, pp. 468–72.

13. This is the title and theme of Jacobs, *Modernisation without Development*; see esp. chap. 1. Within the economic context, note the title and see R. Clower *et al.*, *Growth without Development: An Economic Survey of Liberia* (Evanston, Ill., 1966), esp. chap. 1.
14. This is examined in detail in Jacobs, *Modernisation without Development*, chap. 13. Some pertinent references are cited there.

The Policies, Interests and Attitudes of Donor and Recipient Countries, and the Role of Multilateral Aid

DAVID HIRSCHMANN

1. DONOR COUNTRIES: WHY AID?

> The Clyde shipbuilder, the French *ouvrier*, the American in the hard hat, do not easily realise that they owe a part of what they already consider to be their threatened standard of living to peasants in Bengal, Benin or Brazil.[1]

The motives underlying the transfer of resources from a developed country to a developing country for the purpose of development are both complex and interrelated. These motives, further, tend to become blurred and confused by the fact that so much of what is said about them is not meant, so much of what is meant is not said; and that emphases on goals and objectives change not only from one audience (e.g. the donor country's electorate or legislature) to another (e.g. a delegation from a developing country or a U.N. development agency), but also from time to time; similarly, the interrelationship of motives does not remain static.

Nevertheless, it is possible to list briefly some of the principal motives for foreign assistance:

1. *Moral motives*: based on the humanitarian's repugnance of the fact of a world in which a minority lives in affluence and a majority in deprivation, and on the consequent determination to improve the lot of the latter.

2. *Political motives*: to protect a certain structure of political and economic establishment beneficial, or at least not

inimical, to the interests of the donor, and to prevent an antagonistic power establishing or increasing its influence.

3. *Military motives*: closely related to political motives; for instance, strengthening a government which allows military bases on its territory or bolstering a military commitment.

4. *Short-term economic motives*: to protect, maintain and and expand investments, trade, markets and preferences.

5. *Long-term economic motives*: to assist and accelerate the development of economies of countries which, when more advanced, should become increasingly significant trading partners in a more buoyant world economy.[2]

6. *World peace motives*: to prevent the poverty and frustration of the poorer nations, angered at the ever-widening gap between themselves and the richer nations, from erupting in a continuous sequence of violence, revolutions and wars which endanger the relatively peaceful progress of the developed countries.

7. *Historic responsibility motives*: countries such as the United Kingdom and France have accepted a degree of responsibility for the welfare of their former colonies which reached political independence lacking many of the human and physical resources necessary for healthy economic growth.

8. *Cultural motives*: related to historic responsibility and with obvious political and economic connotations, the purpose is to broaden the influence of the culture, language and way of life of the donor country.

Yet for all these seemingly significant motivating forces the mid-1960s saw a so-called 'crisis of aid' or 'weakening of the will' on the part of the donor countries, occasioned by their own balance-of-payments difficulties, growing concern with domestic problems of poverty and race relations, and widening disillusionment – even boredom – of public opinion at the apparent failure of aid to induce significant benefits and at the apparent lack of appreciation by some of the recipients.

There are development analysts and a few leaders of developing countries who deny that foreign aid assists the developmental process and assert that on the contrary it is more likely to retard progress. But this is not chiefly what the crisis of aid is about. Rather it is about the failure of foreign aid to guarantee in any substantial way the interests of the aid-giving country, leading one commentator to conclude that foreign aid programmes, subjected to close scrutiny, 'would probably emerge as a clumsy, expensive and counter-productive method of carrying out a foreign policy'.[3]

If it is difficult to prove that external assistance has substantially assisted economic development, or that statistical economic advancement leads to widespread and healthy development, so is it also difficult to demonstrate that economic progress, where this does occur, leads necessarily to political stability. 'This depends on how societies will react to the achievement of certain economic objectives (assuming foreign aid is successful in realising or helping to realise these objectives) and upon the impact of these social relations in turn on the character and policies of their governments.'[4]

Still less can it be convincingly shown that economic growth determines the international behaviour of the recipient government or its attitudes towards the political objectives of the donor country; nor does it guarantee to elicit any feelings of gratitude. These lessons were strikingly illustrated by the voting of many recipients of U.S. aid on the question of the representation of China in the U.N. in 1971. Both the Israel–Arab war of 1967 and the India–Pakistan war of December 1971 also demonstrated the limitations on the control exercised by the big-power donor countries. Moreover, when an aid-giving country does find a sympathetic recipient government, foreign aid cannot ensure that that government will not be replaced at very short notice by one less sympathetic.

Further, serious doubt has been cast on whether any national economic benefits accrue to donor countries, in consequence of their assistance to user countries. It is the view of Raymond F. Mikesell that if there are in fact such benefits (other than export credits), they are 'largely indirect, highly tenuous, and of such a long-term nature that their discounted value will almost surely be exceeded by present costs'.[5] He also argues that even if frustrated economically poorer nations are more prone to violent revolutions than wealthier nations, this hardly constitutes a serious threat to a country like the United States with its overwhelming military power.[6]

This weakening of the will to assist coincided with increased demands for support as the number of countries calling for aid rose, as their ability to absorb and utilise aid improved and as the rate of growth to which they aspired accelerated. In these circumstances of aid weariness and growing need, Mr Robert McNamara of the World Bank requested Mr Lester B. Pearson to lead a Commission on International Development to inquire into the consequences of twenty years of development assistance and to make recommendations for the future.

The resultant report, entitled *Partners in Development*,[7] in looking at the question of 'Why, aid?', and more specifically at the question of why the advanced countries, saddled with their own heavy social and economic problems, should seek to assist other nations, commences by explaining what foreign aid should not be expected to do: it cannot guarantee that the recipient government will choose 'any particular ideology or value system'; nor is it a 'guarantee of political stability or an antidote to violence' ('Change is, itself, intrinsically disruptive'); nor is it an 'assurance of peaceful and responsible international behaviour' (similar points to those made by Mikesell above); nor will it close all gaps or eliminate inequality. 'The simplest answer to the question is a moral one: that it is only right for those who have to share with those who have not.' Concern with the needs of poorer nations arises from a recent awareness that we belong to a world community and amounts to a recognition that 'concern with the improvement of the human condition is no longer divisible'. In addition, there is the appeal of enlightened self-interest: 'The fullest possible utilisation of all the world's resources, human and physical, which can be brought about only by international co-operation, helps not only those countries now economically weak, but also those strong and healthy.' He warns, however, that donor countries must not expect any economic windfalls; nor should they attempt, through aid, to buy dependable friends.[8]

Professor Harry G. Johnson of the London School of Economics and Political Science has been one among a number who have criticised the Report severely. Referring to it as a 'public relations exercise on behalf of increased aid, and especially of official and multilateral aid',[9] he maintains that it failed in its principal objective, that of providing a new motivation for the giving of aid by the developed world. 'Especially it has failed to provide any arguments likely to appeal to the aid-weary and domestically-preoccupied American public.'[10]

> The failure of the Pearson Report to provide a persuasive new reason for aid-giving is the inevitable result of the conflict between moral conception and the facts of reality that arises with any charitable operation such as development aid or the relief of poverty: the moral conception stresses the inherent dignity and worth of man as man, and hence leads to resentment on the one side and uneasiness on the other about the reality of economic difference, which is the occasion of the charity itself. This conflict is exacerbated when the participants in the charitable transfer are not individuals but nation-states jealous of their sovereignty. It can only be resolved by resort to the fiction on both sides of the charity transaction that the need for charity is temporary. Hence any effort to resolve the conflict within a general and consistent philosophy of sustained charity must prove self-defeating: charity can only be a continuing process if new reasons are continually being discovered as to why it will be temporary, and this precludes a general philosophy.[11]

Johnson lists further criticisms, some in the detail of, other in the conception of, the Report, and does not see grounds for believing that official aid, supported by more favourable public opinion, will increase substantially. His view, however, is that even a decline in official aid will not seriously hamper development as it will mean greater dependence on private market mechanisms of economic development, as contrasted with governmental planning and control.

The importance of this whole topic of mobilising public opinion in the economically advanced countries is verified by the fact that the final section of the International Development Strategy for the Second United Nations Development Decade states that an essential part of the work of the Decade will consist in mobilising such opinion. Governments are called on to intensify their endeavours to deepen public understanding of the interdependent nature of the development effort and of the efforts which the developing countries themselves are making, and to consider giving some degree of development orientation to their education curricula.[12]

The question of 'Why aid?' has obvious relevance to the user-countries of Southern Africa; but there is an additional, potentially important, reason for looking into the reasons for the giving of aid. John Kenneth Galbraith has argued that we should not see the world as divided strictly between developed countries and underdeveloped countries, but rather as spaced along a line representing various levels of advancement. 'No group of countries is uniquely qualified to extend assistance and no other group is similarly condemned to the role of recipients.'[13] Looked at in this way, each country will have something to gain and learn from those that are ahead and something to offer and teach those that follow. The Pearson Report also mentions that the peculiarly relevant experience of recent aid 'graduates' could produce fruitful results when applied to countries a little behind in their stage of development.[14] This idea of assistance from developing nation to developing nation need not only be seen as applying to an overall development lead, but also to sectors of development: one country may be able to teach another about the establishment of small industries or the functioning of a national development corporation and learn in return about water utilisation and soil conservation.

2. RECIPIENT COUNTRIES: THE KIND OF AID

At the 1966 Conference on International Co-operation in Aid, held at Cambridge University, Dr I. G. Patel, then Chief Economic Adviser to the Indian government, listed the components of an aid-recipient's ideal of how aid should be given.[15] His version of the ideal may be summarised as follows:

1. Determination of the requirements of assistance would be based on the needs of the developing countries as measured in relation to certain minimum standards, e.g. nutrition, education, etc.
2. Priority for such aid would be given to those countries furthest removed from accepted world standards of minimum social and economic well-being.
3. Minimum needs would be sought to be satisfied in the shortest possible time and the assistance given would be

aimed at increasing productivity and employment opportunities.

4. Funds required for foreign aid would be collected by taxation of all nation-states in accordance with their capacity to pay and would not be dependent on periodic vetoes by national legislatures.

5. Both donors and recipients would have a say in deciding the total quantum of foreign aid.

6. No considerations of political ideology, race or creed would interfere with distribution according to need.

7. Criteria of national performance would become largely irrelevant. ('If the sins of the fathers should not be visited on the sons, there is no reason why the sins of the leaders and the privileged élite in any country should be visited upon the large mass of the poor who may have little effective say in the governance of their country.')

8. Donor countries would receive no rewards for their efforts and recipients would feel no obligation to make recompense except in terms of their own efforts towards the common endeavour.

That remains an ideal.

It is not the intention in this section to deal with the very considerable arguments about aid amounting to a negative factor in the development process; nor to deal with the more complex psychological problems inherent in the relations of an aid-giver and an aid-receiver. Rather the intention is to discuss some of the major difficulties which those developing countries that wish to receive external economic support – that is, the majority of them – face in their dealings with donor countries.

For a start, many developing lands see aid from a very different angle from that of their benefactors. Based on past exploitation of their people and natural resources, which impaired their progress, these new states feel that it is an obligation of the rich nations, in recompense for past wrongs and in partial expiation of guilt, to give substantial aid to the poorer countries. If these countries are not economically advanced, it is not through any fault of their own, but is rather an injustice of the world. Therefore, the amount of assistance should be determined by their needs, not by any charitable measure of the more fortunate countries.

Irritation is caused by the habit of donor countries of exaggerating the amount of real aid given. Their definition of aid lumps together with actual grants, loans with varying concessionary and less concessionary terms, various kinds of private investment, the dispatch of domestically unsaleable goods and agricultural surpluses, without deducting capital that streams back to, or never leaves, the donor country, namely: repayment of loans and interest, returns from capital investment, exports and services attached to tied aid and the salaries of experts, advisers and administrators, a fair proportion of which is paid in their home country.

In the field of foreign private investment, frustration is experienced at the developing countries' inability to control the flow of capital. J. F. Rweyemamu, of the University of Dar-es-Salaam, in an article in the *African Review*, makes this point:

> There are in addition to the recorded adverse effects of foreign private investment on these economies, other forms of transfers which invariably go unrecorded. These include profits on the importation of machinery, over-invoicing of other imports bought from or through affiliated companies or branches, under-invoicing of exports sold to or through affiliated companies or branches and remittances of payments to overseas head offices for management fees, royalty fees, agency fees, etc.[16]

The undependability of aid provides a further source of unease. Whenever one of the developed countries experiences balance-of-payments pressures, invariably one of the first items to suffer a cut is foreign aid – witness President Nixon's 1971 cut in overseas assistance by 10 per cent. For satisfactory and effective long-term planning, user countries need an assured and steady flow of assistance which can be appropriated in terms of three- or five-year development plans. Annual budgeting by donor legislatures and continual chopping and changing of budgets and allowances for external aid – while a matter of course to the donors – do not give the recipient the necessary assurance that assistance will not fall away when it may be most needed.

Recipients, further, are suspicious of the motives of aiding governments, most particularly of their latent and patent expectations of political and economic returns for assistance. And the wealthy states, by withholding aid here and increasing it there, depending on internal governmental or economic changes in, or the strategic position of, the recipient, have done little to allay suspicions that the goal of buying political allies is an important motive behind aid.

All forms of intervention in the recipient country's domestic affairs provide a constant source of friction. For example, recipients do not necessarily see their economic problems, or their solutions, in terms of external ideologies, whereas donors are quick to categorise policy decisions in such terms and to express approval or disapproval accordingly. Aid, in general, can be said to constitute an involvement in the domestic policies of the user country going far beyond normal contacts between sovereign states: when an aid-giving government consents to support a share of a development plan, but does this subject to certain conditions and controls – however sensible these may appear – this does amount to a substantial encroachment on the recipient's field of authority. The donor's wish to be consulted on matters of economic policy central to development and the threat of withdrawal which they covertly or overtly wield at all times constitute further instances of such intrusion: a more beneficent example is the policy of tying aid to criteria of self-help or standards of development performance.

The concept of granting assistance on the basis of performance, however, is beset with problems. Firstly, those lands whose needs are most urgent will protest that this is hardly a moral philosophy of aid – although those that are making greater headway might support it. Further, if such standards are to be applied, they must be practised consistently, using the same criteria for countries at similar levels of economic development. If this is not done, and aid continues to be conferred or denied for a variety of other reasons, the policy loses its credibility. Recipients detect a further inconsistency in the wealthier countries, which are themselves falling short of the international standards of foreign assistance required of them, continuing to demand standards of performance from the less developed world.

Differences over development policies in general constitute a further abundant source of potential antagonism. Donors may feel that, not being caught up in the day-to-day internal political struggles of recipient governments, they are able to see problems more clearly and objectively; recipient authorities argue that it is they who truly understand, and in any case have to cope with, the real problems of the development process; probably neither has a monopoly of wisdom. For example, aided governments accuse donors of looking for prestige projects, or for quick results or quick profits, and of neglecting the longer-term and less dramatic needs of the country; or if they do support these latter needs they attempt so to control their progress that they will still be around when the profits are eventually realised. Similarly, donors accuse recipient leaders of trying to gain short-term political advantage and personal prestige from ostentatious, rather than necessary, projects, and by limiting benefits to a small privileged élite, not allowing a healthy spread of development.

A basic dislocation in the donor–recipient relationship arises from the fact that countries that are sufficiently advanced to offer assistance do in many instances offer a technology that is too sophisticated and not oriented to the requirements or structure of the country, e.g. capital-intensive industry, where what is needed is labour-intensive industry. Barbara Ward makes this point: 'They are plumping down great gobbets of advanced industrial technology into countries where there is neither the market nor the skills nor the managerial capacity nor indeed any of the preconditions for such a technology to work successfully.'[17] Donors, satisfied with the superiority of their methods, are often too rigid and fail to see the necessity for adapting to changed circumstances, ignoring, for example, the fact that incentives which are relevant to the pattern of personal relations in industrialised societies might well be non-incentives, even disincentives, in unindustrialised societies.

Similarly, contacts between volunteers from wealthier countries and those whom they are meant to assist or teach can easily become seriously strained. Some cannot overcome the barrier, created by their status as advisers, between themselves and those whom they advise – a problem for which there is a singularly apt African proverb: 'I cannot hear what you are saying, for who you are is thundering in my ears.'[18] Ukpabi Asika, Governor of the East Central State of Nigeria, speaks of an influx of expatriate personnel – some 'unteachable', others 'working out their private neuroses' – who must be expensively housed and transported. As a result, he contends, most of the money 'goes into administering the administrators'.[19] The transmission by volunteers of the values and habits of an affluent consumer society to an economically deprived society can have confusing and unhappy consequences. Further alienation results from the youth of many of the volunteers who are cast in the roles of mentors in a society with strong traditions of gerontocracy.[20]

Annoyance, even hurt, is felt at the continuing 'brain drain' to the richer countries, which are 'siphoning off' at an alarming rate the very educated and talented people that the developing countries so desperately need. In 1970 the total of 'professional, technical and kindred workers' (obviously not all from less developed countries) to the United States reached 44,328.[21] Aiding countries bear some responsibility for this serious depletion of the human resources of the developing nations, for the training which they give to students from those countries frequently has little relation to their people's needs.

Accepting, for all this, that aid does bring some benefits, the new states feel that what is given is then promptly taken away, with interest, on the international trade markets. There is an urgent need for some protection of their long-term development plans from the adverse consequences of fluctuating trends in world trade over which they exercise no control. Urgent in this respect are the needs for some stabilisation of prices for their primary products, as also greater access to the markets of industrialised countries. The O.E.C.D. has admitted the danger of the export-promotion and agricultural diversification programmes which its members are supporting in the developing lands being seriously jeopardised by those same members pursuing inconsistent trade policies which deny entry of competitively priced products from developing countries.[22]

Finally, there are the disadvantages of tied aid, which results in some cases not only in recipients having to pay for more expensive commodities than necessary, but also in them having to accept – even become reliant upon – inappropriate technology. It also increases the difficulties involved in arranging for and organising assistance:

> First you prepare a plan, then you submit it to the potential donors for scrutiny as to whether it is such as they will support, then you submit to all of them a documented list of the projects

making up the plan so that they can each say which they will help finance, then you have to reconcile their conflicting choices as best you can, then you have to make sure that the import materials to be used for each project are bought by your contractor from the country that is going to produce the money for the project. And you must not start with the carrying out of the project until the financing agreement with the donor in respect of its share of the cost has been signed![23]

3. THE ROLE OF MULTILATERAL AID

Spokesmen for developing countries regularly assert that many of the most serious of these difficulties are inherent in a bilateral aid relationship and they would be considerably eased by assistance being channelled through multilateral agencies.

By their nature, mutilateral aid institutions are far less able, and decidedly less interested in, exerting pressure on the domestic political patterns and foreign policy behaviour of recipients. Because they represent less of a threat to the sovereignty of the new states and thus attract less suspicion of their motives, advice and performance monitoring by such agencies is more readily accepted by aided countries. Leaders who act in accordance with such advice – as contrasted with bilateral advice – particularly where the action taken might prove unpopular, are in a stronger position to defend themselves against accusations of forfeiting their country's independence and submitting to the pressures of neo-colonialism.

Great advantage is seen furthermore in removing the entire assistance process from the unsettling arena of world power politics, as the infusion of external conflicts into the less developed world seriously hinders their constructive development. Okwudiba Nnoli, discussing the implications of contemporary world politics for African development, argues that development is 'the creation of a better life in which contradictions, tensions and conflicts are continuously and progressively minimised' and therefore involves a decrease 'in the number and effects of the multiple poles of conflict and conflict potential within African States'.[24] Increasing use of multilateral channels will serve to weaken the impact of extra-African antagonisms as a source of conflict potential in the new states.

Ideally, in the same way as internationalised aid is less likely to bear political strings, so is it less prone to be conditional on economic ties. As has been pointed out, untied assistance allows a better utilisation of foreign resources and enables the recipient, on advice of a disinterested agency, to select technological assistance most appropriate to its requirements.

In place of the somewhat awkward bilateral contacts, with overtones of charity and paternalism on one side, and harmful effects on feelings of self-reliance and independence on the other, multilateralism offers far greater scope for mutuality and co-operation. Aided countries are represented in such organisations, are able to make their point of view heard with effect, have representatives serving on executive staffs and governing councils, and fully participate in policy-making and the distribution of aid. This participation, and the accompanying responsibility for the whole process of aid, assists in diffusing the conflicts of donor–recipient relations and, again, eases the way for recipients to accept advice on development.

The multiplicity of bilateral aid agencies is in itself a severe hindrance to the realisation of benefits by user countries in proportion to the input of manpower and capital by the aiding states. Limited, as they are, in qualified organisational and managerial personnel, the authorities of a developing country are faced with a battery of agencies, in wasteful competition, each proffering its own project or projects which might overlap with others, or be unrelated to an overall national programme. It would greatly help these authorities in identifying priorities and time-schedules, if they were in a position to deal with one donor agency, fully aware of the extent of its capacity for assistance.

Recipients believe, too, that multilateral agencies are able to introduce a significant element of objectivity in aid allocation. Less concerned about immediate favourable or unfavourable reactions and better able to resist pressures from donors and recipients, they will be able to allocate assistance on more consistent bases, utilising criteria agreed to by the less developed world. Hence they might be able to counter some of the imbalances resultant upon the inconsistencies of bilateral aid.

Because it is not subject to the vagaries of domestic politics and the veto of legislative assemblies at annual budgetary sessions, multilateral assistance promises greater continuity and security to the receiving authorities. Further, an international body, by virtue of its own experience, and having no need of political rewards, will be more likely to concentrate its efforts on the structuring of regional projects, which are vital to the economically weaker states.

Finally, a strategy of assistance must be related to the development process in its totality, and must take account of such significant factors as fluctuations in export earnings, the burden of debts already incurred, etc.

> By their nature, however, these other problems cannot be solved through bilateral arrangements but must be tackled through some concerted international action. If, for instance, a developing country experiences difficulties in meeting its debt service obligations and if debts are owed to a number of creditor countries, an effective debt settlement is virtually impossible unless at least several, if not all, creditors agree to such an arrangement. Even if one creditor country were able and willing to make arrangements unilaterally to postpone debt service payments or to relieve the debt burden by some other method, it would be most reluctant to do so without some assurance that other creditor countries would not continue to resume lending on terms which would threaten to bring about another debt service crisis. Multilateral action is also needed to provide relief when a country experiences an unexpected shortfall in its export earnings. No single country would want to take on alone the financial burden of making up the shortfall. Moreover it would run the risk that another country or group of other countries would offset by their action the effect of its unilateral efforts.[25]

Proponents of multilateralism claim further that the advantages consequent on the increasing internationalisation of aid would serve not only the interests of the recipients, but those of the donor as well. It would in the first place expand the humanitarian element of the process; assistance would be allocated more in accordance with the needs of the less developed world than any politico-economic strategy requirements of the more developed nations, and would therefore make donors less vulnerable to accusations of neo-colonialism and a variety of other sinister motives.

Further, and of greater significance, it would advance the

donor's interests by better utilisation of the assistance, because recipients are more likely to accept and follow the guidance of multilateral representatives; because these representatives are in a stronger position to insist on the recipients living up to their commitments and to monitor their development performance; and because they are more able to channel the numerous contributions into an integrated and effective programme of development.

This is what Eugene Black, former President of the World Bank, meant when he spoke of economic development diplomacy in which aid could be used to induce the adoption of improved development programmes and which could most effectively be carried out by multilateral agencies. The accelerated rate of growth consequent on such diplomacy would promote the economic and non-economic objectives of donor governments more effectively and durably than the tactical use of aid for purposes unrelated to economic development.[26]

Opponents of these views assert for a start that, if recipients were pushed to decide exclusively between accepting aid from bilateral sources or from multilateral sources, many would in fact choose the former. In the first place, many of the vices attributed to bilateral aid also accompany the assistance of multilateral agencies; they, too, are guilty of multiplicity, wasteful competition and lack of co-ordination; they, too, are dependent on the generosity of wealthy contributing governments as well as on access to capital markets controlled by those governments; they too, are served by many of those same nationals who are a cause of protest against bilateral aid; they, too, are guilty of proffering assistance inappropriate to the recipients' needs; and they, too, are not free from political pressures.

Secondly, the very number of bilateral sources, and the great variety of motives behind them, result in substantially greater quantities of aid being available and leave the recipient greater room for manoeuvre and greater independence of choice than would be possible in dealing with one all-embracing agency.

Thirdly, by choosing multilateral assistance, recipients would forfeit the extra advantages of special relationships with certain of the donors, or the aid-attracting factors of their geographical or strategic positions, or the benefits of playing on world power rivalries.

Countries in the Southern African region, such as Botswana, Lesotho, Swaziland and Malawi, stand to receive additional aid – in theory, at least – from Britain because of the historic colonial connection and lingering British responsibility; from the United States which may wish to balance its continuing relations with South Africa by demonstrating its support for the non-racial structures of these countries; and from South Africa because of its wish to prove its policy of friendship towards, and its need for friends in Africa. Madagascar stands to gain from its ties with France and its strategic position in the Indian Ocean. These possible advantages would disappear under an objective, global multilateral system of aid allocation.

Finally, because it serves the interests of the donor countries most directly, and thus more readily elicits support from public opinion in those countries, bilateral aid offers, and promises to continue offering, overwhelmingly larger quantities of aid than can feasibly be hoped for from multilateral sources.

For this same reason – that donor governments see foreign aid as a tangible and positive instrument of foreign policy which serves their national interests – they refuse to relinquish control over aid to an international organisation over which their influence is limited. They maintain that they need control over the allocation, direction and amount of aid, in order to relate it to their own national ends, political, economic and strategic. Aid, it is argued, not only provides a substantial source of prestige, power and influence, but also serves to spread the culture and language of the donor.

Professor Harry G. Johnson makes the point that the essence of increased multilateralism is to increase the taxation of the donor countries for the benefit of the recipients, while depriving the donors of control over the spending of their own money – a process unlikely to prove acceptable to the citizens of those countries.[27] Lester Pearson admitted in his lectures to the Council on Foreign Relations that it was idle to imagine that donor countries, particularly the major ones, would surrender their control: 'The United States, for instance, is no more likely to disengage itself from a direct aid relationship with certain developing countries than the Soviet Union is to allow the World Bank to handle its aid relations with the United Arab Republic.'[28]

Further, there are those who argue that the performance of international aid agencies has given the donor authorities scant reason for upgrading the level of their multilateral contributions. Donors who feel a special responsibility based on historical connections, or have some other special interest, or who have some experience with the problems in a particular country, or who have large field missions of their own, believe that they are in a better position to assist with the developmental needs of recipients than international bodies whose capacity to channel aid effectively has been over-strained.

The major criticism of international organisations has been their proliferation and inability to co-operate and co-ordinate aid projects and policy, both at headquarters level and at the country level where the need for co-ordination is urgent. The wastage and frustration caused by a multiplicity of agencies has been discussed above, and the battery of organisations and agencies of the U.N. family was widely recognised to be in dire need of central control.

The second trenchant criticism has been levelled at the staffing of the U.N. development system. Firstly, weakness has arisen from the quota system in accordance with which the agencies attempt to recruit a proportionate number of personnel from each member country. Selection based on geography rather than ability must have adverse effects on the standard of the personnel recruited. Secondly, as contracts of employment are short-term, the most qualified persons are not attracted to the posts, and the recipient countries are denied the advantages of continuity and experience. Thirdly, the various agencies have been unwilling to contract with private organisations and firms which have access to greater technical and professional skills.

That these criticisms were well grounded and apposite, and that they found their mark, was attested to by the U.N. Development Programme's appointment of a commission under Sir Robert Jackson. The commission was given the task of recommending ways and means for the U.N. development system to free itself from the paralysis of fragmentation, overcome the above-mentioned criticisms, and equip itself to handle effectively not only the existing resources channelled through it, but also a doubling of those resources envisaged for the U.N. Second Development Decade.

Late in 1969 Sir Robert submitted the commission's report,

entitled *A Study of the Capacity of the United Nations Development System*, which called for a strategy, the essential element of
which was the need 'to *centralise* responsibility for *policy-making*
and *decentralise* the responsibility for *operations* intended to put
those policies into effect',[29] involving major alterations and
improvements in structure.

Firstly, limits must be placed on the independence of the
organisations of the U.N. development system and their role
should become that of partners under the leadership of the
U.N.D.P., headed by the Administrator. All funds should be
channelled through the U.N.D.P. and responsibility for U.N.
development programmes and projects, as well as for the proper
utilisation of funds, should be firmly centred on the U.N.D.P.
Administrator.

Secondly, in order to stress the essentially operational character
of the U.N.D.P., the shortest line of authority between U.N.D.P.'s
Governing Council and user governments must be secured. To
this end it is essential to decentralise authority and delegate the
major responsibility for projects at the country level to the
Resident Representative.

Thirdly, the Resident Representative, as the direct representative of the Administrator, must become the key figure in the
U.N. system at the country level. He must shoulder overall responsibility for U.N. programmes and act as the main instrument
of co-operation with the recipient government and as the sole
spokesman for all the agencies.

Greater use should be made of subcontracting to independent
commercial firms, particularly for larger projects, and the policy
of automatically using U.N. special agencies should be discontinued.

The roles of the U.N.D.P. and the World Bank group should
be clearly delineated to prevent any duplication, and there should
be collaboration to ensure that their activities complement each
other and also forge the necessary links between pre-investment
and investment.

A Staff College should be established to train U.N. employees
in planning, administration and field work. A U.N. development
service should be built on a career basis, comprising a relatively
small international force of highly qualified, experienced long-
term specialists. Recruitment of personnel should be based on

merit, while an equitable geographical distribution could eventually be achieved through careful selection of junior officers.

Central to the new structure is the concept of the country programme. This involves discussion, co-operation and planning between the components of the U.N. system on the one hand and the recipient government on the other. It must be based on a prior and comprehensive socio-economic study of the country and on the priorities and plans identified by the government concerned. The assistance of the various U.N. agencies should be integrated and their combined assistance should dovetail into the country's national development plan.

The commission further recommended that programming of assistance be based on five phases of a development cycle. In the first phase, representatives of the U.N. development system would meet with the government to discuss its development plan and the assistance which it could offer, taking account of all other offers of aid as well as international monetary and trade policies. In the second phase the programme would be submitted to the Governing Council for its appraisal and approval, after which funds would be allocated for the duration of the approved projects. Thirdly, this would be followed by implementation of the projects under the supervision of the Resident Representative, greater freedom being allowed him in selecting methods and agents for executing the projects. Fourthly, there is the role of evaluation which is not to be considered a phase, but rather as a constant thread running through the cycle. Finally, there should be an effective follow-up support of completed projects in order to maximise their value.

Though not considered one of the phases of the cycle, a significant role would be that of the annual review. This would involve a major annual evaluation within the cycle which would provide the Governing Council with a progress report and, by advancing the programme one year ahead, increase its flexibility.

The major principles of the Jackson Report were accepted by the Governing Council (although in the words of its President it took into account what was possible and what was not[30]) and country programming has been introduced into a number of countries, including recipient countries in Southern Africa. A useful analysis of, and judgement on, the reality and efficacy of the innovations must await the elapse of a year or two. (Further information on the role of the U.N.D.P. in Southern Africa is contained in an appendix to this paper.)

Although there has been an increase in the proportion of aid flowing through multilateral channels – from an annual average of 10·2 per cent for the years 1960–2 to 16·5 per cent in 1970 – there is nevertheless little likelihood of the bulk of aid being internationalised in the near future. Jacob J. Kaplan argues that a more realistic objective would be the delineation of distinctive roles for the numerous programmes, multilateral and bilateral, and the establishment of international machinery for allocating responsibilities, reaching decisions and reconciling conflicts. (Both D.A.C. and ECOSOC introduced mechanisms for increased co-operation, the former for bilateral agencies, the latter for multilateral, but both have met with limited success.) The objective must be to structure a co-ordinating machinery under which 'anarchism in aid-giving can be mitigated without endangering the persistence of pluralism'.[31]

Experience with or serious efforts towards multilateral assistance and multi-national economic co-operation in the form of regional economic, technical or developmental agencies in Southern Africa has, since the demise of C.C.T.A. (Commission for Technical Co-operation in Africa South of the Sahara) and C.S.A. (Scientific Council of Africa South of the Sahara), been limited to the customs union agreement between South Africa, Lesotho, Swaziland and Botswana on the sharing of customs and tax revenues; the Southern African Regional Commission for the Conservation and Utilisation of the Soil (SARCCUS) – a government-sponsored agency for the promotion of inter-territorial co-operation in Southern Africa within the broad field of agriculture and natural resources; and the embryonic Southern African Regional Tourism Council (SARTOC) with its headquarters in Malawi.

SARCCUS, because it has functioned uninterruptedly since 1950, because it is voluntary (as compared with the customs union which approaches necessity), because of its effectiveness, and because of its broad membership – Angola, Botswana, Lesotho, Malawi, Mozambique, South Africa, South West Africa (Namibia), Rhodesia, SãoTomé and Principe, and Swaziland – presents the most interesting example. Among its principal functions are the following:

to assure adequate interchange of information among the different territories in regard to:
(i) the action taken by each to promote the conservation and rational untilisation of soil, vegetation and water supplies, and (ii) the research and field techniques adopted in this connection;
to promote the exchange of visits among the technicians of the different territories, so that they may obtain first-hand information regarding the organisation and execution of local conservation programmes;
to ensure a concerted study of and approach to common problems of direct concern to several or all territories, as for example the safeguarding of a common hydrological network;
to promote reciprocal aid among territories as regards personnel and material;
to promote inter-territorial co-operation in the training of personnel for dealing with problems connected with conservation and utilisation of the soil, vegetation and water resources.[32]

There have been a number of serious recommendations for the institutionalisation of regional economic co-operation in Southern Africa by prominent academics, businessmen and journalists. Professor J. L. Sadie, for example, has spoken of an Economic Commission for Southern Africa (E.C.S.A.), the functions of which would be to promote members' regional and foreign trade, to provide development assistance, to establish an institute of development studies, and to realise the economies of scale. Mr Otto Krause, in September 1967, called for the acceptance of Southern Africa as a 'Development Community'. 'Where trade has brought Europe together, so can the goal of development bring Southern Africa together. Development is the one aim that all its people have in common, and it should be the guiding strand.'[33]

Dr Frans Cronjé and others have called for a free-trade area, and Mr J. J. Williams, the managing director of the South African Foreign Trade Organisation (SAFTO), in 1969 elaborated on the concept of a regional development bank, able to promote vigorous mobilisation of both domestic and external monetary resources; identify sound development projects; influence the allotment of monetary resources to various economic sectors so as to facilitate balanced growth; focus attention on – and channel resources to – those areas which are depressed in relation to the region as a whole; and promote projects that would serve the region as a whole in the form of infrastructural ventures and industrial projects that might not be viable in terms of a single market.[34]

The concept of a regional development bank is not new to Africa. The original agreement establishing the African Development Bank (to which Swaziland acceded last year as the 33rd member and to which Botswana will accede this years as the 34th) was signed in Khartoum in August 1963. It was set up as an agency of the U.N. Economic Commission for Africa (E.C.A.) with the object of becoming an important agency in helping to overcome the economic difficulties caused by national boundaries bequeathed by the colonial powers, particularly by backing projects which affect more than one state, by harmonising development plans of member countries and by assisting weaker states when in difficulty.

The initiative came from E.C.A. which produced a document emphasising the need for economic co-operation in development finance. The document pointed out that, excluding Egypt, South Africa and Nigeria, there were about forty countries or countries-to-be in Africa, averaging about 4 million people per country. Of these people only half, i.e. 2 million, had any contact with a market economy, and their average cash purchasing power corresponded to approximately one-twentieth of that of an average inhabitant of Western Europe. Thus they represented a cash-market equivalent to a moderate-size European town of 100,000 inhabitants. The argument concluded therefore that, in the same way that it did not make sense in Europe to have separate plans and financing institutions for each individual town of 100,000, regardless of what went on in the next town, so a purely national approach to planning and financing economic development in Africa was no more sensible.

While the usual arguments for regional inter-governmental machinery of this nature are as strong in Southern Africa as they are in the rest of the continent, yet a broad impetus towards institutionalised regional arrangements is lacking. This is not to say that co-operation and trade are not in fact increasing in the region, but rather to suggest that proposals for formal permanent institutions purporting to bind signatories more closely will have to take account of, and will certainly be subject to, the numerous centrifugal political forces at play in this part of the continent.

NOTES

1. 'Nations in Need', a special report on aid to developing countries, published with *The Times* (London), 14 Sep 1971, p. i.
2. See J. Audibert, 'Bilateral Aid', in Ronald Robinson (ed.), *International Cooperation in Aid* (Cambridge: Cambridge University Overseas Studies Committee, 1966) pp. 96–8.
3. Nigel Lawson, 'Foreign Aid: The Wrong Thing for the Right Reasons', *The Times* (London), 3 Nov 1971, p. 14.
4. Raymond F. Mikesell, *The Economics of Foreign Aid* (London: Weidenfeld & Nicolson, 1968) p. 8.
5. Ibid., p. 11.
6. Ibid., p. 9.
7. Lester B. Pearson *et al.*, *Partners in Development: Report of the Commission on International Development* (London: Pall Mall Press, 1969).
8. Ibid., pp. 7–11.
9. Harry G. Johnson, *The 'Crisis of Aid' and the Pearson Report* (Edinburgh Univ. Press, 1970) p. 10. See also P. T. Bauer and B. S. Yamey, 'The Economics of the Pearson Report', *Journal of Development Studies*, VIII 2 (Jan 1972) 319; R. H. Green, 'Anatomy of Two Assessments: Pearson, Jackson and Development Partnership', *African Review*, I 2 (Sep 1971) 137; and Michael Monroe, 'A Lost Opportunity: A Comment on the Pearson Commission Report', *International Affairs*, XLVI I (Jan 1970) 30.
10. Ibid., p. 21.
11. Ibid., p. 11–12.
12. United Nations General Assembly, Resolutions of the General Assembly at its 25th Regular Session, Press Release GA/4355, 17 Dec 1970.
13. John Kenneth Galbraith, *Economic Development in Perspective* (Oxford Univ. Press, 1963) p. 19.
14. Pearson, op. cit., p. 134.
15. I. G. Patel, 'How to Give Aid: A Recipient's Point of View', in Robinson (ed.), *International Co-operation in Aid*, pp. 88–90.
16. J. F. Rweyemamu, 'The Political Economy of Foreign Private Investment in the Underdeveloped Countries', *African Review*, I I (Mar 1971) 115.
17. Barbara Ward, 'The Decade of Development: A Study in Frustration?', in *Two Views on Aid to Developing Countries*, Occasional Paper No. 9 (London: Institute of Economic Affairs, 1966) p. 17.
18. In David R. Abernethy, 'Bureaucracy and Economic Development in Africa', *African Review*, I I (Mar 1971) 101.

638   *Accelerated Development in Southern Africa*

19. Ukpabi Asika, in Frederick Hunter, 'On Learning from Relief', *Christian Science Monitor* (Boston), 20 Oct 1971, p. 1.
20. Stanislav L. Andreski, *The African Predicament: A Study in the Pathology of Modernisation* (London: Michael Joseph, 1968) p. 168.
21. Daniel Quinn, 'The Brain Drain: Robbing the Poor, Aiding the Rich', *Christian Science Monitor* (Boston), 8 Nov 1971, p. 7.
22. Organisation for Economic Co-operation and Development, Development Assistance Committee, *Development Assistance Efforts and Policies of the Members of the Development Assistance Committee, 1969 Review*, report by Edwin M. Martin (Paris: O.E.C.D., 1969).
23. S. O. Adebo, 'Why Aid?', in Robinson (ed.), *International Co-operation in Aid*, p. 61.
24. Okwudiba Nnoli, 'Some Implications of Contemporary World Politics for African Development', *African Review*, 1 1 (Mar 1971) 50.
25. J. Adler, 'Multilateral Aid', in Robinson (ed.), *International Co-operation in Aid*, p. 77.
26. Jacob J. Kaplan, *The Challenge of Foreign Aid: Policies, Problems, and Possibilities* (New York: Praeger, 1967) p. 347.
27. Johnson, op. cit., p. 21.
28. Lester B. Pearson, *The Crisis of Development*, Russell C. Lefingwell Lectures, Council on Foreign Relations (New York: Praeger, 1969) p. 74.
29. R. G. A. Jackson, *A Study of the Capacity of the United Nations Development System*, vols I–II (Geneva: United Nations, 1969) p. 102.
30. *United Nations Monthly Chronicle*, VII 2 (July 1970) 81.
31. Kaplan, op. cit., p. 346.
32. D. M. Joubert, 'The Southern African Regional Commission for the Conservation and Utilisation of the Soil', appendix 1 to *The Use and Protection of Natural Resources in Southern Africa* (Johannesburg: South African Institute of International Affairs, 1973).
33. *Newscheck*, 20 Sep 1967, p. 17.
34. *Rand Daily Mail* (Johannesburg), 8 Apr 1969.

UNITED NATIONS DEVELOPMENT PROGRAMME IN SOUTHERN AFRICA

This appendix is based directly on answers given to the author by Mr Antony C. Gilpin, Regional Representative of U.N.D.P. in South-east Africa, who is based in Lusaka, Zambia.

1. STRUCTURE OF U.N.D.P. IN SOUTHERN AFRICA

The Regional Office in Lusaka (set up in 1964) originally covered Botswana, Lesotho, Malawi and Swaziland in addition to Zambia. Since 1964, separate U.N.D.P. offices have been set up in all these countries, and these are virtually autonomous in their day-to-day operations. The Regional Office, however, retains a co-ordinating role, and the U.N.D.P. Representatives from the five countries meet two or three times each year to discuss questions of mutual interest, including in particular existing and new regional projects, that is to say, projects covering more than one country of the region. As economic and other links have developed between the five countries, this aspect of U.N.D.P. work has gradually become more important. In this and other respects, the Regional Office co-operates closely with the United Nations Economic Commission for Africa, and Dr Robert Gardiner, the Executive Secretary of E.C.A., has attended meetings on more than one occasion.

2. INNOVATIONS IN U.N.D.P. ORGANISATION

The Jackson Report undoubtedly had an influence on the recent reorganisation of U.N.D.P. and on the introduction of country programming; it is difficult, however, to be more specific. The country programming exercise of U.N.D.P. assistance is a definite step forward since it represents a fundamental shift in allocating assistance from a project basis to a programme basis. In effect, this will mean that U.N.D.P. assistance will be related more directly and effectively to a country's national development plan; such a relationship will enable participating agencies and the government to engage in forward planning of the type and volume of assistance which will be required and thus act more expeditiously in providing the expert personnel required by government.

While some of the Specialised Agencies retain separate national or regional missions, an important recent innovation has been the appointment by F.A.O. and UNIDO of Senior Advisers (who are also their Country Representatives) within the U.N.D.P. Office. This arrangement, apart from making for improved co-operation and co-ordination within the U.N. family, also provides the U.N.D.P. Resident Representative with a fund of easily available and necessary expertise in the fields of agricultural and industrial development. The F.A.O. Representative was first based in this office but has recently moved to the U.N.D.P. office in Swaziland. At present, he covers all five countries; however, in the near future, a new Representative will be appointed in Lusaka who will cover Zambia and Botswana. The F.A.O. Representative in Swaziland will then cover only Lesotho, Malawi and Swaziland. The UNIDO Representative, based in Lusaka, covers not only the five countries mentioned above but also Mauritius, Madagascar, the Seychelles and the Comoro Islands. Ideally, a Representative of this kind should probably cover only one country, and eventually U.N.D.P. programmes may perhaps be large enough to justify this.

The authority of the U.N.D.P. Resident Representative has been gradually strengthened, and he is now generally regarded as the senior representative of the UN family of agencies wherever he may be stationed. The only exception is a place like Addis Ababa, where there is a Regional Economic Commission of the United Nations and, in that case, the Executive Secretary of the Commission is the senior U.N. Representative. One important new authority recently given to the Resident Representative is the ability to approve new projects, within the country's Indicative Planning Figure (I.P.F.), costing up to $100,000. This should make for more expeditious handling of relatively small requests from governments.

3. ASSISTANCE TO THE COUNTRIES OF SOUTHERN AFRICA

In money terms the simplest way to measure this assistance is by showing the I.P.F.s for the current five-year period. The I.P.F. (Indicative Planning Figure) provides the financial order of magnitude within which U.N.D.P. assistance – ongoing as well as new – can be programmed in advance. It is initially approved for a five-year period, commencing 1 January 1972, but will be reviewed annually on a 'roll-over' basis in the light of the pledges made by member countries and an estimate of other U.N.D.P. resources. The I.P.F.s for the five countries are as follows (in U.S. $):

Botswana	5·8 million
Lesotho	8·3 million
Malawi	7.5 million
Swaziland	5.7 million
Zambia	15 million

In addition, Botswana, Lesotho and Malawi have been included in a U.N. list of 'least developed' developing countries and, as such, have a further claim on additional U.N. regular funds. In terms of numbers of expert personnel, financed by U.N.D.P. and provided by the Participating Agencies, and currently in the five countries, approximate figures are as follows:

Botswana	41
Lesotho	50
Malawi	35
Swaziland	45
Zambia	150

As regards current projects in Botswana, mention may be made of the surveys and training for development of water resources and agricultural production (U.N.D.P.–F.A.O.), a co-operative development centre (U.N.D.P.–I.L.O.), a national vocational training centre (U.N.D.P.–I.L.O.), and UNESCO assistance to the Teacher Training College at Francistown. In Lesotho there is a pilot agricultural team in the Leribe area (U.N.D.P.–F.A.O.) and a project for the exploration for diamonds (U.N.D.P.–U.N.). An important earlier project (U.N.D.P.–World Bank) related to a feasibility study of the Oxbow complex. In Malawi there are three large U.N.D.P./F.A.O.-assisted projects, namely in fisheries training, improvement of livestock and dairy industry, and the Kasinthula demonstration farm. There is also a U.N.D.P./I.L.O.-assisted project on manpower assessment and utilisation, and World Bank experts are assisting with the Lilongwe Land

Development Project. Current projects in Swaziland consist entirely of individual experts provided by various agencies of the U.N. family, notably F.A.O., the I.L.O., I.T.U., UNESCO and UNIDO.

Examples of U.N.D.P. work in Zambia are a pilot irrigation scheme for the production of fruit and vegetables at Chapula, near Kitwe (U.N.D.P.–F.A.O.); a nutritional status survey (U.N.D.P.–F.A.O.); the establishment of a national industrial vocational training scheme with its main centre at the David Kaunda School in Lusaka (U.N.D.P.–I.L.O.); and the training of secondary-school teachers at the University of Zambia (U.N.D.P.–UNESCO).

There are also important regional projects, notably the U.N.D.P.–UNESCO assistance to the University of Botswana, Lesotho and Swaziland; and a Telecommunications and Postal Training Project (U.N.D.P.–I.T.U.–U.P.U), based in Malawi, but also serving Botswana, Lesotho and Swaziland.

4. THE PARTICULAR ROLE OF U.N.D.P.

Two commonly cited features of U.N.D.P., as distinct from bilateral aid agencies, are:

(i) the fact that no political 'strings' are attached as is sometimes the case with bilateral aid;

(ii) the fact that the U.N. agencies are able to recruit their experts from all over the world.

In practice, there is increasing co-operation between U.N.D.P. and most of the bilateral aid agencies. This is particularly important in the current country programming exercises, as U.N.D.P. assistance has to be seen in the light of assistance being requested from all other sources. Moreover, some countries, e.g. Sweden, have chosen to channel some of their aid through U.N.D.P. and the Specialised Agencies.

Policies and Interests of a Donor Country: The Commonwealth Development Corporation

F. R. WILSON

1. GENERAL

This paper deals exclusively with the operations of the Commonwealth Development Corporation, a U.K. statutory body. As the following paragraphs will show, the Corporation is not an aid-provider in the commonly accepted sense, and it operates rather differently from the development organisations of most aid-giving countries. It is thought, however, that a brief description of its methods and interests may be of value in the discussion of this topic.

The Commonwealth Development Corporation (C.D.C.) is a development agency established in 1948 by Act of the U.K. Parliament. Its task is to assist the economic development of the countries of the Commonwealth, both dependent and independent, and it can also operate, with ministerial approval, in countries outside the Commonwealth. To date approval has been given for operations in Thailand, Indonesia, Cameroun and Ethiopia. C.D.C. has long- and medium-term borrowing powers of up to £225 million, of which up to £205 million may be borrowed from U.K. Exchequer funds. It receives no grants, only loans; it operates on commercial lines and has a statutory obligation to pay its way. It is empowered to undertake, either alone or in association with others, projects for the promotion or expansion of a wide range of economic enterprises, including agriculture, forestry, mining, factories, electricity and water undertakings, transport, housing, hotels, building and engineering. In Swaziland, for example, C.D.C. is involved in the financing, and in some cases also the management, of a sugar mill and estate, an irrigation scheme, a settlement of Swazi farmers, an iron-ore mine, a railway, a hotel, a packaging plant, a cannery, two forestry schemes and a pulp mill. So as to ensure that its activities are directed in the best interests of the economic development of the territories in which it operates, C.D.C. maintains close relations with the territorial governments through its six Regional Offices, situated in Kingston (Jamaica), Lagos, Nairobi, Lusaka, Johannesburg and Singapore.

C.D.C. does not choose its investments either for maximum commercial returns or for the greatest assistance to U.K. exports. It does choose them for their development value to the country concerned, provided that the projects are viable in themselves and give C.D.C. the expectation of a return sufficient to cover all its costs, including the service of its loan capital, as well as its administrative expenses and an element to cover commercial risks. In order to meet these criteria, and particularly to be assured of capital recoveries to enable it to repay the U.K. Treasury, C.D.C. must be afforded all exchange-control consents, and all practicable facilities, to enable it to remit to the U.K. all net income, loan-service payments and capital realisations, as they arise from its investments. As to tax, C.D.C. seeks to be given full relief in respect of interest payable by it on U.K. government loans from which the invested funds derive, as well as the normal relief for expenses. C.D.C. is nevertheless a major contributor to the tax revenues of the overseas countries in which it operates.

The keynote of C.D.C.'s investment policy is flexibility, as to the types of project (so long as they fall within its statutory terms of reference), as to its partners and associates in development enterprises, and as to the methods by which it is prepared to provide finance. Apart from the need to be commercially viable, projects in which C.D.C. will be prepared to invest must have good development value for the host country and the approval of its government, and they must have management of high calibre, either provided or procured by the sponsors. C.D.C. itself provides management and technical services for many of its projects, and in such cases expects entry visas and work permits to be granted without undue delay for individual staff members whom it requires to fill approved management or administrative posts, until such time as these can be filled by competent local substitutes.

As a U.K. statutory corporation, C.D.C.'s investments form part of the British government's aid programme, but its loans for development projects are not tied so as to restrict borrowers to use them only for financing plant and goods produced in the United Kingdom. However, by the very nature of its projects, C.D.C. does in fact contribute materially to the credit of the United Kingdom's balance of payments.

As a final point, C.D.C. aims to revolve its funds and, when a project has been successfully established, it is prepared to consider offering participations on suitable terms, particularly to buyers resident in the country where the project is situated.

2. TRAINING FOR DEVELOPMENT

The training and equipping of its nationals to play the fullest possible part at the earliest possible moment in any development scheme is a political priority with the governments of most newly independent territories. It is particularly in this sphere, therefore, that any development agency must identify itself closely with government policy from the inception of any new scheme. It is most important to establish at the outset both the extent to which expatriate skills will be necessary, and for how long, and the training requirements to enable locally recruited employees to play an initial and then an increasingly important part in the progress of schemes. Here there is a need for understanding between the agency and the government, for without goodwill on both sides a new scheme may be launched with inadequate expatriate staff, or a scheme which is well established may fall foul of the local government through failure to make acceptable progress with the training of nationals for the more responsible posts.

Training for posts not requiring professional or advanced technical skills is normally carried out 'on the job', with supplementary instruction at central training establishments. Some of these are set up by governments, often with overseas technical assistance, and cater for such skills as mechanics, building, secretarial, book-keeping, etc. Often the sponsor of a scheme will establish a training centre to cover skills particularly relevant to his business.

Training in the higher skills is, of course, a much more difficult problem and depends largely on the availability of basically educated candidates, suitable training facilities and adequate finance. Qualified engineers, agronomists and accountants, for instance, are at a premium the world over, not only in the developing countries, and donor governments are rightly devoting increasing quantities of their technical aid to providing the means by which nationals in these countries can be trained to fill the gaps as quickly as possible.

An important and widening gap which faces developing countries is that of agricultural management. In most of these countries improved agriculture is the sphere in which the greatest impact can be made on both human and animal populations. Much is being done to train people in the techniques of growing better crops, and to this end agricultural colleges, farmers' training centres and research stations have been established. However, management of agricultural projects, initially in the hands of expatriates, has tended to devolve upon their local successors on the strength of their practical experience with crops, rather than their knowledge of management techniques and requirements.

Training of nationals in all the countries in which it operates is a major preoccupation of C.D.C. For example, in Swaziland C.D.C. has its own qualified training officer to direct the training programme for its agricultural and industrial projects in the area. Under him, training courses cater for driving instruction, secretarial work, mill techniques, etc., and adult education classes are also organised.

With its growing agricultural commitments all over the world, C.D.C. is finding it increasingly difficult to recruit management-trained agriculturalists to initiate and direct new schemes. Its recruitment field was for several years the cadre of ex-colonial government staff who had handed over their jobs to local people. This field is now barren, and C.D.C. looks for its future agricultural scheme managers among newly graduated men of all nationalities. These men need both practical experience and management training, and to meet this latter need C.D.C. has decided to set up in Swaziland an agricultural management training centre, details of which are given in an appendix to this paper. Building started in February 1972, and it is hoped to run a first course towards the end of the year. A principal has been appointed and is in post.

Training for development is as important to developing countries as new development schemes themselves. Sponsors must be ready to provide local citizens with training for management, professional and technical posts up to top levels, as well as training on the job for the less responsible tasks. In return, the governments of these countries must accept that in asking outside agencies to invest in new schemes and to manage them in their initial stages, and often longer, they must permit – and indeed encourage – expatriates with the necessary skills to remain and work in their countries, until they can be replaced by nationals of the requisite qualifications. While all these countries are impatient at the apparently slow pace of 'localisation', it is to their credit that in the main they understand the present need for expatriate participation in their development and make arrangements accordingly.

APPENDIX

MANANGA AGRICULTURAL MANAGEMENT CENTRE

In most countries of the tropics and subtropics, future economic and social development depends largely on improved agricultural production. Agricultural development has to be fostered to produce commodities for the export markets and for the rapidly growing domestic markets, which requires modernisation of agriculture, with greater productivity. To achieve this needs not only inputs in capital for land improvement and equipment, but also specialised skills, including those of management.

1. REQUIREMENTS FOR TRAINING IN AGRICULTURAL MANAGEMENT

1. The Commonwealth Development Corporation (C.D.C.) has wide experience in agricultural production in developing countries both on an estate scale and in smallholder schemes. It is one of C.D.C.'s principles that in all its development projects it either bears responsibility for management or ensures that efficient management is available. C.D.C. has been successful in its projects in providing local citizens with training for management, professional and technical posts up to top levels. There is, however, a growing need for management training:

(*a*) to improve the management capacity of the young nationals who now form an increasingly important part of project staff in C.D.C.'s own agricultural projects and also in the projects which it finances; and

(*b*) to provide middle management training for national staff to fit them for higher management responsibilities on larger agricultural projects which, with the increasing scope for C.D.C.'s activities, will in future be likely to make considerable demands for agricultural management staff.

2. Experience indicates that there is a similar need for improving management capacity of young nationals in commercial companies, as well as in government and statutory bodies, in the territories in which C.D.C. operates, and it is thought that a service can be provided which will in part meet this need. Where

agricultural qualifications are required, academic or practical, it is assumed that those will have already been attained. What C.D.C. has in mind is to provide practical training for management of agricultural projects and services, which would be complementary to academic qualifications and field experience. The training will cover every aspect of agricultural management, including project programming, budgeting, administration of finance, crop operations, use of livestock, irrigation, machinery and equipment, the handling of staff and labour, and the processing and marketing of agricultural products. It is intended that the principles taught will be equally of value in management of arable, tree-crop, livestock or forestry projects.

2. PROPOSAL TO ESTABLISH AN AGRICULTURAL MANAGEMENT TRAINING CENTRE

1. C.D.C. has therefore decided to set up and to finance the cost of an agricultural management training centre in Swaziland, based on the irrigation complex of its Swaziland Irrigation Scheme, designed to provide training not only for C.D.C. staff, but also for nationals of countries in which C.D.C. operates.

2. It is proposed that the training centre should develop its own irrigated farm of 915 acres, growing sugar cane as a plantation crop on about 500 acres, together with a programme of annual rotational crops under irrigation. The arable crops which are most likely to fit reasonably well into the farming system are maize, wheat, cotton, beans and potatoes. Maize and cotton would be grown as summer crops, the others as winter crops.

3. MANAGEMENT TRAINING FACILITIES AVAILABLE

1. Since the mid-1950's C.D.C. has developed in the lowlands of Swaziland an irrigation system, together with a reservoir for the storage of 33,000 acre-feet of water, for the development of some 32,000 acres under irrigated crops, with some 27,000 acres so far developed, the farming of which involves both labour-intensive and mechanically intensive cropping systems. The complex which has evolved from the development provides good examples of large-scale crop development and processing, notably sugar cane and rice, ranch management, smallholder scheme development, management and financial control, irrigation and

drainage systems, and plantation and annual crop operations. These include:

(a) the Swaziland Irrigation Scheme (S.I.S.), which developed and administers the overall irrigation scheme, with citrus as a tree crop (700 acres), mechanised irrigated rice (3,500 acres) and sugar cane (2,500 acres), and a ranch (65,000 acres) with some 7,000 head of beef cattle;

(b) the Mhlume Sugar Company growing 9,000 acres of sugar cane and milling 87,000 tons of sugar, and processing cane supplied by estate and smallholder outgrowers who draw water from S.I.S.;

(c) the Vuvulane Irrigated Farms, a settlement scheme on which to date 168 Swazi farmers have been settled on holdings varying in size from 8 to 60 acres growing a range of crops with sugar cane as the principal cash crop and cotton, hybrid maize, beans, potatoes and vegetables grown in rotation on about 25 per cent of each holding. The settlement is being expanded progressively.

2. The projects making up the complex will assist in the management training programme by practical demonstration, by participation in the programme of instruction and by providing the basis for project studies by students.

4. COURSES

1. *Two main courses* are proposed to cater for two main types of trainee. These are:

(a) *Junior course.* A six months' course for young men with basic educational qualifications of at least school certificate and from three to five years' experience in junior agricultural management positions, largely for nationals of countries in which C.D.C. operates.

(b) *Senior course.* A four months' course for persons in middle management to fit them for higher management responsibilities on larger agricultural projects; it would follow the main lines of the junior course with greater emphasis on higher management problems, economic and marketing management, and detailed project identification, preparation and appraisal.

Early courses are expected to take about twelve trainees, but later courses could be increased to take up to twenty. It is hoped to start the first course in late 1972.

2. Junior course outline:

(a) The course deals with farm and estate management only; it does not deal with project identification, preparation and appraisal, which will be dealt with in the senior course. The course cannot cover the whole subject of farm management in detail. It is concerned rather to instruct farm or agricultural project managers (of junior status) in the contribution that business management can make to their overall function and tasks.

(b) One of the main aims of the course will be to provide an understanding of the underlying principles and concepts in the process of making decisions and the techniques available for use in the processes of planning, decision-making and control. Examples of management techniques and the attitudes that underlie them will be used in case studies, involving both managers of estates (or sections) and the students. Record-keeping, both physical and financial, and the use and significance of records will constitute an important part of the training.

(c) Economic principles will be dealt with only briefly and touching only on those that are essential to the proper understanding of business management.

(d) The syllabus for the course will include the following: farming objectives; basic economic concepts; financial and physical records; budgeting and planning; budgetary and other controls; capital; labour and machinery planning and control; marketing; general agricultural, livestock and afforestation policies; agricultural smallholder schemes; case studies and field exercise.

5. COURSE ACCOMMODATION AND STAFFING

1. Courses will be residential and the necessary buildings (administration, instruction and mess blocks, staff and student accommodation, farm buildings and village) are now being erected on a suitable site. Student acommodation will include a few married quarters for senior course students and their wives.

2. C.D.C. will provide staff for the training unit, which will comprise a principal experienced in developing training projects, a senior farm manager and a senior accountant (all of whom would be teaching staff as well as having executive functions), together with an assistant farm manager and the necessary supporting staff.

3. It is hoped to arrange visits from staff of other training institutions, to assist in developing the training programmes and also to do some specific teaching, for example, long vacation visits of two to three months by an agricultural management training staff member from a university, which would be of mutual benefit particularly where the university concerned runs tropical agricultural or management courses.

6. COST OF COURSES

1. The fee for a course will include the cost of providing accommodation, subsistence, etc., together with a share of the cost of the training provided. Preliminary consideration of the costs involved and the probable number of students leads towards the conclusion of a cost of up to £Stg500 for the junior course.

2. Employers sponsoring students will be responsible for the payment of course fees. They will also be responsible for all arrangements (including cost) for the student's travel to and from the centre, and for any emoluments or allowances while they are attending a course.

3. It may be possible in some cases to secure assistance from aid sources, national or international, towards travel costs or course fees.

COMMENTS

D. Z. Kadzamira and Henri Razafindratovo

Mr Kadzamira began by stating that he would like to discuss economic co-operation in Southern Africa, specifically distinguishing it from economic integration involving the reduction of national control of economic policy. Economic co-operation could be considered with reference to trade, aid and technology.

The level of intra-African trade was low, largely because of the similarity of products and the absence of facilities for the processing of raw materials. In Southern Africa, on the other hand, there existed a wide range of technological sophistication and a wide range of primary commodities being produced, which facilitated inter-state trade, not only between South Africa and her less developed neighbours, but between the latter themselves, for example, Zambia–Malawi.

He defined the prime function of aid as allowing for the exploitation of development opportunities at an earlier time than would be the case otherwise. He pointed out, however, that tied aid in particular gave greater benefit to the donor than to the recipient. An important element of aid was the transfer of skills and intellectual resources in the form of technical assistance. He stressed that donor countries which were geographically close to recipients might be more aware of the latter's needs than were more distant countries.

He pointed out the dangers of importing advanced technology into less advanced economies, but stressed that these dangers were frequently exaggerated; sometimes advanced technology was essential in the infrastructure. Once again he stated that it was possible that geographically close donors might be more sensitive to the appropriateness of new techniques.

In conclusion, he stressed the symbiotic relationship of donor and recipient countries. He emphasised that in the ultimate instance the success of such relationships depended upon mutual respect of the parties concerned.

Mr Razafindratovo pointed out that the importation of technical advice and skills into Madagascar dated from the 1820s. He related the attitude towards aid from France in the post-independence period to the manner in which independence had been achieved by the francophone states. Where independence had been achieved in an atmosphere of hostility (such as in Algeria and Guinea), such aid was accepted purely on a financial basis, while in those cases where independence had been achieved in a fraternal manner, technical assistance, in addition to financial aid, was accepted.

Aid was understood in part as compensation for exploitation during colonial times, but in practice it was also in accord with the cultural, economic, political and strategic interests of France. He pointed out that Madagascar was one of the largest recipients of aid per capita in the Third World; this aid came largely from France, but the E.E.C., the World Bank and individual countries (recently including South Africa) also fulfilled a role in this direction. However, French aid was characterised by controversy on both sides: in France there was a feeling that internal development should be given priority over foreign assistance, while in Madagascar there was a preference for increasing the world prices of primary products, rather than simply for the provision of aid.

Part Three

Evaluation and Prospects

Chapter Thirteen

Rapporteurs' Report

A. Political Questions and Governmental Structure

KURT GLASER

This general report cannot, within the scope allotted, enter into the details of the foregoing papers and discussions. Instead, your rapporteurs propose to concentrate on a few significant perceptions and consensuses that emerged during the Conference.

It is almost a truism to observe at this point that many of the discussions were strongly policy-oriented, and that they brought to light a variety of criticisms and proposals. But your rapporteurs will refrain from policy recommendations of their own since these would necessarily be personal. Members of the Conference and readers of the book resulting from it will be able to draw their own policy conclusions from the material presented.

The three parts of this report will deal with broad topics rather than specific sessions, as ideas and themes were often carried over from one session to another. Generally, this part will deal with political questions and problems of governmental structure. Part B, by Professor Brand, will concentrate on economic matters, and Part C, by Mr Schlemmer, will deal with social and educational problems, as well as research needs identified during the Conference.

Your rapporteurs wish to emphasise that all contributions to the Conference, including those coming from the floor, were carefully reviewed, even though it proved possible to mention only a few speakers by name.

BASIC CONCEPTS AND GOALS

Professor Weidner set the tone for the Conference by pointing to the all-embracing nature of development, involving the blue ball of earth as seen from space as a whole, and man, who lives on this ball, considered as a total personality – as a *Gestalt*. This concept formed the basis for our further deliberations.

All people all over the world, Professor Weidner continued, are interrelated. Development is therefore not only a national problem, but an individual and an international matter at the same time. The philosophy of development combines belief in the dignity of man with the desire to improve his condition. It is also manipulative, since it is based on the assumption that man can change his environment. Professor Louw developed this concept further, describing development as a revolution in which 'haves' and 'have nots' join and both sides win.

The presentations by Professors Weidner and Louw and the ensuing discussion focused attention on two points that were reiterated in later sessions. First of all, basic development decisions are political in nature: heads of government, ministers and parliaments must answer for them to their constituencies. A professional planner must not, therefore, overstep his *staff* capacity. His function is to assemble the data needed for rational choices and to compose scenarios of development within available resources. But the plan adopted must be acceptable to the public agencies and communities that will carry it out. Professor Weidner emphasised that plans must have a *support base*, while Professor Knall, in the session on planning, spoke of the need for *commitment*.

The second important point is that planning, as a goal-setting activity, is intimately linked with social justice. The connection was brought out by the response to a statement by Professor Weidner that development is fundamentally an equalitarian goal. Professor Arkin and Mr Thahane commented that the practical results of development did not always lead towards equality. Professor Weidner then explained that his statement was normative, meaning that greater equality was an important aim of development. The principle of reducing existing inequalities appeared to evoke universal consensus among Conference participants. The idea of concentrating development in the most primitive, and hence poorest, areas of Southern Africa, involving necessarily a redistribution of social product, seemed implicit in most of what was said about specific needs and programmes.

At the same time, however, the Conference as a whole seemed disposed to agree with the introductory speakers that development was a multiplex process requiring the rational use of human and material resources. Professor Weidner spoke of the choices to be made, such as balanced versus unbalanced development and the extent of government control over business. Professor Louw showed that development has a number of distinct functional areas, which form the subject-matters of economics, sociology, political science and other disciplines. He underlined the need for governmental structures capable of managing complex development programmes.

PROBLEMS OF ETHNIC COEXISTENCE

The papers and discussions on political dynamics centred for the most part on the fact of multi-ethnicity and the adaptation of governmental system to that fact. The underlying problem might be stated as follows: What kinds of governmental structure – given the ethnic composition of Southern Africa – can best create a stable base for development by assuring domestic peace and removing causes of inter-ethnic friction?

In his comprehensive essay, Professor Possony dealt with the social dynamics as well as the politics of development. He laid particular stress on the insight that *development must be accomplished by the developing people themselves.* It cannot be handed to them by others, however well intentioned. Development policy must therefore start from the premise that people can be helped but not 'developed from above'. The remarks of several discussants, however, suggested that there may still be officials who yield to the latter temptation.

In his verbal presentation, Professor Possony focused on the rights of nationalities. He had already made it apparent in his written discussion that he regards nationalities or ethnic groups as self-defining except to the extent that a group defines itself by excluding other groups. Two groups may, however, merge *if both groups so desire.*

The key point of Professor Possony's lecture was the *right of ethnic integrity*: the right of each nationality to self-preservation and the pursuit of its own culture. Such integrity, he declared, is a *sine qua non* of regional development. Over and above assurance of its ethnic integrity, Professor Possony continued, each group desiring to develop also needs (*a*) capital, (*b*) entrepreneurial attitudes and abilities, (*c*) intfrastructure and (*d*) security. Outsiders may help in achieving these, but they cannot provide the grass-roots motive power. That can only be done by the people desiring to develop.

To assure development in a multi-ethnic region, Possony reasoned, the political structure must provide an active role for each people.

Dr Worrall's presentation analysed the variant types of political system that exist in Southern Africa and their distinctive approaches to modernisation. He focused attention on the multiple nature of Southern Africa's political system – the juxtaposition of dominant and subordinate elements – and the failure to take decisions that would vitalise the Black homelands.

The discussion that followed dealt with the possibilities of an expanded common market or federation. The latter, Mr Thahane observed, would need to have empathy for the different ethnic groups. The point was also made that within the existing customs union, South Africa sometimes made unilateral tariff decisions in the interest of its own producers. A recent case in point involved a Swazi fertiliser plant that threatened to compete with South African production. The Republic placed this plant at a disadvantage by raising the common external tariff on the raw materials it imported.

Professor Vosloo offered a factual description of the administrative structure and methods of separate development. He admitted quite frankly the existence of an 'overarching and dominant White power structure' and the present (though not necessarily future) role of agencies such as the Bantu Development Corporation and the Xhosa Development Corporation as *de facto* parts of that structure. He did not, however, editorialise about his findings of fact – an ommission that earned him criticism by a few Conference members.

Your rapporteur, however, feels that Professor Vosloo did well to limit himself to a factual description of the *status quo*. In so doing, he laid the groundwork for a lively discussion of improvements that would promote development and self-government. Mr Mapena, for instance, suggested modernisation of the political structure in the homelands, involving wider use of the elective principle and possibly moving the chiefs upstairs to a 'House of Lords'. The principle that the urban Bantu is a temporary resident, he observed, needs re-examination. Professor Ngcobo suggested that the policy that Bantu be educated 'in accordance with their own principles' was administered under a White interpretation of these principles. A Black discussant from within the Republic then pointed out that the homelands were not yet able to change school syllabuses, issue bus franchises or float loans for public purposes.

Further discussion indicated a consensus which may not have been unanimous, but seemed to be shared by many White as well as Black participants, that the time had come – as Professor Ntsanwisi said – for a substantial further delegation of powers to the homeland governments.

In the session on multi-ethnic societies – actually the second on structural problems – your present rapporteur discussed the experience of Austria–Hungary and compared the rationalist-territorial idea of the nation as the people of a state with Herder's ethnic-linguistic or *Volk* concept of the nation as a collective personality. He stated his views:

(*a*) that the Herder model is more applicable to the African situation; and

(*b*) that the unitary state will not work in a multi-ethnic region.

Your rapporteur also emphasised the need for 'existential security' – analogous to Professor Possony's 'ethnic integrity'. His paper can properly be interpreted as an endorsement of separate development, but with important qualifications:

(*a*) Nationalities must, as rapidly as possible, be given genuine self-government. This includes, as Mr Thahane puts it, the right to make one's own mistakes. To keep these to the minimum, however, a massive effort is needed to train administrators and planners.

(*b*) The process of decision-making on matters affecting non-European nationalities should be converted to the model of negotiation and bargaining – on an informal basis at first, but moving towards formal institutions based on experience.

(*c*) A mode of representation and self-administration must be found for the urban Black, as well as for Coloureds and

Indians. This might well be based on Karl Renner's concept of 'personal autonomy'.

(d) Nationalities should enjoy shares of resources permitting the optimum development of each nationality and of the region of Southern Africa as a whole.

Insistence on the existential security of each nationality, it should be emphasised, is not a qualification of the philosophy of separate development, but inherent in that philosophy.

THE SPECTRUM OF POLITICAL CONSENSUS

The Conference did not reach a single consensus on what is the best political structure for South Africa or Southern Africa as a whole. To do so was not its purpose nor the expectation of its organisers. The intention was rather to analyse problems of development and to find ways of working together to solve them. This the Conference did most effectively.

So far as political structure is concerned, your rapporteur gained the impression – for which no infallibity is claimed – that *in so far as members of the Conference expressed preferences for particular political arrangements*, directly or by implication, they could be grouped into three main categories, each of which cuts across racial and national lines. These may for convenience be called groups A, B and C. They may be defined generally as follows, always allowing for the possibility that particular Conference participants will have opinions that do not fall clearly within any of the groups defined:

Group A

This rather large group believes in the workability of plural governmental structures, especially those of federal type. So far as South Africa is concerned, they favour reforms ranging in scope from very moderate to very considerable and in speed from gradual to quite rapid. Participants who simply favoured the *status quo* without any changes were hardly in evidence. On the relation of desired reforms to existing policy, it appears to your rapporteur that changes increasing the autonomy of nationalities and bettering their development opportunities are implementations of separate development. Changes removing barriers to co-operation do not violate the principle, which has never required isolation.

Group B

The members of this group, which is also quite large, are sceptical about the workability of plural organisation. They would prefer some other system for South Africa, but they recognise that existing policy is not likely to change in the near future. They are therefore willing to work within it for the maximum advantage of their own people and others. There is also probably an intermediate group, who could be designated as A/B's, who do not like separate development as now conceived and administered, but would accept a perfected model.

Group C

This group, which was represented by a rather smaller number at the Conference, think separate development so abhorrent that no good can come from working within it.

It should be noted that the foregoing groups, including all their possible combinations and permutations, are limited to those who expressed an opinion on governmental structure. There is a fourth group, including several Americans and several others, who deliberately and explicitly refrained from expressing any preferences whatever concerning structural arrangements in South Africa or Southern Africa. It need hardly be added that the three sponsoring organisations are not committed to any of the opinions expressed in the Conference, nor is any participant identified with any view he did not himself express.

So far as shades of opinion emerged at the Conference, however, it is clear that a firm basis for co-operation exists between members of groups A and B. It is to be hoped that friendships made or strengthened during our days together will result in co-operative development efforts. Quite naturally, A's are inclined to hope that as concrete improvements are achieved, some B's may be converted to A's. And it is likely that B's have analogous hopes of conversion.

Whether the co-operation of C's on specific projects can be

secured depends on the C's. Certainly, no person of goodwill would want to exclude them.

So far as the Southern African region as a whole is concerned, the Conference manifested a clear consensus on the need for co-operation and sharing resources. There was little indication of desire for a formal organisation beyond the functional bodies (such as the regional Conservation Commission) that now exist. There is, however, general recognition of the common interests of Southern Africa as a region and of the need for continued and intensified private as well as government co-operation on development questions.

B. Economic Aspects

SIMON S. BRAND

The procedure adopted in drawing up this report was, first, to try to identify both those issues on which a clear consensus emerged in the course of the Conference and those on which it did not. Where a consensus did not emerge, it was nevertheless attempted to indicate points on which the opposing views appeared to converge. Also, rather than trying to stick closely to the sequence in which topics appeared on the programme, the report is presented in a thematic sequence.

DEFINITIONS AND GOALS OF DEVELOPMENT

Definitions of economic development which were presented by various main participants and discussants ranged all the way from agnostic statements, justified both in terms of conceptual difficulties and of the shortcomings of the available statistical measures, to positive definitions in terms of the growth of real output per capita or employment opportunities, or in terms of less quantifiable concepts such as 'more of the good things of life' or a widening of scope. In the various statements on what development is about, perhaps the most frequently recurring concept was that of *choice*, variously qualified by such adjectives as 'informed', 'effective', 'voluntary', and 'individual'. The kind of definition about which the widest agreement was apparent at the Conference is that formulated some years ago by Bauer and Yamey, and quoted by Professor Leistner in a contribution from the floor, viz. 'the widening of the range of effective choice is the most valuable single objective of economic development as well as the best single criterion of its attainment'.*

The Economics of Underdeveloped Countries (Cambridge, 1957) pp. 149–50.

Most definitions of development have a normative content, in the sense that particular development goals are either explicitly or implicitly stated in them. Apart from the development goals implied in the definitions already referred to, equalitarianism was put forward as a goal of development at various points in the programme of the Conference, with some variation in opinions on the priority it should be given relative to competing goals. However, there was wide, if not complete, agreement that whether or not the ultimate goals of development should be framed in equalitarian terms, operational goals should be chosen pragmatically in the light of given situations, and would necessarily have to fall short of ideal objectives. A proximate goal which appeared to enjoy fairly general acceptance was the narrowing of disparities between groups and regions, with some participants insisting on the explicit condition that this should not be done by drawing down groups or regions that are now at the higher end of the spectrum of attained development, but rather by uplifting those that are now at the lower end. The position was also stated that in a world of finite resources this last condition cannot be met, but, as will appear below, this conclusion was not widely supported at the Conference.

THE MANIPULATION OF DEVELOPMENT

In close relationship to the question of goals, a rather fundamental division of opinion became apparent on the question of whether explicitly formulated goals can indeed be purposively attained over specified time-spans. On the one hand, it was held that social scientists and policy-makers cannot identify the strategic variables of which development is a function, or assign proper weights to them, and in particular that conventional economic models do not give appropriate guidance in this respect; that even if those variables can be identified, they cannot be controlled effectively; and that attempts to control them can only be harmful. On the other hand, it was pointed out that the concept of *accelerated* development itself implies that man can control not only his physical but also his social environment, and that he possesses both the knowledge to identify under- or slow development and the techniques to bring about accelerated development.

At the root of this division, contrasting views were apparent as to the nature of the physical and social environment in which development must take place. Those who held with the intractability of development to conscious manipulation tended to lay stress on the persistence of differences in individual and socio-cultural traits, and of differential control over resources as between groups, leading on to persistent differences in economic performance. While the importance of these intervening variables was not fundamentally at issue, others were more ready to assume that they can be purposively influenced in predetermined directions. As regards the physical environment in particular, the position that the world's physical resources are absolutely limited, and therefore a severe constraint on development, was stated and discussed at some length, but the majority view seemed to be that technological development should effectively continue to lift this constraint, as has been the case in the past.

SOCIAL CONTROL VIS-À-VIS PRIVATE DECISIONS

The division of opinion about the merits of attempting to manipulate development led on directly to the question of the respective roles of the government and private sectors in the process of development. It was forcefully argued by some that most, perhaps even all, historical examples of successful development were unplanned, and that the best attainable rate of development in any given situation would result if individuals, as individuals or in voluntary association, should act and dispose of the resources at their command as they see fit. While it was conceded by some proponents of this viewpoint that not all kinds of government intervention are equally harmful, it was emphasised that none is subject to the discipline of the market; that restrictions on private economic activities tend to reinforce the zero-sum-game philosophy, which is anathema to development; that interventions usually lead to the misallocation of resources; that they tend to affect adversely the spread of ideas, and so on. According to this viewpoint, it is consequently best to limit the role of government to the classic functions in the fields of law and order, external affairs, monetary and fiscal management, health and education, which functions would in any event stretch the resources at the command of governments in most less developed countries.

As against this viewpoint, various justifications were submitted for defining the role of government in wider terms than allowed for in the classic government functions. The first, most general, argument was that 'political man' is as pervasive a phenomenon as 'economic man', and that harmful government intervention can therefore best be avoided by precisely defining the areas in which there is a clear need for government intervention. Secondly, the well-known technical-economic arguments for intervention were put forward, in particular that the free price system cannot adequately handle the kinds of structural adjustments required in less developed countries, even assuming that it is the best mechanism for handling the more marginal, or continuous, adjustments typically taking place in developed economies. Other arguments based on the existence of market imperfections drew attention to distortions in the structure of relative prices in less developed countries, so that market prices do not correctly reflect relative scarcities, with resulting misallocation of resources.

A third kind of argument in favour of government intervention was that the outcome of free market processes is not necessarily compatible with wider socio-political objectives. Examples of areas in which such divergencies are common were pointed out, e.g. the regional distribution of economic activity, and income distribution.

FORMS OF DEVELOPMENT PLANNING

Given the need for some government intervention beyond the classic functions, various degrees of such intervention can, of course, still be visualised. While the 'classical' position was forcefully stated, no one explicitly took the completely opposite position. The point was positively made by several participants that the actual degree of social control over, or government intervention in, economic activity in a given situation would depend on the value system of the society in question: in the United States, for example, the tolerance of intervention would be much lower than in less developed countries without a similarly strong tradition of free enterprise. Also, in respect of South Africa it was pointed out that the strong tradition of private decision-making in economic matters has effectively constrained the degree of government intervention, even in the face of strong demands for such intervention, deriving from other socio-political objectives.

In so far as a need for government intervention in economic development in Southern Africa was accepted, the general preference was not for imperative planning, but rather for utilising the market mechanism by manipulating the system of incentives and disincentives, e.g. through the use of a system of differential subsidies and taxes to encourage a desired regional distribution of economic activities. This, it was held, would still leave the largest part of the actual economic calculation and decision-making with private entrepreneurs and individual owners of production factors, and would retain to a large extent the disciplining effect of market forces. As a means towards introducing a parallel discipline into the economic functions of the government sector itself, the advantages of applying planning-programming-budgeting systems in fiscal administration were mentioned by several participants, while the educative effect that the use of such systems can have on community leaders was stressed as a benefit in itself.

The fact that no specific attention was given in the programme to planning in other spheres than the economic was deplored by participants from the floor, especially in view of the general agreement at the Conference that the orthodox economic variables and models are not adequate for understanding and as a basis for manipulating the development process.

THE ROLE OF PLANNING COMMISSIONS

There was general agreement at the Conference that planning bodies should not be given an independent existence outside the mainstream of the machinery of government. There can be no assurance that development strategies put forward by independent planning bodies will be compatible with the political system of the country in question, as such bodies have no way of legitimising goals; they can therefore be no more than the generators of one particular kind of input with which political leaders must deal, along with other inputs, in coming to decisions. The corollary of this is the plans put out by planning commissions cannot be effective unless they are linked directly to the political-administrative decision-making process, e.g. to ensure that once the goals assumed in the plan have been accepted, budgeting will be consistent with the attainment of those goals within the plan framework.

It was also agreed that the setting of goals cannot properly be a function of planning bodies, but that their role in goal formulation should simply be to articulate alternative goals and their respective implications, in particular in respect of the commitment of resources; but it was also recognised that in practice the role of planning bodies often turns out to be more active in this respect.

The South African experience with regard to the development of the Bantu homelands was cited as an example of inadequate utilisation of a planning commission in the process of goal formulation, in that the government committed itself to certain explicit objectives, such as certain population distribution patterns, without first having obtained a realistic assessment of the resources that would be required to attain those objectives. The task of the planning commission was thereby reduced to working backwards from the given objectives to the required resources and instruments. The actual mobilisation of resources and plan implementation remained within the political-administrative system, whereby the commitment of resources inevitably tended to be eroded in relation to the claims of competing objectives.

The session on planning brought forward many other specific views on various technical aspects of the planning process, in particular on criteria for effective planning, which it would serve no purpose to repeat in summarised form. The most generally stressed among these criteria was perhaps the need for building flexibility into the planning process.

STRATEGIES AND INSTRUMENTS OF DEVELOPMENT

The important role of agriculture, both in the present economic situation of the less developed parts of Southern Africa and in the context of development strategy, was generally accepted at the Conference. Apart from the purely quantitative aspect, especially in respect of employment, the role of agriculture as a bridge in the changing of attitudes and skills through commercialisation was also stressed. It was also evident in various papers, and in contributions from the floor, that agricultural development alone cannot be sufficient to ensure the attainment of policy objectives such as improved levels of living or desired settlement patterns. Since, furthermore, mineral developments and potentials are unevenly distributed, the attainment of such goals in the respective economies of the subcontinent will necessarily depend to an important extent on the diversion of some part of the overall industrial growth from the established industrial concentrations towards outlying areas, and on the attendant multiplier effects. Related to this conclusion, the agreement among the sociologists at the Conference on the modernising influence of urbanisation was also striking.

With regard to *agricultural development*, it was fairly generally accepted that the responses of tribal farmers to market forces can be adequate to justify a strategy relying on market incentives, within a smallholder pattern of farming, and supported by appropriate institutions to provide supporting services such as extension services, agriculture research, marketing channels and credit. The evidence of the East African experience in this regard, which was presented to the Conference, had a very significant impact on the proceedings, although several participants expressed their doubts as to the suitability of individual tenure systems in tribal areas in Southern Africa. That the applicability of the Kenyan model to agricultural development in Southern Africa merits intensive research was, however, clearly indicated.

It was pointed out by several participants that up till now *industrial and mining development* has led to increasing inequalities between both regions and population groups. The hypothesis was also put forward that further industrial and mining development would automatically lead to a narrowing of such disparities, but this was widely disputed on the basis of empirical experience of polarisation in the subcontinent. To some extent this conflict of views revolves around the question of the acceptable time-span within which the gaps should start narrowing, but it did not appear as if the opposing views could be reconciled simply by agreeing on such a time-span. Thus there was strong support for the position that countervailing mechanisms and measures are required to offset the polarisation tendencies. Such measures would include deliberate manipulation of comparative cost structures to effect a desired dispersal of industrial activities, intensified programmes of education and training, and policies aimed at a fuller utilisation of the subcontinent's labour resources.

Related to the last point, it was also stressed that *population policy* should be aimed not only at quantitative but also at qualitative aspects. However, the relationships between population tendencies and economic growth parameters which were put before the Conference made it clear that in general the nations of Southern Africa can gain significantly from reduced rates of population growth. That population control policies cannot be pursued in isolation from general socio-economic policies was also agreed.

ECONOMIC CO-OPERATION IN SOUTHERN AFRICA

The continued dependence of all countries in the region, including South Africa, on external trade was duly emphasised, and it was pointed out that the definition of Southern Africa as a region is based to a large extent on economic ties between the various countries, such as intra-regional trade and labour movements. It was recognised, however, that the large degree of complementarity between the exports of the countries in the region, and the small domestic markets of most of these countries, impose limits on the further development of intra-regional trade. The advantages and disadvantages of the existing customs union and of possible wider co-operation, for the respective member countries, were discussed at length, and there was wide agreement that without such countervailing measures against spontaneous polarisation of economic activities as referred to above, the prior attainment of comparable levels of development in the various countries tends to become a condition for mutually beneficial co-operation in the form of customs unions, free-trade areas or other arrangements of this nature.

The kind of strategy towards closer economic co-operation in Southern Africa which enjoyed the widest support at the Conference was one of starting at lower levels of co-operation in specific areas of common interest, such as soil conservation, and gradually working up towards formal overall institutions on the analogy of the O.E.C.D. Also, a point that was strongly emphasised at several sessions was that, to be viable, economic co-operation must presuppose true participation of all communities, groups and regions in all decisions affecting their respective interests, and must preclude the subordination of some of the participating entities to centralised decision-making vested in one or a few of them.

FORMS OF DEVELOPMENT ASSISTANCE

Attention was given by Conference participants to both technical and financial forms of development assistance, and to both official and private channels of assistance. In close correspondence with the factual situation in Southern Africa with regard to intra-regional aid flows, official or inter-governmental development assistance was discussed mainly in terms of technical assistance, and the point made that this should by no means be seen as a one-way flow from the more advanced to the less developed countries in the region, while financial assistance was discussed mainly in relation to international private investment.

The usual economic reservations about such private investment flows were voiced, to the effect that the multiplier and linkage effects in the recipient country tend to be limited. These reservations were severely discounted by several speakers, and interestingly enough the detailed case study of one such investment project which was presented to the Conference can be interpreted in favour of both viewpoints. On the one hand, it provided a clear illustration of specific measures which can be taken to ensure at least a certain minimum of positive spillover effects in the host country, and on the other, the implication is that those spillover effects would not have eventuated had the measures in question not been taken. In the final instance, this provided an extremely informative illustration of the operation of a factor, the importance of which emerged at several points during the Conference, viz. the effective, informed participation in development decisions of autonomous local leaders of the communities affected by those decisions.

C. Major Social, Cultural and Psychological Factors which Bear upon Problems of and Prospects for Accelerated Development in Southern Africa

LAWRENCE SCHLEMMER

In this report on part of the proceedings of the Conference, I have not attempted to summarise much of the important theoretical arguments advanced, since these have been mainly political and economic in content. My focus, rather, has been on what is practically and empirically of direct relevance to Southern Africa.

The material summarised here does not necessarily always represent a broad consensus of opinion among delegates. In some cases there was a clear polarisation of views, and this has been indicated. In other cases important points were made without any dissent being voiced within the time available for discussion, and here I have had to assume that no significant disagreement existed.

Obviously, considerable overlap in the social, political and economic subject-matter existed, and it has not been possible to avoid reflecting this in the points presented below.

As far as possible I have used terminology which, although much less impressive than some of the academic terminology used during the Conference, hopefully is readily comprehensible to a lay audience.

Unfortunately I have had to omit a great deal of valuable material from this necessarily brief report.

It has been necessary, very often, to draw together scattered points made at different sessions in the Conference in order to present a systematic and coherent statement of the social and cultural subject-matter of the Conference. Points which were not necessarily linked during the discussion have been combined in this presentation in order to draw out the significance of the material.

THE HUMAN FACTOR AND THE GOALS AND MEANS OF DEVELOPMENT

The needs of people, in addition to the necessity for favourable growth statistics, were emphasised by many speakers, discussants and participants. Development was variously seen as an increase in the options and alternatives open to people; an improvement in the quality of the lives of human beings in the fullest sense (as opposed to people viewed as labour or consumption units); and as the manner in which mankind seeks its identity and attains the fullest human stature.

In line with these goals, it was emphasised that overall development plans and specific schemes should carry the approval of the majority of people to be affected and, ideally, that people should participate in the formulation and implementation of development plans or, at the very least, enjoy full consultation. Pleas were made for planners to pay heed to the social costs of some forms of economic development: costs such as, for example, the destruction of the environment, the breakdown of existing family patterns, the growth of landless proletariats in rural areas, the growth of competitiveness and exploitative behaviour, etc.

Although by no means everyone was optimistic, it was generally agreed that development in Southern Africa must involve a trend towards the equalisation of the incomes and status of people. Not only poverty, but the relative gap in the material standards of different groups and regions, was considered likely to cause unrest which would further undermine stability and development in the whole subcontinent. 'If some don't eat, others don't sleep' was a warning accepted by most delegates.

Then again, a prominent homeland politician, in relating one of South Africa's sick race jokes, very eloquently made the point that what Africans feel they need most is to have their dignity and humanity recognised in full.

FACTORS IN THE TRADITIONAL AND IN THE CHANGING CULTURES OF SOUTHERN AFRICA WHICH BEAR UPON THE PROCESS OF MODERNISATION

African traditional culture and social structure does not generally allow scope for innovation, and does not encourage behaviour oriented towards personal achievement or dissent. Social prestige and status, attitudes to work and livestock, individual life-goals, the system of communal land tenure, the family system and the integrating and unifying factors in traditional societies are all tightly interwoven in a kinship-based social system which rigidly prescribes roles and ascribes status.

Occupations are largely undifferentiated, as are the pre-literary forms of education and social training. A quality of fatalism and an absence of rational planning and rational anticipation of problems is encouraged by the traditional religious beliefs.

Such societies are virtually the complete antithesis of the model of a modern or modernising society which, above all, is characterised by the inbuilt facility to adapt to changing conditions and to ensure its own survival in changing circumstances.

However, vast and sweeping changes have occurred as a result of the growth of a modern industrial economy in South Africa and as a result of missionary influences, colonial rule and the modern administration of territories.

The money economy has penetrated everywhere, most tribal people have become convinced of the value of modern education, and increasingly the African (and other) populations are becoming urbanised and gaining experience of industrialised labour. Christian beliefs or certain values which are broadly associated with modern Christianity and/or with rational-scientific thinking are sweeping away traditional supernatural beliefs, although some aspects of these beliefs, like the fear of witchcraft, for example, are proving to be fairly resilient.

These changes have given rise to a number of specific factors which have both positive and negative implications for accelerated development. The positive influences are:

(i) Urbanisation, in itself, is generally positively associated with changes in attitudes, values and patterns of response to social situations – changes which are generally favourable to development. This relationship, however, depends on the urbanising society acquiring the formal and informal organisations for dealing with complex administrative tasks and for resolving internal conflicts.

(ii) Urban African workers, and, in some cases and areas, seasonal migrant workers as well, are generally committed to industrial employment and usually form a stable workforce, even though relatively few as yet appear to have acquired carreer orientations or an acceptance of the value of self-expression through achievement for its own sake.

(iii) It was suggested that growing occupational, material and prestige differentiation among urbanising and modernising groups could spur the initially less successful members or groups to greater efforts. A contradictory view was also expressed which will be noted presently.

(iv) Numbers of voluntary associations have come into existence spontaneously to provide mutual assistance and to provide immigrants to cities and towns with support and security in a new environment. Such associations teach new and appropriate ways of behaving and take the place of those traditional institutions which do not function adequately in the new milieu.

(v) When rapid change occurs, as with urbanisation, individuals, acting in a changing cultural context, become aware of dissatisfying features, inconsistencies and discrepancies in their social environment, often as a result of some changes occurring faster than others. Once aware of these inconsistencies, provided conditions of leadership are favourable, individuals and groups take action to correct the inconsistencies, and such change-oriented behaviour becomes established as a positive, often dynamic feature in the modernising society.

The process of rapid urbanisation, however, has also resulted in some very serious social problems:

(i) The breakdown of the traditional family, and of the norms and sanctions associated with it, has resulted in certain transitional features like, for example, a relatively unstable single or nuclear family system, high illegitimacy rates and juvenile delinquency.

(ii) Poverty, overcrowding and unemployment have led to rising crime rates.

(iii) In some territories in particular and in Southern Africa as a whole, the large numbers of unskilled work-seekers – the surplus labour – tend to work with other factors in keeping wage rates exceptionally low, exacerbating the problems mentioned above. On the other hand, shortages of skilled workers have, in part, contributed to wide income disparities between skilled and unskilled workers, which seriously impede the struggle for prosperity among Black people and Black states in Southern Africa.

(iv) Many better-educated Africans reveal a tendency to distance themselves from less educated people and from rural people, contributing towards a weakening of social cohesion and leadership in urban areas. This is, in part, a reflection on one function of the conventional educational system which (in one of the education groups at least) was considered to be a negative feature in that the values and form of education encourage the stratification of African communities.

(v) Migrant labour has meant that rural subsistence agriculture is deprived of a considerable proportion of able-bodied male workers, contributing to the exceptionally poor efficiency in subsistence farming.

Despite the seriousness and urgency of these problems, the view was expressed that in certain cases the very seriousness of the problems acts as a powerful political incentive to efforts to overcome such problems, which in turn act as a spur to development. Even the breakdown of moral values and resulting social disorganisation, for example, can speed up the process of detribalisation.

SOME SOCIAL AND CULTURAL FACTORS WHICH
INFLUENCE POLITICAL DEVELOPMENT

(i) In many parts of Africa, ethnic group identity has proved
to be a serious dividing factor, emerging after the unity
achieved in independence struggles has become attenuated
in the post-independence period.

(ii) Certain territories in Southern Africa are characterised
by potentially disruptive tribal divisions which are coun-
tered by attempts to regenerate unifying mass political
movements, which can have other effects beneficial to the
process of modernisation as well.

(iii) There did not appear to be unanimity among delegates
in regard to the salience of tribal divisions in South Africa.
One point of view, broadly, was that feelings of solidarity
among Africans across tribal divisions were a temporary
response to the broader pattern of colour-based discrimination in South African society, and that powerful historical and contemporary analogies suggested that tribal
conflict would reappear if other conflicts were to pass.
Another view, briefly, was that subjective patterns of
group identity were, to an important degree, a response
to objective factors affecting the interests of people in
society, and that no hard-and-fast predictions could be
made as to whether or not tribal hostility would reappear
in a hypothetical future. Yet another view was that strong
subjective feelings of group identity existed to unite most
Africans in South Africa, and that tribal identities were
in large measure a result of political policies of the present
government and could not be regarded as autonomous
social movements. The view was expressed that it was
extremely difficult for Whites to understand fully the
authentic responses of Africans in situations like the
present.

(iv) On another issue, it was considered that the traditional
role and status of the African chief have been distorted
by present policies which entail the nomination of chiefs
as political leaders of the African people in South Africa.
These policies result in a weakening of the chief's prestige

and an exposure of chiefs to the indignities of the hurly-burly of politics.

(v) Evidence from Malawi and Germany suggested that the morale and initiative of peasants was greatly improved by political 'liberation' and by the feeling among people that they were able to participate in deciding their own affairs. Black consciousness programmes in South Africa were seen by some as potentially able to improve morale among Africans, whereas others considered that they would be disruptive of harmonious relations between Black and White.

(vi) Two speakers and a few participants expressed the view that race attitudes and self-interest among members of the White electorate (or among political party support groups) placed a definite limit on the extent to which material assistance for the developmente of African people could be provided by the White government. Such attitudes also stood in the way of Africans in South Africa enjoying improvements in occupational status.

(vii) The point was made that an important segment of poorer Black people in South Africa resided permanently in the common area of South Africa, and that their development could not be considered in isolation from political and economic issues in the developed sector of South African society.

SOCIAL AND CULTURAL FACTORS WHICH INFLUENCE AGRICULTURAL DEVELOPMENT PROGRAMMES

(i) Two divergent views emerged on whether or not subsistence peasants should be encouraged to undertake communal farming activity, on the one hand, or should be given the opportunity to own or lease individual plots and become small-scale entrepreneurial farmers on the other. One view was that private African smallholders had proved themselves in Kenya and elsewhere, and that no successful communal ventures existed outside of the very special circumstances in Israel. Difficulties facing communal ven-

tures, in particular, were the generally inefficient management which seemed inevitable unless there was very strong
authority, as well as the difficulty of a general inability to
discipline labour without personal income incentives for
the food producers.

(ii) An alternative view was that the social costs of private-
enterprise farming were high, since this tended to result
in growing inequality and in a landless proleteriat coming
into existence. In view of the extreme pressure on land
in some parts of Southern Africa, it was suggested that
successful communal farming was a challenge which had
to be faced. However, in defence of individual tenure the
point was made that many landless peasants were usually
given employment on the private small farms of relatives
and that a general average improvement in material standards for all could result, relative to what the standard of
living would be on inefficient communal farms.

It was emphasised that in most types of settlement schemes,
however, three conditions appeared to be necessary for success:

(*a*) that strong guidance and authority should be present in
the early stages;

(*b*) that initial rewards should be high in order to overcome
the understandable reluctance of peasants to take risks and
sacrifice leisure; and

(*c*) that well-organised co-operative marketing and credit
schemes (either public or private) should exist. The benefits
of individual tenure on leasehold with public 'landlords',
with the authority to ensure sustained effort, were mentioned (cf. Professor Ruthenberg). However, specific mention was made of two successful co-operative farming
schemes in Lesotho, although both schemes were admittedly
fairly new.

SOCIAL FACTORS RELATING TO DEMOGRAPHIC TRENDS

Ideally, the need for family-planning schemes was fully endorsed,
since mounting pressure of population numbers cancelled econo-

mic growth, led to a high number of dependants per family, and was a factor contributing to political and social instability.

Severe impediments to family planning exist in Southern Africa, however, and some of these are:

(i) The low cost of bringing up children in subsistence agriculture.

(ii) Children are the only form of social security for parents where no state welfare benefits or social security exist.

(iii) A political factor is also present in South Africa, and this manifests itself in the belief that family-planning schemes are suggested by Whites to reduce the numbers of Africans who, on the other hand, see their numbers as a potential source of political strength. It was suggested that family-planning schemes should be made applicable to all, irrespective of race.

SOCIAL FACTORS RELATING TO EDUCATION

Note: This is not a summary of the report on the Education Workshop which appears elsewhere. It is merely a selection of aspects emerging from the discussions which are relevant to this summary of social and cultural factors in accelerated development.

(i) Doubts were expressed as to the benefits of primary-school attainments in conventional education. Functional literacy and numeracy were felt to be possibly more effective as a stimulant to development.

(ii) The function of conventional education in contributing to sharp status distinctions in the community has already been noted. The desire on the part of school-goers to achieve white-collar status and the tendency for them to disparage agriculture, and manual and technical work, is a related feature. It was considered that these features might result in part from values embedded in conventional education and that developing countries should make attempts to discourage these values, where they exist.

(iii) Education should be rooted in the familiar culture of children, but should aim at preparing every child for adjustment to the demands of a changing, developing society.

(iv) The importance of school feeding was emphasised, in combating the poor performance of hungry children.

(v) In a developing society, lifelong education (adult education) had a particularly important place, and its major concern should be literacy training of a type which would encourage an intelligent, thoughtful awareness of community issues and the individual's own life-goals.

(vi) 'Terminal' primary-school courses should have the effect of encouraging further progress of the pupil on his or her own, making use of adult educational or correspondence-school facilities. Primary-school courses should provide children with useful skills instead of being a preparation for further academic studies.

(vii) Dedicated volunteers from better-educated sections of the South African community should devote themselves to providing part-time instruction to adults in less fortunate educational circumstances, and such efforts should be encouraged, not discouraged, by the South African government.

MAJOR BROAD SUGGESTIONS EMERGING AS REGARDS STRATEGIES FOR SOCIAL DEVELOPMENT

(i) Urbanisation should be carefully studied, the problems assessed, and development planning should include urban planning and social and community development programmes to deal with urban problems. The mobilisation of community members to assist in solving their own problems is particularly important.

(ii) Socially active people in underdeveloped communities should be encouraged to assume leading roles, implying some form of leadership training.

(iii) Many planning attempts have failed because of communication problems. Experts experience difficulty in operating at the grass roots, and agricultural extension officers, for example, have difficulty in understanding farmers. Generally, difficulties exist in overcoming the natural suspicion and caution of peasants, and this difficulty is probably aggravated in the political climate of South Africa. Sustained efforts should be made to improve the quality of technical assistance, particularly in regard to the aspect of communication. The role of the social scientist here is paramount.

SOME RESEARCH PROPOSALS ARISING OUT OF THE NEEDS AND PROBLEMS RAISED DURING THE CONFERENCE

The following are some areas in which research appears to be urgently required. For the most part they represent my own assessment of research needs, since very few concrete suggestions for research were made at the Conference.

I have been parsimonious in suggesting research topics, limiting myself to what I see as very high-priority needs, because of the fact that research is expensive, and generally has to be replicated in different situations before the validity of findings can be fully established. The following are regarded as essential projects:

(i) A study of peasant communities, with a view to exploring those factors which lead to urban migration and to a failure on the part of migrants to return to the land or to maintain ties with or responsibility for dependants in rural areas.

(ii) Studies of traditional and modern élites in rural areas, and of the conflicts between such élites, specifically incorporating experimental studies of group dynamics approaches to conflict resolution and of institutional arrangements to resolve or minimise such conflicts. A study of conflicts between generations as they relate to development should also be included in such projects.

(iii) In the light of realities of population pressure, the high density in certain areas like, say, Zululand or Lesotho, for example, we need careful and exhaustive studies of the prospects for group farming and for communal village farming, with particular emphasis on the sort of social institutions that might be encouraged to develop which could help lessen some of the difficulties associated with group farming programmes.

(iv) Collation of all possible data, and of the records of success or failure and the reasons for success or failure (where possible), on all ongoing development schemes in Southern Africa. There is a great need for some sort of handbook – a guide to what is happening in the field of development. This would have to be kept up to date.

(v) Study of school drop-outs with particular emphasis on personal motivation and on the social and other factors predisposing children to failure.

(vi) Experimental studies of methods of improving teaching without the necessity for the recruitment of more teachers (who are likely to be in short supply for many years to come). For example, resource books are needed which will overcome second-language learning difficulties, and teaching aids using simple technology are required. All these possible methods require considerable researching before their effectiveness can be established.

(vii) Experimental studies of community development schemes and of self-help techniques and organisations which could assist unemployed or underemployed migrants to avoid dangers of social dislocation, and enable them to help themselves and the community by working on community projects which could provide money or subsistence for the unemployed while being useful, none the less, for the community as a whole.

(viii) (Suggested by Professor Kurt Glaser.) Since discussion on population policy showed marked disagreement, it is evident that data are needed as a basis for rational choice. Therefore research should be undertaken projecting expected rates of development (per capita G.N.P.), on the basis of various assumed rates of population growth, for different groups within the Southern African population separately.

The study would have to assume a range of alternative policies on allocation of resources – since that is a political question. For each policy, it should assess the effects of various birth rates and immigration balances on the ability of White South Africa to divert resources to non-White communities and the ability of the latter to attain optimum economic growth and social development.

Chapter 14
Epilogue

Epilogue*

G. VAN N. VILJOEN

I am personally very grateful for the predominant tone of serious scholarship that has marked this Conference. I should like to emphasise particularly the dispassionateness and the objectivity of the scholarship with which our speakers dealt with often very thorny and potentially very explosive topics. Let this also be an example to us of the spirit in which the work of this Conference ought to be continued.

I should, as a question of particular importance, like to suggest that the scholarship perhaps did not quite come to grips with the concept of ethnicity, the ethnic factor. We have been speaking about it and around it, but it seems to me that a lot of confusion still remains, and that this in particular is a topic on which in future we might expend some more intellectual energy. It struck me how, in the final discussions, parallels were again drawn between territories which are, on the one hand, multi-ethnic and, on the other hand, practically uni-ethnic or nation-states. The fact is that all the states of Southern Africa are different in this regard. I am sure that the Republic of South Africa would set about its inter-human relations, its political thinking and practice, in quite a different way, if it had a population composed in the same way as, for instance, Malawi or Lesotho or Madagascar. I think it is necessary that, if we think about these things again, we should perhaps be clearer in our analyses.

As a matter of personal conviction, you will perhaps allow me to say something about the concept of separate development which is often flung up in discussions, and is perhaps understood as a sort of final solution, as a sort of dogma. As I see it, separate development is, or at least in its pure concept should be, an open-

* The text of Professor Viljoen's concluding remarks at the closing session of the Conference.

ended method, a road towards an eventual solution and not a dogma or an end in itself. It is an open-ended method which could lead to any possible final solution, which will have to be left to the different groups to decide upon by themselves at the moment when they can really take a considered and well-informed decision about the matter. But, on the other hand, it seems to me that an approach which prefers the multi-racial or the integrated point of departure is really not open-ended, but is a closed and a final solution, and in that sense perhaps more of a dogma than separate development is. I think this is what we need in our thinking, whether we accept the one or the other, or think out something different. We have to find a road with an open end, where the ingenuity of the human mind and the increasing experience of human generations can find better solutions than perhaps we can at this stage finally formulate – rather than finding a road which leads to a final set-up, to which very little change can be introduced later on.

Another feature, which I think has pleased all of us, was the tremendously wide range of views expressed by the speakers, as has been so excellently brought out by the rapporteurs. Not only were these views wide-ranging, they were also frank and open in their formulation. The word 'dialogue' has been used, but I should prefer the word 'interaction'. Dialogue basically means an exchange of words; interaction I should say perhaps adds a dimension to an exchange of words, which has the effect of bringing about changes in the attitudes of people. Moreover, in the interaction of this Conference all of us were gratified to note the concentration on points of agreement rather than on points of difference, and to note the fact that this concentration on points of agreement enables us, I think, to eliminate or at least to reduce the points of difference that we might have thought existed. I am quite sure that, if on this note of interacting dialogue we were to move forward, we should find that this process of reduction, of elimination, might surprise us.

I should like to emphasise again what one of the speakers at the previous session said, namely that this Conference, as a conference, has not expressed any view, has not reached any conclusion or any agreement. Any attempt towards creating an impression that this Conference was in favour of a particular view or tended towards favouring a particular view would be a distortion of the facts. There was a continuous interaction of ideas maintained.

I should like to refer to a point made by Professor Possony, which has struck all of us, namely the unavailability of information on the problem of accelerated development. This has made us deeply conscious of the need for this kind of information. In many ways this Conference entails an accusation against the scholars, particularly the social scientists, of South Africa, for their failure to make available in published form a systematised presentation of the vitally important information on both the theory and the practice of development. I hope the challenge that has been thrown out will be taken up by our scholars, and that particularly our universities will here do a sterling task in the years ahead. We owe this not only to ourselves, but we owe this to the world, because Southern Africa, as a veritable laboratory of inter-human relations, has a store of experience which we are not entitled to keep to ourselves.

We have had interaction on several levels. There was an interaction between the scholars, the university people, on the one side, and the practical administrators, managers, on the other side. We have had exemplified in one of the participants to this Conference the ability to combine what one of our colleagues called having his head in the clouds of theory and his feet right down on the earth of reality. This metaphor showed us, I think, a measure of the dimensions of the man, and you will allow me to say that we really envy Lesotho for having its planning in such hands. But we also had the opportunity of bringing together the planners, the administrators, on the one hand, and the people for whom they are doing it on the other hand. In this field, in particular, I think it has been emphasised – and I should like to associate myself with that point of view – that South Africa has a lot to learn about how to bring the people for whom development is being planned into the preparation of the planning and into the working-out of development. We have in this regard had a valuable exercise in bringing these people together to talk to each other.

We have also had the interaction between scholars from abroad, from the United States, Germany, Great Britain, and South Africans – South Africans from both racial groups, Blacks and Whites – and this has been a valuable opportunity for interaction. In this regard we recall the very well-justified warning of Professor Kgware about the responsibility of all of us to make sure that, as this interaction takes place in everyday life in South Africa, it should be on an improved basis of the acceptance and appreciation of each other's human dignity.

We have also had interaction between South Africans and Southern Africans, which has been very stimulating, because, while South Africa has its multi-ethnic set-up, most of the other states in Southern Africa have a more unitary population composition. I am rather sorry that we did not have the privilege of more active contributions on the part of the participants here from Angola, Mozambique and Madagascar. I am sure that these participants have a store of valuable information, and I know that they exchanged much of their experience in the informal meetings between sessions. But I should like to express the hope that at a future convention of this nature we shall be able to widen the dialogue and perhaps overcome understandable language barriers, so as to have an even greater diversity of opinion.

We have also had interaction between the disciplines. This has been emphasised over and over and we are all very grateful for it. However, I think it is fair to state that, when we actually start planning for development, it remains almost exclusively economic, in spite of the emphasis on the total or comprehensive, interdisciplinary concept which we subscribe to in theory. I think also that in a future repetition of this kind of exercise we should try to bring down the theory more practically to the operational level, and that in particular the theory of the interdisciplinary approach should on the operational level be given concrete form by applying our minds to concrete case studies.

If we were to repeat something of this nature in future, we might make good use of the Germanic seminar method, where participants are perhaps confined to smaller groups, where they have had proper opportunity of studying beforehand the basic tenets to be applied, and where they could work on a really interdisciplinary basis – where the political scientist, the economist, the sociologist, the anthropologist, the educationalist, could have their minds clashing on a specific stated problem of development in a specific territory. I think this has been one of the great needs that have been shown up by this Conference.

Now, in conclusion, what about the future? What about continuation? I should like to take up Professor Beekman's suggestion that we should not just leave things here. At the same time, certain reservations have been heard about a formally structured continuation. But I should like to say here that from my side I shall do my best, together with the other sponsors, to try to set up an informal working group of experts in development from Southern Africa who could meet at least once a year and, if the need is sufficiently strong, perhaps even more frequently. People who could continue to exchange their experience, their information, their insights, and who could get to know each other, who could introduce each other to colleagues and so on, and who could really keep this sort of flow of thought, of experience, of exchange of ideas, going.

Should we consider on the other hand perhaps having another conference? Personally, I sincerely hope so. The Institute here has of course considerable experience in this field, and so has the Foundation. From my point of view it seems that there are a number of problems which I as a layman could identify. I am sure that there are many more, and that you could specify these problems far more clearly than I can – problems around which I am sure future conferences focused upon accelerated development could very usefully do some work. There is, for instance, the whole question of urbanisation. We are perhaps two generations behind the United States of America in respect of urbanisation. We can learn from their, in many ways, disconcerting experience, and we can investigate in far more detail the concepts put forward by Professor Dotson and others here about the role of urbanisation in modernisation and development. This is, in particular, a field that could require a whole conference to be properly thrashed out.

Several speakers suggested the need for arriving at a clearer concept of consultation within Southern Africa, and particularly within the Republic of South Africa itself – consultation on the political level, and consultation particularly in respect of the role of the Bantu outside the homelands. This calls for urgent attention, and we cannot simply state that there is a need for it; we must thrash out and define the problems, and try to arrive at a solution.

I should like to suggest furthermore that a conference could be held on small-scale industrialisation, or small-scale technology. We are perhaps too easily inclined to think of development in terms of large-scale industrial set-ups, mining conglomerates and all the rest of it, while what we really want is a type of development that would lead to more opportunities of employment, more diversity of ways of life for people. This I am sure could be found in a field with which at least the White South Africans are not very well acquainted, namely small-scale industry, small-scale technological development. I know that this has been done in Kenya and in Tanzania too. We could very well, I think, devote some more attention to this.

Finally, as has been briefly suggested once – and I should like to take this up – there is the vitally important role of modern communication methods in training people for development and, in particular, motivating them towards development.

So I am sure that this Conference has not been a final result. It has only been the beginning of something good: in the different fields of interaction that I have suggested to you, but also towards the continuation of the work perhaps by way of future conferences and, in particular, I hope, by way of a working group which would bring together again some of the people who have enjoyed these past few days together.

ANNEXURE

Contributors

(including authors of main papers, discussants and editors)

Professor Stanislav Andreski, Sociology, University of Reading, U.K.

Professor Marcus Arkin, Economics, Rhodes University, South Africa.

Mr John Barratt, Director, South African Institute of International Affairs.

Professor P. T. Bauer, Economics, London School of Economics and Political Science, U.K.

Mr W. H. Beatty, Vice-President, Chase Manhattan Bank, New York, U.S.A.

Professor Jan F. Beekman, Public Administration, University of Cape Town, South Africa.

Professor Simon S. Brand, Economics, Rand Afrikaans University, South Africa.

Professor J. H. Coetzee, Anthropology, Potchefstroom University, South Africa.

Dr David S. Collier, Director, Foundation for Foreign Affairs, Inc., Chicago, U.S.A.

Mr B. I. Dladla, Executive Councillor (Community Development), KwaZulu Government, South Africa.

Professor Arch Dotson, Political Science, Cornell University, U.S.A.

Dr Leif Egeland, National Chairman, South African Institute of International Affairs.

Mr A. Erwin, Economics, University of Natal, South Africa.

Professor L. Fourie, Economics and Public Administration, University of Durban–Westville, South Africa.

Professor Kurt Glaser, Political Science, Southern Illinois University, U.S.A.

Dr Athyr Guimarães, Director, E.I.A.P., Fundação Getulio Vargas, Brazil.

Mr Badal Sen Gupta, Sociology, University of Erlangen–Nürnberg, Germany.

Mr David Hirschmann, International Relations, South African Institute of International Affairs.

Professor Norman Jacobs, Sociology, University of Illinois, U.S.A.

Dr C. J. Jooste, Director, South African Bureau for Racial Affairs.

Mr D. Z. Kadzamira, Political Science, University of Malawi.

Professor Arthur Kemp, Economics, Clarement Men's College, U.S.A.

Professor W. M. Kgware, Comparative Education, University of the North, South Africa.

Professor Bruno Knall, Economics, University of Heidelberg, Germany.

Professor G. M. E. Leistner, Economics, University of South Africa.

Professor Jan A. Lombard, Economics, University of Pretoria, South Africa.

Professor Michael H. H. Louw, International Relations, University of the Witwatersrand, South Africa.

Mr I. O. H. M. Mapena, Native Law and Administration, University of the North, South Africa.

Mr R. F. Margo, South African Institute of Race Relations.

Professor S. B. Ngcobo, Economics, University of Botswana, Lesotho and Swaziland.

Professor H. W. E. Ntsanwisi, Chief Councillor, Gazankulu Government, South Africa.

Mr D. M. Ntusi, Ministry of Education, Transkei Government, South Africa.

The Hon. Sishayi S. Nxumalo, Minister of Commerce, Industry and Mines, Swaziland.

Mr F. Taylor Ostrander, American Metal Climax, Inc., U.S.A.

Professor Don Paarlberg, Agricultural Economics, Purdue University, U.S.A.

Professor Franklin Parker, Education, West Virginia University, U.S.A.

Professor Svetozar Pejovich, Director, Economic Research Division, Ohio University, U.S.A.

Dr Ben J. Piek, Demography, Rand Afrikaans University, South Africa.

Professor Stefan T. Possony, Hoover Institution on War, Revolution and Peace, Stanford University, U.S.A.

Mr Henri Razafindratovo, Counsellor, Foreign Ministry, Madagascar.

Professor D. H. Reader, Sociology, University of Rhodesia.

Professor N. J. Rhoodie, Sociology, University of Pretoria, South Africa.

Professor Hans Ruthenberg, Agricultural Economics, University of Hohenheim, Germany.

Professor J. L. Sadie, Demography and Economics, University of Stellenbosch, South Africa.

Mr Lawrence Schlemmer, Sociology, Institute for Social Research, University of Natal.

Mr Siegfried Schönherr, Sociology, University of Erlangen-Nürnberg, Germany.

Mr L. L. Sebe, Executive Councillor (Agriculture), Ciskei Government, South Africa.

Professor Theodore L. Shay, Political Science, Willamette University, U.S.A.

Dr A. W. Stadler, Political Science, University of the Witwatersrand, South Africa.

Professor J. J. Stadler, Economics, University of Pretoria, South Africa.

Professor Anna F. Steyn, Sociology, Rand Afrikaans University, South Africa.

Mr T. T. Thahane, Director of Planning, Government of Lesotho.

Professor B. S. van As, Public Administration, University of South Africa.

Mr F. J. van Wyk, Director, South African Institute of Race Relations.

Professor G. van N. Viljoen, Rector, Rand Afrikaans University, South Africa.

Professor W. B. Vosloo, Political Science and Public Administration, University of Stellenbosch, South Africa.

Professor Edward W. Weidner, Chancellor, University of Wisconsin (Green Bay), U.S.A.

Mr F. R. Wilson, Southern African Representative, Commonwealth Development Corporation, U.K.

Dr Denis Worrall, International Relations, University of the Witwatersrand, South Africa.

Professor Gerhard Wurzbacher, Sociology, University of Erlangen–Nürnberg, Germany.

Index

QUEEN MARY
COLLEGE
LIBRARY

WITHDRAWN
FROM STOCK
QMUL LIBRARY